OXFORD WORLD'S CLASSICS

THE LIVES OF THE POETS

SAMUEL JOHNSON was born in 1709 in Lichfield, Staffordshire. The son of an impecunious bookseller, he experienced poverty throughout the first part of his life, and, in spite of his formidable mental endowments, was able to attend Pembroke College, Oxford, for only a year. After moving to London in 1737, he earned his living by miscellaneous journalism for many years, until his *Rambler* essays and the first historical dictionary of the English language brought him fame. A government pension of £300 a year relieved him from necessity, and in the later part of his life he came to be regarded as the greatest literary figure of his time in England. Among his most noted works are his poem 'The Vanity of Human Wishes', his periodical essays, his moral tale *Rasselas*, his edition of Shakespeare's plays, and *The Lives of the Poets*. He died in 1784 and was buried in Westminster Abbey.

ROGER LONSDALE, formerly Professor of English Literature at the University of Oxford, is an Emeritus Fellow of Balliol College. His publications include *The New Oxford Book of Eighteenth-Century Verse* (1984) and *Eighteenth-Century Women Poets: An Oxford Anthology* (1989). His four-volume edition of *The Lives of the Poets* appeared in 2006.

JOHN MULLAN is Professor of English at University College London. His publications include *How Novels Work* (2006), *Anonymity: A Secret History of English Literature* (2007), and editions of Daniel Defoe. A broadcaster and literary journalist, he writes a weekly column on fiction for the *Guardian* newspaper.

OXFORD WORLD'S CLASSICS

For over 100 years Oxford World's Classics have brought readers closer to the world's great literature. Now with over 700 titles—from the 4,000-year-old myths of Mesopotamia to the twentieth century's greatest novels—the series makes available lesser-known as well as celebrated writing.

The pocket-sized hardbacks of the early years contained introductions by Virginia Woolf, T. S. Eliot, Graham Greene, and other literary figures which enriched the experience of reading. Today the series is recognized for its fine scholarship and reliability in texts that span world literature, drama and poetry, religion, philosophy, and politics. Each edition includes perceptive commentary and essential background information to meet the changing needs of readers.

OXFORD WORLD'S CLASSICS

SAMUEL JOHNSON

The Lives of the Poets

A Selection

Text edited by
ROGER LONSDALE

Selected with an Introduction and Notes by
JOHN MULLAN

OXFORD
UNIVERSITY PRESS

OXFORD
UNIVERSITY PRESS

Great Clarendon Street, Oxford OX2 6DP

Oxford University Press is a department of the University of Oxford.
It furthers the University's objective of excellence in research, scholarship,
and education by publishing worldwide in

Oxford New York

Auckland Cape Town Dar es Salaam Hong Kong Karachi
Kuala Lumpur Madrid Melbourne Mexico City Nairobi
New Delhi Shanghai Taipei Toronto

With offices in

Argentina Austria Brazil Chile Czech Republic France Greece
Guatemala Hungary Italy Japan Poland Portugal Singapore
South Korea Switzerland Thailand Turkey Ukraine Vietnam

Oxford is a registered trade mark of Oxford University Press
in the UK and in certain other countries

Published in the United States
by Oxford University Press Inc., New York

First published as an Oxford World's Classics paperback 2009

British Library Cataloguing in Publication Data

Data available

Library of Congress Cataloging-in-Publication Data

Data available

Typeset by Cepha Imaging Private Ltd., Bangalore, India
Printed in Great Britain
on acid-free paper by
Clays Ltd, Elcograf S.p.A.

ISBN 978-0-19-922674-0

9

CONTENTS

THE LIVES OF THE POETS

INTRODUCTION

The Lives of the Most Eminent English Poets; with Critical Observations on Their Works (to use its eventual full title) was the last major work that Samuel Johnson undertook. Its title page might have led unwary readers to expect that the nation's greatest man of letters was providing a celebratory survey of its literary culture. For by the 1770s genteel readers and book purchasers had begun to revere what we now call 'English Literature'. During the eighteenth century it had gradually become possible to speak of Shakespeare and Milton in terms that had once been reserved for Homer and Virgil. English could be as good a language for poetry as Greek or Latin. In his two greatest undertakings, his *Dictionary of the English Language* (1755) and his edition of the plays of Shakespeare (1765), Johnson had himself made a major contribution to establishing a national literary culture. His *Dictionary*, in some ways his greatest work of literary criticism, had illustrated his minutely subdivided definitions of words with thousands of extracts from what he thought the best of English poetry, drama, and prose. The language was now illuminated by its literature. His edition of Shakespeare had played a major role in establishing Shakespeare as the equal of any 'ancient', and the central figure in a canon of vernacular writing. Johnson had himself proclaimed, in the Preface to his *Dictionary*, that 'the chief glory of every people arises from its authors'.[1] No one could have done more than him to honour his country's literature.

Yet Johnson's *Lives of the Poets* is intrigued by everything inglorious about the life of writing. A contemporary reviewer complained that 'the general tendency of Dr. Johnson's work is rather to diminish than to exalt our writers', sounding as if the Great Cham had performed less than his patriotic duty.[2] The complaint was not without reason. The *Lives* is still provoking and frequently funny because it is so unenchanted about the writers whose lives and writings it describes. There is nothing supercilious, however, in

[1] Johnson, Preface to *A Dictionary of the English Language*, in Samuel Johnson, *The Major Works*, ed. Donald Greene (Oxford, 1984), 327.

[2] See Samuel Johnson, *The Lives of the Most Eminent English Poets*, ed. Roger Lonsdale (Oxford, 2006) (hereafter Lonsdale), iv. 537.

Johnson's observation of his authors' failings. In a *Rambler* essay he noted how disappointment was the likely reflex of any admiring reader who discovered something of the life of the writer. 'Those whom the appearance of virtue, or the evidence of genius, have tempted to a nearer knowledge of the writer in whose performances they may be found, have indeed had frequent reason to repent their curiosity.'[3] But Johnson's conclusion is not cynical. The life does not belie the work, even if it fails to match it. There are good reasons why 'a man writes much better than he lives'. Johnson wrote this from experience. In the *Lives of the Poets* he looks back down more than a century of English poetry, but he is also looking back through his own 'life of writing', ruefully cataloguing the occupational self-delusions of authors. It often seems from his condensed biographies that a writer is the best human exemplum: authorship focuses the most essential human aspirations and vanities. Perhaps this is especially true of poets, who supposedly aspire higher than all other writers, and many of whom hanker after a vindication of which they must always be uncertain: the admiration of posterity. All the authors whose lives Johnson narrated were dead. In most cases, their literary achievements had begun to shrink; in some cases they had already been forgotten. To bring back to life their ambitions and endeavours was to witness in close-up the vanity of human wishes. As Johnson says in 'Pope', 'let no man dream of influence beyond his life' (p. 406): even the most famous and successful of poets cannot know his posthumous fate. When he wrote this, Pope was still the most widely admired poet of the century and a proper subject for a high-minded critic. But Johnson's biographical format allowed him to make Pope a kind of psychological case study, an extreme example of the 'voracity of fame' (p. 378). His picture of the poet as a man who 'pleased himself with being important and formidable, and gratified sometimes his pride, and sometimes his resentment' is, we might say, hardly sympathetic (p. 399). Yet it is not just disapproving. These are the inevitable self-consolations of an author. As the greatest author of the age, it was natural that Pope's vanities be the most powerful and his self-delusions the most elaborate. Johnson skewers his affectations: his faked 'contempt of his own poetry', his pretended 'insensibility to censure and criticism', and

[3] *Rambler*, no. 14, (5 May 1750).

the 'gloomy indignation' with which he looked on 'the world' (p. 413). He declares, with a confidence that a modern biographer would never hazard, that these attitudes were certainly 'counterfeited'. This is not because Johnson has particular counter-evidence to offer, but simply because he is sure he understands the psychology of a writer who was so hungry for the regard of his readers.

Johnson's 'Pope' is the culmination of his *Lives*, the last one he wrote. In Johnson's version, Pope was, as Byron would disapprovingly put it, '*all author*', his every gesture a contribution to his imagined reputation.[4] We hear how the 16-year-old Pope, performing his poetic tricks for superannuated men of letters like William Wycherley, was already learning to behave like a poet—adopting the poet's disdain for the mere critic. 'It is pleasant to remark how soon Pope learned the cant of an author, and began to treat criticks with contempt, though he had yet suffered nothing from them' (p. 351). But authorial self-regard is inevitably masochistic. Johnson preserved the memorable anecdote of Pope's self-torment as a satirist who claimed to relish his enmities. Handed one of Colly Cibber's pamphlets against him, he supposedly declared, '*These things are my diversion*'—but those who watched as he read it saw 'his features writhen with anguish' (p. 403). The greater the writer, the more tender the sense of self. So, elsewhere in the *Lives*, we find Dryden, his 'supremacy of reputation' on the London stage apparently threatened by Settle's absurd *Empress of Morocco*, drawn in to a contest of abuse that Johnson explicates in wondering detail (pp. 126-31). Dryden is of course foolish to give critics and rivals 'the power of vexing him'. But it is an occupational folly. 'He is always angry at some past, or afraid of some future censure' (p. 144). This is what being an author, especially a successful author, is like. At the opening of his life of Savage, Johnson talks of the 'mournful narratives' of 'the heroes of literary history' (p. 238). The *Lives of the Poets* are 'mournful narratives' in a double sense. They chronicle 'the miseries of the learned', the thwarted ambitions and the gnawing doubts of even the best writers. They also speak for Johnson's own particular melancholy—his mournful sensitivity to human disappointment. The reader of Richard Savage's life will know that its mournfulness is inextricable from its humour. Savage's talents are unappreciated and

[4] See Byron, *Beppo: A Venetian Story*, st. 75, l. 593.

his best creations neglected, but then the poet becomes expert in comic self-solace. When his ambitious poem *On Public Spirit* sells only seventy-two copies, Savage tells himself that was 'unluckily published two days after the prorogation of the parliament', just when 'all those who could be expected to regard it' were distracted (p. 290). No wonder it did not sell. The special skill of authors is explaining away their failures.

A Commercial Venture

Savage is an anomaly for the modern reader, the only subject of one of Johnson's major lives who is now forgotten as a poet. He is there because Johnson knew him well and published an extraordinary life of him in 1744 that was later incorporated into the *Lives*. But the original collection included many other minor figures. Johnson's original *Lives of the Poets* was an odder survey than this present selection might make it seem. The first part, which appeared in 1779, included his accounts not just of Milton and Dryden, but also of the likes of John Pomfret, Edmund Smith, and George Stepney. When the second part of his work appeared two years later, it added not just Pope and Gray, but also William Broome, John Hughes, and Thomas Yalden. The complete collection comprised fifty-two lives (one of which, the account of Edward Young, was contributed by Young's relative Herbert Croft). It covered writers who were active from the mid-seventeenth century onwards. Some of these were poets who are now little known, but whose standing was high when Johnson was writing, authors like Waller, Denham, or Thomson. However, there were also names in the collection that would have been obscure to most of Johnson's contemporaries. His sometimes very brief *Lives* of these men hardly seem designed to rescue them from obscurity. Take his account of the late seventeenth-century poet Richard Duke. It begins with the fatalistic 'Of Mr. Richard Duke I can find few memorials' and ends with 'His death is mentioned in Swift's Journal'—a footnote in literary history.[5] In between are a few short paragraphs that name some of Duke's works but do not recommend them. 'His poems are not below mediocrity; nor have I found much in them to be praised.'

[5] See Lonsdale, iv. 181.

The strivings of such minor literary characters are briefly recognized before they disappear from view.

Reading the *Lives* in a selection like this Oxford World's Classics edition, we must lose these minor figures, but we need not lose Johnson's most engaged criticism, nor any of those essays where he has entered into a biographical narrative with most curiosity or imaginative sympathy. Johnson's accounts of those whom we now consider the major post-Restoration English poets—Milton, Dryden, and Pope—were amongst the most substantial of his *Lives*. It is not coincidental that, in his *Dictionary*, completed more than twenty years earlier, these three had been the most frequently quoted authors after Shakespeare. Two other *Lives* were particularly long: 'Cowley', which involved Johnson's engagement with metaphysical poetry and included some close consideration of the poetry of Donne, and 'Savage'. All of these long *Lives* are included in the present selection. Also given here are his lives of Rochester, Congreve, Gay, Swift, and Gray, writers chosen because they continue to engage readers in the twenty-first century. Altogether these lives make up a large proportion of Johnson's original work. Yet the work was also characterized by its survey of all those minor figures, none of whom matters on his own.

To understand how and why particular authors were chosen for Johnson's *Lives*, we need to know about the commercial origins of the project and the role played in it by the eighteenth-century entrepreneurs of print: the booksellers. Appropriately for the son of a provincial bookseller, who from the first knew of literature as commerce, Johnson's own largest literary undertakings were booksellers' commissions—books dreamt up by businessmen. His greatest work, his *Dictionary*, was one such. He was hired for the project by a group of leading London booksellers, who shared the financial risk. We would now call these men 'publishers', though their roles were more various than those of modern publishers. Not only would they commission and finance a new publication, they would often have a shop where it could be sold, and perhaps a press where it could be printed. Johnson's edition of Shakespeare was also a project brought to him by booksellers, keen to cash in on the expanding market for prestigious editions of the author who was becoming the national poet. The *Dictionary* and the Shakespeare edition were expensive prestige productions, designed to impress; they were also intended to turn a good profit. Johnson's last great work may have been a project for which he may have had an inclination but it was another entrepreneurial venture.

He was approached in March 1777 by representatives of a consortium of some forty-two London booksellers who had decided to publish an edition of *The Works of the English Poets*. It was an undertaking born of new commercial opportunities and, for the booksellers, new commercial anxieties. Despite the Copyright Act of 1710, which had specified that copyright could be owned for only fourteen years, renewable for another fourteen if the author were still alive, London booksellers had continued to behave as if they possessed permanent copyrights in the works that had been assigned to them. However, this assumption had recently become untenable. In March 1774, the House of Lords had ruled that a Scottish bookseller, Alexander Donaldson, had the right to reprint James Thomson's *The Seasons*, one of the most popular poetical works of the eighteenth century. The ruling established that there could be no such thing as perpetual copyright. The way was clear to the unhampered production of editions of literary classics. One of the literary entrepreneurs liberated by this legal ruling was the opportunistic young Edinburgh bookseller John Bell. In 1776 Bell began publishing his collection of English drama, *Bell's British Theatre* (21 vols., 1776–80), and in the same year set out on what was to be a huge and relatively cheap edition of *The Poets of Great Britain Complete from Chaucer to Churchill*. The edition for which Johnson was to write biographical prefaces was devised to meet the threat of Bell's collection. Bell had included anonymously contributed biographies of his poets. Johnson was the nation's greatest man of letters and his name would add prestige to the rival edition and therefore greatly help sales. In advance of its appearance, the booksellers advertised it as 'Dr. JOHNSON'S EDITION of the ENGLISH POETS'.[6] The booksellers, and not Johnson, decided to begin their list of poets in the mid-seventeenth century, partly because some of the earlier seventeenth-century poets had appeared in recent editions published by members of their group. Johnson's *Lives* were to be prefaces to each section of this multi-volume edition.

[6] Ibid i. 24.

Yet the more substantial *Lives* outgrew the booksellers' expectations and apparently Johnson's initial intentions. The first thing that the final work was to tell the reader, in its prefatory Advertisement, was that Johnson had been 'led beyond my intention' (p. 3). Instead of uniform short prefaces there was a range of essays, from the perfunctory to the lengthy and elaborate. Eighteenth-century readers encountered Johnson's *Lives* as we do now: pieces detached from the pages of poetry that they were supposed to adorn. Johnson was simply too slow to produce the promised prefaces to the individual poets, and the booksellers had to adopt the drastic measure of publishing the volumes of poetry before these prefaces were completed. The fifty-six-volume sets of the *English Poets* were from the first physically separate from Johnson's *Prefaces, Biographical and Critical, to the Works of the English Poets*, as they were originally titled. The first four volumes of these *Prefaces*, containing twenty-two lives, appeared in March 1779, though they were officially available only to those who had already purchased the complete set of the *English Poets*. Soon a single-volume Dublin piracy of the *Lives* was produced. The public had to wait for the remaining *Lives*. There was considerable anticipation, and occasional prophecies of completion, in contemporary periodicals. It was not until May 1781, more than two years after the first *Lives*, that the remaining *Prefaces*, as they were still being called, appeared in six volumes. A month later, the booksellers also published a four-volume edition of Johnson's complete *Lives*, now available separately from the sets of the *English Poets* and given the title *The Lives of the Most Eminent English Poets*.

Johnson was always happy to associate himself with the booksellers and their interest in the market for literature. 'He considered them as the patrons of literature,' recalled Boswell in his *Life of Johnson*.[7] Boswell had said that he was sorry that they had not paid Johnson more for the *Dictionary*, but Johnson rejected the idea that the booksellers had exploited him. They were, he said, 'generous, liberal-minded men'. 'He, upon all occasions, did ample justice to their character in this respect', Boswell added, identifying a conviction that was both deep-seated and unconventional. In the mid-eighteenth century it was still usual to regret that literature had

[7] James Boswell, *Life of Johnson*, ed. Pat Rogers (Oxford World's Classics), 217.

become a business, controlled by vulgar entrepreneurs. The great satirists of a previous generation, Pope and Swift, had scorned the influence of the booksellers. Swift's *A Tale of a Tub* presents itself as a text mutilated at the behest of booksellers, and published without authority by one of them. In early versions of Pope's satiric magnum opus *The Dunciad*, first published in 1728, one of the three books is given over to a parody of Homeric games, in which London booksellers compete to dominate the dirty world of print. Instead of the running and discus-throwing of ancient epic, these modern competitors test themselves in pissing contests or in diving into the Fleet Ditch, London's largest sewer. In his life of Pope, Johnson scorned the poet's disdain for those who write for money. We remember Johnson for his unillusioned aphorism about authorship in Boswell's *Life*: 'No man but a blockhead ever wrote, except for money'.[8] Thus the wry humour in his summary of Richard Savage's predicament, denied financial sustenance by his own mother. 'He was therefore obliged to seek some other means of support; and, having no profession, became by necessity an author' (p. 243). Authorship is the occupation for those who have no proper occupation. Vocation it is not. Johnson is consistently sceptical about the role of inspiration. Most authors, he said elsewhere, do not write because they feel in themselves 'some peculiar impulse of genius'; 'they perceive no particular summons to composition, except the sound of the clock'.[9] He describes as 'a fantastick foppery' Thomas Gray's notion 'that he could not write but at certain times, or at happy moments' (p. 457). These are the pretensions of the academic poet, dining in his Cambridge college and knowing nothing of the bookseller's requirements.

Johnson vindicated the literary marketplace in preference to the culture of patronage that it was replacing. To annotate Johnson's *Lives* is to realize how important patrons had been over the previous century. Any reader can still see that the work is thronged with the names of lords and ladies. For any literary historian inclined to believe that the eighteenth century saw the demise of patronage, it is salutary to see how important the favours of 'the great' remained. In several of the *Lives*, Johnson describes how writers were made dishonest or absurd by their patrons. His comment about the booksellers being the 'patrons of literature' implies his preference of the

[8] Ibid. 731. [9] *Rambler*, no. 145 (6 Aug. 1751).

market to what it had largely replaced: the culture of patronage. The frustrations and indignities that accompanied the quest for patronage—the exchange of praise for money, as he bluntly defines it in 'Pope' (p. 418)—feature in many of Johnson's accounts. When we hear of John Gay, quitting his apprenticeship to a silk mercer to become secretary to the Duchess of Monmouth, a woman 'remarkable for inflexible perseverance in her demand to be treated as a princess', the implication is that one kind of 'servility' has but been exchanged for another (p. 229). And perhaps a worse one: 'by quitting a shop for such service, he might gain leisure, but he certainly advanced little in the boast of independence'. Johnson expresses his scorn for the postures of admiration into which the needy writer is twisted by his desire to please a potential patron. In his *Life of Savage* he had chronicled the life of a man who, while never grateful for the favour he was granted, spent much of his life pursuing patrons. Here Johnson had been almost amused by his subject's 'literary hypocrisy' (p. 264). For twenty guineas, Savage had composed 'a panegyrick on Sir Robert Walpole', even though in conversation (as Johnson would have known first-hand) he spoke of him 'generally with contempt' (p. 265). (Characteristically, he lost a vital pension a few years later by speaking to Walpole with angry 'roughness' when a little tact would have assured him of its continuance (p. 298).) Questioned on this, Savage was ever 'ready to lament the misery of living at the tables of other men', making his hypocrisy seem a burden for which Johnson felt compassion.

The other flatterers in Johnson's collection did not have the chance to make their excuses so disarmingly to their biographer, and elsewhere there is less sympathy for the needy poet who turns to obsequiousness. Edmund Waller was a skilled writer as he was a skilled politician, switching his allegiances from Charles I to Cromwell to Charles II, but in Johnson's cameo one who had 'flattery ready for all whom the vicissitudes of the world happen to exalt', and therefore 'a prostituted mind'.[10] Johnson tells the story of Samuel Butler being denied the favour of the Duke of Buckingham because, as Butler was about to make his address to the great man, 'his Grace' noticed 'a pimp of his acquaintance (the creature too was a knight) trip by with a brace of ladies'.[11] Off went the lascivious aristocratic connoisseur, 'to follow another kind of business, at which he was

[10] Lonsdale, ii. 40. [11] Ibid. 3.

more ready than in doing good offices to men of desert'. He catches the 'servile absurdity' of Addison's dedication of his opera *Rosamond* to the Duchess of Marlborough, a woman without skill, or pretensions to skill, in poetry or literature.'[12] In his life of the courtier-poet Charles Sackville, Earl of Dorset, Johnson scornfully cites Dryden's choice of 'authors of our own country superior to those of antiquity'. Who were the greatest modern writers? In his dedicatory address to Dorset in his 'Discourse of the Original and Progress of Satire' (1693) Dryden nominated Shakespeare for tragedy, and '*your Lordship in satire*'. Johnson is delightedly amazed. 'Would it be imagined that, of this rival to antiquity, all the satires were little personal invectives, and that his longest composition was a song of eleven stanzas?' Here is simply a client fawning on his patron, a dilettante writer who never produced more than the occasional 'effusions of a man of wit'.

Dryden is Johnson's main character study of the deforming effects of patronage—a 'great poet' who became an expert flatterer of the rich and powerful (p. 121). He may be a man 'whom every English generation must mention with reverence as a critick and a poet', but irreverence characterizes Johnson's account of his professional life (p. 165). After conceding that his 'dramatick immorality' might have been the common tendency of the age, he adds, 'but in the meanness and servility of hyperbolical adulation, I know not whether, since the days in which the Roman emperors were deified, he has ever been equalled' (p. 160). Dryden, Johnson thinks, took easily and happily to the business of celebrating patrons, and potential patrons; 'he considers the great as entitled to encomiastick homage, and brings praise rather as a tribute than a gift'. Patrons themselves are invariably distinguished by vanity as well as wealth. Johnson enjoys retelling the story, obtained from Joseph Spence's then unpublished record of Pope's conversations, of how Pope read draft passages of his translation of the *Iliad* aloud to Lord Halifax, who several times stopped the poet to tell him that 'something in that passage' was not quite right (p. 372). A few months later he returned to Halifax, thanked him for his 'kind observations', and read out the same passages as if rewritten, but in fact unaltered. He was told by the great man that they were now just right. The potentate preened

12 Ibid. iii. 5.

himself as a literary patron, but was a mere pretender to taste. The relationship between Pope and Halifax is given as a diagram of the rationale of patronage. 'Their commerce had its beginning in hope of praise on one side, and of money on the other, and ended because Pope was less eager of money than Halifax of praise' (p. 373). Pope's friend John Gay, in contrast, was doomed to solicit favours from 'the great'. He made a thousand pounds when he published his *Poems* by subscription in 1720, but, seduced by dreams of 'dignity and splendour', he invested the money in South Sea stock and lost it all (p. 232). Back he was thrown into the old quest for patrons, paying his 'diligent court' to Henrietta Howard, Countess of Suffolk, George II's mistress, but to no end: 'solicitations, verses, and flatteries were thrown away; the lady heard them, and did nothing' (p. 232).

The corrosive influence of patronage had long been a theme for Johnson. Nos. 26 and 27 of his periodical essay the *Rambler* had consisted of imagined letters from Eubulus, a young would-be writer who comes up to London and seeks to advance himself into the favour of patrons. All his lessons are bitter ones, especially his final success with Eutyches, the statesman. 'His measures were censured; I wrote in his defence, and was recompensed with a place, of which the profits were never received by me without the pangs of remembering that they were the reward of wickedness.'[13] Johnson had had his own experience of uselessly flattering a potential patron when he set out on his *Dictionary*. On the advice of the bookseller Robert Dodsley, he had dedicated his *Plan of a Dictionary of the English Language* (1747) to the Earl of Chesterfield, a statesman and noted man of taste. Initially Chesterfield had appeared pleased to be associated with the project and had sent Johnson £10, but before long he lost interest and neglected even to receive the needy editor when he visited him. After nine years of hard editorial labour, 'amidst inconvenience and distraction, in sickness and in sorrow', the *Dictionary* was published with a Preface that declared it to have been completed 'with little assistance of the learned, and without any patronage of the great'.[14] Chesterfield, notified by Dodsley that the great work was finished, had recalled his own connection to it and written two

13 *The Rambler*, no. 27 (19 June 1750).

14 Johnson, Preface, in *The Major Works*, ed. Greene, 328.

letters to the elegant periodical the *World* celebrating its imminent appearance. Johnson responded with a letter that was to become famous, in which he described a patron as 'one who looks with unconcern on a man struggling for life in the water, and, when he has reached ground, encumbers him with help'.[15] By the time that Johnson began the *Lives*, he was financially secure. In 1762, in his mid-fifties, he had been awarded a government pension of £300 per annum as a mark of the status of his *Dictionary*, already a kind of national literary monument. The pension rescued him from the anxiety about money, and occasionally the actual poverty, that had dominated his life as a writer. His past experiences of having to write for pay continued to influence him, however. In the *Lives* he is attentive to how authors managed or failed to earn money. He is interested in the details of Milton's contract with his bookseller for the publication of *Paradise Lost* (p. 85), or the minutiae of Pope's brilliantly successful scheme to sell copies of his *Iliad* by subscription (pp. 360–1 and 364–5).

Pope may have been obsessed by money, and ready to mock rival authors who lacked it, but Johnson pauses to concede that his 'fortune . . . as it arose from publick approbation was very honourably obtained' (p. 411). Pope made his money from selling books. He was a snob and a name-dropper, but he was never a client. 'Pope never set his genius to sale.' He profited by pleasing readers, and the verdict of ordinary readers is never scorned by Johnson. When he says that Pope's *The Rape of the Lock* has been praised over the years 'by readers of every class, from the critick to the waiting-maid', he implies that the waiting-maid's verdict should make the critic more confident (p. 426). Those works of the imagination that have appealed to 'readers of every class' have a special status in Johnson's judgement. Indeed, Johnson coined the phrase 'the common reader' for the character whom literature did best to please. He had first used the term in his *Plan of the Dictionary* (1747). He is explaining how his definitions of words will not be designed to satisfy specialists: 'it will be required by common readers, that the explications should be sufficient for common use'.[16] He goes on to say that this is

[15] Letter of 7 February 1755, in *The Letters of Samuel Johnson*, ed. Bruce Redford, 5 vols. (Oxford, 1992), i. 96.

[16] See *Johnson: Prose and Poetry*, ed. Mona Wilson (1963), 132.

just why he will use quotes from 'the best writers'. His *Dictionary* is a cornucopia of quotes from what we would call 'Literature' because this is, he assumes, what will reach to 'common readers'. The phrase returns memorably in his life of Gray. 'In the character of his Elegy I rejoice to concur with the common reader; for by the common sense of readers uncorrupted with literary prejudices, after all the refinements of subtilty and the dogmatism of learning, must be finally decided all claim to poetical honours' (p. 461). The 'common reader' is a new measure of literary reach, a being created by the commerce of print. The common reader is what we get when books are written not for special people but for what we call 'the public'.

By omitting some of Johnson's less significant lives in this selection, we perhaps sacrifice the accumulated sense of how the life of writing is shaped by the struggle for money, and how often the achievement of financial security is provisional or belated. John Hughes, having 'suffered the mortifications of a narrow fortune' for most of his life, eventually achieved affluence when he received a sinecure from a powerful patron; 'but such is human life, that he had it when his declining health could neither allow him long possession nor quick enjoyment'.[17] James Thomson, after a life of some 'indigence', finally received a lucrative sinecure through one of his patrons, but promptly caught a cold while being rowed across the Thames 'which, with some careless exasperation, ended in a fever that put an end to his life'.[18] In his short life of another writer whom he knew personally, William Collins, Johnson is actually present when the impecunious 'literary adventurer' is 'immured by a bailiff, that was prowling in the street'.[19] A bookseller bails him out on the promise of a translation of Aristotle's *Poetics*, but Collins is suddenly left a large sum of money by an uncle and thoughts of the translation evaporate. Materially secure, he succumbs to 'depression of mind'. His very poetic bent seems an affliction. Learned and inventive, he was 'delighted with those flights of the imagination which pass the bounds of nature'. 'He loved fairies, genii, giants, and monsters; he delighted to rove through the meanders of inchantment, to gaze on the magnificence of golden palaces, to repose by the waterfalls of Elysian gardens.' Johnson expresses no admiration for his poetry, but

[17] Lonsdale, iii. 41. [18] Ibid. iv. 101. [19] Ibid. 120.

there is an outreach of sympathy in his 'character' of this poetic dreamer.

Johnson the Critic

'The biographical part of literature is what I love most,' Johnson had once told Boswell.[20] Johnson is a brilliant biographer because the genre makes him succumb to unexpected sympathies. He had had an early schooling in biography in his thirties when he had earned his living writing anonymously for Edward Cave's *Gentleman's Magazine*. He had written miscellaneous short lives of eminent men for the magazine, beginning with a life of the Dutch physician Herman Boerhaave (January–April 1739), and ranging from Sir Francis Drake to Confucius.[21] These lives were fabricated hastily from previous accounts. His earliest truly individual work was a biography, his *Life of Savage*, written in 1743 and published in 1744. Savage was one of the poets already chosen by the booksellers, so it was natural to include this earlier work amongst the *Lives of the Poets*. Yet it is anomalous, the work not only of a young man, but of a writer still striving for success, still writing hard for money. The bond between writer and subject is close not just because Johnson had known Savage very well, but because he too was an author trying to make a name for himself. (The *Life of Savage* was published anonymously.) In its structure it is different from the other lives: there is no 'examination' of Savage's major works to conclude the piece; it is all biography. Vivid in its depiction of its disarming, exasperating subject, 'Savage' is however notoriously full of errors, and written without scepticism of Savage's own version of things. Rarely do we go to the *Lives* for indisputable fact. Johnson was candidly careless of biographical research. At the opening of his life of Roscommon, he characteristically says that he has taken most of his information from a long note by Elijah Fenton in his edition of the works of Edmund Waller, 'though I know not whether all that he relates is certain'.[22]

[20] *Life of Johnson*, ed. Rogers, 301.

[21] These lives are collected in *Early Biographical Writings of Dr Johnson*, ed. J. D. Fleeman (Farnborough, 1973).

[22] Lonsdale, ii. 17.

Yet the more sustained *Lives* have an extraordinary narrative force. Partly this is a consequence of Johnson's moralism. For him, biography provides corrective lessons. In 'Milton' this is striking still, and was controversial in his own day. Since the late seventeenth century, the effort of admirers had been to detach Milton the poet from his political views and actions. Addison's *Spectator* papers on *Paradise Lost* had successfully celebrated the poem as the great English epic and the proper reading for a cultured Christian. In one of his own *Idler* essays, Johnson had mocked a contemporary reverence for the poet: his vacuous *littérateur* Dick Minim prospers by parroting the platitudes of the day, one of which is Milton's pre-eminence. '*Milton* is the only writer whose books *Minim* can read for ever without weariness.'[23] Johnson had himself confirmed Milton's pre-eminence only a few years earlier, when he had added to the new (1773) edition of his *Dictionary* a tissue of further, often lengthy, quotations from *Paradise Lost*.[24] In the *Lives*, he was determined to return his genteel readers to the 'surly and acrimonious republican' of the past. In the biographical section of 'Milton' he insists on the poet's appetite for intolerant ideological controversy, sticking closer than he needs to the pamphlet battles of the 1640s and 1650s, making the reader follow the progress of Milton's disputes and outbursts. He was pleased to discover in Milton's private life the traits that would explain his political affiliations. He was 'severe and arbitrary' in his 'domestic relations', treating his wife and daughters 'as subordinate and inferior beings' (p. 93). 'It has been observed, that they who most loudly clamour for liberty do not most liberally grant it.' In a different way this is also true of 'Swift'. His life of Swift is almost all biography, his poetry amounting, in Johnson's view, to rather little. More than any other of the *Lives*, Johnson's 'Swift' chooses to be 'unfair'. In its very opening he takes the complexity of Swift's sense of national identity—a celebrated Irish patriot who called himself an Englishman—as a sign of bad faith. Was he English or Irish? 'The question may, without much regret, be left in the obscurity in which he delighted to involve it' (p. 318). He takes Swift's habit of travelling on foot as evidence of 'a passion which seems to

[23] *Idler*, no. 61 (16 June 1759).

[24] See Allen Reddick, *The Making of Johnson's Dictionary 1746–1773* (Cambridge, 1990), 122–30.

have been deep fixed in his heart, the love of a shilling' (p. 320). Such biographical ill will is visible to any reader, but Johnson also conflated incidents and juggled chronology to make. Swift seem politically mercenary.[25] He was determined that there was something wrong with Swift. His satirical output betokened some unnatural condition, some warping of humanity. Isolated as an old man, his thoughts 'being neither renovated by discourse, nor increased by reading, wore gradually away, and left his mind vacant to the vexations of the hour, till at last his anger was heightened into madness'. This is where satirical misanthropy leads, Johnson is almost glad to say.

But the *Lives* is not all biography. Johnson also provided what his original title page called 'critical observations' on his poets. In fact, each substantial life follows a tripartite pattern. First there is a biographical narrative, then a brief 'character' of the writer concerned, then an 'examination' of his major works. Johnson's 'examinations' aroused as much controversy as his biographies, and have given us some famous quotations concerning English poetry. On metaphysical poetry: 'heterogeneous ideas are yoked by violence together' (p. 16). On Milton, 'Milton's delight was to sport in the wide regions of possibility; reality was a scene too narrow for his mind' (p. 104). On *The Rape of the Lock*: 'New things are made familiar, and familiar things are made new' (p. 427). On Gray's odes: 'He has a kind of strutting dignity, and is tall by walking on tiptoe' (p. 460). For all his wonder at *Paradise Lost*, what we recall is his 'None ever wished it longer than it is' (p. 108). This is sometimes quoted as if it were dismissive, but in fact it is the line with which Johnson calls himself back from the poem's sublimity to ordinary 'recreation'. The influence of the *Lives* on later generations has partly been a consequence of this quotability: arguments are refined and concentrated by such summings up. Johnson was not the first to describe the features of metaphysical poetry, but, after the *Lives*, it is invariably his verdict with which critics have contended. Equally, Johnson did not invent the interest in what we might call 'national biography' (his own work was greatly facilitated by William Oldys's recent multi-volume reference work *Biographia Britannica*), yet he

[25] Martin Maner, *The Philosophical Biographer. Doubt and Dialectic in Johnson's Lives of the Poets* (Athens, Ga. 1988), ch. 5.

did show the power of the 'literary life' as a genre. Many of the most memorable anecdotes in the *Lives* are lifted from earlier printed sources, but it is thanks to Johnson that they became so well known.

Johnson's critical judgements are often sceptical, and would have seemed subversive of the booksellers' project if his *Lives* had appeared as prefaces to the works they described, as originally intended. The modern reader who reads the minor lives is struck by his low estimation of many of his authors, and his aspersions on some of the writing of even the authors he admired. He begins his critical survey of John Gay's work with 'As a poet, he cannot be rated very high' (p. 235). Of James Hammond, 'It would be hard to find in all his productions three stanzas that deserve to be remembered'.[26] Of Ambrose Philips, 'He has added nothing to English poetry'.[27] Some of this is the consequence of Johnson being contracted to pronounce on poets he had not chosen and did not admire, but it is more than this. The discovery of 'faults' was part of his business. When he examines *Paradise Lost*, he can hardly give it greater praise. It is 'a poem, which, considered with respect to design, may claim the first place, and with respect to performance the second, among the productions of the human mind' (p. 99). Yet even here appreciation must give way to deprecation. 'The defects and faults of *Paradise Lost*, for faults and defects every work of man must have, it is the business of impartial criticism to discover' (p. 106). Johnson then devotes as many pages to these 'faults and defects' as he has done to achievement of the poem. It is sometimes thought that Johnson's antagonism to Milton's politics and religious enthusiasm might explain this anatomy of failings. In fact, the business of finding fault is a constitutional habit of Johnson's criticism. His Preface to Shakespeare, published a decade-and-a-half earlier, famously vindicated the playwright from the 'petty cavils' of neoclassical critics and helped establish Shakespeare as the greatest of English writers. Yet it then dedicated several pages to Shakespeare's 'faults'.

Why was fault finding so important? Johnson gave his own answer in a *Rambler* essay when he said that the faults of a good writer were 'dangerous' because of 'the influence of his example', and that they needed to be 'discovered and stigmatized, before they have the

[26] Lonsdale, iii. 117. [27] Ibid. iv. 116.

sanction of antiquity conferred upon them'.[28] This is a symptom of Johnson's concern with 'correctness', a critical criterion that belonged to his age and that we find difficult to recognize. There were conventions governing diction, allusion, poetic form, and generic consistency that a poet should try to observe. But it is also a more personal concern. Like some of the greatest literary critics of the twentieth century—one thinks of William Empson or Christopher Ricks—Johnson believed that poetry must pass the tests of reason and experience. He would not be blinded by technique or fooled by a blur of fine-sounding words. Thus his sardonic version of Thomas Gray's poetical extravagance. 'In 1757 he published *The Progress of Poetry* and *The Bard*, two compositions at which the readers of poetry were at first content to gaze in mute amazement' (p. 454). It was thanks to a few critics who championed these poems that their status was assured, and 'many were content to be shewn beauties which they could not see'. His subsequent close reading of 'the two Sister Odes' acknowledges the 'cumbrous splendour' of Gray's odes, but catalogues the examples of incoherence, illogicality, and even meaninglessness that he finds as he reads through them. Sometimes this sceptical spirit amounts to a suspicion that poetry is out to trick the reader. When Johnson 'examines' Pope's *Essay on Man*, he shakes his head at the evidence of the poet's 'genius' (p. 453). Here are 'the dazzling splendour of imagery, and the seductive powers of eloquence', but they are deployed exactly in order to 'dazzle' and to 'seduce'. The poem consists of commonplaces made to seem wonderful by the poet's 'ornaments'. 'Never were penury of knowledge and vulgarity of sentiment so happily disguised.' With his 'blaze of embellishment' and 'sweetness of melody', Pope, in effect, sets about deceiving the reader.

The belief that good criticism involves undeceiving the reader is behind his treatment of metaphysical poetry in 'Cowley'. When Johnson refers to 'a race of writers that may be termed the metaphysical poets' he was not coining a phrase but confirming a category. Dryden and Pope had both recognized this type of poetry. But Johnson sought to make 'metaphysical' a pejorative term. There is something almost excessive in his quarrel with metaphysical poetry, which sometimes amounts to a recognition of its qualities.

[28] *The Rambler*, no. 93 (5 Feb. 1751).

The suspicion is strengthened by his tussle with Donne, a bad example to others in Johnson's opinion, but clearly a powerful one. His first comment on Donne—'a man of very extensive and various knowledge'—is a candid compliment. Displaying lines from Donne's 'To the Countess of Bedford IV' as being 'too scholastick', he concedes 'they are not inelegant' (p. 19); lines from another Donne poem are 'yet more abstruse and profound'. The last adjective wavers between exasperation and unwilling admiration. Quoting Donne's analogy between two lovers and the two feet of a pair of compasses, he doubts 'whether absurdity or ingenuity has the better claim' (p. 30). 'Who but Donne would have thought that a good man is a telescope' (p. 22). Is this disapproval or concealed admiration?

In 'Cowley' he also makes apparent his low estimation of certain traditional genres, notably pastoral ('which requires no acquaintance of the living world') and love poetry ('amorous ditties'). These prejudices persist. He disdainfully characterizes *Epitaphium Damonis*, Milton's commemorative poem in Latin, occasioned by the death of his friend Charles Diodati, as 'the common but childish imitation of pastoral life' (p. 60). He is famously unimpressed by Milton's greatest elegiac poem, *Lycidas*, gruffly dismissing its allusions to classical mythology: 'Where there is leisure for fiction there is little grief' (p. 95). Oddly enough, the modern reader may find it easier to take pleasure in the lyrical artificiality of Milton's poem, and not to worry about the putative feelings of the poet. Johnson characterizes the pastoral form of *Lycidas* as 'easy, vulgar, and therefore disgusting' (p. 95). The word 'disgusting' is a milder one than it has since become, but it is clear that the poem's very genre is enough to diminish it in Johnson's eyes.[29] Pastoral drama, he says in 'Gay', is inherently contemptible. 'Such scenes please Barbarians in the dawn of literature, and children in the dawn of life; but will be for the most part thrown away, as men grow wise, and nations grow learned' (p. 237). What now seem his odder critical judgements are often shaped by his disdain for certain genres or poetic forms. In 'Milton' he dismisses the poet's sonnet about the death of his wife, 'Methought I saw my late espoused saint', a beautiful and subtle revisiting of the Alcestis myth. When he calls it a 'poor sonnet' (p. 70) he may be thinking of the triviality of the form rather than

[29] See his discussion of pastoral in the *Rambler*, nos. 36 and 37 (July 1750).

the quality of Milton's use of it. Later in 'Milton' he observes, as if it were beyond argument, that the 'fabrick of a sonnet', while suited to Italian, a language with easy and frequent rhymes, has 'never succeeded' in English.

Some of his fixed prejudices about particular genres are, and are felt to be, personal. The most significant is his discomfort about religious, and in particular devotional, verse. In the eighteenth century this would have included a large part of the output of living poets. He is best known for the comments in 'Waller'. 'Contemplative piety, or the intercourse between God and the human soul, cannot be poetical.' It is a useful corrective to the assumption that the believer warms to religious poetry in a way that the unbeliever cannot. Some of the poets of the seventeenth century whose religious verse is now universally admired, Donne, Herbert, or Vaughan, address God poetically in a manner that Johnson deplored. 'Man admitted to implore the mercy of his Creator, and plead the merits of his Redeemer, is already in a higher state than poetry can confer.'[30] The topics of Christian devotion are few and universal, and the 'novelty' that good poetry promises is inappropriate decoration and distraction. The thought returns frequently in the *Lives*. He expresses, for instance, his undisguised admiration for the piety of Isaac Watts, even though he was an obdurate Dissenter. He commends all his writing except his religious verse: 'his devotional poetry is, like that of others, unsatisfactory'. The failure is inevitable, for 'the sanctity of the matter rejects the ornaments of figurative diction'.[31]

A more positive prejudice that shapes his judgements would have seemed uncontroversial to most of his readers. This was the belief that writing in English—and particularly poetry in English—was fit to be admired because it had been improved by the efforts of outstanding writers. There is a narrative of increasing refinement that runs under the *Lives*. Johnson quotes with approbation Prior's judgement that Denham and Waller 'improved our versification'.[32] Denham ought to be read with 'gratitude' because he 'improved our taste, and advanced our language'.[33] After an 'examination' of Waller's verse that is mostly a catalogue of his deficiencies, Johnson concedes, 'it cannot be denied that he added something to our

[30] Lonsdale, ii. 53. [31] Ibid. iv. 110. [32] Ibid. i. 237. [33] Ibid. 241.

elegance of diction, and something to our propriety of thought'.[34] The arithmetical metaphor is telling: Waller has made his contribution to the progress of 'our' poetry. He and Denham, he says in his life of Dryden, began a poetic 'reformation' that cured poets of their itch for irrational conceits (p. 121). Metaphysical ingenuity was a phase that English poetry had to grow out of. Though Johnson is not consistent on this, he sometimes writes as if poetry, indeed literary English more generally, had been steadily improved over the preceding two centuries. It was conventional in the eighteenth century to believe that different cultural forms had become more polished, more refined, more 'polite' (to use a favoured term of the period) during the seventeenth and eighteenth centuries. The very edition to which Johnson had been asked to contribute his prefaces was evidence of this belief. The booksellers were not expecting prospective purchasers to believe that Granville, Pitt, or Somerville were poets to rank with Dryden and Pope, but they were investing in the idea that, by the late eighteenth century, there existed a respectable body of elegant, sophisticated English poetry.

Dryden is venerated, says Johnson, because 'he refined the language, improved the sentiments, and tuned the numbers of English Poetry' (p. 172). The 'ruggedness' of early seventeenth-century poets such as Donne and Jonson cannot be thought a virtue. Johnson may have confessed some unwilling admiration of Donne's ingenuity in his metaphysical lyrics, but in his 'Pope' he talks of the 'imbecillity' of his satires (p. 397). Dryden, being 'elegant' and 'easy' and 'smooth', is evidently more advanced. In particular he successfully arrived at 'poetical diction', a 'system of words . . . refined from the grossness of domestick use' (p. 172). (It will be just this establishment of 'poetical diction' against which Wordsworth rebels in his Preface to *Lyrical Ballads*, only a couple of decades later.) Dryden rescued English poetry from 'savageness', no less, and made English an appropriate language into which to translate classical verse (p. 173). 'Whatever subjects employed his pen, he was still improving our measures and embellishing our language' (p. 198). When the now forgotten Earl of Roscommon, who translated Horace's *Ars Poetica* and wrote his own poetic *Essay on Translated Verse*, is praised as 'the only correct writer in verse before Addison'[35] the praise is

[34] Ibid. ii. 55. [35] Ibid. 20.

clearly limited. 'He is elegant, but not great.'[36] He is all smoothness and precision: never an inexact rhyme or a hitch in the rhythm. And this is enough to have made him an agent of progress. 'He improved taste, if he did not enlarge knowledge, and may be numbered among the benefactors to English literature.' Johnson never explicitly questions the narrative of refinement, but there is some faint praise. He calls Addison's prose 'the model of the middle style', but expands the judgement in an almost disappointed manner. 'Addison never deviates from the track to snatch a grace; he seeks no ambitious ornaments, and tries no hazardous innovations.'[37] Johnson's sense of improvement is strongest when he is looking at translation. When he examines Pope's individual poems, he delights in *The Rape of the Lock* and *Eloisa to Abelard*, but it is only when he reaches Pope's *Iliad* that he finds English poetry in Pope's debt. 'He cultivated our language with so much diligence and art, that he has left in his *Homer* a treasure of poetical elegances to posterity' (p. 429).

The narrative of improvement was of its age, but Johnson's biographical attention to human and poetic failure goes against this official story. Even his extraordinary prose style carries the energy of contradiction, often mirroring the self-bafflement of one of his authors. Here is a characteristic sentence, describing Swift's increasing isolation in the latter part of his life. 'After the death of Stella, his benevolence was contracted, and his severity exasperated; he drove his acquaintance from his table, and wondered why he was deserted.' The pairings of antitheses and synonyms have the neatness of a rhyming couplet, but the pattern clinches a human contrariness. The bifurcations of Johnson's prose more often describe contradiction than balance, as when he sketches Swift's painful state of mind: 'the rage of neglected pride and the languishment of unsatisfied desire' (p. 344). In 'Savage', these patterns are comic as well as contradictory. 'It was his peculiar happiness, that he scarcely ever found a stranger, whom he did not leave a friend; but it must likewise be added, that he had not often a friend long, without obliging him to become a stranger' (p. 269). '[H]e contented himself with the applause of men of judgement, and was somewhat disposed to exclude all those from the character of men of judgement who did

[36] Ibid. 23. [37] Ibid. iii. 38.

not applaud him' (p. 276). Behind the elegant chiasmus of these sentences (Johnson's favourite *abba* pattern) is an ordinary human nature that we can imagine very well.

It was in the early *Life of Savage* that Johnson developed a kind of mock-verbosity, casting ignoble human behaviour into the form of resounding euphemism. Responding to the accusation that Savage would satirize in print those whom he cultivated as friends, Johnson observes, 'it must be confessed, that Mr. Savage's esteem was no very certain possession' (p. 262). The impersonal circumlocution is all the funnier because we realize that personal observation of Savage lies behind it. Later Johnson explains that a pension from the Queen, though it might have 'kept an exact œconomist from want', was 'very far from being sufficient for Mr. Savage, who had never been accustomed to dismiss any of his appetites without the gratification which they solicited' (p. 285). The periphrasis makes a show of avoiding the vulgar truth: Savage was a spendthrift. This technique is revived in the later *Lives*. Pope's letters 'exhibit a perpetual and unclouded effulgence of general benevolence and particular fondness' (p. 412). The nebulous words mock the poet's disingenuous wordiness. Gray's indolence as a Professor of History who never got round to giving any lectures left the poet 'uneasy at his neglect of duty, and appeasing his uneasiness with designs of reformation, and with a resolution which he believed himself to have made of resigning the office, if he found himself unable to discharge it' (p. 455). The syntax drolly mimics the twists of Gray's pretensions. For the best writers have the most ability to deceive themselves. No wonder that Johnson's eloquently 'mournful narratives' of their lives have proved so entertaining. Johnson would have us see that authors do what we all would do.

NOTE ON THE TEXT

The text is taken from Roger Lonsdale's Oxford University Press edition *The Lives of the Most Eminent English Poets; with Critical Observations on their Works*, 4 vols. (2006). This is based on the 4-volume 1783 edition of *The Lives of the Most Eminent English Poets*, the last to be published in Johnson's lifetime. As Lonsdale argues in his introduction (vol. i., pp. 182-4), it is clear that Johnson himself undertook thorough revision of the previous (1781) edition for this edition. Furthermore, there is evidence from a surviving section of the text marked up for amendment by Johnson that all the revisions for the 1783 edition were authorial.

All footnotes are by Johnson. Asterisks in the text indicate an explanatory note at the back of the book.

The following authors were included in Johnson's original *Lives of the Poets* but are not included in the present selection:

ADDISON
AKENSIDE
BLACKMORE
BROOME
BUTLER
COLLINS
DENHAM
DORSET
DUKE
DYER
FENTON
GARTH
GRANVILLE
HALIFAX
HAMMOND
HUGHES
KING
LYTTELTON
MALLET
OTWAY
PARNELL
PHILIPS, A.
PHILIPS, J.
PITT
POMFRET
PRIOR
ROSCOMMON
ROWE
SHEFFIELD
SHENSTONE
SMITH
SOMERVILE
SPRAT
STEPNEY
THOMSON
TICKELL
WALLER
WALSH
WATTS
WEST
YALDEN
TOUNG

SELECT BIBLIOGRAPHY

Editions and Collections

Fleeman, J. D., ed., *Early Biographical Writings of Dr Johnson* (Farnborough, 1973).
Lonsdale, Roger, ed., *The Lives of the Most Eminent English Poets; with Critical Observations on their Works*, 4 vols. (Oxford, 2006).
Redford, Bruce, ed., *The Letters of Samuel Johnson*, 5 vols. (Oxford, 1992–4).
Tracy, Clarence, ed., *Life of Savage* (Oxford, 1971).

Biography

Bate, W. J., *Samuel Johnson* (New York, 1977).
Boswell, James, *Life of Johnson*, ed. Pat Rogers (Oxford, 1980).
Brack, O. M., and Kelley, Robert E. (eds.), *The Early Biographies of Samuel Johnson* (Iowa City, Iowa, 1974).
De Maria, Robert, *The Life of Samuel Johnson* (Oxford, 1993).
Hill, G. B., ed., *Johnsonian Miscellanies* (Oxford, 1897).

General Criticism

The Age of Johnson: A Scholarly Annual (New York, 1987–).
Bate, W. J., *The Achievement of Samuel Johnson* (Chicago, 1955).
Boulton, James T. (ed.), *Johnson: The Critical Heritage* (London, 1971).
Brown, Joseph Epes, *The Critical Opinions of Samuel Johnson* (New York, 1961).
Clingham, Greg (ed.), *The Cambridge Companion to Samuel Johnson* (Cambridge, 1997).
Damrosch, Leopold, *The Uses of Johnson's Criticism* (Charlottesville, Va., 1976).
Fussell, P., *Samuel Johnson and the Life of Writing* (London, 1972).
Greene, Donald, *Samuel Johnson's Library: An Annotated Guide* (Victoria, BC, 1975).
Grundy, Isobel (ed.), *Samuel Johnson: New Critical Essays* (London, 1984).
Kernan, Alvin, *Printing Technology, Letters and Samuel Johnson* (Princeton, 1987).

Korshin, Paul J. (ed.), *Johnson After Two Hundred Years* (Philadelphia, 1986).
Lipking, Lawrence, *Samuel Johnson. The Life of an Author* (Cambridge, Mass., 1998).
Wimsatt, W. K., *The Prose Style of Samuel Johnson* (New Haven, 1941).

Studies of Johnson's Lives

Folkenfluk, Robert, *Samuel Johnson, Biographer* (Ithaca, NY, 1978).
Kirkley, Harriet, *A Biographer at Work: Samuel Johnson's Notes for the Life of Pope* (Lewisburg, Pa., 2002).
London, April, 'Johnson's Lives and the Genealogy of Late Eighteenth-Century Literary History', in Philip Smallwood (ed.), *Critical Pasts: Writing Criticism, Writing History* (Lewisburg, Pa., 2004).
Lynch, Jack, 'Betwixt Two Ages Cast: Milton, Johnson, and the English Renaissance', *Journal of the History of Ideas*, 61/3 (July 2000).
Maner, Martin, *The Philosophical Biographer: Doubt and Dialectic in Johnson's Lives of the Poets* (Athens, Ga., 1988).
Parke, Catherine, *Samuel Johnson and Biographical Thinking* (Columbia, Mo., 1991).
Parker, Fred, 'Johnson and the *Lives of the Poets*', *Cambridge Quarterly*, 29/4 (2000).
Parrinder, Patrick, *Authors and Authority: English and American Criticism 1750–1990* (London, 1991), ch. 1.
Rogers, Pat, 'Johnson's *Lives* of the Poets and the Biographic Dictionaries', *Review of English Studies*, 31 (1980).
Wheeler, David (ed.), *Domestick Privacies: Samuel Johnson and the Art of Biography* (Lexington, Kentucky, 1987).

Further Reading in Oxford World's Classics

Johnson, Samuel, *The Major Works*, ed. Donald Greene.
—— *Rasselas*, ed. Tom Keymer.

A CHRONOLOGY OF SAMUEL JOHNSON

1709 Samuel Johnson born (7 September, OS; 18, NS) at Lichfield, Staffordshire.

1712 Taken to London to be touched by Queen Anne for 'the Evil' (scrofula). Nathanael Johnson (brother) born.

1717 Enters Lichfield Grammar School.

1726 Visits his cousin, the Revd Cornelius Ford, at Stourbridge, Worcestershire; attends school there.

1728 Enters Pembroke College, Oxford, in October; leaves December 1729.

1731 Michael Johnson (father) dies.

1732 Teaches for some months at Market Bosworth, Leicestershire.

1733 At Birmingham. Translates Lobo's *Voyage to Abyssinia* (published 1735).

1735 Marries Elizabeth Porter (widow of Harry Porter, and mother of Jervis, Joseph, and Lucy Porter).

1736 Opens school at Edial, near Lichfield. Begins *Irene*.

1737 Nathanael Johnson dies. Moves to London (March) with David Garrick.

1738 Begins writing for Edward Cave's *Gentleman's Magazine*; publishes *London: A Poem in Imitation of the Third Satire of Juvenal.*

1739 *Marmor Norfolciense, A Complete Vindication of the Licensers of the Stage* (anti-government pamphlets). 'Life of Boerhaave'; translation of Crousaz's *Commentary* on Pope's *Essay on Man*.

1740 Lives of Admiral Robert Blake, Sir Francis Drake, Jean-Philippe Barretier.

1741–4 'Life of Sydenham'. Contributions to *Harleian Miscellany* and catalogue of the Harleian library. 'Debates in the Senate of Lilliput' and other journalism for the *Gentleman's Magazine. Life of Savage.*

1745 Proposals (abortive) for an edition of Shakespeare. *Miscellaneous Observations on Macbeth.*

1746 Signs contract for *Dictionary*.

1749 *The Vanity of Human Wishes. Irene* performed and published.

1750 Begins *The Rambler* (to 1752).

1752 Elizabeth ('Tetty') Johnson (wife) dies.

1753 Contributes to *The Adventurer*.

1754 Publishes biography of Edward Cave.

1755 *Dictionary of the English Language* published; awarded honorary MA degree by Oxford University.

1758 Begins *The Idler* (to 1760).

1759 Sarah Johnson (mother) dies. *Rasselas*.

1762 Awarded annual pension of £300 by government.

1763 Meets James Boswell.

1764 Founds 'the Club': members include Sir Joshua Reynolds, Oliver Goldsmith, and Edmund Burke.

1765 Edition of Shakespeare published. Meets Mr and Mrs Henry Thrale. Honorary LL D, Trinity College, Dublin.

1766 Severe depression; recovers with help of Mrs Thrale.

1770 *The False Alarm*.

1771 *Thoughts on Falkland's Islands*.

1773 Revised editions of *Dictionary* and Shakespeare published. Tours Scotland (August to November) with Boswell.

1774 Tours Wales with the Thrales. *The Patriot*.

1775 *Journey to the Western Islands of Scotland. Taxation No Tyranny*. Honorary DCL, Oxford. Visits France with the Thrales.

1777 Agreement with booksellers to write prefaces to works of English poets (*The Lives of the Poets*). Unsuccessful campaign to reprieve the Revd William Dodd, condemned to be hanged for forgery.

1779 First four volumes of *Lives of the Poets* published.

1781 Henry Thrale dies. Last six volumes of *Lives* published.

1782 'On the Death of Dr Robert Levet'.

1783 Stroke, temporary loss of speech. Recovers; during winter of 1783–4 ill and depressed.

1784 Dies 13 December. Buried in Westminster Abbey, 20 December.

THE LIVES OF THE POETS

ADVERTISEMENT

THE Booksellers having determined to publish a Body of English Poetry, I was persuaded to promise them a Preface to the Works of each Author; an undertaking, as it was then presented to my mind, not very extensive or difficult.

My purpose was only to have allotted to every Poet an Advertisement, like those which we find in the French Miscellanies,* containing a few dates and a general character; but I have been led beyond my intention, I hope, by the honest desire of giving useful pleasure.

In this minute kind of History, the succession of facts is not easily discovered; and I am not without suspicion that some of Dryden's works are placed in wrong years. I have followed Langbaine,* as the best authority for his plays: and if I shall hereafter obtain a more correct chronology, will publish it; but I do not yet know that my account is erroneous.

Dryden's Remarks on Rymer* have been somewhere printed before. The former edition I have not seen. This was transcribed for the press from his own manuscript.

As this undertaking was occasional and unforeseen, I must be supposed to have engaged in it with less provision of materials than might have been accumulated by longer premeditation. Of the later writers at least I might, by attention and enquiry, have gleaned many particulars, which would have diversified and enlivened my Biography. These omissions, which it is now useless to lament, have been often supplied by the kindness of Mr. STEEVENS* and other friends; and great assistance has been given me by Mr. SPENCE's Collections,* of which I consider the communication as a favour worthy of publick acknowledgement.

COWLEY

THE Life of Cowley, notwithstanding the penury of English biography, has been written by Dr. Sprat,* an author whose pregnancy of imagination and elegance of language have deservedly set him high in the ranks of literature; but his zeal of friendship, or ambition of eloquence, has produced a funeral oration rather than a history: he has given the character, not the life of Cowley; for he writes with so little detail, that scarcely any thing is distinctly known, but all is shewn confused and enlarged through the mist of panegyrick.

ABRAHAM COWLEY was born in the year one thousand six hundred and eighteen. His father was a grocer, whose condition Dr. Sprat conceals under the general appellation of a citizen; and, what would probably not have been less carefully suppressed, the omission of his name in the register of St. Dunstan's parish gives reason to suspect that his father was a sectary.* Whoever he was, he died before the birth of his son, and consequently left him to the care of his mother; whom Wood* represents as struggling earnestly to procure him a literary education, and who, as she lived to the age of eighty, had her solicitude rewarded by seeing her son eminent, and, I hope, by seeing him fortunate, and partaking his prosperity. We know at least, from Sprat's account, that he always acknowledged her care, and justly paid the dues of filial gratitude.

In the window of his mother's apartment lay Spenser's Fairy Queen; in which he very early took delight to read, till, by feeling the charms of verse, he became, as he relates, irrecoverably a poet. Such are the accidents, which, sometimes remembered, and perhaps sometimes forgotten, produce that particular designation of mind, and propensity for some certain science or employment, which is commonly called Genius. The true Genius is a mind of large general powers, accidentally determined to some particular direction. Sir Joshua Reynolds,* the great Painter of the present age, had the first fondness for his art excited by the perusal of Richardson's treatise.

By his mother's solicitation he was admitted into Westminster school, where he was soon distinguished. He was wont, says Sprat, to relate, "That he had this defect in his memory at that time, that his teachers never could bring it to retain the ordinary rules of grammar."

This is an instance of the natural desire of man to propagate a wonder. It is surely very difficult to tell any thing as it was heard, when Sprat could not refrain from amplifying a commodious incident, though the book to which he prefixed his narrative contained its confutation. A memory admitting some things, and rejecting others, an intellectual digestion that concocted the pulp of learning, but refused the husks, had the appearance of an instinctive elegance, of a particular provision made by Nature for literary politeness. But in the author's own honest relation, the marvel vanishes: he was, he says, such "an enemy to all constraint, that his master never could prevail on him to learn the rules without book." He does not tell that he could not learn the rules, but that, being able to perform his exercises without them, and being an "enemy to constraint," he spared himself the labour.

Among the English poets, Cowley, Milton, and Pope, might be said "to lisp in numbers;"* and have given such early proofs, not only of powers of language, but of comprehension of things, as to more tardy minds seems scarcely credible. But of the learned puerilities of Cowley there is no doubt, since a volume of his poems was not only written but printed in his thirteenth year; containing, with other poetical compositions, "The tragical History of Pyramus and Thisbe," written when he was ten years old; and "Constantia and Philetus," written two years after.

While he was yet at school he produced a comedy called "Love's Riddle," though it was not published till he had been some time at Cambridge. This comedy is of the pastoral kind, which requires no acquaintance with the living world, and therefore the time at which it was composed adds little to the wonders of Cowley's minority.

In 1636, he was removed to Cambridge, where he continued his studies with great intenseness; for he is said to have written, while he was yet a young student, the greater part of his Davideis; a work of which the materials could not have been collected without the study of many years, but by a mind of the greatest vigour and activity.

Two years after his settlement at Cambridge he published "Love's Riddle," with a poetical dedication to Sir Kenelm Digby;* of whose acquaintance all his contemporaries seem to have been ambitious; and "Naufragium Joculare," a comedy written in Latin, but without due attention to the ancient models: for it is not loose verse, but mere prose. It was printed, with a dedication in verse to Dr. Comber,* master of the college; but having neither the facility of a popular nor the accuracy of a learned work, it seems to be now universally neglected.

At the beginning of the civil war, as the Prince passed through Cambridge in his way to York, he was entertained with the representation of the "Guardian," a comedy, which Cowley says was neither written nor acted, but rough-drawn by him, and repeated by the scholars. That this comedy was printed during his absence from his country, he appears to have considered as injurious to his reputation; though, during the suppression of the theatres, it was sometimes privately acted with sufficient approbation.

In 1643, being now master of arts, he was, by the prevalence* of the parliament, ejected from Cambridge, and sheltered himself at St. John's College in Oxford;* where, as is said by Wood, he published a satire called "The Puritan and Papist," which was only inserted in the last collection of his works; and so distinguished himself by the warmth of his loyalty, and the elegance of his conversation, that he gained the kindness and confidence of those who attended the King, and amongst others of Lord Falkland,* whose notice cast a lustre on all to whom it was extended.

About the time when Oxford was surrendered to the parliament, he followed the Queen to Paris, where he became secretary to the Lord Jermin,* afterwards Earl of St. Albans, and was employed in such correspondence as the royal cause required, and particularly in cyphering and decyphering the letters that passed between the King and Queen; an employment of the highest confidence and honour. So wide was his province of intelligence, that, for several years, it filled all his days and two or three nights in the week.

In the year 1647, his "Mistress" was published; for he imagined, as he declared in his preface to a subsequent edition, that "poets are scarce thought freemen of their company without paying some duties, or obliging themselves to be true to Love."

This obligation to amorous ditties owes, I believe, its original to the fame of Petrarch, who, in an age rude and uncultivated, by his tuneful homage to his Laura,* refined the manners of the lettered world, and filled Europe with love and poetry. But the basis of all excellence is truth: he that professes love ought to feel its power. Petrarch was a real lover, and Laura doubtless deserved his tenderness.

Of Cowley, we are told by Barnes[1],* who had means enough of information, that, whatever he may talk of his own inflammability, and the variety of characters by which his heart was divided, he in reality was in love but once, and then never had resolution to tell his passion.

This consideration cannot but abate, in some measure, the reader's esteem for the work and the author. To love excellence, is natural; it is natural likewise for the lover to solicit reciprocal regard by an elaborate display of his own qualifications. The desire of pleasing has in different men produced actions of heroism, and effusions of wit; but it seems as reasonable to appear the champion as the poet of an "airy nothing,"* and to quarrel as to write for what Cowley might have learned from his master Pindar to call the "dream of a shadow."*

It is surely not difficult, in the solitude of a college, or in the bustle of the world, to find useful studies and serious employment. No man needs to be so burthened with life as to squander it in voluntary dreams of fictitious occurrences. The man that sits down to suppose himself charged with treason or peculation, and heats his mind to an elaborate purgation of his character from crimes which he was never within the possibility of committing, differs only by the infrequency of his folly from him who praises beauty which he never saw, complains of jealousy which he never felt; supposes himself sometimes invited, and sometimes forsaken; fatigues his fancy, and ransacks his memory, for images which may exhibit the gaiety of hope, or the gloominess of despair, and dresses his imaginary Chloris or Phyllis sometimes in flowers fading as her beauty, and sometimes in gems lasting as her virtues.

At Paris, as secretary to Lord Jermin, he was engaged in transacting things of real importance with real men and real women, and at that time did not much employ his thoughts upon phantoms of gallantry. Some of his letters to Mr. Bennet, afterwards Earl of Arlington, from April to December in 1650, are preserved in "Miscellanea Aulica," a collection of papers published by Brown.* These letters, being written like those of other men whose mind is more on things than words, contribute no otherwise to his reputation than as they shew him to have been above the affectation of unseasonable elegance, and to have known that the business of a statesman can be little forwarded by flowers of rhetorick.

[1] V. Barnesii Anacreontem.

One passage, however, seems not unworthy of some notice. Speaking of the Scotch treaty then in agitation:

"The Scotch treaty," says he, "is the only thing now in which we are vitally concerned; I am one of the last hopers, and yet cannot now abstain from believing, that an agreement will be made: all people upon the place incline to that of union. The Scotch will moderate something of the rigour of their demands; the mutual necessity of an accord is visible, the King is persuaded of it. And to tell you the truth (which I take to be an argument above all the rest), Virgil has told the same thing to that purpose."

This expression from a secretary of the present time would be considered as merely ludicrous, or at most as an ostentatious display of scholarship; but the manners of that time were so tinged with superstition, that I cannot but suspect Cowley of having consulted on this great occasion the Virgilian lots,* and to have given some credit to the answer of his oracle.

Some years afterwards, "business," says Sprat, "passed of course into other hands;" and Cowley, being no longer useful at Paris, was in 1656 sent back into England, that, "under pretence of privacy and retirement, he might take occasion of giving notice of the posture of things in this nation."

Soon after his return to London, he was seized by some messengers of the usurping powers, who were sent out in quest of another man; and, being examined, was put into confinement, from which he was not dismissed without the security of a thousand pounds given by Dr. Scarborow.*

This year he published his poems, with a preface, in which he seems to have inserted something, suppressed in subsequent editions, which was interpreted to denote some relaxation of his loyalty. In this preface he declares, that "his desire had been for some days past, and did still very vehemently continue, to retire himself to some of the American plantations, and to forsake this world for ever."

From the obloquy which the appearance of submission to the usurpers brought upon him, his biographer has been very diligent to clear him, and indeed it does not seem to have lessened his reputation. His wish for retirement we can easily believe to be undissembled; a man harrassed in one kingdom, and persecuted in another, who, after a course of business that employed all his days and half his nights in cyphering and decyphering, comes to his own country and steps into a prison, will be willing enough to retire to some place of quiet, and of safety. Yet let neither our reverence for a genius, nor our pity for a sufferer, dispose us to forget that, if his activity was virtue, his retreat was cowardice.

He then took upon himself the character of Physician, still, according to Sprat, with intention "to dissemble the main design of his coming over," and, as Mr. Wood relates, "complying with the men then in power (which was much taken notice of by the royal party), he obtained an order to be created Doctor of Physick, which being done to his mind (whereby he gained the ill-will of some of his friends), he went into France again, having made a copy of verses on Oliver's death."

This is no favourable representation, yet even in this not much wrong can be discovered. How far he complied with the men in power, is to be enquired before he can be blamed. It is not said that he told them any secrets, or assisted them by intelligence, or any other act. If he only promised to be quiet, that they in whose hands he was might free him from confinement, he did what no law of society prohibits.

The man whose miscarriage in a just cause has put him in the power of his enemy may, without any violation of his integrity, regain his liberty, or preserve his life, by a promise of neutrality: for the stipulation gives the enemy nothing which he had not before; the neutrality of a captive may be always secured by his imprisonment or death. He that is at the disposal of another may not promise to aid him in any injurious act, because no power can compel active obedience. He may engage to do nothing, but not to do ill.

There is reason to think that Cowley promised little. It does not appear that his compliance gained him confidence enough to be trusted without security, for the bond of his bail was never cancelled; nor that it made him think himself secure, for at that dissolution of government, which followed the death of Oliver,* he returned into France, where he resumed his former station, and staid till the Restoration.

"He continued," says his biographer, "under these bonds till the general deliverance;" it is therefore to be supposed, that he did not go to France, and act again for the King, without the consent of his bondsman; that he did not shew his loyalty at the hazard of his friend, but by his friend's permission.

Of the verses on Oliver's death, in which Wood's narrative seems to imply something encomiastick, there has been no appearance. There is a discourse concerning his government, indeed, with verses intermixed, but such as certainly gained its author no friends among the abettors of usurpation.

A doctor of physick however he was made at Oxford, in December 1657; and in the commencement of the Royal Society, of which an account has been published by Dr. Birch,* he appears busy among the experimental philosophers with the title of Doctor Cowley.

There is no reason for supposing that he ever attempted practice; but his preparatory studies have contributed something to the honour of his country. Considering Botany as necessary to a physician, he retired into Kent to gather plants; and as the predominance of a favourite study affects all subordinate operations of the intellect, Botany in the mind of Cowley turned into poetry. He composed in Latin several books on Plants, of which the first and second display the qualities of Herbs, in elegiac verse; the third and fourth the beauties of Flowers in various measures; and in the fifth and sixth, the uses of Trees in heroick numbers.

At the same time were produced from the same university, the two great Poets, Cowley and Milton, of dissimilar genius, of opposite principles; but concurring in the cultivation of Latin poetry, in which the English, till their works and May's poem* appeared, seemed unable to contest the palm with any other of the lettered nations.

If the Latin performances of Cowley and Milton be compared, for May I hold to be superior to both, the advantage seems to lie on the side of Cowley. Milton is generally content to express the thoughts of the ancients in their language; Cowley, without much loss of purity or elegance, accommodates the diction of Rome to his own conceptions.

At the Restoration, after all the diligence of his long service, and with consciousness not only of the merit of fidelity, but of the dignity of great abilities, he naturally expected ample preferments; and, that he might not be forgotten by his own fault, wrote a Song of Triumph.* But this was a time of such general hope, that great numbers were inevitably disappointed; and Cowley found his reward very tediously delayed. He had been promised by both Charles the first and second the Mastership of the Savoy;* but "he lost it," says Wood, "by certain persons, enemies to the Muses."

The neglect of the court was not his only mortification; having, by such alteration as he thought proper, fitted his old Comedy of the Guardian for the stage, he produced it to the publick under the title of the "Cutter of Coleman-street." It was treated on the stage with great severity, and was afterwards censured as a satire on the king's party.

Mr. Dryden, who went with Mr. Sprat to the first exhibition, related to Mr. Dennis, "that when they told Cowley how little favour had been shewn him, he received the news of his ill success, not with so much firmness as might have been expected from so great a man."

What firmness they expected, or what weakness Cowley discovered, cannot be known. He that misses his end will never be as much pleased as he that attains it, even when he can impute no part of his failure to himself; and when the end is to please the multitude, no man perhaps has a right, in things admitting of gradation and comparison, to throw the whole blame upon his judges, and totally to exclude diffidence and shame by a haughty consciousness of his own excellence.

For the rejection of this play, it is difficult now to find the reason: it certainly has, in a very great degree, the power of fixing attention and exciting merriment. From the charge of disaffection he exculpates himself in his preface, by observing how unlikely it is that, having followed the royal family through all their distresses, "he should chuse the time of their restoration to begin a quarrel with them." It appears, however, from the Theatrical Register of Downes the prompter,* to have been popularly considered as a satire on the Royalists.

That he might shorten this tedious suspense, he published his pretensions and his discontent, in an ode called "The Complaint;" in which he styles himself the *melancholy* Cowley. This met with the usual fortune of complaints, and seems to have excited more contempt than pity.

These unlucky incidents are brought, maliciously enough, together in some stanzas, written about that time, on the choice of a laureat; a mode of satire, by which, since it was first introduced by Suckling,* perhaps every generation of poets has been teazed:

> Savoy-missing Cowley came into the court,
> Making apologies for his bad play;

Every one gave him so good a report,
That Apollo gave heed to all he could say;
Nor would he have had, 'tis thought, a rebuke,
Unless he had done some notable folly;
Writ verses unjustly in praise of Sam Tuke,
Or printed his pitiful Melancholy.

His vehement desire of retirement now came again upon him. "Not finding," says the morose Wood, "that preferment conferred upon him which he expected, while others for their money carried away most places, he retired discontented into Surrey."

"He was now," says the courtly Sprat, "weary of the vexations and formalities of an active condition. He had been perplexed with a long compliance to foreign manners. He was satiated with the arts of a court; which sort of life, though his virtue made it innocent to him, yet nothing could make it quiet. Those were the reasons that moved him to follow the violent inclination of his own mind, which, in the greatest throng of his former business, had still called upon him, and represented to him the true delights of solitary studies, of temperate pleasures, and a moderate revenue below the malice and flatteries of fortune."

So differently are things seen, and so differently are they shown; but actions are visible, though motives are secret. Cowley certainly retired; first to Barn-elms, and afterwards to Chertsey, in Surrey. He seems, however, to have lost part of his dread of the [1]*hum of men*. He thought himself now safe enough from intrusion, without the defence of mountains and oceans; and, instead of seeking shelter in America, wisely went only so far from the bustle of life as that he might easily find his way back, when solitude should grow tedious. His retreat was at first but slenderly accommodated; yet he soon obtained, by the interest of the Earl of St. Albans and the duke of Buckingham,* such a lease of the Queen's lands as afforded him an ample income.

By the lover of virtue and of wit it will be solicitously asked, if he now was happy. Let them peruse one of his letters accidentally preserved by Peck, which I recommend to the consideration of all that may hereafter pant for solitude.

[1] L'Allegro of Milton.

"To Dr. Thomas Sprat*

Chertsey, 21 May, 1665.

The first night that I came hither I caught so great a cold, with a defluxion of rheum, as made me keep my chamber ten days. And, two after, had such a bruise on my ribs with a fall, that I am yet unable to move or turn myself in my bed. This is my personal fortune here to begin with. And, besides, I can get no money from my tenants, and have my meadows eaten up every night by cattle put in by my neighbours. What this signifies, or may come to in time, God knows; if it be ominous, it can end in nothing less than hanging. Another misfortune has been, and stranger than all the rest, that you have broke your word with me, and failed to come, even though you told Mr. Bois that you would. This is what they call *Monstri simile*.* I do hope to recover my late hurt so farre within five or six days (though it be uncertain yet whether I shall ever recover it) as to walk about again. And then, methinks, you and I and *the Dean** might be very merry upon S. Anne's Hill. You might very conveniently come hither the way of Hampton Town, lying there one night. I write this in pain, and can say no more: *Verbum sapienti*."*

He did not long enjoy the pleasure or suffer the uneasiness of solitude; for he died at the Porch-house[1] in Chertsey in 1667, in the 49th year of his age.

He was buried with great pomp near Chaucer and Spenser; and king Charles pronounced, "That Mr. Cowley had not left a better man behind him in England." He is represented by Dr. Sprat as the most amiable of mankind; and this posthumous praise may be safely credited, as it has never been contradicted by envy or by faction.

Such are the remarks and memorials which I have been able to add to the narrative of Dr. Sprat; who, writing when the feuds of the civil war were yet recent, and the minds of either party easily irritated, was obliged to pass over many transactions in general expressions, and to leave curiosity often unsatisfied. What he did not tell, cannot however now be known. I must therefore recommend the perusal of his work, to which my narration can be considered only as a slender supplement.

COWLEY, like other poets who have written with narrow views, and, instead of tracing intellectual pleasure to its natural sources in

[1] Now in the possession of Mr. Clarke, Alderman of London.

the mind of man, paid their court to temporary prejudices, has been at one time too much praised, and too much neglected at another.

Wit, like all other things subject by their nature to the choice of man, has its changes and fashions, and at different times takes different forms. About the beginning of the seventeenth century appeared a race of writers that may be termed the metaphysical poets;* of whom, in a criticism on the works of Cowley, it is not improper to give some account.

The metaphysical poets were men of learning, and to shew their learning was their whole endeavour; but, unluckily resolving to shew it in rhyme, instead of writing poetry, they only wrote verses, and very often such verses as stood the trial of the finger better than of the ear; for the modulation was so imperfect, that they were only found to be verses by counting the syllables.

If the father of criticism* has rightly denominated poetry τέχνη μιμητική, *an imitative art*, these writers will, without great wrong, lose their right to the name of poets; for they cannot be said to have imitated any thing; they neither copied nature nor life; neither painted the forms of matter, nor represented the operations of intellect.

Those, however who deny them to be poets, allow them to be wits. Dryden confesses* of himself and his contemporaries, that they fall below Donne in wit, but maintains that they surpass him in poetry.

If Wit be well described by Pope, as being, "that which has been often thought, but was never before so well expressed,"* they certainly never attained, nor ever sought it; for they endeavoured to be singular in their thoughts, and were careless of their diction. But Pope's account of wit is undoubtedly erroneous: he depresses it below its natural dignity, and reduces it from strength of thought to happiness of language.

If by a more noble and more adequate conception that be considered as Wit, which is at once natural and new, that which, though not obvious, is, upon its first production, acknowledged to be just; if it be that, which he that never found it, wonders how he missed; to wit of this kind the metaphysical poets have seldom risen. Their thoughts are often new, but seldom natural; they are not obvious, but neither are they just; and the reader, far from wondering that he missed them, wonders more frequently by what perverseness of industry they were ever found.

But Wit, abstracted from its effects upon the hearer, may be more rigorously and philosophically considered as a kind of *discordia concors*;* a combination of dissimilar images, or discovery of occult resemblances in things apparently unlike. Of wit, thus defined, they have more than enough. The most heterogeneous ideas are yoked by violence together; nature and art are ransacked for illustrations, comparisons, and allusions; their learning instructs, and their subtilty surprises; but the reader commonly thinks his improvement dearly bought, and, though he sometimes admires, is seldom pleased.

From this account of their compositions it will be readily inferred, that they were not successful in representing or moving the affections. As they were wholly employed on something unexpected and surprising, they had no regard to that uniformity of sentiment which enables us to conceive and to excite the pains and the pleasure of other minds: they never enquired what, on any occasion, they should have said or done; but wrote rather as beholders than partakers of human nature; as Beings looking upon good and evil, impassive and at leisure; as Epicurean deities* making remarks on the actions of men, and the vicissitudes of life, without interest and without emotion. Their courtship was void of fondness, and their lamentation of sorrow. Their wish was only to say what they hoped had been never said before.

Nor was the sublime more within their reach than the pathetick; for they never attempted that comprehension and expanse of thought which at once fills the whole mind, and of which the first effect is sudden astonishment, and the second rational admiration. Sublimity is produced by aggregation, and littleness by dispersion. Great thoughts are always general, and consist in positions not limited by exceptions, and in descriptions not descending to minuteness. It is with great propriety that Subtlety, which in its original import means exility of particles, is taken in its metaphorical meaning for nicety of distinction. Those writers who lay on the watch for novelty could have little hope of greatness; for great things cannot have escaped former observation. Their attempts were always analytick; they broke every image into fragments: and could no more represent, by their slender conceits and laboured particularities, the prospects of nature, or the scenes of life, than he, who dissects a sun-beam with a prism, can exhibit the wide effulgence of a summer noon.

What they wanted however of the sublime, they endeavoured to supply by hyperbole; their amplification had no limits; they left not only reason but fancy behind them; and produced combinations of confused magnificence, that not only could not be credited, but could not be imagined.

Yet great labour, directed by great abilities, is never wholly lost: if they frequently threw away their wit upon false conceits, they likewise sometimes struck out unexpected truth: if their conceits were far-fetched, they were often worth the carriage. To write on their plan, it was at least necessary to read and think. No man could be born a metaphysical poet, nor assume the dignity of a writer, by descriptions copied from descriptions, by imitations borrowed from imitations, by traditional imagery, and hereditary similies, by readiness of rhyme, and volubility of syllables.

In perusing the works of this race of authors, the mind is exercised either by recollection or inquiry; either something already learned is to be retrieved, or something new is to be examined. If their greatness seldom elevates, their acuteness often surprises; if the imagination is not always gratified, at least the powers of reflection and comparison are employed; and in the mass of materials which ingenious absurdity has thrown together, genuine wit and useful knowledge may be sometimes found, buried perhaps in grossness of expression, but useful to those who know their value; and such as, when they are expanded to perspicuity, and polished to elegance, may give lustre to works which have more propriety though less copiousness of sentiment.

This kind of writing, which was, I believe, borrowed from Marino* and his followers, had been recommended by the example of Donne, a man of very extensive and various knowledge; and by Jonson, whose manner resembled that of Donne more in the ruggedness* of his lines than in the cast of his sentiments.

When their reputation was high, they had undoubtedly more imitators, than time has left behind. Their immediate successors, of whom any remembrance can be said to remain, were Suckling, Waller, Denham, Cowley, Cleiveland, and Milton. Denham and Waller sought another way to fame, by improving the harmony of our numbers. Milton tried the metaphysick style only in his lines upon Hobson the Carrier.* Cowley adopted it, and excelled his predecessors, having as much sentiment, and more musick. Suckling neither improved versification, nor abounded in conceits.

The fashionable style remained chiefly with Cowley; Suckling could not reach it, and Milton disdained it.

Critical Remarks are not easily understood without examples; and I have therefore collected instances of the modes of writing by which this species of poets, for poets they were called by themselves and their admirers, was eminently distinguished.

As the authors of this race were perhaps more desirous of being admired than understood, they sometimes drew their conceits from recesses of learning not very much frequented by common readers of poetry. Thus Cowley on *Knowledge*:

> The sacred tree midst the fair orchard grew;
> The phœnix Truth did on it rest,
> And built his perfum'd nest,
> That right Porphyrian tree which did true logick shew.
> Each leaf did learned notions give,
> And th' apples were demonstrative:
> So clear their colour and divine,
> The very shade they cast did other lights outshine.*

On Anacreon continuing a lover in his old age:

> Love was with thy life entwin'd,
> Close as heat with fire is join'd,
> A powerful brand prescrib'd the date
> Of thine, like Meleager's fate.
> Th' antiperistasis of age
> More enflam'd thy amorous rage.*

In the following verses we have an allusion to a Rabbinical opinion concerning Manna:

> Variety I ask not: give me one
> To live perpetually upon.
> The person Love does to us fit,
> Like manna, has the taste of all in it.*

Thus *Donne* shews his medicinal knowledge in some encomiastic verses:

> In every thing there naturally grows
> A Balsamum to keep it fresh and new,
> If 'twere not injur'd by extrinsique blows;

Your youth and beauty are this balm in you.
  But you, of learning and religion,
And virtue and such ingredients, have made
  A mithridate, whose operation
Keeps off, or cures what can be done or said.*

Though the following lines of Donne, on the last night of the year, have something in them too scholastick, they are not inelegant:

This twilight of two years, not past nor next,
  Some emblem is of me, or I of this,
Who, meteor-like, of stuff and form perplext,
  Whose what and where, in disputation is,
  If I should call me any thing, should miss.

I sum the years and me, and find me not
  Debtor to th' old, nor creditor to th' new,
That cannot say, my thanks I have forgot,
  Nor trust I this with hopes; and yet scarce true
  This bravery is, since these times shew'd me you.*
DONNE.

Yet more abstruse and profound is *Donne's* reflection upon Man as a Microcosm:

If men be worlds, there is in every one
Something to answer in some proportion
All the world's riches: and in good men, this
Virtue, our form's form, and our soul's soul is.*

OF thoughts so far-fetched, as to be not only unexpected, but unnatural, all their books are full.

To a lady, who wrote poesies for rings.

They, who above do various circles find,
Say, like a ring th' æquator heaven does bind.
When heaven shall be adorn'd by thee,
(Which then more heaven than 'tis, will be)
'Tis thou must write the poesy there,
For it wanteth one as yet,
Though the sun pass through't twice a year,
The sun, which is esteem'd the god of wit.*
COWLEY.

The difficulties which have been raised about identity in philosophy, are by Cowley with still more perplexity applied to Love:

Five years ago (says story) I lov'd you,
For which you call me most inconstant now;
Pardon me, madam, you mistake the man;
For I am not the same that I was then;
No flesh is now the same 'twas then in me,
And that my mind is chang'd yourself may see.

The same thoughts to retain still, and intents,
Were more inconstant far; for accidents
Must of all things most strangely inconstant prove,
If from one subject they t'another move:
My members then, the father members were
From whence these take their birth, which now are here.
If then this body love what th'other did,
'Twere incest, which by nature is forbid.*

The love of different women is, in geographical poetry, compared to travels through different countries:

Hast thou not found, each woman's breast
(The lands where thou hast travelled)
Either by savages possest,
Or wild, and uninhabited?
What joy could'st take, or what repose,
In countries so uncivilis'd as those?

Lust, the scorching dog star, here
Rages with immoderate heat;
Whilst Pride, the rugged Northern Bear,
In others makes the cold too great.
And where these are temperate known,
The soil's all barren sand, or rocky stone.*

COWLEY.

A lover, burnt up by his affection, is compared to Egypt:

The fate of Egypt I sustain,
And never feel the dew of rain,
From clouds which in the head appear;
But all my too much moisture owe
To overflowings of the heart below.*

COWLEY.

The lover supposes his lady acquainted with the ancient laws of augury and rites of sacrifice:

And yet this death of mine, I fear,
Will ominous to her appear:
  When sound in every other part,
Her sacrifice is found without an heart.
  For the last tempest of my death
Shall sigh out that too, with my breath.*

That the chaos was harmonised, has been recited of old; but whence the different sounds arose, remained for a modern to discover:

Th' ungovern'd parts no correspondence knew,
An artless war from thwarting motions grew;
Till they to number and fixt rules were brought,
Water and air he for the Tenor chose,
Earth made the Base, the Treble flame arose.*
COWLEY.

The tears of lovers are always of great poetical account; but Donne has extended them into worlds. If the lines are not easily understood, they may be read again.

On a round ball
A workman, that hath copies by, can lay
An Europe, Afric, and an Asia,
And quickly make that, which was nothing, all
  So doth each tear,
  Which thee doth wear,
A globe, yea world, by that impression grow,
Till thy tears mixt with mine do overflow
This world, by waters sent from thee my heaven dissolved so.*

On reading the following lines, the reader may perhaps cry out—*Confusion worse confounded.*

Here lies a she sun, and a he moon here,
  She gives the best light to his sphere,
  Or each is both, and all, and so
They unto one another nothing owe.*
DONNE.

Who but Donne would have thought that a good man is a telescope?

Though God be our true glass, through which we see
All, since the being of all things is he,
Yet are the trunks, which do to us derive
Things, in proportion fit, by perspective
Deeds of good men; for by their living here,
Virtues, indeed remote, seem to be near.*

Who would imagine it possible that in a very few lines so many remote ideas could be brought together?

Since 'tis my doom, Love's undershrieve,
  Why this reprieve?
Why doth my She Advowson fly
  Incumbency?
To sell thyself dost thou intend
  By candle's end,
And hold the contrast thus in doubt,
  Life's taper out?
Think but how soon the market fails,
Your sex lives faster than the males;
As if to measure age's span,
The sober Julian were th' acount of man,
Whilst you live by the fleet Gregorian.*

CLEIVELAND.

OF enormous and disgusting hyberboles, these may be examples:

By every wind, that comes this way,
Send me at least a sigh or two,
Such and so many I'll repay
As shall themselves make winds to get to you.*

COWLEY.

In tears I'll waste these eyes,
By Love so vainly fed;
So lust of old the Deluge punished.*

COWLEY.

All arm'd in brass the richest dress of war,
(A dismal glorious fight) he shone afar.
The sun himself started with sudden fright,
To see his beams return so dismal bright.*

COWLEY.

An universal consternation:

His bloody eyes he hurls round, his sharp paws
Tear up the ground; then runs he wild about,
Lashing his angry tail and roaring out.
Beasts creep into their dens, and tremble there;
Trees, though no wind is stirring, shake with fear;
Silence and horror fill the place around:
Echo itself dares scarce repeat the sound.*

COWLEY.

THEIR fictions were often violent and unnatural.

Of his Mistress bathing:

The fish around her crouded, as they do
To the false light that treacherous fishers shew,
And all with as much ease might taken be,
As she at first took me:
For ne'er did light so clear
Among the waves appear,
Though every night the sun himself set there.*

COWLEY.

The poetical effect of a Lover's name upon glass:

My name engrav'd herein
Doth contribute my firmness to this glass;
Which, ever since that charm, hath been
As hard as that which grav'd it was.*

DONNE.

THEIR conceits were sometimes slight and trifling.

On an inconstant woman:

He enjoys thy calmy sunshine now,
And no breath stirring hears,
In the clear heaven of thy brow,
No smallest cloud appears.
He sees thee gentle, fair and gay,
And trusts the faithless April of thy May.*

COWLEY.

Upon a paper written with the juice of lemon, and read by the fire:

Nothing yet in thee is seen;
But when a genial heat warms thee within,
A new-born wood of various lines there grows;
Here buds an L, and there a B,
Here sprouts a V, and there a T,
And all the flourishing letters stand in rows.*
COWLEY.

As they sought only for novelty, they did not much enquire whether their allusions were to things high or low, elegant or gross; whether they compared the little to the great, or the great to the little.

Physick and Chirurgery for a Lover.

Gently, ah gently, madam, touch
The wound, which you yourself have made;
That pain must needs be very much,
Which makes me of your hand afraid.
Cordials of pity give me now,
For I too weak for purgings grow.*
COWLEY.

The World and a Clock.

Mahol, th' inferior world's fantastic face,
Through all the turns of matter's maze did trace;
Great Nature's well-set clock in pieces took;
On all the springs and smallest wheels did look
Of life and motion; and with equal art
Made up again the whole of every part.*
COWLEY.

A coal-pit has not often found its poet; but, that it may not want its due honour, Cleiveland has paralleled it with the Sun:

The moderate value of our guiltless ore
Makes no man atheist, nor no woman whore;
Yet why should hallow'd vestal's sacred shrine
Deserve more honour than a flaming mine?
These pregnant wombs of heat would fitter be
Than a few embers, for a deity.
Had he our pits, the Persian would admire

No sun, but warm's devotion at our fire:
He'd leave the trotting whipster, and prefer
Our profound Vulcan 'bove that waggoner.
For wants he heat, or light? or would have store
Or both? 'tis here: and what can suns give more?
Nay, what's the sun but, in a different name,
A coal-pit rampant, or a mine on flame!
Then let this truth reciprocally run,
The sun's heaven's coalery, and coals our sun.*

Death, a Voyage:

No family
Ere rigg'd a soul for heaven's discovery,
With whom more venturers might boldly dare
Venture their stakes, with him in joy to share.*
DONNE.

THEIR thoughts and expressions were sometimes grossly absurd, and such as no figures or licence can reconcile to the understanding.

A Lover neither dead nor alive:

Then down I laid my head,
Down on cold earth; and for a while was dead,
And my freed soul to a strange somewhere fled:
Ah, sottish soul, said I,
When back to its cage again I saw it fly:
Fool to resume her broken chain!
And row her galley here again!
Fool, to that body to return
Where it condemn'd and destin'd is to burn!
Once dead, how can it be,
Death should a thing so pleasant seem to thee,
That thou should'st come to live it o'er again in me?*
COWLEY.

A Lover's heart, a hand grenado.

Wo to her stubborn heart, if once mine come
Into the self-same room,
'Twill tear and blow up all within,

Like a grenado shot into a magazin.
Then shall Love keep the ashes, and torn parts,
Of both our broken hearts:
Shall out of both one new one make;
From her's th' allay; from mine, the metal take.*

COWLEY.

The poetical Propagation of Light:

The Prince's favour is diffus'd o'er all,
From which all fortunes, names, and natures fall;
Then from those wombs of stars, the Bride's bright eyes,
At every glance a constellation flies,
And sowes the court with stars, and doth prevent
In light and power, the all-ey'd firmament:
First her eye kindles other ladies' eyes,
Then from their beams their jewels lustres rise;
And from their jewels torches do take fire,
And all is warmth, and light, and good desire.*

DONNE.

THEY were in very little care to clothe their notions with elegance of dress, and therefore miss the notice and the praise which are often gained by those, who think less, but are more diligent to adorn their thoughts.

That a mistress beloved is fairer in idea than in reality, is by Cowley thus expressed:

Thou in my fancy dost much higher stand,
Than women can be plac'd by Nature's hand;
And I must needs, I'm sure, a loser be,
To change thee, as thou'rt there, for very thee.*

That prayer and labour should co-operate, are thus taught by Donne:

In none but us, are such mixt engines found,
As hands of double office: for the ground
We till with them; and them to heaven we raise;
Who prayerless labours, or without this, prays,
Doth but one half, that's none.*

By the same author, a common topick, the danger of procrastination, is thus illustrated:

—That which I should have begun
In my youth's morning, now late must be done;
And I, as giddy travellers must do,
Which stray or sleep all day, and having lost
Light and strength, dark and tir'd must then ride post.*

All that Man has to do is to live and die; the sum of humanity is comprehended by Donne in the following lines:

Think in how poor a prison thou didst lie;
After, enabled but to suck and cry.
Think, when 'twas grown to most, 'twas a poor inn,
A province pack'd up in two yards of skin,
And that usurp'd, or threaten'd with a rage
Of sicknesses, or their true mother, age.
But think that death hath now enfranchis'd thee;
Thou hast thy expansion now, and liberty;
Think, that a rusty piece discharg'd is flown
In pieces, and the bullet is his own,
And freely flies: this to thy soul allow,
Think thy shell broke, think thy soul hatch'd but now.*

THEY were sometimes indelicate and disgusting. Cowley thus apostrophises beauty:

—Thou tyrant, which leav'st no man free!
Thou subtle thief, from whom nought safe can be!
Thou murtherer, which hast kill'd, and devil, which would'st
damn me.*

Thus he addresses his Mistress:

Thou who, in many a propriety,
So truly art the sun to me,
Add one more likeness, which I'm sure you can,
And let me and my sun beget a man.*

Thus he represents the meditations of a Lover:

Though in thy thoughts scarce any tracts have been
So much as of original sin,
Such charms thy beauty wears as might

Desires in dying confest saints excite.
  Thou with strange adultery
Dost in each breast a brothel keep;
  Awake, all men do lust for thee,
And some enjoy thee when they sleep.*

The true taste of Tears:

Hither with crystal vials, lovers, come,
  And take my tears, which are Love's wine,
And try your mistress' tears at home;
  For all are false, that taste not just like mine.*

DONNE.

This is yet more indelicate:

As the sweet sweat of roses in a still,
As that which from chaf'd musk-cat's pores doth trill,
As the almighty balm of th' early East,
Such are the sweet drops of my mistress' breast.
And on her neck her skin such lustre sets,
They seem no sweat-drops, but pearl coronets:
Rank sweaty froth thy mistress' brow defiles.*

DONNE.

THEIR expressions sometimes raise horror, when they intend perhaps to be pathetic:

As men in hell are from diseases free,
  So from all other ills am I,
  Free from their known formality:
But all pains eminently lie in thee.*

COWLEY.

THEY were not always strictly curious, whether the opinions from which they drew their illustrations were true; it was enough that they were popular. Bacon remarks, that some falsehoods are continued by tradition, because they supply commodious allusions.

It gave a piteous groan, and so it broke;
In vain it something would have spoke:
The love within too strong for 't was,
Like poison put into a Venice-glass.*

COWLEY.

In forming descriptions, they looked out not for images, but for conceits. Night has been a common subject, which poets have contended to adorn. Dryden's Night* is well known; Donne's is as follows:

Thou seest me here at midnight, now all rest:
Time's dead low-water; when all minds divest
To-morrow's business, when the labourers have
Such rest in bed, that their last church-yard grave,
Subject to change, will scarce be a type of this,
Now when the client, whose last hearing is
To-morrow, sleeps; when the condemned man,
Who when he opes his eyes, must shut them then
Again by death, although sad watch he keep,
Doth practise dying by a little sleep,
Thou at this midnight seest me.*

It must be however confessed of these writers, that if they are upon common subjects often unnecessarily and unpoetically subtle; yet where scholastick speculation can be properly admitted, their copiousness and acuteness may justly be admired. What Cowley has written upon Hope, shews an unequalled fertility of invention:

Hope, whose weak being ruin'd is,
Alike if it succeed, and if it miss;
Whom good or ill does equally confound,
And both the horns of Fate's dilemma wound.
Vain shadow, which dost vanish quite,
Both at full noon and perfect night!
The stars have not a possibility
Of blessing thee;
If things then from their end we happy call,
'Tis Hope is the most hopeless thing of all.
Hope, thou bold taster of delight,
Who, whilst thou should'st but taste, devour'st it quite!
Thou bring'st us an estate, yet leav'st us poor,
By clogging it with legacies before!
The joys which we entire should wed,
Come deflower'd virgins to our bed;
Good fortunes without gain imported be,
Such mighty custom's paid to thee:

For joy, like wine, kept close does better taste;
If it take air before, its spirits waste.*

To the following comparison of a man that travels, and his wife that stays at home, with a pair of compasses, it may be doubted whether absurdity or ingenuity has the better claim:

Our two souls therefore, which are one,
  Though I must go, endure not yet
A breach, but an expansion,
  Like gold to airy thinness beat.

If they be two, they are two so
  As stiff twin-compasses are two,
Thy soul the fixt foot, makes no show
  To move, but doth, if th' other do.

And though it in the centre sit,
  Yet when the other far doth roam,
It leans, and hearkens after it,
  And grows erect, as that comes home.

Such wilt thou be to me, who must
  Like th' other foot, obliquely run.
Thy firmness makes my circle just,
  And makes me end where I begun.*

DONNE.

In all these examples it is apparent, that whatever is improper or vicious, is produced by a voluntary deviation from nature in pursuit of something new and strange; and that the writers fail to give delight, by their desire of exciting admiration.

HAVING thus endeavoured to exhibit a general representation of the style and sentiments of the metaphysical poets, it is now proper to examine particularly the works of Cowley, who was almost the last of that race, and undoubtedly the best.

His Miscellanies contain a collection of short compositions, written some as they were dictated by a mind at leisure, and some as they were called forth by different occasions; with great variety of style and sentiment, from burlesque levity to awful grandeur. Such an assemblage of diversified excellence no other poet has hitherto afforded. To choose the best, among many good, is one of the most hazardous attempts of criticism. I know not whether Scaliger himself has persuaded many readers to join with him in his preference of the two favourite odes, which he estimates in his raptures at the value of a kingdom. I will however venture to recommend Cowley's first piece, which ought to be inscribed *To my muse*, for want of which the second couplet is without reference. When the title is added, there will still remain a defect; for every piece ought to contain in itself whatever is necessary to make it intelligible. Pope has some epitaphs without names; which are therefore epitaphs to be let, occupied indeed for the present, but hardly appropriated.

The ode on Wit is almost without a rival. It was about the time of Cowley that *Wit*, which had been till then used for *Intellection*, in contradistinction to *Will*, took the meaning, whatever it be, which it now bears.

Of all the passages in which poets have exemplified their own precepts, none will easily be found of greater excellence than that in which Cowley condemns exuberance of Wit:

> Yet 'tis not to adorn and gild each part,
>   That shews more cost than art.
> Jewels at nose and lips but ill appear;
>   Rather than all things wit, let none be there.
>   Several lights will not be seen,
>   If there be nothing else between.
> Men doubt, because they stand so thick i' th' sky,
> If those be stars which paint the galaxy.*

In his verses to lord Falkland,* whom every man of his time was proud to praise, there are, as there must be in all Cowley's compositions, some striking thoughts; but they are not well wrought. His elegy on Sir Henry Wotton* is vigorous and happy, the series of thoughts is easy and natural, and the conclusion, though a little weakened by the intrusion of Alexander, is elegant and forcible.

It may be remarked, that in this Elegy, and in most of his encomiastic poems, he has forgotten or neglected to name his heroes.

In his poem on the death of Hervey,* there is much praise, but little passion, a very just and ample delineation of such virtues as a studious privacy admits, and such intellectual excellence as a mind not yet called forth to action can display. He knew how to distinguish, and how to commend the qualities of his companion; but when he wishes to make us weep, he forgets to weep himself, and diverts his sorrow by imagining how his crown of bays, if he had it, would *crackle* in the *fire*. It is the odd fate of this thought to be worse for being true. The bay-leaf crackles remarkably as it burns; as therefore this property was not assigned it by chance, the mind must be thought sufficiently at ease that could attend to such minuteness of physiology. But the power of Cowley is not so much to move the affections, as to exercise the understanding.

The *Chronicle* is a composition unrivalled and alone: such gaiety of fancy, such facility of expression, such varied similitude, such a succession of images, and such a dance of words, it is vain to expect except from Cowley. His strength always appears in his agility; his volatility is not the flutter of a light, but the bound of an elastick mind. His levity never leaves his learning behind it; the moralist, the politician, and the critick, mingle their influence even in this airy frolick of genius. To such a performance Suckling could have brought the gaiety, but not the knowledge; Dryden could have supplied the knowledge, but not the gaiety.

The verses to Davenant,* which are vigorously begun, and happily concluded, contain some hints of criticism very justly conceived and happily expressed. Cowley's critical abilities have not been sufficiently observed: the few decisions and remarks which his prefaces and his notes on the Davideis supply, were at that time accessions to English literature, and shew such skill as raises our wish for more examples.

The lines from Jersey are a very curious and pleasing specimen of the familiar descending to the burlesque.

His two metrical disquisitions* *for* and *against* Reason, are no mean specimens of metaphysical poetry. The stanzas against knowledge produce little conviction. In those which are intended to exalt the human faculties, Reason has its proper task assigned it; that of judging, not of things revealed, but of the reality of revelation. In the verses *for* Reason is a passage which Bentley,* in the only English verses which he is known to have written, seems to have copied, though with the inferiority of an imitator.

> The holy Book like the eighth sphere does shine
> With thousand lights of truth divine,
> So numberless the stars that to our eye
> It makes all but one galaxy:
> Yet Reason must assist too; for in seas
> So vast and dangerous as these,

> Our course by stars above we cannot know
> Without the compass too below,

After this says Bentley:

> Who travels in religious jars,
> Truth mix'd with error, clouds with rays,
> With Whiston wanting pyx and stars,
> In the wide ocean sinks or strays.

Cowley seems to have had, what Milton is believed to have wanted, the skill to rate his own performances by their just value, and has therefore closed his Miscellanies with the verses upon Crashaw, which apparently excel all that have gone before them, and in which there are beauties which common authors may justly think not only above their attainment, but above their ambition.

To the Miscellanies succeed the *Anacreontiques*, or paraphrastical translations of some little poems, which pass, however justly, under the name of Anacreon. Of those songs dedicated to festivity and gaiety, in which even the morality is voluptuous, and which teach nothing but the enjoyment of the present day, he has given rather a pleasing than a faithful representation, having retained their spriteliness, but lost their simplicity. The Anacreon of Cowley, like the Homer of Pope, has admitted the decoration of some modern graces, by which he is undoubtedly made more amiable to common readers, and perhaps, if they would honestly declare their own perceptions, to far the greater part of those whom courtesy and ignorance are content to style the Learned.

These little pieces will be found more finished in their kind than any other of Cowley's works. The diction shews nothing of the mould of time, and the sentiments are at no great distance from our present habitudes of thought. Real mirth must be always natural, and nature is uniform. Men have been wise in very different modes; but they have always laughed the same way.

Levity of thought naturally produced familiarity of language, and the familiar part of language continues long the same: the dialogue of comedy, when it is transcribed from popular manners and real life, is read from age to age with equal pleasure. The artifice of inversion, by which the established order of words is changed, or of innovation, by which new words or new meanings of words are introduced, is practised, not by those who talk to be understood, but by those who write to be admired.

The Anacreontiques therefore of Cowley give now all the pleasure which they ever gave. If he was formed by nature for one kind of writing more than for another, his power seems to have been greatest in the familiar and the festive.

The next class of his poems is called *The Mistress*, of which it is not necessary to select any particular pieces for praise or censure. They have all the same beauties and faults, and nearly in the same proportion. They are written with exuberance of wit, and with copiousness of learning; and it is truly asserted by Sprat, that the plenitude of the writer's knowledge flows in upon his page, so that the reader is commonly surprised into some improvement. But, considered as the verses of a lover, no man that has ever loved will much commend them. They are neither courtly nor pathetick, have neither gallantry nor fondness. His praises are too far-sought, and too hyperbolical, either to express love, or to excite it: every stanza is crouded with darts and flames, with wounds and death, with mingled souls, and with broken hearts.

The principal artifice by which *The Mistress* is filled with conceits is very copiously displayed by Addison.* Love is by Cowley, as by other poets, expressed metaphorically by flame and fire; and that which is true of real fire is said of love, or figurative fire, the same word in the same sentence retaining both significations. Thus, "observing the cold regard of his mistress's eyes, and at the same time their power of producing love in him, he considers them as burning-glasses made of ice. Finding himself able to live in the greatest extremities of love, he concludes the torrid zone to be habitable. Upon the dying of a tree, on which he had cut his loves, he observes, that his flames had burnt up and withered the tree."

These conceits Addison calls mixed wit; that is, wit which consists of thoughts true in one sense of the expression, and false in the other. Addison's representation is sufficiently indulgent. That confusion of images may entertain for a moment; but being unnatural, it soon grows wearisome. Cowley delighted in it, as much as if he had invented it; but, not to mention the ancients, he might have found it full-blown in modern Italy. Thus Sanazarro;

Aspice quam variis distringar Vesbia curis,
  Uror, & heu! nostro manat ab igne liquor;
Sum Nilus, sumque Ætna simul; restringite flammas
  O lacrimæ, aut lacrimas ebibe flamma meas.*

One of the severe theologians of that time censured him as having published *a book of profane and lascivious Verses*. From the charge of profaneness, the constant tenour of his life, which seems to have been eminently virtuous, and the general tendency of his opinions, which discover no irreverence of religion, must defend him; but that the accusation of lasciviousness is unjust, the perusal of his works will sufficiently evince.

Cowley's *Mistress* has no power of seduction; "she plays round the head, but comes not at the heart." Her beauty and absence, her kindness and cruelty, her disdain and inconstancy, produce no correspondence of emotion. His poetical account of the virtues of plants, and colours of flowers, is not perused with more sluggish frigidity. The compositions are such as might have been written for penance by a hermit, or for hire by a philosophical rhymer who had only heard of another sex; for they turn the mind only on the writer, whom, without thinking on a woman but as the subject for his task, we sometimes esteem as learned, and sometimes despise as trifling, always admire as ingenious, and always condemn as unnatural.

The Pindarique Odes are now to be considered; a species of composition, which Cowley thinks Pancirolus* might have counted *in his list of the lost inventions of antiquity*, and which he has made a bold and vigorous attempt to recover.

The purpose with which he has paraphrased an Olympick and Nemeæan Ode, is by himself sufficiently explained. His endeavour was, not to shew *precisely what Pindar spoke, but his manner of speaking*. He was therefore not at all restrained to his expressions, nor much to his sentiments; nothing was required of him, but not to write as Pindar would not have written.

Of the Olympick Ode the beginning is, I think, above the original in elegance, and the conclusion below it in strength. The connection is supplied with great perspicuity, and the thoughts, which to a reader of less skill seem thrown together by chance, are concatenated without any abruption. Though the English ode cannot be called a translation, it may be very properly consulted as a commentary.

The spirit of Pindar is indeed not every where equally preserved. The following pretty lines are not such as his *deep mouth* was used to pour:

Great Rhea's son,
If in Olympus' top where thou
Sitt'st to behold thy sacred show,
If in Alpheus' silver flight,
If in my verse thou take delight,
My verse, great Rhea's son, which is
Lofty as that, and smooth as this.

In the Nemeæan ode* the reader must, in mere justice to Pindar, observe that whatever is said of *the original new moon, her tender forehead and her horns*, is superadded by his paraphrast, who has many other plays of words and fancy unsuitable to the original, as,

The table, free for every guest,
No doubt will thee admit,
And feast more upon thee, than thou on it.

He sometimes extends his author's thoughts without improving them. In the Olympionick* an oath is mentioned in a single word, and Cowley spends three lines in swearing by the *Castalian Stream*. We are told of Theron's bounty, with a hint that he had enemies, which Cowley thus enlarges in rhyming prose:

But in this thankless world the giver
Is envied even by the receiver;
'Tis now the cheap and frugal fashion
Rather to hide than own the obligation:
Nay, 'tis much worse than so;
It now an artifice does grow
Wrongs and injuries to do,
Lest men should think we owe.

It is hard to conceive that a man of the first rank in learning and wit, when he was dealing out such minute morality in such feeble diction, could imagine, either waking or dreaming, that he imitated Pindar.

In the following odes, where Cowley chooses his own subjects, he sometimes rises to dignity truly Pindarick, and, if some deficiencies of language be forgiven, his strains are such as those of the Theban bard were to his contemporaries:

> Begin the song, and strike the living lyre:
> Lo how the years to come, a numerous and well-fitted quire,
> All hand in hand do decently advance,
> And to my song with smooth and equal measure dance;
> While the dance lasts, how long soe'er it be,
> My musick's voice shall bear it company;
> Till all gentle notes be drown'd
> In the last trumpet's dreadful sound.*

After such enthusiasm, who will not lament to find the poet conclude with lines like these!

> But stop, my Muse—
> Hold thy Pindarick Pegasus closely in,
> Which does to rage begin—
> —'Tis an unruly and a hard-mouth'd horse—
> 'Twill no unskilful touch endure,
> But flings writer and reader too that sits not sure.

The fault of Cowley, and perhaps of all the writers of the metaphysical race, is that of pursuing his thoughts to their last ramifications, by which he loses the grandeur of generality; for of the greatest things the parts are little; what is little can be but pretty, and by claiming dignity becomes ridiculous. Thus all the power of description is destroyed by a scrupulous enumeration; and the force of metaphors is lost, when the mind by the mention of particulars is turned more upon the original than the secondary sense, more upon that from which the illustration is drawn than that to which it is applied.

Of this we have a very eminent example in the ode intituled *The Muse*, who goes to *take the air* in an intellectual chariot, to which he harnesses Fancy and Judgement, Wit and Eloquence, Memory and Invention: how he distinguished Wit from Fancy, or how Memory could properly contribute to Motion, he has not explained; we are however content to suppose that he could have justified his own fiction, and wish to see the Muse begin her career; but there is yet more to be done.

> Let the *postilion* Nature mount, and let
> The *coachman* Art be set;
> And let the airy *footmen*, running all beside,

Make a long row of goodly pride;
Figures, conceits, raptures, and sentences,
In a well-worded dress,
And innocent loves, and pleasant truths, and useful lies,
In all their gaudy *liveries*.

Every mind is now disgusted with this cumber of magnificence; yet I cannot refuse myself the four next lines:

Mount, glorious queen, thy travelling throne,
And bid it to put on;
For long though cheerful is the way,
And life alas allows but one ill winter's day.

In the same ode, celebrating the power of the Muse, he gives her prescience, or, in poetical language, the foresight of events hatching in futurity; but having once an egg in his mind, he cannot forbear to shew us that he knows what an egg contains:

Thou into the close nests of Time dost peep,
And there with piercing eye
Through the firm shell and the thick white dost spy
Years to come a-forming lie,
Close in their sacred secundine* asleep.

The same thought is more generally, and therefore more poetically, expressed by Casimir, a writer who has many of the beauties and faults of Cowley:

Omnibus mundi Dominator horis
Aptat urgendas per inane pennas,
Pars adhuc nido latet, & futuros
Crescit in annos.*

Cowley, whatever was his subject, seems to have been carried, by a kind of destiny, to the light and the familiar, or to conceits which require still more ignoble epithets. A slaughter in the Red Sea, *new dies the waters name*;* and England, during the Civil War, was *Albion no more, nor to be named from white.** It is surely by some fascination not easily surmounted, that a writer professing to revive *the noblest and highest writing in verse*,* makes this address to the new year:

Nay, if thou lov'st me, gentle year,
Let not so much as love be there,

Vain fruitless love I mean; for, gentle year,
  Although I fear,
There's of this caution little need,
  Yet, gentle year, take heed
  How thou dost make
  Such a mistake;
Such love I mean alone
As by thy cruel predecessors has been shewn;
For, though I have too much cause to doubt it,
I fain would try, for once, if life can live without it.*

The reader of this will be inclined to cry out with Prior—

—Ye Criticks, say,
*How poor to this was Pindar's style!**

Even those who cannot perhaps find in the Isthmian or Nemeæan songs what Antiquity has disposed them to expect, will at least see that they are ill represented by such puny poetry; and all will determine that if this be the old Theban strain, it is not worthy of revival.

To the disproportion and incongruity of Cowley's sentiments must be added the uncertainty and looseness of his measures. He takes the liberty of using in any place a verse of any length, from two syllables to twelve. The verses of Pindar have, as he observes, very little harmony to a modern ear; yet by examining the syllables we perceive them to be regular, and have reason enough for supposing that the ancient audiences were delighted with the sound. The imitator ought therefore to have adopted what he found, and to have added what was wanting; to have preserved a constant return of the same numbers, and to have supplied smoothness of transition and continuity of thought.

It is urged by Dr. Sprat, that the *irregularity of numbers is the very thing* which makes *that kind of poesy fit for all manner of subjects.* But he should have remembered, that what is fit for every thing can fit nothing well. The great pleasure of verse arises from the known measure of the lines, and uniform structure of the stanzas, by which the voice is regulated, and the memory relieved.

If the Pindarick style be, what Cowley thinks it, *the highest and noblest kind of writing in verse*,* it can be adapted only to high and noble subjects; and it will not be easy to reconcile the poet with the critick, or to conceive how that can be the highest kind of writing in verse, which, according to Sprat, *is chiefly to be preferred for its near affinity to prose*.

This lax and lawless versification so much concealed the deficiencies of the barren, and flattered the laziness of the idle, that it immediately overspread our books of poetry; all the boys and girls caught the pleasing fashion, and they that could do nothing else could write like Pindar. The rights of antiquity were invaded, and disorder tried to break into the Latin: a poem on the Sheldonian Theatre,* in which all kinds of verse are shaken together, is unhappily inserted in the *Musæ Anglicanæ*. Pindarism prevailed above half a century; but at last died gradually away, and other imitations supply its place.

The Pindarique Odes have so long enjoyed the highest degree of poetical reputation, that I am not willing to dismiss them with unabated censure; and surely though the mode of their composition be erroneous, yet many parts deserve at least that admiration which is due to great comprehension of knowledge, and great fertility of fancy. The thoughts are often new, and often striking; but the greatness of one part is disgraced by the littleness of another; and total negligence of language gives the noblest conceptions the appearance of a fabric august in the plan, but mean in the materials. Yet surely those verses are not without a just claim to praise; of which it may be said with truth, that no man but Cowley could have written them.

The Davideis now remains to be considered; a poem which the author designed to have extended to twelve books, merely, as he makes no scruple of declaring, because the Æneid had that number; but he had leisure or perseverance only to write the third part.* Epick poems have been left unfinished by Virgil, Statius, Spenser, and Cowley. That we have not the whole Davideis is, however, not much to be regretted; for in this undertaking Cowley is, tacitly at least, confessed to have miscarried. There are not many examples of so great a work, produced by an author generally read, and generally praised, that has crept through a century with so little regard. Whatever is said of Cowley, is meant of his other works. Of the Davideis no mention is made; it never appears in books, nor emerges in conversation. By the *Spectator* it has once been quoted, by *Rymer** it has once been praised, and by *Dryden*, in

Mac Flecknoe, it has once been imitated; nor do I recollect much other notice from its publication till now, in the whole succession of English literature.

Of this silence and neglect, if the reason be inquired, it will be found partly in the choice of the subject, and partly in the performance of the work.

Sacred History has been always read with submissive reverence, and an imagination over-awed and controlled. We have been accustomed to acquiesce in the nakedness and simplicity of the authentick narrative, and to repose on its veracity with such humble confidence, as suppresses curiosity. We go with the historian as he goes, and stop with him when he stops. All amplification is frivolous and vain; all addition to that which is already sufficient for the purposes of religion, seems not only useless, but in some degree profane.

Such events as were produced by the visible interposition of Divine Power are above the power of human genius to dignify. The miracle of Creation, however it may teem with images, is best described with little diffusion of language: *He spake the word, and they were made.**

We are told that Saul *was troubled with an evil spirit*;* from this Cowley takes an opportunity of describing hell, and telling the history of Lucifer, who was, he says,

> Once general of a gilded host of sprites,
> Like Hesper leading forth the spangled nights;
> But down like lightning, which him struck, he came,
> And roar'd at his first plunge into the flame.

Lucifer makes a speech to the inferior agents of mischief, in which there is something of heathenism, and therefore of impropriety; and, to give efficacy to his words, concludes by lashing *his breast with his long tail*. Envy, after a pause, steps out, and among other declarations of her zeal utters these lines:

> Do thou but threat, loud storms shall make reply,
> And thunder echo't to the trembling sky.
> Whilst raging seas swell to so bold an height,
> As shall the fire's proud element affright.
> Th' old drudging Sun, from his long-beaten way,
> Shall at thy voice start, and misguide the day.

The jocund orbs shall break their measur'd pace,
And stubborn Poles change their allotted place.
Heaven's gilded troops shall flutter here and there,
Leaving their boasting songs tun'd to a sphere.

Every reader feels himself weary with this useless talk of an allegorical Being.

It is not only when the events are confessedly miraculous, that fancy and fiction lose their effect: the whole system of life, while the Theocracy was yet visible, has an appearance so different from all other scenes of human action, that the reader of the Sacred Volume habitually considers it as the peculiar mode of existence of a distinct species of mankind, that lived and acted with manners uncommunicable; so that it is difficult even for imagination to place us in the state of them whose story is related, and by consequence their joys and griefs are not easily adopted, nor can the attention be often interested in any thing that befals them.

To the subject, thus originally indisposed to the reception of poetical embellishments, the writer brought little that could reconcile impatience, or attract curiosity. Nothing can be more disgusting than a narrative spangled with conceits, and conceits are all that the Davideis supplies.

One of the great sources of poetical delight is description, or the power of presenting pictures to the mind. Cowley gives inferences instead of images, and shews not what may be supposed to have been seen, but what thoughts the sight might have suggested. When Virgil describes the stone which Turnus lifted against Æneas, he fixes the attention on its bulk and weight:

Saxum circumspicit ingens,
Saxum antiquum, ingens, campo quod forte jacebat
Limes agro positus, litem ut discerneret arvis.*

Cowley says of the stone with which Cain slew his brother,

I saw him fling the stone, as if he meant
At once his murther and his monument.

Of the sword taken from Goliah, he says,

A sword so great, that it was only fit
To cut off his great head that came with it.

Other poets describe death by some of its common appearances; Cowley says, with a learned allusion to sepulchral lamps real or fabulous,

> 'Twixt his right ribs deep pierc'd the furious blade,
> And open'd wide those secret vessels where
> Life's light goes out, when first they let in air.

But he has allusions vulgar as well as learned. In a visionary succession of kings:

> Joas at first does bright and glorious show,
> In life's fresh morn his fame does early crow.

Describing an undisciplined army, after having said with elegance,

> His forces seem'd no army, but a crowd
> Heartless, unarm'd, disorderly, and loud;

he gives them a fit of the ague.

The allusions however are not always to vulgar things: he offends by exaggeration as much as by diminution:

> The king was plac'd alone, and o'er his head
> A well-wrought heaven of silk and gold was spread.

Whatever he writes is always polluted with some conceit:

> Where the sun's fruitful beams give metals birth,
> Where he the growth of fatal gold does see,
> Gold, which alone more influence has than he.

In one passage he starts a sudden question, to the confusion of philosophy:

> Ye learned heads, whom ivy garlands grace,
> Why does that twining plant the oak embrace?
> The oak, for courtship most of all unfit,
> And rough as are the winds that fight with it.

His expressions have sometimes a degree of meanness that surpasses expectation:

> Nay, gentle guests, he cries, since now you're in,
> The story of your gallant friend begin.

In a simile descriptive of the Morning:

> As glimmering stars just at th' approach of day,
> Cashier'd by troops, at last drop all away.

The dress of Gabriel deserves attention:

> He took for skin a cloud most soft and bright,
> That e'er the midday sun pierc'd through with light,
> Upon his cheeks a lively blush he spread,
> Wash'd from the morning beauties deepest red;
> An harmless flattering meteor shone for hair,
> And fell adown his shoulders with loose care;
> He cuts out a silk mantle from the skies,
> Where the most sprightly azure pleas'd the eyes;
> This he with starry vapours sprinkles all,
> Took in their prime ere they grow ripe and fall,
> Of a new rainbow, ere it fret or fade,
> The choicest piece cut out, a scarfe is made.

This is a just specimen of Cowley's imagery: what might in general expressions be great and forcible, he weakens and makes ridiculous by branching it into small parts. That Gabriel was invested with the softest or brightest colours of the sky, we might have been told, and been dismissed to improve the idea in our different proportions of conception; but Cowley could not let us go till he had related where Gabriel got first his skin, and then his mantle, then his lace, and then his scarfe, and related it in the terms of the mercer and taylor.

Sometimes he indulges himself in a digression, always conceived with his natural exuberance, and commonly, even where it is not long, continued till it is tedious:

> I' th' library a few choice authors stood,
> Yet 'twas well stor'd, for that small store was good;
> Writing, man's spiritual physic, was not then
> Itself, as now, grown a disease of men.
> Learning (young virgin) but few suitors knew;
> The common prostitute she lately grew,
> And with the spurious brood loads now the press;
> Laborious effects of idleness.

As the Davideis affords only four books, though intended to consist of twelve, there is no opportunity for such criticisms as Epick poems commonly supply. The plan of the whole work is very imperfectly shewn by the third part. The duration of an unfinished action cannot be known. Of characters either not yet introduced, or shewn but upon few occasions, the full extent and the nice discriminations cannot be ascertained. The fable is plainly implex, formed rather from the Odyssey than the Iliad; and many artifices of diversification are employed, with the skill of a man acquainted with the best models. The past is recalled by narration, and the future anticipated by vision: but he has been so lavish of his poetical art, that it is difficult to imagine how he could fill eight books more without practising again the same modes of disposing his matter; and perhaps the perception of this growing incumbrance inclined him to stop. By this abruption, posterity lost more instruction than delight. If the continuation of the Davideis can be missed, it is for the learning that had been diffused over it, and the notes in which it had been explained.

Had not his characters been depraved like every other part by improper decorations, they would have deserved uncommon praise. He gives Saul both the body and mind of a hero:

> His way once chose, he forward thrust outright,
> Nor turn'd aside for danger or delight.

And the different beauties of the lofty Merab and the gentle Michol are very justly conceived and strongly painted.

Rymer has declared the Davideis superior to the *Jerusalem of Tasso*, "which," says he, "the poet, with all his care, has not totally purged from pedantry."* If by pedantry is meant that minute knowledge which is derived from particular sciences and studies, in opposition to the general notions supplied by a wide survey of life and nature, Cowley certainly errs, by introducing pedantry far more frequently than Tasso. I know not, indeed, why they should be compared; for the resemblance of Cowley's work to Tasso's is only that they both exhibit the agency of celestial and infernal spirits, in which however they differ widely; for Cowley supposes them commonly to operate upon the mind by suggestion; Tasso represents them as promoting or obstructing events by external agency.

Of particular passages that can be properly compared, I remember only the description of Heaven, in which the different manner of the two writers is sufficiently discernible. Cowley's is scarcely description, unless it be possible to describe by negatives; for he tells us only what there is not in heaven. Tasso endeavours to represent the splendours and pleasures of the regions of happiness. Tasso affords images, and Cowley sentiments. It happens, however, that Tasso's description affords some reason for Rymer's censure. He says of the Supreme Being,

> Hà sotto i piedi e fato e la natura
> Ministri humili, e'l moto, e ch'il misura.

The second line has in it more of pedantry than perhaps can be found in any other stanza of the poem.

In the perusal of the Davideis, as of all Cowley's works, we find wit and learning unprofitably squandered. Attention has no relief; the affections are never moved; we are sometimes surprised, but never delighted, and find much to admire, but little to approve. Still however it is the work of Cowley, of a mind capacious by nature, and replenished by study.

In the general review of Cowley's poetry it will be found, that he wrote with abundant fertility, but negligent or unskilful selection; with much thought; but with little imagery; that he is never pathetick, and rarely sublime, but always either ingenious or learned, either acute or profound.

It is said by Denham in his elegy,*

> To him no author was unknown;
> Yet what he writ was all his own.

This wide position requires less limitation, when it is affirmed of Cowley, than perhaps of any other poet—He read much, and yet borrowed little.

His character of writing was indeed not his own: he unhappily adopted that which was predominant. He saw a certain way to present praise, and not sufficiently enquiring by what means the ancients have continued to delight through all the changes of human manners, he contented himself with a deciduous laurel, of which the verdure in its spring was bright and gay, but which time has been continually stealing from his brows.

He was in his own time considered as of unrivalled excellence. Clarendon represents him as having taken a flight beyond all that went before him;* and Milton is said to have declared, that the three greatest English poets were Spenser, Shakspeare, and Cowley.

His manner he had in common with others: but his sentiments were his own. Upon every subject he thought for himself; and such was his copiousness of knowledge, that something at once remote and applicable rushed into his mind; yet it is not likely that he always rejected a commodious idea merely because another had used it: his known wealth was so great, that he might have borrowed without loss of credit.

In his elegy on Sir Henry Wotton, the last lines have such resemblance to the noble epigram of Grotius upon the death of Scaliger,* that I cannot but think them copied from it, though they are copied by no servile hand.

One passage in his *Mistress* is so apparently borrowed from Donne, that he probably would not have written it, had it not mingled with his own thoughts, so as that he did not perceive himself taking it from another.

Although I think thou never found wilt be,
  Yet I'm resolv'd to search for thee;
  The search itself rewards the pains.
So, though the chymic his great secret miss,
(For neither it in Art nor Nature is)
  Yet things well worth his toil he gains:
  And does his charge and labour pay
With good unsought experiments by the way.*
COWLEY.

Some that have deeper digg'd Love's mine than I,
Say, where his centric happiness doth lie:
  I have lov'd, and got, and told;
But should I love, get, tell, till I were old,
I should not find that hidden mystery;
  Oh, 'tis imposture all:
And as no chymic yet th' elixir got,
  But glorifies his pregnant pot,
  If by the way to him befal
Some odoriferous thing, or medicinal,
  So lovers dream a rich and long delight,
  But get a winter-seeming summer's night.*
DONNE.

Jonson and Donne, as Dr. Hurd* remarks, were then in the highest esteem.

It is related by Clarendon, that Cowley always acknowledged his obligation to the learning and industry of Jonson; but I have found no traces of Jonson in his works: to emulate Donne, appears to have been his purpose; and from Donne he may have learned that familiarity with religious images, and that light allusion to sacred things, by which readers far short of sanctity are frequently offended; and which would not be born in the present age, when devotion, perhaps not more fervent, is more delicate.

Having produced one passage taken by Cowley from Donne, I will recompense him by another which Milton seems to have borrowed from him. He says of Goliah,

> His spear, the trunk was of a lofty tree,
> Which Nature meant some tall ship's mast should be.*

Milton of Satan,

> His spear, to equal which the tallest pine
> Hewn on Norwegian hills, to be the mast
> Of some great admiral, were but a wand,
> He walk'd with.*

His diction was in his own time censured as negligent. He seems not to have known, or not to have considered, that words being arbitrary must owe their power to association, and have the influence, and that only, which custom has given them. Language is the dress of thought; and as the noblest mien, or most graceful action, would be degraded and obscured by a garb appropriated to the gross employments of rusticks or mechanicks, so the most heroick sentiments will lose their efficacy, and the most splendid ideas drop their magnificence, if they are conveyed by words used commonly upon low and trivial occasions, debased by vulgar mouths, and contaminated by inelegant applications.

Truth indeed is always truth, and reason is always reason; they have an intrinsick and unalterable value, and constitute that intellectual gold which defies destruction: but gold may be so concealed in baser matter, that only a chymist can recover it; sense may be so hidden in unrefined and plebeian words, that none but philosophers can distinguish it; and both may be so buried in impurities, as not to pay the cost of their extraction.

The diction, being the vehicle of the thoughts, first presents itself to the intellectual eye: and if the first appearance offends, a further knowledge is not often sought. Whatever professes to benefit by pleasing, must please at once. The pleasures of the mind imply something sudden and unexpected; that which elevates must always surprise. What is perceived by slow degrees may gratify us with the consciousness of improvement, but will never strike with the sense of pleasure.

Of all this, Cowley appears to have been without knowledge, or without care. He makes no selection of words, nor seeks any neatness of phrase: he has no elegances either lucky or elaborate; as his endeavours were rather to impress sentences upon the understanding than images on the fancy, he has few epithets, and those scattered without peculiar propriety or nice adaptation. It seems to follow from the necessity of the subject, rather than the care of the writer, that the diction of his heroick poem is less familiar than that of his slightest writings. He has given not the same numbers, but the same diction, to the gentle Anacreon and the tempestuous Pindar.

His versification seems to have had very little of his care; and if what he thinks be true, that his numbers are unmusical only when they are ill read, the art of reading them is at present lost; for they are commonly harsh to modern ears. He has indeed many noble lines, such as the feeble care of Waller never could produce. The bulk of his thoughts sometimes swelled his verse to unexpected and inevitable grandeur; but his excellence of this kind is merely fortuitous: he sinks willingly down to his general carelessness, and avoids with very little care either meanness or asperity.

His contractions are often rugged and harsh:

> One flings a mountain, and its rivers too
> Torn up with't.*

His rhymes are very often made by pronouns or particles, or the like unimportant words, which disappoint the ear, and destroy the energy of the line.

His combination of different measures is sometimes dissonant and unpleasing; he joins verses together, of which the former does not slide easily into the latter.

The words *do* and *did*, which so much degrade in present estimation the line that admits them, were in the time of Cowley little censured or avoided; how often he used them, and with how bad an effect, at least to our ears, will appear by a passage, in which every reader will lament to see just and noble thoughts defrauded of their praise by inelegance of language:

> Where honour or where conscience *does* not bind,
> No other law shall shackle me;
> Slave to myself I ne'er will be;
> Nor shall my future actions be confin'd
> By my own present mind.
> Who by resolves and vows engag'd *does* stand
> For days, that yet belong to fate,
> *Does* like an unthrift mortgage his estate,
> Before it falls into his hand,
> The bondman of the cloister so,
> All that he *does* receive *does* always owe.
> And still as Time comes in, it goes away,
> Not to enjoy, but debts to pay!
> Unhappy slave, and pupil to a bell!
> Which his hours' work as well as hours *does* tell:
> Unhappy till the last, the kind releasing knell.*

His heroick lines are often formed of monosyllables; but yet they are sometimes sweet and sonorous.

He says of the Messiah,

> Round the whole earth his dreaded name shall sound,
> *And reach to worlds that must not yet be found.**

In another place, of David,

> Yet bid him go securely, when he sends;
> *'Tis Saul that is his foe, and we his friends.*
> *The man who has his God, no aid can lack;*
> *And we who bid him go, will bring him back.**

Yet amidst his negligence he sometimes attempted an improved and scientifick versification; of which it will be best to give his own account subjoined to this line,

Nor can the glory contain itself in th' endless space.*

"I am sorry that it is necessary to admonish the most part of readers, that it is not by negligence that this verse is so loose, long, and, as it were, vast; it is to paint in the number the nature of the thing which it describes, which I would have observed in divers other places of this poem, that else will pass for very careless verses: as before,

And over-runs the neighb'ring fields with violent course.

In the second book;

Down a precipice deep, down he casts them all.—

—And,

And fell a-down his shoulders with loose care.

In the third,

Brass was his helmet, his boots brass, and o'er
His breast a thick plate of strong brass he wore.

In the fourth,

Like some fair pineo'er-looking all th' ignobler wood.

And,

Some from the rocks cast themselves down headlong.

"And many more: but it is enough to instance in a few. The thing is, that the disposition of words and numbers should be such, as that, out of the order and sound of them, the things themselves may be represented. This the Greeks were not so accurate as to bind themselves to; neither have our English poets observed it, for aught I can find. The Latins *(qui musas colunt severiores)** sometimes did it, and their prince, Virgil, always: in whom the examples are innumerable, and taken notice of by all judicious men, so that it is superfluous to collect them."

I know not whether he has, in many of these instances, attained the representation or resemblance that he purposes. Verse can imitate only sound and motion. A *boundless* verse, a *headlong* verse, and a verse of *brass* or of *strong brass*, seem to comprise very incongruous and unsociable ideas. What there is peculiar in the sound of the line expressing *loose care*, I cannot discover; nor why the *pine* is *taller* in an Alexandrine than in ten syllables.

But, not to defraud him of his due praise, he has given one example of representative versification, which perhaps no other English line can equal:

> Begin, be bold, and venture to be wise.
> He who defers this work from day to day,
> Does on a river's bank expecting stay
> Till the whole stream that stopp'd him shall be gone,
> *Which runs, and as it runs, for ever shall run on.**

Cowley was, I believe, the first poet that mingled Alexandrines at pleasure with the common heroick of ten syllables, and from him Dryden borrowed the practice, whether ornamental or licentious. He considered the verse of twelve syllables as elevated and majestick, and has therefore deviated into that measure when he supposes the voice heard of the Supreme Being.

The Author of the Davideis is commended by Dryden for having written it in couplets, because he discovered that any staff was too lyrical for an heroick poem; but this seems to have been known before by *May* and *Sandys*,* the translators of the Pharsalia and the Metamorphoses.

In the Davideis are some hemistichs, or verses left imperfect by the author, in imitation of Virgil, whom he supposes not to have intended to complete them: that this opinion is erroneous, may be probably concluded, because this truncation is imitated by no subsequent Roman poet; because Virgil himself filled up one broken line in the heat of recitation; because in one the sense is now unfinished; and because all that can be done by a broken verse, a line intersected by a *cæsura* and a full stop will equally effect.

Of triplets in his Davideis he makes no use, and perhaps did not at first think them allowable; but he appears afterwards to have changed his mind, for in the verses on the government of Cromwell he inserts them liberally with great happiness.

After so much criticism on his Poems, the Essays which accompany them must not be forgotten. What is said by Sprat of his conversation, that no man could draw from it any suspicion of his excellence in poetry, may be applied to these compositions. No author ever kept his verse and his prose at a greater distance from each other. His thoughts are natural, and his style has a smooth and placid equability, which has never yet obtained its due commendation. Nothing is far-sought, or hard-laboured; but all is easy without feebleness, and familiar without grossness.

It has been observed by Felton,* in his Essay on the Classicks, that Cowley was beloved by every Muse that he courted; and that he has rivalled the Ancients in every kind of poetry but tragedy.

It may be affirmed, without any encomiastick fervour, that he brought to his poetick labours a mind replete with learning, and that his pages are embellished with all the ornaments which books could supply; that he was the first who imparted to English numbers the enthusiasm of the greater ode, and the gaiety of the less; that he was equally qualified for spritely sallies, and for lofty flights; that he was among those who freed translation from servility, and, instead of following his author at a distance, walked by his side; and that if he left versification yet improvable, he left likewise from time to time such specimens of excellence as enabled succeeding poets to improve it.

MILTON

THE Life of Milton has been already written in so many forms, and with such minute enquiry, that I might perhaps more properly have contented myself with the addition of a few notes to Mr. Fenton's elegant Abridgement,* but that a new narrative was thought necessary to the uniformity of this edition.

JOHN MILTON was by birth a gentleman, descended from the proprietors of Milton near Thame in Oxfordshire, one of whom forfeited his estate in the times of York and Lancaster. Which side he took I know not; his descendant inherited no veneration for the White Rose.

His grandfather John was keeper of the forest of Shotover, a zealous papist, who disinherited his son, because he had forsaken the religion of his ancestors.

His father, John, who was the son disinherited, had recourse for his support to the profession of a scrivener. He was a man eminent for his skill in musick, many of his compositions being still to be found; and his reputation in his profession was such, that he grew rich, and retired to an estate. He had probably more than common literature,* as his son addresses him in one of his most elaborate Latin poems. He married a gentlewoman of the name of Caston, a Welsh family, by whom he had two sons, John the poet, and Christopher who studied the law, and adhered, as the law taught him, to the King's party, for which he was awhile persecuted; but having, by his brother's interest, obtained permission to live in quiet, he supported himself so honourably by chamber-practice, that soon after the accession of King James, he was knighted and made a Judge; but, his constitution being too weak for business, he retired before any disreputable compliances became necessary.

He had likewise a daughter Anne, whom he married with a considerable fortune to Edward Philips, who came from Shrewsbury, and rose in the Crown-office to be secondary:* by him she had two sons, John and Edward, who were educated by the poet, and from whom is derived the only authentick account of his domestick manners.

John, the poet, was born in his father's house, at the Spread-Eagle in Bread-street, Dec. 9, 1608, between six and seven in the morning. His father appears to have been very solicitous about his education; for he was instructed at first by private tuition under the care of Thomas Young,* who was afterwards chaplain to the English merchants at Hamburgh; and of whom we have reason to think well, since his scholar considered him as worthy of an epistolary Elegy.

He was then sent to St. Paul's School, under the care of Mr. Gill;* and removed, in the beginning of his sixteenth year, to Christ's College in Cambridge, where he entered a sizar,* Feb. 12, 1624.

He was at this time eminently skilled in the Latin tongue; and he himself, by annexing the dates to his first compositions, a boast of which the learned *Politian** had given him an example, seems to commend the earliness of his own proficiency to the notice of posterity. But the products of his vernal fertility have been surpassed by many, and particularly by his contemporary Cowley. Of the powers of the mind it is difficult to form an estimate: many have excelled Milton in their first essays, who never rose to works like *Paradise Lost*.

At fifteen, a date which he uses till he is sixteen, he translated or versified two Psalms, 114 and 136, which he thought worthy of the publick eye; but they raise no great expectations: they would in any numerous school have obtained praise, but not excited wonder.

Many of his elegies appear to have been written in his eighteenth year, by which it appears that he had then read the Roman authors with very nice discernment. I once heard Mr. Hampton, the translator of Polybius,* remark what I think is true, that Milton was the first Englishman who, after the revival of letters, wrote Latin verses with classick elegance. If any exceptions can be made, they are very few: Haddon and Ascham,* the pride of Elizabeth's reign, however they may have succeeded in prose, no sooner attempt verses than they provoke derision. If we produced any thing worthy of notice before the elegies of Milton, it was perhaps *Alabaster's Roxana*.*

Of the exercises which the rules of the University required, some were published by him in his maturer years. They had been undoubtedly applauded; for they were such as few can perform: yet there is reason to suspect that he was regarded in his college with no great fondness. That he obtained no fellowship is certain; but the unkindness with which he was treated was not merely negative. I am ashamed to relate what I fear is true, that Milton was one of the last students in either university that suffered the publick indignity of corporal correction.

It was, in the violence of controversial hostility, objected to him, that he was expelled: this he steadily denies, and it was apparently not true; but it seems plain from his own verses to *Diodati*,* that he had incurred *Rustication*; a temporary dismission into the country, with perhaps the loss of a term:

> Me tenet urbs refluâ quam Thamesis alluit undâ,
> Meque nec invitum patria dulcis habet.
> Jam nec arundiferum mihi cura revisere Camum,
> Nec dudum *vetiti* me *laris* angit amor.—
> Nec duri libet usque minas perferre magistri,
> Cæteraque ingenio non subeunda meo.
> Si sit hoc *exilium* patrias adiisse penates,
> Et vacuum curis otia grata sequi,
> Non ego vel *profugi* nomen sortemve recuso,
> Lætus et *exilii* conditione fruor.*

I cannot find any meaning but this, which even kindness and reverence can give to the term, *vetiti laris*, "a habitation from which he is excluded;" or how *exile* can be otherwise interpreted. He declares yet more, that he is weary of enduring *the threats of a rigorous master, and something else, which a temper like his cannot undergo*. What was more than threat was probably punishment. This poem, which mentions his *exile*, proves likewise that it was not perpetual; for it concludes with a resolution of returning some time to Cambridge. And it may be conjectured from the willingness with which he has perpetuated the memory of his exile, that its cause was such as gave him no shame.

He took both the usual degrees; that of Batchelor in 1628, and that of Master in 1632; but he left the university with no kindness for its institution, alienated either by the injudicious severity of his governors, or his own captious perverseness. The cause cannot now be known, but the effect appears in his writings. His scheme of education, inscribed to *Hartlib*,* supersedes all academical instruction, being intended to comprise the whole time which men usually spend in literature, from their entrance upon grammar, *till they proceed, as it is called, masters of arts*. And in his Discourse* *on the* *likeliest Way to remove Hirelings out of the Church*, he ingeniously proposes, that *the profits of the lands forfeited by the act for superstitious uses, should be applied to such academies all over the land, where languages and arts may be taught together; so that youth may be at once brought up to a competency of learning and an honest trade, by which means such of them as had the gift, being enabled to support themselves (without titles) by the latter, may, by the help of the former, become worthy preachers.*

One of his objections to academical education, as it was then conducted, is, that men designed for orders in the Church were permitted to act plays, *writhing and unboning their clergy limbs to all the antick and dishonest gestures of Trincalos, buffoons and bawds, prostituting the shame of that ministry which they had, or were near having, to the eyes of courtiers and court-ladies, their grooms and mademoiselles.*

This is sufficiently peevish in a man, who, when he mentions his exile from the college, relates, with great luxuriance, the compensation which the pleasures of the theatre afford him. Plays were therefore only criminal when they were acted by academicks.

He went to the university with a design of entering into the church, but in time altered his mind; for he declared, that whoever became a clergyman must "subscribe slave, and take an oath withal, which, unless he took with a conscience that could retch, he must straight perjure himself. He thought it better to prefer a blameless silence before the office of speaking, bought and begun with servitude and forswearing."*

These expressions are, I find, applied to the subscription of the Articles; but it seems more probable that they relate to canonical obedience. I know not any of the Articles* which seem to thwart his opinions: but the thoughts of obedience, whether canonical or civil, raised his indignation.

His unwillingness to engage in the ministry, perhaps not yet advanced to a settled resolution of declining it, appears in a letter to one of his friends, who had reproved his suspended and dilatory life, which he seems to have imputed to an insatiable curiosity, and fantastick luxury of various knowledge. To this he writes a cool and plausible answer, in which he endeavors to persuade him that the delay proceeds not from the delights of desultory study, but from the desire of obtaining more fitness for his task; and that he goes on, *not taking thought of being late, so it give advantage to be more fit.*

When he left the university, he returned to his father, then residing at Horton in Buckinghamshire, with whom he lived five years; in which time he is said to have read all the Greek and Latin writers. With what limitations this universality is to be understood, who shall inform us?

It might be supposed that he who read so much should have done nothing else; but Milton found time to write the Masque of *Comus*, which was presented at Ludlow, then the residence of the Lord President of Wales, in 1634; and had the honour of being acted by the Earl of Bridgewater's sons and daughter. The fiction is derived from Homer's *Circe*;* but we never can refuse to any modern the liberty of borrowing from Homer:

—a quo ceu fonte perenni
Vatum Pieriis ora rigantur aquis.*

His next production was *Lycidas*, an elegy, written in 1637, on the death of Mr. King,* the son of Sir John King, secretary for Ireland in the time of Elizabeth, James, and Charles. King was much a favourite at Cambridge, and many of the wits joined to do honour to his memory. Milton's acquaintance with the Italian writers may be discovered by a mixture of longer and shorter verses, according to the rules of Tuscan poetry, and his malignity to the Church by some lines which are interpreted as threatening its extermination.

He is supposed about this time to have written his *Arcades*; for while he lived at Horton he used sometimes to steal from his studies a few days, which he spent at Harefield, the house of the countess dowager of Derby, where the *Arcades* made part of a dramatick entertainment.*

He began now to grow weary of the country; and had some purpose of taking chambers in the Inns of Court, when the death of his mother set him at liberty to travel, for which he obtained his father's consent, and Sir Henry Wotton's directions,* with the celebrated precept of prudence, *i pensieri stretti, ed il viso sciolto*; "thoughts close, and looks loose."

In 1638 he left England, and went first to Paris; where, by the favour of Lord *Scudamore*,* he had the opportunity of visiting *Grotius*,* then residing at the French court as ambassador from Christina of Sweden. From Paris he hasted into Italy, of which he had with particular diligence studied the language and literature: and, though he seems to have intended a very quick perambulation of the country, staid two months at Florence; where he found his way into the academies, and produced his compositions with such applause as appears to have exalted him in his own opinion, and confirmed him in the hope, that, "by labour and intense study, which," says he, "I take to be my portion in this life, joined with a strong propensity of nature," he might "leave something so written to after-times, as they should not willingly let it die."*

It appears, in all his writings, that he had the usual concomitant of great abilities, a lofty and steady confidence in himself, perhaps not without some contempt of others; for scarcely any man ever wrote so much, and praised so few. Of his praise he was very frugal; as he set its value high, and considered his mention of a name as a security against the waste of time, and a certain preservative from oblivion.

At Florence he could not indeed complain that his merit wanted distinction. Carlo Dati presented him with an encomiastick inscription, in the tumid lapidary style; and Francini* wrote him an ode, of which the first stanza is only empty noise; the rest are perhaps too diffuse on common topicks: but the last is natural and beautiful.

From Florence he went to Sienna, and from Sienna to Rome, where he was again received with kindness by the Learned and the Great. Holstenius, the keeper of the Vatican Library, who had resided three years at Oxford, introduced him to Cardinal Barberini;* and he, at a musical entertainment, waited for him at the door, and led him by the hand into the assembly. Here Selvaggi praised him in a distich, and Salsilli* in a tetrastich: neither of them of much value. The Italians were gainers by this literary commerce; for the encomiums with which Milton repaid Salsilli, though not secure against a stern grammarian, turn the balance indisputably in Milton's favour.

Of these Italian testimonies, poor as they are, he was proud enough to publish them before his poems; though he says, he cannot be suspected but to have known that they were said *non tam de se, quam supra se*.*

At Rome, as at Florence, he staid only two months; a time indeed sufficient, if he desired only to ramble with an explainer of its antiquities, or to view palaces and count pictures; but certainly too short for the contemplation of learning, policy, or manners.

From Rome he passed on to Naples, in company of a hermit; a companion from whom little could be expected, yet to him Milton owed his introduction to Manso* marquis of Villa, who had been before the patron of Tasso. Manso was enough delighted with his accomplishments to honour him with a sorry distich, in which he commends him for every thing but his religion; and Milton, in return, addressed him in a Latin poem, which must have raised an high opinion of English elegance and literature.

His purpose was now to have visited Sicily and Greece; but, hearing of the differences between the king and parliament, he thought it proper to hasten home, rather than pass his life in foreign amusements while his countrymen were contending for their rights. He therefore came back to Rome, though the merchants informed him of plots laid against him by the Jesuits, for the liberty of his conversations on religion. He had sense enough to judge that there was no danger, and therefore kept on his way, and acted as before, neither obtruding nor shunning controversy. He had perhaps given some offence by visiting Galileo,* then a prisoner in the Inquisition for philosophical heresy; and at Naples he was told by Manso, that, by his declarations on religious questions, he had excluded himself from some distinctions which he should otherwise have paid him. But such conduct, though it did not please, was yet sufficiently safe; and Milton staid two months more at Rome, and went on to Florence without molestation.

From Florence he visited Lucca. He afterwards went to Venice; and having sent away a collection of musick and other books, travelled to Geneva, which he probably considered as the metropolis of orthodoxy. Here he reposed, as in a congenial element, and became acquainted with John Diodati and Frederick Spanheim,* two learned professors of Divinity. From Geneva he passed through France; and came home, after an absence of a year and three months.

At his return he heard of the death of his friend Charles Diodati;* a man whom it is reasonable to suppose of great merit, since he was thought by Milton worthy of a poem, intituled, *Epitaphium Damonis*, written with the common but childish imitation of pastoral life.

He now hired a lodging at the house of one Russel, a taylor in St. Bride's Church-yard, and undertook the education of John and Edward Philips, his sister's sons. Finding his rooms too little, he took a house and garden in Aldersgate-street, which was not then so much out of the world as it is now; and chose his dwelling at the upper end of a passage, that he might avoid the noise of the street. Here he received more boys, to be boarded and instructed.

Let not our veneration for Milton forbid us to look with some degree of merriment on great promises and small performance, on the man who hastens home, because his countrymen are contending for their liberty, and, when he reaches the scene of action, vapours away his patriotism in a private boarding-school. This is the period of his life from which all his biographers seem inclined to shrink. They are unwilling that Milton should be degraded to a school-master; but, since it cannot be denied that he taught boys, one finds out that he taught for nothing, and another that his motive was only zeal for the propagation of learning and virtue; and all tell what they do not know to be true, only to excuse an act which no wise man will consider as in itself disgraceful. His father was alive; his allowance was not ample; and he supplied its deficiences by an honest and useful employment.

It is told, that in the art of education he performed wonders; and a formidable list is given of the authors, Greek and Latin, that were read in Aldersgate-street, by youth between ten and fifteen or sixteen years of age. Those who tell or receive these stories should consider that nobody can be taught faster than he can learn. The speed of the horseman must be limited by the power of his horse. Every man, that has ever undertaken to instruct others, can tell what slow advances he has been able to make, and how much patience it requires to recall vagrant inattention, to stimulate sluggish indifference, and to rectify absurd misapprehension.

The purpose of Milton, as it seems, was to teach something more solid than the common literature of Schools, by reading those authors that treat of physical subjects; such as the Georgick,* and astronomical treatises of the ancients. This was a scheme of improvement which seems to have busied many literary projectors* of that age. Cowley, who had more means than Milton of knowing what was wanting to the embellishments of life, formed the same plan of education in his imaginary College.

But the truth is, that the knowledge of external nature, and the sciences which that knowledge requires or includes, are not the great or the frequent business of the human mind. Whether we provide for action or conversation, whether we wish to be useful or pleasing, the first requisite is the religious and moral knowledge of right and wrong; the next is an acquaintance with the history of mankind, and with those examples which may be said to embody truth, and prove by events the reasonableness of opinions. Prudence and Justice are virtues, and excellences, of all times and of all places; we are perpetually moralists, but we are geometricians only by chance. Our intercourse with intellectual nature is necessary; our speculations upon matter are voluntary, and at leisure. Physiological learning is of such rare emergence, that one man may know another half his life without being able to estimate his skill in hydrostaticks or astronomy; but his moral and prudential character immediately appears.

Those authors, therefore, are to be read at schools that supply most axioms of prudence, most principles of moral truth, and most materials for conversation; and these purposes are best served by poets, orators, and historians.

Let me not be censured for this digression as pedantick or paradoxical; for if I have Milton against me, I have Socrates on my side. It was his labour to turn philosophy from the study of nature to speculations upon life; but the innovators whom I oppose are turning off attention from life to nature. They seem to think, that we are placed here to watch the growth of plants, or the motions of the stars. Socrates was rather of opinion, that what we had to learn was, how to do good, and avoid evil.

Ὅττι τοι ἐν μεγάροισι κακόν τ᾽ ἀγαθόντε τέτυκται*

Of institutions we may judge by their effects. From this wonder-working academy, I do not know that there ever proceeded any man very eminent for knowledge: its only genuine product,* I believe, is a small History of Poetry, written in Latin by his nephew Philips, of which perhaps none of my readers has ever heard.

That in his school, as in every thing else which he undertook, he laboured with great diligence, there is no reason for doubting. One part of his method deserves general imitation. He was careful to instruct his scholars in religion. Every Sunday was spent upon theology, of which he dictated a short system, gathered from the writers that were then fashionable in the Dutch universities.

He set his pupils an example of hard study and spare diet; only now and then he allowed himself to pass a day of festivity and indulgence with some gay gentlemen of Gray's Inn.

He now began to engage in the controversies of the times, and lent his breath to blow the flames of contention. In 1641 he published a treatise of *Reformation*,* in two books, against the established Church; being willing to help the Puritans, who were, he says, *inferior to the Prelates in learning*.

Hall bishop of Norwich* had published an *Humble Remonstrance*, in defence of Episcopacy; to which, in 1641, six ministers, of whose names the first letters made the celebrated word *Smectymnuus*, gave their Answer. Of this answer a Confutation was attempted by the learned *Usher*;* and to the Confutation Milton published a Reply, intituled, *Of Prelatical Episcopacy, and whether it may be deduced from the Apostolical Times, by virtue of those testimonies which are alledged to that purpose in some late treatises, one whereof goes under the name of James Lord Bishop of Armagh.*

I have transcribed this title, to shew, by his contemptuous mention of Usher, that he had now adopted the puritanical savageness of manners. His next work was, *The Reason of Church Government urged against Prelacy, by Mr. John Milton*, 1642. In this book he discovers, not with ostentatious exultation, but with calm confidence, his high opinion of his own powers; and promises to undertake something, he yet knows not what, that may be of use and honour to his country. "This," says he, "is not to be obtained but by devout prayer to that Eternal Spirit that can enrich with all utterance and knowledge, and sends out his Seraphim with the hallowed fire of his altar, to touch and purify the lips of whom he pleases. To this must be added, industrious and select reading, steady observation, and insight into all seemly and generous arts and affairs; till which in some measure be compast, I refuse not to sustain this expectation."* From a promise like this, at once fervid, pious, and rational, might be expected the *Paradise Lost*.

He published the same year two more pamphlets,* upon the same question. To one of his antagonists, who affirms that he was *vomited out of the university*, he answers, in general terms; "The Fellows of the College wherein I spent some years, at my parting, after I had taken two degrees, as the manner is, signified many times how much better it would content them that I should stay.—As for the common approbation or dislike of that place, as now it is, that I should esteem or disesteem myself the more for that, too simple is the answerer, if he think to obtain with me. Of small practice were the physician who could not judge, by what she and her sister have of long time vomited, that the worser stuff she strongly keeps in her stomach, but the better she is ever kecking at, and is queasy: she vomits now out of sickness; but before it be well with her, she must vomit by strong physick.—The university, in the time of her better health, and my younger judgement, I never greatly admired, but now much less."

This is surely the language of a man who thinks that he has been injured. He proceeds to describe the course of his conduct, and the train of his thoughts; and, because he has been suspected of incontinence, gives an account of his own purity: "That if I be justly charged," says he, "with this crime, it may come upon me with tenfold shame."

The style of his piece is rough, and such perhaps was that of his antagonist. This roughness he justifies, by great examples, in a long digression. Sometimes he tries to be humorous: "Lest I should take him for some chaplain in hand, some squire of the body to his prelate, one who serves not at the altar only but at the Court-cupboard, he will bestow on us a pretty model of himself; and sets me out half a dozen ptisical mottos, wherever he had them, hopping short in the measure of convulsion fits; in which labour the agony of his wit having scaped narrowly, instead of well-sized periods, he greets us with a quantity of thumbring posies.—And thus ends this section, or rather dissection of himself." Such is the controversial merriment of Milton; his gloomy seriousness is yet more offensive. Such is his malignity, *that hell grows darker at his frown*.*

His father, after Reading was taken by *Essex*,* came to reside in his house; and his school increased. At Whitsuntide, in his thirty-fifth year, he married Mary, the daughter of Mr. Powel,* a justice of the Peace in Oxfordshire. He brought her to town with him, and expected all the advantages of a conjugal life. The lady, however, seems not much to have delighted in the pleasures of spare diet and hard study; for, as Philips relates,* "having for a month led a philosophical life, after having been used at home to a great house, and much company and joviality, her friends, possibly by her own desire, made earnest suit to have her company the remaining part of the summer; which was granted, upon a promise of her return at Michaelmas."

Milton was too busy to much miss his wife: he pursued his studies; and now and then visited the Lady Margaret Leigh,* whom he has mentioned in one of his sonnets. At last Michaelmas arrived; but the Lady had no inclination to return to the sullen gloom of her husband's habitation, and therefore very willingly forgot her promise. He sent her a letter, but had no answer; he sent more with the same success. It could be alleged that letters miscarry; he therefore dispatched a messenger, being by this time too angry to go himself. His messenger was sent back with some contempt. The family of the Lady were Cavaliers.

In a man whose opinion of his own merit was like Milton's, less provocation than this might have raised violent resentment. Milton soon determined to repudiate her for disobedience; and, being one of those who could easily find arguments to justify inclination, published (in 1644) *The Doctrine and Discipline of Divorce*; which was followed by *The Judgement of Martin Bucer, concerning Divorce*; and the next year, his Tetrachordon, *Expositions upon the four chief Places of Scripture which treat of Marriage*.

This innovation was opposed, as might be expected, by the clergy; who, then holding their famous assembly at Westminster, procured that the author should be called before the Lords; "but that House," says Wood, "whether approving the doctrine, or not favouring his accusers, did soon dismiss him."*

There seems not to have been much written against him, nor any thing by any writer of eminence. The antagonist that appeared is styled by him, *a Serving man turned Solicitor.* *Howel* in his letters* mentions the new doctrine with contempt; and it was, I suppose, thought more worthy of derision than of confutation. He complains of this neglect in two sonnets,* of which the first is contemptible, and the second not excellent.

From this time it is observed that he became an enemy to the Presbyterians, whom he had favoured before. He that changes his party by his humour, is not more virtuous than he that changes it by his interest; he loves himself rather than truth.

His wife and her relations now found that Milton was not an unresisting sufferer of injuries; and perceiving that he had begun to put his doctrine in practice, by courting a young woman of great accomplishments, the daughter of one Doctor Davis, who was however not ready to comply, they resolved to endeavour a re-union. He went sometimes to the house of one Blackborough, his relation, in the lane of St. Martin's-le-Grand, and at one of his usual visits was surprised to see his wife come from another room, and implore forgiveness on her knees. He resisted her intreaties for a while; "but partly," says Philips, "his own generous nature, more inclinable to reconciliation than to perseverance in anger or revenge, and partly the strong intercession of friends on both sides, soon brought him to an act of oblivion and a firm league of peace." It were injurious to omit, that Milton afterwards received her father and her brothers in his own house, when they were distressed, with other Royalists.

He published about the same time his *Areopagitica, a Speech of Mr.* John Milton *for the liberty of unlicensed Printing.** The danger of such unbounded liberty, and the danger of bounding it, have produced a problem in the science of Government, which human understanding seems hitherto unable to solve. If nothing may be published but what civil authority shall have previously approved, power must always be the standard of truth; if every dreamer of innovations may propagate his projects, there can be no settlement; if every murmurer at government may diffuse discontent, there can be no peace; and if every sceptick in theology may teach his follies, there can be no religion. The remedy against these evils is to punish the authors; for it is yet allowed that every society may punish, though not prevent, the publication of opinions, which that society shall think pernicious; but this punishment, though it may crush the author, promotes the book; and it seems not more reasonable to leave the right of printing unrestrained, because writers may be afterwards censured, than it would be to sleep with doors unbolted, because by our laws we can hang a thief.

But whatever were his engagements, civil or domestick, poetry was never long out of his thoughts. About this time (1645) a collection of his Latin and English poems appeared, in which the *Allegro* and *Penseroso*, with some others, were first published.

He had taken a larger house in Barbican for the reception of scholars; but the numerous relations of his wife, to whom he generously granted refuge for a while, occupied his rooms. In time, however, they went away; "and the house again," says Philips, "now looked like a house of the Muses only, though the accession of scholars was not great. Possibly his having proceeded so far in the education of youth, may have been the occasion of his adversaries calling him pedagogue and school-master; whereas it is well known he never set up for a publick school, to teach all the young fry of a parish; but only was willing to impart his learning and knowledge to relations, and the sons of gentlemen who were his intimate friends; and that neither his writings nor his way of teaching ever savoured in the least of pedantry."

Thus laboriously does his nephew extenuate what cannot be denied, and what might be confessed without disgrace. Milton was not a man who could become mean by a mean employment. This, however, his warmest friends seem not to have found; they therefore shift and palliate. He did not sell literature to all comers at an open shop; he was a chamber-milliner, and measured his commodities only to his friends.

Philips, evidently impatient of viewing him in this state of degradation, tells us that it was not long continued; and, to raise his character again, has a mind to invest him with military splendour: "He is much mistaken," he says, "if there was not about this time a design of making him an adjutant-general in Sir William Waller's army. But the new modelling of the army proved an obstruction to the design." An event cannot be set at a much greater distance than by having been only *designed, about some time*, if a man *be not much mistaken*. Milton shall be a pedagogue no longer; for, if Philips be not much mistaken, somebody at some time designed him for a soldier.

About the time that the army was new-modelled (1645) he removed to a smaller house in Holbourn, which opened backward into Lincoln's-Inn-Fields.* He is not known to have published any thing afterwards till the King's death, when, finding his murderers condemned by the Presbyterians, he wrote a treatise to justify it,* and *to compose the minds of the people*.

He made some *Remarks on the Articles of Peace between Ormond and the Irish Rebels*. While he contented himself to write, he perhaps did only what his conscience dictated; and if he did not very vigilantly watch the influence of his own passions, and the gradual prevalence of opinions, first willingly admitted and then habitually indulged, if objections, by being overlooked, were forgotten, and desire superinduced conviction; he yet shared only the common weakness of mankind, and might be no less sincere than his opponents. But as faction seldom leaves a man honest, however it might find him, Milton is suspected of having interpolated the book called *Icon Basilike*,* which the Council of State, to whom he was now made Latin secretary, employed him to censure, by inserting a prayer taken from *Sidney's Arcadia*, and imputing it to the King; whom he charges, in his *Iconoclastes*, with the use of this prayer as with a heavy crime, in the indecent language with which prosperity had emboldened the advocates for rebellion to insult all that is venerable or great: "Who would have imagined so little fear in him of the true all-seeing Deity—as, immediately before his death, to pop into the hands of the grave bishop that attended him, as a special relique of his saintly exercises, a prayer stolen word for word from the mouth of a heathen woman praying to a heathen god?"

The papers which the King gave to Dr. Juxon* on the scaffold the regicides took away, so that they were at least the publishers of this prayer; and Dr. Birch, who had examined the question with great care, was inclined to think them the forgers. The use of it by adaptation was innocent; and they who could so noisily censure it, with a little extension of their malice could contrive what they wanted to accuse.

King Charles the Second, being now sheltered in Holland, employed Salmasius,* professor of Polite Learning at Leyden, to write a defence of his father and of monarchy; and, to excite his industry, gave him, as was reported, a hundred Jacobuses. Salmasius was a man of skill in languages, knowledge of antiquity, and sagacity of emendatory criticism, almost exceeding all hope of human attainment; and having, by excessive praises, been confirmed in great confidence of himself, though he probably had not much considered the principles of society or the rights of government, undertook the employment without distrust of his own qualifications; and, as his expedition in writing was wonderful, in 1649 published *Defensio Regis*.

To this Milton was required to write a sufficient answer; which he performed (1651) in such a manner, that Hobbes declared himself unable to decide whose language was best, or whose arguments were worst. In my opinion, Milton's periods are smoother, neater, and more pointed; but he delights himself with teizing his adversary as much as with confuting him. He makes a foolish allusion of Salmasius, whose doctrine he considers as servile and unmanly, to the stream of *Salmacis*, which whoever entered left half his virility behind him. Salmasius was a Frenchman, and was unhappily married to a scold. *Tu es Gallus*, says Milton, *et, ut aiunt, nimium gallinaceus.** But his supreme pleasure is to tax his adversary, so renowned for criticism, with vitious Latin. He opens his book with telling that he has used *Persona*, which, according to Milton, signifies only a *Mask*, in a sense not known to the Romans, by applying it as we apply *Person*. But as Nemesis is always on the watch, it is memorable that he has enforced the charge of a solecism by an expression in itself grossly solecistical, when, for one of those supposed blunders, he says, as *Ker*,* and I think some one before him, has remarked, *propino te grammatistis tuis* vapulandum. From *vapulo*, which has a passive sense, *vapulandus* can never be derived. No man forgets his original trade: the rights of nations, and of kings, sink into questions of grammar, if grammarians discuss them.

Milton when he undertook this answer was weak of body, and dim of sight; but his will was forward, and what was wanting of health was supplied by zeal. He was rewarded with a thousand pounds, and his book was much read; for paradox, recommended by spirit and elegance, easily gains attention; and he who told every man that he was equal to his King, could hardly want an audience.

That the performance of Salmasius was not dispersed with equal rapidity, or read with equal eagerness, is very credible. He taught only the stale doctrine of authority, and the unpleasing duty of submission; and he had been so long not only the monarch but the tyrant of literature, that almost all mankind were delighted to find him defied and insulted by a new name, not yet considered as any one's rival. If Christina,* as is said, commended the *Defence of the People*, her purpose must be to torment Salmasius, who was then at her Court; for neither her civil station nor her natural character could dispose her to favour the doctrine, who was by birth a queen, and by temper despotick.

That Salmasius was, from the appearance of Milton's book, treated with neglect, there is not much proof; but to a man so long accustomed to admiration, a little praise of his antagonist would be sufficiently offensive, and might incline him to leave Sweden, from which, however, he was dismissed, not with any mark of contempt, but with a train of attendance scarce less than regal.

He prepared a reply, which, left as it was imperfect, was published by his son in the year of the Restauration. In the beginning, being probably most in pain for his Latinity, he endeavours to defend his use of the word *persona*; but, if I remember right, he misses a better authority than any that he has found, that of Juvenal in his fourth satire:

—Quid agis cum dira & fœdior omni
Crimine *Persona* est?*

As Salmasius reproached Milton with losing his eyes in the quarrel, Milton delighted himself with the belief that he had shortened Salmasius's life, and both perhaps with more malignity than reason.

Salmasius died at the Spa, Sept. 3, 1653; and as controvertists are commonly said to be killed by their last dispute, Milton was flattered with the credit of destroying him.

Cromwell had now dismissed the parliament by the authority of which he had destroyed monarchy, and commenced monarch himself, under the title of protector, but with kingly and more than kingly power. That his authority was lawful, never was pretended; he himself founded his right only in necessity; but Milton, having now tasted the honey of publick employment, would not return to hunger and philosophy, but, continuing to exercise his office under a manifest usurpation, betrayed to his power that liberty which he had defended. Nothing can be more just than that rebellion should end in slavery; that he, who had justified the murder of his king, for some acts which to him seemed unlawful, should now sell his services, and his flatteries, to a tyrant, of whom it was evident that he could do nothing lawful.

He had now been blind for some years; but his vigour of intellect was such, that he was not disabled to discharge his office of Latin secretary, or continue his controversies. His mind was too eager to be diverted, and too strong to be subdued.

About this time his first wife died in childbed, having left him three daughters. As he probably did not much love her, he did not long continue the appearance of lamenting her; but after a short time married Catherine, the daughter of one captain Woodcock of Hackney; a woman doubtless educated in opinions like his own. She died within a year, of childbirth, or some distemper that followed it; and her husband has honoured her memory with a poor sonnet.*

The first Reply to Milton's *Defensio Populi* was published in 1651, called *Apologia pro Rege & Populo Anglicano, contra Johannis Polypragmatici (alias Miltoni) defensionem destructivam Regis & Populi*. Of this the author was not known;* but Milton and his nephew Philips, under whose name he published an answer so much corrected by him that it might be called his own, imputed it to Bramhal; and, knowing him no friend to regicides, thought themselves at liberty to treat him as if they had known what they only suspected.

Next year appeared *Regii Sanguinis clamor ad Cœlum*. Of this the author was Peter du Moulin, who was afterwards prebendary of Canterbury; but Morus, or More, a French minister, having the care of its publication, was treated as the writer by Milton in his

Defensio Secunda,* and overwhelmed by such violence of invective, that he began to shrink under the tempest, and gave his persecutors the means of knowing the true author. Du Moulin was now in great danger; but Milton's pride operated against his malignity; and both he and his friends were more willing that Du Moulin should escape than that he should be convicted of mistake.

In this second Defence he shews that his eloquence is not merely satirical; the rudeness of his invective is equalled by the grossness of his flattery. "Deserimur, Cromuelle, tu solus superes, ad te summa nostrarum rerum rediit, in te solo consistit, insuperabili tuæ virtuti cedimus cuncti, nemine vel obloquente, nisi qui æquales inæqualis ipse honores sibi quærit, aut digniori concessos invidet, aut non intelligit nihil esse in societate hominum magis vel Deo gratum, vel rationi consentaneum, esse in civitate nihil æquius, nihil utilius, quam potiri rerum dignissimum. Eum te agnoscunt omnes, Cromuelle, ea tu civis maximus et[1] gloriosissimus, dux publici consilii, exercituum fortissimorum imperator, pater patriæ gessisti. Sic tu spontanea bonorum omnium et animitus missa voce salutaris."*

Cæsar, when he assumed the perpetual dictatorship, had not more servile or more elegant flattery. A translation may shew its servility; but its elegance is less attainable. Having exposed the unskilfulness or selfishness of the former government, "We were left," says Milton, "to ourselves: the whole national interest fell into your hands, and subsists only in your abilities. To your virtue, overpowering and resistless, every man gives way, except some who, without equal qualifications, aspire to equal honours, who envy the distinctions of merit greater than their own, or who have yet to learn, that in the coalition of human society nothing is more pleasing to God, or more agreeable to reason, than that the highest mind should have the sovereign power. Such, Sir, are you by general confession; such are the things atchieved by you, the greatest and most glorious of our countrymen, the director of our publick councils, the leader of unconquered armies, the father of your country; for by that title does every good man hail you, with sincere and voluntary praise."

[1] It may be doubted whether *gloriosissimus* be here used with Milton's boasted purity. *Res gloriosa* is an *illustrious thing*; but *vir gloriosus* is commonly a *braggart*, as in *miles gloriosus*.

Next year, having defended all that wanted defence, he found leisure to defend himself. He undertook his own vindication against More, whom he declares in his title to be justly called the author of the *Regii Sanguinis clamor.* In this there is no want of vehemence nor eloquence, nor does he forget his wonted wit. "Morus es? an Momus? an uterque idem est?" He then remembers that *Morus* is Latin for a Mulberry-tree, and hints at the known transformation:

—Poma alba ferebat
Quæ post nigra tulit Morus.*

With this piece ended his controversies; and he from this time gave himself up to his private studies and his civil employment.

As secretary to the Protector he is supposed to have written the Declaration of the reasons for a war with Spain. His agency was considered as of great importance; for when a treaty with Sweden was artfully suspended, the delay was publickly imputed to Mr. Milton's indisposition; and the Swedish agent was provoked to express his wonder, that only one man in England could write Latin, and that man blind.

Being now forty-seven years old, and seeing himself disencumbered from external interruptions, he seems to have recollected his former purposes, and to have resumed three great works which he had planned for his future employment: an epick poem, the history of his country, and a dictionary of the Latin tongue.

To collect a dictionary, seems a work of all others least practicable in a state of blindness, because it depends upon perpetual and minute inspection and collation. Nor would Milton probably have begun it, after he had lost his eyes; but, having had it always before him, he continued it, says Philips, *almost to his dying-day; but the papers were so discomposed and deficient, that they could not be fitted for the press.** The compilers of the Latin dictionary, printed at Cambridge, had the use of those collections in three folios; but what was their fate afterwards is not known.

To compile a history from various authors, when they can only be consulted by other eyes, is not easy, nor possible, but with more skilful and attentive help than can be commonly obtained; and it was probably the difficulty of consulting and comparing that stopped Milton's narrative at the Conquest; a period at which affairs were not yet very intricate, nor authors very numerous.

For the subject of his epick poem, after much deliberation, *long chusing, and beginning late*,* he fixed upon *Paradise Lost*; a design so comprehensive, that it could be justified only by success. He had once designed to celebrate King Arthur, as he hints in his verses to Mansus;* but *Arthur was reserved*, says Fenton, *to another destiny*.

It appears, by some sketches of poetical projects left in manuscript,* and to be seen in a library at Cambridge, that he had digested his thoughts on this subject into one of those wild dramas which were anciently called Mysteries; and Philips had seen what he terms part of a tragedy, beginning with the first ten lines of Satan's address to the Sun. These Mysteries consist of allegorical persons; such as *Justice, Mercy, Faith*. Of the tragedy or mystery of *Paradise Lost* there are two plans:

The Persons.

Michael.
Chorus of Angels.
Heavenly Love.
Lucifer.
Adam, } with the
Eve, } Serpent.
Conscience.
Death.
Labour, }
Sickness, }
Discontent, } Mutes.
Ignorance, }
with others; }
Faith.
Hope.
Charity.

The Persons.

Moses.
Divine Justice, Wisdom,
Heavenly Love.
The Evening Star,
Hesperus.
Chorus of Angels.
Lucifer.
Adam.
Eve.
Conscience.
Labour, }
Sickness, }
Discontent, }
Ignorance, } Mutes.
Fear, }
Death; }
Faith.
Hope.
Charity.

Paradise Lost.

The Persons.

Moses, προλογίζει,* recounting how he assumed his true body; that it corrupts not, because it is with God in the mount; declares the like of Enoch and Eliah; besides the purity of the place, that certain pure winds, dews, and clouds, preserve it from corruption; whence exhorts to the sight of God; tells, they cannot see Adam in the state of innocence, by reason of their sin.

Justice,
Mercy,
Wisdom, } debating what should become of man, if he fall.

Chorus of Angels singing a hymn of the Creation.

ACT II

Heavenly Love.

Evening Star.

Chorus sing the marriage-song, and describe Paradise.

ACT III

Lucifer, contriving Adam's ruin.

Chorus fears for Adam, and relates Lucifer's rebellion and fall.

ACT IV

Adam,
Eve, } fallen.

Conscience cites them to God's examination.

Chorus bewails, and tells the good Adam has lost.

ACT V

Adam and Eve driven out of Paradise.

——— presented by an angel with

Labour, Grief, Hatred, Envy,
War, Famine, Pestilence, Sickness,
Discontent, Ignorance, Fear, Death, } Mutes.

To whom he gives their names. Likewise Winter, Heat, Tempest, &c.

Faith,
Hope,
Charity, } comfort him, and instruct him.

Chorus briefly concludes.

Such was his first design, which could have produced only an allegory, or mystery. The following sketch seems to have attained more maturity.

Adam unparadised:

The angel Gabriel, either descending or entering; shewing, since this globe was created, his frequency as much on earth as in heaven; describes Paradise. Next, the Chorus, shewing the reason of his coming to keep his watch in Paradise, after Lucifer's rebellion, by command from God; and withal expressing his desire to see and know more concerning this excellent new creature, man. The angel Gabriel, as by his name signifying a prince of power, tracing Paradise with a more free office, passes by the station of the Chorus, and, desired by them, relates what he knew of man; as the creation of Eve, with their love and marriage. After this, Lucifer appears; after his overthrow, bemoans himself, seeks revenge on man. The Chorus prepare resistance at his first approach. At last, after discourse of enmity on either side, he departs: whereat the Chorus sings of the battle and victory in heaven, against him and his accomplices: as before, after the first act, was sung a hymn of the creation. Here again may appear Lucifer, relating and insulting in what he had done to the destruction of man. Man next, and Eve having by this time been seduced by the Serpent, appears confusedly covered with leaves. Conscience, in a shape, accuses him; Justice cites him to the place whither Jehovah called for him. In the mean while, the Chorus entertains the stage, and is informed by some angel the manner of the Fall. Here the Chorus bewails Adam's fall; Adam then and Eve return; accuse one another; but especially Adam lays the blame to his wife; is stubborn in his offence. Justice appears, reasons with him, convinces him. The Chorus admonisheth Adam, and bids him beware Lucifer's example of impenitence. The angel is sent to banish them out of Paradise; but before causes to pass before his eyes, in shapes, a mask of all the evils of this life and world. He is humbled, relents, despairs: at last appears Mercy, comforts him, promises the Messiah; then calls in Faith, Hope, and Charity; instructs him; he repents, gives God the glory, submits to his penalty. The Chorus briefly concludes. Compare this with the former draught.

These are very imperfect rudiments of *Paradise Lost*; but it is pleasant to see great works in their seminal state, pregnant with latent possibilities of excellence; nor could there be any more delightful entertainment than to trace their gradual growth and expansion, and to observe how they are sometimes suddenly advanced by accidental hints, and sometimes slowly improved by steady meditation.

Invention is almost the only literary labour which blindness cannot obstruct, and therefore he naturally solaced his solitude by the indulgence of his fancy, and the melody of his numbers. He had done what he knew to be necessarily previous to poetical excellence; he had made himself acquainted with *seemly arts and affairs*;* his comprehension was extended by various knowledge, and his memory stored with intellectual treasures. He was skilful in many languages, and had by reading and composition attained the full mastery of his own. He would have wanted little help from books, had he retained the power of perusing them.

But while his greater designs were advancing, having now, like many other authors, caught the love of publication, he amused himself, as he could, with little productions. He sent to the press (1658) a manuscript of Raleigh, called the *Cabinet Council*; and next year gratified his malevolence to the clergy, by a *Treatise of Civil Power in Ecclesiastical Cases, and the Means of removing Hirelings out of the Church*.*

Oliver was now dead; Richard was constrained to resign:* the system of extemporary government, which had been held together only by force, naturally fell into fragments when that force was taken away; and Milton saw himself and his cause in equal danger. But he had still hope of doing something. He wrote letters, which Toland has published, to such men as he thought friends to the new commonwealth; and even in the year of the Restoration he *bated no jot of heart or hope*,* but was fantastical enough to think that the nation, agitated as it was, might be settled by a pamphlet, called *A ready and easy way to establish a Free Commonwealth*; which was, however, enough considered to be both seriously and ludicrously answered.*

The obstinate enthusiasm of the commonwealthmen was very remarkable. When the King was apparently returning, Harrington,* with a few associates as fanatical as himself, used to meet, with all the gravity of political importance, to settle an equal government by rotation; and Milton, kicking when he could strike no longer, was foolish enough to publish, a few weeks before the Restoration, *Notes* upon a sermon preached by one Griffiths, intituled, *The Fear of God* *and the King*. To these notes an answer was written by L'Estrange, in a pamphlet petulantly called *No blind Guides*.*

But whatever Milton could write, or men of greater activity could do, the King was now about to be restored with the irresistible approbation of the people. He was therefore no longer secretary, and was consequently obliged to quit the house which he held by his office; and proportioning his sense of danger to his opinion of the importance of his writings, thought it convenient to seek some shelter, and hid himself for a time in Bartholomew-Close by West Smithfield.

I cannot but remark a kind of respect, perhaps unconsciously, paid to this great man by his biographers: every house in which he resided is historically mentioned, as if it were an injury to neglect naming any place that he honoured by his presence.

The King, with lenity of which the world has had perhaps no other example, declined to be the judge or avenger of his own or his father's wrongs; and promised to admit into the Act of Oblivion all, except those whom the parliament should except; and the parliament doomed none to capital punishment but the wretches who had immediately co-operated in the murder of the King. Milton was certainly not one of them; he had only justified what they had done.

This justification was indeed sufficiently offensive; and (June 16) an order was issued to seize Milton's *Defence*, and Goodwin's *Obstructors of Justice*,* another book of the same tendency, and burn them by the common hangman. The attorney-general was ordered to prosecute the authors; but Milton was not seized, nor perhaps very diligently pursued.

Not long after (August 19) the flutter of innumerable bosoms was stilled by an act, which the King, that his mercy might want no recommendation of elegance, rather called an *act of oblivion* than of grace. Goodwin was named, with nineteen more, as incapacitated for any publick trust; but of Milton there was no exception.

Of this tenderness shewn to Milton, the curiosity of mankind has not forborn to enquire the reason. Burnet thinks he was forgotten; but this is another instance which may confirm Dalrymple's observation,* who says, "that whenever Burnet's narrations are examined, he appears to be mistaken."

Forgotten he was not; for his prosecution was ordered; it must be therefore by design that he was included in the general oblivion.

He is said to have had friends in the House, such as Marvel, Morrice, and Sir Thomas Clarges;* and undoubtedly a man like him must have had influence. A very particular story of his escape is told by Richardson in his Memoirs, which he received from Pope, as delivered by Betterton, who might have heard it from Davenant.* In the war between the King and Parliament, Davenant was made prisoner, and condemned to die; but was spared at the request of Milton. When the turn of success brought Milton into the like danger, Davenant repaid the benefit by appearing in his favour. Here is a reciprocation of generosity and gratitude so pleasing, that the tale makes its own way to credit. But if help were wanted, I know not where to find it. The danger of Davenant is certain from his own relation; but of his escape there is no account. Betterton's narration can be traced no higher; it is not known that he had it from Davenant. We are told that the benefit exchanged was life for life; but it seems not certain that Milton's life ever was in danger. Goodwin, who had committed the same kind of crime, escaped with incapacitation; and as exclusion from publick trust is a punishment which the power of government can commonly inflict without the help of a particular law, it required no great interest to exempt Milton from a censure little more than verbal. Something may be reasonably ascribed to veneration and compassion; to veneration of his abilities, and compassion for his distresses, which made it fit to forgive his malice for his learning. He was now poor and blind; and who would pursue with violence an illustrious enemy, depressed by fortune, and disarmed by nature?

The publication of the act of oblivion put him in the same condition with his fellow-subjects. He was, however, upon some pretence not now known, in the custody of the serjeant in December; and, when he was released, upon his refusal of the fees demanded, he and the serjeant were called before the House. He was now safe within the shade of oblivion, and knew himself to be as much out of the power of a griping officer as any other man. How the question was determined is not known. Milton would hardly have contended, but that he knew himself to have right on his side.

He then removed to Jewin-street, near Aldersgate-street; and being blind, and by no means wealthy, wanted a domestick companion and attendant; and therefore, by the recommendation of Dr. Paget, married Elizabeth Minshul,* of a gentleman's family in

Cheshire, probably without a fortune. All his wives were virgins; for he has declared that he thought it gross and indelicate to be a second husband: upon what other principles his choice was made, cannot now be known; but marriage afforded not much of his happiness. The first wife left him in disgust, and was brought back only by terror; the second, indeed, seems to have been more a favourite, but her life was short. The third, as Philips relates, oppressed his children in his life-time, and cheated them at his death.

Soon after his marriage, according to an obscure story, he was offered the continuance of his employment; and, being pressed by his wife to accept it, answered, "You, like other women, want to ride in your coach; my wish is to live and die an honest man."* If he considered the Latin secretary as exercising any of the powers of government, he that had shared authority either with the parliament or Cromwell, might have forborn to talk very loudly of his honesty; and if he thought the office purely ministerial, he certainly might have honestly retained it under the king. But this tale has too little evidence to deserve a disquisition; large offers and sturdy rejections are among the most common topicks of falsehood.

He had so much either of prudence or gratitude, that he forbore to disturb the new settlement with any of his political or ecclesiastical opinions, and from this time devoted himself to poetry and literature. Of his zeal for learning, in all its parts, he gave a proof by publishing, the next year (1661), *Accidence commenced Grammar*; a little book which has nothing remarkable, but that its author, who had been lately defending the supreme powers of his country, and was then writing *Paradise Lost*, could descend from his elevation to rescue children from the perplexity of grammatical confusion, and the trouble of lessons unnecessarily repeated.

About this time Elwood the quaker,* being recommended to him as one who would read Latin to him, for the advantage of his conversation; attended him every afternoon, except on Sundays. Milton, who, in his letter to Hartlib, had declared, that *to read Latin with an English mouth is as ill a hearing as Law French*, required that Elwood should learn and practise the Italian pronunciation, which, he said, was necessary, if he would talk with foreigners. This seems to have been a task troublesome without use. There is little reason for preferring the Italian pronunciation to our own, except that it is more general; and to teach it to an Englishman is only to make him a foreigner at home. He who travels, if he speaks Latin, may so soon learn the sounds which every native gives it, that he need make no provision before his journey; and if strangers visit us, it is their business to practise such conformity to our modes as they expect from us in their own countries. Elwood complied with the directions, and improved himself by his attendance; for he relates, that Milton, having a curious ear, knew by his voice when he read what he did not understand, and would stop him, and *open the most difficult passages.*

In a short time he took a house in the *Artillery Walk*, leading to *Bunhill Fields*; the mention of which concludes the register of Milton's removals and habitations. He lived longer in this place than in any other.

He was now busied by *Paradise Lost.* Whence he drew the original design has been variously conjectured, by men who cannot bear to think themselves ignorant of that which, at last, neither diligence nor sagacity can discover. Some find the hint in an Italian tragedy. Voltaire tells a wild and unauthorised story of a farce seen by Milton in Italy, which opened thus: *Let the Rainbow be the Fiddlestick of the Fiddle of Heaven.** It has been already shewn, that the first conception was a tragedy or mystery, not of a narrative, but a dramatick work, which he is supposed to have begun to reduce to its present form about the time (1655) when he finished his dispute with the defenders of the king.

He long before had promised to adorn his native country by some great performance, while he had yet perhaps no settled design, and was stimulated only by such expectations as naturally arose from the survey of his attainments, and the consciousness of his powers. What he should undertake, it was difficult to determine. He was *long chusing, and began late.**

While he was obliged to divide his time between his private studies and affairs of state, his poetical labour must have been often interrupted; and perhaps he did little more in that busy time than construct the narrative, adjust the episodes, proportion the parts, accumulate images and sentiments, and treasure in his memory, or preserve in writing, such hints as books or meditation would supply. Nothing particular is known of his intellectual operations while he was a statesman; for, having every help and accommodation at hand, he had no need of uncommon expedients.

Being driven from all publick stations, he is yet too great not to be traced by curiosity to his retirement; where he has been found by Mr. Richardson, the fondest of his admirers, sitting *before his door in a grey coat of coarse cloth, in warm sultry weather, to enjoy the fresh air; and so, as well as in his own room, receiving the visits of people of distinguished parts as well as quality.** His visitors of high quality must now be imagined to be few; but men of parts might reasonably court the conversation of a man so generally illustrious, that foreigners are reported, by Wood, to have visited the house in Bread-street where he was born.

According to another account, he was seen in a small house, *neatly enough dressed in black cloaths, sitting in a room hung with rusty green; pale but not cadaverous, with chalkstones in his hands. He said, that if it were not for the gout, his blindness would be tolerable.*

In the intervals of his pain, being made unable to use the common exercises, he used to swing in a chair, and sometimes played upon an organ.

He was now confessedly and visibly employed upon his poem, of which the progress might be noted by those with whom he was familiar; for he was obliged, when he had composed as many lines as his memory would conveniently retain, to employ some friend in writing them, having, at least for part of the time, no regular attendant. This gave opportunity to observations and reports.

Mr. Philips observes, that there was a very remarkable circumstance in the composure of *Paradise Lost*, "which I have a particular reason," says he, "to remember; for whereas I had the perusal of it from the very beginning, for some years, as I went from time to time to visit him, in parcels of ten, twenty, or thirty verses at a time (which, being written by whatever hand came next, might possibly want correction as to the orthography and pointing), having, as the summer came on, not been shewed any for a considerable while, and desiring the reason thereof, was answered, that his vein never happily flowed but from the Autumnal Equinox to the Vernal; and that whatever he attempted at other times was never to his satisfaction, though he courted his fancy never so much; so that, in all the years he was about this poem, he may be said to have spent half his time therein."*

Upon this relation Toland remarks, that in his opinion Philips has mistaken the time of the year; for Milton, in his Elegies, declares that with the advance of the Spring he feels the increase of his poetical force, *redeunt in carmina vires.** To this it is answered, that Philips could hardly mistake time so well marked; and it may be added, that Milton might find different times of the year favourable to different parts of life. Mr. Richardson conceives it impossible that *such a work should be suspended for six months, or for one. It may go on faster or slower, but it must go on*. By what necessity it must continually go on, or why it might not be laid aside and resumed, it is not easy to discover.

This dependance of the soul upon the seasons, those temporary and periodical ebbs and flows of intellect, may, I suppose, justly be derided as the fumes of vain imagination. *Sapiens dominabitur astris.** The author that thinks himself weather-bound will find, with a little help from hellebore, that he is only idle or exhausted. But while this notion has possession of the head, it produces the inability which it supposes. Our powers owe much of their energy to our hopes; *possunt quia posse videntur.** When success seems attainable, diligence is enforced; but when it is admitted that the faculties are suppressed by a cross wind, or a cloudy sky, the day is given up without resistance; for who can contend with the course of Nature?

From such prepossessions Milton seems not to have been free. There prevailed in his time an opinion that the world was in its decay, and that we have had the misfortune to be produced in the decrepitude of Nature. It was suspected that the whole creation languished, that neither trees nor animals had the height or bulk of their predecessors, and that every thing was daily sinking by gradual diminution. Milton appears to suspect that souls partake of the general degeneracy, and is not without some fear that his book is to be written in *an age too late** for heroick poesy.

Another opinion wanders about the world, and sometimes finds reception among wise men; an opinion that restrains the operations of the mind to particular regions, and supposes that a luckless mortal may be born in a degree of latitude too high or too low for wisdom or for wit. From this fancy, wild as it is, he had not wholly cleared his head, when he feared lest the *climate* of his country might be *too cold* for flights of imagination.

Into a mind already occupied by such fancies, another not more reasonable might easily find its way. He that could fear lest his genius had fallen upon too old a world, or too chill a climate, might consistently magnify to himself the influence of the seasons, and believe his faculties to be vigorous only half the year.

His submission to the seasons was at least more reasonable than his dread of decaying Nature, or a frigid zone; for general causes must operate uniformly in a general abatement of mental power; if less could be performed by the writer, less likewise would content the judges of his work. Among this lagging race of frosty grovellers he might still have risen into eminence by producing something which *they should not willingly let die*.* However inferior to the heroes who were born in better ages, he might still be great among his contemporaries, with the hope of growing every day greater in the dwindle of posterity. He might still be the giant of the pygmies, the one-eyed monarch of the blind.

Of his artifices of study, or particular hours of composition, we have little account, and there was perhaps little to be told. Richardson, who seems to have been very diligent in his enquiries, but discovers always a wish to find Milton discriminated from other men, relates, that "he would sometimes lie awake whole nights, but not a verse could he make; and on a sudden his poetical faculty would rush upon him with an *impetus* or *œstrum*, and his daughter was immediately called to secure what came. At other times he would dictate perhaps forty lines in a breath, and then reduce them to half the number."

These bursts of lights, and involutions of darkness; these transient and involuntary excursions and retrocessions of invention, having some appearance of deviation from the common train of Nature, are eagerly caught by the lovers of a wonder. Yet something of this inequality happens to every man in every mode of exertion, manual or mental. The mechanick cannot handle his hammer and his file at all times with equal dexterity; there are hours, he knows not why, when *his hand is out*. By Mr. Richardson's relation, casually conveyed, much regard cannot be claimed. That, in his intellectual hour, Milton called for his daughter *to secure what came*, may be questioned; for unluckily it happens to be known that his daughters were never taught to write; nor would he have been obliged, as is universally confessed, to have employed any casual visiter in disburthening his memory, if his daughter could have performed the office.

The story of reducing his exuberance has been told of other authors, and, though doubtless true of every fertile and copious mind, seems to have been gratuitously transferred to Milton.

What he has told us, and we cannot now know more, is, that he composed much of his poem in the night and morning, I suppose before his mind was disturbed with common business; and that he poured out with great fluency his *unpremeditated verse*.* Versification, free, like his, from the distresses of rhyme, must, by a work so long, be made prompt and habitual; and, when his thoughts were once adjusted, the words would come at his command.

At what particular times of his life the parts of his work were written, cannot often be known. The beginning of the third book shews that he had lost his sight; and the Introduction to the seventh, that the return of the King had clouded him with discountenance; and that he was offended by the licentious festivity of the Restoration. There are no other internal notes of time. Milton, being now cleared from all effects of his disloyalty, had nothing required from him but the common duty of living in quiet, to be rewarded with the common right of protection: but this, which, when he sculked from the approach of his King, was perhaps more than he hoped, seems not to have satisfied him; for no sooner is he safe, than he finds himself in danger, *fallen on evil days and evil tongues, and with darkness and with danger compass'd round*.* This darkness, had his eyes been better employed, had undoubtedly deserved compassion: but to add the mention of danger was ungrateful and unjust. He was fallen indeed on *evil days*; the time was come in which regicides could no longer boast their wickedness. But of *evil tongues* for Milton to complain, required impudence at least equal to his other powers; Milton, whose warmest advocates must allow, that he never spared any asperity of reproach or brutality of insolence.

But the charge itself seems to be false; for it would be hard to recollect any reproach cast upon him, either serious or ludicrous, through the whole remaining part of his life. He pursued his studies, or his amusements, without persecution, molestation, or insult. Such is the reverence paid to great abilities, however misused: they who contemplated in Milton the scholar and the wit, were contented to forget the reviler of his King.

When the plague (1665) raged in London, Milton took refuge at Chalfont in Bucks; where Elwood,* who had taken the house for him, first saw a complete copy of *Paradise Lost*, and, having perused it, said to him, "Thou hafs said a great deal upon *Paradise Lost*; what hast thou to say upon *Paradise Found*?"

Next year, when the danger of infection had ceased, he returned to Bunhill-fields, and designed the publication of his poem. A license was necessary, and he could expect no great kindness from a chaplain of the archbishop of Canterbury.* He seems, however, to have been treated with tenderness; for though objections were made to particular passages, and among them to the simile of the sun eclipsed in the first book, yet the license was granted; and he sold his copy, April 27, 1667, to Samuel Simmons, for an immediate payment of five pounds, with a stipulation to receive five pounds more when thirteen hundred should be sold of the first edition: and again, five pounds after the sale of the same number of the second edition: and another five pounds after the same sale of the third. None of the three editions were to be extended beyond fifteen hundred copies.

The first edition was ten books, in a small quarto. The titles were varied from year to year; and an advertisement and the arguments of the books were omitted in some copies, and inserted in others.

The sale gave him in two years a right to his second payment, for which the receipt was signed April 26, 1669. The second edition was not given till 1674; it was printed in small octavo; and the number of books was increased to twelve, by a division of the seventh and twelfth; and some other small improvements were made. The third edition was published in 1678; and the widow, to whom the copy was then to devolve, sold all her claims to Simmons for eight pounds, according to her receipt given Dec. 21, 1680. Simmons had already agreed to transfer the whole right to Brabazon Aylmer for twenty-five pounds; and Aylmer sold to Jacob Tonson* half, August 17, 1683, and half, March 24, 1690, at a price considerably enlarged. In the history of *Paradise Lost* a deduction thus minute will rather gratify than fatigue.

The slow sale and tardy reputation of this poem have been always mentioned as evidences of neglected merit, and of the uncertainty of literary fame; and enquiries have been made, and conjectures offered, about the causes of its long obscurity and late reception. But has the case been truly stated? Have not lamentation and wonder been lavished on an evil that was never felt?

That in the reigns of Charles and James the *Paradise Lost* received no publick acclamations, is readily confessed. Wit and literature were on the side of the Court: and who that solicited favour or fashion would venture to praise the defender of the regicides? All that he himself could think his due, from *evil tongues* in *evil days*, was that reverential silence which was generously preserved. But it cannot be inferred that his poem was not read, or not, however unwillingly, admired.

The sale, if it be considered, will justify the publick. Those who have no power to judge of past times but by their own, should always doubt their conclusions. The call for books was not in Milton's age what it is in the present. To read was not then a general amusement; neither traders, nor often gentlemen, thought themselves disgraced by ignorance. The women had not then aspired to literature, nor was every house supplied with a closet of knowledge. Those, indeed, who professed learning, were not less learned than at any other time; but of that middle race of students who read for pleasure or accomplishment, and who buy the numerous products of modern typography, the number was then comparatively small. To prove the paucity of readers, it may be sufficient to remark, that the nation had been satisfied, from 1623 to 1664, that is, forty-one years, with only two editions of the works of Shakspeare,* which probably did not together make one thousand copies.

The sale of thirteen hundred copies in two years, in opposition to so much recent enmity, and to a style of versification new to all and disgusting to many, was an uncommon example of the prevalence of genius. The demand did not immediately increase; for many more readers than were supplied at first the nation did not afford. Only three thousand were sold in eleven years; for it forced its way without assistance: its admirers did not dare to publish their opinion; and the opportunities now given of attracting notice by advertisements were then very few; the means of proclaiming the publication of new books have been produced by that general literature which now pervades the nation through all its ranks.

But the reputation and price of the copy still advanced, till the Revolution* put an end to the secrecy of love, and *Paradise Lost* broke into open view with sufficient security of kind reception.

Fancy can hardly forbear to conjecture with what temper Milton surveyed the silent progress of his work, and marked his reputation stealing its way in a kind of subterraneous current through fear and silence. I cannot but conceive him calm and confident, little disappointed, not at all dejected, relying on his own merit with steady consciousness, and waiting, without impatience, the vicissitudes of opinion, and the impartiality of a future generation.

In the mean time he continued his studies, and supplied the want of sight by a very odd expedient, of which Philips gives the following account:

Mr. Philips tells us, "that though our author had daily about him one or other to read, some persons of man's estate, who, of their own accord, greedily catched at the opportunity of being his readers, that they might as well reap the benefit of what they read to him, as oblige him by the benefit of their reading; and others of younger years were sent by their parents to the same end: yet excusing only the eldest daughter, by reason of her bodily infirmity, and difficult utterance of speech, (which, to say truth, I doubt was the principal cause of excusing her), the other two were condemned to the performance of reading, and exactly pronouncing of all the languages of whatever book he should, at one time or other, think fit to peruse, viz. the Hebrew (and I think the Syriac), the Greek, the Latin, the Italian, Spanish, and French. All which sorts of books to be confined to read, without understanding one word, must needs be a trial of patience almost beyond endurance. Yet it was endured by both for a long time, though the irksomeness of this employment could not be always concealed, but broke out more and more into expressions of uneasiness; so that at length they were all, even the eldest also, sent out to learn some curious and ingenious sorts of manufacture, that are proper for women to learn; particularly embroideries in gold or silver."*

In the scene of misery which this mode of intellectual labour sets before our eyes, it is hard to determine whether the daughters or the father are most to be lamented. A language not understood can never be so read as to give pleasure, and very seldom so as to convey meaning. If few men would have had resolution to write books with such embarrassments, few likewise would have wanted ability to find some better expedient.

Three years after his *Paradise Lost* (1667), he published his *History of England*, comprising the whole fable of Geoffry of Monmouth, and continued to the Norman invasion. Why he should have given the first part, which he seems not to believe, and which is universally rejected, it is difficult to conjecture. The style is harsh; but it has something of rough vigour, which perhaps may often strike, though it cannot please.

On this history the licenser again fixed his claws, and before he would transmit it to the press tore out several parts. Some censures of the Saxon monks were taken away, lest they should be applied to the modern clergy; and a character of the Long Parliament, and Assembly of Divines, was excluded; of which the author gave a copy to the earl of Anglesea,* and which, being afterwards published, has been since inserted in its proper place.

The same year were printed *Paradise Regained*, and *Sampson Agonistes*, a tragedy written in imitation of the Ancients, and never designed by the author for the stage. As these poems were published by another bookseller, it has been asked, whether Simmons was discouraged from receiving them by the slow sale of the former. Why a writer changed his bookseller a hundred years ago, I am far from hoping to discover. Certainly, he who in two years sells thirteen hundred copies of a volume in quarto, bought for two payments of five pounds each, has no reason to repent his purchase.

When Milton shewed *Paradise Regained* to Elwood, "This," said he, "is owing to you; for you put it in my head by the question you put to me at Chalfont, which otherwise I had not thought of."

His last poetical offspring was his favourite. He could not, as Elwood relates, endure to hear *Paradise Lost* preferred to *Paradise Regained*. Many causes may vitiate a writer's judgement of his own works. On that which has cost him much labour he sets a high value, because he is unwilling to think that he has been diligent in vain; what has been produced without toilsome efforts is considered with delight, as a proof of vigorous faculties and fertile invention; and the last work, whatever it be, has necessarily most of the grace of novelty. Milton, however it happened, had this prejudice, and had it to himself.

To that multiplicity of attainments, and extent of comprehension, that entitle this great author to our veneration, may be added a kind of humble dignity, which did not disdain the meanest services to literature. The epic poet, the controvertist, the politician, having already descended to accommodate children with a book of rudiments, now, in the last years of his life, composed a book of Logick, for the initiation of students in philosophy: and published (1672) *Artis Logicae plenior Institutio ad Petri Rami methodum concinnata*; that is, "A new Scheme of Logick, according to the Method of Ramus." I know not whether, even in this book, he did not intend an act of hostility against the Universities; for Ramus* was one of the first oppugners of the old philosophy, who disturbed with innovations the quiet of the schools.

His polemical disposition again revived. He had now been safe so long, that he forgot his fears, and published a *Treatise of true Religion, Heresy, Schism, Toleration, and the best Means to prevent the Growth of Popery*.

But this little tract is modestly written, with respectful mention of the Church of England, and an appeal to the thirty-nine articles. His principle of toleration is, agreement in the sufficiency of the Scriptures; and he extends it to all who, whatever their opinions are, profess to derive them from the sacred books. The papists appeal to other testimonies, and are therefore in his opinion not to be permitted the liberty of either publick or private worship; for though they plead conscience, *we have no warrant*, he says, *to regard conscience which is not grounded in Scripture*.

Those who are not convinced by his reasons, may be perhaps delighted with his wit. The term *Roman catholick* is, he says, *one of the Pope's bulls; it is particular universal, or catholick schismatick*.

He has, however, something better. As the best preservative against Popery, he recommends the diligent perusal of the Scriptures; a duty, from which he warns the busy part of mankind not to think themselves excused.

He now reprinted his juvenile poems, with some additions.

In the last year of his life he sent to the press, seeming to take delight in publication, a collection of Familiar Epistles in Latin; to which, being too few to make a volume, he added some academical exercises, which perhaps he perused with pleasure, as they recalled to his memory the days of youth; but for which nothing but veneration for his name could now procure a reader.

When he had attained his sixty-sixth year, the gout, with which he had been long tormented, prevailed over the enfeebled powers of nature. He died by a quiet and silent expiration, about the tenth of November 1674, at his house in Bunhill-fields; and was buried next his father in the chancel of St. Giles at Cripplegate. His funeral was very splendidly and numerously attended.

Upon his grave there is supposed to have been no memorial; but in our time a monument has been erected in Westminster-Abbey *To the Author of Paradise Lost*, by Mr. Benson,* who has in the inscription bestowed more words upon himself than upon Milton.

When the inscription for the monument of Philips, in which he was said to be *soli Miltono secundus*, was exhibited to Dr. Sprat, then dean of Westminster, he refused to admit it; the name of Milton was, in his opinion, too detestable to be read on the wall of a building dedicated to devotion. Atterbury, who succeeded him, being author of the inscription, permitted its reception. "And such has been the change of publick opinion," said Dr. Gregory, from whom I heard this account, "that I have seen erected in the church a statue of that man, whose name I once knew considered as a pollution of its walls."*

Milton has the reputation of having been in his youth eminently beautiful, so as to have been called the Lady of his college. His hair, which was of a light brown, parted at the foretop, and hung down upon his shoulders, according to the picture which he has given of Adam. He was, however, not of the heroick stature, but rather below the middle size, according to Mr. Richardson, who mentions him as having narrowly escaped from being *short and thick*. He was vigorous and active, and delighted in the exercise of the sword, in which he is related to have been eminently skilful. His weapon was, I believe, not the rapier, but the backsword, of which he recommends the use in his book on Education.

His eyes are said never to have been bright; but, if he was a dexterous fencer, they must have been once quick.

His domestick habits, so far as they are known, were those of a severe student. He drank little strong drink of any kind, and fed without excess in quantity, and in his earlier years without delicacy of choice. In his youth he studied late at night; but afterwards changed his hours, and rested in bed from nine to four in the summer, and five in winter. The course of his day was best known after he was blind. When he first rose, he heard a chapter in the Hebrew Bible, and then studied till twelve; then took some exercise for an hour; then dined; then played on the organ, and sung, or heard another sing; then studied to six; then entertained his visiters till eight; then supped, and, after a pipe of tobacco and a glass of water, went to bed.

So is his life described; but this even tenour appears attainable only in Colleges. He that lives in the world will sometimes have the succession of his practice broken and confused. Visiters, of whom Milton is represented to have had great numbers, will come and stay unseasonably; business, of which every man has some, must be done when others will do it.

When he did not care to rise early, he had something read to him by his bedside; perhaps at this time his daughters were employed.

He composed much in the morning, and dictated in the day, sitting obliquely in an elbow-chair, with his leg thrown over the arm.

Fortune appears not to have had much of his care. In the civil wars he lent his personal estate to the parliament; but when, after the contest was decided, he solicited repayment, he met not only with neglect, but *sharp rebuke*; and, having tired both himself and his friends, was given up to poverty and hopeless indignation, till he shewed how able he was to do greater service. He was then made Latin secretary, with two hundred pounds a year; and had a thousand pounds for his *Defence of the People*. His widow, who, after his death, retired to Namptwich in Cheshire, and died about 1729, is said to have reported that he lost two thousand pounds by entrusting it to a scrivener; and that, in the general depredation upon the Church, he had grasped an estate of about sixty pounds a year belonging to Westminster-Abbey, which, like other sharers of the plunder of rebellion, he was afterwards obliged to return. Two thousand pounds, which he had placed in the Excise-office, were also lost. There is yet no reason to believe that he was ever reduced to indigence. His wants, being few, were competently supplied. He sold his library before his death, and left his family fifteen hundred pounds, on which his widow laid hold, and only gave one hundred to each of his daughters.

His literature was unquestionably great. He read all the languages which are considered either as learned or polite; Hebrew, with its two dialects, Greek, Latin, Italian, French, and Spanish. In Latin his skill was such as places him in the first rank of writers and criticks; and he appears to have cultivated Italian with uncommon diligence. The books in which his daughter, who used to read to him, represented him as most delighting, after Homer, which he could almost repeat, were Ovid's Metamorphoses and Euripides. His Euripides is, by Mr. Cradock's kindness,* now in my hands: the margin is sometimes noted; but I have found nothing remarkable.

Of the English poets he set most value upon Spenser, Shakspeare, and Cowley. Spenser was apparently his favourite: Shakspeare he may easily be supposed to like, with every other skilful reader; but I should not have expected that Cowley, whose ideas of excellence were so different from his own, would have had much of his approbation. His character of Dryden, who sometimes visited him, was, that he was a good rhymist, but no poet.

His theological opinions are said to have been first Calvinistical; and afterwards, perhaps when he began to hate the Presbyterians, to have tended towards Arminianism.* In the mixed questions of theology and government, he never thinks that he can recede far enough from popery, or prelacy; but what Baudius says of Erasmus seems applicable to him, *magis habuit quod fugeret, quam quod sequeretur.** He had determined rather what to condemn, than what to approve. He has not associated himself with any denomination of Protestants: we know rather what he was not, than what he was. He was not of the church of Rome; he was not of the church of England.

To be of no church, is dangerous. Religion, of which the rewards are distant, and which is animated only by Faith and Hope, will glide by degrees out of the mind, unless it be invigorated and reimpressed by external ordinances, by stated calls to worship, and the salutary influence of example. Milton, who appears to have had full conviction of the truth of Christianity, and to have regarded the Holy Scriptures with the profoundest veneration, to have been untainted by any heretical peculiarity of opinion, and to have lived in a confirmed belief of the immediate and occasional agency of Providence, yet grew old without any visible worship. In the distribution of his hours, there was no hour of prayer, either solitary, or with his household; omitting publick prayers, he omitted all.

Of this omission the reason has been sought, upon a supposition which ought never to be made, that men live with their own approbation, and justify their conduct to themselves. Prayer certainly was not thought superfluous by him, who represents our first parents as praying acceptably in the state of innocence, and efficaciously after their fall. That he lived without prayer can hardly be affirmed; his studies and meditations were an habitual prayer. The neglect of it in his family was probably a fault for which he condemned himself, and which he intended to correct, but that death, as too often happens, intercepted his reformation.

His political notions were those of an acrimonious and surly republican, for which it is not known that he gave any better reason than that *a popular government was the most frugal; for the trappings of a monarchy would set up an ordinary commonwealth.** It is surely very shallow policy, that supposes money to be the chief good; and even this, without considering that the support and expence of a Court is, for the most part, only a particular kind of traffick, by which money is circulated, without any national impoverishment.

Milton's republicanism was, I am afraid, founded in an envious hatred of greatness, and a sullen desire of independence; in petulance impatient of controul, and pride disdainful of superiority. He hated monarchs in the state, and prelates in the church; for he hated all whom he was required to obey. It is to be suspected, that his predominant desire was to destroy rather than establish, and that he felt not so much the love of liberty as repugnance to authority.

It has been observed, that they who most loudly clamour for liberty do not most liberally grant it. What we know of Milton's character, in domestick relations, is, that he was severe and arbitrary. His family consisted of women; and there appears in his books something like a Turkish contempt of females, as subordinate and inferior beings. That his own daughters might not break the ranks, he suffered them to be depressed by a mean and penurious education. He thought woman made only for obedience, and man only for rebellion.

Of his family some account may be expected. His sister, first married to Mr. Philips, afterwards married Mr. Agar, a friend of her first husband, who succeeded him in the Crown-office. She had by her first husband Edward and John, the two nephews whom Milton educated; and by her second, two daughters.

His brother, Sir Christopher, had two daughters, Mary and Catherine, and a son Thomas, who succeeded Agar in the Crown-office, and left a daughter living in 1749 in Grosvenor-street.*

Milton had children only by his first wife; Anne, Mary, and Deborah. Anne, though deformed, married a master-builder, and died of her first child. Mary died single. Deborah married Abraham Clark, a weaver in Spital-fields, and lived seventy-six years, to August 1727. This is the daughter of whom publick mention has been made. She could repeat the first lines of Homer, the Metamorphoses, and some of Euripides, by having often read them. Yet here incredulity is ready to make a stand. Many repetitions are necessary to fix in the memory lines not understood; and why should Milton wish or want to hear them so often! These lines were at the beginning of the poems. Of a book written in a language not understood, the beginning raises no more attention than the end; and as those that understand it know commonly the beginning best, its rehearsal will seldom be necessary. It is not likely that Milton required any passage to be so much repeated as that his daughter could learn it; nor likely that he desired the initial lines to be read at all: nor that the daughter, weary of the drudgery of pronouncing unideal* sounds, would voluntarily commit them to memory.

To this gentlewoman Addison made a present, and promised some establishment; but died soon after. Queen Caroline sent her fifty guineas. She had seven sons and three daughters; but none of them had any children, except her son Caleb and her daughter Elizabeth. Caleb went to Fort St. George in the East Indies, and had two sons, of whom nothing is now known. Elizabeth married Thomas Foster, a weaver in Spital-fields, and had seven children, who all died. She kept a petty grocer's or chandler's shop, first at Holloway, and afterwards in Cock-lane near Shoreditch Church. She knew little of her grandfather, and that little was not good. She told of his harshness to his daughters, and his refusal to have them taught to write; and, in opposition to other accounts, represented him as delicate, though temperate, in his diet.

In 1750, April 5, *Comus* was played for her benefit.* She had so little acquaintance with diversion or gaiety, that she did not know what was intended when a benefit was offered her. The profits of the night were only one hundred and thirty pounds, though Dr. Newton brought a large contribution; and twenty pounds were given by Tonson, a man who is to be praised as often as he is named. Of this sum one hundred pounds was placed in the stocks, after some debate between her and her husband in whose name it should be entered; and the rest augmented their little stock, with which they removed to Islington. This was the greatest benefaction that *Paradise Lost* ever procured the author's descendents; and to this he who has now attempted to relate his Life, had the honour of contributing a Prologue.

IN the examination of Milton's poetical works, I shall pay so much regard to time as to begin with his juvenile productions. For his early pieces he seems to have had a degree of fondness not very laudable: what he has once written he resolves to preserve, and gives to the publick an unfinished poem, which he broke off because he was *nothing satisfied with what he had done*,* supposing his readers less nice than himself. These preludes to his future labours are in Italian,

Latin, and English. Of the Italian I cannot pretend to speak as a critick; but I have heard them commended by a man well qualified to decide their merit. The Latin pieces are lusciously elegant; but the delight which they afford is rather by the exquisite imitation of the ancient writers, by the purity of the diction, and the harmony of the numbers, than by any power of invention, or vigour of sentiment. They are not all of equal value; the elegies excell the odes; and some of the exercises on Gunpowder Treason might have been spared.

The English poems, though they make no promises of *Paradise Lost*, have this evidence of genius, that they have a cast original and unborrowed. But their peculiarity is not excellence: if they differ from the verses of others, they differ for the worse; for they are too often distinguished by repulsive harshness; the combinations of words are new, but they are not pleasing; the rhymes and epithets seem to be laboriously sought, and violently applied.

That in the early parts of his life he wrote with much care appears from his manuscripts, happily preserved at Cambridge, in which many of his smaller works are found as they were first written, with the subsequent corrections. Such reliques shew how excellence is acquired; what we hope ever to do with ease, we may learn first to do with diligence.

Those who admire the beauties of this great poet, sometimes force their own judgement into false approbation of his little pieces, and prevail upon themselves to think that admirable which is only singular. All that short compositions can commonly attain is neatness and elegance. Milton never learned the art of doing little things with grace; he overlooked the milder excellence of suavity and softness; he was a *Lion* that had no skill *in dandling the Kid.**

One of the poems on which much praise has been bestowed is *Lycidas*; of which the diction is harsh, the rhymes uncertain, and the numbers unpleasing. What beauty there is, we must therefore seek in the sentiments and images. It is not to be considered as the effusion of real passion; for passion runs not after remote allusions and obscure opinions. Passion plucks no berries from the myrtle and ivy, nor calls upon Arethuse and Mincius, nor tells of rough *satyrs* and *fauns with cloven heel.** Where there is leisure for fiction there is little grief.

In this poem there is no nature, for there is no truth; there is no art, for there is nothing new. Its form is that of a pastoral, easy, vulgar, and therefore disgusting: whatever images it can supply, are long ago exhausted; and its inherent improbability always forces dissatisfaction on the mind. When Cowley tells of Hervey that they studied together,* it is easy to suppose how much he must miss the companion of his labours, and the partner of his discoveries; but what image of tenderness can be excited by these lines!

> We drove a field, and both together heard
> What time the grey fly winds her sultry horn,
> Battening our flocks with the fresh dews of night.*

We know that they never drove a field, and that they had no flocks to batten; and though it be allowed that the representation may be allegorical, the true meaning is so uncertain and remote, that it is never sought because it cannot be known when it is found.

Among the flocks, and copses, and flowers, appear the heathen deities; Jove and Phœbus, Neptune and Æolus, with a long train of mythological imagery, such as a College easily supplies. Nothing can less display knowledge, or less exercise invention, than to tell how a shepherd has lost his companion, and must now feed his flocks alone, without any judge of his skill in piping; and how one god asks another god what is become of Lycidas, and how neither god can tell. He who thus grieves will excite no sympathy; he who thus praises will confer no honour.

This poem has yet a grosser fault. With these trifling fictions are mingled the most awful and sacred truths, such as ought never to be polluted with such irreverend combinations. The shepherd likewise is now a feeder of sheep, and afterwards an ecclesiastical pastor, a superintendent of a Christian flock. Such equivocations are always unskilful; but here they are indecent, and at least approach to impiety, of which, however, I believe the writer not to have been conscious.

Such is the power of reputation justly acquired, that its blaze drives away the eye from nice examination. Surely no man could have fancied that he read *Lycidas* with pleasure, had he not known its author.

Of the two pieces, *L'Allegro* and *Il Penseroso*, I believe opinion is uniform; every man that reads them, reads them with pleasure. The author's design is not, what Theobald has remarked,* merely to shew how objects derive their colours from the mind, by representing the operation of the same things upon the gay and the melancholy temper, or upon the same man as he is differently disposed; but rather how, among the successive variety of appearances, every disposition of mind takes hold on those by which it may be gratified.

The *chearful* man hears the lark in the morning; the *pensive* man hears the nightingale in the evening. The *chearful* man sees the cock strut, and hears the horn and hounds echo in the wood; then walks *not unseen** to observe the glory of the rising sun, or listen to the singing milk-maid, and view the labours of the plowman and the mower; then casts his eyes about him over scenes of smiling plenty, and looks up to the distant tower, the residence of some fair inhabitant; thus he pursues rural gaiety through a day of labour or of play, and delights himself at night with the fanciful narratives of superstitious ignorance.

The *pensive* man, at one time, walks *unseen* to muse at midnight; and at another hears the sullen curfew. If the weather drives him home, he sits in a room lighted only by *glowing embers*;* or by a lonely lamp outwatches the North Star, to discover the habitation of separate souls, and varies the shades of meditation, by contemplating the magnificent or pathetick scenes of tragick and epic poetry. When the morning comes, a morning gloomy with rain and wind, he walks into the dark trackless woods, falls asleep by some murmuring water, and with melancholy enthusiasm expects some dream of prognostication, or some musick played by aerial performers.

Both Mirth and Melancholy are solitary, silent inhabitants of the breast that neither receive nor transmit communication; no mention is therefore made of a philosophical friend, or a pleasant companion. The seriousness does not arise from any participation of calamity, nor the gaiety from the pleasures of the bottle.

The man of *chearfulness*, having exhausted the country, tries what *towered cities** will afford, and mingles with scenes of splendor, gay assemblies, and nuptial festivities; but he mingles a mere spectator, as, when the learned comedies of Jonson, or the wild dramas of Shakspeare, are exhibited, he attends the theatre.

The *pensive* man never loses himself in crowds, but walks the cloister, or frequents the cathedral. Milton probably had not yet forsaken the Church.

Both his characters delight in musick; but he seems to think that chearful notes would have obtained from Pluto a compleat dismission of Eurydice, of whom solemn sounds only procured a conditional release.

For the old age of Chearfulness he makes no provision; but Melancholy he conducts with great dignity to the close of life. His Chearfulness is without levity, and his Pensiveness without asperity.

Through these two poems the images are properly selected, and nicely distinguished; but the colours of the diction seem not sufficiently discriminated. I know not whether the characters are kept sufficiently apart. No mirth can, indeed, be found in his melancholy; but I am afraid that I always meet some melancholy in his mirth. They are two noble efforts of imagination.

The greatest of his juvenile performances is the *Mask of Comus*; in which may very plainly be discovered the dawn or twilight of *Paradise Lost*. Milton appears to have formed very early that system of diction, and mode of verse, which his maturer judgement approved, and from which he never endeavoured nor desired to deviate.

Nor does *Comus* afford only a specimen of his language; it exhibits likewise his power of description and his vigour of sentiment, employed in the praise and defence of virtue. A work more truly poetical is rarely found; allusions, images, and descriptive epithets, embellish almost every period with lavish decoration. As a series of lines, therefore, it may be considered as worthy of all the admiration with which the votaries have received it.

As a drama it is deficient. The action is not probable. A Masque, in those parts where supernatural intervention is admitted, must indeed be given up to all the freaks of imagination; but, so far as the action is merely human, it ought to be reasonable, which can hardly be said of the conduct of the two brothers; who, when their sister sinks with fatigue in a pathless wilderness, wander both away together in search of berries too far to find their way back, and leave a helpless Lady to all the sadness and danger of solitude. This however is a defect overbalanced by its convenience.

What deserves more reprehension is, that the prologue spoken in the wild wood by the attendant Spirit is addressed to the audience; a mode of communication so contrary to the nature of dramatick representation, that no precedents can support it.

The discourse of the Spirit is too long; an objection that may be made to almost all the following speeches: they have not the spriteliness of a dialogue animated by reciprocal contention, but seem rather declamations deliberately composed, and formally repeated, on a moral question. The auditor therefore listens as to a lecture, without passion, without anxiety.

The song of Comus has airiness and jollity; but, what may recommend Milton's morals as well as his poetry, the invitations to pleasure are so general, that they excite no distinct images of corrupt enjoyment, and take no dangerous hold on the fancy.

The following soliloquies of Comus and the Lady are elegant, but tedious. The song must owe much to the voice, if it ever can delight. At last the Brothers enter, with too much tranquillity; and when they have feared lest their sister should be in danger, and hoped that she is not in danger, the Elder makes a speech in praise of chastity, and the Younger finds how fine it is to be a philosopher.

Then descends the Spirit in form of a shepherd; and the Brother, instead of being in haste to ask his help, praises his singing, and enquires his business in that place. It is remarkable, that at this interview the Brother is taken with a short fit of rhyming. The Spirit relates that the Lady is in the power of Comus; the Brother moralises again; and the Spirit makes a long narration, of no use because it is false, and therefore unsuitable to a good Being.

In all these parts the language is poetical, and the sentiments are generous; but there is something wanting to allure attention.

The dispute between the Lady and Comus is the most animated and affecting scene of the drama, and wants nothing but a brisker reciprocation of objections and replies, to invite attention, and detain it.

The songs are vigorous, and full of imagery; but they are harsh in their diction, and not very musical in their numbers.

Throughout the whole, the figures are too bold, and the language too luxuriant for dialogue. It is a drama in the epic style, inelegantly splendid, and tediously instructive.

The *Sonnets* were written in different parts of Milton's life, upon different occasions. They deserve not any particular criticism; for of the best it can only be said, that they are not bad; and perhaps only the eighth and the twenty-first are truly entitled to this slender commendation. The fabrick of a sonnet, however adapted to the Italian language, has never succeeded in ours, which, having greater variety of termination, requires the rhymes to be often changed.

Those little pieces may be dispatched without much anxiety; a greater work calls for greater care. I am now to examine *Paradise Lost*; a poem, which, considered with respect to design, may claim the first place, and with respect to performance the second, among the productions of the human mind.

By the general consent of criticks, the first praise of genius is due to the writer of an epick poem, as it requires an assemblage of all the powers which are singly sufficient for other compositions. Poetry is the art of uniting pleasure with truth, by calling imagination to the help of reason. Epick poetry undertakes to teach the most important truths by the most pleasing precepts, and therefore relates some great event in the most affecting manner. History must supply the writer with the rudiments of narration, which he must improve and exalt by a nobler art, must animate by dramatick energy, and diversify by retrospection and anticipation; morality must teach him the exact bounds, and different shades, of vice and virtue; from policy, and the practice of life, he has to learn the discriminations of character, and the tendency of the passions, either single or combined; and physiology must supply him with illustrations and images. To put these materials to poetical use, is required an imagination capable of painting nature, and realizing fiction. Nor is he yet a poet till he has attained the whole extension of his language, distinguished all the delicacies of phrase, and all the colours of words, and learned to adjust their different sounds to all the varieties of metrical modulation.

Bossu* is of opinion that the poet's first work is to find a *moral*, which his fable is afterwards to illustrate and establish. This seems to have been the process only of Milton; the moral of other poems is incidental and consequent; in Milton's only it is essential and intrinsick. His purpose was the most useful and the most arduous; *to vindicate the ways of God to man*;* to shew the reasonableness of religion, and the necessity of obedience to the Divine Law.

To convey this moral, there must be a *fable*, a narration artfully constructed, so as to excite curiosity, and surprise expectation. In this part of his work, Milton must be confessed to have equalled every other poet. He has involved in his account of the Fall of Man the events which preceded, and those that were to follow it: he has interwoven the whole system of theology with such propriety, that every part appears to be necessary; and scarcely any recital is wished shorter for the sake of quickening the progress of the main action.

The subject of an epic poem is naturally an event of great importance. That of Milton is not the destruction of a city, the conduct of a colony, or the foundation of an empire. His subject is the fate of worlds, the revolutions of heaven and of earth; rebellion against the Supreme King, raised by the highest order of created beings; the overthrow of their host, and the punishment of their crime; the creation of a new race of reasonable creatures; their original happiness and innocence, their forfeiture of immortality, and their restoration to hope and peace.

Great events can be hastened or retarded only by persons of elevated dignity. Before the greatness displayed in Milton's poem, all other greatness shrinks away. The weakest of his agents are the highest and noblest of human beings, the original parents of mankind; with whose actions the elements consented; on whose rectitude, or deviation of will, depended the state of terrestrial nature, and the condition of all the future inhabitants of the globe.

Of the other agents in the poem, the chief are such as it is irreverence to name on slight occasions. The rest were lower powers;

> —of which the least could wield
> Those elements, and arm him with the force
> Of all their regions;*

powers, which only the controul of Omnipotence restrains from laying creation waste, and filling the vast expanse of space with ruin and confusion. To display the motives and actions of beings thus superiour, so far as human reason can examine them, or human imagination represent them, is the task which this mighty poet has undertaken and performed.

In the examination of epick poems much speculation is commonly employed upon the *characters*. The characters in the *Paradise Lost*, which admit of examination, are those of angels and of man; of angels good and evil; of man in his innocent and sinful state.

Among the angels, the virtue of Raphael is mild and placid, of easy condescension and free communication; that of Michael is regal and lofty, and, as may seem, attentive to the dignity of his own nature. Abdiel and Gabriel appear occasionally, and act as every incident requires; the solitary fidelity of Abdiel is very amiably painted.

Of the evil angels the characters are more diversified. To Satan, as Addison observes,* such sentiments are given as suit *the most exalted and most depraved being*. Milton has been censured, by Clarke[1], for

[1] Essay on Study.

the impiety which sometimes breaks from Satan's mouth. For there are thoughts, as he justly remarks, which no observation of character can justify, because no good man would willingly permit them to pass, however transiently, through his own mind. To make Satan speak as a rebel, without any such expressions as might taint the reader's imagination, was indeed one of the great difficulties in Milton's undertaking, and I cannot but think that he has extricated himself with great happiness. There is in Satan's speeches little that can give pain to a pious ear. The language of rebellion cannot be the same with that of obedience. The malignity of Satan foams in haughtiness and obstinacy; but his expressions are commonly general, and no otherwise offensive than as they are wicked.

The other chiefs of the celestial rebellion are very judiciously discriminated in the first and second books; and the ferocious character of Moloch appears, both in the battle and the council, with exact consistency.

To Adam and to Eve are given, during their innocence, such sentiments as innocence can generate and utter. Their love is pure benevolence and mutual veneration; their repasts are without luxury, and their diligence without toil. Their addresses to their Maker have little more than the voice of admiration and gratitude. Fruition left them nothing to ask, and Innocence left them nothing to fear.

But with guilt enter distrust and discord, mutual accusation, and stubborn self-defence; they regard each other with alienated minds, and dread their Creator as the avenger of their transgression. At last they seek shelter in his mercy, soften to repentance, and melt in supplication. Both before and after the Fall, the superiority of Adam is diligently sustained.

Of the *probable* and the *marvellous*, two parts of a vulgar epic poem, which immerge the critick in deep consideration, the *Paradise Lost* requires little to be said. It contains the history of a miracle, of Creation and Redemption; it displays the power and the mercy of the Supreme Being; the probable therefore is marvellous, and the marvellous is probable. The substance of the narrative is truth; and as truth allows no choice, it is, like necessity, superior to rule. To the accidental or adventitious parts, as to every thing human, some slight exceptions may be made. But the main fabrick is immovably supported.

It is justly remarked by Addison, that this poem has, by the nature of its subject, the advantage above all others, that it is universally and perpetually interesting. All mankind will, through all ages, bear the same relation to Adam and to Eve, and must partake of that good and evil which extend to themselves.

Of the *machinery*, so called from Θεὸς ἀπο μηχανῆς,* by which is meant the occasional interposition of supernatural power, another fertile topic of critical remarks, here is no room to speak, because every thing is done under the immediate and visible direction of Heaven; but the rule is so far observed, that no part of the action could have been accomplished by any other means.

Of *episodes*, I think there are only two, contained in Raphael's relation of the war in heaven, and Michael's prophetick account of the changes to happen in this world. Both are closely connected with the great action; one was necessary to Adam as a warning, the other as a consolation.

To the compleatness or *integrity* of the design nothing can be objected; it has distinctly and clearly what Aristotle requires, a beginning, a middle, and an end. There is perhaps no poem, of the same length, from which so little can be taken without apparent mutilation. Here are no funeral games, nor is there any long description of a shield. The short digressions at the beginning of the third, seventh, and ninth books, might doubtless be spared; but superfluities so beautiful, who would take away? or who does not wish that the author of the *Iliad* had gratified succeeding ages with a little knowledge of himself? Perhaps no passages are more frequently or more attentively read than those extrinsick paragraphs; and, since the end of poetry is pleasure, that cannot be unpoetical with which all are pleased.

The questions, whether the action of the poem be strictly *one*, whether the poem can be properly termed *heroick*, and who is the hero, are raised by such readers as draw their principles of judgement rather from books than from reason. Milton, though he intituled *Paradise Lost* only a *poem*, yet calls it himself *heroick song*. Dryden, petulantly and indecently, denies the heroism of Adam, because he was overcome;* but there is no reason why the hero should not be unfortunate, except established practice, since success and virtue do not go necessarily together. Cato is the hero of Lucan; but Lucan's authority will not be suffered by Quintilian to decide.* However, if success be necessary, Adam's deceiver was at last crushed; Adam was restored to his Maker's favour, and therefore may securely resume his human rank.

After the scheme and fabrick of the poem, must be considered its component parts, the sentiments and the diction.

The *sentiments*, as expressive of manners, or appropriated to characters, are, for the greater part, unexceptionably just.

Splendid passages, containing lessons of morality, or precepts of prudence, occur seldom. Such is the original formation of this poem, that as it admits no human manners till the Fall, it can give little assistance to human conduct. Its end is to raise the thoughts above sublunary cares or pleasures. Yet the praise of that fortitude, with which Abdiel maintained his singularity of virtue against the scorn of multitudes, may be accommodated to all times; and Raphael's reproof of Adam's curiosity after the planetary motions, with the answer returned by Adam, may be confidently opposed to any rule of life which any poet has delivered.

The thoughts which are occasionally called forth in the progress, are such as could only be produced by an imagination in the highest degree fervid and active, to which materials were supplied by incessant study and unlimited curiosity. The heat of Milton's mind might be said to sublimate his learning, to throw off into his work the spirit of science, unmingled with its grosser parts.

He had considered creation in its whole extent, and his descriptions are therefore learned. He had accustomed his imagination to unrestrained indulgence, and his conceptions therefore were extensive. The characteristick quality of his poem is sublimity. He sometimes descends to the elegant, but his element is the great. He can occasionally invest himself with grace; but his natural port is gigantick loftiness.[1] He can please when pleasure is required; but it is his peculiar power to astonish.

He seems to have been well acquainted with his own genius, and to know what it was that Nature had bestowed upon him more bountifully than upon others; the power of displaying the vast, illuminating the splendid, enforcing the awful, darkening the gloomy, and aggravating the dreadful: he therefore chose a subject on which too much could not be said, on which he might tire his fancy without the censure of extravagance.

The appearances of nature, and the occurrences of life, did not satiate his appetite of greatness. To paint things as they are, requires

[1] Algarotti terms it *gigantesca sublimità Miltoniana*.

a minute attention, and employs the memory rather than the fancy. Milton's delight was to sport in the wide regions of possibility; reality was a scene too narrow for his mind. He sent his faculties out upon discovery, into worlds where only imagination can travel, and delighted to form new modes of existence, and furnish sentiment and action to superior beings, to trace the counsels of hell, or accompany the choirs of heaven.

But he could not be always in other worlds: he must sometimes revisit earth, and tell of things visible and known. When he cannot raise wonder by the sublimity of his mind, he gives delight by its fertility.

Whatever be his subject, he never fails to fill the imagination. But his images and descriptions of the scenes or operations of Nature do not seem to be always copied from original form, nor to have the freshness, raciness, and energy of immediate observation. He saw Nature, as Dryden expresses it, *through the spectacles of books*;* and on most occasions calls learning to his assistance. The garden of Eden brings to his mind the vale of *Enna*, where Proserpine was gathering flowers. Satan makes his way through fighting elements, like *Argo* between the *Cyanean* rocks, or *Ulysses* between the two *Sicilian* whirlpools, when he shunned *Charybdis* on the *larboard*. The mythological allusions have been justly censured, as not being always used with notice of their vanity; but they contribute variety to the narration, and produce an alternate exercise of the memory and the fancy.

His similies are less numerous, and more various, than those of his predecessors. But he does not confine himself within the limits of rigorous comparison: his great excellence is amplitude, and he expands the adventitious image beyond the dimensions which the occasion required. Thus, comparing the shield of Satan to the orb of the Moon, he crouds the imagination with the discovery of the telescope, and all the wonders which the telescope discovers.

Of his moral sentiments it is hardly praise to affirm that they excel those of all other poets; for this superiority he was indebted to his acquaintance with the sacred writings. The ancient epick poets, wanting the light of Revelation, were very unskilful teachers of virtue: their principal characters may be great, but they are not amiable. The reader may rise from their works with a greater degree of active or passive fortitude, and sometimes of prudence; but he will be able to carry away few precepts of justice, and none of mercy.

From the Italian writers it appears, that the advantages of even Christian knowledge may be possessed in vain. Ariosto's pravity* is generally known; and though the *Deliverance of Jerusalem* may be considered as a sacred subject, the poet has been very sparing of moral instruction.

In Milton every line breathes sanctity of thought, and purity of manners, except when the train of the narration requires the introduction of the rebellious spirits; and even they are compelled to acknowledge their subjection to God, in such a manner as excites reverence, and confirms piety.

Of human beings there are but two; but those two are the parents of mankind, venerable before their fall for dignity and innocence, and amiable after it for repentance and submission. In their first state their affection is tender without weakness, and their piety sublime without presumption. When they have sinned, they shew how discord begins in mutual frailty, and how it ought to cease in mutual forbearance; how confidence of the divine favour is forfeited by sin, and how hope of pardon may be obtained by penitence and prayer. A state of innocence we can only conceive, if indeed, in our present misery, it be possible to conceive it; but the sentiments and worship proper to a fallen and offending being, we have all to learn, as we have all to practise.

The poet, whatever be done, is always great. Our progenitors, in their first state, conversed with angels; even when folly and sin had degraded them, they had not in their humiliation *the port of mean suitors*;* and they rise again to reverential regard, when we find that their prayers were heard.

As human passions did not enter the world before the Fall, there is in the *Paradise Lost* little opportunity for the pathetick; but what little there is has not been lost. That passion which is peculiar to rational nature, the anguish arising from the consciousness of transgression, and the horrours attending the sense of the Divine Displeasure, are very justly described and forcibly impressed. But the passions are moved only on one occasion; sublimity is the general and prevailing quality in this poem; sublimity variously modified, sometimes descriptive, sometimes argumentative.

The defects and faults of *Paradise Lost*, for faults and defects every work of man must have, it is the business of impartial criticism to discover. As, in displaying the excellence of Milton, I have not made long quotations, because of selecting beauties there had been no end, I shall in the same general manner mention that which seems to deserve censure; for what Englishman can take delight in transcribing passages, which, if they lessen the reputation of Milton, diminish in some degree the honour of our country?

The generality of my scheme does not admit the frequent notice of verbal inaccuracies; which Bentley,* perhaps better skilled in grammar than in poetry, has often found, though he sometimes made them, and which he imputed to the obtrusions of a reviser whom the author's blindness obliged him to employ. A supposition rash and groundless, if he thought it true; and vile and pernicious, if, as is said, he in private allowed it to be false.

The plan of *Paradise Lost* has this inconvenience, that it comprises neither human actions nor human manners. The man and woman who act and suffer, are in a state which no other man or woman can ever know. The reader finds no transaction in which he can be engaged; beholds no condition in which he can by any effort of imagination place himself; he has, therefore, little natural curiosity or sympathy.

We all, indeed, feel the effects of Adam's disobedience; we all sin like Adam, and like him must all bewail our offences; we have restless and insidious enemies in the fallen angels, and in the blessed spirits we have guardians and friends; in the Redemption of mankind we hope to be included; and in the description of heaven and hell we are surely interested, as we are all to reside hereafter either in the regions of horror or of bliss.

But these truths are too important to be new; they have been taught to our infancy; they have mingled with our solitary thoughts and familiar conversation, and are habitually interwoven with the whole texture of life. Being therefore not new, they raise no unaccustomed emotion in the mind; what we knew before, we cannot learn; what is not unexpected, cannot surprise.

Of the ideas suggested by these awful scenes, from some we recede with reverence, except when stated hours require their association; and from others we shrink with horrour, or admit them only as salutary inflictions, as counterpoises to our interests and passions. Such images rather obstruct the career of fancy than incite it.

Pleasure and terrour are indeed the genuine sources of poetry; but poetical pleasure must be such as human imagination can at least conceive, and poetical terrour such as human strength and fortitude may combat. The good and evil of Eternity are too ponderous for the wings of wit; the mind sinks under them in passive helplessness, content with calm belief and humble adoration.

Known truths, however, may take a different appearance, and be conveyed to the mind by a new train of intermediate images. This Milton has undertaken, and performed with pregnancy and vigour of mind peculiar to himself. Whoever considers the few radical positions which the Scriptures afforded him, will wonder by what energetick operation he expanded them to such extent, and ramified them to so much variety, restrained as he was by religious reverence from licentiousness of fiction.

Here is a full display of the united force of study and genius; of a great accumulation of materials, with judgement to digest, and fancy to combine them: Milton was able to select from nature, or from story, from ancient fable, or from modern science, whatever could illustrate or adorn his thoughts. An accumulation of knowledge impregnated his mind, fermented by study, and exalted by imagination.

It has been therefore said, without an indecent hyperbole, by one of his encomiasts, that in reading *Paradise Lost* we read a book of universal knowledge.

But original deficience cannot be supplied. The want of human interest is always felt. *Paradise Lost* is one of the books which the reader admires and lays down, and forgets to take up again. None ever wished it longer than it is. Its perusal is a duty rather than a pleasure. We read Milton for instruction, retire harrassed and over-burdened, and look elsewhere for recreation; we desert our master, and seek for companions.

Another inconvenience of Milton's design is, that it requires the description of what cannot be described, the agency of spirits. He saw that immateriality supplied no images, and that he could not show angels acting but by instruments of action; he therefore invested them with form and matter. This, being necessary, was therefore defensible; and he should have secured the consistency of his system, by keeping immateriality out of sight, and enticing his reader to drop it from his thoughts. But he has unhappily perplexed his poetry with his philosophy. His infernal and celestial powers are sometimes pure spirit, and sometimes animated body. When Satan walks with his lance upon the *burning marle*, he has a body; when, in his passage between hell and the new world, he is in danger of sinking in the vacuity, and is supported by a gust of rising vapours, he has a body; when he animates the toad, he seems to be mere spirit, that can penetrate matter at pleasure; when he *starts up in his own shape*, he has at least a determined form; and when he is brought before Gabriel, he has a *spear and a shield*,* which he had the power of hiding in the toad, though the arms of the contending angels are evidently material.

The vulgar inhabitants of Pandæmonium, being *incorporeal spirits*, are *at large, though without number*, in a limited space; yet in the battle, when they were overwhelmed by mountains, their armour hurt them, *crushed in upon their substance, now grown gross by sinning*. This likewise happened to the uncorrupted angels, who were overthrown *the sooner for their arms, for unarmed they might easily as spirits have evaded by contraction or remove*.* Even as spirits they are hardly spiritual; for *contraction* and *remove* are images of matter; but if they could have escaped without their armour, they might have escaped from it, and left only the empty cover to be battered. Uriel, when he rides on a sun-beam, is material; Satan is material when he is afraid of the prowess of Adam.

The confusion of spirit and matter which pervades the whole narration of the war of heaven fills it with incongruity; and the book, in which it is related, is, I believe, the favourite of children, and gradually neglected as knowledge is increased.

After the operation of immaterial agents, which cannot be explained, may be considered that of allegorical persons, which have no real existence. To exalt causes into agents, to invest abstract ideas with form, and animate them with activity, has always been the right of poetry. But such airy beings are, for the most part, suffered only to do their natural office, and retire. Thus Fame tells a tale, and Victory hovers over a general, or perches on a standard; but Fame and Victory can do no more. To give them any real employment, or ascribe to them any material agency, is to make them allegorical no longer, but to shock the mind by ascribing effects to nonentity. In the *Prometheus* of Æschylus, we see *Violence* and *Strength*, and in the *Alcestis* of Euripides, we see *Death*, brought upon the stage, all as active persons of the drama; but no precedents can justify absurdity.

Milton's allegory of Sin and Death is undoubtedly faulty. Sin is indeed the mother of Death, and may be allowed to be the portress of hell; but when they stop the journey of Satan, a journey described as real, and when Death offers him battle, the allegory is broken. That Sin and Death should have shewn the way to hell, might have been allowed; but they cannot facilitate the passage by building a bridge, because the difficulty of Satan's passage is described as real and sensible, and the bridge ought to be only figurative. The hell assigned to the rebellious spirits is described as not less local than the residence of man. It is placed in some distant part of space, separated from the regions of harmony and order by a chaotick waste and an unoccupied vacuity; but *Sin* and *Death* worked up a *mole* of *aggregated soil*, cemented with *asphaltus*;* a work too bulky for ideal architects.

This unskilful allegory appears to me one of the greatest faults of the poem; and to this there was no temptation, but the author's opinion of its beauty.

To the conduct of the narrative some objections may be made. Satan is with great expectation brought before Gabriel in Paradise, and is suffered to go away unmolested. The creation of man is represented as the consequence of the vacuity left in heaven by the expulsion of the rebels; yet Satan mentions it as a report *rife in heaven* before his departure.

To find sentiments for the state of innocence, was very difficult; and something of anticipation perhaps is now and then discovered. Adam's discourse of dreams seems not to be the speculation of a new-created being. I know not whether his answer to the angel's reproof for curiosity does not want something of propriety: it is the speech of a man acquainted with many other men. Some philosophical notions, especially when the philosophy is false, might have been better omitted. The angel, in a comparison, speaks of *timorous deer*,* before deer were yet timorous, and before Adam could understand the comparison.

Dryden remarks, that Milton has some flats among his elevations.* This is only to say, that all the parts are not equal. In every work, one part must be for the sake of others; a palace must have passages; a poem must have transitions. It is no more to be required that wit should always be blazing, than that the sun should always stand at noon. In a great work there is a vicissitude of luminous and opaque parts, as there is in the world a succession of day and night. Milton, when he has expatiated in the sky, may be allowed sometimes to revisit earth; for what other author ever soared so high, or sustained his flight so long?

Milton, being well versed in the Italian poets, appears to have borrowed often from them; and, as every man catches something from his companions, his desire of imitating Ariosto's levity has disgraced his work with the *Paradise of Fools*;* a fiction not in itself ill-imagined, but too ludicrous for its place.

His play on words, in which he delights too often; his equivocations, which Bentley endeavours to defend by the example of the ancients; his unnecessary and ungraceful use of terms of art; it is not necessary to mention, because they are easily remarked, and generally censured, and at last bear so little proportion to the whole, that they scarcely deserve the attention of a critick.

Such are the faults of that wonderful performance *Paradise Lost*; which he who can put in balance with its beauties must be considered not as nice* but as dull, as less to be censured for want of candour, than pitied for want of sensibility.

Of *Paradise Regained*, the general judgement seems now to be right, that it is in many parts elegant, and every-where instructive. It was not to be supposed that the writer of *Paradise Lost* could ever write without great effusions of fancy, and exalted precepts of wisdom. The basis of *Paradise Regained* is narrow; a dialogue without action can never please like an union of the narrative and dramatic powers. Had this poem been written not by Milton, but by some imitator, it would have claimed and received universal praise.

If *Paradise Regained* has been too much depreciated, *Sampson Agonistes* has in requital been too much admired. It could only be by long prejudice, and the bigotry of learning, that Milton could prefer the ancient tragedies, with their encumbrance of a chorus, to the exhibitions of the French and English stages; and it is only by a blind confidence in the reputation of Milton, that a drama can be praised in which the intermediate parts have neither cause nor consequence, neither hasten nor retard the catastrophe.

In this tragedy are however many particular beauties, many just sentiments and striking lines; but it wants that power of attracting the attention which a well-connected plan produces.

Milton would not have excelled in dramatick writing; he knew human nature only in the gross, and had never studied the shades of character, nor the combinations of concurring, or the perplexity of contending passions. He had read much, and knew what books could teach; but had mingled little in the world, and was deficient in the knowledge which experience must confer.

Through all his greater works there prevails an uniform peculiarity of *Diction*, a mode and cast of expression which bears little resemblance to that of any former writer, and which is so far removed from common use, that an unlearned reader, when he first opens his book, finds himself surprised by a new language.

This novelty has been, by those who can find nothing wrong in Milton, imputed to his laborious endeavours after words suitable to the grandeur of his ideas. *Our language*, says Addison, *sunk under him.** But the truth is, that, both in prose and verse, he had formed his style by a perverse and pedantick principle. He was desirous to use English words with a foreign idiom. This in all his prose is discovered and condemned; for there judgment operates freely, neither softened by the beauty, nor awed by the dignity of his thoughts; but such is the power of his poetry, that his call is obeyed without resistance, the reader feels himself in captivity to a higher and a nobler mind, and criticism sinks in admiration.

Milton's style was not modified by his subject: what is shown with greater extent in *Paradise Lost*, may be found in *Comus*. One source of his peculiarity was his familiarity with the Tuscan poets: the disposition of his words is, I think, frequently Italian; perhaps sometimes combined with other tongues. Of him, at last, may be said what Jonson says of Spenser, that *he wrote no language*,* but has formed what *Butler* calls a *Babylonish Dialect*,* in itself harsh and barbarous, but made by exalted genius, and extensive learning, the vehicle of so much instruction and so much pleasure, that, like other lovers, we find grace in its deformity.

Whatever be the faults of his diction, he cannot want the praise of copiousness and variety: he was master of his language in its full extent; and has selected the melodious words with such diligence, that from his book alone the Art of English Poetry might be learned.

After his diction, something must be said of his *versification. The measure*, he says, *is the English heroick verse without rhyme.** Of this mode he had many examples among the Italians, and some in his own country. The Earl of Surrey is said to have translated one of Virgil's books without rhyme; and, besides our tragedies, a few short poems had appeared in blank verse; particularly one tending to reconcile the nation to Raleigh's wild attempt upon Guiana, and probably written by Raleigh himself.* These petty performances cannot be supposed to have much influenced Milton, who more probably took his hint from Trisino's *Italia Liberata*;* and, finding blank verse easier than rhyme, was desirous of persuading himself that it is better.

Rhyme, he says, and says truly, *is no necessary adjunct of true poetry*.* But perhaps, of poetry as a mental operation, metre or musick is no necessary adjunct: it is however by the musick of metre that poetry has been discriminated in all languages; and in languages melodiously constructed with a due proportiona of long and short syllables, metre is sufficient. But one language cannot communicate its rules to another: where metre is scanty and imperfect, some help is necessary. The musick of the English heroick line strikes the ear so faintly that it is easily lost, unless all the syllables of every line co-operate together: this co-operation can be only obtained by the preservation of every verse unmingled with another, as a distinct system of sounds; and this distinctness is obtained and preserved by the artifice of rhyme. The variety of pauses, so much boasted by the lovers of blank verse, changes the measures of an English poet to the periods of a declaimer; and there are only a few skilful and happy readers of Milton, who enable their audience to perceive where the lines end or begin. *Blank verse*, said an ingenious critick, *seems to be verse only to the eye*.*

Poetry may subsist without rhyme, but English poetry will not often please; nor can rhyme ever be safely spared but where the subject is able to support itself. Blank verse makes some approach to that which is called the *lapidary style*; has neither the easiness of prose, nor the melody of numbers, and therefore tires by long continuance. Of the Italian writers without rhyme, whom Milton alleges as precedents, not one is popular; what reason could urge in its defence, has been confuted by the ear.

But, whatever be the advantage of rhyme, I cannot prevail on myself to wish that Milton had been a rhymer; for I cannot wish his work to be other than it is; yet, like other heroes, he is to be admired rather than imitated. He that thinks himself capable of astonishing, may write blank verse; but those that hope only to please, must condescend to rhyme.

The highest praise of genius is original invention. Milton cannot be said to have contrived the structure of an epick poem, and therefore owes reverence to that vigour and amplitude of mind to which all generations must be indebted for the art of poetical narration, for the texture of the fable, the variation of incidents, the interposition of dialogue, and all the stratagems that surprise and enchain attention. But, of all the borrowers from Homer, Milton is perhaps the least indebted. He was naturally a thinker for himself, confident of his own abilities, and disdainful of help or hindrance: he did not refuse admission to the thoughts or images of his predecessors, but he did not seek them. From his contemporaries he neither courted nor received support; there is in his writings nothing by which the pride of other authors might be gratified, or favour gained; no exchange of praise, nor solicitation of support. His great works were performed under discountenance, and in blindness, but difficulties vanished at his touch; he was born for whatever is arduous; and his work is not the greatest of heroick poems, only because it is not the first.

ROCHESTER

JOHN WILMOT, afterwards Earl of Rochester, the son of Henry Earl of Rochester, better known by the title of Lord Wilmot, so often mentioned in Clarendon's History, was born April 10, 1647, at Ditchley in Oxfordshire.* After a grammatical education at the school of Burford, he entered a nobleman into Wadham College in 1659, only twelve years old; and in 1661, at fourteen, was, with some other persons of high rank, made master of arts by Lord Clarendon in person.

He travelled afterwards into France and Italy; and, at his return, devoted himself to the Court. In 1665 he went to sea with Sandwich, and distinguished himself at Bergen by uncommon interpidity; and the next summer served again on board [the ship commanded by] Sir Edward Spragge, who, in the heat of the engagement, having a message of reproof to send to one of his captains, could find no man ready to carry it but Wilmot, who, in an open boat, went and returned amidst the storm of shot.*

But his reputation for bravery was not lasting: he was reproached with slinking away in street quarrels, and leaving his companions to shift as they could without him; and Sheffield Duke of Buckingham* has left a story of his refusal to fight him.

He had very early an inclination to intemperance, which he totally subdued in his travels; but, when he became a courtier, he unhappily addicted himself to dissolute and vitious company, by which his principles were corrupted, and his manners depraved. He lost all sense of religious restraint; and, finding it not convenient to admit the authority of laws which he was resolved not to obey, sheltered his wickedness behind infidelity.

As he excelled in that noisy and licentious merriment which wine incites, his companions eagerly encouraged him in excess, and he willingly indulged it; till, as he confessed to Dr. Burnet,* he was for five years together continually drunk, or so much inflamed by frequent ebriety, as in no interval to be master of himself.

In this state he played many frolicks, which it is not for his honour that we should remember, and which are not now distinctly known. He often pursued low amours in mean disguises, and always acted with great exactness and dexterity the characters which he assumed.

He once erected a stage on Tower-hill, and harangued the populace as a mountebank; and, having made physick part of his study, is said to have practised it successfully.

He was so much in favour with King Charles, that he was made one of the gentlemen of the bedchamber, and comptroller of Woodstock Park.*

Having an active and inquisitive mind, he never, except in his paroxysms of intemperance, was wholly negligent of study: he read what is considered as polite learning so much, that he is mentioned by Wood* as the greatest scholar of all the nobility. Sometimes he retired into the country, and amused himself with writing libels, in which he did not pretend to confine himself to truth.

His favourite author in French was Boileau, and in English Cowley.

Thus in a course of drunken gaiety, and gross sensuality, with intervals of study perhaps yet more criminal, with an avowed contempt of all decency and order, a total disregard to every moral, and a resolute denial of every religious obligation, he lived worthless and useless, and blazed out his youth and his health in lavish voluptuousness; till, at the age of one and thirty, he had exhausted the fund of life, and reduced himself to a state of weakness and decay.

At this time he was led to an acquaintance with Dr. Burnet, to whom he laid open with great freedom the tenour of his opinions, and the course of his life, and from whom he received such conviction of the reasonableness of moral duty, and the truth of Christianity, as produced a total change both of his manners and opinions. The account of those salutary conferences is given by Burnet, in a book intituled, *Some Passages of the Life and Death of* John *Earl of* Rochester; which the critick ought to read for its elegance, the philosopher for its arguments, and the saint for its piety. It were an injury to the reader to offer him an abridgement.

He died July 26, 1680, before he had completed his thirty-fourth year; and was so worn away by a long illness, that life went out without a struggle.

Lord Rochester was eminent for the vigour of his colloquial wit, and remarkable for many wild pranks and sallies of extravagance. The glare of his general character diffused itself upon his writings; the compositions of a man whose name was heard so often, were certain of attention, and from many readers certain of applause.

This blaze of reputation is not yet quite extinguished; and his poetry still retains some splendour beyond that which genius has bestowed.

Wood and Burnet give us reason to believe, that much was imputed to him which he did not write. I know not by whom the original collection was made, or by what authority its genuineness was ascertained. The first edition was published in the year of his death, with an air of concealment, professing in the title page to be printed at *Antwerp*.*

Of some of the pieces, however, there is no doubt. The Imitation of Horace's Satire, the Verses to Lord Mulgrave, the Satire against Man, the Verses upon *Nothing*, and perhaps some others, are I believe genuine, and perhaps most of those which the late collection exhibits.

As he cannot be supposed to have found leisure for any course of continued study, his pieces are commonly short, such as one fit of resolution would produce.

His songs have no particular character: they tell, like other songs, in smooth and easy language, of scorn and kindness, dismission and desertion, absence and inconstancy, with the common places of artificial courtship. They are commonly smooth and easy; but have little nature, and little sentiment.

His imitation of Horace on Lucilius is not inelegant or unhappy.* In the reign of Charles the Second began that adaptation, which has since been very frequent, of ancient poetry to present times; and perhaps few will be found where the parallelism is better preserved than in this. The versification is indeed sometimes careless, but it is sometimes vigorous and weighty.

The strongest effort of his Muse is his poem upon *Nothing*. He is not the first who has chosen this barren topick for the boast of his fertility. There is a poem called *Nihil* in Latin by *Passerat*,* a poet and critick of the sixteenth century in France; who, in his own epitaph, expresses his zeal for good poetry thus:

—Molliter ossa quiescent
Sint modo carminibus non onerata malis.*

His works are not common, and therefore I shall subjoin his verses.

In examining this performance, *Nothing* must be considered as having not only a negative but a kind of positive signification; as I need not fear thieves, I have *nothing*; and *nothing* is a very powerful protector. In the first part of the sentence it is taken negatively; in the second it is taken positively, as an agent. In one of Boileau's lines it was a question, whether he should use *à rien faire*, or *à ne rien faire*; and the first was preferred, because it gave *rien* a sense in some sort positive.* *Nothing* can be a subject only in its positive sense, and such a sense is given it in the first line:

Nothing, thou elder brother ev'n to shade.

In this line, I know not whether he does not allude to a curious book *de Umbra*, by Wowerus, which, having told the qualities of *Shade*, concludes with a poem in which are these lines:

Jam primum terram validis circumspice claustris
Suspensam totam, decus admirabile mundi
Terrasque tractusque maris, camposque liquentes
Aeris & vasti laqueata palatia cœli—
Omnibus UMBRA prior.*

The positive sense is generally preserved, with great skill, through the whole poem; though sometimes, in a subordinate sense, the negative *nothing* is injudiciously mingled. Passerat confounds the two senses.

Another of his most vigorous pieces is his Lampoon on Sir Car Scroop, who, in a poem called *The Praise of Satire*, had some lines like these[1];

He who can push into a midnight fray
His brave companion, and then run away,
Leaving him to be murder'd in the street,
Then put it off with some buffoon conceit;
Him, thus dishonour'd, for a wit you own,
And court him as top fidler of the town.*

This was meant of Rochester, whose *buffoon conceit** was, I suppose, a saying often mentioned, that *every Man would be a Coward if he durst*;* and drew from him those furious verses; to which Scroop made in reply an epigram, ending with these lines:

Thou canst hurt no man's fame with thy ill word;
Thy pen is full as harmless as thy sword.*

[1] I quote from memory

Of the satire against *Man*, Rochester can only claim what remains when all Boileau's part is taken away.*

In all his works there is sprightliness and vigour, and every where may be found tokens of a mind which study might have carried to excellence. What more can be expected from a life spent in ostentatious contempt of regularity, and ended before the abilities of many other men began to be displayed?

Poema Cl. V. JOANNIS PASSERATII,
Regii in Academia Parisiensi Professoris.
Ad ornatissimum virum ERRICUM MEMMIUM.

Janus adest, festæ poscunt sua dona Kalendæ,
Munus abest festis quod possim offerre Kalendis.
Siccine Castalius nobis exaruit humor?
Usque adeò ingenii nostri est exhausta facultas,
Immunem ut videat redeuntis janitor anni?
Quod nusquam est, potius nova pervestigia quæram.

Ecce autem partes dum sese versat in omnes
Invenit mea Musa NIHIL, ne despice munus.
Nam NIHIL est gemmis, NIHIL est pretiosius auro.
Huc animum, huc igitur vultus adverte benignos:
Res nova narratur quæ nulli audita priorum,
Ausonii & Graii dixerunt cætera vates,
Ausoniæ indictum NIHIL est Græcæque Camœnæ.

E cœlo quacunque Ceres sua prospicit arva,
Aut genitor liquidis orbem complectitur ulnis
Oceanus, NIHIL interitus & originis expers.
Immortale NIHIL, NIHIL omni parte beatum.
Quòd si hinc majestas & vis divina probatur,
Num quid honore deûm, num quid dignabimur aris?
Conspectu lucis NIHIL est jucundius almæ,
Vere NIHIL, NIHIL irriguo formosius horto,
Floridius pratis, Zephyri clementius aura;
In bello sanctum NIHIL est, Martisque tumultu:
Justum in pace NIHIL, NIHIL est in fœdere tutum.
Felix cui NIHIL est, (fuerant hæc vota Tibullo)
Non timet insidias: fures, incendia temnit:
Sollicitas sequitur nullo sub judice lites.
Ille ipse invictis qui subjicit omnia fatis
Zenonis sapiens, NIHIL admiratur & optat.

Socraticique gregis fuit ista scientia quondam,
Scire NIHIL, studio cui nunc incumbitur uni.
Nec quicquam in ludo mavult didicisse juventus,
Ad magnas quia ducit opes, & culmen honorum.
Nosce NIHIL, nosces fertur quod Pythagoreæ
Grano hærere fabæ, cui vox adjuncta negantis.
Multi Mercurio freti duce viscera terræ
Pura liquefaciunt simul, & patrimonia miscent,
Arcano instantes operi, & carbonibus atris,
Qui tandem exhausti damnis, fractique labore,
Inveniunt atque inventum NIHIL usque requirunt.
Hoc dimetiri non ulla decempeda possit:
Nec numeret Libycæ numerum qui callet arenæ:
Et Phœbo ignotum NIHIL est, NIHIL altius astris.
Tuque, tibi licet eximium sit mentis acumen,
Omnem in naturam penetrans, & in abdita rerum,
Pace tua, Memmi, NIHIL ignorare vidêris.
Sole tamen NIHIL est, & puro clarius igne.
Tange NIHIL, dicesque NIHIL sine corpore tangi.
Cerne NIHIL, cerni dices NIHIL absque colore.
Surdum audit loquitúrque NIHIL sine voce, volátque
Absque ope pennarum, & graditur sine cruribus ullis.
Absque loco motuque NIHIL per inane vagatur.
Humano generi utilius NIHIL arte medendi.
Ne rhombos igitur, neu Thessala murmura tentet
Idalia vacuum trajectus arundine pectus,
Neu legat Idæo Dictæum in vertice gramen.
Vulneribus sævi NIHIL auxiliatur amoris.
Vexerit & quemvis trans mœstas portitor undas,
Ad superos imo NIHIL hunc revocabit ab orco.
Inferni NIHIL inflectit præcordia regis,
Parcarúmque colos, & inexorabile pensum.
Obruta Phlegræis campis Titania pubes
Fulmineo sensit NIHIL esse potentius ictu:
Porrigitur magni NIHIL extra mœnia mundi:
Diíque NIHIL metuunt. Quid longo carmine plura
Commemorem? virtute NIHIL præstantius ipsa,
Splendidius NIHIL est; NIHIL est Jove denique majus.
Sed tempus finem argutis imponere nugis:
Ne tibi si multa laudem mea carmina charta,
De NIHILO NIHILI pariant fastidia versus.*

DRYDEN

OF the great poet whose life I am about to delineate, the curiosity which his reputation must excite, will require a display more ample than can now be given. His contemporaries, however they reverenced his genius, left his life unwritten; and nothing therefore can be known beyond what casual mention and uncertain tradition have supplied.

JOHN DRYDEN was born August 9, 1631, at Aldwincle near Oundle, the son of Erasmus Dryden of Tichmersh; who was the third son of Sir Erasmus Dryden, Baronet, of Canons Ashby. All these places are in Northamptonshire; but the original stock of the family was in the county of Huntingdon.

He is reported by his last biographer, Derrick,* to have inherited from his father an estate of two hundred a year, and to have been bred, as was said, an Anabaptist.* For either of these particulars no authority is given. Such a fortune ought to have secured him from that poverty which seems always to have oppressed him; or if he had wasted it, to have made him ashamed of publishing his necessities. But though he had many enemies, who undoubtedly examined his life with a scrutiny sufficiently malicious, I do not remember that he is ever charged with waste of his patrimony. He was indeed sometimes reproached for his first religion. I am therefore inclined to believe that Derrick's intelligence was partly true, and partly erroneous.

From Westminster School, where he was instructed as one of the king's scholars by Dr. Busby,* whom he long after continued to reverence, he was in 1650 elected to one of the Westminster scholarships at Cambridge.

Of his school performances has appeared only a poem on the death of Lord Hastings,* composed with great ambition of such conceits as, notwithstanding the reformation begun by Waller and Denham, the example of Cowley still kept in reputation. Lord Hastings died of the small-pox, and his poet has made of the pustules first rosebuds, and then gems; at last exalts them into stars; and says,

> No comet need foretell his change drew on,
> Whose corps might seem a constellation.

At the university he does not appear to have been eager of poetical distinction, or to have lavished his early wit either on fictitious subjects or public occasions. He probably considered that he who purposed to be an author, ought first to be a student. He obtained, whatever was the reason, no fellowship in the College. Why he was excluded cannot now be known, and it is vain to guess; had he thought himself injured, he knew how to complain. In the Life of Plutarch he mentions his education in the College with gratitude; but in a prologue at Oxford, he has these lines:

> Oxford to him a dearer name shall be
> Than his own mother-university;
> Thebes did his rude unknowing youth engage;
> He chooses Athens in his riper age.*

It was not till the death of Cromwell, in 1658, that he became a public candidate for fame, by publishing *Heroic Stanzas on the late Lord Protector*; which, compared with the verses of Sprat and Waller on the same occasion, were sufficient to raise great expectations of the rising poet.

When the king was restored, Dryden, like the other panegyrists of usurpation, changed his opinion, or his profession, and published ASTREA REDUX, *a poem on the happy restoration and return of his most sacred Majesty King Charles the Second.*

The reproach of inconstancy was, on this occasion, shared with such numbers, that it produced neither hatred nor disgrace; if he changed, he changed with the nation. It was, however, not totally forgotten when his reputation raised him enemies.

The same year he praised the new king in a second poem on his restoration.* In the ASTREA was the line,

> An horrid *stillness* first *invades* the *ear*,
> And in that silence we a tempest fear.*

for which he was persecuted with perpetual ridicule, perhaps with more than was deserved. *Silence* is indeed mere privation; and, so considered, cannot *invade*; but privation likewise certainly is *darkness*, and probably *cold*; yet poetry has never been refused the right of ascribing effects or agency to them as to positive powers. No man scruples to say that *darkness* hinders him from his work; or that *cold* has killed the plants. Death is also privation, yet who has made any difficulty of assigning to Death a dart and the power of striking?

In settling the order of his works, there is some difficulty; for, even when they are important enough to be formally offered to a patron, he does not commonly date his dedication; the time of writing and publishing is not always the same; nor can the first editions be easily found, if even from them could be obtained the necessary information.

The time at which his first play was exhibited is not certainly known, because it was not printed till it was some years afterwards altered and revived; but since the plays are said to be printed in the order in which they were written, from the dates of some, those of others may be inferred; and thus it may be collected that in 1663, in the thirty-second year of his life, he commenced a writer for the stage; compelled undoubtedly by necessity, for he appears never to have loved that exercise of his genius, or to have much pleased himself with his own dramas.

Of the stage, when he had once invaded it, he kept possession for many years; not indeed without the competition of rivals who sometimes prevailed, or the censure of criticks, which was often poignant and often just; but with such a degree of reputation as made him at least secure of being heard, whatever might be the final determination of the public.

His first piece was a comedy called the *Wild Gallant*.* He began with no happy auguries; for his performance was so much disapproved, that he was compelled to recall it, and change it from its imperfect state to the form in which is now appears, and which is yet sufficiently defective to vindicate the criticks.

I wish that there were no necessity of following the progress of his theatrical fame, or tracing the meanders of his mind through the whole series of his dramatick performances; it will be fit however to enumerate them, and to take especial notice of those that are distinguished by any peculiarity intrinsick or concomitant; for the composition and fate of eight and twenty dramas include too much of a poetical life to be omitted.

In 1664 he published the *Rival Ladies*, which he dedicated to the Earl of Orrery, a man of high reputation both as a writer and a statesman.* In this play he made his essay of dramatick rhyme, which he defends in his dedication, with sufficient certainty of a favourable hearing; for Orrery was himself a writer of rhyming tragedies.

He then joined with Sir Robert Howard* in the *Indian Queen*, a tragedy in rhyme. The parts which either of them wrote are not distinguished.

The *Indian Emperor* was published in 1667. It is a tragedy in rhyme, intended for a sequel to *Howard's Indian Queen*. Of this connection notice was given to the audience by printed bills, distributed at the door; an expedient supposed to be ridiculed in the *Rehearsal*, when Bayes tells how many reams he has printed, to instill into the audience some conception of his plot.*

In this play is the description of Night, which *Rymer* has made famous by preferring it to those of all other poets.*

The practice of making tragedies in rhyme was introduced soon after the Restoration, as it seems, by the earl of Orrery, in compliance with the opinion of Charles the Second, who had formed his taste by the French theatre; and Dryden, who wrote, and made no difficulty of declaring that he wrote, only to please, and who perhaps knew that by his dexterity of versification he was more likely to excel others in rhyme than without it, very readily adopted his master's preference. He therefore made rhyming tragedies, till, by the prevalence of manifest propriety, he seems to have grown ashamed of making them any longer.

To this play is prefixed a very vehement defence of dramatick rhyme, in confutation of the preface to the *Duke of Lerma*, in which Sir Robert Howard had censured it.

In 1667, he published *Annus Mirabilis*, the *Year of Wonders*, which may be esteemed one of his most elaborate works.

It is addressed to Sir Robert Howard by a letter, which is not properly a dedication; and, writing to a poet, he has interspersed many critical observations, of which some are common, and some perhaps ventured without much consideration. He began, even now, to exercise the domination of conscious genius, by recommending his own performance: "I am satisfied that as the Prince and General [Rupert and Monk] are incomparably the best subjects I ever had, so what I have written on them is much better than what I have performed on any other. As I have endeavoured to adorn my poem with noble thoughts, so much more to express those thoughts with elocution."*

It is written in quatrains, or heroick stanzas of four lines; a measure which he had learned from the *Gondibert* of Davenant,* and which he then thought the most majestick that the English language affords. Of this stanza he mentions the encumbrances, encreased as they were by the exactness which the age required. It was, throughout his life, very much his custom to recommend his works, by representation of the difficulties that he had encountered, without appearing to have sufficiently considered, that where there is no difficulty there is no praise.

There seems to be in the conduct of Sir Robert Howard and Dryden towards each other, something that is not now easily to be explained. Dryden, in his dedication to the earl of Orrery, had defended dramatick rhyme; and Howard, in the preface to a collection of plays, had censured his opinion.* Dryden vindicated himself in his *Dialogue on Dramatick Poetry*;* Howard, in his Preface to the *Duke of Lerma*, animadverted on the Vindication; and Dryden, in a Preface to the *Indian Emperor*, replied to the Animadversions with great asperity, and almost with contumely. The dedication to this play is dated the year in which the *Annus Mirabilis* was published. Here appears a strange inconsistency; but Langbaine* affords some help, by relating that the answer to Howard was not published in the first edition of the play, but was added when it was afterwards reprinted; and as the *Duke of Lerma* did not appear till 1668, the same year in which the Dialogue was published, there was time enough for enmity to grow up between authors, who, writing both for the theatre, were naturally rivals.

He was now so much distinguished, that in 1668 he succeeded Sir William Davenant as poet-laureat. The salary of the laureat had been raised in favour of Jonson, by Charles the First, from an hundred marks to one hundred pounds a year, and a tierce* of wine; a revenue in those days not inadequate to the conveniencies of life.

The same year he published his Essay on Dramatick Poetry, an elegant and instructive dialogue; in which we are told by Prior, that the principal character is meant to represent the duke of Dorset. This work seems to have given Addison a model for his Dialogues upon Medals.

Secret Love, or the Maiden Queen, is a tragi-comedy. In the preface he discusses a curious question, whether a poet can judge well of his own productions: and determines very justly, that, of the plan and disposition, and all that can be reduced to principles of science, the author may depend upon his own opinion; but that, in those parts where fancy predominates, self-love may easily deceive. He might have observed, that what is good only because it pleases, cannot be pronounced good till it has been found to please.

Sir Martin Marall is a comedy, published without preface or dedication, and at first without the name of the author. Langbaine charges it, like most of the rest, with plagiarism; and observes that the song is translated from Voiture, allowing however that both the sense and measure are exactly observed.

The Tempest is an alteration of Shakspeare's play, made by Dryden in conjunction with Davenant, "whom," says he, "I found of so quick a fancy, that nothing was proposed to him in which he could not suddenly produce a thought extremely pleasant and surprising; and those first thoughts of his, contrary to the Latin proverb, were not always the least happy; and as his fancy was quick, so likewise were the products of it remote and new. He borrowed not of any other, and his imaginations were such as could not easily enter into any other man."*

The effect produced by the conjunction of these two powerful minds was, that to Shakspeare's monster Caliban is added a sister-monster Sicorax; and a woman, who, in the original play, had never seen a man, is in this brought acquainted with a man that had never seen a woman.

About this time, in 1673, Dryden seems to have had his quiet much disturbed by the success of the *Empress of Morocco*, a tragedy written in rhyme by *Elkanah Settle*;* which was so much applauded, as to make him think his supremacy of reputation in some danger. Settle had not only been prosperous on the stage, but, in the confidence of success, had published his play, with sculptures and a preface of defiance. Here was one offence added to another; and, for the last blast of inflammation, it was acted at Whitehall by the court-ladies.

Dryden could not now repress these emotions, which he called indignation, and others jealousy; but wrote upon the play and the dedication such criticism as malignant impatience could pour out in haste.

Of Settle he gives this character. "He's an animal of a most deplored understanding, without conversation. His being is in a twilight of sense, and some glimmering of thought, which he can never fashion into wit or English. His style is boisterous and rough-hewn, his rhyme incorrigibly lewd, and his numbers perpetually harsh and ill-sounding. The little talent which he has, is fancy. He sometimes labours with a thought; but, with the pudder he makes to bring it into the world, 'tis commonly still-born; so that, for want of learning and elocution, he will never be able to express any thing either naturally or justly!"*

This is not very decent; yet this is one of the pages in which criticism prevails most over brutal fury. He proceeds: "He has a heavy hand at fools, and a great felicity in writing nonsense for them. Fools they will be in spite of him. His King, his two Empresses, his villain, and his sub-villain, nay his hero, have all a certain natural cast of the father—their folly was born and bred in them, and something of the Elkanah will be visible."

This is Dryden's general declamation; I will not withhold from the reader a particular remark. Having gone through the first act he says, "To conclude this act with the most rumbling piece of nonsense spoken yet,

> To flattering lightning our feign'd smiles conform,
> Which back'd with thunder do but gild a storm.

Conform a smile to lightning, make a *smile* imitate *lightning*, and *flattering lightning*: lightning sure is a threatening thing. And this lightning must *gild a storm*. Now if I must conform my smiles to lightning, then my smiles must gild a storm too: to *gild* with *smiles* is a new invention of gilding. And gild a storm by being *backed with thunder*. Thunder is part of the storm; so one part of the storm must help to *gild* another part, and help by *backing*; as if a man would gild a thing the better for being backed, or having a load upon his back. So that here is *gilding* by *conforming, smiling, lightning, backing*, and *thundering*. The whole is as if I should say thus, I will make my counterfeit smiles look like a flattering stone-horse, which, being backed with a trooper, does but gild the battle. I am mistaken if nonsense is not here pretty thick sown. Sure the poet writ these two lines aboard some smack in a storm, and, being sea-sick, spewed up a good lump of clotted nonsense at once."

Here is perhaps a sufficient specimen; but as the pamphlet, though Dryden's, has never been thought worthy of republication, and is not easily to be found, it may gratify curiosity to quote it more largely.

Whene'er she bleeds,
He no severer a damnation needs,
That dares pronounce the sentence of her death,
Than the infection that attends that breath.

"*That attends that breath.*—The poet is at *breath* again; *breath* can never 'scape him; and here he brings in a *breath* that must be *infectious* with *pronouncing* a sentence; and this sentence is not to be pronounced till the condemned party *bleeds*; that is, she must be executed first, and sentenced after; and the *pronouncing* of this *sentence* will be infectious; that is, others will catch the disease of that sentence, and this infecting of others will torment a man's self. The whole is thus; *when she bleeds, thou needest no greater hell or torment to thyself, than infecting of others by pronouncing a sentence upon her.* What hodge-podge does he make here! Never was Dutch grout such clogging, thick, indigestible stuff. But this is but a taste to stay the stomach; we shall have a more plentiful mess presently.

"Now to dish up the poet's broth, that I promised:

For when we're dead, and our freed souls enlarg'd,
Of nature's grosser burden we're discharg'd,
Then gently, as a happy lover's sigh,
Like wandering meteors through the air we'll fly,
And in our airy walk, as subtle guests,
We'll steal into our cruel fathers breasts,
There read their souls, and track each passion's sphere:
See how Revenge moves there, Ambition here.
And in their orbs view the dark characters
Of sieges, ruins, murders, blood and wars.
We'll blot out all those hideous draughts, and write
Pure and white forms; then with a radiant light
Their breasts encircle, till their passions be
Gentle as nature in its infancy:
Till soften'd by our charms their furies cease,
And their revenge resolves into a peace.
Thus by our death their quarrel ends,
Whom living we made foes, dead we'll make friends.

If this be not a very liberal mess, I will refer myself to the stomach of any moderate guest. And a rare mess it is, far excelling any Westminster white-broth. It is a kind of gibblet porridge, made of the gibblets of a couple of young geese, stodged full of *meteors, orbs, spheres, track, hideous draughts, dark characters, white forms*, and *radiant light*, designed not only to please appetite, and indulge luxury; but it is also physical, being an approved medicine to purge choler: for it is propounded by Morena, as a receipt to cure their fathers of their choleric humours: and were it written in characters as barbarous as the words, might very well pass for a doctor's bill. To conclude, it is porridge, 'tis a receipt, 'tis a pig with a pudding in the belly, 'tis I know not what: for, certainly, never any one that pretended to write sense, had the impudence before to put such stuff as this, into the mouths of those that were to speak it before an audience, whom he did not take to be all fools; and after that to print it too, and expose it to the examination of the world. But let us see, what we can make of this stuff:

For when we're dead, and our freed souls enlarg'd—

Here he tells us what it is to be *dead*; it is to have *our freed souls set free*. Now if to have a soul set free is to be dead, then to have a *freed soul* set free, is to have a dead man die.

Then gentle, as a happy lover's sigh—

They two like one *sigh*, and that one *sigh* like two wandering meteors,

—shall flie through the air—

That is, they shall mount above like falling stars, or else they shall skip like two Jacks with lanthorns, or Will with a wisp, and Madge with a candle."

And in their airy walk steal into their cruel fathers breasts, like subtle guests. So "that their *fathers breasts* must be in an *airy walk*, an airy *walk* of a *flier*. *And there they will read their souls, and track the spheres of their passions*. That is, these walking fliers, Jack with a lanthorn, &c. will put on his spectacles, and fall a *reading souls*, and put on his pumps and fall a *tracking of spheres*; so that he will read and run, walk and fly at the same time! Oh! Nimble Jack. *Then he will see, how revenge here, how ambition there*—The birds will hop about. *And then view the dark characters of sieges, ruins, murders, blood, and wars, in their orbs: Track the characters* to their forms! Oh! rare sport for Jack. Never was place so full of game as these breasts! You cannot stir but you flush a sphere, start a character, or unkennel an orb!"

Settle's is said to have been the first play embellished with sculptures;* those ornaments seem to have given poor Dryden great disturbance. He tries however to ease his pain, by venting his malice in a parody.

"The poet has not only been so impudent to expose all this stuff, but so arrogant to defend it with an epistle; like a saucy booth-keeper, that, when he had put a cheat upon the people, would wrangle and fight with any that would not like it, or would offer to discover it; for which arrogance our poet receives this correction; and to jerk him a little the sharper, I will not transpose his verse, but by the help of his own words trans-non-sense sense, that, by my stuff, people may judge the better what his is:

> Great Boy, thy tragedy and sculptures done
> From press, and plates in fleets do homeward come:
> And in ridiculous and humble pride,
> Their course in ballad-singers baskets guide,
> Whose greasy twigs do all new beauties take,
> From the gay shews thy dainty sculptures make.
> Thy lines a mess of rhiming nonsense yield,
> A senseless tale, with flattering fustian fill'd.
> No grain of sense does in one line appear,
> Thy words big bulks of boisterous bombast bear.
> With noise they move, and from players mouths rebound,
> When their tongues dance to thy words empty sound.
> By thee inspir'd the rumbling verses roll,
> As if that rhyme and bombast lent a soul:
> And with that soul they seem taught duty too,
> To huffing words does humble nonsense bow,
> As if it would thy worthless worth enhance,
> To th' lowest rank of fops thy praise advance;
> To whom, by instinct, all thy stuff is dear;
> Their loud claps echo to the theatre.
> From breaths of fools thy commendation spreads,
> Fame sings thy praise with mouths of loggerheads.
> With noise and laughing each thy fustian greets,
> 'Tis clapt by quires of empty-headed cits,
> Who have their tribute sent, and homage given,
> As men in whispers send loud noise to heaven.

"Thus I have daubed him with his own puddle: and now we are come from aboard his dancing, masking, rebounding, breathing fleet; and as if we had landed at Gotham, we meet nothing but fools and nonsense."

Such was the criticism to which the genius of Dryden could be reduced, between rage and terrour; rage with little provocation, and terrour with little danger. To see the highest minds thus levelled with the meanest, may produce some solace to the consciousness of weakness, and some mortification to the pride of wisdom. But let it be remembered, that minds are not levelled in their powers but when they are first levelled in their desires. Dryden and Settle had both placed their happiness in the claps of multitudes.

The *Mock Astrologer*, a comedy, is dedicated to the illustrious duke of Newcastle,* whom he courts by adding to his praises those of his lady, not only as a lover but a partner of his studies. It is unpleasing to think how many names, once celebrated, are since forgotten. Of Newcastle's works nothing is now known but his treatise on horsemanship.

The Preface seems very elaborately written, and contains many just remarks on the Fathers of the English drama. Shakspeare's plots, he says, are in the hundred novels of *Cinthio*;* those of Beaumont and Fletcher in Spanish Stories; Jonson only made them for himself. His criticisms upon tragedy, comedy, and farce, are judicious and profound. He endeavours to defend the immorality of some of his comedies by the example of former writers; which is only to say, that he was not the first nor perhaps the greatest offender. Against those that accused him of plagiarism, he alleges a favourable expression of the king: "He only desired that they, who accuse me of thefts, would steal him plays like mine;"* and then relates how much labour he spends in fitting for the English stage what he borrows from others.

Tyrannick Love, or the Virgin Martyr, was another tragedy in rhyme, conspicuous for many passages of strength and elegance, and many of empty noise and ridiculous turbulence. The rants of Maximin have been always the sport of criticism; and were at length, if his own confession may be trusted, the shame of the writer.*

Of this play he takes care to let the reader know, that it was contrived and written in seven weeks. Want of time was often his excuse, or perhaps shortness of time was his private boast in the form of an apology.

It was written before the *Conquest of Granada*, but published after it. The design is to recommend piety. "I considered that pleasure was not the only end of poesy, and that even the instructions of morality were not so wholly the business of a poet, as that precepts and examples of piety were to be omitted; for to leave that employment altogether to the clergy, were to forget that religion was first taught in verse, which the laziness or dulness of succeeding priesthood turned afterwards into prose."* Thus foolishly could Dryden write, rather than not shew his malice to the parsons.

The two parts of the *Conquest of Granada* are written with a seeming determination to glut the public with dramatick wonders; to exhibit in its highest elevation a theatrical meteor of incredible love and impossible valour, and to leave no room for a wilder flight to the extravagance of posterity. All the rays of romantick heat, whether amorous or warlike, glow in Almanzor by a kind of concentration.* He is above all laws; he is exempt from all restraints; he ranges the world at will, and governs wherever he appears. He fights without enquiring the cause, and loves in spite of the obligations of justice, of rejection by his mistress, and of prohibition from the dead. Yet the scenes are, for the most part, delightful; they exhibit a kind of illustrious depravity, and majestick madness: such as, if it is sometimes despised, is often reverenced, and in which the ridiculous is mingled with the astonishing.

In the Epilogue to the second part of the *Conquest of Granada*, Dryden indulges his favourite pleasure of discrediting his predecessors; and this Epilogue he has defended by a long postscript. He had promised a second dialogue, in which he should more fully treat of the virtues and faults of the English poets, who have written in the dramatick, epick, or lyrick way. This promise was never formally performed; but, with respect to the dramatick writers, he has given us in his prefaces, and in this postscript, something equivalent; but his purpose being to exalt himself by the comparison, he shews faults distinctly, and only praises excellence in general terms.

A play thus written, in professed defiance of probability, naturally drew down upon itself the vultures of the theatre. One of the criticks that attacked it was *Martin Clifford*,* to whom *Sprat* addressed the Life of Cowley, with such veneration of his critical powers as might naturally excite great expectations of instruction from his remarks.

But let honest credulity beware of receiving characters from contemporary writers. Clifford's remarks, by the favour of Dr. *Percy*,* were at last obtained; and, that no man may ever want them more, I will extract enough to satisfy all reasonable desire.

In the first Letter his observation is only general: "You do live," says he, "in as much ignorance and darkness as you did in the womb: your writings are like a Jack-of-all-trades shop; they have variety, but nothing of value; and if thou art not the dullest plant-animal that ever the earth produced, all that I have conversed with are strangely mistaken in thee."

In the second, he tells him that Almanzor is not more copied from Achilles than from Ancient Pistol. "But I am," says he, "strangely mistaken if I have not seen this very *Almanzor* of yours in some disguise about this town, and passing under another name. Pr'ythee tell me true, was not this Huffcap once the *Indian Emperor*, and at another time did he not call himself *Maximin*? Was not *Lyndaraxa* once called *Almeria*? I mean under *Montezuma* the Indian Emperor. I protest and vow they are either the same, or so alike that I cannot, for my heart, distinguish one from the other. You are therefore a strange unconscionable thief; thou art not content to steal from others, but dost rob thy poor wretched self too."

Now was *Settle's* time to take his revenge. He wrote a vindication of his own lines; and, if he is forced to yield any thing, makes reprisals upon his enemy. To say that his answer is equal to the censure, is no high commendation. To expose Dryden's method of analysing his expressions, he tries the same experiment upon the description of the ships in the *Indian Emperor*, of which however he does not deny the excellence; but intends to shew, that by studied misconstruction every thing may be equally represented as ridiculous. After so much of Dryden's elegant animadversions, justice requires that something of Settle's should be exhibited. The following observations are therefore extracted from a quarto pamphlet of ninety-five pages:

> Fate after him below with pain did move,
> And victory could scarce keep pace above.

These two lines, if he can shew me any sense or thought in, or any thing but bombast and noise, he shall make me believe every word in his observations on *Morocco* sense.

"In the *Empress of Morocco* were these lines:

> I'll travel then to some remoter sphere,
> Till I find out new worlds, and crown you there.

"On which Dryden made this remark:

"*I believe our learned author takes a sphere for a country: the sphere of Morocco, as if Morocco were the globe of earth and water; but a globe is no sphere neither, by his leave,*" &c. So *sphere* must not be sense, unless it relate to a circular motion about a globe, in which sense the astronomers use it. I would desire him to expound those lines in *Granada*:

> I'll to the turrets of the palace go,
> And add new fire to those that fight below.
> Thence, hero-like, with torches by my side,
> (Far be the omen tho') my Love I'll guide.
> No, like his better fortune I'll appear,
> With open arms, loose vail and flowing hair,
> Just flying forward from my rowling sphere.*

I wonder, if he be so strict, how he dares make so bold with *sphere* himself, and be so critical in other men's writings. Fortune is fancied standing on a globe, not on a *sphere*, as he told us in the first Act.

"Because *Elkanah's Similies are the most unlike things to what they are compared in the world*, I'll venture to start a simile in his *Annus Mirabilis*: he gives this poetical description of the ship called the *London*:

> The goodly London in her gallant trim,
> The Phenix-daughter of the vanquisht old,
> Like a rich bride does to the ocean swim,
> And on her shadow rides in floating gold.
>
> Her flag aloft spread ruffling in the wind,
> And sanguine streamers seem'd the flood to fire:
> The weaver, charm'd with what his loom design'd,
> Goes on to sea, and knows not to retire.
>
> With roomy decks, her guns of mighty strength,
> Whose low-laid mouths each mounting billow laves,
> Deep in her draught, and warlike in her length,
> She seems a sea-wasp flying on the waves.*

What a wonderful pother is here, to make all these poetical beautifications of a ship! that is, a *phenix* in the first stanza, and but a *wasp* in the last: nay, to make his humble comparison of a *wasp* more ridiculous, he does not say it flies upon the waves as nimbly as a wasp, or the like, but it seemed a *wasp*. But our author at the writing of this was not in his altitudes, to compare ships to floating palaces; a comparison to the purpose, was a perfection he did not arrive to, till his *Indian Emperor's* days. But perhaps his similitude has more in it than we imagine; this ship had a great many guns in her, and they, put all together, made the sting in the wasp's tail: for this is all the reason I can guess, why it seem'd a *wasp*. But, because we will allow him all we can to help out, let it be a *phenix sea-wasp*, and the rarity of such an animal may do much towards the heightening the fancy.

"It had been much more to his purpose, if he had designed to render the senseless play little, to have searched for some such pedantry as this:

> Two ifs scarce make one possibility.
> If justice will take all and nothing give,
> Justice, methinks, is not distributive.
> To die or kill you, is the alternative,
> Rather than take your life, I will not live.*

"Observe, how prettily our author chops logick in heroick verse. Three such fustian canting words as *distributive, alternative*, and *two ifs*, no man but himself would have come within the noise of. But he's a man of general learning, and all comes into his play.

" 'Twould have done well too, if he could have met with a rant or two, worth the observation: such as,

> Move swiftly, Sun, and fly a lover's pace,
> Leave months and weeks behind thee in thy race.*

"But surely the Sun, whether he flies a lover's or not a lover's pace, leaves weeks and months, nay years too, behind him in his race.

"Poor Robin, or any other of the Philomathematicks, would have given him satisfaction in the point.

> If I could kill thee now, thy fate's so low,
> That I must stoop, ere I can give the blow.
> But mine is fixt so far above thy crown,
> That all thy men,
> Piled on thy back, can never pull it down.*

"Now where that is, Almanzor's fate is fixt, I cannot guess; but wherever it is, I believe Almanzor, and think that all Abdalla's subjects, piled upon one another, might not pull down his fate so well as without piling: besides, I think Abdalla so wise a man, that if Almanzor had told him piling his men upon his back might do the feat, he would scarce bear such a weight, for the pleasure of the exploit; but it is a huff, and let Abdalla do it if he dare.

> The people like a headlong torrent go,
> And every dam they break or overflow.
> But, unoppos'd, they either lose their force,
> Or wind in volumes to their former course.*

A very pretty allusion, contrary to all sense or reason. Torrents, I take it, let them wind never so much, can never return to their former course, unless he can suppose that fountains can go upwards, which is impossible: nay more, in the foregoing page he tells us so too. A trick of a very unfaithful memory.

> But can no more than fountains upward flow.*

Which of a *torrent*, which signifies a rapid stream, is much more impossible. Besides, if he goes to quibble, and say that it is possible by art water may be made return, and the same water run twice in one and the same channel: then he quite confutes what he says; for, it is by being opposed, that it runs into its former course: for all engines that make water so return, do it by compulsion and opposition. Or, if he means a headlong torrent for a tide, which would be ridiculous, yet they do not wind in volumes, but come fore-right back (if their upright lies straight to their former course), and that by opposition of the sea-water, that drives them back again.

"And for fancy, when he lights of any thing like it, 'tis a wonder if it be not borrowed. As here, for example of, I find this fanciful thought in his *Ann. Mirab.*

> Old father Thames raised up his reverend head;
> But feared the fate of Simoeis would return;
> Deep in his ooze he sought his sedgy bed;
> And shrunk his waters back into his urn.

This is stolen from Cowley's *Davideis*, p. 9.

Swift Jordan started, and strait backward fled,
Hiding amongst thick reeds his aged head.
And when the Spaniards their assault begin,
At once beat those without and those within.*

This Almanzor speaks of himself; and sure for one man to conquer an army within the city, and another without the city, at once, is something difficult; but this flight is pardonable, to some we meet with in *Granada*. Osmin, speaking of Almanzor:

Who, like a tempest that outrides the wind,
Made a just battle, ere the bodies join'd.*

Pray what does this honourable person mean by a *tempest that outrides the wind!* A tempest that outrides itself. To suppose a tempest without wind, is as bad as supposing a man to walk without feet; for if he supposes the tempest to be something distinct from the wind, yet as being the effect of wind only, to come before the cause is a little preposterous: so that, if he takes it one way, or if he takes it the other, those two *ifs* will scarce make one *possibility*." Enough of Settle.

Marriage Alamode is a comedy, dedicated to the Earl of Rochester; whom he acknowledges not only as the defender of his poetry, but the promoter of his fortune. Langbaine places this play in 1673. The earl of Rochester therefore was the famous Wilmot, whom yet tradition always represents as an enemy to Dryden, and who is mentioned by him with some disrespect in the preface to Juvenal.

The Assignation, or Love in a Nunnery, a comedy, was driven off the stage, *against the opinion*, as the author says, *of the best judges*. It is dedicated, in a very elegant address, to Sir Charles Sedley;* in which he finds an opportunity for his usual complaint of hard treatment and unreasonable censure.

Amboyna is a tissue of mingled dialogue in verse and prose, and was perhaps written in less time than *The Virgin Martyr*; though the author thought not fit either ostentatiously or mournfully to tell how little labour it cost him, or at how short a warning he produced it. It was a temporary performance, written in the time of the Dutch war, to inflame the nation against their enemies; to whom he hopes, as he declares in his Epilogue, to make his poetry not less destructive than that by which Tyrtæus of old animated the Spartans. This play was written in the second Dutch war in 1673.

Troilus and Cressida, is a play altered from Shakspeare; but so altered that even in Langbaine's opinion, *the last scene in the third act is a masterpiece*. It is introduced by a discourse on *the grounds of criticism in tragedy*; to which I suspect that Rymer's book had given occasion.*

The *Spanish Fryar* is a tragi-comedy, eminent for the happy coincidence and coalition of the two plots. As it was written against the Papists, it would naturally at that time have friends and enemies; and partly by the popularity which it obtained at first, and partly by the real power both of the serious and risible part, it continued long a favourite of the publick.

It was Dryden's opinion, at least for some time, and he maintains it in the dedication of this play, that the drama required an alternation of comick and tragick scenes, and that it is necessary to mitigate by alleviations of merriment the pressure of ponderous events, and the fatigue of toilsome passions. "Whoever," says he, "cannot perform both parts, *is but half a writer for the stage*."

The *Duke of Guise*, a tragedy written in conjunction with Lee,* as *Oedipus* had been before, seems to deserve notice only for the offence which it gave to the remnant of the Covenanters, and in general to the enemies of the court, who attacked him with great violence, and were answered by him; though at last he seems to withdraw from the conflict, by transferring the greater part of the blame or merit to his partner. It happened that a contract had been made between them, by which they were to join in writing a play; and *he happened*, says Dryden, *to claim the promise just upon the finishing of a poem, when I would have been glad of a little respite.*—Two *thirds of it belonged to him; and to me only the first scene of the play, the whole fourth act, and the first half or somewhat more of the fifth.**

This was a play written professedly for the party of the duke of York, whose succession was then opposed. A parallel is intended between the Leaguers of France and the Covenanters of England; and this intention produced the controversy.*

Albion and Albania is a musical drama or opera, written, like the *Duke of Guise*, against the Republicans. With what success it was performed, I have not found.

The State of Innocence and Fall of Man is termed by him an opera: it is rather a tragedy in heroick rhyme, but of which the personages are such as cannot decently be exhibited on the stage. Some such production was foreseen by Marvel, who writes thus to Milton:

> Or if a work so infinite be spann'd,
> Jealous I was least some less skilful hand,
> Such as disquiet always what is well,
> And by ill-imitating would excel,
> Might hence presume the whole creation's day,
> To change in scenes, and show it in a play.*

It is another of his hasty productions for the heat of his imagination raised it in a month.

This composition is addressed to the princess of Modena, then dutchess of York, in a strain of flattery which disgraces genius, and which it was wonderful that any man that knew the meaning of his own words, could use without self-detestation. It is an attempt to mingle earth and heaven, by praising human excellence in the language of religion.

The preface contains an apology for heroick verse, and poetick licence; by which is meant not any liberty taken in contracting or extending words, but the use of bold fictions and ambitious figures.

The reason which he gives for printing what was never acted, cannot be overpassed: "I was induced to it in my own defence, many hundred copies of it being dispersed abroad without my knowledge or consent, and every one gathering new faults, it became at length a libel against me." These copies as they gathered faults were apparently manuscript; and he lived in an age very unlike ours, if many hundred copies of fourteen hundred lines were likely to be transcribed. An author has a right to print his own works, and needs not seek an apology in falsehood; but he that could bear to write the dedication felt no pain in writing the preface.

Aureng Zebe is a tragedy founded on the actions of a great prince then reigning, but over nations not likely to employ their criticks upon the transactions of the English stage. If he had known and disliked his own character, our trade was not in those times secure from his resentment. His country is at such a distance, that the manners might be safely falsified, and the incidents feigned; for remoteness of place is remarked by Racine, to afford the same conveniencies to a poet as length of time.*

This play is written in rhyme; and has the appearance of being the most elaborate of all the dramas. The personages are imperial; but the dialogue is often domestick, and therefore susceptible of sentiments accommodated to familiar incidents. The complaint of life is celebrated, and there are many other passages that may be read with pleasure.

This play is addressed to the earl of Mulgrave, afterwards duke of Buckingham, himself, if not a poet, yet a writer of verses, and a critick.* In this address Dryden gave the first hints of his intention to write an epick poem. He mentions his design in terms so obscure, that he seems afraid lest his plan should be purloined, as, he says, happened to him when he told it more plainly in his preface to Juvenal. "The design," says he, "you know is great, the story English, and neither too near the present times, nor too distant from them."

All for Love, or the World well lost, a tragedy founded upon the story of Antony and Cleopatra, he tells us, *is the only play which he wrote for himself*;* the rest were given to the people. It is by universal consent accounted the work in which he has admitted the fewest improprieties of style or character; but it has one fault equal to many, though rather moral than critical, that by admitting the romantick omnipotence of Love, he has recommended as laudable and worthy of imitation that conduct which, through all ages, the good have censured as vicious, and the bad despised as foolish.

Of this play the prologue and the epilogue, though written upon the common topicks of malicious and ignorant criticism, and without any particular relation to the characters or incidents of the drama, are deservedly celebrated for their elegance and spriteliness.

Limberham, or the kind Keeper, is a comedy, which, after the third night, was prohibited as too indecent for the stage. What gave offence, was in the printing, as the author says, altered or omitted. Dryden confesses that its indecency was objected to; but Langbaine, who yet seldom favours him, imputes its expulsion to resentment, because it *so much exposed the keeping part of the town.**

Oedipus is a tragedy formed by Dryden and Lee, in conjunction, from the works of Sophocles, Seneca, and Corneille. Dryden planned the scenes, and composed the first and third acts.

Don Sebastian is commonly esteemed either the first or second of his dramatick performances. It is too long to be all acted, and has many characters and many incidents; and though it is not without sallies of frantick dignity, and more noise than meaning, yet as it makes approaches to the possibilities of real life, and has some sentiments which leave a strong impression, it continued long to attract attention. Amidst the distresses of princes, and the vicissitudes of empire, are inserted several scenes which the writer intended for comick; but which, I suppose, that age did not much commend, and this would not endure. There are, however, passages of excellence universally acknowledged; the dispute and the reconciliation of Dorax and Sebastian has always been admired.

This play was first acted in 1690, after Dryden had for some years discontinued dramatick poetry.

Amphitryon is a comedy derived from Plautus and Moliere. The dedication is dated Oct. 1690. This play seems to have succeeded at its first appearance; and was, I think, long considered as a very diverting entertainment.

Cleomenes is a tragedy, only remarkable as it occasioned an incident related in the *Guardian*, and allusively mentioned by Dryden in his preface. As he came out from the representation, he was accosted thus by some airy stripling: *Had I been left alone with a young beauty, I would not have spent my time like your Spartan. That, Sir*, said Dryden, *perhaps is true; but give me leave to tell you, that you are no hero.**

King Arthur is another opera. It was the last work that Dryden performed for King Charles, who did not live to see it exhibited; and it does not seem to have been ever brought upon the stage. In the dedication to the marquis of Halifax, there is a very elegant character of Charles, and a pleasing account of his latter life. When this was first brought upon the stage, news that the duke of Monmouth had landed was told in the theatre, upon which the company departed, and *Arthur* was exhibited no more.*

His last drama was *Love triumphant*, a tragi-comedy. In his dedication to the earl of Salisbury* he mentions *the lowness of fortune to which he has voluntarily reduced himself, and of which he has no reason to be ashamed.*

This play appeared in 1694. It is said to have been unsuccessful. The catastrophe, proceeding merely from a change of mind, is confessed by the author to be defective. Thus he began and ended his dramatick labours with ill success.

From such a number of theatrical pieces it will be supposed, by most readers, that he must have improved his fortune; at least, that such diligence with such abilities must have set penury at defiance. But in Dryden's time the drama was very far from that universal approbation which it has now obtained. The playhouse was abhorred by the Puritans, and avoided by those who desired the character of seriousness or decency. A grave lawyer would have debased his dignity, and a young trader would have impaired his credit, by appearing in those mansions of dissolute licentiousness. The profits of the theatre, when so many classes of the people were deducted from the audience, were not great; and the poet had for a long time but a single night. The first that had two nights was *Southern*, and the first that had three was *Rowe*.* There were however, in those days, arts of improving a poet's profit, which Dryden forbore to practise; and a play therefore seldom produced him more than a hundred pounds, by the accumulated gain of the third night, the dedication, and the copy.

Almost every piece had a dedication, written with such elegance and luxuriance of praise, as neither haughtiness nor avarice could be imagined able to resist. But he seems to have made flattery too cheap. That praise is worth nothing of which the price is known.

To increase the value of his copies, he often accompanied his work with a preface of criticism; a kind of learning then almost new in the English language, and which he, who had considered with great accuracy the principles of writing, was able to distribute copiously as occasions arose. By these dissertations the publick judgment must have been much improved; and Swift, who conversed with Dryden, relates that he regretted the success of his own instructions, and found his readers made suddenly too skilful to be easily satisfied.*

His prologues had such reputation, that for some time a play was considered as less likely to be well received, if some of his verses did not introduce it. The price of a prologue was two guineas, till being asked to write one for Mr. Southern, he demanded three; *Not*, said he, *young man, out of disrespect to you, but the players have had my goods too cheap*.*

Though he declares, that in his own opinion his genius was not dramatick, he had great confidence in his own fertility; for he is said to have engaged, by contract, to furnish four plays a year.

It is certain that in one year, 1678, he published *All for Love, Assignation*, two parts of the *Conquest of Granada, Sir Martin Marall*, and the *State of Innocence*, six complete plays, with a celerity of performance, which, though all Langbaine's charges of plagiarism should be allowed, shews such facility of composition, such readiness of language, and such copiousness of sentiment, as, since the time of Lopez de Vega,* perhaps no other author has possessed.

He did not enjoy his reputation, however great, nor his profits, however small, without molestation. He had criticks to endure, and rivals to oppose. The two most distinguished wits of the nobility, the duke of Buckingham and earl of Rochester, declared themselves his enemies.

Buckingham characterised him in 1671, by the name of *Bayes* in the *Rehearsal*; a farce which he is said to have written with the assistance of Butler the author of *Hudibras*,* Martin Clifford of the Charterhouse, and Dr. Sprat, the friend of Cowley, then his chaplain.* Dryden and his friends laughed at the length of time, and the number of hands employed upon this performance; in which, though by some artifice of action it yet keeps possession of the stage, it is not possible now to find any thing that might not have been written without so long delay, or a confederacy so numerous.

To adjust the minute events of literary history, is tedious and troublesome; it requires indeed no great force of understanding, but often depends upon enquiries which there is no opportunity of making, or is to be fetched from books and pamphlets not always at hand.

The *Rehearsal* was played in 1671, and yet is represented as ridiculing passages in the *Conquest of Granada* and *Assignation*, which were not published till 1678, in *Marriage Alamode* published in 1673, and in *Tyrannick Love* of 1677. These contradictions shew how rashly satire is applied.

It is said that this farce was originally intended against Davenant, who in the first draught was characterised by the name of *Bilboa*. Davenant had been a soldier and an adventurer.

There is one passage in the *Rehearsal* still remaining, which seems to have related originally to Davenant. *Bayes* hurts his nose, and comes in with brown paper applied to the bruise; how this affected Dryden, does not appear. Davenant's nose had suffered such diminution by mishaps among the women, that a patch upon that part evidently denoted him.

It is said likewise that Sir Robert Howard was once meant. The design was probably to ridicule the reigning poet, whoever he might be.

Much of the personal satire, to which it might owe its first reception, is now lost or obscured. *Bayes* probably imitated the dress, and mimicked the manner, of Dryden; the cant words which are so often in his mouth may be supposed to have been Dryden's habitual phrases, or customary exclamations. *Bayes*, when he is to write, is blooded and purged: this, as Lamotte relates himself to have heard, was the real practice of the poet.*

There were other strokes in the *Rehearsal* by which malice was gratified: the debate between Love and Honour, which keeps prince *Volscius* in a single boot, is said to have alluded to the misconduct of the duke of Ormond, who lost Dublin to the rebels while he was toying with a mistress.

The earl of Rochester, to suppress the reputation of Dryden, took Settle into his protection, and endeavoured to persuade the publick that its approbation had been to that time misplaced. Settle was a while in high reputation: his *Empress of Morocco*, having first delighted the town, was carried in triumph to Whitehall, and played by the ladies of the court. Now was the poetical meteor at the highest; the next moment began its fall. Rochester withdrew his patronage; seeming resolved, says one of his biographers, *to have a judgement contrary to that of the town.** Perhaps being unable to endure any reputation beyond a certain height, even when he had himself contributed to raise it.

Neither criticks nor rivals did Dryden much mischief, unless they gained from his own temper the power of vexing him, which his frequent bursts of resentment give reason to suspect. He is always angry at some past, or afraid of some future censure; but he lessens the smart of his wounds by the balm of his own approbation, and endeavours to repel the shafts of criticism by opposing a shield of adamantine confidence.

The perpetual accusation produced against him, was that of plagiarism, against which he never attempted any vigorous defence; for, though he was perhaps sometimes injuriously censured, he would by denying part of the charge have confessed the rest; and as his adversaries had the proof in their own hands, he, who knew that wit had little power against facts, wisely left in that perplexity which generality produces a question which it was his interest to suppress, and which, unless provoked by vindication, few were likely to examine.

Though the life of a writer, from about thirty-five to sixty-three, may be supposed to have been sufficiently busied by the composition of eight and twenty pieces for the stage, Dryden found room in the same space for many other undertakings.

But, how much soever he wrote, he was at least once suspected of writing more; for in 1679 a paper of verses, called *an Essay on Satire*, was shewn about in manuscript, by which the earl of Rochester, the dutchess of Portsmouth,* and others, were so much provoked, that, as was supposed, for the actors were never discovered, they procured Dryden, whom they suspected as the author, to be waylaid and beaten. This incident is mentioned by the duke of Buckinghamshire, the true writer, in his Art of Poetry; where he says of Dryden,

> Though prais'd and beaten for another's rhymes,
> His own deserves as great applause sometimes.

His reputation in time was such, that his name was thought necessary to the success of every poetical or literary performance, and therefore he was engaged to contribute something, whatever it might be, to many publications. He prefixed the Life of Polybius to the translation of Sir Henry Sheers; and those of Lucian and Plutarch to versions of their works by different hands. Of the English Tacitus he translated the first book; and, if Gordon be credited, translated it from the French.* Such a charge can hardly be mentioned without some degree of indignation; but it is not, I suppose, so much to be inferred that Dryden wanted the literature necessary to the perusal of Tacitus, as that, considering himself as hidden in a crowd, he had no awe of the publick; and writing merely for money, was contented to get it by the nearest way.

In 1680, the Epistles of Ovid being translated by the poets of the time, among which one was the work of Dryden, and another of Dryden and Lord Mulgrave, it was necessary to introduce them by a preface; and Dryden, who on such occasions was regularly summoned, prefixed a discourse upon translation, which was then struggling for the liberty that it now enjoys. Why it should find any difficulty in breaking the shackles of verbal interpretation, which must for ever debar it from elegance, it would be difficult to conjecture, were not the power of prejudice every day observed. The authority of Jonson, Sandys, and Holiday, had fixed the judgement of the nation; and it was not easily believed that a better way could be found than they had taken, though Fanshaw, Denham, Waller, and Cowley, had tried to give examples of a different practice.*

In 1681, Dryden became yet more conspicuous by uniting politicks with poetry, in the memorable satire called *Absalom and Achitophel*, written against the faction which, by lord Shaftesbury's incitement, set the duke of Monmouth at its head.*

Of this poem, in which personal satire was applied to the support of publick principles, and in which therefore every mind was interested, the reception was eager, and the sale so large, that my father, an old bookseller, told me, he had not known it equalled but by *Sacheverell's* trial.*

The reason of this general perusal Addison has attempted to derive from the delight which the mind feels in the investigation of secrets; and thinks that curiosity to decypher the names procured readers to the poem. There is no need to enquire why those verses were read, which, to all the attractions of wit, elegance, and harmony, added the co-operation of all the factious passions, and filled every mind with triumph or resentment.

It could not be supposed that all the provocation given by Dryden would be endured without resistance or reply. Both his person and his party were exposed in their turns to the shafts of satire, which, though neither so well pointed nor perhaps so well aimed, undoubtedly drew blood.

One of these poems is called *Dryden's Satire on his Muse*; ascribed; though, as Pope says, falsely, to *Somers*, who was afterwards Chancellor.* The poem, whose soever it was, has much virulence, and some spriteliness. The writer tells all the ill that he can collect both of Dryden and his friends.

The poem of *Absalom and Achitophel* had two answers, now both forgotten; one called *Azaria and Hushai*; the other *Absalom senior*. Of these hostile compositions, Dryden apparently imputes *Absalom senior* to *Settle*, by quoting in his verses against him the second line. *Azaria and Hushai* was, as *Wood* says, imputed to him, though it is somewhat unlikely that he should write twice on the same occasion. This is a difficulty which I cannot remove, for want of a minuter knowledge of poetical transactions.

The same year he published the *Medal*, of which the subject is a medal struck on lord Shaftesbury's escape from a prosecution, by the *ignoramus* of a grand jury of Londoners.*

In both poems he maintains the same principles, and saw them both attacked by the same antagonist. Elkanah Settle, who had answered *Absalom*, appeared with equal courage in opposition to the *Medal*, and published an answer called *The Medal reversed*, with so much success in both encounters, that he left the palm doubtful, and divided the suffrages of the nation. Such are the revolutions of fame, or such is the prevalence of fashion, that the man whose works have not yet been thought to deserve the care of collecting them; who died forgotten in an hospital; and whose latter years were spent in contriving shows for fairs, and carrying an elegy or epithalamium, of which the beginning and end were occasionally varied, but the intermediate parts were always the same, to every house where there was a funeral or a wedding; might, with truth, have had inscribed upon his stone,

Here lies the Rival and Antagonist of Dryden.

Settle was, for this rebellion, severely chastised by Dryden under the name of *Doeg*, in the second part of *Absalom and Achitophel*, and was perhaps for his factious audacity made the city poet, whose annual office was to describe the glories of the Mayor's day. Of these bards he was the last, and seems not much to have deserved even this degree of regard, if it was paid to his political opinions; for he afterwards wrote a panegyrick on the virtues of judge Jefferies,* and what more could have been done by the meanest zealot for prerogative?

Of translated fragments, or occasional poems, to enumerate the titles, or settle the dates would be tedious, with little use. It may be observed, that as Dryden's genius was commonly excited by some personal regard, he rarely writes upon a general topick.

Soon after the accession of king James, when the design of reconciling the nation to the church of Rome became apparent, and the religion of the court gave the only efficacious title to its favours, Dryden declared himself a convert to popery. This at any other time might have passed with little censure. Sir *Kenelm Digby* embraced popery; the two *Rainolds* reciprocally converted one another; and *Chillingworth** himself was a while so entangled in the wilds of controversy, as to retire for quiet to an infallible church. If men of argument and study can find such difficulties, or such motives, as may either unite them to the church of Rome, or detain them in uncertainty, there can be no wonder that a man, who perhaps never enquired why he was a protestant, should by an artful and experienced disputant be made a papist, overborn by the sudden violence of new and unexpected arguments, or deceived by a representation which shews only the doubts on one part, and only the evidence on the other.

That conversion will always be suspected that apparently concurs with interest. He that never finds his error till it hinders his progress towards wealth or honour, will not be thought to love Truth only for herself. Yet it may easily happen that information may come at a commodious time; and as truth and interest are not by any fatal necessity at variance, that one may by accident introduce the other. When opinions are struggling into popularity, the arguments by which they are opposed or defended become more known; and he that changes his profession would perhaps have changed it before, with the like opportunities of instruction. This was then the state of popery; every artifice was used to shew it in its fairest form; and it must be owned to be a religion of external appearance sufficiently attractive.

It is natural to hope that a comprehensive is likewise an elevated soul, and that whoever is wise is also honest. I am willing to believe that Dryden, having employed his mind, active as it was, upon different studies, and filled it, capacious as it was, with other materials, came unprovided to the controversy, and wanted rather skill to discover the right than virtue to maintain it. But enquiries into the heart are not for man; we must now leave him to his Judge.

The priests, having strengthened their cause by so powerful an adherent, were not long before they brought him into action. They engaged him to defend the controversial papers found in the strong-box of Charles the Second, and, what yet was harder, to defend them against Stillingfleet.*

With hopes of promoting popery, he was employed to translate Maimbourg's History of the League; which he published with a large introduction.* His name is likewise prefixed to the English Life of Francis Xavier; but I know not that he ever owned himself the translator.* Perhaps the use of his name was a pious fraud, which however seems not to have had much effect; for neither of the books, I believe, was ever popular.

The version of Xavier's Life is commended by Brown, in a pamphlet not written to flatter;* and the occasion of it is said to have been, that the Queen, when she solicited a son, made vows to him as her tutelary saint.

He was supposed to have undertaken to translate *Varillas's History of Heresies*;* and when *Burnet* published Remarks upon it, to have written an *Answer*; upon which Burnet makes the following observation:

"I have been informed from England, that a gentleman, who is famous both for poetry and several other things, had spent three months in translating M. Varillas's History; but that, as soon as my Reflections appeared, he discontinued his labour, finding the credit of his author was gone. Now, if he thinks it is recovered by his Answer, he will perhaps go on with his translation; and this may be, for aught I know, as good an entertainment for him as the conversation that he had set on between the Hinds and Panthers, and all the rest of animals, for whom M. Varillas may serve well enough as an author: and this history and that poem are such extraordinary things of their kind, that it will be but suitable to see the author of the worst poem become likewise the translator of the worst history that the age has produced. If his grace and his wit improve both proportionably, he will hardly find that he has gained much by the change he has made, from having no religion to chuse one of the worst. It is true, he had somewhat to sink from in matter of wit; but as for his morals, it is scarce possible for him to grow a worse man than he was. He has lately wreaked his malice on me for spoiling his three months labour; but in it he has done me all the honour that any man can receive from him, which is to be railed at by him. If I had ill-nature enough to prompt me to wish a very bad wish for him, it should be, that he would go on and finish his translation. By that it will appear, whether the English nation, which is the most competent judge in this matter, has, upon the seeing our debate, pronounced in M. Varillas's favour, or in mine. It is true, Mr. D. will suffer a little by it; but at least it will serve to keep him in from other extravagancies; and if he gains little honour by this work, yet he cannot lose so much by it as he has done by his last employment."*

Having probably felt his own inferiority in theological controversy, he was desirous of trying whether, by bringing poetry to aid his arguments, he might become a more efficacious defender of his new profession. To reason in verse was, indeed, one of his powers; but subtilty and harmony united are still feeble, when opposed to truth.

Actuated therefore by zeal for Rome, or hope of fame, he published the *Hind and Panther*, a poem in which the church of Rome, figured by the *milk-white Hind*, defends her tenets against the church of England, represented by the *Panther*, a beast beautiful, but spotted.

A fable which exhibits two beasts talking Theology, appears at once full of absurdity; and it was accordingly ridiculed in the *City Mouse* and *Country Mouse*, a parody, written by Montague, afterwards earl of Halifax, and Prior, who then gave the first specimen of his abilities.*

The conversion of such a man, at such a time, was not likely to pass uncensured. Three dialogues were published by the facetious *Thomas Brown*,* of which the two first were called *Reasons of Mr. Bayes's changing his religion*: and the third *The Reasons of Mr. Hains the player's conversion and re-conversion*. The first was printed in 1688, the second not till 1690, the third in 1691. The clamour seems to have been long continued, and the subject to have strongly fixed the publick attention.

In the two first dialogues *Bayes* is brought into the company of *Crites* and *Eugenius*, with whom he had formerly debated on dramatick poetry. The two talkers in the third are Mr. *Bayes* and Mr. *Hains*.

Brown was a man not deficient in literature, nor destitute of fancy; but he seems to have thought it the pinnacle of excellence to be a *merry fellow*; and therefore laid out his powers upon small jests or gross buffoonery, so that his performances have little intrinsick value, and were read only while they were recommended by the novelty of the event that occasioned them.

These dialogues are like his other works: what sense or knowledge they contain, is disgraced by the garb in which it is exhibited. One great source of pleasure is to call Dryden *little Bayes*. *Ajax*, who happens to be mentioned, is *he that wore as many cowhides upon his shield as would have furnished half the king's army with shoe-leather*.

Being asked whether he has seen the *Hind and Panther*, Crites answers: *Seen it! Mr.* Bayes, *why I can stir no where but it persues me; it haunts me worse than a pewter-buttoned serjeant does a decayed cit. Sometimes I meet it in a band-box, when my laundress brings home my linen; sometimes, whether I will or no, it lights my pipe at a coffee-house; sometimes it surprises me in a trunkmaker's shop; and sometimes it refreshes my memory for me on the backside of a Chancery-lane parcel. For your comfort too, Mr. Bayes, I have not only seen it, as you may perceive, but have read it too, and can quote it as freely upon occasion as a frugal tradesman can quote that noble treatise the* Worth of a Penny *to his extravagant 'prentice, that revels in stewed apples, and penny custards.*

The whole animation of these compositions arises from a profusion of ludicrous and affected comparisons. *To secure one's chastity*, says Bayes, *little more is necessary than to leave off a correspondence with the other sex, which, to a wise man, is no greater a punishment than it would be to a fanatic parson to be forbid* seeing *the* Cheats *and the* Committee; *or for my Lord Mayor and Aldermen to be interdicted the sight of the* London Cuckold.—This is the general strain, and therefore I shall be easily excused the labour of more transcription.

Brown does not wholly forget past transactions: *You began*, says Crites to Bayes, *with a very indifferent religion, and have not mended the matter in your last choice. It was but reason that your Muse, which appeared first in a Tyrant's quarrel, should employ her last efforts to justify the usurpations of the* Hind.

Next year the nation was summoned to celebrate the birth of the Prince.* Now was the time for Dryden to rouse his imagination, and strain his voice. Happy days were at hand, and he was willing to enjoy and diffuse the anticipated blessings. He published a poem, filled with predictions of greatness and prosperity; predictions of which it is not necessary to tell how they have been verified.

A few months passed after these joyful notes, and every blossom of popish hope was blasted for ever by the Revolution. A papist now could be no longer Laureat. The revenue, which he had enjoyed with so much pride and praise, was transferred to Shadwell, an old enemy, whom he had formerly stigmatised by the name of *Og*.* Dryden could not decently complain that he was deposed; but seemed very angry that Shadwell succeeded him, and has therefore celebrated the intruder's inauguration in a poem exquisitely satirical, called *Mac Flecknoe*; of which the *Dunciad*, as Pope himself declares, is an imitation, though more extended in its plan, and more diversified in its incidents.

It is related by Prior, that Lord Dorset,* when, as chamberlain, he was constrained to eject Dryden from his office, gave him from his own purse an allowance equal to the salary. This is no romantick or incredible act of generosity; an hundred a year is often enough given to claims less cogent, by men less famed for liberality. Yet Dryden always represented himself as suffering under a public infliction; and once particularly demands respect for the patience with which he endured the loss of his little fortune. His patron might, indeed, enjoin him to suppress his bounty; but if he suffered nothing, he should not have complained.

During the short reign of king James he had written nothing for the stage, being, in his own opinion, more profitably employed in controversy and flattery. Of praise he might perhaps have been less lavish without inconvenience, for James was never said to have much regard for poetry: he was to be flattered only by adopting his religion.

Times were now changed: Dryden was no longer the court-poet, and was to look back for support to his former trade; and having waited about two years, either considering himself as discountenanced by the publick, or perhaps expecting a second revolution, he produced *Don Sebastian* in 1690; and in the next four years four dramas more.

In 1693 appeared a new version of Juvenal and Persius. Of Juvenal he translated the first, third, sixth, tenth, and sixteenth satires; and of Persius the whole work. On this occasion he introduced his two sons to the publick, as nurselings of the Muses. The fourteenth of Juvenal was the work of John, and the seventh of Charles Dryden. He prefixed a very ample preface in the form of a dedication to lord Dorset; and there gives an account of the design which he had once formed to write an epic poem on the actions either of Arthur or the Black Prince. He considered the epick as necessarily including some kind of supernatural agency, and had imagined a new kind of contest between the guardian angels of kingdoms, of whom he conceived that each might be represented zealous for his charge, without any intended opposition to the purposes of the Supreme Being, of which all created minds must in part be ignorant.

This is the most reasonable scheme of celestial interposition that ever was formed. The surprizes and terrors of enchantments, which have succeeded to the intrigues and oppositions of pagan deities, afford very striking scenes, and open a vast extent to the imagination; but, as Boileau observes, and Boileau will be seldom found mistaken, with this incurable defect, that in a contest between heaven and hell we know at the beginning which is to prevail; for this reason we follow Rinaldo to the enchanted wood with more curiosity than terror.*

In the scheme of Dryden there is one great difficulty, which yet he would perhaps have had address enough to surmount. In a war justice can be but on one side; and to entitle the hero to the protection of angels, he must fight in the defence of indubitable right. Yet some of the celestial beings, thus opposed to each other, must have been represented as defending guilt.

That this poem was never written, is reasonably to be lamented. It would doubtless have improved our numbers, and enlarged our language, and might perhaps have contributed by pleasing instruction to rectify our opinions, and purify our manners.

What he required as the indispensable condition of such an undertaking, a publick stipend, was not likely in those times to be obtained. Riches were not become familiar to us, nor had the nation yet learned to be liberal.

This plan he charged Blackmore with stealing; only, says he, *the guardian angels of kingdoms were machines too ponderous for him to manage*.*

In 1694, he began the most laborious and difficult of all his works, the translation of Virgil; from which he borrowed two months, that he might turn Fresnoy's Art of Painting* into English prose. The preface, which he boasts to have written in twelve mornings, exhibits a parallel of poetry and painting, with a miscellaneous collection of critical remarks, such as cost a mind stored like his no labour to produce them.

In 1697, he published his version of the works of Virgil; and that no opportunity of profit might be lost, dedicated the Pastorals to the lord Clifford, the Georgics to the earl of Chesterfield, and the Eneid to the earl of Mulgrave.* This œconomy of flattery, at once lavish and discreet, did not pass without observation.

This translation was censured by Milbourne, a clergyman, styled by Pope *the fairest of criticks*, because he exhibited his own version to be compared with that which he condemned.*

His last work was his Fables, published in 1699, in consequence, as is supposed, of a contract now in the hands of Mr. Tonson; by which he obliged himself, in consideration of three hundred pounds, to finish for the press ten thousand verses.

In this volume is comprised the well-known ode on St. Cecilia's day, which, as appeared by a letter communicated to Dr. Birch,* he spent a fortnight in composing and correcting. But what is this to the patience and diligence of Boileau, whose *Equivoque*, a poem of only three hundred forty-six lines, took from his life eleven months to write it, and three years to revise it!

Part of this book of Fables is the first Iliad in English, intended as a specimen of a version of the whole. Considering into what hands Homer was to fall, the reader cannot but rejoice that this project went no further.

The time was now at hand which was to put an end to all his schemes and labours. On the first of May 1701,* having been some time, as he tells us, a cripple in his limbs, he died in Gerard-street of a mortification in his leg.

There is extant a wild story relating to some vexatious events that happened at his funeral, which, at the end of Congreve's Life, by a writer of I know not what credit, are thus related, as I find the account transferred to a biographical dictionary:*

"Mr. Dryden dying on the Wednesday morning, Dr. Thomas Sprat, then bishop of Rochester and dean of Westminster, sent the next day to the lady Elizabeth Howard, Mr. Dryden's widow, that he would make a present of the ground, which was forty pounds, with all the other Abbey-fees. The lord Halifax likewise sent to the lady Elizabeth, and Mr. Charles Dryden her son, that, if they would give him leave to bury Mr. Dryden, he would inter him with a gentleman's private funeral, and afterwards bestow five hundred pounds on a monument in the Abbey; which, as they had no reason to refuse, they accepted. On the Saturday following the company came: the corpse was put into a velvet hearse, and eighteen mourning coaches, filled with company, attended. When they were just ready to move, the lord Jefferies, son of the lord chancellor Jefferies, with some of his rakish companions coming by, asked whose funeral it was: and being told Mr. Dryden's, he said, "What, shall Dryden, the greatest honour and ornament of the nation, be buried after this private manner! No, gentlemen, let all that loved Mr. Dryden, and honour his memory, alight and join with me in gaining my lady's consent to let me have the honour of his interment, which shall be after another manner than this; and I will bestow a thousand pounds on a monument in the Abbey for him." The gentlemen in the coaches, not knowing of the bishop of Rochester's favour, nor of the lord Halifax's generous design (they both having, out of respect to the family, enjoined the lady Elizabeth and her son to keep their favour concealed to the world, and let it pass for their own expence) readily came out of the coaches, and attended lord Jefferies up to the lady's bedside, who was then sick; he repeated the purport of what he had before said; but she absolutely refusing, he fell on his knees, vowing never to rise till his request was granted. The rest of the company by his desire kneeled also; and the lady, being under a sudden surprize, fainted away. As soon as she recovered her speech, she cried, *No, no*. Enough, gentlemen, replied he; my lady is very good, she says, *Go, go*. She repeated her former words with all her strength, but in vain; for her feeble voice was lost in their acclamations of joy; and the lord Jefferies ordered the hearsemen to carry the corpse to Mr. Russel's, an undertaker's in Cheapside, and leave it there till he should send orders for the embalment, which, he added, should be after the royal manner. His directions were obeyed, the company dispersed, and lady Elizabeth and her son remained inconsolable. The next day Mr. Charles Dryden waited on the lord Halifax and the bishop, to excuse his mother and himself, by relating the real truth. But neither his lordship nor the bishop would admit of any plea; especially the latter, who had the Abbey lighted, the ground opened, the choir attending, an anthem ready set, and himself waiting for some time without any corpse to bury. The undertaker, after three days expectance of orders for embalment without receiving any, waited on the lord Jefferies; who pretending ignorance of the matter, turned it off with an ill-natured jest, saying, That those who observed the orders of a drunken frolick deserved no better; that he remembered nothing at all of it; and that he might do what he pleased with the corpse. Upon this, the undertaker waited upon the lady Elizabeth and her son, and threatened to bring the corpse home, and set it before the door. They desired a day's respite, which was granted. Mr. Charles Dryden wrote a handsome letter to the lord Jefferies, who returned it with this cool answer, "That he knew nothing of the matter, and would be troubled no more about it." He then addressed the lord

Halifax and the bishop of Rochester, who absolutely refused to do any thing in it. In this distress Dr. Garth sent for the corpse to the College of Physicians, and proposed a funeral by subscription, to which himself set a most noble example. At last a day, about three weeks after Mr. Dryden's decease, was appointed for the interment: Dr. Garth pronounced a fine Latin oration, at the College, over the corpse; which was attended to the Abbey by a numerous train of coaches. When the funeral was over, Mr. Charles Dryden sent a challenge to the lord Jefferies, who refusing to answer it, he sent several others, and went often himself; but could neither get a letter delivered, nor admittance to speak to him: which so incensed him, that he resolved, since his lordship refused to answer him like a gentleman, that he would watch an opportunity to meet, and fight off-hand, though with all the rules of honour; which his lordship hearing, left the town: and Mr. Charles Dryden could never have the satisfaction of meeting him, though he sought it till his death with the utmost application."

This story I once intended to omit, as it appears with no great evidence; nor have I met with any confirmation, but in a letter of Farquhar,* and he only relates that the funeral of Dryden was tumultuary and confused.

Supposing the story true, we may remark that the gradual change of manners, though imperceptible in the process, appears great when different times, and those not very distant, are compared. If at this time a young drunken Lord should interrupt the pompous regularity of a magnificent funeral, what would be the event, but that he would be justled out of the way, and compelled to be quiet? If he should thrust himself into a house, he would be sent roughly away; and what is yet more to the honour of the present time, I believe, that those who had subscribed to the funeral of a man like Dryden, would not, for such an accident, have withdrawn their contributions.

He was buried among the poets in Westminster Abbey, where, though the duke of Newcastle had, in a general dedication prefixed by Congreve to his dramatick works, accepted thanks for his intention of erecting him a monument, he lay long without distinction, till the duke of Buckinghamshire gave him a tablet, inscribed only with the name of DRYDEN.*

He married the lady Elizabeth Howard, daughter of the earl of Berkshire, with circumstances, according to the satire imputed to lord Somers,* not very honourable to either party: by her he had three sons, Charles, John, and Henry. Charles was usher of the palace to pope Clement the XIth, and visiting England in 1704, was drowned in an attempt to swim cross the Thames at Windsor.

John was author of a comedy called *The Husband his own Cuckold.* He is said to have died at Rome. Henry entered into some religious order. It is some proof of Dryden's sincerity in his second religion, that he taught it to his sons. A man conscious of hypocritical profession in himself, is not likely to convert others; and as his sons were qualified in 1693 to appear among the translators of Juvenal, they must have been taught some religion before their father's change.

Of the person of Dryden I know not any account; of his mind, the portrait which has been left by Congreve, who knew him with great familiarity, is such as adds our love of his manners to our admiration of his genius. "He was," we are told, "of a nature exceedingly humane and compassionate, ready to forgive injuries, and capable of a sincere reconciliation with those that had offended him. His friendship, where he professed it, went beyond his professions. He was of a very easy, of very pleasing access; but somewhat slow, and, as it were, diffident in his advances to others: he had that in his nature which abhorred intrusion into any society whatever. He was therefore less known, and consequently his character became more liable to misapprehensions and misrepresentations: he was very modest, and very easily to be discountenanced in his approaches to his equals or superiors. As his reading had been very extensive, so was he very happy in a memory tenacious of every thing that he had read. He was not more possessed of knowledge than he was communicative of it; but then his communication was by no means pedantick, or imposed upon the conversation, but just such, and went so far as, by the natural turn of the conversation in which he was engaged, it was necessarily promoted or required. He was extreme ready, and gentle in his correction of the errors of any writer who thought fit to consult him, and full as ready and patient to admit of the reprehensions of others, in respect of his own oversights or mistakes."*

To this account of Congreve nothing can be objected but the fondness of friendship; and to have excited that fondness in such a mind is no small degree of praise. The disposition of Dryden, however, is shewn in this character rather as it exhibited itself in cursory conversation, than as it operated on the more important parts of life. His placability and his friendship indeed were solid virtues; but courtesy and good-humour are often found with little real worth. Since Congreve, who knew him well, has told us no more, the rest must be collected as it can from other testimonies, and particularly from those notices which Dryden has very liberally given us of himself.

The modesty which made him so slow to advance, and so easy to be repulsed, was certainly no suspicion of deficient merit, or unconsciousness of his own value: he appears to have known, in its whole extent, the dignity of his character, and to have set a very high value on his own powers and performances. He probably did not offer his conversation, because he expected it to be solicited; and he retired from a cold reception, not submissive but indignant, with such reverence of his own greatness as made him unwilling to expose it to neglect or violation.

His modesty was by no means inconsistent with ostentatiousness: he is diligent enough to remind the world of his merit, and expresses with very little scruple his high opinion of his own powers; but his self-commendations are read without scorn or indignation; we allow his claims, and love his frankness.

Tradition, however, has not allowed that his confidence in himself exempted him from jealousy of others. He is accused of envy and insidiousness; and is particularly charged with inciting Creech to translate Horace, that he might lose the reputation which Lucretius had given him.*

Of this charge we immediately discover that it is merely conjectural; the purpose was such as no man would confess; and a crime that admits no proof, why should we believe?

He has been described as magisterially presiding over the younger writers, and assuming the distribution of poetical fame; but he who excels has a right to teach, and he whose judgement is incontestable may, without usurpation, examine and decide.

Congreve represents him as ready to advise and instruct; but there is reason to believe that his communication was rather useful than entertaining. He declares of himself that he was saturnine, and not one of those whose spritely sayings diverted company; and one of his censurers makes him say,

> Nor wine nor love could ever see me gay;
> To writing bred, I knew not what to say.*

There are men whose powers operate only at leisure and in retirement, and whose intellectual vigour deserts them in conversation; whom merriment confuses, and objection disconcerts; whose bashfulness restrains their exertion, and suffers them not to speak till the time of speaking is past; or whose attention to their own character makes them unwilling to utter at hazard what has not been considered, and cannot be recalled.

Of Dryden's sluggishness in conversation it is vain to search or to guess the cause. He certainly wanted neither sentiments nor language; his intellectual treasures were great, though they were locked up from his own use. *His thoughts*, when he wrote, *flowed in upon him so fast, that his only care was which to chuse, and which to reject.** Such rapidity of composition naturally promises a flow of talk, yet we must be content to believe what an enemy says of him, when he likewise says it of himself. But whatever was his character as a companion, it appears that he lived in familiarity with the highest persons of his time. It is related by Carte of the duke of Ormond, that he used often to pass a night with Dryden, and those with whom Dryden consorted:* who they were, Carte has not told; but certainly the convivial table at which Ormond sat was not surrounded with a plebeian society. He was indeed reproached with boasting of his familiarity with the great; and Horace will support him in the opinion, that to please superiours is not the lowest kind of merit.

The merit of pleasing must, however, be estimated by the means. Favour is not always gained by good actions or laudable qualities. Caresses and preferments are often bestowed on the auxiliaries of vice, the procurers of pleasure, or the flatterers of vanity. Dryden has never been charged with any personal agency unworthy of a good character: he abetted vice and vanity only with his pen. One of his enemies has accused him of lewdness in his conversation; but if accusation without proof be credited, who shall be innocent?

His works afford too many examples of dissolute licentiousness, and abject adulation; but they were probably, like his merriment, artificial and constrained; the effects of study and meditation, and his trade rather than his pleasure.

Of the mind that can trade in corruption, and can deliberately pollute itself with ideal wickedness for the sake of spreading the contagion in society, I wish not to conceal or excuse the depravity.—Such degradation of the dignity of genius, such abuse of superlative abilities, cannot be contemplated but with grief and indignation. What consolation can be had, Dryden has afforded, by living to repent, and to testify his repentance.

Of dramatick immorality he did not want examples among his predecessors, or companions among his contemporaries; but in the meanness and servility of hyperbolical adulation, I know not whether, since the days in which the Roman emperors were deified, he has been ever equalled, except by Afra Behn in an address to Eleanor Gwyn.* When once he has undertaken the task of praise, he no longer retains shame in himself, nor supposes it in his patron. As many odoriferous bodies are observed to diffuse perfumes from year to year, without sensible diminution of bulk or weight, he appears never to have impoverished his mint of flattery by his expences, however lavish. He had all the forms of excellence, intellectual and moral, combined in his mind, with endless variation; and when he had scattered on the hero of the day the golden shower of wit and virtue, he had ready for him, whom he wished to court on the morrow, new wit and virtue with another stamp. Of this kind of meanness he never seems to decline the practice, or lament the necessity: he considers the great as entitled to encomiastick homage, and brings praise rather as a tribute than a gift, more delighted with the fertility of his invention than mortified by the prostitution of his judgement. It is indeed not certain, that on these occasions his judgement much rebelled against his interest. There are minds which easily sink into submission, that look on grandeur with undistinguishing reverence, and discover no defect where there is elevation of rank and affluence of riches.

With his praises of others and of himself is always intermingled a strain of discontent and lamentation, a sullen growl of resentment, or a querulous murmur of distress. His works are under-valued, his merit is unrewarded, and *he has few thanks to pay his stars that he was born among Englishmen.** To his criticks he is sometimes contemptuous, sometimes resentful, and sometimes submissive. The writer who thinks his works formed for duration, mistakes his interest when he mentions his enemies. He degrades his own dignity by shewing that he was affected by their censures, and gives lasting importance to names, which, left to themselves, would vanish from remembrance. From this principle Dryden did not oft depart; his complaints are for the greater part general; he seldom pollutes his page with an adverse name. He condescended indeed to a controversy with Settle, in which he perhaps may be considered rather as assaulting than repelling; and since Settle is sunk into oblivion, his libel remains injurious only to himself.

Among answers to criticks, no poetical attacks, or altercations, are to be included; they are, like other poems, effusions of genius, produced as much to obtain praise as to obviate censure. These Dryden practised, and in these he excelled.

Of Collier,* Blackmore,* and Milbourne,* he has made mention in the preface to his Fables. To the censure of Collier, whose remarks may be rather termed admonitions than criticisms, he makes little reply; being, at the age of sixty-eight, attentive to better things than the claps of a playhouse. He complains of Collier's rudeness, and the *horse-play of his raillery*; and asserts that *in many places he has perverted by his glosses the meaning* of what he censures; but in other things he confesses that he is justly taxed; and says, with great calmness and candour, *I have pleaded guilty to all thoughts or expressions of mine that can be truly accused of obscenity, immorality, or profaneness, and retract them. If he be my enemy, let him triumph; if he be my friend, he will be glad of my repentance.* Yet, as our best dispositions are imperfect, he left standing in the same book a reflection on Collier of great asperity, and indeed of more asperity than wit.

Blackmore he represents as made his enemy by the poem of *Absalom and Achitophel*, which *he thinks a little hard upon his fanatick patrons*; and charges him with borrowing the plan of his *Arthur* from the preface to Juvenal, *though he had*, says he, *the baseness not to acknowledge his benefactor, but instead of it to traduçe me in a libel.*

The libel in which Blackmore traduced him was a *Satire upon Wit*; in which, having lamented the exuberance of false wit and the deficiency of true, he proposes that all wit should be re-coined before it is current, and appoints masters of assay who shall reject all that is light or debased.

> 'Tis true, that when the coarse and worthless dross
> Is purg'd away, there will be mighty loss;
> Ev'n Congreve, Southern, manly Wycherley,
> When thus refin'd, will grievous sufferers be;
> Into the melting-pot when Dryden comes,

What horrid stench will rise, what noisome fumes!
How will he shrink, when all his lewd allay,
And wicked mixture, shall be purg'd away!

Thus stands the passage in the last edition; but in the original there was an abatement of the censure, beginning thus:

But what remains will be so pure, 'twill bear
Th' examination of the most severe.

Blackmore, finding the censure resented, and the civility disregarded, ungenerously omitted the softer part. Such variations discover a writer who consults his passions more than his virtue; and it may be reasonably supposed that Dryden imputes his enmity to its true cause.

Of Milbourne he wrote only in general terms, such as are always ready at the call of anger, whether just or not: a short extract will be sufficient. *He pretends a quarrel to me, that I have fallen foul upon priesthood; if I have, I am only to ask pardon of good priests, and am afraid his share of the reparation will come to little. Let him be satisfied that he shall never be able to force himself upon me for an adversary; I contemn him too much to enter into competition with him.*

As for the rest of those who have written against me, they are such scoundrels that they deserve not the least notice to be taken of them. Blackmore and Milbourne are only distinguished from the crowd by being remembered to their infamy.

Dryden indeed discovered, in many of his writings, an affected and absurd malignity to priests and priesthood, which naturally raised him many enemies, and which was sometimes as unseasonably resented as it was exerted. Trapp* is angry that he calls the sacrificer in the *Georgicks* the *holy butcher*: the translation is indeed ridiculous; but Trapp's anger arises from his zeal, not for the author, but the priest; as if any reproach of the follies of paganism could be extended to the preachers of truth.

Dryden's dislike of the priesthood is imputed by Langbaine, and I think by Brown, to a repulse which he suffered when he solicited ordination; but he denies, in the preface to his Fables, that he ever designed to enter into the church; and such a denial he would not have hazarded, if he could have been convicted of falsehood.

Malevolence to the clergy is seldom at a great distance from irreverence of religion, and Dryden affords no exception to this observation. His writings exhibit many passages, which, with all the allowance that can be made for characters and occasions, are such as piety would not have admitted, and such as may vitiate light and unprincipled minds. But there is no reason for supposing that he disbelieved the religion which he disobeyed. He forgot his duty rather than disowned it. His tendency to profaneness is the effect of levity, negligence, and loose conversation, with a desire of accommodating himself to the corruption of the times, by venturing to be wicked as far as he durst. When he professed himself a convert to Popery, he did not pretend to have received any new conviction of the fundamental doctrines of Christianity.

The persecution of criticks was not the worst of his vexations; he was much more disturbed by the importunities of want. His complaints of poverty are so frequently repeated, either with the dejection of weakness sinking in helpless misery, or the indignation of merit claiming its tribute from mankind, that it is impossible not to detest the age which could impose on such a man the necessity of such solicitations, or not to despise the man who could submit to such solicitations without necessity.

Whether by the world's neglect, or his own imprudence, I am afraid that the greatest part of his life was passed in exigences. Such outcries were surely never uttered but in severe pain. Of his supplies or his expences no probable estimate can now be made. Except the salary of the Laureate, to which king James added the office of Historiographer, perhaps with some additional emoluments, his whole revenue seems to have been casual; and it is well known that he seldom lives frugally who lives by chance. Hope is always liberal, and they that trust her promises make little scruple of revelling to-day on the profits of the morrow.

Of his plays the profit was not great, and of the produce of his other works very little intelligence can be had. By discoursing with the late amiable Mr. Tonson,* I could not find that any memorials of the transactions between his predecessor and Dryden had been preserved, except the following papers:

"I do hereby promise to pay John Dryden, Esq; or order, on the 25th of March 1699, the sum of two hundred and fifty guineas, in consideration of ten thousand verses, which the said John Dryden, Esq; is to deliver to me Jacob Tonson, when finished, whereof seven thousand five hundred verses, more or less, are already in the said

Jacob Tonson's possession. And I do hereby farther promise, and engage myself, to make up the said sum of two hundred and fifty guineas three hundred pounds sterling to the said John Dryden, Esq; his executors, administrators, or assigns, at the beginning of the second impression of the said ten thousand verses.

"In witness whereof I have hereunto set my hand and seal, this 20th day of March, $169\frac{8}{9}$.

Jacob Tonson.

Sealed and delivered, being first
duly stampt, pursuant to the acts
of parliament for that purpose,
in the presence of
Ben. Portlock.
Will. Congreve."

"March 24th, 1698.

"Received then of Mr. Jacob Tonson the sum of two hundred sixty-eight pounds fifteen shillings, in pursuance of an agreement for ten thousand verses, to be delivered by me to the said Jacob Tonson, whereof I have already delivered to him about seven thousand five hundred, more or less; he the said Jacob Tonson being obliged to make up the foresaid sum of two hundred sixty-eight pounds fifteen shillings three hundred pounds, at the beginning of the second impression of the foresaid ten thousand verses;

I say, received by me
John Dryden.
Witness Charles Dryden."

Two hundred and fifty guineas, at 1*l.* 1*s.* 6*d.* is 268*l.* 15*s.*

It is manifest from the dates of this contract, that it relates to the volume of Fables, which contains about twelve thousand verses, and for which therefore the payment must have been afterwards enlarged.

I have been told of another letter yet remaining, in which he desires Tonson to bring him money, to pay for a watch which he had ordered for his son, and which the maker would not leave without the price.

The inevitable consequence of poverty is dependence. Dryden had probably no recourse in his exigencies but to his bookseller. The particular character of Tonson I do not know; but the general conduct of traders was much less liberal in those times than in our own; their views were narrower, and their manners grosser. To the mercantile ruggedness of that race, the delicacy of the poet was sometimes exposed. Lord Bolingbroke,* who in his youth had cultivated poetry, related to Dr. King of Oxford,* that one day, when he visited Dryden, they heard, as they were conversing, another person entering the house. "This," said Dryden, "is Tonson. You will take care not to depart before he goes away; for I have not completed the sheet which I promised him; and if you leave me unprotected, I must suffer all the rudeness to which his resentment can prompt his tongue."

What rewards he obtained for his poems, besides the payment of the bookseller, cannot be known: Mr. Derrick,* who consulted some of his relations, was informed that his Fables obtained five hundred pounds from the dutchess of Ormond;* a present not unsuitable to the magnificence of that splendid family; and he quotes Moyle,* as relating that forty pounds were paid by a musical society for the use of *Alexander's Feast.*

In those days the œconomy of government was yet unsettled, and the payments of the Exchequer were dilatory and uncertain: of this disorder there is reason to believe that the Laureat sometimes felt the effects; for in one of his prefaces he complains of those, who, being intrusted with the distribution of the Prince's bounty, suffer those that depend upon it to languish in penury.

Of his petty habits or slight amusements, tradition has retained little. Of the only two men whom I have found to whom he was personally known, one told me that at the house which he frequented, called Will's Coffee-house,* the appeal upon any literary dispute was made to him; and the other related, that his armed chair, which in the winter had a settled and prescriptive place by the fire, was in the summer placed in the balcony, and that he called the two places his winter and his summer seat. This is all the intelligence which his two survivors afforded me.

One of his opinions will do him no honour in the present age, though in his own time, at least in the beginning of it, he was far from having it confined to himself. He put great confidence in the prognostications of judicial astrology. In the Appendix to the Life of Congreve is a narrative of some of his predictions wonderfully fulfilled; but I know not the writer's means of information, or character of veracity. That he had the configurations of the horoscope in his mind, and considered them as influencing the affairs of men, he does not forbear to hint.

> The utmost malice of the stars is past.—
> Now frequent *trines* the happier lights among,
> And *high-rais'd Jove*, from his dark prison freed,
> Those weights took off that on his planet hung,
> Will gloriously the new-laid works succeed.*

He has elsewhere shewn his attention to the planetary powers; and in the preface to his Fables has endeavoured obliquely to justify his superstition, by attributing the same to some of the Ancients. The letter, added to this narrative, leaves no doubt of his notions or practice.

So slight and so scanty is the knowledge which I have been able to collect concerning the private life and domestick manners of a man, whom every English generation must mention with reverence as a critick and a poet.

DRYDEN may be properly considered as the father of English criticism, as the writer who first taught us to determine upon principles the merit of composition. Of our former poets, the greatest dramatist wrote without rules, conducted through life and nature by a genius that rarely misled, and rarely deserted him. Of the rest, those who knew the laws of propriety had neglected to teach them.

Two *Arts of English Poetry* were written in the days of Elizabeth by Webb and Puttenham,* from which something might be learned, and a few hints had been given by Jonson and Cowley; but Dryden's *Essay on Dramatick Poetry* was the first regular and valuable treatise on the art of writing.

He who, having formed his opinions in the present age of English literature, turns back to peruse this dialogue, will not perhaps find much increase of knowledge, or much novelty of instruction; but he is to remember that critical principles were then in the hands of a few, who had gathered them partly from the Ancients, and partly from the Italians and French. The structure of dramatick poems was not then generally understood. Audiences applauded by instinct, and poets perhaps often pleased by chance.

A writer who obtains his full purpose loses himself in his own lustre. Of an opinion which is no longer doubted, the evidence ceases to be examined. Of an art universally practised, the first teacher is forgotten. Learning once made popular is no longer learning; it has the appearance of something which we have bestowed upon ourselves, as the dew appears to rise from the field which it refreshes.

To judge rightly of an author, we must transport ourselves to his time, and examine what were the wants of his contemporaries, and what were his means of supplying them. That which is easy at one time was difficult at another. Dryden at least imported his science, and gave his country what it wanted before; or rather, he imported only the materials, and manufactured them by his own skill.

The dialogue on the Drama was one of his first essays of criticism, written when he was yet a timorous candidate for reputation, and therefore laboured with that diligence which he might allow himself somewhat to remit, when his name gave sanction to his positions, and his awe of the public was abated, partly by custom, and partly by success. It will not be easy to find, in all the opulence of our language, a treatise so artfully variegated with successive representations of opposite probabilities, so enlivened with imagery, so brightened with illustrations. His portraits of the English dramatists are wrought with great spirit and diligence. The account of Shakspeare may stand as a perpetual model of encomiastick criticism; exact without minuteness, and lofty without exaggeration. The praise lavished by Longinus, on the attestation of the heroes of Marathon, by Demosthenes, fades away before it. In a few lines is exhibited a character, so extensive in its comprehension, and so curious in its limitations, that nothing can be added, diminished, or reformed; nor can the editors and admirers of Shakspeare, in all their emulation of reverence, boast of much more than of having diffused and paraphrased this epitome of excellence, of having changed Dryden's gold for baser metal, of lower value though of greater bulk.

In this, and in all his other essays on the same subject, the criticism of Dryden is the criticism of a poet; not a dull collection of theorems, nor a rude detection of faults, which perhaps the censor was not able to have committed; but a gay and vigorous dissertation, where delight is mingled with instruction, and where the author proves his right of judgement, by his power of performance.

The different manner and effect with which critical knowledge may be conveyed, was perhaps never more clearly exemplified than in the performances of Rymer and Dryden. It was said of a dispute between two mathematicians, "malim cum Scaligero errare, quam cum Clavio recte sapere;" that *it was more eligible to go wrong with one than right with the other.** A tendency of the same kind every mind must feel at the perusal of Dryden's prefaces and Rymer's discourses. With Dryden we are wandering in quest of Truth; whom we find, if we find her at all, drest in the graces of elegance; and if we miss her, the labour of the pursuit rewards itself; we are led only through fragrance and flowers: Rymer, without taking a nearer, takes a rougher way; every step is to be made through thorns and brambles; and Truth, if we meet her, appears repulsive by her mien, and ungraceful by her habit. Dryden's criticism has the majesty of a queen; Rymer's has the ferocity of a tyrant.

As he had studied with great diligence the art of poetry, and enlarged or rectified his notions, by experience perpetually increasing, he had his mind stored with principles and observations; he poured out his knowledge with little labour; for of labour, notwithstanding the multiplicity of his productions, there is sufficient reason to suspect that he was not a lover. To write *con amore*, with fondness for the employment, with perpetual touches and retouches, with unwillingness to take leave of his own idea, and an unwearied pursuit of unattainable perfection, was, I think, no part of his character.

His Criticism may be considered as general or occasional. In his general precepts, which depend upon the nature of things, and the structure of the human mind, he may doubtless be safely recommended to the confidence of the reader; but his occasional and particular positions were sometimes interested, sometimes negligent, and sometimes capricious. It is not without reason that Trapp, speaking of the praises which he bestows on Palamon and Arcite, says, "Novimus judicium Drydeni de poemate quodam *Chauceri*, pulchro sane illo, et admodum laudando, nimirum quod non modo vere epicum sit, sed Iliada etiam atque Æneada æquet, imo superet. Sed novimus eodem tempore viri illius maximi non semper accuratissimas esse censuras, nec ad severissimam critices normam exactas: illo judice id plerumque optimum est, quod nunc præ manibus habet, & in quo nunc occupatur."*

He is therefore by no means constant to himself. His defence and desertion of dramatick rhyme is generally known. *Spence*, in his remarks on Pope's Odyssey,* produces what he thinks an unconquerable quotation from Dryden's preface to the Eneid, in favour of translating an epic poem into blank verse; but he forgets that when his author attempted the Iliad, some years afterwards, he departed from his own decision, and translated into rhyme.

When he has any objection to obviate, or any license to defend, he is not very scrupulous about what he asserts, nor very cautious, if the present purpose be served, not to entangle himself in his own sophistries. But when all arts are exhausted, like other hunted animals, he sometimes stands at bay; when he cannot disown the grossness of one of his plays, he declares that he knows not any law that prescribes morality to a comick poet.

His remarks on ancient or modern writers are not always to be trusted. His parallel of the versification of Ovid with that of Claudian has been very justly censured by *Sewel*[1]. His comparison of the first line of Virgil with the first of Statius is not happier: Virgil, he says, is soft and gentle, and would have thought Statius mad if he had heard him thundering out

Quæ superimposito moles geminata colosso.*

Statius perhaps heats himself, as he proceeds, to exaggerations somewhat hyperbolical; but undoubtedly Virgil would have been too hasty, if he had condemned him to straw for one sounding line. Dryden wanted an instance, and the first that occurred was imprest into the service.

What he wishes to say, he says at hazard; he cited *Gorbuduc*,* which he had never seen; gives a false account of *Chapman's* versification;* and discovers, in the preface to his Fables, that he translated the first book of the Iliad, without knowing what was in the second.

It will be difficult to prove that Dryden ever made any great advances in literature. As having distinguished himself at Westminster under the tuition of Busby, who advanced his scholars to a height of knowledge very rarely attained in grammar-schools, he resided afterwards at Cambridge, it is not to be supposed, that his skill in the ancient languages was deficient, compared with that of common students; but his scholastick acquisitions seem not proportionate to his opportunities and abilities. He could not, like Milton or Cowley,

[1] Preface to Ovid's Metamorphoses.

have made his name illustrious merely by his learning. He mentions but few books, and those such as lie in the beaten track of regular study; from which if ever he departs, he is in danger of losing himself in unknown regions.

In his Dialogue on the Drama, he pronounces with great confidence that the Latin tragedy of Medea is not Ovid's, because it is not sufficiently interesting and pathetick. He might have determined the question upon surer evidence; for it is quoted by Quintilian as the work of Seneca; and the only line which remains of Ovid's play, for one line is left us, is not there to be found.* There was therefore no need of the gravity of conjecture, or the discussion of plot or sentiment, to find what was already known upon higher authority than such discussions can ever reach.

His literature, though not always free from ostentation, will be commonly found either obvious, and made his own by the art of dressing it; or superficial, which, by what he gives, shews what he wanted; or erroneous, hastily collected, and negligently scattered.

Yet it cannot be said that his genius is ever unprovided of matter, or that his fancy languishes in penury of ideas. His works abound with knowledge, and sparkle with illustrations. There is scarcely any science or faculty that does not supply him with occasional images and lucky similitudes; every page discovers a mind very widely acquainted both with art and nature, and in full possession of great stores of intellectual wealth. Of him that knows much, it is natural to suppose that he has read with diligence; yet I rather believe that the knowledge of Dryden was gleaned from accidental intelligence and various conversation, by a quick apprehension, a judicious selection, and a happy memory, a keen appetite of knowledge, and a powerful digestion; by vigilance that permitted nothing to pass without notice, and a habit of reflection that suffered nothing useful to be lost. A mind like Dryden's, always curious, always active, to which every understanding was proud to be associated, and of which every one solicited the regard, by an ambitious display of himself, had a more pleasant, perhaps a nearer way, to knowledge than by the silent progress of solitary reading. I do not suppose that he despised books, or intentionally neglected them; but that he was carried out, by the impetuosity of his genius, to more vivid and speedy instructors; and that his studies were rather desultory and fortuitous than constant and systematical.

It must be confessed that he scarcely ever appears to want book-learning but when he mentions books; and to him may be transferred the praise which he gives his master Charles.

> His conversation, wit, and parts,
> His knowledge in the noblest useful arts,
> Were such, dead authors could not give,
> But habitudes of those that live;
> Who, lighting him, did greater lights receive:
> He drain'd from all, and all they knew,
> His apprehension quick, his judgement true:
> That the most learn'd with shame confess
> His knowledge more, his reading only less.*

Of all this, however, if the proof be demanded, I will not undertake to give it; the atoms of probability, of which my opinion has been formed, lie scattered over all his works; and by him who thinks the question worth his notice, his works must be perused with very close attention.

Criticism, either didactick or defensive, occupies almost all his prose, except those pages which he has devoted to his patrons; but none of his prefaces were ever thought tedious. They have not the formality of a settled style, in which the first half of the sentence betrays the other. The clauses are never balanced, nor the periods modelled; every word seems to drop by chance, though it falls into its proper place. Nothing is cold or languid; the whole is airy, animated, and vigorous; what is little, is gay; what is great, is splendid. He may be thought to mention himself too frequently; but while he forces himself upon our esteem, we cannot refuse him to stand high in his own. Every thing is excused by the play of images and the spriteliness of expression. Though all is easy, nothing is feeble; though all seems careless, there is nothing harsh; and though, since his earlier works, more than a century has passed, they have nothing yet uncouth or obsolete.

He who writes much, will not easily escape a manner, such a recurrence of particular modes as may be easily noted. Dryden is always *another and the same*,* he does not exhibit a second time the same elegances in the same form, nor appears to have any art other than that of expressing with clearness what he thinks with vigour. His style could not easily be imitated, either seriously or ludicrously;

for, being always equable and always varied, it has no prominent or discriminative characters. The beauty who is totally free from disproportion of parts and features, cannot be ridiculed by an over-charged resemblance.

From his prose, however, Dryden derives only his accidental and secondary praise; the veneration with which his name is pronounced by every cultivator of English literature, is paid to him as he refined the language, improved the sentiments, and tuned the numbers of English Poetry.

After about half a century of forced thoughts, and rugged metre, some advances towards nature and harmony had been already made by Waller and Denham; they had shewn that long discourses in rhyme grew more pleasing when they were broken into couplets, and that verse consisted not only in the number but the arrangement of syllables.

But though they did much, who can deny that they left much to do? Their works were not many, nor were their minds of very ample comprehension. More examples of more modes of composition were necessary for the establishment of regularity, and the introduction of propriety in word and thought.

Every language of a learned nation necessarily divides itself into diction scholastick and popular, grave and familiar, elegant and gross; and from a nice distinction of these different parts, arises a great part of the beauty of style. But if we except a few minds, the favourites of nature, to whom their own original rectitude was in the place of rules, this delicacy of selection was little known to our authors; our speech lay before them in a heap of confusion, and every man took for every purpose what chance might offer him.

There was therefore before the time of Dryden no poetical diction, no system of words at once refined from the grossness of domestick use, and free from the harshness of terms appropriated to particular arts. Words too familiar, or too remote, defeat the purpose of a poet. From those sounds which we hear on small or on coarse occasions, we do not easily receive strong impressions, or delightful images; and words to which we are nearly strangers, whenever they occur, draw that attention on themselves which they should transmit to things.

Those happy combinations of words which distinguish poetry from prose, had been rarely attempted; we had few elegances or flowers of speech, the roses had not yet been plucked from the bramble, or different colours had not been joined to enliven one another.

It may be doubted whether Waller and Denham could have overborn the prejudices which had long prevailed, and which even then were sheltered by the protection of Cowley. The new versification, as it was called, may be considered as owing its establishment to Dryden; from whose time it is apparent that English poetry has had no tendency to relapse to its former savageness.

The affluence and comprehension of our language is very illustriously displayed in our poetical translations of Ancient Writers; a work which the French seem to relinquish in despair, and which we were long unable to perform with dexterity. Ben Jonson thought it necessary to copy Horace almost word by word; Feltham, his contemporary and adversary, considers it as indispensably requisite in a translation to give line for line. It is said that Sandys, whom Dryden calls the best versifier of the last age, has struggled hard to comprise every book of his English Metamorphoses in the same number of verses with the original. Holyday had nothing in view but to shew that he understood his author, with so little regard to the grandeur of his diction, or the volubility of his numbers, that his metres can hardly be called verses; they cannot be read without reluctance, nor will the labour always be rewarded by understanding them. Cowley saw that such *copyers* were a *servile race*; he asserted his liberty, and spread his wings so boldly that he left his authors. It was reserved for Dryden to fix the limits of poetical liberty, and give us just rules and examples of translation.

When languages are formed upon different principles, it is impossible that the same modes of expression should always be elegant in both. While they run on together, the closest translation may be considered as the best; but when they divaricate, each must take its natural course. Where correspondence cannot be obtained, it is necessary to be content with something equivalent. *Translation therefore*, says Dryden, *is not so loose as paraphrase, nor so close as metaphrase.**

All polished languages have different styles; the concise, the diffuse, the lofty, and the humble. In the proper choice of style consists the resemblance which Dryden principally exacts from the translator. He is to exhibit his author's thoughts in such a dress of diction as the author would have given them, had his language been English: rugged magnificence is not to be softened: hyperbolical ostentation is not to be repressed, nor sententious affectation to have its points blunted. A translator is to be like his author: it is not his business to excel him.

The reasonableness of these rules seems sufficient for their vindication; and the effects produced by observing them were so happy, that I know not whether they were ever opposed but by Sir Edward Sherburne,* a man whose learning was greater than his powers of poetry; and who, being better qualified to give the meaning than the spirit of Seneca, has introduced his version of three tragedies by a defence of close translation. The authority of Horace, which the new translators cited in defence of their practice, he has, by a judicious explanation, taken fairly from them; but reason wants not Horace to support it.

It seldom happens that all the necessary causes concur to any great effect: will is wanting to power, or power to will, or both are impeded by external obstructions. The exigences in which Dryden was condemned to pass his life, are reasonably supposed to have blasted his genius, to have driven out his works in a state of immaturity, and to have intercepted the full-blown elegance which longer growth would have supplied.

Poverty, like other rigid powers, is sometimes too hastily accused. If the excellence of Dryden's works was lessened by his indigence, their number was increased; and I know not how it will be proved, that if he had written less he would have written better; or that indeed he would have undergone the toil of an author, if he had not been solicited by something more pressing than the love of praise.

But as is said by his Sebastian,

What had been, is unknown; what is, appears.*

We know that Dryden's several productions were so many successive expedients for his support; his plays were therefore often borrowed, and his poems were almost all occasional.

In an occasional performance no height of excellence can be expected from any mind, however fertile in itself, and however stored with acquisitions. He whose work is general and arbitrary, has the choice of his matter, and takes that which his inclination and his studies have best qualified him to display and decorate. He is at liberty to delay his publication, till he has satisfied his friends and himself; till he has reformed his first thoughts by subsequent examination; and polished away those faults which the precipitance of ardent composition is likely to leave behind it. Virgil is related to have poured out a great number of lines in the morning, and to have passed the day in reducing them to fewer.

The occasional poet is circumscribed by the narrowness of his subject. Whatever can happen to man has happened so often, that little remains for fancy or invention. We have been all born; we have most of us been married; and so many have died before us, that our deaths can supply but few materials for a poet. In the fate of princes the publick has an interest; and what happens to them of good or evil, the poets have always considered as business for the Muse. But after so many inauguratory gratulations, nuptial hymns, and funeral dirges, he must be highly favoured by nature, or by fortune, who says any thing not said before. Even war and conquest, however splendid, suggest no new images; the triumphal chariot of a victorious monarch can be decked only with those ornaments that have graced his predecessors.

Not only matter but time is wanting. The poem must not be delayed till the occasion is forgotten. The lucky moments of animated imagination cannot be attended; elegances and illustrations cannot be multiplied by gradual accumulation: the composition must be dispatched while conversation is yet busy, and admiration fresh; and haste is to be made, lest some other event should lay hold upon mankind.

Occasional compositions may however secure to a writer the praise both of learning and facility; for they cannot be the effect of long study, and must be furnished immediately from the treasures of the mind.

The death of Cromwell was the first publick event which called forth Dryden's poetical powers. His heroick stanzas have beauties and defects; the thoughts are vigorous, and though not always proper, shew a mind replete with ideas; the numbers are smooth, and the diction, if not altogether correct, is elegant and easy.

Davenant was perhaps at this time his favourite author, though Gondibert never appears to have been popular; and from Davenant he learned to please his ear with the stanza of four lines alternately rhymed.

Dryden very early formed his versification: there are in this early production no traces of Donne's or Jonson's ruggedness; but he did not so soon free his mind from the ambition of forced conceits. In his verses on the Restoration, he says of the King's exile,

> He, toss'd by Fate—
> Could taste no sweets of youth's desired age,
> But found his life too true a pilgrimage.*

And afterwards, to shew how virtue and wisdom are increased by adversity, he makes this remark:

> Well might the ancient poets then confer
> On Night the honour'd name of *counsellor*,
> Since, struck with rays of prosperous fortune blind,
> We light alone in dark afflictions find.

His praise of Monk's dexterity comprises such a cluster of thoughts unallied to one another, as will not elsewhere be easily found:

> 'Twas Monk, whom Providence design'd to loose
> Those real bonds false freedom did impose.
> The blessed saints that watch'd this turning scene,
> Did from their stars with joyful wonder lean,
> To see small clues draw vastest weights along,
> Not in their bulk, but in their order strong.
> Thus pencils can by one slight touch restore
> Smiles to that changed face that wept before.
> With ease such fond chimæras we pursue,
> As fancy frames for fancy to subdue:
> But, when ourselves to action we betake,
> It shuns the mint like gold that chymists make:
> How hard was then his task, at once to be
> What in the body natural we see!
> Man's Architect distinctly did ordain
> The charge of muscles, nerves, and of the brain,
> Through viewless conduits spirits to dispense
> The springs of motion from the seat of sense.
> 'Twas not the hasty product of a day,
> But the well-ripen'd fruit of wise delay.
> He, like a patient angler, ere he strook,
> Would let them play a-while upon the hook.

Our healthful food the stomach labours thus,
At first embracing what it straight doth crush.
Wise leaches will not vain receipts obtrude,
While growing pains pronounce the humours crude;
Deaf to complaints, they wait upon the ill,
Till some safe crisis authorize their skill.

He had not yet learned, indeed he never learned well, to forbear the improper use of mythology. After having rewarded the heathen deities for their care,

With *Alga* who the sacred altar strows?
To all the sea-gods Charles an offering owes;
A bull to thee, Portunus, shall be slain;
A ram to you, ye Tempests of the Main.

He tells us, in the language of religion,

Prayer storm'd the skies, and ravish'd Charles from thence,
As heaven itself is took by violence.

And afterwards mentions one of the most awful passages of Sacred History.

Other conceits there are, too curious to be quite omitted; as,

For by example most we sinn'd before,
And, glass-like, clearness mix'd with frailty bore.

How far he was yet from thinking it necessary to found his sentiments on Nature, appears from the extravagence of his fictions and hyperboles:

The winds, that never moderation knew,
Afraid to blow too much, too faintly blew;
Or, out of breath with joy, could not enlarge
Their straiten'd lungs.—
It is no longer motion cheats your view;
As you meet it, the land approacheth you;
The land returns, and in the white it wears
The marks of penitence and sorrow bears.

I know not whether this fancy, however little be its value, was not borrowed. A French poet read to Malherbe some verses, in which he represents France as moving out of its place to receive the king.

"Though this," said Malherbe, "was in my time, I do not remember it."*

His poem on the *Coronation* has a more even tenour of thought. Some lines deserve to be quoted:

> You have already quench'd sedition's brand,
> And zeal, that burnt it, only warms the land;
> The jealous sects that durst not trust their cause
> So far from their own will as to the laws,
> Him for their umpire, and their synod take,
> And their appeal alone to Cæsar make.*

Here may be found one particle of that old versification, of which, I believe, in all his works, there is not another:

> Nor is it duty, or our hope alone,
> Creates that joy, but full *fruition*.*

In the verses to the lord chancellor Clarendon, two years afterwards, is a conceit so hopeless at the first view, that few would have attempted it; and so successfully laboured, that though at last it gives the reader more perplexity than pleasure, and seems hardly worth the study that it costs, yet it must be valued as a proof of a mind at once subtle and comprehensive:

> In open prospect nothing bounds our eye,
> Until the earth seems join'd unto the sky:
> So in this hemisphere our outmost view
> Is only bounded by our king and you:
> Our sight is limited where you are join'd,
> And beyond that no farther heaven can find.
> So well your virtues do with his agree,
> That, though your orbs of different greatness be,
> Yet both are for each other's use dispos'd,
> His to enclose, and yours to be enclos'd.
> Nor could another in your room have been,
> Except an emptiness had come between.*

The comparison of the Chancellor to the Indies leaves all resemblance too far behind it:

> And as the Indies were not found before
> Those rich perfumes which from the happy shore
> The winds upon their balmy wings convey'd,

Whose guilty sweetness first their world betray'd;
So by your counsels we are brought to view
A new and undiscover'd world in you.

There is another comparison, for there is little else in the poem, of which, though perhaps it cannot be explained into plain prosaick meaning, the mind perceives enough to be delighted, and readily forgives its obscurity, for its magnificence:

How strangely active are the arts of peace,
Whose restless motions less than wars do cease:
Peace is not freed from labour, but from noise;
And war more force, but not more pains employs:
Such is the mighty swiftness of your mind,
That, like the earth's, it leaves our sense behind,
While you so smoothly turn and rowl our sphere,
That rapid motion does but rest appear.
For as in nature's swiftness, with the throng
Of flying orbs while ours is borne along,
All seems at rest to the deluded eye,
Mov'd by the soul of the same harmony:
So carry'd on by our unwearied care,
We rest in peace, and yet in motion share.

To this succeed four lines, which perhaps afford Dryden's first attempt at those penetrating remarks on human nature, for which he seems to have been peculiarly formed:

Let envy then those crimes within you see,
From which the happy never must be free;
Envy that does with misery reside,
The joy and the revenge of ruin'd pride.

Into this poem he seems to have collected all his powers; and after this he did not often bring upon his anvil such stubborn and unmalleable thoughts; but, as a specimen of his abilities to unite the most unsociable matter, he has concluded with lines, of which I think not myself obliged to tell the meaning:

Yet unimpair'd with labours, or with time,
Your age but seems to a new youth to climb.
Thus heavenly bodies do our time beget,
And measure change, but share no part of it:

And still it shall without a weight increase,
Like this new year, whose motions never cease.
For since the glorious course you have begun,
Is led by Charles, as that is by the sun,
It must both weightless and immortal prove,
Because the centre of it is above.

In the *Annus Mirabilis* he returned to the quatrain, which from that time he totally quitted, perhaps from this experience of its inconvenience, for he complains of its difficulty. This is one of his greatest attempts. He had subjects equal to his abilities, a great naval war, and the Fire of London. Battles have always been described in heroick poetry; but a sea-fight and artillery had yet something of novelty. New arts are long in the world before poets describe them; for they borrow every thing from their predecessors, and commonly derive very little from nature or from life. Boileau was the first French writer that had ever hazarded in verse the mention of modern war, or the effects of gunpowder. We, who are less afraid of novelty, had already possession of those dreadful images: Waller had described a sea-fight.* Milton had not yet transferred the invention of fire-arms to the rebellious angels.

This poem is written with great diligence, yet does not fully answer the expectation raised by such subjects and such a writer. With the stanza of Davenant he has sometimes his vein of parenthesis, and incidental disquisition, and stops his narrative for a wise remark.

The general fault is, that he affords more sentiment than description, and does not so much impress scenes upon the fancy, as deduce consequences and make comparisons.

The initial stanzas have rather too much resemblance to the first lines of Waller's poem on the war with Spain; perhaps such a beginning is natural, and could not be avoided without affectation. Both Waller and Dryden might take their hint from the poem on the civil war of Rome, *Orbem jam totum*, &c.*

Of the king collecting his navy, he says,

It seems as every ship their sovereign knows,
His awful summons they so soon obey;
So hear the scaly herds when Proteus blows,
And so to pasture follow through the sea.*

It would not be hard to believe that Dryden had written the two first lines seriously, and that some wag had added the two latter in burlesque. Who would expect the lines that immediately follow, which are indeed perhaps indecently hyperbolical, but certainly in a mode totally different?

> To see this fleet upon the ocean move,
> Angels drew wide the curtains of the skies;
> And heaven, as if there wanted lights above,
> For tapers made two glaring comets rise.

The description of the attempt at Bergen will afford a very compleat specimen of the descriptions in this poem:

> And now approach'd their fleet from India, fraught
> With all the riches of the rising sun:
> And precious sand from southern climates brought,
> The fatal regions where the war begun.
>
> Like hunted castors, conscious of their store,
> Their way-laid wealth to Norway's coast they bring;
> Then first the North's cold bosom spices bore,
> And winter brooded on the eastern spring.
>
> By the rich scent we found our perfum'd prey,
> Which, flank'd with rocks, did close in covert lie:
> And round about their murdering cannon lay,
> At once to threaten and invite the eye.
>
> Fiercer than cannon, and than rocks more hard,
> The English undertake th' unequal war:
> Seven ships alone, by which the port is barr'd,
> Besiege the Indies, and all Denmark dare.
>
> These fight like husbands, but like lovers those:
> These fain would keep, and those more fain enjoy:
> And to such height their frantic passion grows,
> That what both love, both hazard to destroy:
>
> Amidst whole heaps of spices lights a ball,
> And now their odours arm'd against them fly:
> Some preciously by shatter'd porcelain fall,
> And some by aromatic splinters die.
>
> And though by tempests of the prize bereft,
> In heaven's inclemency some ease we find:
> Our foes we vanquish'd by our valour left,
> And only yielded to the seas and wind.*

In this manner is the sublime too often mingled with the ridiculous. The Dutch seek a shelter for a wealthy fleet: this surely needed no illustration; yet they must fly, not like all the rest of mankind on the same occasion, but *like hunted castors*; and they might with strict propriety be hunted; for we winded them by our noses—their *perfumes* betrayed them. The *Husband* and the *Lover*, though of more dignity than the Castor, are images too domestick to mingle properly with the horrors of war. The two quatrains that follow are worthy of the author.

The account of the different sensations with which the two fleets retired, when the night parted them, is one of the fairest flowers of English poetry.

> The night comes on, we eager to pursue
> The combat still, and they asham'd to leave:
> 'Till the last streaks of dying day withdrew,
> And doubtful moon-light did our rage deceive.
>
> In th' English fleet each ship resounds with joy,
> And loud applause of their great leader's fame:
> In firy dreams the Dutch they still destroy,
> And, slumbering, smile at the imagin'd flame.
>
> Not so the Holland fleet, who, tir'd and done,
> Stretch'd on their decks like weary oxen lie;
> Faint sweats all down their mighty members run,
> (Vast bulks, which little souls but ill supply.)
>
> In dreams they fearful precipices tread,
> Or, shipwreck'd, labour to some distant shore:
> Or, in dark churches, walk among the dead;
> They wake with horror, and dare sleep no more.*

It is a general rule in poetry, that all appropriated terms of art should be sunk in general expressions, because poetry is to speak an universal language. This rule is still stronger with regard to arts not liberal, or confined to few, and therefore far removed from common knowledge; and of this kind, certainly, is technical navigation. Yet Dryden was of opinion that a sea-fight ought to be described in the nautical language; *and certainly,* says he, *as those who in a logical disputation keep to general terms would hide a fallacy, so those who do it in any poetical description would veil their ignorance.**

Let us then appeal to experience; for by experience at last we learn as well what will please as what will profit. In the battle, his terms seem to have been blown away; but he deals them liberally in the dock:

So here some pick out bullets from the side,
Some drive old *okum* thro' each *seam* and rift:
Their left-hand does the *calking-iron* guide,
The rattling *mallet* with the right they lift.

With boiling pitch another near at hand
(From friendly Sweden brought) the *seams instops*:
Which, well laid o'er, the salt-sea waves withstand,
And shake them from the rising beak in drops.

Some the *gall'd* ropes with dawby *marling* blind,
Or sear-cloth masts with strong *tarpawling* coats:
To try new *shrouds* one mounts into the wind,
And one below, their ease or stiffness notes.*

I suppose here is not one term which every reader does not wish away.

His digression to the original and progress of navigation, with his prospect of the advancement which it shall receive from the Royal Society, then newly instituted, may be considered as an example seldom equalled of seasonable excursion and artful return.

One line, however, leaves me discontented; he says, that by the help of the philosophers,

Instructed ships shall sail to quick commerce,
By which remotest regions are allied.—*

Which he is constrained to explain in a note, *By a more exact measure of longitude*. It had better become Dryden's learning and genius to have laboured science into poetry, and have shewn, by explaining longitude, that verse did not refuse the ideas of philosophy.

His description of the Fire is painted by resolute meditation, out of a mind better formed to reason than to feel. The conflagration of a city, with all its tumults of concomitant distress, is one of the most dreadful spectacles which this world can offer to human eyes; yet it seems to raise little emotion in the breast of the poet; he watches the flame coolly from street to street, with now a reflection, and now a simile, till at last he meets the king, for whom he makes a speech, rather tedious in a time so busy; and then follows again the progress of the fire.

There are, however, in this part some passages that deserve attention; as in the beginning:

The diligence of trades and noiseful gain
  And luxury more late asleep were laid;
All was the night's, and in her silent reign
  No sound the rest of Nature did invade

In this deep quiet—*

The expression *All was the night's* is taken from Seneca, who remarks on Virgil's line.

Omnia noctis erant placida composita quiete,*

that he might have concluded better,

Omnia noctis erant.

The following quatrain is vigorous and animated:

The ghosts of traytors from the bridge descend
  With bold fanatick spectres to rejoice;
About the fire into a dance they bend,
  And sing their sabbath notes with feeble voice.

His prediction of the improvements which shall be made in the new city, is elegant and poetical, and, with an event which Poets cannot always boast, has been happily verified. The poem concludes with a simile that might have better been omitted.

Dryden, when he wrote this poem, seems not yet fully to have formed his versification, or settled his system of propriety.

From this time, he addicted himself almost wholly to the stage, *to which*, says he, *my genius never much inclined me*,* merely as the most profitable market for poetry. By writing tragedies in rhyme, he continued to improve his diction and his numbers. According to the opinion of *Harte*,* who had studied his works with great attention, he settled his principles of versification in 1676, when he produced the play of *Aureng Zebe*; and according to his own account of the short time in which he wrote *Tyrannick Love*, and the *State of Innocence*, he soon obtained the full effect of diligence, and added facility to exactness.*

Rhyme has been so long banished from the theatre, that we know not its effect upon the passions of an audience; but it has this convenience, that sentences stand more independent on each other, and striking passages are therefore easily selected and retained. Thus the description of Night in the *Indian Emperor*, and the rise and fall of empire in the *Conquest of Granada*, are more frequently repeated than any lines in *All for Love*, or *Don Sebastian*.

To search his plays for vigorous sallies, and sententious elegances, or to fix the dates of any little pieces which he wrote by chance, or by solicitation, were labour too tedious and minute.

His dramatic labours did not so wholly absorb his thoughts, but that he promulgated the laws of translation in a preface to the English Epistles of Ovid; one of which he translated himself, and another in conjunction with the Earl of Mulgrave.

Absalom and Achitophel is a work so well known, that particular criticism is superfluous. If it be considered as a poem political and controversial, it will be found to comprise all the excellences of which the subject is susceptible; acrimony of censure, elegance of praise, artful delineation of characters, variety and vigour of sentiment, happy turns of language, and pleasing harmony of numbers; and all these raised to such a height as can scarcely be found in any other English composition.

It is not, however, without faults; some lines are inelegant or improper, and too many are irreligiously licentious. The original structure of the poem was defective; allegories drawn to great length will always break; Charles could not run continually parallel with David.

The subject had likewise another inconvenience: it admitted little imagery or description, and a long poem of mere sentiments easily becomes tedious; though all the parts are forcible, and every line kindles new rapture, the reader, if not relieved by the interposition of something that sooths the fancy, grows weary of admiration, and defers the rest.

As an approach to historical truth was necessary, the action and catastrophe were not in the poet's power; there is therefore an unpleasing disproportion between the beginning and the end. We are alarmed by a faction formed out of many sects various in their principles, but agreeing in their purpose of mischief, formidable for their numbers, and strong by their supports, while the king's friends are few and weak. The chiefs on either part are set forth to view; but when expectation is at the height, the king makes a speech, and

> Henceforth a series of new times began.*

Who can forbear to think of an enchanted castle, with a wide moat and lofty battlements, walls of marble and gates of brass, which vanishes at once into air, when the destined knight blows his horn before it?

In the second part, written by *Tate*,* there is a long insertion, which, for poignancy of satire, exceeds any part of the former. Personal resentment, though no laudable motive to satire, can add great force to general principles. Self-love is a busy prompter.

The *Medal*, written upon the same principles with *Absalom and Achitophel*, but upon a narrower plan, gives less pleasure, though it discovers equal abilities in the writer. The superstructure cannot extend beyond the foundation; a single character or incident cannot furnish as many ideas, as a series of events, or multiplicity of agents. This poem therefore, since time has left it to itself, is not much read, nor perhaps generally understood, yet it abounds with touches both of humorous and serious satire. The picture of a man whose propensions to mischief are such, that his best actions are but inability of wickedness, is very skilfully delineated and strongly coloured.

> Power was his aim: but, thrown from that pretence,
> The wretch turn'd loyal in his own defence,
> And malice reconcil'd him to his Prince.
> Him, in the anguish of his soul, he serv'd;
> Rewarded faster still than he deserv'd:
> Behold him now exalted into trust;
> His counsels oft convenient, seldom just.
> Ev'n in the most sincere advice he gave,
> He had a grudging still to be a knave.
> The frauds he learnt in his fanatic years,
> Made him uneasy in his lawful gears;
> At least as little honest as he cou'd:
> And, like white witches, mischievously good.
> To his first bias, longingly, he leans;
> And rather would be great by wicked means.*

The *Threnodia*, which, by a term I am afraid neither authorized nor analogical,* he calls *Augustalis*, is not among his happiest productions. Its first and obvious defect is the irregularity of its metre, to which the ears of that age, however, were accustomed. What is worse, it has neither tenderness nor dignity, it is neither magnificent nor pathetick. He seems to look round him for images which he cannot find, and what he has he distorts by endeavouring to enlarge them. He is, he says, *petrified with grief*; but the marble sometimes relents, and trickles in a joke.

> The sons of art all med'cines try'd,
> And every noble remedy apply'd;
> With emulation each essay'd
> His utmost skill; *nay more they pray'd*:
> Was never losing game with better conduct play'd.*

He had been a little inclined to merriment before upon the prayers of a nation for their dying sovereign, nor was he serious enough to keep heathen fables out of his religion.

> With him th' innumberable croud of armed prayers
> Knock'd at the gates of heaven, and knock'd aloud;
> *The first well-meaning rude petitioners*,
> All for his life assail'd the throne,
> All would have brib'd the skies by offering up their own.
> So great a throng not heaven itself could bar;
> 'Twas almost borne by force *as in the giants war*.
> The prayers, at least, for his reprieve were heard;
> His death, like Hezekiah's, was deferr'd.*

There is throughout the composition a desire of splendor without wealth. In the conclusion he seems too much pleased with the prospect of the new reign to have lamented his old master with much sincerity.

He did not miscarry in this attempt for want of skill either in lyrick or elegiack poetry. His poem *on the death* of Mrs. *Killigrew*, is undoubtedly the noblest ode that our language ever has produced. The first part flows with a torrent of enthusiasm. *Fervet immensusque ruit*.* All the stanzas indeed are not equal. An imperial crown cannot be one continued diamond; the gems must be held together by some less valuable matter.

In his first ode for Cecilia's day, which is lost in the splendor of the second, there are passages which would have dignified any other poet. The first stanza is vigorous and elegant, though the word *diapason* is too technical, and the rhymes are too remote from one another.

From harmony, from heavenly harmony,
  This universal frame began:
When nature underneath a heap of jarring atoms lay,
  And could not heave her head,
The tuneful voice was heard from high,
  Arise ye more than dead.
Then cold and hot, and moist and dry,
In order to their stations leap,
  And musick's power obey.
From harmony, from heavenly harmony,
  This universal frame began:
  From harmony to harmony
Through all the compass of the notes it ran,
  The diapason closing full in man.*

The conclusion is likewise striking, but it includes an image so awful in itself, that it can owe little to poetry; and I could wish the antithesis of *musick untuning* had found some other place.

As from the power of sacred lays
  The spheres began to move,
And sung the great Creator's praise
  To all the bless'd above.
So when the last and dreadful hour
This crumbling pageant shall devour,
The trumpet shall be heard on high,
The dead shall live, the living die,
And musick shall untune the sky.*

Of his skill in Elegy he has given a specimen in his *Eleonora*, of which the following lines discover their author.

Though all these rare endowments of the mind
Were in a narrow space of life confin'd,
The figure was with full perfection crown'd;
Though not so large an orb, as truly round:
As when in glory, through the public place,
The spoils of conquer'd nations were to pass,
And but one day for triumph was allow'd,
The consul was constrain'd his pomp to crowd;
And so the swift procession hurry'd on,
That all, though not distinctly, might be shown:
So in the straiten'd bounds of life confin'd,

She gave but glimpses of her glorious mind:
And multitudes of virtues pass'd along;
Each pressing foremost in the mighty throng,
Ambitious to be seen, and then make room
For greater multitudes that were to come.
Yet unemploy'd no minute slipp'd away;
Moments were precious in so short a stay.
The haste of heaven to have her was so great,
That some were single acts, though each compleat;
And every act stood ready to repeat.*

This piece, however, is not without its faults; there is so much likeness in the initial comparison, that there is no illustration. As a king would be lamented, Eleonora was lamented.

As when some great and gracious monarch dies,
Soft whispers, first, and mournful murmurs rise
Among the sad attendants; then the sound
Soon gathers voice, and spreads the news around,
Through town and country, till the dreadful blast
Is blown to distant colonies at last;
Who, then, perhaps, were offering vows in vain,
For his long life, and for his happy reign:
So slowly by degrees, unwilling fame
Did matchless Eleonora's fate proclaim,
Till publick as the loss the news became.*

This is little better than to say in praise of a shrub, that it is as green as a tree, or of a brook, that it waters a garden, as a river waters a country.

Dryden confesses that he did not know the lady whom he celebrates; the praise being therefore inevitably general, fixes no impression upon the reader, nor excites any tendency to love, nor much desire of imitation. Knowledge of the subject is to the poet, what durable materials are to the architect.

The *Religio Laici*, which borrows its title from the *Religio Medici* of Browne, is almost the only work of Dryden which can be considered as a voluntary effusion; in this, therefore, it might be hoped, that the full effulgence of his genius would be found. But unhappily the subject is rather argumentative than poetical: he intended only a specimen of metrical disputation.

And this unpolish'd rugged verse I chose,
As fittest for discourse, and nearest prose.*

This, however, is a composition of great excellence in its kind, in which the familiar is very properly diversified with the solemn, and the grave with the humorous; in which metre has neither weakened the force, nor clouded the perspicuity of argument; nor will it be easy to find another example equally happy of this middle kind of writing, which, though prosaick in some parts, rises to high poetry in others, and neither towers to the skies, nor creeps along the ground.

Of the same kind, or not far distant from it, is the *Hind and Panther*, the longest of all Dryden's original poems; an allegory intended to comprize and to decide the controversy between the Romanists and Protestants. The scheme of the work is injudicious and incommodious; for what can be more absurd than that one beast should counsel another to rest her faith upon a pope and council? He seems well enough skilled in the usual topicks of argument, endeavours to shew the necessity of an infallible judge, and reproaches the Reformers with want of unity; but is weak enough to ask, why since we see without knowing how, we may not have an infallible judge without knowing where.

The *Hind* at one time is afraid to drink at the common brook, because she may be worried; but walking home with the *Panther*, talks by the way of the *Nicene Fathers*, and at last declares herself to be the Catholic church.

This absurdity was very properly ridiculed in the *City Mouse* and *Country Mouse* of *Montague* and *Prior*;* and in the detection and censure of the incongruity of the fiction, chiefly consists the value of their performance, which, whatever reputation it might obtain by the help of temporary passions, seems to readers almost a century distant, not very forcible or animated.

Pope, whose judgment was perhaps a little bribed by the subject, used to mention this poem as the most correct specimen of Dryden's versification. It was indeed written when he had completely formed his manner, and may be supposed to exhibit, negligence excepted, his deliberate and ultimate scheme of metre.

We may therefore reasonably infer, that he did not approve the perpetual uniformity which confines the sense to couplets, since he has broken his lines in the initial paragraph.

A milk-white Hind, immortal and unchang'd,
Fed on the lawns, and in the forest rang'd;
Without unspotted, innocent within,
She fear'd no danger, for she knew no sin.
Yet had she oft been chac'd with horns and hounds
And Scythian shafts, and many winged wounds
Aim'd at her heart; was often forc'd to fly,
And doom'd to death, though fated not to die.*

These lines are lofty, elegant, and musical, notwithstanding the interruption of the pause, of which the effect is rather increase of pleasure by variety, than offence by ruggedness.

To the first part it was his intention, he says, *to give the majestick turn of heroick poesy*;* and perhaps he might have executed his design not unsuccessfully, had not an opportunity of satire, which he cannot forbear, fallen sometimes in his way. The character of a Presbyterian, whose emblem is the *Wolf*, is not very heroically majestick.

More haughty than the rest, the wolfish race
Appear with belly gaunt and famish'd face:
Never was so deform'd a beast of grace.
His ragged tail betwixt his legs he wears,
Close clapp'd for shame; but his rough crest he rears,
And pricks up his predestinating ears.*

His general character of the other sorts of beasts that never go to church, though spritely and keen, has, however, not much of heroick poesy.

These are the chief; to number o'er the rest,
And stand like Adam naming every beast,
Were weary work; nor will the Muse describe
A slimy-born, and sun-begotten tribe;
Who, far from steeples and their sacred sound,
In fields their sullen conventicles found.
These gross, half-animated, lumps I leave;
Nor can I think what thoughts they can conceive;
But if they think at all, 'tis sure no higher
Than matter, put in motion, may aspire;
Souls that can scarce ferment their mass of clay;
So drossy, so divisible are they,
As would but serve pure bodies for allay:
Such souls as shards produce, such beetle things

As only buz to heaven with evening wings;
Strike in the dark, offending but by chance;
Such are the blindfold blows of ignorance.
They know not beings, and but hate a name;
To them the Hind and Panther are the same.*

One more instance, and that taken from the narrative part, where style was more in his choice, will show how steadily he kept his resolution of heroick dignity.

For when the herd, suffic'd, did late repair
To ferny heaths, and to their forest laire,
She made a mannerly excuse to stay,
Proffering the Hind to wait her half the way:
That, since the sky was clear, an hour of talk
Might help her to beguile the tedious walk.
With much good-will the motion was embrac'd,
To chat awhile on their adventures past:
Nor had the grateful Hind so soon forgot
Her friend and fellow-sufferer in the plot.
Yet, wondering how of late she grew estrang'd,
Her forehead cloudy and her count'nance chang'd,
She thought this hour th' occasion would present
To learn her secret cause of discontent,
Which well she hop'd, might be with ease redress'd,
Considering her a well-bred civil beast,
And more a gentlewoman than the rest.
After some common talk what rumours ran,
The lady of the spotted muff began.*

The second and third parts he professes to have reduced to diction more familiar and more suitable to dispute and conversation; the difference is not, however, very easily perceived; the first has familiar, and the two others have sonorous, lines. The original incongruity runs through the whole; the king is now *Cæsar*, and now the *Lyon*; and the name *Pan* is given to the Supreme Being.

But when this constitutional absurdity is forgiven, the poem must be confessed to be written with great smoothness of metre, a wide extent of knowledge, and an abundant multiplicity of images; the controversy is embellished with pointed sentences, diversified by illustrations, and enlivened by sallies of invective. Some of the facts to which allusions are made, are now become obscure, and perhaps there may be many satirical passages little understood.

As it was by its nature a work of defiance, a composition which would naturally be examined with the utmost acrimony of criticism, it was probably laboured with uncommon attention; and there are, indeed, few negligences in the subordinate parts. The original impropriety, and the subsequent unpopularity of the subject, added to the ridiculousness of its first elements, has sunk it into neglect; but it may be usefully studied, as an example of poetical ratiocination, in which the argument suffers little from the metre.

In the poem on *the Birth of the Prince of Wales*, nothing is very remarkable but the exorbitant adulation, and that insensibility of the precipice on which the king was then standing, which the laureate apparently shared with the rest of the courtiers. A few months cured him of controversy, dismissed him from court, and made him again a play-wright and translator.

Of Juvenal there had been a translation by Stapylton, and another by Holiday; neither of them is very poetical.* Stapylton is more smooth, and Holiday's is more esteemed for the learning of his notes. A new version was proposed to the poets of that time, and undertaken by them in conjunction. The main design was conducted by Dryden, whose reputation was such that no man was unwilling to serve the Muses under him.

The general character of this translation will be given, when it is said to preserve the wit, but to want the dignity of the original. The peculiarity of Juvenal is a mixture of gaiety and stateliness, of pointed sentences and declamatory grandeur. His points have not been neglected; but his grandeur none of the band seemed to consider as necessary to be imitated, except *Creech*,* who undertook the thirteenth satire. It is therefore perhaps possible to give a better representation of that great satirist, even in those parts which Dryden himself has translated, some passages excepted, which will never be excelled.

With Juvenal was published Persius, translated wholly by Dryden. This work, though like all the other productions of Dryden it may have shining parts, seems to have been written merely for wages, in an uniform mediocrity, without any eager endeavour after excellence, or laborious effort of the mind.

There wanders an opinion among the readers of poetry, that one of these satires is an exercise of the school. Dryden says that he once translated it at school; but not that he preserved or published the juvenile performance.

Not long afterwards he undertook perhaps the most arduous work of its kind, a translation of Virgil, for which he had shewn how well he was qualified by his version of the Pollio, and two episodes, one of Nisus and Euryalus, the other of Mezentius and Lausus.

In the comparison of Homer and Virgil, the discriminative excellence of Homer is elevation and comprehension of thought, and that of Virgil is grace and splendor of diction. The beauties of Homer are therefore difficult to be lost, and those of Virgil difficult to be retained. The massy trunk of sentiment is safe by its solidity, but the blossoms of elocution easily drop away. The author, having the choice of his own images, selects those which he can best adorn: the translator must, at all hazards, follow his original, and express thoughts which perhaps he would not have chosen. When to this primary difficulty is added the inconvenience of a language so much inferior in harmony to the Latin, it cannot be expected that they who read the Georgick and the Eneid should be much delighted with any version.

All these obstacles Dryden saw, and all these he determined to encounter. The expectation of his work was undoubtedly great; the nation considered its honour as interested in the event. One gave him the different editions of his author, and another helped him in the subordinate parts. The arguments of the several books were given him by Addison.

The hopes of the publick were not disappointed. He produced, says Pope, *the most noble and spirited translation that I know in any language*.* It certainly excelled whatever had appeared in English, and appears to have satisfied his friends, and, for the most part, to have silenced his enemies. Milbourne, indeed, a clergyman, attacked it;* but his outrages seem to be the ebullitions of a mind agitated by stronger resentment than bad poetry can excite, and previously resolved not to be pleased.

His criticism extends only to the Preface, Pastorals, and Georgicks; and, as he professes, to give his antagonist an opportunity of reprisal, he has added his own version of the first and fourth Pastorals, and the first Georgick. The world has forgotten his book; but since his attempt has given him a place in literary history, I will preserve a specimen of his criticism, by inserting his remarks on the invocation before the first Georgick, and of his poetry, by annexing his own version.*

Ver. 1. "*What makes a plenteous harvest, when to turn, The fruitful soil, and when to sow the corn*—It's *unlucky*, they say, *to stumble at the threshold*, but what has a *plenteous harvest* to do here? *Virgil* would not pretend to prescribe *rules* for *that* which depends not on the *husbandman's* care, but the *disposition of Heaven* altogether. Indeed, the *plenteous crop* depends somewhat on the *good method of tillage*, and where the *land*'s ill manur'd, the *corn*, without a miracle, can be but *indifferent*; but the *harvest* may be *good*, which is its *properest* epithet, tho' the *husbandman's skill* were never so *indifferent*. The next *sentence* is *too literal*, and *when to plough* had been *Virgil's* meaning, and intelligible to every body; and *when to sow the corn*, is a needless *addition*."

Ver. 3. "*The care of sheep, of oxen, and of kine, And when to geld the lambs, and sheer the swine*, would as well have fallen under the *cura boum, qui cultus habendo sit pecori*, as Mr. *D's deduction* of particulars."

Ver. 5. "*The birth and genius of the frugal bee, I sing*, Mæcenas, *and I sing to thee*.—But where did *experientia* ever signify *birth and genius*? or what ground was there for such a *figure* in this place? How much more manly is Mr. *Ogylby's* version!

> What makes rich grounds, in what celestial signs,
> 'Tis good to plough, and marry elms with vines.
> What best fits cattle, what with sheep agrees,
> And several arts improving frugal bees,
> I sing, *Mæcenas*.

Which four lines, tho' faulty enough, are yet much more to the purpose than Mr. *D's* six."

Ver. 22. "*From fields and mountains to my song repair*. For *patrium linquens nemus, saltusque Lycæi*—Very well explained!"

Ver. 23, 24. "*Inventor* Pallas, *of the fattening oil, Thou founder of the plough, and ploughman's toil*! Written as if *these* had been *Pallas's invention. The ploughman's toil*'s impertinent."

Ver. 25. "—*The shroud-like cypress*—Why *shroud-like*? Is a *cypress* pulled up by the *roots*, which the *sculpture* in the *last Eclogue* fills *Silvanus's* hand with, so very like a *shroud*? Or did not Mr. *D*. think of that kind of *cypress* us'd often for *scarves and hatbands* at funerals formerly, or for *widow's vails*, &c. if so, 'twas a *deep good thought*."

Ver. 26. "—*That wear the royal honours, and increase the year*—What's meant by *increasing the year*? Did the *gods* or *goddesses* add more *months*, or *days*, or *hours* to it? Or how can *arva tueri*—signify to *wear rural honours*? Is this to *translate*, or *abuse* an *author*? The next *couplet* are borrow'd from *Ogylby*, I suppose, because *less to the purpose* than ordinary."

Ver. 33. "*The patron of the world, and* Rome's *peculiar guard*—*Idle*, and none of *Virgil's*, no more than the sense of the *precedent couplet*; so again, he *interpolates Virgil* with that and *the round circle of the year to guide powerful of blessings, which thou strew'st around*. A ridiculous *Latinism*, and an *impertinent addition*; indeed the whole *period* is but one piece of *absurdity* and *nonsense*, as those who lay it with the *original* must find."

Ver. 42, 43. "*And* Neptune *shall resign the fasces of the sea*. Was he *consul* or *dictator* there? *And watry virgins for thy bed shall strive*. Both absurd *interpolations*."

Ver. 47, 48. "*Where in the void of heaven a place is free*. Ah happy *D—n*, were *that place* for thee! But where is *that void*? Or what does our *translator* mean by it? He knows what *Ovid* says *God* did, to prevent such a *void* in heaven; perhaps, this was then forgotten: but *Virgil* talks more sensibly."

Ver. 49. "*The scorpion ready to receive thy laws*. No, he would not then have *gotten out of his way* so fast."

Ver. 56. "*The Proserpine affects her silent seat*—What made *her* then so *angry* with *Ascalaphus*, for preventing her return? She was now mus'd to *Patience* under the *determinations of Fate*, rather than *fond* of her *residence*."

Ver. 61, 2, 3. "*Pity the poet's, and the ploughman's cares, Interest thy greatness in our mean affairs. And use thyself betimes to hear our prayers*. Which is such a wretched *perversion* of *Virgil's noble thought* as *Vicars* would have blush'd at; but Mr. *Ogylby* makes us some amends, by his better lines:

> O wheresoe'er thou art, from thence incline,
> And grant assistance to my bold design!
> Pity with me, poor husbandmen's affairs,
> And now, as if translated, hear our prayers.

This is *sense*, and *to the purpose*: the other, poor *mistaken stuff*."

Such were the strictures of Milbourne, who found few abettors; and of whom it may be reasonably imagined, that many who favoured his design were ashamed of his insolence.

When admiration had subsided, the translation was more coolly examined, and found like all others, to be sometimes erroneous, and sometimes licentious. Those who could find faults, thought they could avoid them; and Dr. Brady* attempted in blank verse a translation of the Eneid, which, when dragged into the world, did not live long enough to cry. I have never seen it; but that such a version there is, or has been, perhaps some old catalogue informed me.

With not much better success, Trapp, when his Tragedy and his Prelections had given him reputation, attempted another blank version of the Eneid; to which, notwithstanding the slight regard with which it was treated, he had afterwards perseverance enough to add the Eclogues and Georgicks.* His book may continue its existence as long as it is the clandestine refuge of schoolboys.

Since the English ear has been accustomed to the mellifluence* of Pope's numbers, and the diction of poetry has become more splendid, new attempts have been made to translate Virgil; and all his works have been attempted by men better qualified to contend with Dryden. I will not engage myself in an invidious comparison by opposing one passage to another; a work of which there would be no end, and which might be often offensive without use.

It is not by comparing line with line that the merit of great works is to be estimated, but by their general effects and ultimate result. It is easy to note a weak line, and write one more vigorous in its place; to find a happiness of expression in the original, and transplant it by force into the version: but what is given to the parts, may be subducted from the whole, and the reader may be weary, though the critick may commend. Works of imagination excel by their allurement and delight; by their power of attracting and detaining the attention. That book is good in vain, which the reader throws away. He only is the master, who keeps the mind in pleasing captivity; whose pages are perused with eagerness, and in hope of new pleasure are perused again; and whose conclusion is perceived with an eye of sorrow, such as the traveller casts upon departing day.

By his proportion of this predomination I will consent that Dryden should be tried; of this, which, in opposition to reason, makes Ariosto the darling and the pride of Italy; of this, which, in defiance of criticism, continues Shakspeare the sovereign of the drama.

His last work was his *Fables*, in which he gave us the first example of a mode of writing which the Italians call *refaccimento*, a renovation of ancient writers, by modernizing their language. Thus the old poem of *Boiardo* has been new-dressed by *Domenichi* and *Berni*.* The works of Chaucer, upon which this kind of rejuvenescence has been bestowed by Dryden, require little criticism. The tale of the Cock seems hardly worth revival; and the story of *Palamon* and *Arcite*, containing an action unsuitable to the times in which it is placed, can hardly be suffered to pass without censure of the hyperbolical commendation which Dryden has given it in the general Preface, and in a poetical Dedication, a piece where his original fondness of remote conceits seems to have revived.

Of the three pieces borrowed from Boccace, *Sigismunda* may be defended by the celebrity of the story. *Theodore* and *Honoria*, though it contains not much moral, yet afforded opportunities of striking description. And *Cymon* was formerly a tale of such reputation, that, at the revival of letters, it was translated into Latin by one of the *Beroalds*.*

Whatever subjects employed his pen, he was still improving our measures and embellishing our language.

In this volume are interspersed some short original poems, which, with his prologues, epilogues, and songs, may be comprised in Congreve's remark,* that even those, if he had written nothing else, would have entitled him to the praise of excellence in his kind.

One composition must however be distinguished. The ode for *St. Cecilia's* Day,* perhaps the last effort of his poetry, has been always considered as exhibiting the highest flight of fancy, and the exactest nicety of art. This is allowed to stand without a rival. If indeed there is any excellence beyond it, in some other of Dryden's works that excellence must be found. Compared with the Ode on *Killigrew*, it may be pronounced perhaps superiour in the whole; but without any single part, equal to the first stanza of the other.

It is said to have cost Dryden a fortnight's labour; but it does not want its negligences: some of the lines are without correspondent rhymes; a defect, which I never detected but after an acquaintance of many years, and which the enthusiasm of the writer might hinder him from perceiving.

His last stanza has less emotion than the former; but is not less elegant in the diction. The conclusion is vicious; the musick of *Timotheus*, which *raised a mortal to the skies*, had only a metaphorical power; that of *Cecilia*, which *drew an angel down*, had a real effect: the crown therefore could not reasonably be divided.

IN a general survey of Dryden's labours, he appears to have had a mind very comprehensive by nature, and much enriched with acquired knowledge. His compositions are the effects of a vigorous genius operating upon large materials.

The power that predominated in his intellectual operations, was rather strong reason than quick sensibility. Upon all occasions that were presented, he studied rather than felt, and produced sentiments not such as Nature enforces, but meditation supplies. With the simple and elemental passions, as they spring separate in the mind, he seems not much acquainted; and seldom describes them but as they are complicated by the various relations of society, and confused in the tumults and agitations of life.

What he says of love may contribute to the explanation of his character:

> Love various minds does variously inspire;
> It stirs in gentle bosoms gentle fire,
> Like that of incense on the altar laid;
> But raging flames tempestuous souls invade;
> A fire which every windy passion blows,
> With pride it mounts, or with revenge it glows.*

Dryden's was not one of the *gentle bosoms*: Love, as it subsists in itself, with no tendency but to the person loved, and wishing only for correspondent kindness; such love as shuts out all other interest; the Love of the Golden Age, was too soft and subtle to put his faculties in motion. He hardly conceived it but in its turbulent effervescence with some other desires; when it was inflamed by rivalry, or obstructed by difficulties: when it invigorated ambition, or exasperated revenge.

He is therefore, with all his variety of excellence, not often pathetick; and had so little sensibility of the power of effusions purely natural, that he did not esteem them in others. Simplicity gave him no pleasure; and for the first part of his life he looked on *Otway* with contempt, though at last, indeed very late, he confessed that in his play *there* was *Nature, which is the chief beauty*.*

We do not always know our own motives. I am not certain whether it was not rather the difficulty which he found in exhibiting the genuine operations of the heart, than a servile submission to an injudicious audience, that filled his plays with false magnificence. It was necessary to fix attention; and the mind can be captivated only by recollection, or by curiosity; by reviving natural sentiments, or impressing new appearances of things: sentences were readier at his call than images; he could more easily fill the ear with some splendid novelty, than awaken those ideas that slumber in the heart.

The favourite exercise of his mind was ratiocination; and, that argument might not be too soon at an end, he delighted to talk of liberty and necessity, destiny and contingence; these he discusses in the language of the school with so much profundity, that the terms which he uses are not always understood. It is indeed learning, but learning out of place.

When once he had engaged himself in disputation, thoughts flowed in on either side: he was now no longer at a loss; he had always objections and solutions at command; *verbaque provisam rem**—give him matter for his verse, and he finds without difficulty verse for his matter.

In Comedy, for which he professes himself not naturally qualified, the mirth which he excites will perhaps not be found so much to arise from any original humour, or peculiarity of character nicely distinguished and diligently pursued, as from incidents and circumstances, artifices and surprizes; from jests of action rather than of sentiment. What he had of humorous or passionate, he seems to have had not from nature, but from other poets; if not always as a plagiary, at least as an imitator.

Next to argument, his delight was in wild and daring sallies of sentiment, in the irregular and excentrick violence of wit. He delighted to tread upon the brink of meaning, where light and darkness begin to mingle; to approach the precipice of absurdity, and hover over the abyss of unideal vacancy. This inclination sometimes produced nonsense, which he knew; as,

> Move swiftly, sun, and fly a lover's pace,
> Leave weeks and months behind thee in thy race.
>
> Amariel flies
> To guard thee from the demons of the air;
> My flaming sword above them to display,
> All keen, and ground upon the edge of day.*

And sometimes it issued in absurdities, of which perhaps he was not conscious:

> Then we upon our orb's last verge shall go,
> And see the ocean leaning on the sky;
> From thence our rolling neighbours we shall know,
> And on the lunar world securely pry.*

These lines have no meaning; but may we not say, in imitation of Cowley on another book,

> 'Tis so like *sense* 'twill serve the turn as well?*

This endeavour after the grand and the new, produced many sentiments either great or bulky, and many images either just or splendid:

> I am as free as Nature first made man,
> Ere the base laws of servitude began,
> When wild in woods the noble savage ran.
> —'Tis but because the Living death ne'er knew,
> They fear to prove it as a thing that's new:
> Let me th' experiment before you try,
> I'll show you first how easy 'tis to die.
>
> —There with a forest of their darts he strove,
> And stood like *Capaneus* defying Jove;
> With his broad sword the boldest beating down,
> While Fate grew pale lest he should win the town,
> And turn'd the iron leaves of his dark book

To make new dooms, or mend what it mistook.
—I beg no pity for this mouldering clay;
For if you give it burial, there it takes
Possession of your earth;
If burnt, and scatter'd in the air, the winds
That strew my dust diffuse my royalty,
And spread me o'er your clime; for where one atom
Of mine shall light, know there Sebastian reigns.*

Of these quotations the two first may be allowed to be great, the two latter only tumid.

Of such selection there is no end. I will add only a few more passages; of which the first, though it may perhaps not be quite clear in prose, is not too obscure for poetry, as the meaning that it has is noble:

No, there is a necessity in Fate,
Why still the brave bold man is fortunate;
He keeps his object ever full in sight,
And that assurance holds him firm and right;
True, 'tis a narrow way that leads to bliss,
But right before there is no precipice;
Fear makes men look aside, and so their footing miss.*

Of the images which the two following citations afford, the first is elegant, the second magnificent; whether either be just, let the reader judge:

What precious drops are these,
Which silently each other's track pursue,
Bright as young diamonds in their infant dew?

—Resign your castle—
—Enter, brave Sir; for when you speak the word,
The gates shall open of their own accord;
The genius of the place its Lord shall meet,
And bow its towery forehead at your feet.*

These bursts of extravagance, Dryden calls the *Dalilahs* of the Theatre; and owns that many noisy lines of Maximin and Almanzor call out for vengeance upon him; but I *knew*, says he, *that they were bad enough to please, even when I wrote them.** There is surely reason to suspect that he pleased himself as well as his audience; and that these, like the harlots of other men, had his love, though not his approbation.

He had sometimes faults of a less generous and splendid kind. He makes, like almost all other poets, very frequent use of mythology, and sometimes connects religion and fable too closely without distinction.

He descends to display his knowledge with pedantick ostentation; as when, in translating Virgil, he says, *tack to the larboard*—and *veer starboard*;* and talks, in another work, of *virtue spooming before the wind*.* His vanity now and then betrays his ignorance:

> They Nature's king through Nature's opticks view'd;
> Revers'd they view'd him lessen'd to their eyes.*

He had heard of reversing a telescope, and unluckily reverses the object.

He is sometimes unexpectedly mean. When he describes the Supreme Being as moved by prayer to stop the Fire of London, what is his expression?

> A hollow crystal pyramid he takes,
> In firmamental waters dipp'd above,
> Of this a broad *extinguisher* he makes,
> And *hoods* the flames that to their quarry strove.*

When he describes the Last Day, and the decisive tribunal, he intermingles this image:

> When rattling bones together fly,
> From the four quarters of the sky.*

It was indeed never in his power to resist the temptation of a jest. In his Elegy on Cromwell:

> No sooner was the Frenchman's cause embrac'd,
> Than the *light Monsieur* the *grave Don* outweigh'd;
> His fortune turn'd the scale—*

He had a vanity, unworthy of his abilities, to shew, as may be suspected, the rank of the company with whom he lived, by the use of French words, which had then crept into conversation; such as *fraicheur* for *coolness, fougue* for *turbulence*, and a few more, none of which the language has incorporated or retained. They continue only where they stood first, perpetual warnings to future innovators.

These are his faults of affectation; his faults of negligence are beyond recital. Such is the unevenness of his compositions, that ten lines are seldom found together without something of which the reader is ashamed. Dryden was no rigid judge of his own pages; he seldom struggled after supreme excellence, but snatched in haste what was within his reach; and when he could content others, was himself contented. He did not keep present to his mind, an idea of pure perfection; nor compare his works, such as they were, with what they might be made. He knew to whom he should be opposed. He had more musick than Waller, more vigour than Denham, and more nature than Cowley; and from his contemporaries he was in no danger. Standing therefore in the highest place, he had no care to rise by contending with himself; but while there was no name above his own, was willing to enjoy fame on the easiest terms.

He was no lover of labour. What he thought sufficient, he did not stop to make better; and allowed himself to leave many parts unfinished, in confidence that the good lines would overbalance the bad. What he had once written, he dismissed from his thoughts; and, I believe, there is no example to be found of any correction or improvement made by him after publication. The hastiness of his productions might be the effect of necessity; but his subsequent neglect could hardly have any other cause than impatience of study.

What can be said of his versification, will be little more than a dilatation of the praise given it by Pope.

> Waller was smooth; but Dryden taught to join
> The varying verse, the full-resounding line,
> The long majestick march, and energy divine.*

Some improvements had been already made in English numbers; but the full force of our language was not yet felt; the verse that was smooth was commonly feeble. If Cowley had sometimes a finished line, he had it by chance. Dryden knew how to chuse the flowing and the sonorous words; to vary the pauses, and adjust the accents; to diversify the cadence, and yet preserve the smoothness of his metre.

Of Triplets and Alexandrines, though he did not introduce the use, he established it. The triplet has long subsisted among us. Dryden seems not to have traced it higher than to Chapman's Homer; but it is to be found in Phaer's Virgil, written in the reign of Mary, and in Hall's Satires, published five years before the death of Elizabeth.*

The Alexandrine was, I believe, first used by Spenser, for the sake of closing his stanza with a fuller sound. We had a longer measure of fourteen syllables, into which the Eneid was translated by Phaer, and other works of the ancients by other writers; of which Chapman's Iliad was, I believe, the last.

The two first lines of *Phaer*'s third Eneid will exemplify this measure:

> When Asia's state was overthrown, and Priam's kingdom stout,
> All giltless, by the power of gods above was rooted out.

As these lines had their break, or *cæsura*, always at the eighth syllable, it was thought, in time, commodious to divide them; and quatrains of lines, alternately consisting of eight and six syllables, make the most soft and pleasing of our lyrick measures; as,

> Relentless Time, destroying power,
> Which stone and brass obey,
> Who giv'st to every flying hour
> To work some new decay.*

In the Alexandrine, when its power was once felt, some poems, as *Drayton's Polyolbion*,* were wholly written; and sometimes the measures of twelve and fourteen syllables were interchanged with one another. Cowley was the first that inserted the Alexandrine at pleasure among the heroick lines of ten syllables, and from him Dryden professes to have adopted it.

The Triplet and Alexandrine are not universally approved. *Swift* always censured them, and wrote some lines to ridicule them. In examining their propriety, it is to be considered that the essence of verse is regularity, and its ornament is variety. To write verse, is to dispose syllables and sounds harmonically by some known and settled rule; a rule however lax enough to substitute similitude for identity, to admit change without breach of order, and to relieve the ear without disappointing it. Thus a Latin hexameter is formed from dactyls and spondees differently combined; the English heroick admits of acute or grave syllables variously disposed. The Latin never deviates into seven feet, or exceeds the number of seventeen syllables; but the English Alexandrine breaks the lawful bounds, and surprises the reader with two syllables more than he expected.

The effect of the Triplet is the same: the ear has been accustomed to expect a new rhyme in every couplet; but is on a sudden surprized with three rhymes together, to which the reader could not accommodate his voice, did he not obtain notice of the change from the braces of the margins. Surely there is something unskilful in the necessity of such mechanical direction.

Considering the metrical art simply as a science, and consequently excluding all casualty, we must allow that Triplets and Alexandrines, inserted by caprice, are interruptions of that constancy to which science aspires. And though the variety which they produce may very justly be desired, yet to make our poetry exact, there ought to be some stated mode of admitting them.

But till some such regulation can be formed, I wish them still to be retained in their present state. They are sometimes grateful to the reader, and sometimes convenient to the poet. *Fenton* was of opinion that Dryden was too liberal and Pope too sparing in their use.

The rhymes of Dryden are commonly just, and he valued himself for his readiness in finding them; but he is sometimes open to objection.

It is the common practice of our poets to end the second line with a weak or grave syllable:

> Together o'er the Alps methinks we fly,
> Fill'd with ideas of fair *Italy*.*

Dryden sometimes puts the weak rhyme in the first:

> Laugh all the powers that favour *tyranny*,
> And all the standing army of the sky.*

Sometimes he concludes a period or paragraph with the first line of a couplet, which, though the French seem to do it without irregularity, always displeases in English poetry.

The Alexandrine, though much his favourite, is not always very diligently fabricated by him. It invariably requires a break at the sixth syllable; a rule which the modern French poets never violate, but which Dryden sometimes neglected:

> And with paternal thunder vindicates his throne.*

Of Dryden's works it was said by Pope, that *he could select from them better specimens of every mode of poetry than any other English* *writer could supply.** Perhaps no nation ever produced a writer that enriched his language with such variety of models. To him we owe the improvement, perhaps the completion of our metre, the refinement of our language, and much of the correctness of our sentiments. By him we were taught *sapere & fari*, to think naturally and express forcibly. Though Davis has reasoned in rhyme before him, it may be perhaps maintained that he was the first who joined argument with poetry. He shewed us the true bounds of a translator's liberty. What was said of Rome, adorned by Augustus, may be applied by an easy metaphor to English poetry embellished by Dryden, *lateritiam invenit, marmoream reliquit*, he found it brick, and he left it marble.*

THE invocation before the Georgicks is here inserted from Mr. Milbourne's version, that, according to his own proposal, his verses may be compared with those which he censures.*

What makes the richest *tilth*, beneath what signs
To *plough*, and when to match your *elms* and *vines*;
What care with *flocks* and what with *herds* agrees,
And all the management of frugal *bees*,
I sing, *Mæcenas!* Ye immensely clear,
Vast orbs of light which guide the rolling year;
Bacchus, and mother *Ceres*, if by you
We fat'ning *corn* for hungry *mast* pursue,
If, taught by you, we first the *cluster* prest,
And *thin cold streams* with *spritely juice* refresht.
Ye *fawns* the present *numens* of the field,
Woodnymphs and *fawns* your kind assistance yield,
Your gifts I sing! and thou, at whose fear'd stroke
From rending earth the fiery *courser* broke,
Great *Neptune*, O assist my artful song!
And thou to whom the woods and groves belong,
Whose snowy heifers on her flow'ry plains
In mighty herds the *Cæan Isle* maintains!
Pan, happy shepherd, if thy cares divine,
E'er to improve thy *Mænalus* incline;
Leave thy *Lycæan wood* and *native grove*,
And with thy lucky smiles our work approve!
Be *Pallas* too, sweet oil's inventor, kind;
And he, who first the crooked *plough* design'd!
Sylvanus, god of all the woods appear,

Whose hands a new drawn tender *cypress* bear!
Ye *gods* and *goddesses* who e'er with love,
Would guard our pastures, and our fields improve!
You, who new plants from unsown lands supply;
And with condensing clouds obscure the sky,
And drop 'em softly thence in fruitful showers,
Assist my enterprize, ye gentler powers!

And thou, great *Cæsar!* though we know not yet
Among what gods thou'lt fix thy lofty seat,
Whether thou'lt be the kind *tutelar god*
Of thy own *Rome*; or with thy awful nod,
Guide the vast world, while thy great hand shall bear
The fruits and seasons of the turning year,
And thy bright brows thy mother's myrtles wear:
Whether thou'lt all the boundless ocean sway,
And sea-men only to thyself shall pray,
Thule, the farthest island, kneel to thee,
And, that thou may'st her son by marriage be,
Tethys will for the happy purchase yield
To make a *dowry* of her watry field;
Whether thou'lt add to heaven a *brighter sign*,
And o'er the *summer months* serenely shine;
Where between *Cancer* and *Erigone*,
There yet remains a spacious *room* for thee.
Where the hot *Scorpion* too his arms declines,
And more to thee than half his *arch* resigns;
Whate'er thou'lt be; for sure the realms below
No just pretence to thy command can show:
No such ambition sways thy vast desires,
Though *Greece* her own *Elysian fields* admires.
And now, at last, contented *Proserpine*
Can all her mother's earnest prayers decline.
Whate'er thou'lt be, O guide our gentle course,
And with thy smiles our bold attempts enforce;
With me th' unknowing *rustics*' wants relieve,
And, though on earth, our sacred vows receive!

MR. DRYDEN, having received from Rymer his *Remarks on the Tragedies of the last Age*, wrote observations on the blank leaves; which, having been in the possession of Mr. Garrick, are by his favour communicated to the publick, that no particle of Dryden may be lost.*

"That we may the less wonder why pity and terror are not now the only springs on which our tragedies move, and that Shakspeare may be more excused, Rapin confesses that the French tragedies now all run on the *tendre*; and gives the reason, because love is the passion which most predominates in our souls, and that therefore the passions represented become insipid, unless they are conformable to the thoughts of the audience. But it is to be concluded that this passion works not now amongst the French so strongly as the other two did amongst the ancients. Amongst us, who have a stronger genius for writing, the operations from the writing are much stronger: for the raising of Shakspeare's passions is more from the excellency of the words and thoughts, than the justness of the occasion; and if he has been able to pick single occasions, he has never founded the whole reasonably: yet, by the genius of poetry in writing, he has succeeded.

"Rapin attributes more to the *dictio*, that is, to the words and discourse of a tragedy, than Aristotle has done, who places them in the last rank of beauties; perhaps, only last in order, because they are the last product of the design, of the disposition or connection of its parts; of the characters, of the manners of those characters, and of the thoughts proceeding from those manners. Rapin's words are remarkable: 'Tis not the admirable intrigue, the surprising events, and extraordinary incidents, that make the beauty of a tragedy; 'tis the discourses, when they are natural and passionate: so are Shakspeare's.

"The parts of a poem, tragick or heroick, are,

"1. The fable itself.

"2. The order or manner of its contrivance, in relation of the parts to the whole.

"3. The manners, or decency of the characters, in speaking or acting what is proper for them, and proper to be shewn by the poet.

"4. The thoughts which express the manners.

"5. The words which express those thoughts.

"In the last of these, Homer excels Virgil; Virgil all other ancient poets; and Shakspeare all modern poets.

"For the second of these, the order: the meaning is, that a fable ought to have a beginning, middle, and an end, all just and natural: so that that part, *e. g.* which is the middle, could not naturally be the beginning or end, and so of the rest: all depend on one another, like the links of a curious chain. If terror and pity are only to be raised, certainly this author follows Aristotle's rules,* and Sophocles' and Euripides's example: but joy may be raised too, and that doubly; either by seeing a wicked man punished, or a good man at last fortunate; or perhaps indignation, to see wickedness prosperous and goodness depressed: both these may be profitable to the end of tragedy, reformation of manners; but the last improperly, only as it begets pity in the audience: though Aristotle, I confess, places tragedies of this kind in the second form.

"He who undertakes to answer this excellent critique of Mr. Rymer, in behalf of our English poets against the Greek, ought to do it in this manner. Either by yielding to him the greatest part of what he contends for, which consists in this, that the *μύθος*, *i. e.* the design and conduct of it, is more conducing in the Greeks to those ends of tragedy, which Aristotle and he propose, namely, to cause terror and pity; yet the granting this does not set the Greeks above the English poets.

"But the answerer ought to prove two things: first, that the fable is not the greatest master-piece of a tragedy, though it be the foundation of it.

"Secondly, That other ends as suitable to the nature of tragedy may be found in the English, which were not in the Greek.

"Aristotle places the fable first; not *quoad dignitatem, sed quoad fundamentum:** for a fable, never so movingly contrived to those ends of his, pity and terror, will operate nothing on our affections, except the characters, manners, thoughts, and words are suitable.

"So that it remains for Mr. Rymer to prove, that in all those, or the greatest part of them, we are inferior to Sophocles and Euripides: and this he has offered at, in some measure; but, I think, a little partially to the ancients.

"For the fable itself; 'tis in the English more adorned with episodes, and larger than in the Greek poets; consequently more diverting. For, if the action be but one, and that plain, without any counterturn of design or episode, *i.e.* under-plot, how can it be so pleasing as the English, which have both under-plot and a turned design, which keeps the audience in expectation of the catastrophe? whereas in the Greek poets we see through the whole design at first.

"For the characters, they are neither so many nor so various in Sophocles and Euripides, as in Shakspeare and Fletcher; only they are more adapted to those ends of tragedy which Aristotle commends to us, pity and terror.

"The manners flow from the characters, and consequently must partake of their advantages and disadvantages.

"The thoughts and words, which are the fourth and fifth beauties of tragedy, are certainly more noble and more poetical in the English than in the Greek, which must be proved by comparing them, somewhat more equitably than Mr. Rymer has done.

"After all, we need not yield that the English way is less conducing to move pity and terror, because they often shew virtue oppressed and vice punished: where they do not both, or either, they are not to be defended.

"And if we should grant that the Greeks performed this better, perhaps it may admit of dispute, whether pity and terror are either the prime, or at least the only ends of tragedy.

" 'Tis not enough that Aristotle has said so; for Aristotle drew his models of tragedy from Sophocles and Euripides; and, if he had seen ours, might have changed his mind. And chiefly we have to say (what I hinted on pity and terror, in the last paragraph save one), that the punishment of vice and reward of virtue are the most adequate ends of tragedy, because most conducing to good example of life. Now pity is not so easily raised for a criminal, and the ancient tragedy always represents its chief person such, as it is for an innocent man; and the suffering of innocence and punishment of the offender is of the nature of English tragedy: contrarily, in the Greek, innocence is unhappy often, and the offender escapes. Then we are not touched with the sufferings of any sort of men so much as of lovers; and this was almost unknown to the ancients: so that they neither administered poetical justice, of which Mr. Rymer boasts, so well as we; neither knew they the best common-place of pity, which is love.

"He therefore unjustly blames us for not building on what the ancients left us; for it seems, upon consideration of the premises, that we have wholly finished what they began.

"My judgement on this piece is this, that it is extremely learned; but that the author of it is better read in the Greek than in the English poets: that all writers ought to study this critique, as the best account

I have ever seen of the ancients: that the model of tragedy he has here given, is excellent, and extreme correct; but that it is not the only model of all tragedy, because it is too much circumscribed in plot, characters, &c.; and lastly, that we may be taught here justly to admire and imitate the ancients, without giving them the preference with this author, in prejudice to our own country.

"Want of method in this excellent treatise, makes the thoughts of the author sometimes obscure.

"His meaning, that pity and terror are to be moved, is, that they are to be moved as the means conducing to the ends of tragedy, which are pleasure and instruction.

"And these two ends may be thus distinguished. The chief end of the poet is to please; for his immediate reputation depends on it.

"The great end of the poem is to instruct, which is performed by making pleasure the vehicle of that instruction; for poesy is an art, and all arts are made to profit. *Rapin*.

"The pity, which the poet is to labour for, is for the criminal, not for those or him whom he has murdered, or who have been the occasion of the tragedy. The terror is likewise in the punishment of the same criminal; who, if he be represented too great an offender, will not be pitied: if altogether innocent, his punishment will be unjust.

"Another obscurity is, where he says Sophocles perfected tragedy by introducing the third actor; that is, he meant, three kinds of action; one company singing, or another playing on the musick; a third dancing.

"To make a true judgement in this competition betwixt the Greek poets and the English, in tragedy:

"Consider, first, how Aristotle has defined a tragedy. Secondly, what he assigns the end of it to be. Thirdly, what he thinks the beauties of it. Fourthly, the means to attain the end proposed.

"Compare the Greek and English tragick poets justly, and without partiality, according to those rules.

"Then secondly, consider whether Aristotle has made a just definition of tragedy; of its parts, of its ends, and of its beauties; and whether he, having not seen any others but those of Sophocles, Euripides, &c. had or truly could determine what all the excellences of tragedy are, and wherein they consist.

"Next shew in what ancient tragedy was deficient: for example, in the narrowness of its plots, and fewness of persons, and try whether that be not a fault in the Greek poets; and whether their excellency was so great, when the variety was visibly so little; or whether what they did was not very easy to do.

"Then make a judgement on what the English have added to their beauties: as, for example, not only more plot, but also new passions; as, namely, that of love, scarce touched on by the ancients, except in this one example of Phædra, cited by Mr. Rymer; and in that how short they were of Fletcher!

"Prove also that love, being an heroick passion, is fit for tragedy, which cannot be denied, because of the example alledged of Phædra; and how far Shakspeare has outdone them in friendship, &c.

"To return to the beginning of this enquiry; consider if pity and terror be enough for tragedy to move: and I believe, upon a true definition of tragedy, it will be found that its work extends farther, and that it is to reform manners, by a delightful representation of human life in great persons, by way of dialogue. If this be true, then not only pity and terror are to be moved, as the only means to bring us to virtue, but generally love to virtue and hatred to vice; by shewing the rewards of one, and punishments of the other; at least, by rendering virtue always amiable, tho' it be shewn unfortunate; and vice detestable, though it be shewn triumphant.

"If, then, the encouragement of virtue and discouragement of vice be the proper ends of poetry in tragedy, pity and terror, though good means, are not the only. For all the passions, in their turns, are to be set in a ferment: as joy, anger, love, fear, are to be used as the poet's common-places; and a general concernment for the principal actors is to be raised, by making them appear such in their characters, their words, and actions, as will interest the audience in their fortunes.

"And if, after all, in a larger sense, pity comprehends this concernment for the good, and terror includes detestation for the bad, then let us consider whether the English have not answered this end of tragedy, as well as the ancients, or perhaps better.

"And here Mr. Rymer's objections against these plays* are to be impartially weighed, that we may see whether they are of weight enough to turn the balance against our countrymen.

" 'Tis evident those plays, which he arraigns, have moved both those passions in a high degree upon the stage.

"To give the glory of this away from the poet, and to place it upon the actors, seems unjust.

"One reason is, because whatever actors they have found, the event has been the same; that is, the same passions have been always moved: which shews, that there is something of force and merit in the plays themselves, conducing to the design of raising these two passions: and suppose them ever to have been excellently acted, yet action only adds grace, vigour, and more life, upon the stage; but cannot give it wholly where it is not first. But secondly, I dare appeal to those who have never seen them acted, if they have not found these two passions moved within them: and if the general voice will carry it, Mr. Rymer's prejudice will take off his single testimony.

"This, being matter of fact, is reasonably to be established by this appeal; as if one man says 'tis night, the rest of the world conclude it to be day; there needs no farther argument against him, that it is so.

"If he urge, that the general taste is depraved, his arguments to prove this can at best but evince that our poets took not the best way to raise those passions; but experience proves against him, that these means, which they have used, have been successful, and have produced them.

"And one reason of that success is, in my opinion, this, that Shakspeare and Fletcher have written to the genius of the age and nation in which they lived; for though nature, as he objects, is the same in all places, and reason too the same; yet the climate, the age, the disposition of the people, to whom a poet writes, may be so different, that what pleased the Greeks would not satisfy an English audience.

"And if they proceeded upon a foundation of truer reason to please the Athenians than Shakspeare and Fletcher to please the English, it only shews that the Athenians were a more judicious people; but the poet's business is certainly to please the audience.

"Whether our English audience have been pleased hitherto with acorns, as he calls it, or with bread, is the next question; that is, whether the means which Shakspeare and Fletcher have used in their plays to raise those passions before named, be better applied to the ends by the Greek poets than by them. And perhaps we shall not grant him this wholly: let it be granted that a writer is not to run down with the stream, or to please the people by their own usual methods, but rather to reform their judgements, it still remains to prove that our theatre needs this total reformation.

"The faults, which he has found in their designs, are rather wittily aggravated in many places than reasonably urged; and as much may be returned on the Greeks, by one who were as witty as himself.

"2. They destroy not, if they are granted, the foundation of the fabrick; only take away from the beauty of the symmetry: for example, the faults in the character of the King and No-king are not as he makes them, such as render him detestable, but only imperfections which accompany human nature, and are for the most part excused by the violence of his love; so that they destroy not our pity or concernment for him: this answer may be applied to most of his objections of that kind.

"And Rollo committing many murders, when he is answerable but for one, is too severely arraigned by him; for it adds to our horror and detestation of the criminal: and poetick justice is not neglected neither; for we stab him in our minds for every offence which he commits; and the point, which the poet is to gain on the audience, is not so much in the death of an offender as the raising an horror of his crimes.

"That the criminal should neither be wholly guilty, nor wholly innocent, but so participating of both as to move both pity and terror, is certainly a good rule, but not perpetually to be observed; for that were to make all tragedies too much alike, which objection he foresaw, but has not fully answered.

"To conclude, therefore; if the plays of the ancients are more correctly plotted; ours are more beautifully written. And if we can raise passions as high on worse foundations, it shews our genius in tragedy is greater; for, in all other parts of it, the English have manifestly excelled them."

THE original of the following letter is preserved in the Library at Lambeth, and was kindly imparted to the publick by the reverend Dr. Vyse.*

Copy of an original Letter from John Dryden, Esq; to his sons in Italy, from a MS in the Lambeth Library, marked N° 933. p. 56.

(Superscribed)

Al Illustrissimo Sig^{re}
Carlo Dryden Camariere
d'Honore A. S. S.

In Roma.

Franca per Mantoua.

"Sept. the 3d, our style.

"Dear Sons,

"Being now at Sir William Bowyer's* in the country, I cannot write at large, because I find myself somewhat indisposed with a cold, and am thick of hearing, rather worse than I was in town. I am glad to find, by your letter of July 26th, your style, that you are both in health; but wonder you should think me so negligent as to forget to give you an account of the ship in which your parcel is to come. I have written to you two or three letters concerning it, which I have sent by safe hands, as I told you, and doubt not but you have them before this can arrive to you. Being out of town, I have forgotten the ship's name, which your mother will enquire, and put it into her letter, which is joined with mine. But the master's name I remember: he is called Mr. Ralph Thorp; the ship is bound to Leghorn, consigned to Mr. Peter and Mr. Tho. Ball, merchants. I am of your opinion, that by Tonson's means almost all our letters have miscarried for this last year. But, however, he has missed of his design in the Dedication, though he had prepared the book for it; for in every figure of Eneas he has caused him to be drawn like King William, with a hooked nose. After my return to town, I intend to alter a play of Sir Robert Howard's, written long since, and lately put by him into my hands: 'tis called *The Conquest of China by the Tartars.* It will cost me six weeks study, with the probable benefit of an hundred pounds. In the mean time I am writing a song for St. Cecilia's Feast, who, you know, is the patroness of musick. This is troublesome, and no way beneficial; but I could not deny the Stewards of the Feast, who came in a body to me to desire that kindness, one of them being Mr. Bridgman,* whose parents are your mother's friends. I hope to send you thirty guineas between Michaelmass and Christmass, of which I will give you an account when I come to town. I remember the counsel you give me in your letter; but dissembling, though lawful in some cases, is not my talent; yet, for your sake, I will struggle with the plain openness of my nature, and keep-in my just resentments against that degenerate order. In the mean time, I flatter not myself with any manner of hopes, but do my duty, and suffer for God's sake; being assured, beforehand, never to be rewarded, though the times should alter. Towards the latter end of this month, September, Charles will begin to recover his perfect health, according to his nativity, which, casting it myself, I am sure is true, and all things hitherto have happened accordingly to the very time that I predicted them: I hope at the same time to recover more health, according to my age. Remember me to poor Harry, whose prayers I earnestly desire. My Virgil succeeds in the world beyond its desert or my expectation. You know the profits might have been more; but neither my conscience nor my honour would suffer me to take them; but I never can repent of my constancy, since I am thoroughly persuaded of the justice of the cause for which I suffer. It has pleased God to raise up many friends to me amongst my enemies, though they who ought to have been my friends are negligent of me. I am called to dinner, and cannot go on with this letter, which I desire you to excuse; and am

"Your most affectionate father,

"John Dryden."

CONGREVE

WILLIAM CONGREVE descended from a family in Staffordshire, of so great antiquity that it claims a place among the few that extend their line beyond the Norman Conquest; and was the son of William Congreve, second son of Richard Congreve of Congreve and Stratton. He visited, once at least, the residence of his ancestors; and, I believe, more placès than one are still shewn, in groves and gardens, where he is related to have written his *Old Batchelor*.

Neither the time nor place of his birth are certainly known: if the inscription upon his monument be true, he was born in 1672.* For the place; it was said by himself that he owed his nativity to England, and by every body else that he was born in Ireland. Southern* mentioned him with sharp censure, as a man that meanly disowned his native country. The biographers assign his nativity to Bardsa, near Leeds in Yorkshire, from the account given by himself, as they suppose, to Jacob.*

To doubt whether a man of eminence has told the truth about his own birth, is, in appearance, to be very deficient in candour; yet nobody can live long without knowing that falsehoods of convenience or vanity, falsehoods from which no evil immediately visible ensues, except the general degradation of human testimony, are very lightly uttered, and once uttered, are sullenly supported. Boileau, who desired to be thought a rigorous and steady moralist, having told a petty lie to Lewis XIV. continued it afterwards by false dates; thinking himself obliged *in honour*, says his admirer, to maintain what, when he said it, was so well received.

Wherever Congreve was born, he was educated first at Kilkenny, and afterwards at Dublin, his father having some military employment that stationed him in Ireland: but after having passed through the usual preparatory studies, as may be reasonably supposed with great celerity and success, his father thought it proper to assign him a profession, by which something might be gotten; and about the time of the Revolution sent him, at the age of sixteen, to study law in the Middle Temple, where he lived for several years, but with very little attention to Statutes or Reports.

His disposition to become an author appeared very early, as he very early felt that force of imagination, and possessed that copiousness of sentiment, by which intellectual pleasure can be given. His first performance was a novel, called *Incognita, or Love and Duty reconciled*: It is praised by the biographers, who quote some part of the preface, that is indeed, for such a time of life, uncommonly judicious. I would rather praise it than read it.

His first dramatick labour was the *Old Batchelor*; of which he says, in his defence against Collier,* "that comedy was written, as several know, some years before it was acted. When I wrote it, I had little thoughts of the stage; but did it, to amuse myself, in a slow recovery from a fit of sickness. Afterwards, through my indiscretion, it was seen, and in some little time more it was acted; and I, through the remainder of my indiscretion, suffered myself to be drawn in, to the prosecution of a difficult and thankless study, and to be involved in a perpetual war with knaves and fools."

There feems to be a strange affectation in authors of appearing to have done every thing by chance. The *Old Batchelor* was written for amusement, in the languor of convalescence. Yet it is apparently composed with great elaborateness of dialogue, and incessant ambition of wit. The age of the writer considered, it is indeed a very wonderful performance; for, whenever written, it was acted (1693) when he was not more than twenty-one years old; and was then recommended by Mr. Dryden, Mr. Southern, and Mr. Maynwaring.* Dryden said that he never had seen such a first play; but they found it deficient in some things requisite to the success of its exhibition, and by their greater experience fitted it for the stage. Southern used to relate of one comedy, probably of this, that when Congreve read it to the players, he pronounced it so wretchedly that they had almost rejected it; but they were afterwards so well persuaded of its excellence, that, for half a year before it was acted, the manager allowed its author the privilege of the house.

Few plays have ever been so beneficial to the writer; for it procured him the patronage of Halifax,* who immediately made him one of the commissioners for licensing coaches, and soon after gave him a place in the pipe-office, and another in the customs of six hundred pounds a year. Congreve's conversation must surely have been at least equally pleasing with his writings.

Such a comedy, written at such an age, requires some consideration. As the lighter species of dramatick poetry professes the imitation of common life, of real manners, and daily incidents, it apparently presupposes a familiar knowledge of many characters, and exact observation of the passing world; the difficulty therefore is, to conceive how this knowledge can be obtained by a boy.

But if the *Old Batchelor* be more nearly examined, it will be found to be one of those comedies which may be made by a mind vigorous and acute, and furnished with comick characters by the perusal of other poets, without much actual commerce with mankind. The dialogue is one constant reciprocation of conceits, or clash of wit, in which nothing flows necessarily from the occasion, or is dictated by nature. The characters both of men and women are either fictitious and artificial, as those of *Heartwell* and the Ladies; or easy and common, as *Wittol* a tame idiot, *Bluff* a swaggering coward, and *Fondlewife* a jealous puritan; and the catastrophe arises from a mistake not very probably produced, by marrying a woman in a mask.

Yet this gay comedy, when all these deductions are made, will still remain the work of very powerful and fertile faculties: the dialogue is quick and sparkling, the incidents such as seize the attention, and the wit so exuberant that it *o'er-informs its tenement.**

Next year he gave another specimen of his abilities in *The Double Dealer*, which was not received with equal kindness. He writes to his patron the lord Halifax a dedication, in which he endeavours to reconcile the reader to that which found few friends among the audience. These apologies are always useless; *de gustibus non est disputandum*;* men may be convinced, but they cannot be pleased, against their will. But though taste is obstinate, it is very variable, and time often prevails when arguments have failed.

Queen Mary conferred upon both those plays the honour of her presence; and when she died, soon after, Congreve testified his gratitude by a despicable effusion of elegiac pastoral; a composition in which all is unnatural, and yet nothing is new.*

In another year (1695) his prolific pen produced *Love for Love*; a comedy of nearer alliance to life, and exhibiting more real manners, than either of the former. The character of *Foresight* was then common. Dryden calculated nativities; both Cromwell and king

William had their lucky days; and Shaftesbury himself, though he had no religion, was said to regard predictions.* The *Sailor* is not accounted very natural, but he is very pleasant.

With this play was opened the New Theatre, under the direction of Betterton the tragedian;* where he exhibited two years afterwards (1697) *The Mourning Bride*, a tragedy, so written as to shew him sufficiently qualified for either kind of dramatick poetry.

In this play, of which, when he afterwards revised it, he reduced the versification to greater regularity, there is more bustle than sentiment; the plot is busy and intricate, and the events take hold on the attention; but, except a very few passages, we are rather amused with noise, and perplexed with stratagem, than entertained with any true delineation of natural characters. This, however, was received with more benevolence than any other of his works, and still continues to be acted and applauded.

But whatever objections may be made either to his comic or tragick excellence, they are lost at once in the blaze of admiration, when it is remembered that he had produced these four plays before he had passed his twenty-fifth year; before other men, even such as are some time to shine in eminence, have passed their probation of literature, or presume to hope for any other notice than such as is bestowed on diligence and inquiry. Among all the efforts of early genius which literary history records, I doubt whether any one can be produced that more surpasses the common limits of nature than the plays of Congreve.

About this time began the long-continued controversy between Collier and the poets. In the reign of Charles the First the Puritans had raised a violent clamour against the drama, which they considered as an entertainment not lawful to Christians, an opinion held by them in common with the church of Rome; and Prynne published *Histrio-mastix*,* a huge volume, in which stage-plays were censured. The outrages and crimes of the Puritans brought afterwards their whole system of doctrine into disrepute, and from the Restoration the poets and the players were left at quiet; for to have molested them would have had the appearance of tendency to puritanical malignity.

This danger, however, was worn away by time; and Collier, a fierce and implacable Nonjuror,* knew that an attack upon the theatre would never make him suspected for a Puritan; he therefore

(1698) published *A short View of the Immorality and Profaneness of the English Stage*, I believe with no other motive than religious zeal and honest indignation. He was formed for a controvertist; with sufficient learning; with diction vehement and pointed, though often vulgar and incorrect; with unconquerable pertinacity; with wit in the highest degree keen and sarcastick; and with all those powers exalted and invigorated by just confidence in his cause.

Thus qualified, and thus incited, he walked out to battle, and assailed at once most of the living writers, from Dryden to Durfey.* His onset was violent: those passages, which while they stood single had passed with little notice, when they were accumulated and exposed together, excited horror; the wise and the pious caught the alarm, and the nation wondered why it had so long suffered irreligion and licentiousness to be openly taught at the publick charge.

Nothing now remained for the poets but to resist or fly. Dryden's conscience, or his prudence, angry as he was, withheld him from the conflict; Congreve and Vanbrugh* attempted answers. Congreve, a very young man, elated with success, and impatient of censure, assumed an air of confidence and security. His chief artifice of controversy is to retort upon his adversary his own words: he is very angry, and, hoping to conquer Collier with his own weapons, allows himself in the use of every term of contumely and contempt; but he has the sword without the arm of Scanderbeg; he has his antagonist's coarseness, but not his strength. Collier replied; for contest was his delight, he was not to be frighted from his purpose or his prey.

The cause of Congreve was not tenable: whatever glosses he might use for the defence or palliation of single passages, the general tenour and tendency of his plays must always be condemned. It is acknowledged, with universal conviction, that the perusal of his works will make no man better; and that their ultimate effect is to represent pleasure in alliance with vice, and to relax those obligations by which life ought to be regulated.

The stage found other advocates, and the dispute was protracted through ten years; but at last Comedy grew more modest, and Collier lived to see the reward of his labour in the reformation of the theatre.

Of the powers by which this important victory was atchieved, a quotation from *Love for Love*, and the remark upon it, may afford a specimen.*

Sir Samps. *'Sampson's a very good name; for your Sampsons were strong dogs from the beginning.*

Angel. *Have a care—If you remember, the strongest Sampson of your name pull'd an old house over his head at last.*

"Here you have the Sacred History burlesqued, and Sampson once more brought into the house of Dagon, to make sport for the Philistines!"

Congreve's last play was *The Way of the World*; which, though as he hints in his dedication, it was written with great labour and much thought, was received with so little favour, that, being in a high degree offended and disgusted, he resolved to commit his quiet and his fame no more to the caprices of an audience.

From this time his life ceased to be publick; he lived for himself and for his friends; and among his friends was able to name every man of his time whom wit and elegance had raised to reputation. It may be therefore reasonably supposed that his manners were polite, and his conversation pleasing.

He seems not to have taken much pleasure in writing, as he contributed nothing to the *Spectator*, and only one paper to the *Tatler*, though published by men with whom he might be supposed willing to associate; and though he lived many years after the publication of his Miscellaneous Poems, yet he added nothing to them, but lived on in literary indolence; engaged in no controversy, contending with no rival, neither soliciting flattery by publick commendations, nor provoking enmity by malignant criticism, but passing his time among the great and splendid, in the placid enjoyment of his fame and fortune.

Having owed his fortune to Halifax, he continued always of his patron's party, but, as it seems, without violence or acrimony; and his firmness was naturally esteemed, as his abilities were reverenced. His security therefore was never violated; and when, upon the extrusion of the Whigs, some intercession was used lest Congreve should be displaced, the earl of Oxford* made this answer:

> "Non obtusa adeo gestamus pectora Pœni,
> Nec tam aversus equos Tyriâ sol jungit ab urbe."*

He that was thus honoured by the adverse party, might naturally expect to be advanced when his friends returned to power, and he was accordingly made secretary for the island of Jamaica; a place,

I suppose, without trust or care, but which, with his post in the customs, is said to have afforded him twelve hundred pounds a year.*

His honours were yet far greater than his profits. Every writer mentioned him with respect; and, among other testimonies to his merit, Steele made him the patron of his Miscellany,* and Pope inscribed to him his translation of the Iliad.

But he treated the Muses with ingratitude; for, having long conversed familiarly with the great, he wished to be considered rather as a man of fashion than of wit; and, when he received a visit from Voltaire, disgusted him by the despicable foppery of desiring to be considered not as an author but a gentleman; to which the Frenchman replied, "that if he had been only a gentleman, he should not have come to visit him."*

In his retirement he may be supposed to have applied himself to books; for he discovers more literature than the poets have commonly attained. But his studies were in his latter days obstructed by cataracts in his eyes, which at last terminated in blindness. This melancholy state was aggravated by the gout, for which he sought relief by a journey to Bath; but being overturned in his chariot, complained from that time of a pain in his side, and died, at his house in Surrey-street in the Strand, Jan. 29, 1728–9. Having lain in state in the Jerusalem-chamber, he was buried in Westminster-abbey, where a monument is erected to his memory by Henrietta dutchess of Marlborough,* to whom, for reasons either not known or not mentioned, he bequeathed a legacy of about ten thousand pounds; the accumulation of attentive parsimony, which, though to her superfluous and useless, might have given great assistance to the ancient family from which he descended, at that time by the imprudence of his relation reduced to difficulties and distress.

CONGREVE has merit of the highest kind; he is an original writer, who borrowed neither the models of his plot, nor the manner of his dialogue. Of his plays I cannot speak distinctly; for since I inspected them many years have passed; but what remains upon my memory is, that his characters are commonly fictitious and artificial, with very little of nature, and not much of life. He formed a peculiar idea of comick excellence, which he supposed to consist in gay remarks and unexpected answers; but that which he endeavoured, he seldom failed of performing. His scenes exhibit not much of humour, imagery, or passion: his personages are a kind of intellectual gladiators; every sentence is to ward or strike; the contest of smartness is never intermitted; his wit is a meteor playing to and fro with alternate coruscations. His comedies have therefore, in some degree, the operation of tragedies; they surprise rather than divert, and raise admiration oftener than merriment. But they are the works of a mind replete with images, and quick in combination.

Of his miscellaneous poetry, I cannot say any thing very favourable. The powers of Congreve seem to desert him when he leaves the stage, as Antæus* was no longer strong than he could touch the ground. It cannot be observed without wonder, that a mind so vigorous and fertile in dramatick compositions should on any other occasion discover nothing but impotence and poverty. He has in these little pieces neither elevation of fancy, selection of language, nor skill in versification: yet, if I were required to select from the whole mass of English poetry the most poetical paragraph, I know not what I could prefer to an exclamation in *The Mourning Bride:**

ALMERIA.

It was a fancy'd noise; for all is hush'd.

LEONORA.

It bore the accent of a human voice.

ALMERIA.

It was thy fear, or else some transient wind
Whistling thro' hollows of this vaulted isle:
We'll listen—

LEONORA.

Hark!

ALMERIA.

No, all is hush'd, and still as death.—'Tis dreadful!
How reverend is the face of this tall pile;
Whose ancient pillars rear their marble heads,
To bear aloft its arch'd and ponderous roof,
By its own weight made stedfast and immoveable,
Looking tranquillity! It strikes an awe
And terror on my aching sight; the tombs
And monumental caves of death look cold,
And shoot a chilness to my trembling heart.
Give me thy hand, and let me hear thy voice;
Nay, quickly speak to me, and let me hear
Thy voice—my own affrights me with its echoes.

He who reads those lines enjoys for a moment the powers of a poet; he feels what he remembers to have felt before, but he feels it with great increase of sensibility; he recognizes a familiar image, but meets it again amplified and expanded, embellished with beauty, and enlarged with majesty.

Yet could the author, who appears here to have enjoyed the confidence of Nature, lament the death of queen Mary in lines like these:*

> The rocks are cleft, and new-descending rills
> Furrow the brows of all th' impending hills.
> The water-gods to floods their rivulets turn,
> And each, with streaming eyes, supplies his wanting urn.
> The Fauns forsake the woods, the Nymphs the grove,
> And round the plain in sad distractions rove:
> In prickly brakes their tender limbs they tear,
> And leave on thorns their locks of golden hair.
> With their sharp nails, themselves the Satyrs wound,
> And tug their shaggy beards, and bite with grief the ground.
> Lo Pan himself, beneath a blasted oak,
> Dejected lies, his pipe in pieces broke.
> See Pales weeping too, in wild despair,
> And to the piercing winds her bosom bare.
> And see yon fading myrtle, where appears
> The Queen of Love, all bath'd in flowing tears;
> See how she wrings her hands, and beats her breast,
> And tears her useless girdle from her waist:
> Hear the sad murmurs of her sighing doves!
> For grief they sigh, forgetful of their loves.

And many years after, he gave no proof that time had improved his wisdom or his wit; for, on the death of the marquis of Blandford, this was his song:*

> And now the winds, which had so long been still,
> Began the swelling air with sighs to fill:
> The water-nymphs, who motionless remain'd,
> Like images of ice, while she complain'd,
> Now loos'd their streams: as when descending rains
> Roll the steep torrents headlong o'er the plains.
> The prone creation, who so long had gaz'd,

Charm'd with her cries, and at her griefs amaz'd,
Began to roar and howl with horrid yell,
Dismal to hear, and terrible to tell;
Nothing but groans and sighs were heard around,
And Echo multiplied each mournful sound.

In both these funeral poems, when he has *yelled* out many *syllables* of senseless *dolour*, he dismisses his reader with senseless consolation: from the grave of Pastora rises a light that forms a star; and where Amaryllis wept for Amyntas, from every tear sprung up a violet.

But William is his hero, and of William he will sing;*

The hovering winds on downy wings shall wait around,
And catch, and waft to foreign lands, the flying sound.

It cannot but be proper to shew what they shall have to catch and carry:

'Twas now, when flowery lawns the prospect made,
And flowing brooks beneath a forest shade,
A lowing heifer, loveliest of the herd,
Stood feeding by; while two fierce bulls prepar'd
Their armed heads for fight; by fate of war to prove
The victor worthy of the fair-one's love.
Unthought presage of what met next my view;
For soon the shady scene withdrew.
And now, for woods, and fields, and springing flowers,
Behold a town arise, bulwark'd with walls and lofty towers;
Two rival armies all the plain o'erspread,
Each in battalia rang'd, and shining arms array'd;
With eager eyes beholding both from far,
Namur, the prize and mistress of the war.

The *Birth of the Muse* is a miserable fiction. One good line it has, which was borrowed from Dryden. The concluding verses are these:*

This said, no more remain'd. Th' etherial host
Again impatient crowd the crystal coast.
The father, now, within his spacious hands,
Encompass'd all the mingled mass of seas and lands;
And, having heav'd aloft the ponderous sphere,
He launch'd the world to float in ambient air.

Of his irregular poems, that to Mrs. Arabella Hunt* seems to be the best: his ode for Cecilia's Day, however, has some lines which Pope had in his mind when he wrote his own.

His imitations of Horace are feebly paraphrastical, and the additions which he makes are of little value. He sometimes retains what were more properly omitted, as when he talks of *vervain* and *gums* to propitiate Venus.

Of his Translations, the satire of Juvenal was written very early, and may therefore be forgiven, though it have not the massiness and vigour of the original. In all his versions strength and sprightliness are wanting: his Hymn to Venus, from Homer, is perhaps the best. His lines are weakened with expletives, and his rhymes are frequently imperfect.

His petty poems are seldom worth the cost of criticism: sometimes the thoughts are false, and sometimes common. In his verses on lady Gethin,* the latter part is an imitation of Dryden's ode on Mrs. Killigrew; and Doris, that has been so lavishly flattered by Steele, has indeed some lively stanzas, but the expression might be mended; and the most striking part of the character had been already shewn in *Love for Love*. His *Art of Pleasing* is founded on a vulgar but perhaps impracticable principle, and the staleness of the sense is not concealed by any novelty of illustration or elegance of diction.

This tissue of poetry, from which he seems to have hoped a lasting name, is totally neglected, and known only as it is appended to his plays.

While comedy or while tragedy is regarded, his plays are likely to be read; but, except what relates to the stage, I know not that he has ever written a stanza that is sung, or a couplet that is quoted. The general character of his Miscellanies is, that they shew little wit, and little virtue.

Yet to him it must be confessed that we are indebted for the correction of a national error, and for the cure of our Pindarick madness.* He first taught the English writers that Pindar's odes were regular; and though certainly he had not the fire requisite for the higher species of lyrick poetry, he has shewn us that enthusiasm has its rules, and that in mere confusion there is neither grace nor greatness.

GAY

JOHN GAY, descended from an old family that had been long in possession of the manour of[1] Goldworthy in Devonshire, was born in 1688,* at or near Barnstaple, where he was educated by Mr. Luck,* who taught the school of that town with good reputation, and, a little before he retired from it, published a volume of Latin and English verses. Under such a master he was likely to form a taste for poetry. Being born without prospect of hereditary riches, he was sent to London in his youth, and placed apprentice with a silk-mercer.

How long he continued behind the counter, or with what degree of softness and dexterity he received and accommodated the Ladies, as he probably took no delight in telling it, is not known. The report is, that he was soon weary of either the restraint or servility of his occupation, and easily persuaded his master to discharge him.

The dutchess of Monmouth,* remarkable for inflexible perseverance in her demand to be treated as a princess, in 1712 took Gay into her service as secretary: by quitting a shop for such service, he might gain leisure, but he certainly advanced little in the boast of independence. Of his leisure he made so good use, that he published next year a poem on *Rural Sports*, and inscribed it to Mr. Pope, who was then rising fast into reputation. Pope was pleased with the honour; and when he became acquainted with Gay, found such attractions in his manners and conversation, that he seems to have received him into his inmost confidence; and a friendship was formed between them which lasted to their separation by death, without any known abatement on either part. Gay was the general favourite of the whole association of wits; but they regarded him as a play-fellow rather than a partner, and treated him with more fondness than respect.

Next year he published *The Shepherd's Week*, six English Pastorals, in which the images are drawn from real life, such as it appears among the rusticks in parts of England remote from London. Steele, in some papers of the *Guardian*, had praised Ambrose Philips, as the

[1] *Goldworthy* does not appear in the *Villare*.

Pastoral writer that yielded only to Theocritus, Virgil, and Spenser.* Pope, who had also published Pastorals, not pleased to be overlooked, drew up a comparison of his own compositions with those of Philips, in which he covertly gave himself the preference, while he seemed to disown it. Not content with this, he is supposed to have incited Gay to write the *Shepherd's Week*, to shew, that if it be necessary to copy nature with minuteness, rural life must be exhibited such as grossness and ignorance have made it. So far the plan was reasonable; but the Pastorals are introduced by a *Proeme*, written with such imitation as they could attain of obsolete language, and by consequence in a style that was never spoken nor written in any age or in any place.

But the effect of reality and truth became conspicuous, even when the intention was to shew them groveling and degraded. These Pastorals became popular, and were read with delight, as just representations of rural manners and occupations, by those who had no interest in the rivalry of the poets, nor knowledge of the critical dispute.

In 1713 he brought a comedy called *The Wife of Bath* upon the stage, but it received no applause; he printed it, however; and seventeen years after, having altered it, and, as he thought, adapted it more to the publick taste, he offered it again to the town; but, though he was flushed with the success of the *Beggar's Opera*, had the mortification to see it again rejected.

In the last year of queen Anne's life, Gay was made secretary to the earl of Clarendon,* ambassador to the court of Hanover. This was a station that naturally gave him hopes of kindness from every party; but the Queen's death put an end to her favours, and he had dedicated his *Shepherd's Week* to Bolingbroke, which Swift considered as the crime that obstructed all kindness from the house of Hanover.*

He did not, however, omit to improve the right which his office had given him to the notice of the royal family. On the arrival of the princess of Wales, he wrote a poem, and obtained so much favour, that both the Prince and Princess went to see his *What d'ye call it*, a kind of mock-tragedy, in which the images were comick, and the action grave; so that, as Pope relates, Mr. Cromwell, who could not hear what was said, was at a loss how to reconcile the laughter of the audience with the solemnity of the scene.

Of this performance the value certainly is but little; but it was one of the lucky trifles that give pleasure by novelty, and was so much favoured by the audience, that envy appeared against it in the form of criticism; and Griffin a player, in conjunction with Mr. Theobald, a man afterwards more remarkable, produced a pamphlet called the *Key to the What d'ye call it*; which, says Gay, *calls me a blockhead, and Mr. Pope a knave.**

But Fortune has always been inconstant. Not long afterwards (1717) he endeavoured to entertain the town with *Three Hours after Marriage*; a comedy written, as there is sufficient reason for believing, by the joint assistance of Pope and Arbuthnot. One purpose of it was to bring into contempt Dr. Woodward the Fossilist,* a man not really or justly contemptible. It had the fate which such outrages deserve: the scene in which Woodward was directly and apparently ridiculed, by the introduction of a mummy and a crocodile, disgusted the audience, and the performance was driven off the stage with general condemnation.

Gay is represented as a man easily incited to hope, and deeply depressed when his hopes were disappointed. This is not the character of a hero; but it may naturally imply something more generally welcome, a soft and civil companion. Whoever is apt to hope good from others is diligent to please them; but he that believes his powers strong enough to force their own way, commonly tries only to please himself.

He had been simple enough to imagine that those who laughed at the *What d'ye call it* would raise the fortune of its author; and finding nothing done, sunk into dejection. His friends endeavoured to divert him. The earl of Burlington sent him (1716) into Devonshire; the year after, Mr. Pulteney took him to Aix; and in the following year lord Harcourt invited him to his seat, where, during his visit, the two rural lovers were killed with lightning, as is particularly told in Pope's Letters.*

Being now generally known, he published (1720) his Poems by subscription with such success, that he raised a thousand pounds; and called his friends to a consultation, what use might be best made of it. Lewis, the steward of lord Oxford,* advised him to intrust it to the funds, and live upon the interest; Arbuthnot bad him intrust it to Providence, and live upon the principal; Pope directed him, and was seconded by Swift, to purchase an annuity.

Gay in that disastrous year[1] had a present from young Craggs of some South-sea-stock, and once supposed himself to be master of twenty thousand pounds.* His friends persuaded him to sell his share; but he dreamed of dignity and splendour, and could not bear to obstruct his own fortune. He was then importuned to sell as much as would purchase an hundred a year for life, *which*, says Fenton,* *will make you sure of a clean shirt and a shoulder of mutton every day*. This counsel was rejected; the profit and principal were lost, and Gay sunk under the calamity so low that his life became in danger.

By the care of his friends, among whom Pope appears to have shewn particular tenderness, his health was restored; and, returning to his studies, he wrote a tragedy called *The Captives*, which he was invited to read before the princess of Wales. When the hour came, he saw the princess and her ladies all in expectation, and advancing with reverence, too great for any other attention, stumbled at a stool, and falling forwards, threw down a weighty Japan screen. The princess started, the ladies screamed, and poor Gay after all the disturbance was still to read his play.

The fate of *The Captives*, which was acted at Drury-Lane in 1723, I know not; but he now thought himself in favour, and undertook (1726) to write a volume of Fables for the improvement of the young duke of Cumberland.* For this he is said to have been promised a reward, which he had doubtless magnified with all the wild expectations of indigence and vanity.

Next year the Prince and Princess became King and Queen, and Gay was to be great and happy; but upon the settlement of the household he found himself appointed gentleman usher to the princess Louisa. By this offer he thought himself insulted, and sent a message to the Queen, that he was too old for the place. There seem to have been many machinations employed afterwards in his favour; and diligent court was paid to Mrs. Howard,* afterwards countess of Suffolk, who was much beloved by the King and Queen, to engage her interest for his promotion; but solicitations, verses, and flatteries were thrown away; the lady heard them, and did nothing.

All the pain which he suffered from the neglect, or, as he perhaps termed it, the ingratitude of the court, may be supposed to have been

[1] Spence.

driven away by the unexampled success of the *Beggar's Opera*. This play, written in ridicule of the musical Italian Drama, was first offered to Cibber and his brethren at Drury-Lane, and rejected; it being then carried to Rich,* had the effect, as was ludicrously said, of *making* Gay *rich*, and Rich *gay*.

Of this lucky piece, as the reader cannot but wish to know the original and progress, I have inserted the relation which Spence has given in Pope's words.*

"Dr. Swift had been observing once to Mr. Gay, what an odd pretty sort of a thing a Newgate Pastoral might make. Gay was inclined to try at such a thing for some time; but afterwards thought it would be better to write a comedy on the same plan. This was what gave rise to the *Beggar's Opera*. He began on it; and when first he mentioned it to Swift, the Doctor did not much like the project. As he carried it on, he shewed what he wrote to both of us, and we now-and-then gave a correction, or a word or two of advice; but it was wholly of his own writing.—When it was done, neither of us thought it would succeed.—We shewed it to Congreve; who, after reading it over, said, It would either take greatly, or be damned confoundedly.—We were all, at the first night of it, in great uncertainty of the event; till we were very much encouraged by overhearing the duke of Argyle, who sat in the next box to us, say, 'It will do—it must do! I see it in the eyes of them.' This was a good while before the first Act was over, and so gave us ease soon; for that duke (besides his own good taste) has a particular knack, as any one now living, in discovering the taste of the publick. He was quite right in this, as usual; the good nature of the audience appeared stronger and stronger every act, and ended in a clamour of applause."

Its reception is thus recorded in the notes to the *Dunciad*:*

"This piece was received with greater applause than was ever known. Besides being acted in London sixty-three days without interruption, and renewed the next season with equal applause, it spread into all the great towns of England; was played in many places to the thirtieth and fortieth time; at Bath and Bristol fifty, &c. It made its progress into Wales, Scotland, and Ireland, where it was performed twenty-four days successively. The ladies carried about with them the favourite songs of it in fans, and houses were furnished with it in screens. The fame of it was not confined to the author only. The person who acted Polly, till then obscure, became all at once the favourite of the town; her pictures were engraved, and sold in great numbers; her Life written, books of letters and verses to her published, and pamphlets made even of her sayings and jests. Furthermore, it drove out of England (for that season) the Italian Opera, which had carried all before it for ten years."

Of this performance, when it was printed, the reception was different, according to the different opinion of its readers. Swift commended it for the excellence of its morality, as a piece that *placed all kinds of vice in the strongest and most odious light*; but others, and among them Dr. Herring,* afterwards archbishop of Canterbury, censured it as giving encouragement not only to vice but to crimes, by making a highwayman the hero, and dismissing him at last unpunished. It has been even said, that after the exhibition of the *Beggar's Opera* the gangs of robbers were evidently multiplied.

Both these decisions are surely exaggerated. The play, like many others, was plainly written only to divert, without any moral purpose, and is therefore not likely to do good; nor can it be conceived, without more speculation than life requires or admits, to be productive of much evil. Highwaymen and house-breakers seldom frequent the playhouse, or mingle in any elegant diversion; nor is it possible for any one to imagine that he may rob with safety, because he sees Macheath reprieved upon the stage.

This objection however, or some other rather political than moral, obtained such prevalence, that when Gay produced a second part under the name of *Polly*, it was prohibited by the Lord Chamberlain;* and he was forced to recompense his repulse by a subscription, which is said to have been so liberally bestowed, that what he called oppression ended in profit. The ⋆ publication was so much favoured, that though the first part gained him four hundred pounds, near thrice as much was the profit of the second.*

He received yet another recompense for this supposed hardship, in the affectionate attention of the duke and dutchess of Queensberry,* into whose house he was taken, and with whom he passed the remaining part of his life. The ⋆ duke, considering his want of œconomy, undertook the management of his money, and gave it to him as he wanted it. But it is supposed that the discountenance of the Court sunk deep into his heart, and gave him more discontent than the applauses or tenderness of his friends could overpower. He soon

⋆ Spence.

fell into his old distemper, an habitual colick, and languished, though with many intervals of ease and cheerfulness, till a violent fit at last seized him, and hurried him to the grave, as Arbuthnot reported, with more precipitance than he had ever known. He died on the fourth of December 1732, and was buried in Westminster Abbey. The letter which brought an account of his death to Swift was laid by for some days unopened, because when he received it he was imprest with the preconception of some misfortune.

After his death was published a second volume of Fables more political than the former. His opera of *Achilles* was acted, and the profits were given to two widow sisters, who inherited what he left, as his lawful heirs; for he died without a will, though he had gathered * three thousand pounds. There have appeared likewise under his name a comedy called the *Distrest Wife*, and the *Rehearsal at Gotham*, a piece of humour.

The character given him by Pope * is this, that *he was a natural man, without design, who spoke what he thought, and just as he thought it*; and that *he was of a timid temper, and fearful of giving offence to the great;* which caution however, says Pope, was of no avail.

As a poet, he cannot be rated very high. He was, as I once heard a female critick remark, *of a lower order*. He had not in any great degree the *mens divinior*, the dignity of genius. Much however must be allowed to the author of a new species of composition, though it be not of the highest kind. We owe to Gay the Ballad Opera; a mode of comedy which at first was supposed to delight only by its novelty, but has now by the experience of half a century been found so well accommodated to the disposition of a popular audience, that it is likely to keep long possession of the stage. Whether this new drama was the product of judgement or of luck, the praise of it must be given to the inventor; and there are many writers read with more reverence, to whom such merit of originality cannot be attributed.

His first performance, the *Rural Sports*, is such as was easily planned and executed; it is never contemptible, nor ever excellent. The *Fan* is one of those mythological fictions which antiquity delivers ready to the hand; but which, like other things that lie open to every one's use, are of little value. The attention naturally retires from a new tale of Venus, Diana, and Minerva.

* Spence.

His Fables seem to have been a favourite work; for, having published one volume, he left another behind him. Of this kind of Fables, the authors do not appear to have formed any distinct or settled notion. Phædrus* evidently confounds them with *Tales*, and Gay both with *Tales* and *Allegorical Prosopopoeias*. A *Fable* or *Apologue*, such as is now under consideration, seems to be, in its genuine state, a narrative in which beings irrational, and sometimes inanimate, *arbores loquuntur, non tantum feræ*,* are, for the purpose of moral instruction, feigned to act and speak with human interests and passions. To this description the compositions of Gay do not always conform. For a Fable he gives now and then a Tale or an abstracted Allegory; and from some, by whatever name they may be called, it will be difficult to extract any moral principle. They are, however, told with liveliness; the versification is smooth, and the diction, though now-and-then a little constrained by the measure or the rhyme, is generally happy.

To *Trivia* may be allowed all that it claims; it is spritely, various, and pleasant. The subject is of that kind which Gay was by nature qualified to adorn; yet some of his decorations may be justly wished away. An honest blacksmith might have done for Patty what is performed by Vulcan. The appearance of Cloacina is nauseous and superfluous; a shoeboy could have been produced by the casual cohabitation of mere mortals. Horace's rule is broken in both cases; there is no *dignus vindice nodus*,* no difficulty that required any supernatural interposition. A patten* may be made by the hammer of a mortal, and a bastard may be dropped by a human strumpet. On great occasions, and on small, the mind is repelled by useless and apparent falsehood.

Of his little Poems the publick judgement seems to be right; they are neither much esteemed, nor totally despised. The story of the Apparition is borrowed from one of the tales of Poggio. Those that please least are the pieces to which *Gulliver* gave occasion; for who can much delight in the echo of an unnatural fiction?

Dione is a counterpart to *Amynta*, and *Pastor Fido*, and other trifles of the same kind, easily imitated, and unworthy of imitation. What the Italians call comedies from a happy conclusion, Gay calls a tragedy from a mournful event; but the style of the Italians and of Gay is equally tragical. There is something in the poetical *Arcadia* so remote from known reality and speculative possibility, that we can never support its representation through a long work. A Pastoral of an hundred lines may be endured; but who will hear of sheep and goats, and myrtle bowers and purling rivulets, through five acts? Such scenes please Barbarians in the dawn of literature, and children in the dawn of life; but will be for the most part thrown away, as men grow wise, and nations grow learned.

SAVAGE

It has been observed in all ages, that the advantages of nature or of fortune have contributed very little to the promotion of happiness; and that those whom the splendour of their rank, or the extent of their capacity, have placed upon the summits of human life, have not often given any just occasion to envy in those who look up to them from a lower station: whether it be that apparent superiority incites great designs, and great designs are naturally liable to fatal miscarriages; or that the general lot of mankind is misery, and the misfortunes of those whose eminence drew upon them an universal attention, have been more carefully recorded, because they were more generally observed, and have in reality been only more conspicuous than those of others, not more frequent, or more severe.

That affluence and power, advantages extrinsic and adventitious, and therefore easily separable from those by whom they are possessed, should very often flatter the mind with expectations of felicity which they cannot give, raises no astonishment; but it seems rational to hope, that intellectual greatness should produce better effects: that minds qualified for great attainments should first endeavour their own benefit; and that they who are most able to teach others the way to happiness, should with most certainty follow it themselves.

But this expectation, however plausible, has been very frequently disappointed. The heroes of literary as well as civil history have been very often no less remarkable for what they have suffered than for what they have atchieved; and volumes have been written only to enumerate the miseries of the learned, and relate their unhappy lives, and untimely deaths.

To these mournful narratives, I am about to add the Life of Richard Savage, a man whose writings entitle him to an eminent rank in the classes of learning, and whose misfortunes claim a degree of compassion, not always due to the unhappy, as they were often the consequences of the crimes of others, rather than his own.

In the year 1697, Anne Countess of Macclesfield, having lived for some time upon very uneasy terms with her husband, thought a public confession of adultery the most obvious and expeditious method of obtaining her liberty; and therefore declared, that the child, with which she was then great, was begotten by the Earl Rivers. This, as may be easily imagined, made her husband no less desirous of a separation than herself, and he prosecuted his design in the most effectual manner; for he applied not to the ecclesiastical courts for a divorce, but to the parliament for an act, by which his marriage might be dissolved, the nuptial contract totally annulled, and the children of his wife illegitimated. This act, after the usual deliberation, he obtained, though without the approbation of some, who considered marriage as an affair only cognizable by ecclesiastical judges[1]; and on March 3d was separated from his wife, whose fortune, which was very great, was repaid her, and who having, as well as her husband, the liberty of making another choice, was in a short time married to Colonel Brett.*

While the Earl of Macclesfield was prosecuting this affair, his wife was, on the 10th of January 1697–8, delivered of a son, and the Earl Rivers, by appearing to consider him as his own, left none any reason to doubt of the sincerity of her declaration; for he was his godfather, and gave him his own name, which was by his direction inserted in the register of St. Andrew's parish in Holborn, but unfortunately left him to the care of his mother, whom, as she was now set free from her husband, he probably imagined likely to treat with great tenderness the child that had contributed to so pleasing an event.* It is not indeed easy to discover what motives could be found to over-balance that natural affection of a parent, or what interest could be promoted by neglect or cruelty. The dread of shame or of poverty, by which some wretches have been incited to abandon or to murder their children, cannot be supposed to have affected a woman who had proclaimed her crimes and solicited reproach, and on whom the clemency of the legislature had undeservedly bestowed a fortune, which would have been very little diminished by the expences which the care of her child could have

[1] This year was made remarkable by the dissolution of a marriage solemnized in the face of the church. SALMON'S REVIEW.

The following protest is registered in the books of the House of Lords.

Dissentient.

Because we conceive that this is the first bill of that nature that hath passed, where there was not a divorce first obtained in the Spiritual Court; which we look upon as an ill precedent, and may be of dangerous consequence in the future.

HALIFAX. ROCHESTER.

brought upon her. It was therefore not likely that she would be wicked without temptation, that she would look upon her son from his birth with a kind of resentment and abhorrence; and, instead of supporting, assisting, and defending him, delight to see him struggling with misery, or that she would take every opportunity of aggravating his misfortunes, and obstructing his resources, and with an implacable and restless cruelty continue her persecution from the first hour of his life to the last.

But whatever were her motives, no sooner was her son born, than she discovered a resolution of disowning him; and in a very short time removed him from her sight, by committing him to the care of a poor woman, whom she directed to educate him as her own, and injoined never to inform him of his true parents.

Such was the beginning of the life of Richard Savage. Born with a legal claim to honour and to affluence, he was in two months illegitimated by the parliament, and disowned by his mother, doomed to poverty and obscurity, and launched upon the ocean of life, only that he might be swallowed by its quicksands, or dashed upon its rocks.

His mother could not indeed infect others with the same cruelty. As it was impossible to avoid the inquiries which the curiosity or tenderness of her relations made after her child, she was obliged to give some account of the measures that she had taken; and her mother, the Lady Mason, whether in approbation of her design, or to prevent more criminal contrivances, engaged to transact with the nurse, to pay her for her care, and to superintend the education of the child.

In this charitable office she was assisted by his godmother Mrs. Lloyd, who, while she lived, always looked upon him with that tenderness, which the barbarity of his mother made peculiarly necessary; but her death, which happened in his tenth year, was another of the misfortunes of his childhood; for though she kindly endeavoured to alleviate his loss by a legacy of three hundred pounds; yet, as he had none to prosecute his claim, to shelter him from oppression, or call in law to the assistance of justice, her will was eluded by the executors, and no part of the money was ever paid.

He was, however, not yet wholly abandoned. The Lady Mason still continued her care, and directed him to be placed at a small grammar-school near St. Alban's, where he was called by the name of his nurse, without the least intimation that he had a claim to any other.

Here he was initiated in literature, and passed through several of the classes, with what rapidity or what applause cannot now be known. As he always spoke with respect of his master, it is probable that the mean rank, in which he then appeared, did not hinder his genius from being distinguished, or his industry from being rewarded; and if in so low a state he obtained distinction and rewards, it is not likely that they were gained but by genius and industry.

It is very reasonable to conjecture, that his application was equal to his abilities, because his improvement was more than proportioned to the opportunities which he enjoyed; nor can it be doubted, that if his earliest productions had been preserved, like those of happier students, we might in some have found vigorous sallies of that sprightly humour which distinguishes *The Author to be let*, and in others strong touches of that ardent imagination which painted the solemn scenes of *The Wanderer*.*

While he was thus cultivating his genius, his father the Earl Rivers was seized with a distemper, which in a short time put an end to his life. He had frequently inquired after his son, and had always been amused* with fallacious and evasive answers; but, being now in his own opinion on his death-bed, he thought it his duty to provide for him among his other natural children, and therefore demanded a positive account of him, with an importunity not to be diverted or denied. His mother, who could no longer refuse an answer, determined at least to give such as should cut him off for ever from that happiness which competence affords, and therefore declared that he was dead; which is perhaps the first instance of a lye invented by a mother to deprive her son of a provision which was designed him by another, and which she could not expect herself, though he should lose it.

This was therefore an act of wickedness which could not be defeated, because it could not be suspected; the Earl did not imagine there could exist in a human form a mother that would ruin her son without enriching herself, and therefore bestowed upon some other person six thousand pounds, which he had in his will bequeathed to Savage.

The same cruelty which incited his mother to intercept this provision which had been intended him, prompted her in a short time to another project, a project worthy of such a disposition.

She endeavoured to rid herself from the danger of being at any time made known to him, by sending him secretly to the American plantations[1].

By whose kindness this scheme was counteracted, or by what interposition she was induced to lay aside her design, I know not; it is not improbable that the Lady Mason might persuade or compel her to desist, or perhaps she could not easily find accomplices wicked enough to concur in so cruel an action; for it may be conceived, that those who had by a long gradation of guilt hardened their hearts against the sense of common wickedness, would yet be shocked at the design of a mother to expose her son to slavery and want, to expose him without interest, and without provocation; and Savage might on this occasion find protectors and advocates among those who had long traded in crimes, and whom compassion had never touched before.

Being hindered, by whatever means, from banishing him into another country, she formed soon after a scheme for burying him in poverty and obscurity in his own; and, that his station of life, if not the place of his residence, might keep him for ever at a distance from her, she ordered him to be placed with a shoemaker in Holborn, that, after the usual time of trial, he might become his apprentice.[2]

It is generally reported, that this project was for some time successful, and that Savage was employed at the awl longer than he was willing to confess; nor was it perhaps any great advantage to him, that an unexpected discovery determined him to quit his occupation.

About this time his nurse, who had always treated him as her own son, died; and it was natural for him to take care of those effects, which by her death were, as he imagined, become his own; he therefore went to her house, opened her boxes, and examined her papers, among which he found some letters written to her by the Lady Mason, which informed him of his birth, and the reasons for which it was concealed.

He was now no longer satisfied with the employment which had been allotted him, but thought he had a right to share the affluence of his mother; and therefore without scruple applied to her as her son,

[1] Savage's Preface to his Miscellany.
[2] Preface to Savage's Miscellanies.

and made use of every art to awaken her tenderness, and attract her regard. But neither his letters, nor the interposition of those friends which his merit or his distress procured him, made any impression upon her mind. She still resolved to neglect, though she could no longer disown him.

It was to no purpose that he frequently solicited her to admit him to see her; she avoided him with the most vigilant precaution, and ordered him to be excluded from her house, by whomsoever he might be introduced, and what reason soever he might give for entering it.

Savage was at the same time so touched with the discovery of his real mother, that it was his frequent practice to walk in the dark evenings[1] for several hours before her door, in hopes of seeing her as she might come by accident to the window, or cross her apartment with a candle in her hand.

But all his assiduity and tenderness were without effect, for he could neither soften her heart, nor open her hand, and was reduced to the utmost miseries of want, while he was endeavouring to awaken the affection of a mother: He was therefore obliged to seek some other means of support; and, having no profession, became by necessity an author.

At this time the attention of all the literary world was engrossed by the Bangorian controversy, which filled the press with pamphlets, and the coffee-houses with disputants.* Of this subject, as most popular, he made choice for his first attempt, and, without any other knowledge of the question than he had casually collected from conversation, published a poem against the Bishop.

What was the success or merit of this performance, I know not; it was probably lost among the innumerable pamphlets to which that dispute gave occasion. Mr. Savage was himself in a little time ashamed of it, and endeavoured to suppress it, by destroying all the copies that he could collect.

He then attempted a more gainful kind of writing[2], and in his eighteenth year offered to the stage a comedy borrowed from a Spanish plot, which was refused by the players, and was therefore given by him to Mr. Bullock, who, having more interest, made some

[1] See the Plain Dealer.
[2] Jacob's Lives of Dramatic Poets.

slight alterations, and brought it upon the stage, under the title of[1] WOMAN'S A RIDDLE, but allowed the unhappy author no part of the profit.*

Not discouraged however at his repulse, he wrote two years afterwards LOVE IN A VEIL, another comedy, borrowed likewise from the Spanish,* but with little better success than before; for though it was received and acted, yet it appeared so late in the year, that the author obtained no other advantage from it, than the acquaintance of Sir Richard Steele, and Mr. Wilks,* by whom he was pitied, caressed, and relieved.

Sir Richard Steele, having declared in his favour with all the ardour of benevolence which constituted his character, promoted his interest with the utmost zeal, related his misfortunes, applauded his merit, took all the opportunities of recommending him, and asserted, that[2] "the inhumanity of his mother had given him a right to find every good man his father."*

Nor was Mr. Savage admitted to his acquaintance only, but to his confidence, of which he sometimes related an instance too extraordinary to be omitted, as it affords a very just idea of his patron's character.

He was once desired by Sir Richard, with an air of the utmost importance, to come very early to his house the next morning. Mr. Savage came as he had promised, found the chariot at the door, and Sir Richard waiting for him, and ready to go out. What was intended, and whither they were to go, Savage could not conjecture, and was not willing to enquire; but immediately seated himself with Sir Richard; the coachman was ordered to drive, and they hurried with the utmost expedition to Hyde-Park Corner, where they stopped at a petty tavern, and retired to a private room. Sir Richard then informed him, that he intended to publish a pamphlet, and that he had desired him to come thither that he might write for him. They soon sat down to the work. Sir Richard dictated, and Savage wrote, till the dinner that had been ordered was put upon the table. Savage was surprized at the meanness of the entertainment, and after some hesitation ventured to ask for wine, which Sir Richard, not without reluctance, ordered to be brought.

[1] This play was printed first in 8vo; and afterwards in 12mo, the fifth edition.
[2] Plain Dealer.

They then finished their dinner, and proceeded in their pamphlet, which they concluded in the afternoon.

Mr. Savage then imagined his task over, and expected that Sir Richard would call for the reckoning, and return home; but his expectations deceived him, for Sir Richard told him, that he was without money, and that the pamphlet must be sold before the dinner could be paid for; and Savage was therefore obliged to go and offer their new production to sale for two guineas, which with some difficulty he obtained. Sir Richard then returned home, having retired that day only to avoid his creditors, and composed the pamphlet only to discharge his reckoning.

Mr. Savage related another fact equally uncommon, which, though it has no relation to his life, ought to be preserved. Sir Richard Steele having one day invited to his house a great number of persons of the first quality, they were surprized at the number of liveries which surrounded the table; and after dinner, when wine and mirth had set them free from the observation of rigid ceremony, one of them enquired of Sir Richard, how such an expensive train of domestics could be consistent with his fortune. Sir Richard very frankly confessed, that they were fellows of whom he would very willingly be rid. And being then asked, why he did not discharge them, declared that they were bailiffs who had introduced themselves with an execution, and whom, since he could not send them away, he had thought it convenient to embellish with liveries, that they might do him credit while they staid.

His friends were diverted with the expedient, and, by paying the debt, discharged their attendance, having obliged Sir Richard to promise that they should never again find him graced with a retinue of the same kind.

Under such a tutor, Mr. Savage was not likely to learn prudence or frugality; and perhaps many of the misfortunes, which the want of those virtues brought upon him in the following parts of his life, might be justly imputed to so unimproving an example.

Nor did the kindness of Sir Richard end in common favours. He proposed to have established him in some settled scheme of life, and to have contracted a kind of alliance with him, by marrying him to a natural daughter, on whom he intended to bestow a thousand pounds. But though he was always lavish of future bounties, he conducted his affairs in such a manner, that he was very seldom able to keep his promises, or execute his own intentions; and, as he was never able to raise the sum which he had offered, the marriage was delayed. In the mean time he was officiously informed, that Mr. Savage had ridiculed him; by which he was so much exasperated, that he withdrew the allowance which he had paid him, and never afterwards admitted him to his house.

It is not indeed unlikely that Savage might by his imprudence, expose himself to the malice of a tale-bearer; for his patron had many follies, which, as his discernment easily discovered, his imagination might sometimes incite him to mention too ludicrously. A little knowledge of the world is sufficient to discover that such weakness is very common, and that there are few who do not sometimes, in the wantonness of thoughtless mirth, or the heat of transient resentment, speak of their friends and benefactors with levity and contempt, though in their cooler moments they want neither sense of their kindness, nor reverence for their virtue. The fault therefore of Mr. Savage was rather negligence than ingratitude; but Sir Richard must likewise be acquitted of severity, for who is there that can patiently bear contempt from one whom he has relieved and supported, whose establishment he has laboured, and whose interest he has promoted?

He was now again abandoned to fortune, without any other friend than Mr. Wilks; a man, who, whatever were his abilities or skill as an actor, deserves at least to be remembered for his virtues[1], which are not often to be found in the world, and perhaps less often in his profession than in others. To be humane, generous, and candid, is a

[1] As it is a loss to mankind when any good action is forgotten, I shall insert another instance of Mr. Wilks's generosity, very little known. Mr. Smith, a gentleman educated at Dublin, being hindered by an impediment in his pronunciation from engaging in orders, for which his friends designed him, left his own country, and came to London in quest of employment, but found his solicitations fruitless, and his necessities every day more pressing. In this distress he wrote a tragedy, and offered it to the players, by whom it was rejected. Thus were his last hopes defeated, and he had no other prospect than of the most deplorable poverty. But Mr. Wilks thought his performance, though not perfect, at least worthy of some reward, and therefore offered him a benefit. This favour he improved with so much diligence, that the house afforded him a considerable sum, with which he went to Leyden, applied himself to the study of physic; and prosecuted his design with so much diligence and success, that, when Dr. Boerhaave was desired by the Czarina to recommend proper persons to introduce into Russia the practice and study of physic, Dr. Smith was one of those whom he selected. He had a considerable pension settled on him at his arrival, and was one of the chief physicians at the Russian court.

very high degree of merit in any case; but those qualities deserve still greater praise, when they are found in that condition, which makes almost every other man, for whatever reason, contemptuous, insolent, petulant, selfish, and brutal.

As Mr. Wilks was one of those to whom calamity seldom complained without relief, he naturally took an unfortunate wit into his protection, and not only assisted him in any casual distresses, but continued an equal and steady kindness to the time of his death.

By his interposition Mr. Savage once obtained from his mother[1] fifty pounds, and a promise of one hundred and fifty more; but it was the fate of this unhappy man, that few promises of any advantage to him were performed. His mother was infected among others with the general madness of the South Sea traffic;* and, having been disappointed in her expectations, refused to pay what perhaps nothing but the prospect of sudden affluence prompted her to promise.

Being thus obliged to depend upon the friendship of Mr. Wilks, he was consequently an assiduous frequenter of the theatres; and in a short time the amusements of the stage took such possession of his mind, that he never was absent from a play in several years.

This constant attendance naturally procured him the acquaintance of the players, and, among others, of Mrs. Oldfield,* who was so much pleased with his conversation, and touched with his misfortunes, that she allowed him a settled pension of fifty pounds a year, which was during her life regularly paid.

That this act of generosity may receive its due praise, and that the good actions of Mrs. Oldfield may not be sullied by her general character, it is proper to mention what Mr. Savage often declared in the strongest terms, that he never saw her alone, or in any other place than behind the scenes.

At her death he endeavoured to shew his gratitude in the most decent manner, by wearing mourning as for a mother; but did not celebrate her in elegies, because he knew that too great profusion of praise would only have revived those faults which his natural equity did not allow him to think less, because they were committed by one who favoured him; but of which, though his virtue would not endeavour to palliate them, his gratitude would not suffer him to prolong the memory, or diffuse the censure.

[1] This I write upon the credit of the author of his life, which was published 1727.

In his *Wanderer*, he has indeed taken an opportunity of mentioning her, but celebrates her not for her virtue, but her beauty, an excellence which none ever denied her: this is the only encomium with which he has rewarded her liberality, and perhaps he has even in this been too lavish of his praise. He seems to have thought, that never to mention his benefactress would have an appearance of ingratitude, though to have dedicated any particular performance to her memory would have only betrayed an officious partiality, that, without exalting her character, would have depressed his own.

He had sometimes, by the kindness of Mr. Wilks, the advantage of a benefit,* on which occasions he often received uncommon marks of regard and compassion; and was once told by the Duke of Dorset,* that it was just to consider him as an injured nobleman, and that in his opinion the nobility ought to think themselves obliged, without solicitation, to take every opportunity of supporting him by their countenance and patronage. But he had generally the mortification to hear that the whole interest of his mother was employed to frustrate his applications, and that she never left any expedient untried, by which he might be cut off from the possibility of supporting life. The same disposition she endeavoured to diffuse among all those over whom nature or fortune gave her any influence, and indeed succeeded too well in her design; but could not always propagate her effrontery with her cruelty, for some of those, whom she incited against him, were ashamed of their own conduct, and boasted of that relief which they never gave him.

In this censure I do not indiscriminately involve all his relations; for he has mentioned with gratitude the humanity of one Lady, whose name I am now unable to recollect, and to whom therefore I cannot pay the praises which she deserves for having acted well in opposition to influence, precept, and example.

The punishment which our laws inflict upon those parents who murder their infants is well known, nor has its justice ever been contested; but if they deserve death who destroy a child in its birth, what pains can be severe enough for her who forbears to destroy him only to inflict sharper miseries upon him; who prolongs his life only to make it miserable; and who exposes him, without care and without pity, to the malice of oppression, the caprices of chance, and the temptations of poverty; who rejoices to see him overwhelmed with calamities; and, when his own industry, or the charity of others, has enabled him to rise for a short time above his miseries, plunges him again into his former distress?

The kindness of his friends not affording him any constant supply, and the prospect of improving his fortune by enlarging his acquaintance necessarily leading him to places of expence, he found it necessary to[1] endeavour once more at dramatic poetry, for which he was now better qualified by a more extensive knowledge, and longer observation. But having been unsuccessful in comedy, though rather for want of opportunities than genius, he resolved now to try whether he should not be more fortunate in exhibiting a tragedy.

The story which he chose for the subject, was that of Sir Thomas Overbury,* a story well adapted to the stage, though perhaps not far enough removed from the present age, to admit properly the fictions necessary to complete the plan: for the mind, which naturally loves truth, is always most offended with the violation of those truths of which we are most certain; and we of course conceive those facts most certain, which approach nearest to our own time.

Out of this story he formed a tragedy, which, if the circumstances in which he wrote it be considered, will afford at once an uncommon proof of strength of genius, and evenness of mind, of a serenity not to be ruffled, and an imagination not to be suppressed.

During a considerable part of the time in which he was employed upon this performance, he was without lodging, and often without meat; nor had he any other conveniences for study than the fields or the street allowed him; there he used to walk and form his speeches, and afterwards step into a shop, beg for a few moments the use of the pen and ink, and and write down what he had composed, upon paper which he had picked up by accident.

If the performance of a writer thus distressed is not perfect, its faults ought surely to be imputed to a cause very different from want of genius, and must rather excite pity than provoke censure.

But when under these discouragements the tragedy was finished, there yet remained the labour of introducing it on the stage, an undertaking, which, to an ingenuous mind, was in a very high degree vexatious and disgusting; for, having little interest or reputation, he was obliged to submit himself wholly to the players, and

[1] In 1724.

admit, with whatever reluctance, the emendations of Mr. Cibber,* which he always considered as the disgrace of his performance.

He had indeed in Mr. Hill* another critic of a very different class, from whose friendship he received great assistance on many occasions, and whom he never mentioned but with the utmost tenderness and regard. He had been for some time distinguished by him with very particular kindness, and on this occasion it was natural to apply to him as an author of an established character. He therefore sent this tragedy to him, with a short copy of[1] verses, in which he desired his correction. Mr. Hill, whose humanity and politeness are generally known, readily complied with his request; but as he is remarkable for singularity of sentiment, and bold experiments in language, Mr. Savage did not think his play much improved by his innovation, and had even at that time the courage to reject several passages which he could not approve; and, what is still more laudable, Mr. Hill had the generosity not to resent the neglect of his alterations, but wrote the prologue and epilogue, in which he touches on the circumstances of the author with great tenderness.

After all these obstructions and compliances, he was only able to bring his play upon the stage in the summer, when the chief actors had retired, and the rest were in possession of the house for their own advantage. Among these, Mr. Savage was admitted to play the part of Sir Thomas Overbury, by which he gained no great reputation, the theatre being a province for which nature seemed not to have designed him; for neither his voice, look, nor gesture, were such as were expected on the stage; and he was so much ashamed of having been reduced to appear as a player, that he always blotted out his name from the list, when a copy of his tragedy was to be shown to his friends.

In the publication of his performance he was more successful, for the rays of genius that glimmered in it, that glimmered through all the mists which poverty and Cibber had been able to spread over it, procured him the notice and esteem of many persons eminent for their rank, their virtue, and their wit.

Of this play, acted, printed, and dedicated, the accumulated profits arose to an hundred pounds, which he thought at that time a very large sum, having been never master of so much before.

[1] Printed in the late collection of his poems.

In the Dedication[1], for which he received ten guineas, there is nothing remarkable. The Preface contains a very liberal encomium on the blooming excellences of Mr. Theophilus Cibber,* which Mr. Savage could not in the latter part of his life see his friends about to read without snatching the play out of their hands. The generosity of Mr. Hill did not end on this occasion; for afterwards, when Mr. Savage's necessities returned, he encouraged a subscription to a Miscellany of Poems in a very extraordinary manner, by publishing his story in the *Plain Dealer*[2], with some affecting lines, which he asserts to have been written by Mr. Savage upon the treatment received by him from his mother, but of which he was himself the author, as Mr. Savage afterwards declared. These lines, and the paper in which they were inserted, had a very powerful effect upon all but his mother, whom, by making her cruelty more public, they only hardened in her aversion.

Mr. Hill not only promoted the subscription to the Miscellany, but furnished likewise the greatest part of the Poems of which it is composed, and particularly *The Happy Man*, which he published as a specimen.

The subscriptions of those whom these papers should influence to patronize merit in distress, without any other solicitation, were directed to be left at Button's coffee-house; and Mr. Savage going thither a few days afterwards, without expectation of any effect from his proposal, found to his surprise seventy guineas[3], which had been sent him in consequence of the compassion excited by Mr. Hill's pathetic representation.

To this Miscellany he wrote a Preface, in which he gives an account of his mother's cruelty in a very uncommon strain of humour, and

[1] To Herbert Tryst, Esq. of Herefordshire.

[2] The *Plain Dealer* was a periodical paper, written by Mr. Hill and Mr. Bond, whom Mr. Savage called the two contending powers of light and darkness. They wrote by turns each six Essays; and the character of the work was observed regularly to rise in Mr. Hill's weeks, and fall in Mr. Bond's.

[3] The names of those who so generously contributed to his relief, having been mentioned in a former account, ought not to be omitted here. They were the Duchess of Cleveland, Lady Cheyney, Lady Castlemain, Lady Gower, Lady Lechmere, the Dutchess Dowager and Dutchess of Rutland, Lady Strafford, the Countess Dowager of Warwick, Mrs. Mary Floyer, Mrs. Sofuel Noel, Duke of Rutland, Lord Gainsborough, Lord Milsington, Mr. John Savage.

with a gaiety of imagination, which the success of his subscription probably produced.

The Dedication is addressed to the Lady Mary Wortley Montague,* whom he flatters without reserve, and, to confess the truth, with very little[1] art. The same observation may be extended to all his Dedications: his compliments are constrained and violent, heaped together without the grace of order, or the decency of introduction: he seems to have written his panegyrics for the perusal only of his patrons, and to have imagined that he had no other task than to pamper them with praises however gross, and that flattery would make its way to the heart, without the assistance of elegance or invention.

Soon afterwards, the death of the king furnished a general subject for a poetical contest, in which Mr. Savage engaged, and is allowed to have carried the prize of honour from his competitors; but I know not whether he gained by his performance any other advantage than the increase of his reputation; though it must certainly have been with farther views that he prevailed upon himself to attempt a species of writing, of which all the topics had been long before exhausted, and which was made at once difficult by the multitudes that had failed in it, and those that had succeeded.

He was now advancing in reputation, and though frequently involved in very distressful perplexities, appeared however to be gaining upon mankind, when both his fame and his life were endangered by an event, of which it is not yet determined, whether it ought to be mentioned as a crime or a calamity.

On the 20th of November 1727, Mr. Savage came from Richmond, where he then lodged, that he might pursue his studies with less interruption, with an intent to discharge another lodging which he had in Westminster; and accidentally meeting two gentlemen his

[1] This the following extract from it will prove.
—"Since our country has been honoured with the glory of your wit, as elevated and immortal as your soul, it no longer remains a doubt whether your sex have strength of mind in proportion to their sweetness. There is something in your verses as distinguished as your air.—They are as strong as truth, as deep as reason, as clear as innocence, and as smooth as beauty.—They contain a nameless and peculiar mixture of force and grace, which is at once so movingly serene, and so majestically lovely, that it is too amiable to appear any where but in your eyes and in your writings.

"As fortune is not more my enemy than I am the enemy of flattery, I know not how I can forbear this application to your Ladyship, because there is scarce a possibility that I should say more than I believe, when I am speaking of your Excellence."

acquaintances, whose names were Merchant and Gregory, he went in with them to a neighbouring coffee-house, and sat drinking till it was late, it being in no time of Mr. Savage's life any part of his character to be the first of the company that desired to separate. He would willingly have gone to bed in the same house; but there was not room for the whole company, and therefore they agreed to ramble about the streets, and divert themselves with such amusements as should offer themselves till morning.*

In their walk they happened unluckily to discover a light in Robinson's coffee-house, near Charing-cross, and therefore went in. Merchant, with some rudeness, demanded a room, and was told that there was a good fire in the next parlour, which the company were about to leave, being then paying their reckoning. Merchant, not satisfied with this answer, rushed into the room, and was followed by his companions. He then petulantly placed himself between the company and the fire, and soon after kicked down the table. This produced a quarrel, swords were drawn on both sides, and one Mr. James Sinclair was killed. Savage, having wounded likewise a maid that held him, forced his way with Merchant out of the house; but being intimidated and confused, without resolution either to fly or stay, they were taken in a back-court by one of the company and some soldiers, whom he had called to his assistance.

Being secured and guarded that night, they were in the morning carried before three justices, who committed them to the Gatehouse, from whence, upon the death of Mr. Sinclair, which happened the same day, they were removed in the night to Newgate, where they were however treated with some distinction, exempted from the ignominy of chains, and confined, not among the common criminals, but in the Press-yard.

When the day of trial came, the court was crowded in a very unusual manner, and the public appeared to interest itself as in a cause of general concern. The witnesses against Mr. Savage and his friends were, the woman who kept the house, which was a house of ill fame, and her maid, the men who were in the room with Mr. Sinclair, and a woman of the town, who had been drinking with them, and with whom one of them had been seen in bed. They swore in general, that Merchant gave the provocation, which Savage and Gregory drew their swords to justify; that Savage drew first, and that he stabbed

Sinclair when he was not in a posture of defence, or while Gregory commanded his sword; that after he had given the thrust he turned pale, and would have retired, but that the maid clung round him, and one of the company endeavoured to detain him, from whom he broke, by cutting the maid on the head, but was afterwards taken in a court.

There was some difference in their depositions; one did not see Savage give the wound, another saw it given when Sinclair held his point towards the ground; and the woman of the town asserted, that she did not see Sinclair's sword at all: this difference however was very far from amounting to inconsistency; but it was sufficient to shew, that the hurry of the dispute was such, that it was not easy to discover the truth with relation to particular circumstances, and that therefore some deductions were to be made from the credibility of the testimonies.

Sinclair had declared several times before his death, that he received his wound from Savage, nor did Savage at his trial deny the fact, but endeavoured partly to extenuate it, by urging the suddenness of the whole action, and the impossibility of any ill design, or premeditated malice, and partly to justify it by the necessity of self-defence, and the hazard of his own life, if he had lost that opportunity of giving the thrust: he observed, that neither reason nor law obliged a man to wait for the blow which was threatened, and which, if he should suffer it, he might never be able to return; that it was always allowable to prevent an assault, and to preserve life by taking away that of the adversary, by whom it was endangered.

With regard to the violence with which he endeavoured to escape, he declared, that it was not his design to fly from justice, or decline a trial, but to avoid the expences and severities of a prison; and that he intended to have appeared at the bar without compulsion.

This defence, which took up more than an hour, was heard by the multitude that thronged the court with the most attentive and respectful silence: those who thought he ought not be acquitted, owned that applause could not be refused him; and those who before pitied his misfortunes, now reverenced his abilities.

The witnesses which appeared against him were proved to be persons of characters which did not entitle them to much credit; a common strumpet, a woman by whom strumpets were entertained, and a man by whom they were supported; and the character of Savage was by several persons of distinction asserted to be that of a modest inoffensive man, not inclined to broils, or to insolence, and who had, to that time, been only known for his misfortunes and his wit.

Had his audience been his judges, he had undoubtedly been accquitted; but Mr. Page,* who was then upon the bench, treated him with his usual insolence and severity, and when he had summed up the evidence, endeavoured to exasperate the jury, as Mr. Savage used to relate it, with this eloquent harangue:

'Gentlemen of the jury, you are to consider that Mr. Savage is a very great man, a much greater man than you or I, gentlemen of the jury; that he wears very fine clothes, much finer clothes than you or I, gentlemen of the jury; that he has abundance of money in his pocket, much more money than you or I, gentlemen of the jury; but, gentlemen of the jury, is it not a very hard case, gentlemen of the jury, that Mr. Savage should therefore kill you or me, gentlemen of the jury?'

Mr. Savage, hearing his defence thus misrepresented, and the men who were to decide his fate incited against him by invidious comparisons, resolutely asserted, that his cause was not candidly explained, and began to recapitulate what he had before said with regard to his condition, and the necessity of endeavouring to escape the expences of imprisonment; but the judge having ordered him to be silent, and repeated his orders without effect, commanded that he should be taken from the bar by force.

The jury then heard the opinion of the judge, that good characters were of no weight against positive evidence, though they might turn the scale where it was doubtful; and that though, when two men attack each other, the death of either is only manslaughter; but where one is the aggressor, as in the case before them, and, in pursuance of his first attack, kills the other, the law supposes the action, however sudden, to be malicious. They then deliberated upon their verdict, and determined that Mr. Savage and Mr. Gregory were guilty of murder, and Mr. Merchant, who had no sword, only of manslaughter.

Thus ended this memorable trial, which lasted eight hours. Mr. Savage and Mr. Gregory were conducted back to prison, where they were more closely confined, and loaded with irons of fifty pounds weight: four days afterwards they were sent back to the court to receive sentence; on which occasion Mr. Savage made, as far as it could be retained in memory, the following speech.

"It is now, my Lord, too late to offer any thing by way of defence or vindication; nor can we expect from your Lordships, in this court, but the sentence which the law requires you, as judges, to pronounce against men of our calamitous condition.—But we are also persuaded, that as mere men, and out of this seat of rigorous justice, you are susceptive of the tender passions, and too humane, not to commiserate the unhappy situation of those, whom the law sometimes perhaps—exacts—from you to pronounce upon. No doubt you distinguish between offences, which arise out of premeditation, and a disposition habituated to vice or immorality, and transgressions, which are the unhappy and unforeseen effects of casual absence of reason, and sudden impulse of passion: we therefore hope you will contribute all you can to an extension of that mercy, which the gentlemen of the jury have been pleased to shew Mr. Merchant, who (allowing facts as sworn against us by the evidence) has led us into this our calamity. I hope this will not be construed, as if we meant to reflect upon that gentleman, or remove any thing from us upon him, or that we repine the more at our fate, because he has no participation of it: No, my Lord! For my part, I declare nothing could more soften my grief, than to be without any companion in so great a misfortune[1]."

Mr. Savage had now no hopes of life, but from the mercy of the crown, which was very earnestly solicited by his friends, and which, with whatever difficulty the story may obtain belief, was obstructed only by his mother.*

To prejudice the Queen against him, she made use of an incident, which was omitted in the order of time, that it might be mentioned together with the purpose which it was made to serve. Mr. Savage, when he had discovered his birth, had an incessant desire to speak to his mother, who always avoided him in publick, and refused him admission into her house. One evening walking, as it was his custom, in the street that she inhabited, he saw the door of her house by accident open; he entered it, and, finding no person in the passage to hinder him, went up stairs to salute her. She discovered him before he could enter her chamber, alarmed the family with the most distressful outcries, and when she had by her screams gathered them about her, ordered them to drive out of the house that villain, who had

[1] Mr. Savage's Life.

forced himself in upon her, and endeavoured to murder her. Savage, who had attempted with the most submissive tenderness to soften her rage, hearing her utter so detestable an accusation, thought it prudent to retire; and, I believe, never attempted afterwards to speak to her.

But, shocked as he was with her falsehood and her cruelty, he imagined that she intended no other use of her lye, than to set herself free from his embraces and solicitations, and was very far from suspecting that she would treasure it in her memory, as an instrument of future wickedness, or that she would endeavour for this fictitious assault to deprive him of his life.

But when the Queen was solicited for his pardon, and informed of the severe treatment which he had suffered from his judge, she answered, that, however unjustifiable might be the manner of his trial, or whatever extenuation the action for which he was condemned might admit, she could not think that man a proper object of the King's mercy, who had been capable of entering his mother's house in the night, with an intent to murder her.

By whom this atrocious calumny had been transmitted to the Queen; whether she that invented had the front to relate it; whether she found any one weak enough to credit it, or corrupt enough to concur with her in her hateful design, I know not: but methods had been taken to persuade the Queen so strongly of the truth of it, that she for a long time refused to hear any of those who petitioned for his life.

Thus had Savage perished by the evidence of a bawd, a strumpet, and his mother, had not justice and compassion procured him an advocate of rank too great to be rejected unheard, and of virtue too eminent to be heard without being believed. His merit and his calamities happened to reach the ear of the Countess of Hertford,* who engaged in his support with all the tenderness that is excited by pity, and all the zeal which is kindled by generosity; and, demanding an audience of the Queen, laid before her the whole series of his mother's cruelty, exposed the improbability of an accusation by which he was charged with an intent to commit a murder that could produce no advantage, and soon convinced her how little his former conduct could deserve to be mentioned as a reason for extraordinary severity.

The interposition of this Lady was so successful, that he was soon after admitted to bail, and, on the 9th of March 1728, pleaded the King's pardon.

It is natural to enquire upon what motives his mother could prosecute him in a manner so outrageous and implacable; for what reason she could employ all the arts of malice, and all the snares of calumny, to take away the life of her own son, of a son who never injured her, who was never supported by her expence, nor obstructed any prospect of pleasure or advantage; why she should endeavour to destroy him by a lye—a lye which could not gain credit, but must vanish of itself at the first moment of examination, and of which only this can be said to make it probable, that it may be observed from her conduct, that the most execrable crimes are sometimes committed without apparent temptation.

This mother is still alive, and may perhaps even yet, though her malice was so often defeated, enjoy the pleasure of reflecting, that the life, which she often endeavoured to destroy, was at least shortened by her maternal offices; that though she could not transport her son to the plantations, bury him in the shop of a mechanic, or hasten the hand of the public executioner, she has yet had the satisfaction of imbittering all his hours, and forcing him into exigences that hurried on his death.

It is by no means necessary to aggravate the enormity of this woman's conduct, by placing it in opposition to that of the Countess of Hertford; no one can fail to observe how much more amiable it is to relieve, than to oppress, and to rescue innocence from destruction, than to destroy without an injury.

Mr. Savage, during his imprisonment, his trial, and the time in which he lay under sentence of death, behaved with great firmness and equality of mind, and confirmed by his fortitude the esteem of those who before admired him for his abilities. The peculiar circumstances of his life were made more generally known by a short account[1], which was then published, and of which several thousands were in a few weeks dispersed over the nation: and the compassion of mankind operated so powerfully in his favour, that he was enabled, by frequent presents, not only to support himself, but to assist Mr. Gregory in prison; and, when

[1] Written by Mr. Beckingham and another gentleman.

he was pardoned and released, he found the number of his friends not lessened.*

The nature of the act for which he had been tried was in itself doubtful; of the evidences which appeared against him, the character of the man was not unexceptionable, that of the woman notoriously infamous: she, whose testimony chiefly influenced the jury to condemn him, afterwards retracted her assertions. He always himself denied that he was drunk, as had been generally reported. Mr. Gregory, who is now Collector of Antigua, is said to declare him far less criminal than he was imagined, even by some who favoured him: and Page himself afterwards confessed, that he had treated him with uncommon rigour. When all these particulars are rated together, perhaps the memory of Savage may not be much sullied by his trial.

Some time after he had obtained his liberty, he met in the street the woman that had sworn with so much malignity against him. She informed him, that she was in distress, and, with a degree of confidence not easily attainable, desired him to relieve her. He, instead of insulting her misery, and taking pleasure in the calamities of one who had brought his life into danger, reproved her gently for her perjury; and changing the only guinea that he had, divided it equally between her and himself.

This is an action which in some ages would have made a saint, and perhaps in others a hero, and which, without any hyperbolical encomiums, must be allowed to be an instance of uncommon generosity, an act of complicated virtue; by which he at once relieved the poor, corrected the vicious, and forgave an enemy; by which he at once remitted the strongest provocations, and exercised the most ardent charity.

Compassion was indeed the distinguishing quality of Savage; he never appeared inclined to take advantage of weakness, to attack the defenceless, or to press upon the falling: whoever was distressed was certain at least of his good wishes; and when he could give no assistance to extricate them from misfortunes, he endeavoured to sooth them by sympathy and tenderness.

But when his heart was not softened by the sight of misery, he was sometimes obstinate in his resentment, and did not quickly lose the remembrance of an injury. He always continued to speak with anger of the insolence and partiality of Page, and a short time before his death revenged it by a satire[1].

It is natural to enquire in what terms Mr. Savage spoke of this fatal action, when the danger was over, and he was under no necessity of using any art to set his conduct in the fairest light. He was not willing to dwell upon it; and, if he transiently mentioned it, appeared neither to consider himself as a murderer, nor as a man wholly free from the guilt of blood[2]. How much and how long he regretted it, appeared in a poem which he published many years afterwards.* On occasion of a copy of verses, in which the failings of good men were recounted, and in which the author had endeavoured to illustrate his position, that "the best may sometimes deviate from virtue," by an instance of murder committed by Savage in the heat of wine, Savage remarked, that it was no very just representation of a good man, to suppose him liable to drunkenness, and disposed in his riots to cut throats.

He was now indeed at liberty, but was, as before, without any other support than accidental favours and uncertain patronage afforded him; sources by which he was sometimes very liberally supplied, and which at other times were suddenly stopped; so that he spent his life between want and plenty; or, what was yet worse, between beggary and extravagance; for as whatever he received was the gift of chance, which might as well favour him at one time as another, he was tempted to squander what he had, because he always hoped to be immediately supplied.

Another cause of his profusion was the absurd kindness of his friends, who at once rewarded and enjoyed his abilities, by treating him at taverns, and habituating him to pleasures which he could not afford to enjoy, and which he was not able to deny himself, though he purchased the luxury of a single night by the anguish of cold and hunger for a week.

The experience of these inconveniences determined him to endeavour after some settled income, which, having long found submission and intreaties fruitless, he attempted to extort from his mother by rougher methods. He had now, as he acknowledged, lost that tenderness for her, which the whole series of her cruelty had not

[1] Printed in the late collection.

[2] In one of his letters he styles it "a fatal quarrel, but too-well known."

been able wholly to repress, till he found, by the efforts which she made for his destruction, that she was not content with refusing to assist him, and being neutral in his struggles with poverty, but was as ready to snatch every opportunity of adding to his misfortunes, and that she was to be considered as an enemy implacably malicious, whom nothing but his blood could satisfy. He therefore threatened to harass her with lampoons, and to publish a copious narrative of her conduct, unless she consented to purchase an exemption from infamy, by allowing him a pension.

This expedient proved successful. Whether shame still survived, though virtue was extinct, or whether her relations had more delicacy than herself, and imagined that some of the darts which satire might point at her would glance upon them; Lord Tyrconnel,* whatever were his motives, upon his promise to lay aside his design of exposing the cruelty of his mother, received him into his family, treated him as his equal, and engaged to allow him a pension of two hundred pounds a year.

This was the golden part of Mr. Savage's life; and for some time he had no reason to complain of fortune; his appearance was splendid, his expences large, and his acquaintance extensive. He was courted by all who endeavoured to be thought men of genius, and caressed by all who valued themselves upon a refined taste. To admire Mr. Savage, was a proof of discernment; and to be acquainted with him, was a title to poetical reputation. His presence was sufficient to make any place of publick entertainment popular; and his approbation and example constituted the fashion. So powerful is genius, when it is invested with the glitter of affluence! Men willingly pay to fortune that regard which they owe to merit, and are pleased when they have an opportunity at once of gratifying their vanity, and practising their duty.

This interval of prosperity furnished him with opportunities of enlarging his knowledge of human nature, by contemplating life from its highest gradations to its lowest; and, had he afterwards applied to dramatick poetry, he would perhaps not have had many superiors; for as he never suffered any scene to pass before his eyes without notice, he had treasured in his mind all the different combinations of passions, and the innumerable mixtures of vice and virtue, which distinguish one character from another; and, as his conception was strong, his expressions were clear, he easily received impressions from objects, and very forcibly transmitted them to others.

Of his exact observations on human life he has left a proof, which would do honour to the greatest names, in a small pamphlet, called, *The Author to be let*[1], where he introduces Iscariot Hackney, a prostitute scribbler, giving an account of his birth, his education, his disposition and morals, habits of life, and maxims of conduct. In the introduction are related many secret histories of the petty writers of that time, but sometimes mixed with ungenerous reflections on their birth, their circumstances, or those of their relations; nor can it be denied, that some passages are such as Iscariot Hackney might himself have produced.

He was accused likewise of living in an appearance of friendship with some whom he satirised, and of making use of the confidence which he gained by a seeming kindness to discover failings and expose them: it must be confessed, that Mr. Savage's esteem was no very certain possession, and that he would lampoon at one time those whom he had praised at another.

It may be alleged, that the same man may change his principles, and that he, who was once deservedly commended, may be afterwards satirised with equal justice, or that the poet was dazzled with the appearance of virtue, and found the man whom he had celebrated, when he had an opportunity of examining him more narrowly, unworthy of the panegyrick which he had too hastily bestowed; and that, as a false satire ought to be recanted, for the sake of him whose reputation may be injured, false praise ought likewise to be obviated, lest the distinction between vice and virtue should be lost, lest a bad man should be trusted upon the credit of his encomiast, or lest others should endeavour to obtain the like praises by the same means.

But though these excuses may be often plausible, and sometimes just, they are very seldom satisfactory to mankind; and the writer, who is not constant to his subject, quickly sinks into contempt, his satire loses its force, and his panegyrick its value, and he is only considered at one time as a flatterer, and as a calumniator at another.

To avoid these imputations, it is only necessary to follow the rules of virtue, and to preserve an unvaried regard to truth. For though it

[1] Printed in his Works, vol. II. p. 231.

is undoubtedly possible, that a man, however cautious, may be sometimes deceived by an artful appearance of virtue, or by false evidences of guilt, such errors will not be frequent; and it will be allowed, that the name of an author would never have been made contemptible, had no man ever said what he did not think, or misled others but when he was himself deceived.

The Author to be let was first published in a single pamphlet, and afterwards inserted in a collection of pieces relating to the Dunciad, which were addressed by Mr. Savage to the Earl of Middlesex, in a[1] dedication which he was prevailed upon to sign, though he did not write it, and in which there are some positions, that the true author would perhaps not have published under his own name, and on which Mr. Savage afterwards reflected with no great satisfaction;* the enumeration of the bad effects of the uncontroled freedom of the press, and the assertion that the "liberties taken by the writers of Journals with their superiors were exorbitant and unjustifiable," very ill became men, who have themselves not always shewn the exactest regard to the laws of subordination in their writings, and who have often satirised those that at least thought themselves their superiors, as they were eminent for their hereditary rank, and employed in the highest offices of the kingdom. But this is only an instance of that partiality which almost every man indulges with regard to himself; the liberty of the press is a blessing when we are inclined to write against others, and a calamity when we find ourselves overborne by the multitude of our assailants; as the power of the crown is always thought too great by those who suffer by its influence, and too little by those in whose favour it is exerted; and a standing army is generally accounted necessary by those who command, and dangerous and oppressive by those who support it.

Mr. Savage was likewise very far from believing, that the letters annexed to each species of bad poets in the Bathos, were, as he was directed to assert, "set down at random;"* for when he was charged by one of his friends with putting his name to such an improbability, he had no other answer to make, than that "he did not think of it;" and his friend had too much tenderness to reply, that next to the crime of writing contrary to what he thought, was that of writing without thinking.

[1] See his Works, vol. II. p. 233.

After having remarked what is false in this dedication, it is proper that I observe the impartiality which I recommend, by declaring what Savage asserted, that the account of the circumstances which attended the publication of the Dunciad, however strange and improbable, was exactly true.

The publication of this piece at this time raised Mr. Savage a great number of enemies among those that were attacked by Mr. Pope, with whom he was considered as a kind of confederate, and whom he was suspected of supplying with private intelligence and secret incidents: so that the ignominy of an informer was added to the terror of a satirist.

That he was not altogether free from literary hypocrisy, and that he sometimes spoke one thing, and wrote another, cannot be denied; because he himself confessed, that, when he lived in great familiarity with Dennis,* he wrote an epigram[1] against him.

Mr. Savage however set all the malice of all the pigmy writers at defiance, and thought the friendship of Mr. Pope cheaply purchased by being exposed to their censure and their hatred; nor had he any reason to repent of the preference, for he found Mr. Pope a steady and unalienable friend almost to the end of his life.

About this time, notwithstanding his avowed neutrality with regard to party, he published a panegyrick on Sir Robert Walpole,* for which he was rewarded by him with twenty guineas, a sum not very large, if either the excellence of the performance, or the affluence of the patron be considered; but greater than he afterwards obtained from a person of yet higher rank, and more desirous in appearance of being distinguished as a patron of literature.

As he was very far from approving the conduct of Sir Robert Walpole, and in conversation mentioned him sometimes with acrimony, and generally with contempt; as he was one of those who were

[1] This epigram was, I believe, never published.

> Should Dennis publish you had stabb'd your brother,
> Lampoon'd your monarch, or debauch'd your mother;
> Say, what revenge on Dennis can be had,
> Too dull for laughter, for reply too mad?
> On one so poor you cannot take the law,
> On one so old your sword you scorn to draw.
> Uncag'd then, let the harmless monster rage,
> Secure in dulness, madness, want, and age.

always zealous in their assertions of the justice of the late opposition, jealous of the rights of the people, and alarmed by the long-continued triumph of the court; it was natural to ask him what could induce him to employ his poetry in praise of that man who was, in his opinion, an enemy to liberty, and an oppressor of his country? He alleged, that he was then dependent upon the Lord Tyrconnel, who was an implicit follower of the ministry; and that being enjoined by him, not without menaces, to write in praise of his leader, he had not resolution sufficient to sacrifice the pleasure of affluence to that of integrity.

On this, and on many other occasions, he was ready to lament the misery of living at the tables of other men, which was his fate from the beginning to the end of his life; for I know not whether he ever had, for three months together, a settled habitation, in which he could claim a right of residence.

To this unhappy state it is just to impute much of the inconstancy of his conduct; for though a readiness to comply with the inclination of others was no part of his natural character, yet he was sometimes obliged to relax his obstinacy, and submit his own judgement, and even his virtue, to the government of those by whom he was supported: so that, if his miseries were sometimes the consequences of his faults, he ought not yet to be wholly excluded from compassion, because his faults were very often the effects of his misfortunes.

In this gay period[1] of his life, while he was surrounded by affluence and pleasure, he published *The Wanderer*, a moral poem, of which the design is comprised in these lines:

> I fly all public care, all venal strife,
> To try the still compar'd with active life;
> To prove, by these the sons of men may owe
> The fruits of bliss to bursting clouds of woe;
> That ev'n calamity, by thought refin'd,
> Inspirits and adorns the thinking mind.*

And more distinctly in the following passage:

> By woe, the soul to daring action swells;
> By woe, in plaintless patience it excels;

[1] 1729.

From patience, prudent clear experience springs,
And traces knowledge thro' the course of things!
Thence hope is form'd, thence fortitude, success,
Renown:—whate'er men covet and caress.*

This performance was always considered by himself as his masterpiece; and Mr. Pope, when he asked his opinion of it, told him, that he read it once over, and was not displeased with it, that it gave him more pleasure at the second perusal, and delighted him still more at the third.

It has been generally objected to *The Wanderer*, that the disposition of the parts is irregular; that the design is obscure, and the plan perplexed; that the images, however beautiful, succeed each other without order; and that the whole performance is not so much a regular fabrick, as a heap of shining materials thrown together by accident, which strikes rather with the solemn magnificence of a stupendous ruin, than the elegant grandeur of a finished pile.

This criticism is universal, and therefore it is reasonable to believe it at least in a great degree just; but Mr. Savage was always of a contrary opinion, and thought his drift could only be missed by negligence or stupidity, and that the whole plan was regular, and the parts distinct.

It was never denied to abound with strong representations of nature, and just observations upon life; and it may easily be observed, that most of his pictures have an evident tendency to illustrate his first great position, "that good is the consequence of evil." The sun that burns up the mountains, fructifies the vales; the deluge that rushes down the broken rocks with dreadful impetuosity, is separated into purling brooks; and the rage of the hurricane purifies the air.

Even in this poem he has not been able to forbear one touch upon the cruelty of his mother, which, though remarkably delicate and tender, is a proof how deep an impression it had upon his mind.

This must be at least acknowledged, which ought to be thought equivalent to many other excellences, that this poem can promote no other purposes than those of virtue, and that it is written with a very strong sense of the efficacy of religion.

But my province is rather to give the history of Mr. Savage's performances, than to display their beauties, or to obviate the criticisms which they have occasioned; and therefore I shall not dwell upon the particular passages which deserve applause: I shall neither shew the excellence of his descriptions, nor expatiate on the terrifick portrait of suicide, nor point out the artful touches, by which he has distinguished the intellectual features of the rebels, who suffer death in his last canto. It is, however, proper to observe, that Mr. Savage always declared the characters wholly fictitious, and without the least allusion to any real persons or actions.

From a poem so diligently laboured, and so successfully finished, it might be reasonably expected that he should have gained considerable advantage; nor can it, without some degree of indignation and concern, be told, that he sold the copy for ten guineas, of which he afterwards returned two, that the two last sheets of the work might be reprinted, of which he had in his absence intrusted the correction to a friend, who was too indolent to perform it with accuracy.

A superstitious regard to the correction of his sheets was one of Mr. Savage's peculiarities: he often altered, revised, recurred to his first reading or punctuation, and again adopted the alteration; he was dubious and irresolute without end, as on a question of the last importance, and at last was seldom satisfied: the intrusion or omission of a comma was sufficient to discompose him, and he would lament an error of a single letter as a heavy calamity. In one of his letters relating to an impression of some verses, he remarks, that he had, with regard to the correction of the proof, "a spell upon him;" and indeed the anxiety with which he dwelt upon the minutest and most trifling niceties, deserved no other name than that of fascination.

That he sold so valuable a performance for so small a price, was not to be imputed either to necessity, by which the learned and ingenious are often obliged to submit to very hard conditions; or to avarice, by which the booksellers are frequently incited to oppress that genius by which they are supported; but to that intemperate desire of pleasure, and habitual slavery to his passions, which involved him in many perplexities. He happened at that time to be engaged in the pursuit of some trifling gratification, and, being without money for the present occasion, sold his poem to the first bidder, and perhaps for the first price that was proposed, and would probably have been content with less, if less had been offered him.

This poem was addressed to the Lord Tyrconnel, not only in the first lines, but in a formal dedication filled with the highest strains of panegyrick, and the warmest professions of gratitude, but by no means remarkable for delicacy of connection or elegance of style.

These praises in a short time he found himself inclined to retract, being discarded by the man on whom he had bestowed them, and whom he then immediately discovered not to have deserved them. Of this quarrel, which every day made more bitter, Lord Tyrconnel and Mr. Savage assigned very different reasons, which might perhaps all in reality concur, though they were not all convenient to be alleged by either party. Lord Tyrconnel affirmed, that it was the constant practice of Mr. Savage to enter a tavern with any company that proposed it, drink the most expensive wines with great profusion, and when the reckoning was demanded, to be without money: If, as it often happened, his company were willing to defray his part, the affair ended, without any ill consequences; but, if they were refractory, and expected that the wine should be paid for by him that drank it, his method of composition was, to take them with him to his own apartment, assume the government of the house, and order the butler in an imperious manner to set the best wine in the cellar before his company, who often drank till they forgot the respect due to the house in which they were entertained, indulged themselves in the utmost extravagance of merriment, practised the most licentious frolicks, and committed all the outrages of drunkenness.

Nor was this the only charge which Lord Tyrconnel brought against him: Having given him a collection of valuable books, stamped with his own arms, he had the mortification to see them in a short time exposed to sale upon the stalls, it being usual with Mr. Savage, when he wanted a small sum, to take his books to the pawnbroker.

Whoever was acquainted with Mr. Savage easily credited both these accusations: for, having been obliged, from his first entrance into the world, to subsist upon expedients, affluence was not able to exalt him above them; and so much was he delighted with wine and conversation, and so long had he been accustomed to live by chance, that he would at any time go to the tavern without scruple, and trust for his reckoning to the liberality of his company, and frequently of company to whom he was very little known. This conduct indeed very seldom drew upon him those inconveniences that might be feared by any other person; for his conversation was so entertaining, and his address so pleasing, that few thought the pleasure which they received from him dearly purchased, by paying for his wine. It was his peculiar happiness, that he scarcely ever found a stranger, whom he did not leave a friend; but it must likewise be added, that he had not often a friend long, without obliging him to become a stranger.

Mr. Savage, on the other hand, declared, that Lord Tyrconnel[1] quarrelled with him, because he would not substract from his own luxury and extravagance what he had promised to allow him, and that his resentment was only a plea for the violation of his promise: He asserted, that he had done nothing that ought to exclude him from that subsistence which he thought not so much a favour, as a debt, since it was offered him upon conditions, which he had never broken; and that his only fault was, that he could not be supported with nothing.

He acknowledged, that Lord Tyrconnel often exhorted him to regulate his method of life, and not to spend all his nights in taverns, and that he appeared very desirous, that he would pass those hours with him, which he so freely bestowed upon others. This demand Mr. Savage considered as a censure of his conduct, which he could never patiently bear; and which, in the latter and cooler part of his life, was so offensive to him, that he declared it as his resolution, "to spurn that friend who should presume to dictate to him;" and it is not likely, that in his earlier years he received admonitions with more calmness.

He was likewise inclined to resent such expectations, as tending to infringe his liberty, of which he was very jealous, when it was necessary to the gratification of his passions; and declared, that the request was still more unreasonable, as the company to which he was to have been confined was insupportably disagreeable. This assertion affords another instance of that inconsistency of his writings with his conversation, which was so often to be observed. He forgot how lavishly he had, in his Dedication to *The Wanderer*, extolled the delicacy and penetration, the humanity and generosity, the candour and politeness, of the man, whom, when he no longer loved him, he declared to be a wretch without understanding, without good-nature, and without justice; of whose name he thought himself obliged to leave no trace in any future edition of his writings;

[1] His expression in one of his letters was, "that Lord Tyrconnel had involved his estate, and therefore poorly sought an occasion to quarrel with him."

and accordingly blotted it out of that copy of *The Wanderer* which was in his hands.

During his continuance with the Lord Tyrconnel, he wrote *The Triumph of Health and Mirth*, on the recovery of Lady Tyrconnel from a languishing illness. This performance is remarkable, not only for the gaiety of the ideas, and the melody of the numbers, but for the agreeable fiction upon which it is formed. Mirth, overwhelmed with sorrow for the sickness of her favourite, takes a flight in quest of her sister Health, whom she finds reclined upon the brow of a lofty mountain, amidst the fragrance of perpetual spring, with the breezes of the morning sporting about her. Being solicited by her sister Mirth, she readily promises her assistance, flies away in a cloud, and impregnates the waters of Bath with new virtues, by which the sickness of Belinda is relieved.

As the reputation of his abilities, the particular circumstances of his birth and life, the splendour of his appearance, and the distinction which was for some time paid him by Lord Tyrconnel, intitled him to familiarity with persons of higher rank than those to whose conversation he had been before admitted, he did not fail to gratify that curiosity, which induced him to take a nearer view of those whom their birth, their employments, or their fortunes, necessarily place at a distance from the greatest part of mankind, and to examine whether their merit was magnified or diminished by the medium through which it was contemplated; whether the splendour with which they dazzled their admirers was inherent in themselves, or only reflected on them by the objects that surrounded them; and whether great men were selected for high stations, or high stations made great men.

For this purpose he took all opportunities of conversing familiarly with those who were most conspicuous at that time for their power or their influence; he watched their looser moments, and examined their domestick behaviour, with that acuteness which nature had given him, and which the uncommon variety of his life had contributed to increase, and that inquisitiveness which must always be produced in a vigorous mind, by an absolute freedom from all pressing or domestick engagements. His discernment was quick, and therefore he soon found in every person, and in every affair, something that deserved attention; he was supported by others, without any care for himself, and was therefore at leisure to pursue his observations.

More circumstances to constitute a critick on human life could not easily concur; nor indeed could any man, who assumed from accidental advantages more praise than he could justly claim from his real merit, admit an acquaintance more dangerous than that of Savage; of whom likewise it must be confessed, that abilities really exalted above the common level, or virtue refined from passion, or proof against corruption, could not easily find an abler judge, or a warmer advocate.

What was the result of Mr. Savage's enquiry, though he was not much accustomed to conceal his discoveries, it may not be entirely safe to relate, because the persons whose characters he criticised are powerful; and power and resentment are seldom strangers; nor would it perhaps be wholly just, because what he asserted in conversation might, though true in general, be heightened by some momentary ardour of imagination, and, as it can be delivered only from memory, may be imperfectly represented; so that the picture at first aggravated, and then unskilfully copied, may be justly suspected to retain no great resemblance of the original.

It may however be observed, that he did not appear to have formed very elevated ideas of those to whom the administration of affairs, or the conduct of parties, has been intrusted; who have been considered as the advocates of the crown, or the guardians of the people; and who have obtained the most implicit confidence, and the loudest applauses. Of one particular person, who has been at one time so popular as to be generally esteemed, and at another so formidable as to be universally detested, he observed, that his acquisitions had been small, or that his capacity was narrow, and that the whole range of his mind was from obscenity to politicks, and from politicks to obscenity.

But the opportunity of indulging his speculations on great characters was now at an end. He was banished from the table of Lord Tyrconnel, and turned again adrift upon the world, without prospect of finding quickly any other harbour. As prudence was not one of the virtues by which he was distinguished, he had made no provision against a misfortune like this. And though it is not to be imagined but that the separation must for some time have been preceded by coldness, peevishness, or neglect, though it was undoubtedly the consequence of accumulated provocations on both sides; yet every one that knew Savage will readily believe, that to him it was sudden as a stroke of thunder; that, though he might have transiently suspected it, he had never suffered any thought so unpleasing to sink into his mind, but that he had driven it away by amusements, or dreams of future felicity and affluence, and had never taken any measures by which he might prevent a precipitation from plenty to indigence.

This quarrel and separation, and the difficulties to which Mr. Savage was exposed by them, were soon known both to his friends and enemies; nor was it long before he perceived, from the behaviour of both, how much is added to the lustre of genius by the ornaments of wealth.

His condition did not appear to excite much compassion; for he had not always been careful to use the advantages he enjoyed with that moderation which ought to have been with more than usual caution preserved by him, who knew, if he had reflected, that he was only a dependant on the bounty of another, whom he could expect to support him no longer than he endeavoured to preserve his favour by complying with his inclinations, and whom he nevertheless set at defiance, and was continually irritating by negligence or encroachments.

Examples need not be sought at any great distance to prove, that superiority of fortune has a natural tendency to kindle pride, and that pride seldom fails to exert itself in contempt and insult; and if this is often the effect of hereditary wealth, and of honours enjoyed only by the merit of others, it is some extenuation of any indecent triumphs to which this unhappy man may have been betrayed, that his prosperity was heightened by the force of novelty, and made more intoxicating by a sense of the misery in which he had so long languished, and perhaps of the insults which he had formerly borne, and which he might now think himself entitled to revenge. It is too common for those who have unjustly suffered pain, to inflict it likewise in their turn with the same injustice, and to imagine that they have a right to treat others as they have themselves been treated.

That Mr. Savage was too much elevated by any good fortune, is generally known; and some passages of his Introduction to

The Author to be let sufficiently shew, that he did not wholly refrain from such satire as he afterwards thought very unjust, when he was exposed to it himself; for when he was afterwards ridiculed in the character of a distressed poet, he very easily discovered, that distress was not a proper subject for merriment, or topick of invective. He was then able to discern, that, if misery be the effect of virtue, it ought to be reverenced; if of ill-fortune, to be pitied; and if of vice, not to be insulted, because it is perhaps itself a punishment adequate to the crime by which it was produced. And the humanity of that man can deserve no panegyrick, who is capable of reproaching a criminal in the hands of the executioner.

But these reflections, though they readily occurred to him in the first and last parts of his life, were, I am afraid, for a long time forgotten; at least they were, like many other maxims, treasured up in his mind, rather for shew than use, and operated very little upon his conduct, however elegantly he might sometimes explain, or however forcibly he might inculcate, them.

His degradation therefore from the condition which he had enjoyed with such wanton thoughtlessness, was considered by many as an occasion of triumph. Those who had before paid their court to him without success, soon returned the contempt which they had suffered; and they who had received favours from him, for of such favours as he could bestow he was very liberal, did not always remember them. So much more certain are the effects of resentment than of gratitude: it is not only to many more pleasing to recollect those faults which place others below them, than those virtues by which they are themselves comparatively depressed; but it is likewise more easy to neglect, than to recompense; and though there are few who will practise a laborious virtue, there will never be wanting multitudes that will indulge an easy vice.

Savage, however, was very little disturbed at the marks of contempt which his ill-fortune brought upon him, from those whom he never esteemed, and with whom he never considered himself as levelled by any calamities: and though it was not without some uneasiness that he saw some, whose friendship he valued, change their behaviour; he yet observed their coldness without much emotion, considered them as the slaves of fortune and the worshippers of prosperity, and was more inclined to despise them, than to lament himself.

It does not appear that, after this return of his wants, he found mankind equally favourable to him, as at his first appearance in the world. His story, though in reality not less melancholy, was less affecting, because it was no longer new; it therefore procured him no new friends; and those that had formerly relieved him, thought they might now consign him to others. He was now likewise considered by many rather as criminal, than as unhappy; for the friends of Lord Tyrconnel, and of his mother, were sufficiently industrious to publish his weaknesses, which were indeed very numerous; and nothing was forgotten, that might make him either hateful or ridiculous.

It cannot but be imagined, that such representations of his faults must make great numbers less sensible of his distress; many, who had only an opportunity to hear one part, made no scruple to propagate the account which they received; many assisted their circulation from malice or revenge; and perhaps many pretended to credit them, that they might with a better grace withdraw their regard, or withhold their assistance.

Savage however was not one of those, who suffered himself to be injured without resistance, nor was less diligent in exposing the faults of Lord Tyrconnel, over whom he obtained at least this advantage, that he drove him first to the practice of outrage and violence; for he was so much provoked by the wit and virulence of Savage, that he came with a number of attendants, that did no honour to his courage, to beat him at a coffee-house. But it happened that he had left the place a few minutes, and his lordship had, without danger, the pleasure of boasting how he would have treated him. Mr. Savage went next day to repay his visit at his own house; but was prevailed on, by his domesticks, to retire without insisting upon seeing him.

Lord Tyrconnel was accused by Mr. Savage of some actions, which scarcely any provocations will be thought sufficient to justify; such as seizing what he had in his lodgings, and other instances of wanton cruelty, by which he increased the distress of Savage, without any advantage to himself.

These mutual accusations were retorted on both sides, for many years,* with the utmost degree of virulence and rage; and time seemed rather to augment than diminish their resentment. That the anger of Mr. Savage should be kept alive, is not strange, because he felt every day the consequences of the quarrel; but it might reasonably have been hoped, that Lord Tyrconnel might have relented, and at length have forgot those provocations, which, however they might have once inflamed him, had not in reality much hurt him.

The spirit of Mr. Savage indeed never suffered him to solicit a reconciliation; he returned reproach for reproach, and insult for insult; his superiority of wit supplied the disadvantages of his fortune, and enabled him to form a party, and prejudice great numbers in his favour.

But though this might be some gratification of his vanity, it afforded very little relief to his necessities; and he was very frequently reduced to uncommon hardships, of which, however, he never made any mean or importunate complaints, being formed rather to bear misery with fortitude, than enjoy prosperity with moderation.

He now thought himself again at liberty to expose the cruelty of his mother, and therefore, I believe, about this time, published *The Bastard*, a poem remarkable for the vivacious sallies of thought in the beginning, where he makes a pompous enumeration of the imaginary advantages of base birth; and the pathetick sentiments at the end, where he recounts the real calamities which he suffered by the crime of his parents.

The vigour and spirit of the verses, the peculiar circumstances of the author, the novelty of the subject, and the notoriety of the story to which the allusions are made, procured this performance a very favourable reception; great numbers were immediately dispersed, and editions were multiplied with unusual rapidity.

One circumstance attended the publication, which Savage used to relate with great satisfaction. His mother, to whom the poem was with "due reverence" inscribed, happened then to be at Bath, where she could not conveniently retire from censure, or conceal herself from observation; and no sooner did the reputation of the poem begin to spread, than she heard it repeated in all places of concourse, nor could she enter the assembly-rooms, or cross the walks, without being saluted with some lines from *The Bastard*.

This was perhaps the first time that ever she discovered a sense of shame, and on this occasion the power of wit was very conspicuous; the wretch who had, without scruple, proclaimed herself an adulteress, and who had first endeavoured to starve her son, then to transport him, and afterwards to hang him, was not able to bear the representation of her own conduct; but fled from reproach, though she felt no pain from guilt, and left Bath with the utmost haste, to shelter herself among the crowds of London.

Thus Savage had the satisfaction of finding, that, though he could not reform his mother, he could punish her, and that he did not always suffer alone.

The pleasure which he received from this increase of his poetical reputation, was sufficient for some time to overbalance the miseries of want, which this performance did not much alleviate; for it was sold for a very trivial sum to a bookseller, who, though the success was so uncommon that five impressions were sold, of which many were undoubtedly very numerous, had not generosity sufficient to admit the unhappy writer to any part of the profit.

The sale of this poem was always mentioned by Savage with the utmost elevation of heart, and referred to by him as an incontestable proof of a general acknowledgement of his abilities. It was indeed the only production of which he could justly boast a general reception.

But though he did not lose the opportunity which success gave him, of setting a high rate on his abilities, but paid due deference to the suffrages of mankind when they were given in his favour, he did not suffer his esteem of himself to depend upon others, nor found any thing sacred in the voice of the people when they were inclined to censure him; he then readily shewed the folly of expecting that the publick should judge right, observed how slowly poetical merit had often forced its way into the world; he contented himself with the applause of men of judgement, and was somewhat disposed to exclude all those from the character of men of judgement who did not applaud him.

But he was at other times more favourable to mankind than to think them blind to the beauties of his works, and imputed the slowness of their sale to other causes; either they were published at a time when the town was empty, or when the attention of the publick was engrossed by some struggle in the parliament, or some other object of general concern; or they were by the neglect of the publisher not diligently dispersed, or by his avarice not advertised with sufficient frequency. Address, or industry, or liberality, was always wanting; and the blame was laid rather on any person than the author.

By arts like these, arts which every man practises in some degree; and to which too much of the little tranquillity of life is to be ascribed, Savage was always able to live at peace with himself.

Had he indeed only made use of these expedients to alleviate the loss or want of fortune or reputation, or any other advantages, which it is not in man's power to bestow upon himself, they might have been justly mentioned as instances of a philosophical mind, and very properly proposed to the imitation of multitudes, who, for want of diverting their imaginations with the same dexterity, languish under afflictions which might be easily removed.

It were doubtless to be wished, that truth and reason were universally prevalent; that every thing were esteemed according to its real value; and that men would secure themselves from being disappointed in their endeavours after happiness, by placing it only in virtue, which is always to be obtained; but if adventitious and foreign pleasures must be pursued, it would be perhaps of some benefit, since that pursuit must frequently be fruitless, if the practice of Savage could be taught, that folly might be an antidote to folly, and one fallacy be obviated by another.

But the danger of this pleasing intoxication must not be concealed; nor indeed can any one, after having observed the life of Savage, need to be cautioned against it. By imputing none of his miseries to himself, he continued to act upon the same principles, and to follow the same path; was never made wiser by his sufferings, nor preserved by one misfortune from falling into another. He proceeded throughout his life to tread the same steps on the same circle; always applauding his past conduct, or at least forgetting it, to amuse himself with phantoms of happiness, which were dancing before him; and willingly turned his eyes from the light of reason, when it would have discovered the illusion, and shewn him, what he never wished to see, his real state.

He is even accused, after having lulled his imagination with those ideal opiates, of having tried the same experiment upon his conscience; and, having accustomed himself to impute all deviations from the right to foreign causes, it is certain that he was upon every occasion too easily reconciled to himself, and that he appeared very little to regret those practices which had impaired his reputation. The reigning error of his life was, that he mistook the love for the practice of virtue, and was indeed not so much a good man, as the friend of goodness.

This at least must be allowed him, that he always preserved a strong sense of the dignity, the beauty, and the necessity of virtue, and that he never contributed deliberately to spread corruption amongst mankind. His actions, which were generally precipitate, were often blameable; but his writings, being the productions of study, uniformly tended to the exaltation of the mind, and the propagation of morality and piety.

These writings may improve mankind, when his failings shall be forgotten; and therefore he must be considered, upon the whole, as a benefactor to the world; nor can his personal example do any hurt, since, whoever hears of his faults, will hear of the miseries which they brought upon him, and which would deserve less pity, had not his condition been such as made his faults pardonable. He may be considered as a child exposed to all the temptations of indigence, at an age when resolution was not yet strengthened by conviction, nor virtue confirmed by habit; a circumstance which in his *Bastard* he laments in a very affecting manner:

——No Mother's care
Shielded my infant innocence with prayer:
No Father's guardian-hand my youth maintain'd,
Call'd forth my virtues, or from vice restrain'd.*

The Bastard, however it might provoke or mortify his mother, could not be expected to melt her to compassion, so that he was still under the same want of the necessities of life; and he therefore exerted all the interest which his wit, or his birth, or his misfortunes, could procure, to obtain, upon the death of Eusden,* the place of Poet Laureat, and prosecuted his application with so much diligence, that the King publickly declared it his intention to bestow it upon him; but such was the fate of Savage, that even the King, when he intended his advantage, was disappointed in his schemes; for the Lord Chamberlain,* who has the disposal of the laurel, as one of the appendages of his office, either did not know the King's design, or did not approve it, or thought the nomination of the Laureat an encroachment upon his rights, and therefore bestowed the laurel upon Colley Cibber.

Mr. Savage, thus disappointed, took a resolution of applying to the queen, that, having once given him life, she would enable him to support it, and therefore published a short poem on her birth-day, to which he gave the odd title of *Volunteer Laureat*.* The event of this essay he has himself related in the following letter,* which he prefixed to the poem, when he afterwards reprinted it in *The Gentleman's Magazine*, from whence I have copied it intire[1], as this was one of the few attempts in which Mr. Savage succeeded.

"Mr. Urban,

"In your Magazine for February you published the last *Volunteer Laureat*, written on a very melancholy occasion, the death of the royal patroness of arts and literature in general, and of the author of that poem in particular; I now send you the first that Mr. Savage wrote under that title.—This gentleman, notwithstanding a very considerable interest, being, on the death of Mr. Eusden, disappointed of the Laureat's place, wrote the before-mentioned poem; which was no sooner published, but the late Queen sent to a bookseller for it: the author had not at that time a friend either to get him introduced, or his poem presented at court; yet such was the unspeakable goodness of that Princess, that notwithstanding this act of ceremony was wanting, in a few days after publication, Mr. Savage received a Bank-bill of fifty pounds, and a gracious message from her Majesty, by the Lord North and Guilford, to this effect; "That her Majesty was highly pleased with the verses; that she took particularly kind his lines there relating to the King; that he had permission to write annually on the same subject; and that he should yearly receive the like present, till something better (which was her Majesty's intention) could be done for him." After this, he was permitted to present one of his annual poems to her Majesty, had the honour of kissing her hand, and met with the most gracious reception. Yours, &c."

Such was the performance, and such its reception; a reception which, though by no means unkind, was yet not in the highest degree generous: to chain down the genius of a writer to an annual panegyric, shewed in the Queen too much desire of hearing her own praises, and a greater regard to herself than to him on whom her bounty was conferred. It was a kind of avaricious generosity, by which flattery was rather purchased, than genius rewarded.

Mrs. Oldfield had formerly given him the same allowance with much more heroic intention; she had no other view than to enable him to prosecute his studies, and to set himself above the want of

[1] The poem is inserted in the late collection.

assistance, and was contented with doing good without stipulating for encomiums.

Mr. Savage however was not at liberty to make exceptions, but was ravished with the favours which he had received, and probably yet more with those which he was promised; he considered himself now as a favourite of the Queen, and did not doubt but a few annual poems would establish him in some profitable employment.

He therefore assumed the title of *Volunteer Laureat*, not without some reprehensions from Cibber, who informed him, that the title of *Laureat* was a mark of honour conferred by the King, from whom all honour is derived, and which therefore no man has a right to bestow upon himself; and added, that he might, with equal propriety, style himself a Volunteer Lord, or Volunteer Baronet. It cannot be denied that the remark was just; but Savage did not think any title, which was conferred upon Mr. Cibber, so honourable as that the usurpation of it could be imputed to him as an instance of very exorbitant vanity, and therefore continued to write under the same title, and received every year the same reward.

He did not appear to consider these encomiums as tests of his abilities, or as any thing more than annual hints to the Queen of her promise, or acts of ceremony, by the performance of which he was intitled to his pension, and therefore did not labour them with great diligence, or print more than fifty each year, except that for some of the last years he regularly inserted them in *The Gentleman's Magazine*, by which they were dispersed over the kingdom.

Of some of them he had himself so low an opinion, that he intended to omit them in the collection of poems, for which he printed proposals, and solicited subscriptions; nor can it seem strange, that, being confined to the same subject, he should be at some times indolent, and at others unsuccessful; that he should sometimes delay a disagreeable task, till it was too late to perform it well; or that he should sometimes repeat the same sentiment on the same occasion, or at others be misled by an attempt after novelty to forced conceptions and far-fetched images.

He wrote indeed with a double intention, which supplied him with some variety; for his business was to praise the Queen for the favours which he had received, and to complain to her of the delay of those which she had promised: in some of his pieces, therefore, gratitude is predominant, and in some discontent; in some he represents himself as happy in her patronage, and in others as disconsolate to find himself neglected.

Her promise, like other promises made to this unfortunate man, was never performed, though he took sufficient care that it should not be forgotten. The publication of his *Volunteer Laureat* procured him no other reward than a regular remittance of fifty pounds.

He was not so depressed by his disappointments as to neglect any opportunity that was offered of advancing his interest. When the Princess Anne was married, he wrote a poem[1] upon her departure,* only, as he declared, "because it was expected from him," and he was not willing to bar his own prospects by any appearance of neglect.

He never mentioned any advantage gained by this poem, or any regard that was paid to it; and therefore it is likely that it was considered at court as an act of duty to which he was obliged by his dependence, and which it was therefore not necessary to reward by any new favour: or perhaps the Queen really intended his advancement, and therefore thought it superfluous to lavish presents upon a man whom she intended to establish for life.

About this time not only his hopes were in danger of being frustrated, but his pension likewise of being obstructed, by an accidental calumny. The writer of *The Daily Courant*,* a paper then published under the direction of the ministry, charged him with a crime, which, though not very great in itself, would have been remarkably invidious in him, and might very justly have incensed the Queen against him. He was accused by name of influencing elections against the court, by appearing at the head of a tory mob; nor did the accuser fail to aggravate his crime, by representing it as the effect of the most atrocious ingratitude, and a kind of rebellion against the Queen, who had first preserved him from an infamous death, and afterwards distinguished him by her favour, and supported him by her charity. The charge, as it was open and confident, was likewise by good fortune very particular. The place of the transaction was mentioned, and the whole series of the rioter's conduct related. This exactness made Mr. Savage's vindication easy; for he never had in his life seen the place which was declared to be the scene of his wickedness, nor ever had been present in any

[1] Printed in the late collection.

town when its representatives were chosen. This answer he therefore made haste to publish, with all the circumstances necessary to make it credible; and very reasonably demanded, that the accusation should be retracted in the same paper, that he might no longer suffer the imputation of sedition and ingratitude. This demand was likewise pressed by him in a private letter to the author of the paper, who, either trusting to the protection of those whose defence he had undertaken, or having entertained some personal malice against Mr. Savage, or fearing, lest, by retracting so confident an assertion, he should impair the credit of his paper, refused to give him that satisfaction.

Mr. Savage therefore thought it necessary, to his own vindication, to prosecute him in the King's Bench; but as he did not find any ill effects from the accusation, having sufficiently cleared his innocence, he thought any farther procedure would have the appearance of revenge; and therefore willingly dropped it.

He saw soon afterwards a process commenced in the same court against himself, on an information in which he was accused of writing and publishing an obscene pamphlet.

It was always Mr. Savage's desire to be distinguished; and, when any controversy became popular, he never wanted some reason for engaging in it with great ardour, and appearing at the head of the party which he had chosen. As he was never celebrated for his prudence, he had no sooner taken his side, and informed himself of the chief topicks of the dispute, than he took all opportunities of asserting and propagating his principles, without much regard to his own interest, or any other visible design than that of drawing upon himself the attention of mankind.

The dispute between the bishop of London and the chancellor is well known to have been for some time the chief topick of political conversation;* and therefore Mr. Savage, in pursuance of his character, endeavoured to become conspicuous among the controvertists with which every coffee-house was filled on that occasion. He was an indefatigable opposer of all the claims of ecclesiastical power, though he did not know on what they were founded; and was therefore no friend to the Bishop of London. But he had another reason for appearing as a warm advocate for Dr. Rundle; for he was the friend of Mr. Foster and Mr. Thomson,* who were the friends of Mr. Savage.

Thus remote was his interest in the question, which however, as he imagined, concerned him so nearly, that it was not sufficient to harangue and dispute, but necessary likewise to write upon it.

He therefore engaged with great ardour in a new Poem, called by him, *The Progress of a Divine*; in which he conducts a profligate priest by all the gradations of wickedness from a poor curacy in the country, to the highest preferments of the church, and describes with that humour which was natural to him, and that knowledge which was extended to all the diversities of human life, his behaviour in every station; and insinuates, that this priest, thus accomplished, found at last a patron in the Bishop of London.

When he was asked by one of his friends, on what pretence he could charge the bishop with such an action? he had no more to say, than that he had only inverted the accusation, and that he thought it reasonable to believe, that he, who obstructed the rise of a good man without reason, would for bad reasons promote the exaltation of a villain.

The clergy were universally provoked by this satire; and Savage, who, as was his constant practice, had set his name to his performance, was censured in *The Weekly Miscellany*[1] with severity, which he did not seem inclined to forget.

[1] A short satire was likewise published in the same paper, in which were the following lines:

For cruel murder doom'd to hempen death,
Savage, by royal grace, prolong'd his breath.
Well might you think he spent his future years
In prayer, and fasting, and repentant tears.
—But, O vain hope!—the truly Savage cries,
"Priests, and their slavish doctrines, I despise.
Shall I——
Who, by free-thinking to free action fir'd,
In midnight brawls a deathless name acquir'd,
Now stoop to learn of ecclesiastic men?—
—No, arm'd with rhyme, at priests I'll take my aim,
Though prudence bids me murder but their fame."

Weekly Miscellany.

An answer was published in *The Gentleman's Magazine,* written by an unknown hand, from which the following lines are selected:

Transform'd by thoughtless rage, and midnight wine,
From malice free, and push'd without design;

But a return of invective was not thought a sufficient punishment. The Court of King's Bench was therefore moved against him, and he was obliged to return an answer to a charge of obscenity. It was urged, in his defence, that obscenity was criminal when it was intended to promote the practice of vice; but that Mr. Savage had only introduced obscene ideas, with the view of exposing them to detestation, and of amending the age, by shewing the deformity of wickedness. This plea was admitted; and Sir Philip Yorke,* who then presided in that court, dismissed the information with encomiums upon the purity and excellence of Mr. Savage's writings.

The prosecution, however, answered in some measure the purpose of those by whom it was set on foot; for Mr. Savage was so far intimidated by it, that, when the edition of his poem was sold, he did not venture to reprint it; so that it was in a short time forgotten, or forgotten by all but those whom it offended.

It is said, that some endeavours were used to incense the Queen against him: but he found advocates to obviate at least part of their effect; for though he was never advanced, he still continued to receive his pension.

In equal brawl if Savage lung'd a thrust,
And brought the youth a victim to the dust;
So strong the hand of accident appears,
The royal hand from guilt and vengeance clears.

Instead of wasting "all thy future years,
Savage, in prayer and vain repentant tears;"
Exert thy pen to mend a vicious age,
To curb the priest, and sink his high-church rage;
To shew what frauds the holy vestments hide,
The nests of av'rice, lust, and pedant pride;
Then change the scene, let merit brightly shine,
And round the patriot twist the wreath divine;
The heavenly guide deliver down to fame;
In well-tun'd lays transmit a Foster's name;
Touch every passion with harmonious art,
Exalt the genius, and correct the heart.
Thus future times shall royal grace extol;
Thus polish'd lines thy present fame enrol.
—But grant—
—Maliciously that Savage plung'd the steel,
And made the youth its shining vengeance feel;
My soul abhors the act; the man detests,
But more the bigotry in priestly breasts.

GENTLEMAN'S MAGAZINE, May 1735.

This poem drew more infamy upon him than any incident of his life; and, as his conduct cannot be vindicated, it is proper to secure his memory from reproach, by informing those whom he made his enemies, that he never intended to repeat the provocation; and that, though, whenever he thought he had any reason to complain of the clergy, he used to threaten them with a new edition of *The Progress of a Divine*, it was his calm and settled resolution to suppress it for ever.

He once intended to have made a better reparation for the folly or injustice with which he might be charged, by writing another poem, called *The Progress of a Freethinker*, whom he intended to lead through all the stages of vice and folly, to convert him from virtue to wickedness, and from religion to infidelity, by all the modish sophistry used for that purpose; and at last to dismiss him by his own hand into the other world.

That he did not execute this design is a real loss to mankind, for he was too well acquainted with all the scenes of debauchery to have failed in his representations of them, and too zealous for virtue not to have represented them in such a manner as should expose them either to ridicule or detestation.

But this plan was, like others, formed and laid aside, till the vigour of his imagination was spent, and the effervescence of invention had subsided; but soon gave way to some other design, which pleased by its novelty for a while, and then was neglected like the former.

He was still in his usual exigences, having no certain support but the pension allowed him by the Queen, which, though it might have kept an exact œconomist from want, was very far from being sufficient for Mr. Savage, who had never been accustomed to dismiss any of his appetites without the gratification which they solicited, and whom nothing but want of money withheld from partaking of every pleasure that fell within his view.

His conduct with regard to his pension was very particular. No sooner had he changed the bill, than he vanished from the sight of all his acquaintances, and lay for some time out of the reach of all the enquiries that friendship or curiosity could make after him; at length he appeared again pennyless as before, but never informed even those whom he seemed to regard most, where he had been, nor was his retreat ever discovered.

This was his constant practice during the whole time that he received the pension from the Queen: He regularly disappeared and returned. He indeed affirmed that he retired to study, and that the money supported him in solitude for many months; but his friends declared, that the short time in which it was spent sufficiently confuted his own account of his conduct.

His politeness and his wit still raised him friends, who were desirous of setting him at length free from that indigence by which he had been hitherto oppressed; and therefore solicited Sir Robert Walpole in his favour with so much earnestness, that they obtained a promise of the next place that should become vacant, not exceeding two hundred pounds a year. This promise was made with an uncommon declaration, "that it was not the promise of a minister to a petitioner, but of a friend to his friend."

Mr. Savage now concluded himself set at ease for ever, and, as he observes in a poem written on that incident of his life, trusted and was trusted; but soon found that his confidence was ill-grounded, and this friendly promise was not inviolable. He spent a long time in solicitations, and at last despaired and desisted.

He did not indeed deny that he had given the minister some reason to believe that he should not strengthen his own interest by advancing him, for he had taken care to distinguish himself in coffee-houses as an advocate for the ministry of the last years of Queen Anne, and was always ready to justify the conduct, and exalt the character of Lord Bolingbroke,* whom he mentions with great regard in an epistle upon authors, which he wrote about that time, but was too wise to publish, and of which only some fragments have appeared, inserted by him in the *Magazine* after his retirement.

To despair was not, however, the character of Savage; when one patronage failed, he had recourse to another. The prince was now extremely popular, and had very liberally rewarded the merit of some writers whom Mr. Savage did not think superior to himself, and therefore he resolved to address a poem to him.

For this purpose he made choice of a subject, which could regard only persons of the highest rank and highest affluence, and which was therefore proper for a poem intended to procure the patronage of a prince; and having retired for some time to Richmond, that he might prosecute his design in full tranquillity, without the temptations of pleasure, or the solicitations of creditors, by which his meditations were in equal danger of being disconcerted, he produced a poem *On Public Spirit, with regard to Public Works*.

The plan of this poem is very extensive, and comprises a multitude of topicks, each of which might furnish matter sufficient for a long performance, and of which some have already employed more eminent writers; but as he was perhaps not fully acquainted with the whole extent of his own design, and was writing to obtain a supply of wants too pressing to admit of long or accurate enquiries, he passes negligently over many publick works, which, even in his own opinion, deserved to be more elaborately treated.

But though he may sometimes disappoint his reader by transient touches upon these subjects, which have often been considered, and therefore naturally raise expectations, he must be allowed amply to compensate his omissions, by expatiating, in the conclusion of his work, upon a kind of beneficence not yet celebrated by any eminent poet, though it now appears more susceptible of embellishments, more adapted to exalt the ideas, and affect the passions, than many of those which have hitherto been thought most worthy of the ornaments of verse. The settlement of colonies in uninhabited countries, the establishment of those in security, whose misfortunes have made their own country no longer pleasing or safe, the acquisition of property without injury to any, the appropriation of the waste and luxuriant bounties of nature, and the enjoyment of those gifts which heaven has scattered upon regions uncultivated and unoccupied, cannot be considered without giving rise to a great number of pleasing ideas, and bewildering the imagination in delightful prospects; and, therefore, whatever speculations they may produce in those who have confined themselves to political studies, naturally fixed the attention, and excited the applause, of a poet. The politician, when he considers men driven into other countries for shelter, and obliged to retire to forests and deserts, and pass their lives and fix their posterity in the remotest corners of the world, to avoid those hardships which they suffer or fear in their native place, may very properly enquire, why the legislature does not provide a remedy for these miseries, rather than encourage an escape from them. He may conclude, that the flight of every honest man is a loss to the community; that those who are unhappy without guilt ought to be relieved; and the life, which is overburthened by accidental calamities, set at ease by the care of the publick; and that those, who have by misconduct forfeited their claim to favour, ought rather to be made useful to the society which they have injured, than be driven from it. But the poet is employed in a more pleasing undertaking than that of proposing laws, which, however just or expedient, will never be made, or endeavouring to reduce to rational schemes of government societies which were formed by chance, and are conducted by the private passions of those who preside in them. He guides the unhappy fugitive from want and persecution, to plenty, quiet, and security, and seats him in scenes of peaceful solitude, and undisturbed repose.

Savage has not forgotten, amidst the pleasing sentiments which this prospect of retirement suggested to him, to censure those crimes which have been generally committed by the discoverers of new regions, and to expose the enormous wickedness of making war upon barbarous nations because they cannot resist, and of invading countries because they are fruitful; of extending navigation only to propagate vice, and of visiting distant lands only to lay them waste. He has asserted the natural equality of mankind, and endeavoured to suppress that pride which inclines men to imagine that right is the consequence of power.

His description of the various miseries which force men to seek for refuge in distant countries, affords another instance of his proficiency in the important and extensive study of human life; and the tenderness with which he recounts them, another proof of his humanity and benevolence.

It is observable, that the close of this poem discovers a change which experience had made in Mr. Savage's opinions. In a poem written by him in his youth, and published in his Miscellanies, he declares his contempt of the contracted views and narrow prospects of the middle state of life, and declares his resolution either to tower like the cedar, or be trampled like the shrub; but in this poem, though addressed to a prince, he mentions this state of life as comprising those who ought most to attract reward, those who merit most the confidence of power, and the familiarity of greatness; and, accidentally mentioning this passage to one of his friends, declared, that in his opinion all the virtue of mankind was comprehended in that state.

In describing villas and gardens, he did not omit to condemn that absurd custom which prevails among the English, of permitting servants to receive money from strangers for the entertainment that they receive, and therefore inserted in his poem these lines;

> But what the flowering pride of gardens rare,
> However royal, or however fair,
> If gates, which to access should still give way,
> Ope but, like Peter's paradise, for pay?
> If perquisited varlets frequent stand,
> And each new walk must a new tax demand?
> What foreign eye but with contempt surveys?
> What Muse shall from oblivion snatch their praise?*

But before the publication of his performance he recollected, that the Queen allowed her garden and cave at Richmond to be shewn for money, and that she so openly countenanced the practice, that she had bestowed the privilege of shewing them as a place of profit on a man, whose merit she valued herself upon rewarding, though she gave him only the liberty of disgracing his country.

He therefore thought, with more prudence than was often exerted by him, that the publication of these lines might be officiously represented as an insult upon the Queen, to whom he owed his life and his subsistence; and that the propriety of his observation would be no security against the censures which the unseasonableness of it might draw upon him; he therefore suppressed the passage in the first edition, but after the Queen's death thought the same caution no longer necessary, and restored it to the proper place.

The poem was therefore published without any political faults, and inscribed to the Prince; but Mr. Savage, having no friend upon whom he could prevail to present it to him, had no other method of attracting his observation than the publication of frequent advertisements, and therefore received no reward from his patron, however generous on other occasions.

This disappointment he never mentioned without indignation, being by some means or other confident that the Prince was not ignorant of his address to him; and insinuated, that, if any advances in popularity could have been made by distinguishing him, he had not written without notice, or without reward.

He was once inclined to have presented his poem in person, and sent to the printer for a copy with that design; but either his opinion changed, or his resolution deserted him, and he continued to resent neglect without attempting to force himself into regard.

Nor was the publick much more favourable than his patron, for only seventy-two were sold, though the performance was much commended by some whose judgement in that kind of writing is generally allowed. But Savage easily reconciled himself to mankind without imputing any defect to his work, by observing that his poem was unluckily published two days after the prorogation of the parliament, and by consequence at a time when all those who could be expected to regard it were in the hurry of preparing for their departure, or engaged in taking leave of others upon their dismission from publick affairs.

It must be however allowed, in justification of the publick, that this performance is not the most excellent of Mr. Savage's works; and that, though it cannot be denied to contain many striking sentiments, majestic lines, and just observations, it is in general not sufficiently polished in the language, or enlivened in the imagery, or digested in the plan.

Thus his poem contributed nothing to the alleviation of his poverty, which was such as very few could have supported with equal patience; but to which it must likewise be confessed, that few would have been exposed who received punctually fifty pounds a year; a salary which, though by no means equal to the demands of vanity and luxury, is yet found sufficient to support families above want, and was undoubtedly more than the necessities of life require.

But no sooner had he received his pension, than he withdrew to his darling privacy, from which he returned in a short time to his former distress, and for some part of the year generally lived by chance, eating only when he was invited to the tables of his acquaintances, from which the meanness of his dress often excluded him, when the politeness and variety of his conversation would have been thought a sufficient recompence for his entertainment.

He lodged as much by accident as he dined, and passed the night sometimes in mean houses, which are set open at night to any casual wanderers, sometimes in cellars, among the riot and filth of the meanest and most profligate of the rabble; and sometimes, when he had not money to support even the expences of these receptacles, walked about the streets till he was weary, and lay down in the summer upon a bulk,* or in the winter, with his associates in poverty, among the ashes of a glass-house.*

In this manner were passed those days and those nights which nature had enabled him to have employed in elevated speculations, useful studies, or pleasing conversation. On a bulk, in a cellar, or in a glass-house among thieves and beggars, was to be found the Author of *The Wanderer*, the man of exalted sentiments, extensive views, and curious observations; the man whose remarks on life might have assisted the statesman, whose ideas of virtue might have enlightened the moralist, whose eloquence might have influenced senates, and whose delicacy might have polished courts.

It cannot but be imagined that such necessities might sometimes force him upon disreputable practices: and it is probable that these lines in *The Wanderer* were occasioned by his reflections on his own conduct:

> Though misery leads to happiness, and truth,
> Unequal to the load, this languid youth,
> (O, let none censure, if, untried by grief,
> If, amidst woe, untempted by relief,)
> He stoop'd reluctant to low arts of shame,
> Which then, ev'n then he scorn'd, and blush'd to name.*

Whoever was acquainted with him was certain to be solicited for small sums, which the frequency of the request made in time considerable, and he was therefore quickly shunned by those who were become familiar enough to be trusted with his necessities; but his rambling manner of life, and constant appearance at houses of public resort, always procured him a new succession of friends, whose kindness had not been exhausted by repeated requests; so that he was seldom absolutely without resources, but had in his utmost exigences this comfort, that he always imagined himself sure of speedy relief.

It was observed, that he always asked favours of this kind without the least submission or apparent consciousness of dependence, and that he did not seem to look upon a compliance with his request as an obligation that deserved any extraordinary acknowledgements; but a refusal was resented by him as an affront, or complained of as an injury; nor did he readily reconcile himself to those who either denied to lend, or gave him afterwards any intimation that they expected to be repaid.

He was sometimes so far compassionated by those who knew both his merit and distresses, that they received him into their families, but they soon discovered him to be a very incommodious inmate; for, being always accustomed to an irregular manner of life, he could not confine himself to any stated hours, or pay any regard to the rules of a family, but would prolong his conversation till midnight, without considering that business might require his friend's application in the morning; and, when he had persuaded himself to retire to bed, was not, without equal difficulty, called up to dinner; it was therefore impossible to pay him any distinction without the entire subversion of all œconomy, a kind of establishment which, wherever he went, he always appeared ambitious to overthrow.

It must therefore be acknowledged, in justification of mankind, that it was not always by the negligence or coldness of his friends that Savage was distressed, but because it was in reality very difficult to preserve him long in a state of ease. To supply him with money was a hopeless attempt; for no sooner did he see himself master of a sum sufficient to set him free from care for a day, than he became profuse and luxurious. When once he had entered a tavern, or engaged in a scheme of pleasure, he never retired till want of money obliged him to some new expedient. If he was entertained in a family, nothing was any longer to be regarded there but amusements and jollity; wherever Savage entered, he immediately expected that order and business should fly before him, that all should thenceforward be left to hazard, and that no dull principle of domestic management should be opposed to his inclination, or intrude upon his gaiety.

His distresses, however afflictive, never dejected him; in his lowest state he wanted not spirit to assert the natural dignity of wit, and was always ready to repress that insolence which superiority of fortune incited, and to trample on that reputation which rose upon any other basis than that of merit: he never admitted any gross familiarities, or submitted to be treated otherwise than as an equal. Once, when he was without lodging, meat, or clothes, one of his friends, a man not indeed remarkable for moderation in his prosperity, left a message, that he desired to see him about nine in the morning. Savage knew that his intention was to assist him; but was very much disgusted that he should presume to prescribe the hour of his attendance, and, I believe, refused to visit him, and rejected his kindness.

The same invincible temper, whether firmness or obstinacy, appeared in his conduct to the Lord Tyrconnel, from whom he very frequently demanded, that the allowance which was once paid him should be restored; but with whom he never appeared to entertain for a moment the thought of soliciting a reconciliation, and whom he treated at once with all the haughtiness of superiority, and all the bitterness of resentment. He wrote to him, not in a style of supplication or respect, but of reproach, menace, and contempt; and appeared determined, if he ever regained his allowance, to hold it only by the right of conquest.

As many more can discover, that a man is richer than that he is wiser than themselves, superiority of understanding is not so readily acknowledged as that of fortune; nor is that haughtiness, which the consciousness of great abilities incites, born with the same submission as the tyranny of affluence; and therefore Savage, by asserting his claim to deference and regard, and by treating those with contempt whom better fortune animated to rebel against him, did not fail to raise a great number of enemies in the different classes of mankind. Those who thought themselves raised above him by the advantages of riches, hated him because they found no protection from the petulance of his wit. Those who were esteemed for their writings feared him as a critic, and maligned him as a rival, and almost all the smaller wits were his professed enemies.

Among these Mr. Miller so far indulged his resentment as to introduce him in a farce, and direct him to be personated on the stage, in a dress like that which he then wore;* a mean insult, which only insinuated that Savage had but one coat, and which was therefore despised by him rather than resented; for though he wrote a lampoon against Miller, he never printed it: and as no other person ought to prosecute that revenge from which the person who was injured desisted, I shall not preserve what Mr. Savage suppressed: of which the publication would indeed have been a punishment too severe for so impotent an assault.

The great hardships of poverty were to Savage not the want of lodging or of food, but the neglect and contempt which it drew upon him. He complained, that as his affairs grew desperate, he found his reputation for capacity visibly decline; that his opinion in questions of criticism was no longer regarded, when his coat was out of fashion; and that those who, in the interval of his prosperity, were always encouraging him to great undertakings by encomiums on his genius and assurances of success, now received any mention of his designs with coldness, thought that the subjects on which he proposed to write were very difficult, and were ready to inform him, that the event of a poem was uncertain, that an author ought to employ much time in the consideration of his plan, and not presume to sit down to write in confidence of a few cursory ideas, and a superficial knowledge; difficulties were started on all sides, and he was no longer qualified for any performance but *The Volunteer Laureat*.

Yet even this kind of contempt never depressed him; for he always preserved a steady confidence in his own capacity, and believed nothing above his reach which he should at any time earnestly endeavour to attain. He formed schemes of the same kind with regard to knowledge and to fortune, and flattered himself with advances to be made in science, as with riches, to be enjoyed in some distant period of his life. For the acquisition of knowledge he was indeed far better qualified than for that of riches; for he was naturally inquisitive and desirous of the conversation of those from whom any information was to be obtained, but by no means solicitous to improve those opportunities that were sometimes offered of raising his fortune; and he was remarkably retentive of his ideas, which, when once he was in possession of them, rarely forsook him; a quality which could never be communicated to his money.

While he was thus wearing out his life in expectation that the Queen would some time recollect her promise, he had recourse to the usual practice of writers, and published proposals for printing his works by subscription, to which he was encouraged by the success of many who had not a better right to the favour of the publick; but, whatever was the reason, he did not find the world equally inclined to favour him; and he observed with some discontent, that, though he offered his works at half a guinea, he was able to procure but a small number in comparison with those who subscribed twice as much to Duck.*

Nor was it without indignation that he saw his proposals neglected by the Queen, who patronised Mr. Duck's with uncommon ardour, and incited a competition among those who attended the court, who should most promote his interest, and who should first offer a subscription. This was a distinction to which Mr. Savage made no scruple of asserting that his birth, his misfortunes, and his genius, gave him a fairer title, than could be pleaded by him on whom it was conferred.

Savage's applications were however not universally unsuccessful; for some of the nobility countenanced his design, encouraged his proposals, and subscribed with great liberality. He related of the Duke of Chandos* particularly, that, upon receiving his proposals, he sent him ten guineas.

But the money which his subscriptions afforded him was not less volatile than that which he received from his other schemes; whenever a subscription was paid him, he went to a tavern; and, as money so collected is necessarily received in small sums, he never was able to send his poems to the press, but for many years continued his solicitation, and squandered whatever he obtained.

This project of printing his works was frequently revived; and, as his proposals grew obsolete, new ones were printed with fresher dates. To form schemes for the publication was one of his favourite amusements; nor was he ever more at ease than when, with any friend who readily fell in with his schemes, he was adjusting the print, forming the advertisements, and regulating the dispersion of his new edition, which he really intended some time to publish, and which, as long experience had shewn him the impossibility of printing the volume together, he at last determined to divide into weekly or monthly numbers, that the profits of the first might supply the expences of the next.

Thus he spent his time in mean expedients and tormenting suspense, living for the greatest part in the fear of prosecutions from his creditors, and consequently skulking in obscure parts of the town, of which he was no stranger to the remotest corners. But wherever he came, his address secured him friends, whom his necessities soon alienated; so that he had perhaps a more numerous acquaintance than any man ever before attained, there being scarcely any person eminent on any account to whom he was not known, or whose character he was not in some degree able to delineate.

To the acquisition of this extensive acquaintance every circumstance of his life contributed. He excelled in the arts of conversation, and therefore willingly practised them: He had seldom any home, or even a lodging in which he could be private; and therefore was driven into public-houses for the common conveniences of life and supports of nature. He was always ready to comply with every invitation, having no employment to withhold him, and often no money to provide for himself; and by dining with one company, he never failed of obtaining an introduction into another.

Thus dissipated was his life, and thus casual his subsistence; yet did not the distraction of his views hinder him from reflection, nor the uncertainty of his condition depress his gaiety. When he had wandered about without any fortunate adventure by which he was led into a tavern, he sometimes retired into the fields, and was able to employ his mind in study, or amuse it with pleasing imaginations; and seldom appeared to be melancholy, but when some sudden misfortune had just fallen upon him, and even then in a few moments he would disentangle himself from his perplexity, adopt the subject of conversation, and apply his mind wholly to the objects that others presented to it.

This life, unhappy as it may be already imagined, was yet imbittered, in 1738, with new calamities. The death of the Queen deprived him of all the prospects of preferment with which he so long entertained his imagination; and, as Sir Robert Walpole had before given him reason to believe that he never intended the performance of his promise, he was now abandoned again to fortune.

He was however, at that time, supported by a friend;* and as it was not his custom to look out for distant calamities, or to feel any other pain than that which forced itself upon his senses, he was not much afflicted at his loss, and perhaps comforted himself that his pension would be now continued without the annual tribute of a panegyric.

Another expectation contributed likewise to support him: he had taken a resolution to write a second tragedy upon the story of Sir Thomas Overbury, in which he preserved a few lines of his former play, but made a total alteration of the plan, added new incidents, and introduced new characters; so that it was a new tragedy, not a revival of the former.

Many of his friends blamed him for not making choice of another subject; but, in vindication of himself, he asserted, that it was not easy to find a better; and that he thought it his interest to extinguish the memory of the first tragedy, which he could only do by writing one less defective upon the same story; by which he should entirely defeat the artifice of the booksellers, who, after the death of any author of reputation, are always industrious to swell his works, by uniting his worst productions with his best.

In the execution of this scheme, however, he proceeded but slowly, and probably only employed himself upon it when he could find no other amusement; but he pleased himself with counting the profits, and perhaps imagined, that the theatrical reputation which he was about to acquire, would be equivalent to all that he had lost by the death of his patroness.

He did not, in confidence of his approaching riches, neglect the measures proper to secure the continuance of his pension, though some of his favourers thought him culpable for omitting to write on her death; but on her birth-day next year, he gave a proof of the solidity of his judgement, and the power of his genius. He knew that the track of elegy had been so long beaten, that it was impossible to travel in it without treading in the footsteps of those who had gone before him; and that therefore it was necessary, that he might distinguish himself from the herd of encomiasts, to find out some new walk of funeral panegyrick.

This difficult task he performed in such a manner, that his poem may be justly ranked among the best pieces that the death of princes has produced. By transferring the mention of her death to her birth-day, he has formed a happy combination of topicks, which any other man would have thought it very difficult to connect in one view, but which he has united in such a manner, that the relation between them appears natural; and it may be justly said, that what no other man would have thought on, it now appears scarcely possible for any man to miss.

The beauty of this peculiar combination of images is so masterly, that it is sufficient to set this poem above censure; and therefore it is not necessary to mention many other delicate touches which may be found in it, and which would deservedly be admired in any other performance.

To these proofs of his genius may be added, from the same poem, an instance of his prudence, an excellence for which he was not so often distinguished; he does not forget to remind the King, in the most delicate and artful manner, of continuing his pension.

With regard to the success of this address, he was for some time in suspence, but was in no great degree solicitous about it; and continued his labour upon his new tragedy with great tranquillity, till the friend who had for a considerable time supported him, removing his family to another place, took occasion to dismiss him. It then became necessary to enquire more diligently what was determined in his affair, having reason to suspect that no great favour was intended him, because he had not received his pension at the usual time.

It is said, that he did not take those methods of retrieving his interest, which were most likely to succeed; and some of those who were employed in the Exchequer, cautioned him against too much violence in his proceedings; but Mr. Savage, who seldom regulated his conduct by the advice of others, gave way to his passion, and demanded of Sir Robert Walpole, at his levee, the reason of the distinction that was made between him and the other pensioners of the Queen, with a degree of roughness which perhaps determined him to withdraw what had been only delayed.

Whatever was the crime of which he was accused or suspected, and whatever influence was employed against him, he received soon after an account that took from him all hopes of regaining his pension; and he had now no prospect of subsistence but from his play, and he knew no way of living for the time required to finish it.

So peculiar were the misfortunes of this man, deprived of an estate and title by a particular law, exposed and abandoned by a mother, defrauded by a mother of a fortune which his father had allotted him, he entered the world without a friend; and though his abilities forced themselves into esteem and reputation, he was never able to obtain any real advantage, and whatever prospects arose were always intercepted as he began to approach them. The king's intentions in his favour were frustrated; his dedication to the Prince, whose generosity on every other occasion was eminent, procured him no reward; Sir Robert Walpole, who valued himself upon keeping his promise to others, broke it to him without regret; and the bounty of the Queen was, after her death, withdrawn from him, and from him only.

Such were his misfortunes, which yet he bore, not only with decency, but with cheerfulness; nor was his gaiety clouded even by his last disappointments, though he was in a short time reduced to the lowest degree of distress, and often wanted both lodging and food. At this time he gave another instance of the insurmountable obstinacy of his spirit: his clothes were worn out; and he received notice, that at a coffee-house some clothes and linen were left for him: the person who sent them did not, I believe, inform him to whom he was to be obliged, that he might spare the perplexity of acknowledging the benefit; but though the offer was so far generous, it was made with some neglect of ceremonies, which Mr. Savage so much resented, that he refused the present, and declined to enter the house till the clothes that had been designed for him were taken away.

His distress was now publickly known, and his friends, therefore, thought it proper to concert some measures for his relief; and one of them wrote a letter to him,* in which he expressed his concern "for the miserable withdrawing of his pension;" and gave him hopes, that in a short time he should find himself supplied with a competence, "without any dependence on those little creatures which we are pleased to call the Great."

The scheme proposed for this happy and independent subsistence, was, that he should retire into Wales, and receive an allowance of fifty pounds a year, to be raised by a subscription, on which he was to live privately in a cheap place, without aspiring any more to affluence, or having any farther care of reputation.

This offer Mr. Savage gladly accepted, though with intentions very different from those of his friends; for they proposed that he should continue an exile from London for ever, and spend all the remaining part of his life at Swansea; but he designed only to take the opportunity, which their scheme offered him, of retreating for a short time, that he might prepare his play for the stage, and his other works for the press, and then to return to London to exhibit his tragedy, and live upon the profits of his own labour.

With regard to his works, he proposed very great improvements, which would have required much time, or great application; and when he had finished them, he designed to do justice to his subscribers, by publishing them according to his proposals.

As he was ready to entertain himself with future pleasures, he had planned out a scheme of life for the country, of which he had no knowledge but from pastorals and songs. He imagined that he should be transported to scenes of flowery felicity, like those which one poet has reflected to another; and had projected a perpetual round of innocent pleasures, of which he suspected no interruption from pride, or ignorance, or brutality.

With these expectations he was so enchanted, that when he was once gently reproached by a friend for submitting to live upon a subscription, and advised rather by a resolute exertion of his abilities to support himself, he could not bear to debar himself from the happiness which was to be found in the calm of a cottage, or lose the opportunity of listening, without intermission, to the melody of the nightingale, which he believed was to be heard from every bramble, and which he did not fail to mention as a very important part of the happiness of a country life.

While this scheme was ripening, his friends directed him to take a lodging in the liberties of the Fleet,* that he might be secure from his creditors, and sent him every Monday a guinea, which he commonly spent before the next morning, and trusted, after his usual manner, the remaining part of the week to the bounty of fortune.

He now began very sensibly to feel the miseries of dependence. Those by whom he was to be supported, began to prescribe to him with an air of authority, which he knew not how decently to resent, nor patiently to bear; and he soon discovered, from the conduct of most of his subscribers, that he was yet in the hands of "little creatures."

Of the insolence that he was obliged to suffer, he gave many instances, of which none appeared to raise his indignation to a greater height, than the method which was taken of furnishing him with clothes. Instead of consulting him, and allowing him to send a taylor his orders for what they thought proper to allow him, they proposed to send for a taylor to take his measure, and then to consult how they should equip him.

This treatment was not very delicate, nor was it such as Savage's humanity would have suggested to him on a like occasion; but it had scarcely deserved mention, had it not, by affecting him in an uncommon degree, shewn the peculiarity of his character. Upon hearing the design that was formed, he came to the lodging of a friend with the most violent agonies of rage; and, being asked what it could be that gave him such disturbance, he replied with the utmost vehemence of indignation, "That they had sent for a taylor to measure him."

How the affair ended was never enquired, for fear of renewing his uneasiness. It is probable, that, upon recollection, he submitted with a good grace to what he could not avoid, and that he discovered no resentment where he had no power.

He was, however, not humbled to implicit and universal compliance; for when the gentleman, who had first informed him of the design to support him by a subscription, attempted to procure a reconciliation with the Lord Tyrconnel, he could by no means be prevailed upon to comply with the measures that were proposed.

A letter was written for him[1] to Sir William Lemon,* to prevail upon him to interpose his good offices with Lord Tyrconnel, in which he solicited Sir William's assistance, "for a man who really needed it as much as any man could well do;" and informed him, that he was retiring "for ever to a place where he should no more trouble his relations, friends, or enemies;" he confessed, that his passion had betrayed him to some conduct with regard to Lord Tyrconnel, "for which he could not but heartily ask his pardon"; and as he imagined Lord Tyrconnel's passion might be yet so high, that he would not "receive a letter from him," begged that Sir William would endeavour to soften him; and expressed his hopes that he would comply with his request, and that "so small a relation would not harden his heart against him."

That any man should presume to dictate a letter to him, was not very agreeable to Mr. Savage; and therefore he was, before he had opened it, not much inclined to approve it. But when he read it, he found it contained sentiments entirely opposite to his own, and, as he asserted, to the truth; and therefore, instead of copying it, wrote his friend a letter full of masculine resentment and warm expostulations. He very justly observed, that the style was too supplicatory, and the representation too abject, and that he ought at least to have made him complain with "the dignity of a gentleman in distress." He declared that he would not write the paragraph in which he was to ask Lord Tyrconnel's pardon; for, "he despised his pardon, and therefore could not heartily, and would not hypocritically, ask it." He remarked, that his friend made a very unreasonable distinction between himself and him; for, says he, when you mention men of high rank "in your own character," they are "those little creatures whom we are pleased to call the great;" but when you address them "in mine," no servility is sufficiently humble. He then with great propriety explained the ill consequences which might be expected from such a letter, which his relations would print in their own

[1] By Mr. Pope.

defence, and which would for ever be produced as a full answer to all that he should allege against them; for he always intended to publish a minute account of the treatment which he had received. It is to be remembered, to the honour of the gentleman by whom this letter was drawn up, that he yielded to Mr. Savage's reasons, and agreed that it ought to be suppressed.

After many alterations and delays, a subscription was at length raised, which did not amount to fifty pounds a year, though twenty were paid by one gentleman; such was the generosity of mankind, that what had been done by a player without solicitation, could not now be effected by application and interest; and Savage had a great number to court and to obey for a pension less than that which Mrs. Oldfield paid him without exacting any servilities.

Mr. Savage however was satisfied, and willing to retire, and was convinced that the allowance, though scanty, would be more than sufficient for him, being now determined to commence a rigid œconomist, and to live according to the exactest rules of frugality; for nothing was in his opinion more contemptible than a man, who, when he knew his income, exceeded it; and yet he confessed, that instances of such folly were too common, and lamented that some men were not to be trusted with their own money.

Full of these salutary resolutions, he left London in July 1739, having taken leave with great tenderness of his friends, and parted from the author of this narrative with tears in his eyes. He was furnished with fifteen guineas, and informed, that they would be sufficient, not only for the expence of his journey, but for his support in Wales for some time; and that there remained but little more of the first collection. He promised a strict adherence to his maxims of parsimony, and went away in the stage-coach; nor did his friends expect to hear from him, till he informed them of his arrival at Swansea.

But when they least expected, arrived a letter dated the fourteenth day after his departure, in which he sent them word, that he was yet upon the road, and without money; and that he therefore could not proceed without a remittance. They then sent him the money that was in their hands, with which he was enabled to reach Bristol, from whence he was to go to Swansea by water.

At Bristol he found an embargo laid upon the shipping, so that he could not immediately obtain a passage; and being therefore obliged to stay there some time, he with his usual felicity, ingratiated himself with many of the principal inhabitants, was invited to their houses, distinguished at their publick feasts, and treated with a regard that gratified his vanity, and therefore easily engaged his affection.

He began very early after his retirement to complain of the conduct of his friends in London, and irritated many of them so much by his letters, that they withdrew, however honourably, their contributions; and it is believed, that little more was paid him than the twenty pounds a year, which were allowed him by the gentleman who proposed the subscription.

After some stay at Bristol he retired to Swansea, the place originally proposed for his residence, where he lived about a year, very much dissatisfied with the diminution of his salary; but contracted, as in other places, acquaintance with those who were most distinguished in that country, among whom he has celebrated Mr. Powel and Mrs. Jones,* by some verses which he inserted in *The Gentleman's Magazine*[1].

Here he completed his tragedy, of which two acts were wanting when he left London, and was desirous of coming to town to bring it upon the stage. This design was very warmly opposed, and he was advised by his chief benefactor to put it into the hands of Mr. Thomson and Mr. Mallet, that it might be fitted for the stage, and to allow his friends to receive the profits, out of which an annual pension should be paid him.

This proposal he rejected with the utmost contempt. He was by no means convinced that the judgement of those, to whom he was required to submit, was superior to his own. He was now determined, as he expressed it, to be "no longer kept in leading-strings," and had no elevated idea of "his bounty, who proposed to pension him out of the profits of his own labours."

He attempted in Wales to promote a subscription for his works, and had once hopes of success; but in a short time afterwards formed a resolution of leaving that part of the country, to which he thought it not reasonable to be confined for the gratification of those, who, having promised him a liberal income, had no sooner banished him to a remote corner, than they reduced his allowance to a salary scarcely equal to the necessities of life.

[1] Reprinted in the late collection.

His resentment of this treatment, which, in his own opinion at least, he had not deserved, was such, that he broke off all correspondence with most of his contributors, and appeared to consider them as persecutors and oppressors; and in the latter part of his life declared, that their conduct toward him, since his departure from London, "had been perfidiousness improving on perfidiousness, and inhumanity on inhumanity."

It is not to be supposed, that the necessities of Mr. Savage did not sometimes incite him to satirical exaggerations of the behaviour of those by whom he thought himself reduced to them. But it must be granted, that the diminution of his allowance was a great hardship, and that those who withdrew their subscription from a man, who, upon the faith of their promise, had gone into a kind of banishment, and abandoned all those by whom he had been before relieved in his distresses, will find it no easy talk to vindicate their conduct.

It may be alleged, and perhaps justly, that he was petulant and contemptuous; that he more frequently reproached his subscribers for not giving him more, than thanked them for what he received; but it is to be remembered, that his conduct, and this is the worst charge that can be drawn up against him, did them no real injury; and that it therefore ought rather to have been pitied than resented; at least, the resentment it might provoke ought to have been generous and manly; epithets which his conduct will hardly deserve that starves the man whom he has persuaded to put himself into his power.

It might have been reasonably demanded by Savage, that they should, before they had taken away what they promised, have replaced him in his former state, that they should have taken no advantages from the situation to which the appearance of their kindness had reduced him, and that he should have been recalled to London before he was abandoned. He might justly represent, that he ought to have been considered as a lion in the toils, and demand to be released before the dogs should be loosed upon him.

He endeavoured, indeed, to release himself, and, with an intent to return to London, went to Bristol, where a repetition of the kindness which he had formerly found invited him to stay. He was not only caressed and treated, but had a collection made for him of about thirty pounds, with which it had been happy if he had immediately departed for London; but his negligence did not suffer him to consider, that such proofs of kindness were not often to be expected, and that this ardour of benevolence was in a great degree the effect of novelty, and might, probably, be every day less; and therefore he took no care to improve the happy time, but was encouraged by one favour to hope for another, till at length generosity was exhausted, and officiousness wearied.

Another part of his misconduct was the practice of prolonging his visits to unseasonable hours, and disconcerting all the families into which he was admitted. This was an error in a place of commerce which all the charms of his conversation could not compensate; for what trader would purchase such airy satisfaction by the loss of solid gain, which must be the consequence of midnight merriment, as those hours which were gained at night were generally lost in the morning?

Thus Mr. Savage, after the curiosity of the inhabitants was gratified, found the number of his friends daily decreasing, perhaps without suspecting for what reason their conduct was altered; for he still continued to harass, with his nocturnal intrusions, those that yet countenanced him, and admitted him to their houses.

But he did not spend all the time of his residence at Bristol in visits or at taverns, for he sometimes returned to his studies, and began several considerable designs. When he felt an inclination to write, he always retired from the knowledge of his friends, and lay hid in an obscure part of the suburbs, till he found himself again desirous of company, to which it is likely that intervals of absence made him more welcome.

He was always full of his design of returning to London, to bring his tragedy upon the stage; but, having neglected to depart with the money that was raised for him, he could not afterwards procure a sum sufficient to defray the expences of his journey; nor perhaps would a fresh supply have had any other effect, than, by putting immediate pleasures in his power, to have driven the thoughts of his journey out of his mind.

While he was thus spending the day in contriving a scheme for the morrow, distress stole upon him by imperceptible degrees. His conduct had already wearied some of those who were at first enamoured of his conversation; but he might, perhaps, still have devolved to others, whom he might have entertained with equal success, had not the decay of his clothes made it no longer consistent with their vanity to admit him to their tables, or to associate with him in publick places. He now began to find every man from home at whose house he called; and was therefore no longer able to procure the necessaries of life, but wandered about the town, slighted and neglected, in quest of a dinner, which he did not always obtain.

To complete his misery, he was pursued by the officers for small debts which he had contracted; and was therefore obliged to withdraw from the small number of friends from whom he had still reason to hope for favours. His custom was to lie in bed the greatest part of the day, and to go out in the dark with the utmost privacy, and after having paid his visit return again before morning to his lodging, which was in the garret of an obscure inn.

Being thus excluded on one hand, and confined on the other, he suffered the utmost extremities of poverty, and often fasted so long that he was seized with faintness, and had lost his appetite, not being able to bear the smell of meat, till the action of his stomach was restored by a cordial.

In this distress, he received a remittance of five pounds from London, with which he provided himself a decent coat, and determined to go to London, but unhappily spent his money at a favourite tavern. Thus was he again confined to Bristol, where he was every day hunted by bailiffs. In this exigence he once more found a friend, who sheltered him in his house, though at the usual inconveniences with which his company was attended; for he could neither be persuaded to go to bed in the night, nor to rise in the day.

It is observable, that in these various scenes of misery, he was always disengaged and cheerful: he at some times pursued his studies, and at others continued or enlarged his epistolary correspondence; nor was he ever so far dejected as to endeavour to procure an increase of his allowance by any other methods than accusations and reproaches.

He had now no longer any hopes of assistance from his friends at Bristol, who as merchants, and by consequence sufficiently studious of profit, cannot be supposed to have looked with much compassion upon negligence and extravagance, or to think any excellence equivalent to a fault of such consequence as neglect of œconomy. It is natural to imagine, that many of those, who would have relieved his real wants, were discouraged from the exertion of their benevolence by observation of the use which was made of their favours, and conviction that relief would only be momentary, and that the same necessity would quickly return.

At last he quitted the house of his friend, and returned to his lodging at the inn, still intending to set out in a few days for London; but on the 10th of January 1742–3, having been at supper with two of his friends, he was at his return to his lodgings arrested for a debt of about eight pounds, which he owed at a coffee-house, and conducted to the house of a sheriff's officer. The account which he gives of this misfortune, in a letter to one of the gentlemen with whom he had supped, is too remarkable to be omitted.

"It was not a little unfortunate for me, that I spent yesterday's evening with you; because the hour hindered me from entering on my new lodging; however, I have now got one, but such an one as I believe nobody would chuse.

"I was arrested at the suit of Mrs. Read, just as I was going up stairs to bed, at Mr. Bowyer's; but taken in so private a manner, that I believe nobody at the White Lion is apprised of it. Though I let the officers know the strength (or rather weakness) of my pocket, yet they treated me with the utmost civility; and even when they conducted me to confinement, it was in such a manner, that I verily believe I could have escaped, which I would rather be ruined than have done, notwithstanding the whole amount of my finances was but three pence halfpenny.

"In the first place I must insist, that you will industriously conceal this from Mrs. S—s, because I would not have her good-nature suffer that pain, which, I know, she would be apt to feel on this occasion.

"Next, I conjure you, dear Sir, by all the ties of friendship, by no means to have one uneasy thought on my account; but to have the same pleasantry of countenance, and unruffled serenity of mind, which (God be praised!) I have in this, and have had in a much severer calamity. Furthermore, I charge you, if you value my friendship as truly as I do yours, not to utter, or even harbour, the least resentment against Mrs. Read. I believe she has ruined me, but I freely forgive her; and (though I will never more have any intimacy with her) I would, at a due distance, rather do her an act of good, than ill will. Lastly (pardon the expression), I absolutely command you not to offer me any pecuniary assistance, nor to attempt getting me any from any one of your friends. At another time, or on any other occasion, you may, dear friend, be well assured, I would rather write to you in the submissive style of a request, than that of a peremptory command.

"However, that my truly valuable friend may not think I am too proud to ask a favour, let me entreat you to let me have your boy to attend me for this day, not only for the sake of saving me the expence of porters, but for the delivery of some letters to people whose names I would not have known to strangers.

"The civil treatment I have thus far met from those whose prisoner I am, makes me thankful to the Almighty, that, though he has thought fit to visit me (on my birth-night) with affliction, yet (such is his great goodness!) my affliction is not without alleviating circumstances. I murmur not; but am all resignation to the divine will. As to the world, I hope that I shall be endued by Heaven with that presence of mind, that serene dignity in misfortune, that constitutes the character of a true nobleman; a dignity far beyond that of coronets; a nobility arising from the just principles of philosophy, refined and exalted by those of christianity."—

He continued five days at the officer's, in hopes, that he should be able to procure bail, and avoid the necessity of going to prison. The state in which he passed his time, and the treatment which he received, are very justly expressed by him in a letter which he wrote to a friend: "The whole day," says he, "has been employed in various peoples' filling my head with their foolish chimerical systems, which has obliged me coolly (as far as nature will admit) to digest, and accommodate myself to, every different person's way of thinking; hurried from one wild system to another, till it has quite made a chaos of my imagination, and nothing done—promised—disappointed—ordered to send, every hour, from one part of the town to the other."—

When his friends, who had hitherto caressed and applauded, found that to give bail and pay the debt was the same, they all refused to preserve him from a prison at the expence of eight pounds; and therefore, after having been for some time at the officer's house, "at an immense expence," as he observes in his letter, he was at length removed to Newgate.*

This expence he was enabled to support by the generosity of Mr. Nash at Bath,* who, upon receiving from him an account of his condition, immediately sent him five guineas, and promised to promote his subscription at Bath with all his interest.

By his removal to Newgate, he obtained at least a freedom from suspense, and rest from the disturbing vicissitudes of hope and disappointment; he now found that his friends were only companions, who were willing to share his gaiety, but not to partake of his misfortunes; and therefore he no longer expected any assistance from them.

It must however be observed of one gentleman, that he offered to release him by paying the debt; but that Mr. Savage would not consent, I suppose because he thought he had been before too burthensome to him.

He was offered by some of his friends, that a collection should be made for his enlargement; but he "treated the proposal," and declared, "he should again treat it, with disdain. As to writing any mendicant letters, he had too high a spirit, and determined only to write to some ministers of state, to try to regain his pension."

He continued to complain of those that had sent him into the country, and objected to them, that he had "lost the profits of his play, which had been finished three years;" and in another letter declares his resolution to publish a pamphlet, that the world might know how "he had been used."

This pamphlet was never written; for he in a very short time recovered his usual tranquillity, and cheerfully applied himself to more inoffensive studies. He indeed steadily declared, that he was promised a yearly allowance of fifty pounds, and never received half the sum; but he seemed to resign himself to that as well as to other misfortunes, and lose the remembrance of it in his amusements and employments.

The cheerfulness with which he bore his confinement, appears from the following letter, which he wrote, January the 30th, to one of his friends in London:

"I now write to you from my confinement in Newgate, where I have been ever since Monday last was se'nnight, and where I enjoy myself with much more tranquillity than I have known for upwards of a twelvemonth past; having a room entirely to myself, and pursuing the amusement of my poetical studies, uninterrupted, and agreeable to my mind. I thank the Almighty, I am now all collected in myself; and, though my person is in confinement, my mind can expatiate on ample and useful subjects with all the freedom imaginable. I am now more conversant with the Nine than ever; and if, instead of a Newgate-bird, I may be allowed to be a bird of the Muses, I assure you Sir, I sing very freely in my cage; sometimes indeed in the plaintive notes of the nightingale; but, at others, in the cheerful strains of the lark."—

In another letter he observes, that he ranges from one subject to another, without confining himself to any particular task; and that he was employed one week upon one attempt, and the next upon another.

Surely the fortitude of this man deserves, at least, to be mentioned with applause; and, whatever faults may be imputed to him, the virtue of suffering well cannot be denied him. The two powers which, in the opinion of Epictetus, constituted a wise man, are those of bearing and forbearing, which cannot indeed be affirmed to have been equally possessed by Savage; and indeed the want of one obliged him very frequently to practise the other.

He was treated by Mr. Dagg, the keeper of the prison, with great humanity; was supported by him at his own table without any certainty of recompence; had a room to himself, to which he could at any time retire from all disturbance; was allowed to stand at the door of the prison, and sometimes taken out into the fields; so that he suffered fewer hardships in prison than he had been accustomed to undergo in the greatest part of his life.

The keeper did not confine his benevolence to a gentle execution of his office, but made some overtures to the creditor for his release, though without effect; and continued, during the whole time of his imprisonment, to treat him with the utmost tenderness and civility.

Virtue is undoubtedly most laudable in that state which makes it most difficult; and therefore the humanity of a gaoler certainly deserves this public attestation; and the man, whose heart has not been hardened by such an employment, may be justly proposed as a pattern of benevolence. If an inscription was once engraved "to the honest toll-gatherer," less honours ought not to be paid "to the tender gaoler."

Mr. Savage very frequently received visits, and sometimes presents, from his acquaintances: but they did not amount to a subsistence, for the greater part of which he was indebted to the generosity of this keeper; but these favours, however they might endear to him the particular persons from whom he received them, were very far from impressing upon his mind any advantageous ideas of the people of Bristol, and therefore he thought he could not more properly employ himself in prison, than in writing a poem called "London and Bristol delineated."

When he had brought this poem to its present state, which, without considering the chasm, is not perfect, he wrote to London an account of his design, and informed his friend,* that he was determined to print it with his name; but enjoined him not to communicate his intention to his Bristol acquaintance. The gentleman, surprised at his resolution, endeavoured to dissuade him from publishing it, at least from prefixing his name; and declared, that he could not reconcile the injunction of secrecy with his resolution to own it at its first appearance. To this Mr. Savage returned an answer agreeable to his character in the following terms:

"I received yours this morning; and not without a little surprise at the contents. To answer a question with a question, you ask me concerning London and Bristol, Why will I add delineated? Why did Mr. Woolaston add the same word to his RELIGION OF NATURE? I suppose that it was his will and pleasure to add it in his case; and it is mine to do so in my own. You are pleased to tell me, that you understand not why secrecy is enjoined, and yet I intend to set my name to it. My answer is—I have my private reasons, which I am not obliged to explain to any one. You doubt my friend Mr. S— would not approve of it—And what is it to me whether he does or not? Do you imagine that Mr. S—is to dictate to me? If any man who calls himself my friend should assume such an air, I would spurn at his friendship with contempt. You say, I seem to think so by not letting him know it—And suppose I do, what then? Perhaps I can give reasons for that disapprobation, very foreign from what you would imagine. You go on in saying, Suppose I should not put my name to it—My answer is, that I will not suppose any such thing, being determined to the contrary: neither, Sir, would I have you suppose, that I applied to you for want of another press: nor would I have you imagine, that I owe Mr. S—obligations which I do not."

Such was his imprudence, and such his obstinate adherence to his own resolutions, however absurd. A prisoner! supported by charity! and, whatever insults he might have received during the latter part of his stay in Bristol, once caressed, esteemed, and presented with a liberal collection, he could forget on a sudden his danger and his obligations, to gratify the petulance of his wit, or the eagerness of his resentment, and publish a satire, by which he might reasonably expect that he should alienate those who then supported him, and provoke those whom he could neither resist nor escape.

This resolution, from the execution of which it is probable that only his death could have hindered him, is sufficient to shew, how much he disregarded all considerations that opposed his present passions, and how readily he hazarded all future advantages for any immediate gratifications. Whatever was his predominant inclination, neither hope nor fear hindered him from complying with it; nor had opposition any other effect than to heighten his ardour, and irritate his vehemence.

This performance was however laid aside, while he was employed in soliciting assistance from several great persons; and one interruption succeeding another, hindered him from supplying the chasm, and perhaps from retouching the other parts, which he can hardly be imagined to have finished in his own opinion; for it is very unequal, and some of the lines are rather inserted to rhyme to others, than to support or improve the sense; but the first and last parts are worked up with great spirit and elegance.

His time was spent in the prison for the most part in study, or in receiving visits; but sometimes he descended to lower amusements, and diverted himself in the kitchen with the conversation of the criminals; for it was not pleasing to him to be much without company; and though he was very capable of a judicious choice, he was often contented with the first that offered: for this he was sometimes reproved by his friends, who found him surrounded with felons; but the reproof was on that, as on other occasions, thrown away; he continued to gratify himself, and to set very little value on the opinion of others.

But here, as in every other scene of his life, he made use of such opportunities as occurred of benefiting those who were more miserable than himself, and was always ready to perform any offices of humanity to his fellow-prisoners.

He had now ceased from corresponding with any of his subscribers except one, who yet continued to remit him the twenty pounds a year which he had promised him, and by whom it was expected that he would have been in a very short time enlarged, because he had directed the keeper to enquire after the state of his debts.

However, he took care to enter his name according to the forms of the court, that the creditor might be obliged to make him some allowance, if he was continued a prisoner, and when on that occasion he appeared in the hall was treated with very unusual respect.

But the resentment of the city was afterwards raised by some accounts that had been spread of the satire, and he was informed that some of the merchants intended to pay the allowance which the law required, and to detain him a prisoner at their own expence. This he treated as an empty menace; and perhaps might have hastened the publication, only to shew how much he was superior to their insults, had not all his schemes been suddenly destroyed.

When he had been six months in prison, he received from one of his friends[1], in whose kindness he had the greatest confidence, and on whose assistance he chiefly depended, a letter, that contained a charge of very atrocious ingratitude, drawn up in such terms as sudden resentment dictated. Henley, in one of his advertisements, had mentioned *Pope's treatment of Savage*.* This was supposed by Pope to be the consequence of a complaint made by Savage to Henley, and was therefore mentioned by him with much resentment. Mr. Savage returned a very solemn protestation of his innocence, but however appeared much disturbed at the accusation. Some days afterwards he was seized with a pain in his back and side, which, as it was not violent, was not suspected to be dangerous; but growing daily more languid and dejected, on the 25th of July he confined himself to his room, and a fever seized his spirits. The symptoms grew every day more formidable, but his condition did not enable him to procure any assistance. The last time that the keeper saw him was on July the 31st, 1743; when Savage, seeing him at his bed-side, said, with an uncommon earnestness, "I have something to say to you, Sir;" but, after a pause, moved his hand in a melancholy manner; and, finding himself unable to recollect what he was going to communicate, said, " 'Tis gone!" The keeper soon after left him; and the next morning he died. He was buried in the church-yard of St. Peter, at the expence of the keeper.

Such were the life and death of Richard Savage, a man equally distinguished by his virtues and vices; and at once remarkable for his weaknesses and abilities.

[1] Mr. Pope.

He was of a middle stature, of a thin habit of body, a long visage, coarse features, and melancholy aspect; of a grave and manly deportment, a solemn dignity of mien; but which, upon a nearer acquaintance, softened into an engaging easiness of manners. His walk was slow, and his voice tremulous and mournful. He was easily excited to smiles, but very seldom provoked to laughter.

His mind was in an uncommon degree vigorous and active. His judgment was accurate, his apprehension quick, and his memory so tenacious, that he was frequently observed to know what he had learned from others in a short time, better than those by whom he was informed; and could frequently recollect incidents, with all their combination of circumstances, which few would have regarded at the present time, but which the quickness of his apprehension impressed upon him. He had the peculiar felicity, that his attention never deserted him; he was present to every object, and regardful of the most trifling occurrences. He had the art of escaping from his own reflections, and accommodating himself to every new scene.

To this quality is to be imputed the extent of his knowledge, compared with the small time which he spent in visible endeavours to acquire it. He mingled in cursory conversation with the same steadiness of attention as others apply to a lecture; and, amidst the appearance of thoughtless gaiety, lost no new idea that was started, nor any hint that could be improved. He had therefore made in coffee-houses the same proficiency as others in their closets: and it is remarkable, that the writings of a man of little education and little reading have an air of learning scarcely to be found in any other performances, but which perhaps as often obscures as embellishes them.

His judgement was eminently exact both with regard to writings and to men. The knowledge of life was indeed his chief attainment; and it is not without some satisfaction, that I can produce the suffrage of Savage in favour of human nature, of which he never appeared to entertain such odious ideas as some, who perhaps had neither his judgement nor experience, have published, either in ostentation of their sagacity, vindication of their crimes, or gratification of their malice.

His method of life particularly qualified him for conversation, of which he knew how to practise all the graces. He was never vehement or loud, but at once modest and easy, open and respectful; his language was vivacious and elegant, and equally happy upon grave or humourous subjects. He was generally censured for not knowing when to retire; but that was not the defect of his judgement, but of his fortune; when he left his company, he was frequently to spend the remaining part of the night in the street, or at least was abandoned to gloomy reflections, which it is not strange that he delayed as long as he could; and sometimes forgot that he gave others pain to avoid it himself.

It cannot be said, that he made use of his abilities for the direction of his own conduct: an irregular and dissipated manner of life had made him the slave of every passion that happened to be excited by the presence of its object, and that slavery to his passions reciprocally produced a life irregular and dissipated. He was not master of his own motions, nor could promise any thing for the next day.

With regard to his œconomy, nothing can be added to the relation of his life. He appeared to think himself born to be supported by others, and dispensed from all necessity of providing for himself; he therefore never prosecuted any scheme of advantage, nor endeavoured even to secure the profits which his writings might have afforded him. His temper was, in consequence of the dominion of his passions, uncertain and capricious; he was easily engaged, and easily disgusted; but he is accused of retaining his hatred more tenaciously than his benevolence.

He was compassionate both by nature and principle, and always ready to perform offices of humanity; but when he was provoked (and very small offences were sufficient to provoke him), he would prosecute his revenge with the utmost acrimony till his passion had subsided.

His friendship was therefore of little value; for though he was zealous in the support or vindication of those whom he loved, yet it was always dangerous to trust him, because he considered himself as discharged by the first quarrel from all ties of honour or gratitude; and would betray those secrets which, in the warmth of confidence, had been imparted to him. This practice drew upon him an universal accusation of ingratitude: nor can it be denied that he was very ready to set himself free from the load of an obligation; for he could not bear to conceive himself in a state of dependence, his pride being equally powerful with his other passions, and appearing in the form of insolence at one time, and of vanity at another. Vanity, the most innocent species of pride, was most frequently predominant: He could not easily leave off, when he had once begun to mention himself or his works; nor ever read his verses without stealing his eyes from the page, to discover, in the faces of his audience, how they were affected with any favourite passage.

A kinder name than that of vanity ought to be given to the delicacy with which he was always careful to separate his own merit from every other man's, and to reject that praise to which he had no claim. He did not forget, in mentioning his performances, to mark every line that had been suggested or amended; and was so accurate, as to relate that he owed three words in *The Wanderer* to the advice of his friends.

His veracity was questioned, but with little reason; his accounts, though not indeed always the same, were generally consistent. When he loved any man, he suppressed all his faults; and, when he had been offended by him, concealed all his virtues: but his characters were generally true, so far as he proceeded; though it cannot be denied, that his partiality might have sometimes the effect of falsehood.

In cases indifferent, he was zealous for virtue, truth, and justice: he knew very well the necessity of goodness to the present and future happiness of mankind; nor is there perhaps any writer, who has less endeavoured to please by flattering the appetites, or perverting the judgement.

As an author, therefore, and he now ceases to influence mankind in any other character, if one piece which he had resolved to suppress be excepted, he has very little to fear from the strictest moral or religious censure. And though he may not be altogether secure against the objections of the critic, it must however be acknowledged, that his works are the productions of a genius truly poetical; and, what many writers who have been more lavishly applauded cannot boast, that they have an original air, which has no resemblance of any foregoing work, that the versification and sentiments have a cast peculiar to themselves, which no man can imitate with success, because what was nature in Savage, would in another be affectation. It must be confessed, that his descriptions are striking, his images animated, his fictions justly imagined, and his allegories artfully pursued; that his diction is elevated, though sometimes forced, and his numbers sonorous and majestic, though frequently sluggish and encumbered. Of his style, the general fault is harshness, and its general excellence is dignity; of his sentiments, the prevailing beauty is sublimity, and uniformity the prevailing defect.

For his life, or for his writings, none, who candidly consider his fortune, will think an apology either necessary or difficult. If he was not always sufficiently instructed in his subject, his knowledge was at least greater than could have been attained by others in the same state. If his works were sometimes unfinished, accuracy cannot reasonably be exacted from a man oppressed with want, which he has no hope of relieving but by a speedy publication. The insolence and resentment of which he is accused were not easily to be avoided by a great mind, irritated by perpetual hardships, and constrained hourly to return the spurns of contempt, and repress the insolence of prosperity; and vanity may surely readily be pardoned in him, to whom life afforded no other comforts than barren praises, and the consciousness of deserving them.

Those are no proper judges of his conduct, who have slumbered away their time on the down of plenty; nor will any wise man presume to say, "Had I been in Savage's condition, I should have lived or written better than Savage."

This relation will not be wholly without its use, if those, who languish under any part of his sufferings, shall be enabled to fortify their patience, by reflecting that they feel only those afflictions from which the abilities of Savage did not exempt him; or those, who, in confidence of superior capacities or attainments, disregard the common maxims of life, shall be reminded, that nothing will supply the want of prudence; and that negligence and irregularity, long continued, will make knowledge useless, wit ridiculous, and genius contemptible.

SWIFT

AN Account of Dr. Swift has been already collected, with great diligence and acuteness, by Dr. Hawkesworth, according to a scheme which I laid before him in the intimacy of our friendship.* I cannot therefore be expected to say much of a life, concerning which I had long since communicated my thoughts to a man capable of dignifying his narration with so much elegance of language and force of sentiment.

JONATHAN SWIFT was, according to an account said to be written by himself,* the son of Jonathan Swift, an attorney, and was born at Dublin on St. Andrew's day, 1667: according to his own report, as delivered by Pope to Spence, he was born at Leicester, the son of a clergyman, who was minister of a parish in Herefordshire.[1] During his life the place of his birth was undetermined. He was contented to be called an Irishman by the Irish; but would occasionally call himself an Englishman. The question may, without much regret, be left in the obscurity in which he delighted to involve it.

Whatever was his birth, his education was Irish. He was sent at the age of six to the school at Kilkenny, and in his fifteenth year (1682) was admitted into the University of Dublin.*

In his academical studies he was either not diligent or not happy. It must disappoint every reader's expectation, that, when at the usual time he claimed the Bachelorship of Arts, he was found by the examiners too conspicuously deficient for regular admission, and obtained his degree at last by *special favour*; a term used in that university to denote want of merit.

Of this disgrace it may be easily supposed that he was much ashamed, and shame had its proper effect in producing reformation. He resolved from that time to study eight hours a-day, and continued his industry for seven years, with what improvement is sufficiently known. This part of his story well deserves to be remembered; it may afford useful admonition and powerful encouragement to men, whose abilities have been made for a time useless by their passions

[1] Spence's Anecdotes, vol. II. p. 273.

or pleasures, and who, having lost one part of life in idleness, are tempted to throw away the remainder in despair.

In this course of daily application he continued three years longer at Dublin; and in this time, if the observation and memory of an old companion may be trusted, he drew the first sketch of his *Tale of a Tub*.

When he was about one-and-twenty (1688), being by the death of Godwin Swift his uncle, who had supported him, left without subsistence, he went to consult his mother, who then lived at Leicester, about the future course of his life, and by her direction solicited the advice and patronage of Sir William Temple,* who had married one of Mrs. Swift's relations, and whose father Sir John Temple, Master of the Rolls in Ireland, had lived in great familiarity of friendship with Godwin Swift, by whom Jonathan had been to that time maintained.

Temple received with sufficient kindness the nephew of his father's friend, with whom he was, when they conversed together, so much pleased, that he detained him two years in his house. Here he became known to King William, who sometimes visited Temple when he was disabled by the gout, and, being attended by Swift in the garden, shewed him how to cut asparagus in the Dutch way.

King William's notions were all military; and he expressed his kindness to Swift by offering to make him a captain of horse.

When Temple removed to Moor-park, he took Swift with him; and when he was consulted by the Earl of Portland* about the expedience of complying with a bill then depending for making parliaments triennial, against which King William was strongly prejudiced, after having in vain tried to shew the Earl that the proposal involved nothing dangerous to royal power, he sent Swift for the same purpose to the King. Swift, who probably was proud of his employment, and went with all the confidence of a young man, found his arguments, and his art of displaying them, made totally ineffectual by the predetermination of the King; and used to mention this disappointment as his first antidote against vanity.

Before he left Ireland he contracted a disorder, as he thought, by eating too much fruit. The original of diseases is commonly obscure. Almost every boy eats as much fruit as he can get, without any great inconvenience. The disease of Swift was giddiness with deafness, which attacked him from time to time, began very early, pursued him through life, and at last sent him to the grave, deprived of reason.

Being much oppressed at Moor-park by this grievous malady, he was advised to try his native air, and went to Ireland; but, finding no benefit, returned to Sir William, at whose house he continued his studies, and is known to have read, among other books, *Cyprian* and *Irenæus*.* He thought exercise of great necessity, and used to run half a mile up and down a hill every two hours.

It is easy to imagine that the mode in which his first degree was conferred left him no great fondness for the University of Dublin, and therefore he resolved to become a Master of Arts at Oxford. In the testimonial which he produced, the words of disgrace were omitted, and he took his Master's degree (July 5, 1692) with such reception and regard as fully contented him.

While he lived with Temple, he used to pay his mother at Leicester an yearly visit. He travelled on foot, unless some violence of weather drove him into a waggon, and at night he would go to a penny lodging, where he purchased clean sheets for sixpence. This practice Lord Orrery* imputes to his innate love of grossness and vulgarity: some may ascribe it to his desire of surveying human life through all its varieties; and others, perhaps with equal probability, to a passion which seems to have been deep fixed in his heart, the love of a shilling.

In time he began to think that his attendance at Moor-park deserved some other recompence than the pleasure, however mingled with improvement, of Temple's conversation; and grew so impatient, that (1694) he went away in discontent.

Temple, conscious of having given reason for complaint, is said to have made him Deputy Master of the Rolls in Ireland; which, according to his kinsman's account, was an office which he knew him not able to discharge. Swift therefore resolved to enter into the Church, in which he had at first no higher hopes than of the chaplainship to the Factory at Lisbon; but being recommended to Lord Capel, he obtained the prebend of *Kilroot* in *Connor*, of about a hundred pounds a year.*

But the infirmities of Temple made a companion like Swift so necessary, that he invited him back, with a promise to procure him English preferment, in exchange for the prebend which he desired him to resign. With this request Swift complied, having perhaps equally repented their separation, and they lived on together with mutual satisfaction; and, in the four years that passed between his return and Temple's death, it is probable that he wrote the *Tale of a Tub* and the *Battle of the Books*.

Swift began early to think, or to hope, that he was a poet, and wrote Pindarick Odes to Temple, to the King, and to the Athenian Society,* a knot of obscure men, who published a periodical pamphlet of answers to questions, sent, or supposed to be sent, by Letters. I have been told that Dryden, having perused these verses, said, "Cousin Swift,* you will never be a poet;" and that this denunciation was the motive of Swift's perpetual malevolence to Dryden.

In 1699 Temple died, and left a legacy with his manuscripts to Swift, for whom he had obtained, from King William, a promise of the first prebend that should be vacant at Westminster or Canterbury.

That this promise might not be forgotten, Swift dedicated to the King the posthumous works with which he was intrusted; but neither the dedication, nor tenderness for the man whom he once had treated with confidence and fondness, revived in King William the remembrance of his promise. Swift awhile attended the Court; but soon found his solicitations hopeless.

He was then invited by the Earl of Berkeley* to accompany him into Ireland, as his private secretary; but after having done the business till their arrival at Dublin, he then found that one *Bush* had persuaded the Earl that a Clergyman was not a proper secretary, and had obtained the office for himself. In a man like Swift, such circumvention and inconstancy must have excited violent indignation.

But he had yet more to suffer. Lord Berkeley had the disposal of the deanery of Derry, and Swift expected to obtain it; but by the secretary's influence, supposed to have been secured by a bribe, it was bestowed on somebody else; and Swift was dismissed with the livings of *Laracor* and *Rathbeggin* in the diocese of Meath, which together did not equal half the value of the deanery.

At Laracor he increased the parochial duty by reading prayers on Wednesdays and Fridays, and performed all the offices of his profession with great decency and exactness.

Soon after his settlement at Laracor, he invited to Ireland the unfortunate Stella, a young woman whose name was Johnson, the daughter of the steward of Sir William Temple, who, in consideration of her father's virtues, left her a thousand pounds. With her came Mrs. Dingley, whose whole fortune was twenty-seven pounds a year for her life.* With these Ladies he passed his hours of relaxation, and to them he opened his bosom; but they never resided in the same house, nor did he see either without a witness. They lived at the Parsonage, when Swift was away; and when he returned, removed to a lodging, or to the house of a neighbouring clergyman.

Swift was not one of those minds which amaze the world with early pregnancy: his first work, except his few poetical Essays, was the *Dissentions in Athens and Rome*, published (1701) in his thirty-fourth year. After its appearance, paying a visit to some bishop, he heard mention made of the new pamphlet that Burnet had written, replete with political knowledge. When he seemed to doubt Burnet's right to the work, he was told by the Bishop, that he was *a young man*; and, still persisting to doubt, that he was *a very positive young man*.

Three years afterward (1704) was published *The Tale of a Tub:* of this book charity may be persuaded to think that it might be written by a man of a peculiar character, without ill intention; but it is certainly of dangerous example. That Swift was its author, though it be universally believed, was never owned by himself, nor very well proved by any evidence; but no other claimant can be produced, and he did not deny it when Archbishop Sharpe and the Duchess of Somerset, by shewing it to the Queen, debarred him from a bishoprick.*

When this wild work first raised the attention of the publick, Sacheverell, meeting Smalridge,* tried to flatter him, by seeming to think him the author; but Smalridge answered with indignation, "Not all that you and I have in the world, nor all that ever we shall have, should hire me to write the *Tale of a Tub*."

The digressions relating to Wotton and Bentley* must be confessed to discover want of knowledge, or want of integrity; he did not understand the two controversies, or he willingly misrepresented them. But Wit can stand its ground against Truth only a little while. The honours due to learning have been justly distributed by the decision of posterity.

The Battle of the Books is so like the *Combat des Livres*, which the same question concerning the Ancients and Moderns had produced in France, that the improbability of such a coincidence of thoughts without communication is not, in my opinion, balanced by the anonymous protestation prefixed, in which all knowledge of the French book is peremptorily disowned.*

For some time after Swift was probably employed in solitary study, gaining the qualifications requisite for future eminence. How often he visited England, and with what diligence he attended his parishes, I know not. It was not till about four years afterwards that he became a professed author, and then one year (1708) produced *The Sentiments of a Church-of-England Man;* the ridicule of Astrology, under the name of *Bickerstaff;* the *Argument against abolishing Christianity;* and the defence of the *Sacramental Test.*

The Sentiments of a Church-of-England Man is written with great coolness, moderation, ease, and perspicuity. The *Argument against abolishing Christianity* is a very happy and judicious irony. One passage in it deserves to be selected.

"If Christianity were once abolished, how could the free-thinkers, the strong reasoners, and the men of profound learning, be able to find another subject so calculated, in all points, whereon to display their abilities? What wonderful productions of wit should we be deprived of from those, whose genius, by continual practice, hath been wholly turned upon raillery and invectives against religion, and would therefore never be able to shine, or distinguish themselves, upon any other subject? We are daily complaining of the great decline of wit among us, and would take away the greatest, perhaps the only, topick we have left. Who would ever have suspected Asgill for a wit, or Toland for a philosopher, if the inexhaustible stock of Christianity had not been at hand to provide them with materials? What other subject, through all art or nature, could have produced Tindal for a profound author, or furnished him with readers? It is the wise choice of the subject that alone adorns and distinguishes the writer. For had an hundred such pens as these been employed on the side of religion, they would have immediately sunk into silence and oblivion."

The reasonableness of a *Test* is not hard to be proved; but perhaps it must be allowed that the proper test has not been chosen.

The attention paid to the papers published under the name of *Bickerstaff*, induced Steele, when he projected the *Tatler*, to assume an appellation which had already gained possession of the reader's notice.*

In the year following he wrote a *Project for the Advancement of Religion*, addressed to Lady Berkeley; by whose kindness it is not unlikely that he was advanced to his benefices. To this project, which is formed with great purity of intention, and displayed with spriteliness and elegance, it can only be objected, that, like many projects, it is, if not generally impracticable, yet evidently hopeless, as it supposes more zeal, concord, and perseverance, than a view of mankind gives reason for expecting.

He wrote likewise this year a *Vindication of Bickerstaff;* and an explanation of an *Ancient Prophecy*, part written after the facts, and the rest never completed, but well planned to excite amazement.

Soon after began the busy and important part of Swift's life. He was employed (1710) by the primate of Ireland to solicit the Queen for a remission of the First Fruits and Twentieth parts to the Irish Clergy. With this purpose he had recourse to Mr. Harley, to whom he was mentioned as a man neglected and oppressed by the last ministry, because he had refused to co-operate with some of their schemes. What he had refused, has never been told; what he had suffered was, I suppose, the exclusion from a bishoprick by the remonstrances of Sharpe, whom he describes as *the harmless tool of others hate*, and whom he represents as afterwards *suing for pardon*.*

Harley's designs and situation were such as made him glad of an auxiliary so well qualified for his service; he therefore soon admitted him to familiarity, whether ever to confidence some have made a doubt; but it would have been difficult to excite his zeal without persuading him that he was trusted, and not very easy to delude him by false persuasions.

He was certainly admitted to those meetings in which the first hints and original plan of action are supposed to have been formed; and was one of the sixteen Ministers, or agents of the Ministry, who met weekly at each other's houses, and were united by the name of *Brother*.*

Being not immediately considered as an obdurate Tory, he conversed indiscriminately with all the wits, and was yet the friend of Steele; who, in the *Tatler*, which began in 1710, confesses the advantages of his conversation, and mentions something contributed by him to his paper. But he was now immerging into political controversy; for the same year produced the *Examiner*, of which Swift wrote thirty-three papers. In argument he may be allowed to have the advantage; for where a wide system of conduct, and the whole of a publick character, is laid open to enquiry, the accuser having the choice of facts, must be very unskilful if he does not prevail; but with regard to wit, I am afraid none of Swift's papers will be found equal to those by which Addison opposed him.*

Early in the next year he published a *Proposal for correcting, improving, and ascertaining the English Tongue*, in a Letter to the Earl of Oxford;* written without much knowledge of the general nature of language, and without any accurate enquiry into the history of other tongues. The certainty and stability which, contrary to all experience, he thinks attainable, he proposes to secure by instituting an academy; the decrees of which every man would have been willing, and many would have been proud to disobey, and which, being renewed by successive elections, would in a short time have differed from itself.

He wrote the same year a *Letter to the October Club*, a number of Tory Gentlemen sent from the country to Parliament, who formed themselves into a club, to the number of about a hundred, and met to animate the zeal and raise the expectations of each other. They thought, with great reason, that the Ministers were losing opportunities; that sufficient use was not made of the ardour of the nation; they called loudly for more changes, and stronger efforts; and demanded the punishment of part, and the dismission of the rest, of those whom they considered as publick robbers.

Their eagerness was not gratified by the Queen, or by Harley. The Queen was probably slow because she was afraid, and Harley was slow because he was doubtful; he was a Tory only by necessity, or for convenience; and when he had power in his hands, had no settled purpose for which he should employ it; forced to gratify to a certain degree the Tories who supported him, but unwilling to make his reconcilement to the Whigs utterly desperate, he corresponded at once with the two expectants of the Crown, and kept, as has been observed, the succession undetermined. Not knowing what to do, he did nothing; and with the fate of a double-dealer, at last he lost his power, but kept his enemies.

Swift seems to have concurred in opinion with the *October Club;* but it was not in his power to quicken the tardiness of Harley, whom he stimulated as much as he could, but with little effect. He that knows not whither to go, is in no haste to move. Harley, who was perhaps not quick by nature, became yet more slow by irresolution; and was content to hear that dilatoriness lamented as natural, which he applauded in himself as politick.

Without the Tories, however, nothing could be done; and as they were not to be gratified, they must be appeased; and the conduct of the Minister, if it could not be vindicated, was to be plausibly excused.

Swift now attained the zenith of his political importance: he published (1712) the *Conduct of the Allies*, ten days before the

Parliament assembled. The purpose was to persuade the nation to a peace; and never had any writer more success. The people, who had been amused with bonfires and triumphal processions, and looked with idolatry on the General* and his friends, who, as they thought had made England the arbitress of nations, were confounded between shame and rage, when they found that *mines had been exhausted, and millions destroyed*, to secure the Dutch or aggrandize the emperor, without any advantage to ourselves; that we had been bribing our neighbours to fight their own quarrel; and that amongst our enemies we might number our allies.

That is now no longer doubted, of which the nation was then first informed, that the war was unnecessarily protracted to fill the pockets of Marlborough; and that it would have been continued without end, if he could have continued his annual plunder. But Swift, I suppose, did not yet know what he has since written, that a commission was drawn which would have appointed him General for life, had it not become ineffectual by the resolution of Lord Cowper, who refused the seal.

Whatever is received, say the schools, *is received in proportion to the recipient.* The power of a political treatise depends much upon the disposition of the people; the nation was then combustible, and a spark set it on fire. It is boasted, that between November and January eleven thousand were sold; a great number at that time, when we were not yet a nation of readers. To its propagation certainly no agency of power or influence was wanting. It furnished arguments for conversation, speeches for debate, and materials for parliamentary resolutions.

Yet, surely, whoever surveys this wonder-working pamphlet with cool perusal, will confess that its efficacy was supplied by the passions of its readers; that it operates by the mere weight of facts, with very little assistance from the hand that produced them.

This year (1712) he published his *Reflections on the Barrier Treaty*, which carries on the design of his *Conduct of the Allies*, and shews how little regard in that negotiation had been shewn to the interest of England, and how much of the conquered country had been demanded by the Dutch.

This was followed by *Remarks on the Bishop of Sarum's Introduction to his third Volume of the History of the Reformation*; a pamphlet which Burnet* published as an alarm, to warn the nation of the approach of Popery. Swift, who seems to have disliked the Bishop with something more than political aversion, treats him like one whom he is glad of an opportunity to insult.

Swift, being now the declared favourite and supposed confidant of the Tory Ministry, was treated by all that depended on the Court with the respect which dependents know how to pay. He soon began to feel part of the misery of greatness; he that could say he knew him, considered himself as having fortune in his power. Commissions, solicitations, remonstrances, crowded about him; he was expected to do every man's business, to procure employment for one, and to retain it for another. In assisting those who addressed him, he represents himself as sufficiently diligent; and desires to have others believe, what he probably believed himself, that by his interposition many Whigs of merit, and among them Addison and Congreve, were continued in their places. But every man of known influence has so many petitions which he cannot grant, that he must necessarily offend more than he gratifies, because the preference given to one affords all the rest a reason for complaint. *When I give away a place*, said Lewis XIV. *I make an hundred discontented, and one ungrateful.*

Much has been said of the equality and independence which he preserved in his conversation with the Ministers, of the frankness of his remonstrances, and the familiarity of his friendship. In accounts of this kind a few single incidents are set against the general tenour of behaviour. No man, however, can pay a more servile tribute to the Great, than by suffering his liberty in their presence to aggrandize him in his own esteem. Between different ranks of the community there is necessarily some distance: he who is called by his superior to pass the interval, may properly accept the invitation; but petulance and obtrusion are rarely produced by magnanimity; nor have often any nobler cause than the pride of importance, and the malice of inferiority. He who knows himself necessary may set, while that necessity lasts, a high value upon himself; as, in a lower condition, a servant eminently skilful may be saucy; but he is saucy only because he is servile. Swift appears to have preserved the kindness of the great when they wanted him no longer; and therefore it must be allowed, that the childish freedom, to which he seems enough inclined, was overpowered by his better qualities.

His disinterestedness has been likewise mentioned; a strain of heroism, which would have been in his condition romantick and superfluous. Ecclesiastical benefices, when they become vacant, must be given away; and the friends of Power may, if there be no inherent disqualification, reasonably expect them. Swift accepted (1713) the deanery of St. Patrick, the best preferment that his friends could venture to give him. That Ministry was in a great degree supported by the Clergy, who were not yet reconciled to the author of the *Tale of a Tub*, and would not without much discontent and indignation have born to see him installed in an English Cathedral.

He refused, indeed, fifty pounds from Lord Oxford; but he accepted afterwards a draught of a thousand upon the Exchequer, which was intercepted by the Queen's death, and which he resigned, as he says himself, *multa gemens, with many a groan*.*

In the midst of his power and his politicks, he kept a journal of his visits, his walks, his interviews with Ministers, and quarrels with his servant, and transmitted it to Mrs. Johnson and Mrs. Dingley, to whom he knew that whatever befel him was interesting, and no accounts could be too minute. Whether these diurnal trifles were properly exposed to eyes which had never received any pleasure from the presence of the Dean, may be reasonably doubted: they have, however, some odd attraction; the reader, finding frequent mention of names which he has been used to consider as important, goes on in hope of information; and, as there is nothing to fatigue attention, if he is disappointed he can hardly complain. It is easy to perceive, from every page, that though ambition pressed Swift into a life of bustle, the wish for a life of ease was always returning.

He went to take possession of his deanery, as soon as he had obtained it; but he was not suffered to stay in Ireland more than a fortnight before he was recalled to England, that he might reconcile Lord Oxford and Lord Bolingbroke, who began to look on one another with malevolence, which every day increased, and which Bolingbroke appeared to retain in his last years.

Swift contrived an interview, from which they both departed discontented: he procured a second, which only convinced him that the feud was irreconcileable; he told them his opinion, that all was lost. This denunciation was contradicted by Oxford, but Bolingbroke whispered that he was right.

Before this violent dissension had shattered the Ministry, Swift had published, in the beginning of the year (1714), *The publick Spirit of the Whigs*, in answer to *The Crisis*, a pamphlet for which *Steele* was expelled from the House of Commons. Swift was now so far alienated from *Steele* as to think him no longer entitled to decency, and therefore treats him sometimes with contempt, and sometimes with abhorrence.

In this pamphlet the Scotch were mentioned in terms so provoking to that irritable nation, that, resolving *not to be offended with impunity*, the Scotch Lords in a body demanded an audience of the Queen, and solicited reparation. A proclamation was issued, in which three hundred pounds was offered for discovery of the author. From this storm he was, as he relates, *secured by a sleight*; of what kind, or by whose prudence, is not known; and such was the increase of his reputation, that the Scottish *Nation applied again that he would be their friend*.

He was become so formidable to the Whigs, that his familiarity with the Ministers was clamoured at in Parliament, particularly by two men, afterwards of great note, *Aislabie** and *Walpole*.

But, by the disunion of his great friends, his importance and his designs were now at an end; and seeing his services at last useless, he retired about June (1714) into Berkshire, where, in the house of a friend, he wrote what was then suppressed, but has since appeared under the title of *Free Thoughts on the present State of Affairs*.

While he was waiting in this retirement for events which time or chance might bring to pass, the death of the Queen broke down at once the whole system of Tory Politicks; and nothing remained but to withdraw from the implacability of triumphant Whiggism, and shelter himself in unenvied obscurity.

The accounts of his reception in Ireland, given by Lord Orrery and Dr. Delany,* are so different, that the credit of the writers, both undoubtedly veracious, cannot be saved, but by supposing, what I think is true, that they speak of different times. When Delany says that he was received with respect, he means for the first fortnight, when he came to take legal possession; and when Lord Orrery tells that he was pelted by the populace, he is to be understood of the time when, after the Queen's death, he became a settled resident.

The Archbishop of Dublin gave him at first some disturbance in the exercise of his jurisdiction; but it was soon discovered, that between prudence and integrity he was seldom in the wrong; and that, when he was right, his spirit did not easily yield to opposition.

Having so lately quitted the tumults of a party and the intrigues of a court, they still kept his thoughts in agitation, as the sea fluctuates a while when the storm has ceased. He therefore filled his hours with some historical attempts, relating to the *Change of the Ministers* and *the Conduct of the Ministry*. He likewise is said to have written a *History of the Four last Years of Queen Anne*, which he began in her lifetime, and afterwards laboured with great attention, but never published. It was after his death in the hands of Lord Orrery and Dr. King. A book under that title was published, with Swift's name, by Dr. Lucas;* of which I can only say, that it seemed by no means to correspond with the notions that I had formed of it, from a conversation which I once heard between the Earl of Orrery and old Mr. Lewis.*

Swift now, much against his will, commenced Irishman for life, and was to contrive how he might be best accommodated in a country where he considered himself as in a state of exile. It seems that his first recourse was to piety. The thoughts of death rushed upon him, at this time, with such incessant importunity, that they took possession of his mind, when he first waked, for many years together.

He opened his house by a publick table two days a week, and found his entertainments gradually frequented by more and more visitants of learning among the men, and of elegance among the women. Mrs. Johnson had left the country, and lived in lodgings not far from the deanery. On his publick days she regulated the table, but appeared at it as a mere guest, like other Ladies.

On other days he often dined, at a stated price, with Mr. Worral,* a clergyman of his cathedral, whose house was recommended by the peculiar neatness and pleasantry of his wife. To this frugal mode of living, he was first disposed by care to pay some debts which he had contracted, and he continued it for the pleasure of accumulating money. His avarice, however, was not suffered to obstruct the claims of his dignity; he was served in plate, and used to say that he was the poorest gentleman in Ireland that eat upon plate, and the richest that lived without a coach.

How he spent the rest of his time, and how he employed his hours of study, has been enquired with hopeless curiosity. For who can give an account of another's studies? Swift was not likely to admit any to his privacies, or to impart a minute account of his business or his leisure.

Soon after (1716), in his forty-ninth year, he was privately married to Mrs. Johnson by Dr. Ashe, Bishop of Clogher, as Dr. Madden told me, in the garden.* The marriage made no change in their mode of life; they lived in different houses, as before; nor did she ever lodge in the deanery but when Swift was seized with a fit of giddiness. "It would be difficult," says Lord Orrery, "to prove that they were ever afterwards together without a third person."

The Dean of St. Patrick's lived in a private manner, known and regarded only by his friends, till, about the year 1720, he, by a pamphlet, recommended to the Irish the use, and consequently the improvement, of their manufacture. For a man to use the productions of his own labour is surely a natural right, and to like best what he makes himself is a natural passion. But to excite this passion, and enforce this right, appeared so criminal to those who had an interest in the English trade, that the printer was imprisoned; and, as Hawkesworth justly observes, the attention of the publick being by this outrageous resentment turned upon the proposal, the author was by consequence made popular.

In 1723 died Mrs. Van Homrigh,* a woman made unhappy by her admiration of wit, and ignominiously distinguished by the name of *Vanessa*, whose conduct has been already sufficiently discussed, and whose history is too well known to be minutely repeated. She was a young woman fond of literature, whom *Decanus* the *Dean*, called *Cadenus* by transposition of the letters, took pleasure in directing and instructing; till, from being proud of his praise, she grew fond of his person. Swift was then about forty-seven, at an age when vanity is strongly excited by the amorous attention of a young woman. If it be said that Swift should have checked a passion which he never meant to gratify, recourse must be had to that extenuation which he so much despised, *men are but men:** perhaps however he did not at first know his own mind, and, as he represents himself, was undetermined. For his admission of her courtship, and his indulgence of her hopes after his marriage to Stella, no other honest plea can be found, than that he delayed a disagreeable discovery from time to time, dreading the immediate bursts of distress, and watching for a favourable moment. She thought herself neglected, and died of disappointment; having ordered by her will the poem to be published, in which *Cadenus* had proclaimed her excellence, and confessed his love. The effect of the publication upon the Dean and Stella is thus related by Delany.*

"I have good reason to believe, that they both were greatly shocked and distressed (though it may be differently) upon this occasion.

The Dean made a tour to the South of Ireland, for about two months, at this time, to dissipate his thoughts, and give place to obloquy. And Stella retired (upon the earnest invitation of the owner) to the house of a cheerful, generous, good-natured friend of the Dean's, whom she also much loved and honoured. There my informer often saw her; and, I have reason to believe, used his utmost endeavours to relieve, support, and amuse her, in this sad situation.

"One little incident he told me of, on that occasion, I think I shall never forget. As her friend was an hospitable, open-hearted man, well-beloved, and largely acquainted, it happened one day that some gentlemen dropt in to dinner, who were strangers to Stella's situation; and as the poem of *Cadenus and Vanessa* was then the general topic of conversation, one of them said, 'Surely that Vanessa must be an extraordinary woman, that could inspire the Dean to write so finely upon her.' Mrs. Johnson smiled, and answered, "that she thought that point not quite so clear; for it was well known the Dean could write finely upon a broomstick.""*

The great acquisition of esteem and influence was made by the *Drapier's Letters* in 1724. One Wood of Wolverhampton in Staffordshire, a man enterprising and rapacious, had, as is said, by a present to the Duchess of Munster, obtained a patent, empowering him to coin one hundred and eighty thousand pounds of halfpence and farthings for the kingdom of Ireland, in which there was a very inconvenient and embarrassing scarcity of copper coin; so that it was possible to run in debt upon the credit of a piece of money; for the cook or keeper of an alehouse could not refuse to supply a man that had silver in his hand, and the buyer would not leave his money without change.*

The project was therefore plausible. The scarcity, which was already great, Wood took care to make greater, by agents who gathered up the old half-pence; and was about to turn his brass into gold, by pouring the treasures of his new mint upon Ireland, when Swift, finding that the metal was debased to an enormous degree, wrote Letters, under the name of *M. B. Drapier*, to shew the folly of receiving, and the mischief that must ensue, by giving gold and silver for coin worth perhaps not a third part of its nominal value.

The nation was alarmed; the new coin was universally refused: but the governors of Ireland considered resistance to the King's patent as highly criminal; and one Whitshed, then Chief Justice,* who had tried the printer of the former pamphlet, and sent out the Jury nine times, till by clamour and menaces they were frighted into a special verdict, now presented the *Drapier*, but could not prevail on the Grand Jury to find the bill.

Lord Carteret and the Privy Council published a proclamation, offering three hundred pounds for discovering the author of the Fourth Letter.* Swift had concealed himself from his printers, and trusted only his butler, who transcribed the paper. The man, immediately after the appearance of the proclamation, strolled from the house, and staid out all night, and part of the next day. There was reason enough to fear that he had betrayed his master for the reward; but he came home, and the Dean ordered him to put off his livery, and leave the house; "for," says he, "I know that my life is in your power, and I will not bear, out of fear, either your insolence or negligence." The man excused his fault with great submission, and begged that he might be confined in the house while it was in his power to endanger his master; but the Dean resolutely turned him out, without taking farther notice of him, till the term of information had expired, and then received him again. Soon afterwards he ordered him and the rest of the servants into his presence, without telling his intentions, and bade them take notice that their fellow-servant was no longer Robert the butler; but that his integrity had made him Mr. Blakeney, verger of St. Patrick's; an officer whose income was between thirty and forty pounds a year: yet he still continued for some years to serve his old master as his butler.

Swift was known from this time by the appellation of *The Dean*. He was honoured by the populace, as the champion, patron, and instructor of Ireland; and gained such power as, considered both in its extent and duration, scarcely any man has ever enjoyed without greater wealth or higher station.

He was from this important year the oracle of the traders, and the idol of the rabble, and by consequence was feared and courted by all to whom the kindness of the traders or the populace was necessary. The *Drapier* was a sign; the *Drapier* was a health; and which way soever the eye or the ear was turned, some tokens were found of the nation's gratitude to the *Drapier*.

The benefit was indeed great; he had rescued Ireland from a very oppressive and predatory invasion; and the popularity which he had gained he was diligent to keep, by appearing forward and zealous on every occasion where the publick interest was supposed to be involved. Nor did he much scruple to boast his influence; for when, upon some attempts to regulate the coin, Archbishop Boulter,* then one of the Justices, accused him of exasperating the people, he exculpated himself by saying, "If I had lifted up my finger, they would have torn you to pieces."

But the pleasure of popularity was soon interrupted by domestic misery. Mrs. Johnson, whose conversation was to him the great softener of the ills of life, began in the year of the Drapier's triumph to decline; and two years afterwards was so wasted with sickness, that her recovery was considered as hopeless.

Swift was then in England, and had been invited by Lord Bolingbroke to pass the winter with him in France; but this call of calamity hastened him to Ireland, where perhaps his presence contributed to restore her to imperfect and tottering health.

He was now so much at ease, that (1727) he returned to England; where he collected three volumes of Miscellanies in conjunction with Pope, who prefixed a querulous and apologetical Preface.

This important year sent likewise into the world *Gulliver's Travels*, a production so new and strange, that it filled the reader with a mingled emotion of merriment and amazement. It was received with such avidity, that the price of the first edition was raised before the second could be made; it was read by the high and the low, the learned and illiterate. Criticism was for a while lost in wonder; no rules of judgement were applied to a book written in open defiance of truth and regularity. But when distinctions came to be made, the part which gave least pleasure was that which describes the *Flying Island*, and that which gave most disgust must be the history of the *Houyhnhnms*.

While Swift was enjoying the reputation of his new work, the news of the king's death* arrived; and he kissed the hands of the new King and Queen three days after their accession.

By the Queen, when she was Princess, he had been treated with some distinction, and was well received by her in her exaltation; but whether she gave hopes which she never took care to satisfy, or he formed expectations which she never meant to raise, the event was, that he always afterwards thought on her with malevolence, and particularly charged her with breaking her promise of some medals which she engaged to send him.

I know not whether she had not, in her turn, some reason for complaint. A Letter was sent her, not so much entreating as requiring her patronage of Mrs. Barber,* an ingenious Irishwoman, who was then begging subscriptions for her Poems. To this Letter was subscribed the name of *Swift*, and it has all the appearances of his diction and sentiments; but it was not written in his hand, and had some little improprieties. When he was charged with this Letter, he laid hold of the inaccuracies, and urged the improbability of the accusation; but never denied it: he shuffles between cowardice and veracity, and talks big when he says nothing.

He seemed desirous enough of recommencing courtier, and endeavoured to gain the kindness of Mrs. Howard, remembering what Mrs. Masham* had performed in former times; but his flatteries were, like those of the other wits, unsuccessful; the Lady either wanted power, or had no ambition of poetical immortality.

He was seized not long afterwards by a fit of giddiness, and again heard of the sickness and danger of Mrs. Johnson. He then left the house of Pope, as it seems, with very little ceremony, finding that *two sick friends cannot live together*;* and did not write to him till he found himself at Chester.

He returned to a home of sorrow: poor Stella was sinking into the grave, and, after a languishing decay of about two months, died in her forty-fourth year, on January 28, 1728. How much he wished her life, his papers shew; nor can it be doubted that he dreaded the death of her whom he loved most, aggravated by the consciousness that himself had hastened it.

Beauty and the power of pleasing, the greatest external advantages that woman can desire or possess, were fatal to the unfortunate Stella. The man whom she had the misfortune to love was, as Delany observes, fond of singularity, and desirous to make a mode of happiness for himself, different from the general course of things and order of Providence. From the time of her arrival in Ireland he seems resolved to keep her in his power, and therefore hindered a match sufficiently advantageous, by accumulating unreasonable demands, and prescribing conditions that could not be performed. While she was at her own disposal he did not consider his possession as secure; resentment, ambition, or caprice, might separate them; he was therefore resolved to make *assurance double sure*,* and to appropriate her by a private marriage, to which he had annexed the expectation of all the pleasures of perfect friendship, without the uneasiness of conjugal restraint. But with this state poor Stella was not satisfied; she never was treated as a wife, and to the world she had the appearance of a mistress. She lived sullenly on, in hope that in time he would own and receive her; but the time did not come till the change of his manners and depravation of his mind made her tell him, when he offered to acknowledge her, that *it was too late*. She then gave up herself to sorrowful resentment, and died under the tyranny of him, by whom she was in the highest degree loved and honoured.

What were her claims to this excentrick tenderness, by which the laws of nature were violated to retain her, curiosity will enquire; but how shall it be gratified? Swift was a lover; his testimony may be suspected. Delany and the Irish saw with Swift's eyes, and therefore add little confirmation. That she was virtuous, beautiful, and elegant, in a very high degree, such admiration from such a lover makes it very probable; but she had not much literature, for she could not spell her own language; and of her wit, so loudly vaunted, the smart sayings which Swift himself has collected afford no splendid specimen.

The reader of Swift's *Letter to a Lady on her Marriage*, may be allowed to doubt whether his opinion of female excellence ought implicitly to be admitted; for if his general thoughts on women were such as he exhibits, a very little sense in a Lady would enrapture, and a very little virtue would astonish him. Stella's supremacy, therefore, was perhaps only local; she was great, because her associates were little.

In some Remarks lately published on the Life of Swift,* this marriage is mentioned as fabulous, or doubtful; but, alas! poor Stella, as Dr. Madden told me, related her melancholy story to Dr. Sheridan,* when he attended her as a clergyman to prepare her for death; and Delany mentions it not with doubt, but only with regret. Swift never mentioned her without a sigh.

The rest of his life was spent in Ireland, in a country to which not even power almost despotick, nor flattery almost idolatrous, could reconcile him. He sometimes wished to visit England, but always found some reason of delay. He tells Pope, in the decline of life, that he hopes once more to see him; *but if not,* says he, *we must part, as all human beings have parted.**

After the death of Stella, his benevolence was contracted, and his severity exasperated; he drove his acquaintance from his table, and wondered why he was deserted. But he continued his attention to the publick, and wrote from time to time such directions, admonitions, or censures, as the exigency of affairs, in his opinion, made proper; and nothing fell from his pen in vain.

In a short poem on the Presbyterians, whom he always regarded with detestation, he bestowed one stricture upon Bettesworth, a lawyer eminent for his insolence to the clergy, which, from very considerable reputation, brought him into immediate and universal contempt.* Bettesworth, enraged at his disgrace and loss, went to Swift, and demanded whether he was the author of that poem? "Mr. Bettesworth," answered he, "I was in my youth acquainted with great lawyers, who, knowing my disposition to satire, advised me, that, if any scoundrel or blockhead whom I had lampooned should ask, *Are you the author of this paper?* I should tell him that I was not the author; and therefore I tell you, Mr. Bettesworth, that I am not the author of these lines."

Bettesworth was so little satisfied with this account, that he publickly professed his resolution of a violent and corporal revenge; but the inhabitants of St. Patrick's district embodied themselves in the Dean's defence. Bettesworth declared in Parliament, that Swift had deprived him of twelve hundred pounds a year.

Swift was popular a while by another mode of beneficence. He set aside some hundreds to be lent in small sums to the poor, from five shillings, I think, to five pounds. He took no interest, and only required that, at repayment, a small fee should be given to the accomptant; but he required that the day of promised payment should be exactly kept. A severe and punctilious temper is ill qualified for transactions with the poor; the day was often broken, and the loan was not repaid. This might have been easily foreseen; but for this Swift had made no provision of patience or pity. He ordered his debtors to be sued. A severe creditor has no popular character; what then was likely to be said of him who employs the catchpoll under the appearance of charity? The clamour against him was loud, and the resentment of the populace outrageous; he was therefore forced to drop his scheme, and own the folly of expecting punctuality from the poor.

His asperity continually increasing, condemned him to solitude; and his resentment of solitude sharpened his asperity. He was not, however, totally deserted: some men of learning, and some women of elegance, often visited him; and he wrote from time to time either verse or prose; of his verses he willingly gave copies, and is supposed to have felt no discontent when he saw them printed. His favourite maxim was *vive la bagatelle*; he thought trifles a necessary part of life, and perhaps found them necessary to himself. It seems impossible to him to be idle, and his disorders made it difficult or dangerous to be long seriously studious, or laboriously diligent. The love of ease is always gaining upon age, and he had one temptation to petty amusements peculiar to himself; whatever he did, he was sure to hear applauded; and such was his predominance over all that approached, that all their applauses were probably sincere. He that is much flattered, soon learns to flatter himself: we are commonly taught our duty by fear or shame, and how can they act upon the man who hears nothing but his own praises?

As his years increased, his fits of giddiness and deafness grew more frequent, and his deafness made conversation difficult; they grew likewise more severe, till in 1736, as he was writing a poem called *The Legion Club*, he was seized with a fit so painful, and so long continued, that he never after thought it proper to attempt any work of thought or labour.

He was always careful of his money, and was therefore no liberal entertainer; but was less frugal of his wine than of his meat. When his friends of either sex came to him, in expectation of a dinner, his custom was to give every one a shilling, that they might please themselves with their provision. At last his avarice grew too powerful for his kindness; he would refuse a bottle of wine, and in Ireland no man visits where he cannot drink.

Having thus excluded conversation, and desisted from study, he had neither business nor amusement; for having, by some ridiculous resolution or mad vow, determined never to wear spectacles, he could make little use of books in his later years: his ideas, therefore, being neither renovated by discourse, nor increased by reading, wore gradually away, and left his mind vacant to the vexations of the hour, till at last his anger was heightened into madness.

He however permitted one book to be published, which had been the production of former years; *Polite Conversation*, which appeared in 1738. The *Directions for Servants* was printed soon after his death. These two performances shew a mind incessantly attentive, and, when it was not employed upon great things, busy with minute occurrences. It is apparent that he must have had the habit of noting whatever he observed; for such a number of particulars could never have been assembled by the power of recollection.

He grew more violent; and his mental powers declined till (1741) it was found necessary that legal guardians should be appointed of his person and fortune. He now lost distinction. His madness was compounded of rage and fatuity. The last face that he knew was that of Mrs. Whiteway,* and her he ceased to know in a little time. His meat was brought him cut into mouthfuls; but he would never touch it while the servant staid, and at last, after it had stood perhaps an hour, would eat it walking; for he continued his old habit, and was on his feet ten hours a-day.

Next year (1742) he had an inflammation in his left eye, which swelled it to the size of an egg, with boils in other parts; he was kept long waking with the pain, and was not easily restrained by five attendants from tearing out his eye.

The tumour at last subsided; and a short interval of reason ensuing, in which he knew his physician and his family, gave hopes of his recovery; but in a few days he sunk into lethargick stupidity, motionless, heedless, and speechless. But it is said, that, after a year of total silence, when his housekeeper, on the 30th of November, told him that the usual bonfires and illuminations were preparing to celebrate his birth-day, he answered, *It is all folly; they had better let it alone.*

It is remembered that he afterwards spoke now and then, or gave some intimation of a meaning; but at last sunk into perfect silence, which continued till about the end of October 1744, when, in his seventy-eighth year, he expired without a struggle.

WHEN Swift is considered as an author, it is just to estimate his powers by their effects. In the reign of Queen Anne he turned the stream of popularity against the Whigs, and must be confessed to have dictated for a time the political opinions of the English nation. In the succeeding reign he delivered Ireland from plunder and oppression; and shewed that wit, confederated with truth, had such force as authority was unable to resist. He said truly of himself, that Ireland *was his debtor.** It was from the time when he first began to patronize the Irish, that they may date their riches and prosperity. He taught them first to know their own interest, their weight, and their strength, and gave them spirit to assert that equality with their fellow-subjects to which they have ever since been making vigorous advances, and to claim those rights which they have at last established. Nor can they be charged with ingratitude to their benefactor; for they reverenced him as a guardian, and obeyed him as a dictator.

In his works, he has given very different specimens both of sentiment and expression. His *Tale of a Tub* has little resemblance to his other pieces. It exhibits a vehemence and rapidity of mind, a copiousness of images, and vivacity of diction, such as he afterwards never possessed, or never exerted. It is of a mode so distinct and peculiar, that it must be considered by itself; what is true of that, is not true of any thing else which he has written.

In his other works is found an equable tenour of easy language, which rather trickles than flows. His delight was in simplicity. That he has in his works no metaphor, as has been said, is not true; but his few metaphors seem to be received rather by necessity than choice. He studied purity; and though perhaps all his structures are not exact, yet it is not often that solecisms can be found; and whoever depends on his authority may generally conclude himself safe. His sentences are never too much dilated or contracted; and it will not be easy to find any embarrassment in the complication of his clauses, any inconsequence in his connections, or abruptness in his transitions.

His style was well suited to his thoughts, which are never subtilised by nice disquisitions, decorated by sparkling conceits, elevated by ambitious sentences, or variegated by far-sought learning. He pays no court to the passions; he excites neither surprise nor admiration; he always understands himself: and his reader always understands him: the peruser of Swift wants little previous knowledge; it will be sufficient that he is acquainted with common words and common things; he is neither required to mount elevations, nor to explore profundities; his passage is always on a level, along solid ground, without asperities, without obstruction.

This easy and safe conveyance of meaning it was Swift's desire to attain, and for having attained he deserves praise, though perhaps not the highest praise. For purposes merely didactick, when something is to be told that was not known before, it is the best mode, but against that inattention by which known truths are suffered to lie neglected, it makes no provision; it instructs, but does not persuade.

By his political education he was associated with the Whigs; but he deserted them when they deserted their principles, yet without running into the contrary extreme; he continued throughout his life to retain the disposition which he assigns to the *Church-of-England Man*, of thinking commonly with the Whigs of the State, and with the Tories of the Church.

He was a churchman rationally zealous; he desired the prosperity, and maintained the honour of the Clergy; of the Dissenters he did not wish to infringe the toleration, but he opposed their encroachments.

To his duty as Dean he was very attentive. He managed the revenues of his church with exact œconomy; and it is said by Delany, that more money was, under his direction, laid out in repairs than had ever been in the same time since its first erection. Of his choir he was eminently careful; and, though he neither loved nor understood musick, took care that all the singers were well qualified, admitting none without the testimony of skilful judges.

In his church he restored the practice of weekly communion, and distributed the sacramental elements in the most solemn and devout manner with his own hand. He came to church every morning, preached commonly in his turn, and attended the evening anthem, that it might not be negligently performed.

He read the service *rather with a strong nervous voice than in a graceful manner; his voice was sharp and high-toned, rather than harmonious.**

He entered upon the clerical state with hope to excel in preaching; but complained, that, from the time of his political controversies, *he could only preach pamphlets.** This censure of himself, if judgement be made from those sermons which have been published, was unreasonably severe.

The suspicions of his irreligion proceeded in a great measure from his dread of hypocrisy; instead of wishing to seem better, he delighted in seeming worse than he was. He went in London to early prayers, lest he should be seen at church; he read prayers to his servants every morning with such dexterous secrecy, that Dr. Delany was six months in his house before he knew it. He was not only careful to hide the good which he did, but willingly incurred the suspicion of evil which he did not. He forgot what himself had formerly asserted, that hypocrisy is less mischievous than open impiety. Dr. Delany, with all his zeal for his honour, has justly condemned this part of his character.

The person of Swift had not many recommendations. He had a kind of muddy complexion, which, though he washed himself with oriental scrupulosity, did not look clear. He had a countenance sour and severe, which he seldom softened by any appearance of gaiety. He stubbornly resisted any tendency to laughter.

To his domesticks he was naturally rough; and a man of a rigorous temper, with that vigilance of minute attention which his works discover, must have been a master that few could bear. That he was disposed to do his servants good, on important occasions, is no great mitigation; benefaction can be but rare, and tyrannick peevishness is perpetual. He did not spare the servants of others. Once, when he dined alone with the Earl of Orrery, he said, of one that waited in the room, *That man has, since we sat to the table, committed fifteen faults.* What the faults were, Lord Orrery, from whom I heard the story, had not been attentive enough to discover. My number may perhaps not be exact.

In his œconomy he practised a peculiar and offensive parsimony, without disguise or apology. The practice of saving being once necessary, became habitual, and grew first ridiculous, and at last detestable. But his avarice, though it might exclude pleasure, was never suffered to encroach upon his virtue. He was frugal by inclination, but liberal by principle; and if the purpose to which he destined his little accumulations be remembered, with his distribution of occasional charity, it will perhaps appear that he only liked one mode of expence better than another, and saved merely that he might have something to give. He did not grow rich by injuring his successors, but left both Laracor and the Deanery more valuable than he found them.

—With all this talk of his covetousness and generosity, it should be remembered that he was never rich. The revenue of his Deanery was not much more than seven hundred a year.

His beneficence was not graced with tenderness or civility; he relieved without pity, and assisted without kindness, so that those who were fed by him could hardly love him.

He made a rule to himself to give but one piece at a time, and therefore always stored his pocket with coins of different value.

Whatever he did, he seemed willing to do in a manner peculiar to himself, without sufficiently considering that singularity, as it implies a contempt of the general practice, is a kind of defiance which justly provokes the hostility of ridicule; he therefore who indulges peculiar habits is worse than others, if he be not better.

Of his humour, a story told by Pope may afford a specimen.*

[1]"Dr. Swift has an odd, blunt way, that is mistaken, by strangers, for ill-nature. —'Tis so odd, that there's no describing it but by facts. I'll tell you one that first comes into my head. One evening, Gay and I went to see him: you know how intimately we were all acquainted. On our coming in, 'Heyday, gentlemen (says the Doctor), what's the meaning of this visit? How came you to leave all the great Lords, that you are so fond of, to come hither to see a poor Dean?'—Because we would rather see you than any of them.—'Ay, any one that did not know so well as I do, might believe you. But since you are come, I must get some supper for you, I suppose.' No, Doctor, we have supped already.—'Supped already? that's impossible! why, 'tis not eight o'clock yet.— That's very strange; but, if you had not supped, I must have got something for you.—Let me see, what should I have had? A couple of lobsters; ay, that would have done very well; two shillings—tarts, a shilling: but you will drink a glass of wine with me, though you supped so much before your usual time only to spare my pocket?'—No, we had rather talk with you than drink with you.—'But if you had supped with me, as in all reason you ought to have done, you must then have drunk with me.—A bottle of wine, two shillings—two and two is four, and one is five: just two-and-six-pence a-piece. There, Pope, there's half a crown for you, and there's another for you, Sir; for I won't save any thing by you, I am determined.'—This was all said and done with his usual seriousness on such occasions; and, in spite of every thing we could say to the contrary, he actually obliged us to take the money."

In the intercourse of familiar life, he indulged his disposition to petulance and sarcasm, and thought himself injured if the licentiousness of his raillery, the freedom of his censures, or the petulance of his frolicks, was resented or repressed. He predominated over his companions with very high ascendency, and probably would bear none over whom he could not predominate. To give him advice was, in the style of his friend Delany, *to venture to speak to him*. This customary superiority soon grew too delicate for truth; and Swift, with all his penetration, allowed himself to be delighted with low flattery.

On all common occasions, he habitually affects a style of arrogance, and dictates rather than persuades. This authoritative and magisterial language he expected to be received as his peculiar mode

[1] Spence.

of jocularity; but he apparently flattered his own arrogance by an assumed imperiousness, in which he was ironical only to the resentful, and to the submissive sufficiently serious.

He told stories with great felicity, and delighted in doing what he knew himself to do well. He was therefore captivated by the respectful silence of a steady listener, and told the same tales too often.

He did not, however, claim the right of talking alone; for it was his rule, when he had spoken a minute, to give room by a pause for any other speaker. Of time, on all occasions, he was an exact computer, and knew the minutes required to every common operation.

It may be justly supposed that there was in his conversation, what appears so frequently in his Letters, an affectation of familiarity with the Great, an ambition of momentary equality sought and enjoyed by the neglect of those ceremonies which custom has established as the barriers between one order of society and another. This transgression of regularity was by himself and his admirers termed greatness of soul. But a great mind disdains to hold any thing by courtesy, and therefore never usurps what a lawful claimant may take away. He that encroaches on another's dignity, puts himself in his power; he is either repelled with helpless indignity, or endured by clemency and condescension.

Of Swift's general habits of thinking if his Letters can be supposed to afford any evidence, he was not a man to be either loved or envied. He seems to have wasted life in discontent, by the rage of neglected pride, and the languishment of unsatisfied desire. He is querulous and fastidious, arrogant and malignant; he scarcely speaks of himself but with indignant lamentations, or of others but with insolent superiority when he is gay, and with angry contempt when he is gloomy. From the Letters that pass between him and Pope it might be inferred that they, with Arbuthnot and Gay, had engrossed all the understanding and virtue of mankind, that their merits filled the world; or that there was no hope of more. They shew the age involved in darkness, and shade the picture with sullen emulation.

When the Queen's death drove him into Ireland, he might be allowed to regret for a time the interception of his views, the extinction of his hopes, and his ejection from gay scenes, important employment, and splendid friendships; but when time had enabled reason to prevail over vexation, the complaints, which at first were natural, became ridiculous because they were useless.

But querulousness was now grown habitual, and he cried out when he probably had ceased to feel. His reiterated wailings persuaded Bolingbroke that he was really willing to quit his deanery for an English parish; and Bolingbroke procured an exchange, which was rejected, and Swift still retained the pleasure of complaining.

The greatest difficulty that occurs, in analysing his character, is to discover by what depravity of intellect he took delight in revolving ideas, from which almost every other mind shrinks with disgust. The ideas of pleasure, even when criminal, may solicit the imagination; but what has disease, deformity, and filth, upon which the thoughts can be allured to dwell? Delany is willing to think that Swift's mind was not much tainted with this gross corruption before his long visit to Pope. He does not consider how he degrades his hero, by making him at fifty-nine the pupil of turpitude, and liable to the malignant influence of an ascendant mind. But the truth is, that Gulliver had described his *Yahoos* before the visit, and he that had formed those images had nothing filthy to learn.

I have here given the character of Swift as he exhibits himself to my perception; but now let another be heard, who knew him better; Dr. Delany, after long acquaintance, describes him to Lord Orrery in these terms:*

"My Lord, when you consider Swift's singular, peculiar and most variegated vein of wit, always rightly intended (although not always so rightly directed), delightful in many instances, and salutary, even where it is most offensive; when you consider his strict truth, his fortitude in resisting oppression and arbitrary power; his fidelity in friendship, his sincere love and zeal for religion, his uprightness in making right resolutions, and his steadiness in adhering to them; his care of his church, its choir, its œconomy, and its income; his attention to all those that preached in his cathedral, in order to their amendment in pronunciation and style; as also his remarkable attention to the interest of his successors, preferably to his own present emoluments; invincible patriotism, even to a country which he did not love; his very various, well-devised, well-judged, and extensive charities, throughout his life, and his whole fortune (to say nothing of his wife's) conveyed to the same Christian purposes at his death; charities from which he could enjoy no honour, advantage or satisfaction of any kind in this world. When you consider his ironical and humorous, as well as his serious schemes, for the promotion of true religion and virtue; his success in soliciting for the First Fruits and Twentieths, to the unspeakable benefit of the established Church of Ireland; and his felicity (to rate it no higher) in giving occasion to the building of fifty new churches in London.

"All this considered, the character of his life will appear like that of his writings; they will both bear to be re-considered and re-examined with the utmost attention, and always discover new beauties and excellences upon every examination.

"They will bear to be considered as the sun, in which the brightness will hide the blemishes; and whenever petulant ignorance, pride, malice, malignity, or envy, interposes to cloud or sully his fame, I will take upon me to pronounce that the eclipse will not last long.

"To conclude—no man ever deserved better of any country than Swift did of his. A steady, persevering, inflexible friend; a wise, a watchful, and a faithful counsellor, under many severe trials and bitter persecutions, to the manifest hazard both of his liberty and fortune.

"He lived a blessing, he died a benefactor, and his name will ever live an honour to Ireland."

IN the Poetical Works of Dr. Swift there is not much upon which the critick can exercise his powers. They are often humorous, almost always light, and have the qualities which recommend such compositions, easiness and gaiety. They are, for the most part what their author intended. The diction is correct, the numbers are smooth, and the rhymes exact. There seldom occurs a hard-laboured expression, or a redundant epithet; all his verses exemplify his own definition of a good style, they consist of *proper words in proper places*.*

To divide this Collection into classes, and shew how some pieces are gross, and some are trifling, would be to tell the reader what he knows already, and to find faults of which the author could not be ignorant, who certainly wrote often not to his judgement, but his humour.

It was said, in a Preface to one of the Irish editions, that Swift had never been known to take a single thought from any writer, ancient or modern. This is not literally true; but perhaps no writer can easily be found that has borrowed so little, or that in all his excellences and all his defects has so well maintained his claim to be considered as original.

POPE

ALEXANDER POPE was born in London, May 21, 1688, of parents whose rank or station was never ascertained: we are informed that they were of *gentle blood*;* that his father was of a family of which the Earl of Downe was the head, and that his mother was the daughter of William Turner, Esquire, of York, who had likewise three sons, one of whom had the honour of being killed, and the other of dying, in the service of Charles the First; the third was made a general officer in Spain, from whom the sister inherited what sequestrations and forfeitures had left in the family.

This, and this only, is told by Pope; who is more willing, as I have heard observed, to shew what his father was not, than what he was. It is allowed that he grew rich by trade; but whether in a shop or on the Exchange was never discovered, till Mr. Tyers told, on the authority of Mrs. Racket,* that he was a linen-draper in the Strand. Both parents were papists.

Pope was from his birth of a constitution tender and delicate; but is said to have shewn remarkable gentleness and sweetness of disposition. The weakness of his body continued through his life, but the mildness of his mind perhaps ended with his childhood. His voice, when he was young, was so pleasing, that he was called in fondness the *little Nightingale*.*

Being not sent early to school, he was taught to read by an aunt; and when he was seven or eight years old, became a lover of books. He first learned to write by imitating printed books; a species of penmanship in which he retained great excellence through his whole life, though his ordinary hand was not elegant.

When he was about eight, he was placed in Hampshire under Taverner, a Romish priest,* who, by a method very rarely practised, taught him the Greek and Latin rudiments together. He was now first regularly initiated in poetry by the perusal of Ogylby's *Homer*, and Sandys's *Ovid*:* Ogylby's assistance he never repaid with any praise; but of Sandys he declared, in his notes to the *Iliad*, that English poetry owed much of its present beauty to his translations. Sandys very rarely attempted original composition.

From the care of Taverner, under whom his proficiency was considerable, he was removed to a school at Twyford near Winchester, and again to another school about Hyde-park Corner; from which he used sometimes to stroll to the playhouse, and was so delighted with theatrical exhibitions, that he formed a kind of play from Ogylby's *Iliad*, with some verses of his own intermixed, which he persuaded his schoolfellows to act, with the addition of his master's gardener, who personated *Ajax*.

At the two last schools he used to represent himself as having lost part of what Taverner had taught him, and on his master at Twyford he had already exercised his poetry in a lampoon. Yet under those masters he translated more than a fourth part of the *Metamorphoses*. If he kept the same proportion in his other exercises, it cannot be thought that his loss was great.

He tells of himself, in his poems, that *he lisp'd in numbers*;* and used to say that he could not remember the time when he began to make verses. In the style of fiction it might have been said of him as of Pindar, that when he lay in his cradle, *the bees swarmed about his mouth*.*

About the time of the Revolution* his father, who was undoubtedly disappointed by the sudden blast of popish prosperity, quitted his trade, and retired to Binfield in Windsor Forest, with about twenty thousand pounds; for which, being conscientiously determined not to entrust it to the government, he found no better use than that of locking it up in a chest, and taking from it what his expences required; and his life was long enough to consume a great part of it, before his son came to the inheritance.

To Binfield Pope was called by his father when he was about twelve years old; and there he had for a few months the assistance of one Deane, another priest, of whom he learned only to construe a little of *Tully's Offices*.* How Mr. Deane could spend, with a boy who had translated so much of *Ovid*, some months over a small part of *Tully's Offices*, it is now vain to enquire.

Of a youth so successfully employed, and so conspicuously improved, a minute account must be naturally desired; but curiosity must be contented with confused, imperfect, and sometimes improbable intelligence. Pope, finding little advantage from external help, resolved thenceforward to direct himself, and at twelve formed a plan of study which he completed with little other incitement than the desire of excellence.

His primary and principal purpose was to be a poet, with which his father accidentally concurred, by proposing subjects, and obliging him to correct his performances by many revisals; after which the old gentleman, when he was satisfied, would say, *these are good rhymes.*

In his perusal of the English poets he soon distinguished the versification of Dryden, which he considered as the model to be studied, and was impressed with such veneration for his instructer, that he persuaded some friend to take him to the coffee-house which Dryden frequented, and pleased himself with having seen him.

Dryden died May 1, 1701, some days before Pope was twelve; so early must he therefore have felt the power of harmony, and the zeal of genius. Who does not wish that Dryden could have known the value of the homage that was paid him, and foreseen the greatness of his young admirer?

The earliest of Pope's productions is his *Ode on Solitude*, written before he was twelve, in which there is nothing more than other forward boys have attained, and which is not equal to Cowley's performances at the same age.

His time was now spent wholly in reading and writing. As he read the Classicks, he amused himself with translating them; and at fourteen made a version of the first book of the *Thebais*,* which, with some revision, he afterwards published. He must have been at this time, if he had no help, a considerable proficient in the Latin tongue.

By Dryden's Fables, which had then been not long published, and were much in the hands of poetical readers, he was tempted to try his own skill in giving Chaucer a more fashionable appearance, and put *January and May*, and the *Prologue of the Wife of Bath*, into modern English. He translated likewise the Epistle of *Sappho to Phaon* from Ovid, to complete the version, which was before imperfect; and wrote some other small pieces, which he afterwards printed.

He sometimes imitated the English poets, and professed to have written at fourteen his poem upon *Silence*, after Rochester's *Nothing*. He had now formed his versification, and in the smoothness of his numbers surpassed his original: but this is a small part of his praise; he discovers such acquaintance both with human life and public affairs, as is not easily conceived to have been attainable by a boy of fourteen in *Windsor Forest*.

Next year he was desirous of opening to himself new sources of knowledge, by making himself acquainted with modern languages;

and removed for a time to London, that he might study French and Italian, which, as he desired nothing more than to read them, were by diligent application soon dispatched. Of Italian learning he does not appear to have ever made much use in his subsequent studies.

He then returned to Binfield, and delighted himself with his own poetry. He tried all styles, and many subjects. He wrote a comedy, a tragedy, an epick poem, with panegyricks on all the princes of Europe; and, as he confesses, *thought himself the greatest genius that ever was*. Self-confidence is the first requisite to great undertakings; he, indeed, who forms his opinion of himself in solitude, without knowing the powers of other men, is very liable to errour; but it was the felicity of Pope to rate himself at his real value.

Most of his puerile productions were, by his maturer judgement, afterwards destroyed; *Alcander*, the epick poem, was burnt by the persuasion of Atterbury. The tragedy was founded on the legend of *St. Genevieve*. Of the comedy there is no account.

Concerning his studies it is related, that he translated Tully *on old Age*; and that, besides his books of poetry and criticism, he read *Temple's Essays* and *Locke on human Understanding*. His reading, though his favourite authors are not known, appears to have been sufficiently extensive and multifarious; for his early pieces shew, with sufficient evidence, his knowledge of books.

He that is pleased with himself, easily imagines that he shall please others. Sir William Trumbal,* who had been ambassador at Constantinople, and secretary of state, when he retired from business, fixed his residence in the neighbourhood of Binfield. Pope, not yet sixteen, was introduced to the statesman of sixty, and so distinguished himself, that their interviews ended in friendship and correspondence. Pope was, through his whole life, ambitious of splendid acquaintance, and he seems to have wanted neither diligence nor success in attracting the notice of the great; for from his first entrance into the world, and his entrance was very early, he was admitted to familiarity with those whose rank or station made them most conspicuous.

From the age of sixteen the life of Pope, as an author, may be properly computed. He now wrote his pastorals, which were shewn to the Poets and Criticks of that time; as they well deserved, they were read with admiration, and many praises were bestowed upon them and upon the Preface, which is both elegant and learned in a high degree: they were, however, not published till five years afterwards.

Cowley, Milton, and Pope, are distinguished among the English Poets by the early exertion of their powers; but the works of Cowley alone were published in his childhood, and therefore of him only can it be certain that his puerile performances received no improvement from his maturer studies.

At this time began his acquaintance with Wycherley,* a man who seems to have had among his contemporaries his full share of reputation, to have been esteemed without virtue, and caressed without good-humour. Pope was proud of his notice; Wycherley wrote verses in his praise, which he was charged by Dennis* with writing to himself, and they agreed for a while to flatter one another. It is pleasant to remark how soon Pope learned the cant of an author, and began to treat criticks with contempt, though he had yet suffered nothing from them.

But the fondness of Wycherley was too violent to last. His esteem of Pope was such, that he submitted some poems to his revision; and when Pope, perhaps proud of such confidence, was sufficiently bold in his criticisms, and liberal in his alterations, the old scribbler was angry to see his pages defaced, and felt more pain from the detection than content from the amendment of his faults. They parted; but Pope always considered him with kindness, and visited him a little time before he died.

Another of his early correspondents was Mr. Cromwell,* of whom I have learned nothing particular but that he used to ride a-hunting in a tye-wig. He was fond, and perhaps vain, of amusing himself with poetry and criticism; and sometimes sent his performances to Pope, who did not forbear such remarks as were now-and-then unwelcome. Pope, in his turn, put the juvenile version of *Statius* into his hands for correction.

Their correspondence afforded the publick its first knowledge of Pope's Epistolary Powers; for his Letters were given by Cromwell to one Mrs. Thomas, and she many years afterwards sold them to Curll,* who inserted them in a volume of his Miscellanies.

Walsh,* a name yet preserved among the minor poets, was one of his first encouragers. His regard was gained by the Pastorals, and from him Pope received the counsel by which he seems to have regulated his studies. Walsh advised him to correctness, which, as he told him, the English poets had hitherto neglected, and which therefore was left to him as a basis of fame; and, being delighted with rural poems, recommended to him to write a pastoral comedy, like those which are read so eagerly in Italy; a design which Pope probably did not approve, as he did not follow it.

Pope had now declared himself a poet; and, thinking himself entitled to poetical conversation, began at seventeen to frequent Will's, a coffee-house on the north side of Russel-street in Covent-garden, where the wits of that time used to assemble, and where Dryden had, when he lived, been accustomed to preside.

During this period of his life he was indefatigably diligent, and insatiably curious; wanting health for violent, and money for expensive pleasures, and having certainly excited in himself very strong desires of intellectual eminence, he spent much of his time over his books; but he read only to store his mind with facts and images, seizing all that his authors presented with undistinguishing voracity, and with an appetite for knowledge too eager to be nice. In a mind like his, however, all the faculties were at once involuntarily improving. Judgement is forced upon us by experience. He that reads many books must compare one opinion or one style with another; and when he compares, must necessarily distinguish, reject, and prefer. But the account given by himself of his studies was, that from fourteen to twenty he read only for amusement, from twenty to twenty-seven for improvement and instruction; that in the first part of this time he desired only to know, and in the second he endeavoured to judge.

The Pastorals, which had been for some time handed about among poets and criticks, were at last printed (1709) in Tonson's Miscellany,* in a volume which began with the Pastorals of Philips, and ended with those of Pope.

The same year was written the *Essay on Criticism*; a work which displays such extent of comprehension, such nicety of distinction, such acquaintance with mankind, and such knowledge both of ancient and modern learning, as are not often attained by the maturest age and longest experience. It was published about two years afterwards, and being praised by Addison in the *Spectator* with sufficient liberality, met with so much favour as enraged Dennis, "who," he says, "found himself attacked, without any manner of provocation on his side, and attacked in his person, instead of his writings, by one who was wholly a stranger to him, at a time when all the world knew he was persecuted by fortune; and not only saw that this was attempted in a clandestine manner, with the utmost falsehood and calumny, but found that all this was done by a little affected hypocrite, who had nothing in his mouth at the same time but truth, candour, friendship, good-nature, humanity, and magnanimity."*

How the attack was clandestine is not easily perceived, nor how his person is depreciated; but he seems to have known something of Pope's character, in whom may be discovered an appetite to talk too frequently of his own virtues.

The pamphlet is such as rage might be expected to dictate. He supposes himself to be asked two questions; whether the Essay will succeed, and who or what is the author.

Its success he admits to be secured by the false opinions then prevalent; the author he concludes to be *young and raw*.

"First, because he discovers a sufficiency beyond his little ability, and hath rashly undertaken a task infinitely above his force. Secondly, while this little author struts, and affects the dictatorian air, he plainly shews that at the same time he is under the rod; and while he pretends to give laws to others, is a pedantick slave to authority and opinion. Thirdly, he hath, like schoolboys, borrowed both from living and dead. Fourthly, he knows not his own mind, and frequently contradicts himself. Fifthly, he is almost perpetually in the wrong."

All these positions he attempts to prove by quotations and remarks; but his desire to do mischief is greater than his power. He has, however, justly criticised some passages. In these lines,

> There are whom heaven has bless'd with store of wit,
> Yet want as much again to manage it;
> For wit and judgment ever are at strife—*

it is apparent that *wit* has two meanings, and that what is wanted, though called *wit*, is truly judgment. So far Dennis is undoubtedly right; but, not content with argument, he will have a little mirth, and triumphs over the first couplet in terms too elegant to be forgotten.* "By the way, what rare numbers are here! Would not one swear that this youngster had espoused some antiquated Muse, who had sued out a divorce on account of impotence from some superannuated sinner; and, having been p—xed by her former spouse, has got the gout in her decrepit age, which makes her hobble so damnably." This was the man who would reform a nation sinking into barbarity.

In another place Pope himself allowed that Dennis had detected one of those blunders which are called *bulls*. The first edition had this line:

> What is this wit—
> Where wanted, scorn'd; and envied where acquir'd?

"How," says the critick, "can wit be *scorn'd* where it is not? Is not this a figure frequently employed in Hibernian land? The person that wants this wit may indeed be scorned, but the scorn shews the honour which the contemner has for wit." Of this remark Pope made the proper use, by correcting the passage.*

I have preserved, I think, all that is reasonable in Dennis's criticism; it remains that justice be done to his delicacy. "For his acquaintance (says Dennis) he names Mr. Walsh, who had by no means the qualification which this author reckons absolutely necessary to a critick, it being very certain that he was, like this Essayer, a very indifferent poet; he loved to be well-dressed; and I remember a little young gentleman whom Mr. Walsh used to take into his company, as a double foil to his person and capacity.—Enquire between *Sunninghill* and *Oakingham* for a young, short, squab gentleman, the very bow of the God of Love, and tell me whether he be a proper author to make personal reflections?—He may extol the antients, but he has reason to thank the gods that he was born a modern; for had he been born of Grecian parents, and his father consequently had by law had the absolute disposal of him, his life had been no longer than that of one of his poems, the life of half a day.—Let the person of a gentleman of his parts be never so contemptible, his inward man is ten times more ridiculous; it being impossible that his outward form, though it be that of downright monkey, should differ so much from human shape, as his unthinking immaterial part does from human understanding."* Thus began the hostility between Pope and Dennis, which, though it was suspended for a short time, never was appeased. Pope seems, at first, to have attacked him wantonly; but though he always professed to despise him, he discovers, by mentioning him very often, that he felt his force or his venom.

Of this Essay Pope declared that he did not expect the sale to be quick, because *not one gentleman in sixty, even of liberal education, could understand it*. The gentlemen, and the education of that time, seem to have been of a lower character than they are of this. He mentioned a thousand copies as a numerous impression.

Dennis was not his only censurer; the zealous papists thought the monks treated with too much contempt, and Erasmus too studiously praised; but to these objections he had not much regard.

The *Essay* has been translated into French by *Hamilton*, author of the *Comte de Grammont*, whose version was never printed, by *Robotham*, secretary to the King for Hanover, and by *Resnel*; and commented by Dr. Warburton, who has discovered in it such order and connection as was not perceived by Addison, nor, as is said, intended by the author.*

Almost every poem, consisting of precepts, is so far arbitrary and immethodical, that many of the paragraphs may change places with no apparent inconvenience; for of two or more positions, depending upon some remote and general principle, there is seldom any cogent reason why one should precede the other. But for the order in which they stand, whatever it be, a little ingenuity may easily give a reason. *It is possible*, says Hooker, *that by long circumduction, from any one truth all truth may be inferred.** Of all homogeneous truths at least, of all truths respecting the same general end, in whatever series they may be produced, a concatenation by intermediate ideas may be formed, such as, when it is once shewn, shall appear natural; but if this order be reversed, another mode of connection equally specious may be found or made. Aristotle is praised for naming Fortitude first of the cardinal virtues, as that without which no other virtue can steadily be practised; but he might, with equal propriety, have placed Prudence and Justice before it, since without Prudence Fortitude is mad; without Justice, it is mischievous.

As the end of method is perspicuity, that series is sufficiently regular that avoids obscurity; and where there is no obscurity it will not be difficult to discover method.

In the *Spectator* was published the *Messiah*, which he first submitted to the perusal of Steele, and corrected in compliance with his criticisms.

It is reasonable to infer, from his Letters, that the verses on the *Unfortunate Lady* were written about the time when his *Essay* was published. The Lady's name and adventures I have sought with fruitless enquiry.

I can therefore tell no more than I have learned from Mr. Ruffhead,* who writes with the confidence of one who could trust his information. She was a woman of eminent rank and large fortune, the ward of an unkle, who, having given her a proper education, expected like other guardians that she should make at least an equal match; and such he proposed to her, but found it rejected in favour of a young gentleman of inferior condition.

Having discovered the correspondence between the two lovers, and finding the young lady determined to abide by her own choice, he supposed that separation might do what can rarely be done by arguments, and sent her into a foreign country, where she was obliged to converse only with those from whom her unkle had nothing to fear.

Her lover took care to repeat his vows; but his letters were intercepted and carried to her guardian, who directed her to be watched with still greater vigilance; till of this restraint she grew so impatient, that she bribed a woman-servant to procure her a sword, which she directed to her heart.

From this account, given with evident intention to raise the Lady's character, it does not appear that she had any claim to praise, nor much to compassion. She seems to have been impatient, violent, and ungovernable. Her unkle's power could not have lasted long; the hour of liberty and choice would have come in time. But her desires were too hot for delay, and she liked self-murder better than suspence.

Nor is it discovered that the unkle, whoever he was, is with much justice delivered to posterity as a *false Guardian*; he seems to have done only that for which a guardian is appointed; he endeavoured to direct his niece till she should be able to direct herself. Poetry has not often been worse employed than in dignifying the amorous fury of a raving girl.

Not long after, he wrote the *Rape of the Lock*, the most airy, the most ingenious, and the most delightful of all his compositions, occasioned by a frolick of gallantry, rather too familiar, in which Lord Petre cut off a lock of Mrs. Arabella Fermor's hair. This, whether stealth or violence, was so much resented, that the commerce of the two families, before very friendly, was interrupted. Mr. Caryl,* a gentleman who, being secretary to King James's Queen, had followed his Mistress into France, and who being the author of *Sir Solomon Single*, a comedy, and some translations, was entitled to the notice of a Wit, solicited Pope to endeavour a reconciliation by a ludicrous poem, which might bring both the parties to a better temper. In compliance with Caryl's request, though his name was for a long time marked only by the first and last letter, C—l, a poem of two cantos was written (1711), as is said, in a fortnight, and sent to the offended Lady, who liked it well enough to shew it; and, with the usual process of literary transactions, the author, dreading a surreptitious edition, was forced to publish it.

The event is said to have been such as was desired; the pacification and diversion of all to whom it related, except Sir *George Brown*,* who complained with some bitterness that, in the character of *Sir Plume*, he was made to talk nonsense. Whether all this be true, I have some doubt; for at Paris, a few years ago, a niece of Mrs. Fermor, who presided in an English Convent, mentioned Pope's work with very little gratitude, rather as an insult than an honour; and she may be supposed to have inherited the opinion of her family.*

At its first appearance it was termed by Addison *merum sal.** Pope, however, saw that it was capable of improvement; and, having luckily contrived to borrow his machinery from the *Rosicrucians*, imparted the scheme with which his head was teeming to Addison, who told him that his work, as it stood, was *a delicious little thing*, and gave him no encouragement to retouch it.

This has been too hastily considered as an instance of Addison's jealousy; for as he could not guess the conduct of the new design, or the possibilities of pleasure comprised in a fiction of which there had been no examples, he might very reasonably and kindly persuade the author to acquiesce in his own prosperity, and forbear an attempt which he considered as an unnecessary hazard.

Addison's counsel was happily rejected. Pope foresaw the future efflorescence of imagery then budding in his mind, and resolved to spare no art, or industry of cultivation. The soft luxuriance of his fancy was already shooting, and all the gay varieties of diction were ready at his hand to colour and embellish it.

His attempt was justified by its success. The *Rape of the Lock* stands forward, in the classes of literature, as the most exquisite example of ludicrous poetry. Berkeley* congratulated him upon the display of powers more truly poetical than he had shewn before; with elegance of description and justness of precepts, he had now exhibited boundless fertility of invention.

He always considered the intertexture of the machinery with the action as his most successful exertion of poetical art. He indeed could never afterwards produce any thing of such unexampled excellence. Those performances, which strike with wonder, are combinations of skilful genius with happy casualty; and it is not likely that any felicity, like the discovery of a new race of preternatural agents, should happen twice to the same man.

Of this poem the author was, I think, allowed to enjoy the praise for a long time without disturbance. Many years afterwards Dennis published some remarks upon it, with very little force, and with no effect; for the opinion of the publick was already settled, and it was no longer at the mercy of criticism.

About this time he published the *Temple of Fame*, which, as he tells Steele in their correspondence, he had written two years before; that is, when he was only twenty-two years old, an early time of life for so much learning and so much observation as that work exhibits.

On this poem Dennis afterwards published some remarks, of which the most reasonable is, that some of the lines represent *motion* as exhibited by *sculpture*.

Of the Epistle from *Eloisa to Abelard*, I do not know the date. His first inclination to attempt a composition of that tender kind arose, as Mr. Savage told me, from his perusal of Prior's *Nut-brown Maid*. How much he has surpassed Prior's work it is not necessary to mention, when perhaps it may be said with justice, that he has excelled every composition of the same kind. The mixture of religious hope and resignation gives an elevation and dignity to disappointed love, which images merely natural cannot bestow. The gloom of a convent strikes the imagination with far greater force than the solitude of a grove.

This piece was, however, not much his favourite in his latter years, though I never heard upon what principle he slighted it.

In the next year (1713) he published *Windsor Forest*; of which part was, as he relates, written at sixteen, about the same time as his Pastorals, and the latter part was added afterwards: where the addition begins, we are not told. The lines relating to the Peace* confess their own date. It is dedicated to Lord Lansdowne,* who was then high in reputation and influence among the Tories; and it is said, that the conclusion of the poem gave great pain to Addison, both as a poet and a politician. Reports like this are often spread with boldness very disproportionate to their evidence. Why should Addison receive any particular disturbance from the last lines of *Windsor Forest?*

If contrariety of opinion could poison a politician, he would not live a day; and, as a poet, he must have felt Pope's force of genius much more from many other parts of his works.

The pain that Addison might feel it is not likely that he would confess; and it is certain that he so well suppressed his discontent, that Pope now thought himself his favourite; for having been consulted in the revisal of *Cato*,* he introduced it by a Prologue; and, when Dennis published his Remarks, undertook not indeed to vindicate but to revenge his friend, by a *Narrative of the Frenzy of John Dennis.**

There is reason to believe that Addison gave no encouragement to this disingenuous hostility; for, says Pope, in a Letter to him,* "indeed your opinion, that 'tis entirely to be neglected, would be my own in my own case; but I felt more warmth here than I did when I first saw his book against myself (though indeed in two minutes it made me heartily merry)." Addison was not a man on whom such cant of sensibility could make much impression. He left the pamphlet to itself, having disowned it to Dennis, and perhaps did not think Pope to have deserved much by his officiousness.

This year was printed in the *Guardian* the ironical comparison between the Pastorals of Philips and Pope;* a composition of artifice, criticism, and literature, to which nothing equal will easily be found. The superiority of Pope is so ingeniously dissembled, and the feeble lines of Philips so skilfully preferred, that Steele, being deceived, was unwilling to print the paper lest Pope should be offended. Addison immediately saw the writer's design; and, as it seems, had malice enough to conceal his discovery, and to permit a publication which, by making his friend Philips ridiculous, made him for ever an enemy to Pope.

It appears that about this time Pope had a strong inclination to unite the art of Painting with that of Poetry, and put himself under the tuition of Jervas.* He was near-sighted, and therefore not formed by nature for a painter: he tried, however, how far he could advance, and sometimes persuaded his friends to sit. A picture of Betterton, supposed to be drawn by him, was in the possession of Lord Mansfield:* if this was taken from the life, he must have begun to paint earlier; for Betterton* was now dead. Pope's ambition of this new art produced some encomiastick verses to Jervas, which certainly shew his power as a poet, but I have been told that they betray his ignorance of painting.

He appears to have regarded Betterton with kindness and esteem; and after his death published, under his name, a version into modern English of Chaucer's Prologues, and one of his Tales, which, as was related by Mr. Harte, were believed to have been the performance of Pope himself by Fenton,* who made him a gay offer of five pounds, if he would shew them in the hand of Betterton.

The next year (1713) produced a bolder attempt, by which profit was sought as well as praise. The poems which he had hitherto written, however they might have diffused his name, had made very little addition to his fortune. The allowance which his father made him, though, proportioned to what he had, it might be liberal, could not be large; his religion hindered him from the occupation of any civil employment, and he complained that he wanted even money to buy books[1].

He therefore resolved to try how far the favour of the publick extended, by soliciting a subscription to a version of the *Iliad*, with large notes.

To print by subscription was, for some time, a practice peculiar to the English. The first considerable work for which this expedient was employed is said to have been Dryden's *Virgil*; and it had been tried again with great success when the *Tatlers* were collected into volumes.

There was reason to believe that Pope's attempt would be successful. He was in the full bloom of reputation, and was personally known to almost all whom dignity of employment or splendour of reputation had made eminent; he conversed indifferently with both parties, and never disturbed the publick with his political opinions; and it might be naturally expected, as each faction then boasted its literary zeal, that the great men, who on other occasions practised all the violence of opposition, would emulate each other in their encouragement of a poet who had delighted all, and by whom none had been offended.

With those hopes, he offered an English *Iliad* to subscribers, in six volumes in quarto, for six guineas; a sum, according to the value of money at that time, by no means inconsiderable, and greater than I believe to have been ever asked before. His proposal, however, was very favourably received, and the patrons of literature were busy to

[1] Spence.

recommend his undertaking, and promote his interest. Lord Oxford, indeed, lamented that such a genius should be wasted upon a work not original; but proposed no means by which he might live without it: Addison recommended caution and moderation, and advised him not to be content with the praise of half the nation, when he might be universally favoured.

The greatness of the design, the popularity of the author, and the attention of the literary world, naturally raised such expectations of the future sale, that the booksellers made their offers with great eagerness; but the highest bidder was *Bernard Lintot*,* who became proprietor on condition of supplying, at his own expence, all the copies which were to be delivered to subscribers, or presented to friends, and paying two hundred pounds for every volume.

Of the Quartos it was, I believe, stipulated that none should be printed but for the author, that the subscription might not be depreciated; but Lintot impressed the same pages upon a small Folio, and paper perhaps a little thinner; and sold exactly at half the price, for half a guinea each volume, books so little inferior to the Quartos, that, by a fraud of trade, those Folios, being afterwards shortened by cutting away the top and bottom, were sold as copies printed for the subscribers.

Lintot printed two hundred and fifty on royal paper in Folio for two guineas a volume; of the small Folio, having printed seventeen hundred and fifty copies of the first volume, he reduced the number in the other volumes to a thousand.

It is unpleasant to relate that the bookseller, after all his hopes and all his liberality, was, by a very unjust and illegal action, defrauded of his profit. An edition of the English *Iliad* was printed in Holland in Duodecimo, and imported clandestinely for the gratification of those who were impatient to read what they could not yet afford to buy. This fraud could only be counteracted by an edition equally cheap and more commodious; and Lintot was compelled to contract his Folio at once into a Duodecimo, and lose the advantage of an intermediate gradation. The notes, which in the Dutch copies were placed at the end of each book, as they had been in the large volumes, were now subjoined to the text in the same page, and are therefore more easily consulted. Of this edition two thousand five hundred were first printed, and five thousand a few weeks afterwards; but indeed great numbers were necessary to produce considerable profit.

Pope, having now emitted his proposals, and engaged not only his own reputation, but in some degree that of his friends who patronised his subscription, began to be frighted at his own undertaking; and finding himself at first embarrassed with difficulties, which retarded and oppressed him, he was for a time timorous and uneasy; had his nights disturbed by dreams of long journeys through unknown ways, and wished, as he said, *that somebody would hang him*[1].

This misery, however, was not of long continuance; he grew by degrees more acquainted with Homer's images and expressions, and practice increased his facility of versification. In a short time he represents himself as dispatching regularly fifty verses a day, which would shew him by an easy computation the termination of his labour.

His own diffidence was not his only vexation. He that asks a subscription soon finds that he has enemies. All who do not encourage him defame him. He that wants money will rather be thought angry than poor, and he that wishes to save his money conceals his avarice by his malice. Addison had hinted his suspicion that Pope was too much a Tory; and some of the Tories suspected his principles because he had contributed to the *Guardian*, which was carried on by *Steele*.

To those who censured his politicks were added enemies yet more dangerous, who called in question his knowledge of Greek, and his qualifications for a translator of Homer. To these he made no publick opposition; but in one of his Letters escapes from them as well as he can. At an age like his, for he was not more than twenty-five, with an irregular education, and a course of life of which much seems to have passed in conversation, it is not very likely that he overflowed with Greek. But when he felt himself deficient he sought assistance; and what man of learning would refuse to help him? Minute enquiries into the force of words are less necessary in translating Homer than other poets, because his positions are general, and his representations natural, with very little dependence on local or temporary customs, on those changeable scenes of artificial life, which, by mingling original with accidental notions, and crowding the mind with images which time effaces, produce ambiguity in diction, and obscurity in books. To this open display of unadulterated nature it must be

[1] Spence.

ascribed, that Homer has fewer passages of doubtful meaning than any other poet either in the learned or in modern languages. I have read of a man, who being, by his ignorance of Greek, compelled to gratify his curiosity with the Latin printed on the opposite page, declared that from the rude simplicity of the lines literally rendered, he formed nobler ideas of the Homeric majesty than from the laboured elegance of polished versions.

Those literal translations were always at hand, and from them he could easily obtain his author's sense with sufficient certainty; and among the readers of Homer the number is very small of those who find much in the Greek more than in the Latin, except the musick of the numbers.

If more help was wanting, he had the poetical translation of *Eobanus Hessus*, an unwearied writer of Latin verses; he had the French Homers of *La Valterie* and *Dacier*, and the English of *Chapman, Hobbes*, and *Ogylby*.* With Chapman, whose work, though now totally neglected, seems to have been popular almost to the end of the last century, he had very frequent consultations, and perhaps never translated any passage till he had read his version, which indeed he has been sometimes suspected of using instead of the original.

Notes were likewise to be provided; for the six volumes would have been very little more than six pamphlets without them. What the mere perusal of the text could suggest, Pope wanted no assistance to collect or methodize; but more was necessary; many pages were to be filled, and learning must supply materials to wit and judgment. Something might be gathered from Dacier; but no man loves to be indebted to his contemporaries, and Dacier was accessible to common readers. Eustathius* was therefore necessarily consulted. To read Eustathius, of whose work there was then no Latin version, I suspect Pope, if he had been willing, not to have been able; some other was therefore to be found, who had leisure as well as abilities, and he was doubtless most readily employed who would do much work for little money.

The history of the notes has never been traced. Broome,* in his preface to his poems, declares himself the commentator *in part upon the Iliad*; and it appears from Fenton's Letter, preserved in the Museum, that Broome was at first engaged in consulting Eustathius; but that after a time, whatever was the reason, he desisted: another man of Cambridge was then employed, who soon grew weary of the work; and a third, that was recommended by *Thirlby*, is now discovered to have been *Jortin*,* a man since well known to the learned world, who complained that Pope, having accepted and approved his performance, never testified any curiosity to see him, and who professed to have forgotten the terms on which he worked. The terms which Fenton uses are very mercantile:* I *think at first sight that his performance is very commendable, and have sent word for him to finish the 17th book, and to send it with his demands for his trouble. I have here enclosed the specimen; if the rest come before you return, I will keep them till I receive your order.*

Broome then offered his service a second time, which was probably accepted, as they had afterwards a closer correspondence. Parnell* contributed the Life of Homer, which Pope found so harsh, that he took great pains in correcting it; and by his own diligence, with such help as kindness or money could procure him, in somewhat more than five years he completed his version of the *Iliad*, with the notes. He began it in 1712, his twenty-fifth year, and concluded it in 1718, his thirtieth year.

When we find him translating fifty lines a day, it is natural to suppose that he would have brought his work to a more speedy conclusion. The *Iliad*, containing less than sixteen thousand verses, might have been despatched in less than three hundred and twenty days by fifty verses in a day. The notes, compiled with the assistance of his mercenaries, could not be supposed to require more time than the text. According to this calculation, the progress of Pope may seem to have been slow; but the distance is commonly very great between actual performances and speculative possibility. It is natural to suppose, that as much as has been done to-day may be done to-morrow; but on the morrow some difficulty emerges, or some external impediment obstructs. Indolence, interruption, business, and pleasure, all take their turns of retardation; and every long work is lengthened by a thousand causes that can, and ten thousand that cannot, be recounted. Perhaps no extensive and multifarious performance was ever effected within the term originally fixed in the undertaker's mind. He that runs against Time, has an antagonist not subject to casualties.

The encouragement given to this translation, though report seems to have over-rated it, was such as the world has not often seen. The subscribers were five hundred and seventy-five. The copies for which subscriptions were given were six hundred and fifty-four; and only six hundred and sixty were printed. For those copies Pope had nothing to pay; he therefore received, including the two hundred pounds a volume, five thousand three hundred and twenty pounds four shillings, without deduction, as the books were supplied by Lintot.

By the success of his subscription Pope was relieved from those pecuniary distresses with which, notwithstanding his popularity, he had hitherto struggled. Lord Oxford had often lamented his disqualification for publick employment, but never proposed a pension. While the translation of *Homer* was in its progress, Mr. Craggs,* then secretary of state, offered to procure him a pension, which, at least during his ministry, might be enjoyed with secrecy. This was not accepted by Pope, who told him, however, that, if he should be pressed with want of money, he would send to him for occasional supplies. Craggs was not long in power, and was never solicited for money by Pope, who disdained to beg what he did not want.

With the product of this subscription, which he had too much discretion to squander, he secured his future life from want, by considerable annuities. The estate of the Duke of Buckingham* was found to have been charged with five hundred pounds a year, payable to Pope, which doubtless his translation enabled him to purchase.

It cannot be unwelcome to literary curiosity, that I deduce thus minutely the history of the English *Iliad*. It is certainly the noblest version of poetry which the world has ever seen; and its publication must therefore be considered as one of the great events in the annals of Learning.

To those who have skill to estimate the excellence and difficulty of this great work, it must be very desirable to know how it was performed, and by what gradations it advanced to correctness. Of such an intellectual process the knowledge has very rarely been attainable; but happily there remains the original copy of the *Iliad*, which, being obtained by Bolingbroke as a curiosity, descended from him to Mallet, and is now by the solicitation of the late Dr. Maty reposited in the Museum.*

Between this manuscript, which is written upon accidental fragments of paper, and the printed edition, there must have been an intermediate copy, that was perhaps destroyed as it returned from the press.

From the first copy I have procured a few transcripts, and shall exhibit first the printed lines; then, in a smaller print, those of the manuscripts, with all their variations.* Those words in the small print which are given in Italicks, are cancelled in the copy, and the words placed under them adopted in their stead.

The beginning of the first book stands thus:

The wrath of Peleus' son, the direful spring
Of all the Grecian woes, O Goddess, sing;
That wrath which hurl'd to Pluto's gloomy reign
The souls of mighty chiefs untimely slain.

The stern Pelides' *rage*, O Goddess, sing,
wrath
Of all the woes *of Greece* the fatal spring,
Grecian
That strew'd with *warriors* dead the Phrygian plain,
heroes
And *peopled the dark hell with heroes* slain;
fill'd the shady hell with chiefs untimely

Whose limbs, unburied on the naked shore,
Devouring dogs and hungry vultures tore,
Since great Achilles and Atrides strove;
Such was the sovereign doom, and such the will of Jove.

Whose limbs, unburied on the hostile shore,
Devouring dogs and greedy vultures tore,
Since first *Atrides* and *Achilles* strove;
Such was the sovereign doom, and such the will of Jove.

Declare, O Muse, in what ill-fated hour
Sprung the fierce strife, from what offended Power!
Latona's son a dire contagion spread,
And heap'd the camp with mountains of the dead;
The King of Men his reverend priest defy'd,
And for the King's offence the people dy'd.

Declare, O Goddess, what offended Power
Enflam'd their *rage*, in that *ill-omen'd* hour;
anger fatal, hapless
Phœbus himself the *dire* debate procur'd,
fierce
'T' avenge the wrongs his injur'd priest endur'd;
For this the God a dire infection spread,
And heap'd the camp with millions of the dead:
The King of Men the sacred Sire defy'd,
And for the King's offence the people dy'd.

For Chryses sought with costly gifts to gain
His captive daughter from the Victor's chain;
Suppliant the venerable Father stands,
Apollo's awful ensigns grace his hands,
By these he begs, and, lowly bending down,
Extends the sceptre and the laurel crown.

For Chryses sought by *presents to regain*
costly gifts to gain
His captive daughter from the Victor's chain;
Suppliant the venerable Father stands,
Apollo's awful ensigns grac'd his hands,
By these he begs, and lowly bending down
The golden sceptre and the laurel crown,
Presents the sceptre
For these as ensigns of his God he bare,
The God that sends his golden shafts afar;
Then low on earth, the venerable man,
Suppliant before the brother kings began.

He sued to all, but chief implor'd for grace
The brother kings of Atreus' royal race;
Ye kings and warriors, may your vows be crown'd,
And Troy's proud walls lie level with the ground;
May Jove restore you, when your toils are o'er,
Safe to the pleasures of your native shore.

To all he sued, but chief implor'd for grace
The brother kings of Atreus' royal race.
Ye *sons of Atreus*, may your vows be crown'd,
Kings and warriors
Your labours, by the Gods be all your labours crown'd;
So may the Gods your arms with conquest bless,
And Troy's proud walls lie level with the ground;
Till *laid*
And crown your labours with deserv'd success;
May Jove restore you, when your toils are o'er,
Safe to the pleasures of your native shore.

But, oh! relieve a wretched parent's pain,
And give Chryseis to these arms again;
If mercy fail, yet let my present move,
And dread avenging Phœbus, son of Jove.

But, oh! relieve a hapless parent's pain,
And give my daughter to these arms again;
Receive my gifts; if mercy fails, yet let my present move,
And fear *the God that deals his darts around*,
avenging Phœbus, son of Jove.

The Greeks, in shouts, their joint assent declare
The priest to reverence, and release the fair.
Not so Atrides; he, with kingly pride,
Repuls'd the sacred Sire, and thus reply'd.

He said, the Greeks their joint assent declare.
The father said, the gen'rous Greeks relent,
T'accept the ransom, and release the fair:
Revere the priest, and speak their joint assent:
Not so *the tyrant*, he, with kingly pride,
Atrides,
Repuls'd the sacred Sire, and thus reply'd.
[Not so the tyrant. DRYDEN.]

Of these lines, and of the whole first book, I am told that there was yet a former copy, more varied, and more deformed with interlineations.

The beginning of the second book varies very little from the printed page, and is therefore set down without any parallel: the few slight differences do not require to be elaborately displayed.

Now pleasing sleep had seal'd each mortal eye;
Stretch'd in their tents the Grecian leaders lie;
Th' Immortals slumber'd on their thrones above,
All but the ever-watchful eye of Jove.
To honour Thetis' son he bends his care,
And plunge the Greeks in all the woes of war.
Then bids an empty phantom rise to sight,
And thus *commands* the vision of the night:
directs
Fly hence, delusive dream, and, light as air,
To Agamemnon's royal tent repair;
Bid him in arms draw forth th' embattled train,
March all his legions to the dusty plain.
Now tell the King 'tis given him to destroy
Declare ev'n now
The lofty *walls* of wide-extended Troy;
tow'rs
For now no more the Gods with Fate contend;
At Juno's suit the heavenly factions end.
Destruction *hovers* o'er yon devoted wall,
hangs
And nodding Ilium waits th' impending fall.

Invocation to the Catalogue of Ships.

Say, Virgins, seated round the throne divine,
All-knowing Goddesses! immortal Nine!
Since earth's wide regions, heaven's unmeasur'd height,
And hell's abyss, hide nothing from your sight,
(We, wretched mortals! lost in doubts below,
But guess by rumour, and but boast we know)
Oh say what heroes, fir'd by thirst of fame,
Or urg'd by wrongs, to Troy's destruction came!
To count them all, demands a thousand tongues,
A throat of brass and adamantine lungs.

Now, Virgin Goddesses, immortal Nine!
That round Olympus' heavenly summit shine,
Who see through heaven and earth, and hell profound,
And all things know, and all things can resound;
Relate what armies sought the Trojan land,
What nations follow'd, and what chiefs command;
(For doubtful Fame distracts mankind below,
And nothing can we tell, and nothing know)
Without your aid, to count th' unnumber'd train,
A thousand mouths, a thousand tongues were vain.

Book V. *v.* i.

But Pallas now Tydides' soul inspires,
Fills with her force, and warms with all her fires:
Above the Greeks his deathless fame to raise,
And crown her hero with distinguish'd praise,
High on his helm celestial lightnings play,
His beamy shield emits a living ray;
Th' unwearied blaze incessant streams supplies,
Like the red star that fires th' autumnal skies.

But Pallas now Tydides' soul inspires,
Fills with her *rage*, and warms with all her fires;
force,
O'er all the Greeks decrees his fame to raise,
Above the Greeks *her warrior's* fame to raise,
his deathless
And crown her hero with *immortal* praise:
distinguish'd
Bright from his beamy *crest* the lightnings play,
High on helm
From his broad buckler flash'd the living ray,
High on his helm celestial lightnings play,
His beamy shield emits a living ray.

The Goddess with her breath the flame supplies,
Bright as the star whose fires in Autumn rise;
Her breath divine thick streaming flames supplies,
Bright as the star that fires the autumnal skies:
Th' unwearied blaze incessant streams supplies,
Like the red star that fires th' autumnal skies.

When first he rears his radiant orb to sight,
And bath'd in ocean shoots a keener light.
Such glories Pallas on the chief bestow'd,
Such from his arms the fierce effulgence flow'd;
Onward she drives him furious to engage,
Where the fight burns, and where the thickest rage.

When fresh he rears his radiant orb to sight,
And gilds old Ocean with a blaze of light,
Bright as the star that fires th' autumnal skies,
Fresh from the deep, and gilds the seas and skies.
Such glories Pallas on her chief bestow'd,
Such sparkling rays from his bright armour flow'd,
Such from his arms the fierce effulgence flow'd.
Onward she drives him *headlong* to engage,
furious
Where the *war bleeds*, and where the *fiercest* rage.
fight burns, thickest

The sons of Dares first the combat sought,
A wealthy priest, but rich without a fault;
In Vulcan's fane the father's days were led,
The sons to toils of glorious battle bred;

There liv'd a Trojan—Dares was his name,
The priest of Vulcan, rich, yet void of blame;
The sons of Dares first the combat sought,
A wealthy priest, but rich without a fault.

Conclusion of Book VIII. *v.* 687.

As when the moon, refulgent lamp of night,
O'er heaven's clear azure spreads her sacred light;
When not a breath disturbs the deep serene,
And not a cloud o'ercasts the solemn scene;
Around her throne the vivid planets roll,
And stars unnumber'd gild the glowing pole:
O'er the dark trees a yellower verdure shed,
And tip with silver every mountain's head;
Then shine the vales—the rocks in prospect rise,
A flood of glory bursts from all the skies;
The conscious swains, rejoicing in the sight,

Eye the blue vault, and bless the useful light.
So many flames before proud Ilion blaze,
And lighten glimmering Xanthus with their rays;
The long reflexion of the distant fires
Gleam on the walls, and tremble on the spires:
A thousand piles the dusky horrors gild,
And shoot a shady lustre o'er the field;
Full fifty guards each flaming pile attend,
Whose umber'd arms by fits thick flashes send;
Loud neigh the coursers o'er their heaps of corn,
And ardent warriors wait the rising morn.

As when in stillness of the silent night,
As when the moon in all her lustre bright,
As when the moon, refulgent lamp of night,
O'er heaven's *clear* azure *sheds* her *silver* light;
pure spreads sacred
As still in air the trembling lustre stood,
And o'er its golden border shoots a flood;
When *no loose gale* disturbs the deep serene,
not a breath
And *no dim* cloud o'ercasts the solemn scene;
not a
Around her silver throne the planets glow,
And stars unnumber'd trembling beams bestow;
Around her throne the vivid planets roll,
And stars unnumber'd gild the glowing pole:
Clear gleams of light o'er the dark trees are seen,
o'er the dark trees a yellow sheds,
O'er the dark trees a yellower *green* they shed,
gleam
verdure
And tip with silver all the *mountain* heads:
forest
And tip with silver every mountain's head.
The vallies open, and the forests rise,
The vales appear, the rocks in prospect rise,
Then shine the vales, the rocks in prospect rise,
All Nature stands reveal'd before our eyes;
A flood of glory bursts from all the skies.
The conscious shepherd, joyful at the sight,
Eyes the blue vault, and numbers every light.
The conscious *swains rejoicing at the* sight
shepherds gazing with delight
Eye the blue vault, and bless the *vivid* light.
glorious
useful
So many flames before *the navy* blaze,
proud Ilion

And lighten glimmering Xanthus with their rays,
Wide o'er the fields to Troy extend the gleams,
And tip the distant spires with fainter beams;
The long reflexions of the distant fires
Gild the high walls, and tremble on the spires,
Gleam on the walls, and tremble on the spires;
A thousand fires at distant stations bright,
Gild the dark prospect, and dispel the night.

Of these specimens every man who has cultivated poetry, or who delights to trace the mind from the rudeness of its first conceptions to the elegance of its last, will naturally desire a greater number; but most other readers are already tired, and I am not writing only to poets and philosophers.

The *Iliad* was published volume by volume, as the translation proceeded; the four first books appeared in 1715. The expectation of this work was undoubtedly high, and every man who had connected his name with criticism, or poetry, was desirous of such intelligence as might enable him to talk upon the popular topick. Halifax, who, by having been first a poet, and then a patron of poetry, had acquired the right of being a judge, was willing to hear some books while they were yet unpublished. Of this rehearsal Pope afterwards gave the following account[1].

"The famous Lord Halifax was rather a pretender to taste than really possessed of it.—When I had finished the two or three first books of my translation of the *Iliad*, that Lord desired to have the pleasure of hearing them read at his house.—Addison, Congreve, and Garth,* were there at the reading. In four or five places, Lord Halifax stopt me very civilly, and with a speech each time, much of the same kind, 'I beg your pardon, Mr. Pope; but there is something in that passage that does not quite please me.—Be so good as to mark the place, and consider it a little at your leisure.—I'm sure you can give it a little turn.' I returned from Lord Halifax's with Dr. Garth, in his chariot; and, as we were going along, was saying to the Doctor, that my Lord had laid me under a good deal of difficulty by such loose and general observations; that I had been thinking over the passages almost ever since, and could not guess at what it was that offended his Lordship in either of them. Garth laughed heartily at my embarrassment; said, I had not been long enough acquainted with

[1] Spence.

Lord Halifax to know his way yet; that I need not puzzle myself about looking those places over and over, when I got home. 'All you need do (says he) is to leave them just as they are; call on Lord Halifax two or three months hence, thank him for his kind observations on those passages, and then read them to him as altered. I have known him much longer than you have, and will be answerable for the event.' I followed his advice; waited on Lord Halifax some time after; said, I hoped he would find his objections to those passages removed; read them to him exactly as they were at first: and his Lordship was extremely pleased with them, and cried out, *Ay, now they are perfectly right: nothing can be better.*"

It is seldom that the great or the wise suspect that they are despised or cheated. Halifax, thinking this a lucky opportunity of securing immortality, made some advances of favour and some overtures of advantage to Pope, which he seems to have received with sullen coldness. All our knowledge of this transaction is derived from a single Letter (Dec. 1, 1714), in which Pope says, "I am obliged to you, both for the favours you have done me, and those you intend me. I distrust neither your will nor your memory, when it is to do good; and if I ever become troublesome or solicitous, it must not be out of expectation, but out of gratitude. Your Lordship may cause me to live agreeably in the town, or contentedly in the country, which is really all the difference I set between an easy fortune and a small one. It is indeed a high strain of generosity in you to think of making me easy all my life, only because I have been so happy as to divert you some few hours; but, if I may have leave to add it is because you think me no enemy to my native country, there will appear a better reason; for I must of consequence be very much (as I sincerely am) yours &c."*

These voluntary offers, and this faint acceptance, ended without effect. The patron was not accustomed to such frigid gratitude, and the poet fed his own pride with the dignity of independence. They probably were suspicious of each other. Pope would not dedicate till he saw at what rate his praise was valued; he would be *troublesome out of gratitude, not expectation*. Halifax thought himself entitled to confidence; and would give nothing, unless he knew what he should receive. Their commerce had its beginning in hope of praise on one side, and of money on the other, and ended because Pope was less eager of money than Halifax of praise. It is not likely that Halifax had any personal benevolence to Pope; it is evident that Pope looked on Halifax with scorn and hatred.

The reputation of this great work failed of gaining him a patron; but it deprived him of a friend. Addison and he were now at the head of poetry and criticism; and both in such a state of elevation, that, like the two rivals in the Roman state, one could no longer bear an equal, nor the other a superior. Of the gradual abatement of kindness between friends, the beginning is often scarcely discernible by themselves, and the process is continued by petty provocations, and incivilities sometimes peevishly returned, and sometimes contemptuously neglected, which would escape all attention but that of pride, and drop from any memory but that of resentment. That the quarrel of those two wits should be minutely deduced, is not to be expected from a writer to whom, as Homer says, *nothing but rumour has reached, and who has no personal knowledge.**

Pope doubtless approached Addison, when the reputation of their wit first brought them together, with the respect due to a man whose abilities were acknowledged, and who, having attained that eminence to which he was himself aspiring, had in his hands the distribution of literary fame. He paid court with sufficient diligence by his Prologue to *Cato*, by his abuse of Dennis, and, with praise yet more direct, by his poem on the *Dialogues on Medals*, of which the immediate publication was then intended. In all this there was no hypocrisy; for he confessed that he found in Addison something more pleasing than in any other man.

It may be supposed, that as Pope saw himself favoured by the world, and more frequently compared his own powers with those of others, his confidence increased, and his submission lessened; and that Addison felt no delight from the advances of a young wit, who might soon contend with him for the highest place. Every great man, of whatever kind be his greatness, has among his friends those who officiously, or insidiously, quicken his attention to offences, heighten his disgust, and stimulate his resentment. Of such adherents Addison doubtless had many, and Pope was now too high to be without them.

From the emission and reception of the Proposals for the *Iliad*, the kindness of Addison seems to have abated. Jervas the painter once pleased himself (Aug. 20, 1714) with imagining that he had re-established their friendship; and wrote to Pope that Addison once suspected him of too close a confederacy with Swift, but was now satisfied with his conduct. To this Pope answered, a week after, that his engagements to Swift were such as his services in regard to the subscription demanded, and that the Tories never put him under the necessity of asking leave to be grateful. *But,* says he, *as Mr. Addison must be* the judge *in what regards himself, and seems to be no very just one in regard to me, so I must own to you I expect nothing but civility from him.* In the same Letter he mentions Philips, as having been busy to kindle animosity between them; but, in a Letter to Addison, he expresses some consciousness of behaviour, inattentively deficient in respect.

Of Swift's industry in promoting the subscription there remains the testimony of Kennet,* no friend to either him or Pope.

"Nov. 2, 1713, Dr. Swift came into the coffee-house, and had a bow from every body but me, who, I confess, could not but despise him. When I came to the anti-chamber to wait, before prayers, Dr. Swift was the principal man of talk and business, and acted as master of requests.—Then he instructed a young nobleman that the *best Poet in England* was *Mr. Pope* (a papist), who had begun a translation of *Homer* into English verse, for which *he must have them all subscribe*; for, says he, the author *shall not* begin to print till *I have* a thousand guineas for him."

About this time it is likely that Steele, who was, with all his political fury, good-natured and officious, procured an interview between these angry rivals, which ended in aggravated malevolence. On this occasion, if the reports be true, Pope made his complaint with frankness and spirit, as a man undeservedly neglected or opposed; and Addison affected a contemptuous unconcern, and, in a calm even voice, reproached Pope with his vanity, and, telling him of the improvements which his early works had received from his own remarks and those of Steele, said, that he, being now engaged in publick business, had no longer any care for his poetical reputation; nor had any other desire, with regard to Pope, than that his should not, by too much arrogance, alienate the publick.

To this Pope is said to have replied with great keenness and severity, upbraiding Addison with perpetual dependance, and with the abuse of those qualifications which he had obtained at the publick cost, and charging him with mean endeavours to obstruct the progress of rising merit. The contest rose so high, that they parted at last without any interchange of civility.

The first volume of *Homer* was (1715) in time published; and a rival version of the first *Iliad*, for rivals the time of their appearance inevitably made them, was immediately printed, with the name of Tickell.* It was soon perceived that, among the followers of Addison, Tickell had the preference, and the criticks and poets divided into factions. *I*, says Pope, *have the town, that is, the mob, on my side; but it is not uncommon for the smaller party to supply by industry what it wants in numbers.—I appeal to the people as my rightful judges, and, while they are not inclined to condemn me, shall not fear the high-flyers at Button's.* This opposition he immediately imputed to Addison, and complained of it in terms sufficiently resentful to Craggs, their common friend.

When Addison's opinion was asked, he declared the versions to be both good, but Tickell's the best that had ever been written; and sometimes said that they were both good, but that Tickell had more of *Homer*.

Pope was now sufficiently irritated; his reputation and his interest were at hazard. He once intended to print together the four versions of Dryden, Maynwaring,* Pope, and Tickell, that they might be readily compared, and fairly estimated. This design seems to have been defeated by the refusal of Tonson, who was the proprietor of the other three versions.

Pope intended at another time a rigorous criticism of Tickell's translation, and had marked a copy, which I have seen, in all places that appeared defective. But while he was thus meditating defence or revenge, his adversary sunk before him without a blow; the voice of the publick was not long divided, and the preference was universally given to Pope's performance.

He was convinced, by adding one circumstance to another, that the other translation was the work of Addison himself; but if he knew it in Addison's life-time, it does not appear that he told it. He left his illustrious antagonist to be punished by what has been considered as the most painful of all reflections, the remembrance of a crime perpetrated in vain.

The other circumstances of their quarrel were thus related by Pope[1].

"Philips seemed to have been encouraged to abuse me in coffee-houses, and conversations: and Gildon wrote a thing about

[1] Spence.

Wycherley, in which he had abused both me and my relations very grossly. Lord Warwick himself told me one day, that it was in vain for me to endeavour to be well with Mr. Addison; that his jealous temper would never admit of a settled friendship between us: and, to convince me of what he had said, assured me, that Addison had encouraged Gildon to publish those scandals, and had given him ten guineas after they were published. The next day, while I was heated with what I had heard, I wrote a Letter to Mr. Addison, to let him know that I was not unacquainted with this behaviour of his; that if I was to speak severely of him, in return for it, it should not be in such a dirty way, that I should rather tell him, himself, fairly of his faults, and allow his good qualities; and that it should be something in the following manner: I then adjoined the first sketch of what has since been called my satire on Addison. Mr. Addison used me very civilly ever after."

The verses on Addison, when they were sent to Atterbury, were considered by him as the most excellent of Pope's performances; and the writer was advised, since he knew where his strength lay, not to suffer it to remain unemployed.

This year (1715) being, by the subscription, enabled to live more by choice, having persuaded his father to sell their estate at Binfield, he purchased, I think only for his life, that house at Twickenham to which his residence afterwards procured so much celebration, and removed thither with his father and mother.

Here he planted the vines and the quincunx* which his verses mention; and being under the necessity of making a subterraneous passage to a garden on the other side of the road, he adorned it with fossile bodies, and dignified it with the title of a grotto; a place of silence and retreat, from which he endeavoured to persuade his friends and himself that cares and passions could be excluded.

A grotto is not often the wish or pleasure of an Englishman, who has more frequent need to solicit than exclude the sun; but Pope's excavation was requisite as an entrance to his garden, and, as some men try to be proud of their defects, he extracted an ornament from an inconvenience, and vanity produced a grotto where necessity enforced a passage. It may be frequently remarked of the studious and speculative, that they are proud of trifles, and that their amusements seem frivolous and childish; whether it be that men conscious of great reputation think themselves above the reach of censure, and safe in the admission of negligent indulgences, or that mankind expect from elevated genius an uniformity of greatness, and watch its degradation with malicious wonder; like him who having followed with his eye an eagle into the clouds, should lament that she ever descended to a perch.

While the volumes of his *Homer* were annually published, he collected his former works (1717) into one quarto volume, to which he prefixed a Preface, written with great spriteliness and elegance, which was afterwards reprinted, with some passages subjoined that he at first omitted; other marginal additions of the same kind he made in the later editions of his poems. Waller remarks, that poets lose half their praise, because the reader knows not what they have blotted. Pope's voracity of fame taught him the art of obtaining the accumulated honour both of what he had published, and of what he had suppressed.

In this year his father died suddenly, in his seventy-fifth year, having passed twenty-nine years in privacy. He is not known but by the character which his son has given him. If the money with which he retired was all gotten by himself, he had traded very successfully in times when sudden riches were rarely attainable.

The publication of the *Iliad* was at last completed in 1720. The splendor and success of this work raised Pope many enemies, that endeavoured to depreciate his abilities; Burnet,* who was afterwards a Judge of no mean reputation, censured him in a piece called *Homerides* before it was published; Ducket* likewise endeavoured to make him ridiculous. Dennis was the perpetual persecutor of all his studies. But, whoever his criticks were, their writings are lost, and the names which are preserved, are preserved in the *Dunciad*.

In this disastrous year (1720) of national infatuation, when more riches than Peru can boast were expected from the South Sea,* when the contagion of avarice tainted every mind, and even poets panted after wealth, Pope was seized with the universal passion, and ventured some of his money. The stock rose in its price; and he for a while thought himself *the Lord of thousands*. But this dream of happiness did not last long, and he seems to have waked soon enough to get clear with the loss only of what he once thought himself to have won, and perhaps not wholly of that.

Next year he published some select poems of his friend Dr. Parnell, with a very elegant Dedication to the Earl of Oxford;

who, after all his struggles and dangers, then lived in retirement, still under the frown of a victorious faction, who could take no pleasure in hearing his praise.

He gave the same year (1721) an edition of *Shakspeare*. His name was now of so much authority, that Tonson* thought himself entitled, by annexing it, to demand a subscription of six guineas for Shakspeare's plays in six quarto volumes; nor did his expectation much deceive him; for of seven hundred and fifty which he printed, he dispersed a great number at the price proposed. The reputation of that edition indeed sunk afterwards so low, that one hundred and forty copies were sold at sixteen shillings each.

On this undertaking, to which Pope was induced by a reward of two hundred and seventeen pounds twelve shillings, he seems never to have reflected afterwards without vexation; for Theobald, a man of heavy diligence, with very slender powers, first, in a book called *Shakespeare Restored*, and then in a formal edition, detected his deficiencies with all the insolence of victory; and, as he was now high enough to be feared and hated, Theobald had from others all the help that could be supplied, by the desire of humbling a haughty character.*

From this time Pope became an enemy to editors, collaters, commentators, and verbal criticks; and hoped to persuade the world, that he miscarried in this undertaking only by having a mind too great for such minute employment.

Pope in his edition undoubtedly did many things wrong, and left many things undone; but let him not be defrauded of his due praise. He was the first that knew, at least the first that told, by what helps the text might be improved. If he inspected the early editions negligently, he taught others to be more accurate. In his Preface he expanded with great skill and elegance the character which had been given of Shakspeare by Dryden; and he drew the publick attention upon his works, which, though often mentioned, had been little read.

Soon after the appearance of the *Iliad*, resolving not to let the general kindness cool, he published proposals for a translation of the *Odyssey*, in five volumes, for five guineas. He was willing, however, now to have associates in his labour, being either weary with toiling upon another's thoughts, or having heard, as Ruffhead relates, that Fenton and Broome had already begun the work, and liking better to have them confederates than rivals.

In the patent, instead of saying that he had *translated* the *Odyssey*, as he had said of the *Iliad*, he says that he had *undertaken* a translation; and in the proposals the subscription is said to be not solely for his own use, but for that of *two of his friends who have assisted him in this work*.

In 1723, while he was engaged in this new version, he appeared before the Lords at the memorable trial of Bishop Atterbury,* with whom he had lived in great familiarity, and frequent correspondence. Atterbury had honestly recommended to him the study of the popish controversy, in hope of his conversion; to which Pope answered in a manner that cannot much recommend his principles, or his judgement. In questions and projects of learning, they agreed better. He was called at the trial to give an account of Atterbury's domestick life, and private employment, that it might appear how little time he had left for plots. Pope had but few words to utter, and in those few he made several blunders.

His Letters to Atterbury express the utmost esteem, tenderness, and gratitude: *perhaps*, says he, *it is not only in this world that I may have cause to remember the Bishop of Rochester*. At their last interview in the Tower, Atterbury presented him with a Bible.

Of the *Odyssey* Pope translated only twelve books; the rest were the work of Broome and Fenton: the notes were written wholly by Broome, who was not over-liberally rewarded. The Public was carefully kept ignorant of the several shares; and an account was subjoined at the conclusion, which is now known not to be true.

The first copy of Pope's books, with those of Fenton, are to be seen in the Museum. The parts of Pope are less interlined than the *Iliad*, and the latter books of the *Iliad* less than the former. He grew dexterous by practice, and every sheet enabled him to write the next with more facility. The books of Fenton have very few alterations by the hand of Pope. Those of Broome have not been found; but Pope complained, as it is reported, that he had much trouble in correcting them.

His contract with Lintot was the same as for the *Iliad*, except that only one hundred pounds were to be paid him for each volume. The number of subscribers was five hundred and seventy-four, and of copies eight hundred and nineteen; so that his profit, when he had paid his assistants, was still very considerable. The work was finished in 1725, and from that time he resolved to make no more translations.

The sale did not answer Lintot's expectation, and he then pretended to discover something of fraud in Pope, and commenced, or threatened, a suit in Chancery.

On the English *Odyssey* a criticism was published by Spence,* at that time Prelector of Poetry at Oxford; a man whose learning was not very great, and whose mind was not very powerful. His criticism, however, was commonly just; what he thought, he thought rightly; and his remarks were recommended by his coolness and candour. In him Pope had the first experience of a critick without malevolence, who thought it as much his duty to display beauties as expose faults; who censured with respect, and praised with alacrity.

With this criticism Pope was so little offended, that he sought the acquaintance of the writer, who lived with him from that time in great familiarity, attended him in his last hours, and compiled memorials of his conversation. The regard of Pope recommended him to the great and powerful, and he obtained very valuable preferments in the Church.

Not long after Pope was returning home from a visit in a friend's coach, which, in passing a bridge, was overturned into the water; the windows were closed, and being unable to force them open, he was in danger of immediate death, when the postilion snatched him out by breaking the glass, of which the fragments cut two of his fingers in such a manner, that he lost their use.

Voltaire, who was then in England, sent him a Letter of Consolation. He had been entertained by Pope at his table, where he talked with so much grossness that Mrs. Pope was driven from the room. Pope discovered, by a trick, that he was a spy for the Court, and never considered him as a man worthy of confidence.

He soon afterwards (1727) joined with Swift, who was then in England, to publish three volumes of Miscellanies, in which amongst other things he inserted the *Memoirs of a Parish Clerk*, in ridicule of Burnet's importance in his own History,* and a *Debate upon Black and White Horses*, written in all the formalities of a legal process by the assistance, as is said, of Mr. Fortescue,* afterwards Master of the Rolls. Before these Miscellanies is a preface signed by Swift and Pope, but apparently written by Pope; in which he makes a ridiculous and romantick complaint of the robberies committed upon authors by the clandestine seizure and sale of their papers. He tells, in tragick strains, how *the cabinets of the Sick and the closets of the Dead have been* *broke open and ransacked*; as if those violences were often committed for papers of uncertain and accidental value, which are rarely provoked by real treasures; as if epigrams and essays were in danger where gold and diamonds are safe. A cat, hunted for his musk, is, according to Pope's account, but the emblem of a wit winded by booksellers.

His complaint, however, received some attestation; for the same year the Letters written by him to Mr. Cromwell, in his youth, were sold by Mrs. Thomas to Curll, who printed them.

In these Miscellanies was first published the *Art of Sinking in Poetry*, which, by such a train of consequences as usually passes in literary quarrels, gave in a short time, according to Pope's account, occasion to the *Dunciad*.

In the following year (1728) he began to put Atterbury's advice in practice; and shewed his satirical powers by publishing the *Dunciad*, one of his greatest and most elaborate performances, in which he endeavoured to sink into contempt all the writers by whom he had been attacked, and some others whom he thought unable to defend themselves.

At the head of the Dunces he placed poor Theobald, whom he accused of ingratitude; but whose real crime was supposed to be that of having revised *Shakspeare* more happily than himself. This satire had the effect which he intended, by blasting the characters which it touched. Ralph,* who, unnecessarily interposing in the quarrel, got a place in a subsequent edition, complained that for a time he was in danger of starving, as the booksellers had no longer any confidence in his capacity.

The prevalence of this poem was gradual and slow: the plan, if not wholly new, was little understood by common readers. Many of the allusions required illustration; the names were often expressed only by the initial and final letters, and, if they had been printed at length, were such as few had known or recollected. The subject itself had nothing generally interesting, for whom did it concern to know that one or another scribbler was a dunce? If therefore it had been possible for those who were attacked to conceal their pain and their resentment, the *Dunciad* might have made its way very slowly in the world.

This, however, was not to be expected: every man is of importance to himself, and therefore, in his own opinion, to others; and, supposing the world already acquainted with all his pleasures and his pains, is perhaps the first to publish injuries or misfortunes, which had never been known unless related by himself, and at which those that hear them will only laugh; for no man sympathises with the sorrows of vanity.

The history of the *Dunciad* is very minutely related by Pope himself, in a Dedication which he wrote to Lord Middlesex in the name of Savage.*

"I will relate the war of the *Dunces* (for so it has been commonly called), which began in the year 1727, and ended in 1730.

"When Dr. Swift and Mr. Pope thought it proper, for reasons specified in the Preface to their Miscellanies, to publish such little pieces of theirs as had casually got abroad, there was added to them the *Treatise of the Bathos*, or the *Art of Sinking in Poetry*. It happened that in one chapter of this piece the several species of bad poets were ranged in classes, to which were prefixed almost all the letters of the alphabet (the greatest part of them at random); but such was the number of poets eminent in that art, that some one or other took every letter to himself: all fell into so violent a fury, that, for half a year or more, the common newspapers (in most of which they had some property, as being hired writers) were filled with the most abusive falshoods and scurrilities they could possibly devise. A liberty no way to be wondered at in those people, and in those papers, that for many years, during the uncontrouled license of the press, had aspersed almost all the great characters of the age; and this with impunity, their own persons and names being utterly secret and obscure.

"This gave Mr. Pope the thought, that he had now some opportunity of doing good, by detecting and dragging into light these common enemies of mankind; since to invalidate this universal slander, it sufficed to shew what contemptible men were the authors of it. He was not without hopes, that, by manifesting the dulness of those who had only malice to recommend them, either the booksellers would not find their account in employing them, or the men themselves, when discovered, want courage to proceed in so unlawful an occupation. This it was that gave birth to the *Dunciad*; and he thought it an happiness, that, by the late flood of slander on himself, he had acquired such a peculiar right over their names as was necessary to this design.

"On the 12th of March, 1729, at St. James's, that poem was presented to the King and Queen (who had before been pleased to read it) by the right honourable Sir Robert Walpole; and some days after the whole impression was taken and dispersed by several noblemen and persons of the first distinction.

"It is certainly a true observation, that no people are so impatient of censure as those who are the greatest slanderers, which was wonderfully exemplified on this occasion. On the day the book was first vended, a crowd of authors besieged the shop; intreaties, advices, threats of law and battery, nay cries of treason, were all employed to hinder the coming-out of the *Dunciad*: on the other side, the booksellers and hawkers made as great efforts to procure it. What could a few poor authors do against so great a majority as the publick? There was no stopping a torrent with a finger, so out it came.

"Many ludicrous circumstances attended it. The *Dunces* (for by this name they were called) held weekly clubs, to consult of hostilities against the author: one wrote a Letter to a great minister, assuring him Mr. Pope was the greatest enemy the government had; and another bought his image in clay, to execute him in effigy, with which sad sort of satisfactions the gentlemen were a little comforted.

"Some false editions of the book having an owl in their frontispiece, the true one, to distinguish it, fixed in its stead an ass laden with authors. Then another surreptitious one being printed with the same ass, the new edition in octavo returned for distinction to the owl again. Hence arose a great contest of booksellers against booksellers, and advertisements against advertisements; some recommending the edition of the owl, and others the edition of the ass; by which names they came to be distinguished, to the great honour also of the gentlemen of the *Dunciad*."

Pope appears by this narrative to have contemplated his victory over the *Dunces* with great exultation; and such was his delight in the tumult which he had raised, that for a while his natural sensibility was suspended, and he read reproaches and invectives without emotion, considering them only as the necessary effects of that pain which he rejoiced in having given.

It cannot however be concealed that, by his own confession, he was the aggressor; for nobody believes that the letters in the *Bathos* were placed at random; and it may be discovered that, when he thinks himself concealed, he indulges the common vanity of common men, and triumphs in those distinctions which he had affected to despise. He is proud that his book was presented to the King and Queen by the right honourable Sir Robert Walpole; he is proud that they had read it before; he is proud that the edition was taken off by the nobility and persons of the first distinction.

The edition of which he speaks was, I believe, that, which by telling in the text the names and in the notes the characters of those whom he had satirised, was made intelligible and diverting. The criticks had now declared their approbation of the plan, and the common reader began to like it without fear; those who were strangers to petty literature, and therefore unable to decypher initials and blanks, had now names and persons brought within their view; and delighted in the visible effect of those shafts of malice, which they had hitherto contemplated, as shot into the air.

Dennis, upon the fresh provocation now given him, renewed the enmity which had for a time been appeased by mutual civilities; and published remarks, which he had till then suppressed, upon the *Rape of the Lock*. Many more grumbled in secret, or vented their resentment in the newspapers by epigrams or invectives.

Ducket, indeed, being mentioned as loving Burnet with *pious passion*, pretended that his moral character was injured, and for some time declared his resolution to take vengeance with a cudgel. But Pope appeased him, by changing *pious passion* to *cordial friendship*,* and by a note, in which he vehemently disclaims the malignity of meaning imputed to the first expression.

Aaron Hill,* who was represented as diving for the prize, expostulated with Pope in a manner so much superior to all mean solicitation, that Pope was reduced to sneak and shuffle, sometimes to deny, and sometimes to apologize; he first endeavours to wound, and is then afraid to own that he meant a blow.

The *Dunciad*, in the complete edition, is addressed to Dr. Swift: of the notes, part was written by Dr. Arbuthnot, and an apologetical Letter was prefixed, signed by Cleland,* but supposed to have been written by Pope.

After this general war upon dulness, he seems to have indulged himself awhile in tranquillity; but his subsequent productions prove that he was not idle. He published (1731) a poem on *Taste*, in which he very particularly and severely criticises the house, the furniture, the gardens, and the entertainments of *Timon*, a man of great wealth and little taste. By *Timon* he was universally supposed, and by the Earl of Burlington, to whom the poem is addressed, was privately said, to mean the Duke of Chandos;* a man perhaps too much delighted with pomp and show, but of a temper kind and beneficent, and who had consequently the voice of the publick in his favour.

A violent outcry was therefore raised against the ingratitude and treachery of Pope, who was said to have been indebted to the patronage of Chandos for a present of a thousand pounds, and who gained the opportunity of insulting him by the kindness of his invitation.

The receipt of the thousand pounds Pope publickly denied; but from the reproach which the attack on a character so amiable brought upon him, he tried all means of escaping. The name of Cleland was again employed in an apology, by which no man was satisfied; and he was at last reduced to shelter his temerity behind dissimulation, and endeavour to make that disbelieved which he never had confidence openly to deny. He wrote an exculpatory letter to the Duke, which was answered with great magnanimity, as by a man who accepted his excuse without believing his professions. He said, that to have ridiculed his taste, or his buildings, had been an indifferent action in another man; but that in Pope, after the reciprocal kindness that had been exchanged between them, it had been less easily excused.

Pope, in one of his Letters, complaining of the treatment which his poem had found, *owns that such criticks can intimidate him, nay almost persuade him to write no more, which is a compliment this age deserves.* The man who threatens the world is always ridiculous; for the world can easily go on without him, and in a short time will cease to miss him. I have heard of an idiot, who used to revenge his vexations by lying all night upon the bridge. *There is nothing*, says Juvenal, *that a man will not believe in his own favour.** Pope had been flattered till he thought himself one of the moving powers in the system of life. When he talked of laying down his pen, those who sat round him intreated and implored, and self-love did not suffer him to suspect that they went away and laughed.

The following year deprived him of Gay, a man whom he had known early, and whom he seemed to love with more tenderness than any other of his literary friends. Pope was now forty-four years old; an age at which the mind begins less easily to admit new confidence, and the will to grow less flexible, and when therefore the departure of an old friend is very acutely felt.

In the next year he lost his mother, not by an unexpected death, for she had lasted to the age of ninety-three; but she did not die unlamented. The filial piety of Pope was in the highest degree amiable and exemplary; his parents had the happiness of living till he was at the summit of poetical reputation, till he was at ease in his fortune, and without a rival in his fame, and found no diminution of his respect or tenderness. Whatever was his pride, to them he was obedient; and whatever was his irritability, to them he was gentle. Life has, among its soothing and quiet comforts, few things better to give than such a son.

One of the passages of Pope's life, which seems to deserve some enquiry, was a publication of Letters between him and many of his friends, which falling into the hands of *Curll*, a rapacious bookseller of no good fame, were by him printed and sold. This volume containing some Letters from noblemen, Pope incited a prosecution against him in the House of Lords for breach of privilege, and attended himself to stimulate the resentment of his friends. *Curll* appeared at the bar, and, knowing himself in no great danger, spoke of Pope with very little reverence. *He has*, said Curll, *a knack at versifying, but in prose I think myself a match for him*. When the orders of the House were examined, none of them appeared to have been infringed; Curll went away triumphant, and Pope was left to seek some other remedy.

Curll's account was, that one evening a man in a clergyman's gown, but with a lawyer's band, brought and offered to sale a number of printed volumes, which he found to be Pope's epistolary correspondence; that he asked no name, and was told none, but gave the price demanded, and thought himself authorised to use his purchase to his own advantage.

That Curll gave a true account of the transaction, it is reasonable to believe, because no falshood was ever detected; and when some years afterwards I mentioned it to Lintot, the son of Bernard,* he declared his opinion to be, that Pope knew better than any body else how Curll obtained the copies, because another parcel was at the same time sent to himself, for which no price had ever been demanded, as he made known his resolution not to pay a porter, and consequently not to deal with a nameless agent.

Such care had been taken to make them publick, that they were sent at once to two booksellers; to Curll, who was likely to seize them as a prey, and to Lintot, who might be expected to give Pope information of the seeming injury. Lintot, I believe, did nothing; and Curll did what was expected. That to make them publick was the only purpose may be reasonably supposed, because the numbers offered to sale by the private messengers shewed that hope of gain could not have been the motive of the impression.

It seems that Pope, being desirous of printing his Letters, and not knowing how to do, without imputation of vanity, what has in this country been done very rarely, contrived an appearance of compulsion; that when he could complain that his Letters were surreptitiously published, he might decently and defensively publish them himself.

Pope's private correspondence, thus promulgated, filled the nation with praises of his candour, tenderness, and benevolence, the purity of his purposes, and the fidelity of his friendship. There were some Letters which a very good or a very wise man would wish suppressed; but, as they had been already exposed, it was impracticable now to retract them.

From the perusal of those Letters, Mr. Allen* first conceived the desire of knowing him; and with so much zeal did he cultivate the friendship which he had newly formed, that when Pope told his purpose of vindicating his own property by a genuine edition, he offered to pay the cost.

This however Pope did not accept; but in time solicited a subscription for a Quarto volume, which appeared (1737) I believe, with sufficient profit. In the Preface he tells that his Letters were reposited in a friend's library, said to be the Earl of Oxford's, and that the copy thence stolen was sent to the press. The story was doubtless received with different degrees of credit. It may be suspected that the Preface to the Miscellanies was written to prepare the publick for such an incident; and to strengthen this opinion, James Worsdale,* a painter, who was employed in clandestine negotiations, but whose veracity was very doubtful, declared that he was the messenger who carried, by Pope's direction, the books to Curll.

When they were thus published and avowed, as they had relation to recent facts, and persons either then living or not yet forgotten, they may be supposed to have found readers; but as the facts were minute, and the characters being either private or literary, were little known, or little regarded, they awakened no popular kindness or resentment: the book never became much the subject of conversation; some read it as contemporary history, and some perhaps as a model of epistolary language; but those who read it did not talk of it. Not much therefore was added by it to fame or envy; nor do I remember that it produced either publick praise, or publick censure.

It had however, in some degree, the recommendation of novelty. Our language has few Letters, except those of statesmen. Howel indeed, about a century ago, published his Letters, which are commended by *Morhoff*, and which alone of his hundred volumes continue his memory. Loveday's Letters were printed only once; those of Herbert and Suckling are hardly known. Mrs. Phillips's [*Orinda's*] are equally neglected; and those of Walsh seem written as exercises, and were never sent to any living mistress or friend.* Pope's epistolary excellence had an open field; he had no English rival, living or dead.

Pope is seen in this collection as connected with the other contemporary wits, and certainly suffers no disgrace in the comparison; but it must be remembered, that he had the power of favouring himself: he might have originally had publication in his mind, and have written with care, or have afterwards selected those which he had most happily conceived, or most diligently laboured; and I know not whether there does not appear something more studied and artificial in his productions than the rest, except one long Letter by Bolingbroke, composed with all the skill and industry of a professed author. It is indeed not easy to distinguish affectation from habit; he that has once studiously formed a style, rarely writes afterwards with complete ease. Pope may be said to write always with his reputation in his head; Swift perhaps like a man who remembered that he was writing to Pope; but Arbuthnot like one who lets thoughts drop from his pen as they rise into his mind.

Before these Letters appeared, he published the first part of what he persuaded himself to think a system of Ethicks, under the title of an *Essay on Man*; which, if his Letter to Swift (of Sept.14, 1725) be rightly explained by the commentator, had been eight years under his consideration, and of which he seems to have desired the success with great solicitude. He had now many open and doubtless many secret enemies. The *Dunces* were yet smarting with the war; and the superiority which he publickly arrogated, disposed the world to wish his humiliation.

All this he knew, and against all this he provided. His own name, and that of his friend to whom the work is inscribed, were in the first editions carefully suppressed; and the poem, being of a new kind, was ascribed to one or another, as favour determined, or conjecture wandered; it was given, says Warburton, to every man, except him only who could write it. Those who like only when they like the author, and who are under the dominion of a name, condemned it; and those admired it who are willing to scatter praise at random, which while it is unappropriated excites no envy. Those friends of Pope, that were trusted with the secret, went about lavishing honours on the new-born poet, and hinting that Pope was never so much in danger from any former rival.

To those authors whom he had personally offended, and to those whose opinion the world considered as decisive, and whom he suspected of envy or malevolence, he sent his essay as a present before publication, that they might defeat their own enmity by praises, which they could not afterwards decently retract.

With these precautions, in 1733 was published the first part of the *Essay on Man*. There had been for some time a report that Pope was busy upon a System of Morality; but this design was not discovered in the new poem, which had a form and a title with which its readers were unacquainted. Its reception was not uniform; some thought it a very imperfect piece, though not without good lines. While the author was unknown, some, as will always happen, favoured him as an adventurer, and some censured him as an intruder; but all thought him above neglect; the sale increased, and editions were multiplied.

The subsequent editions of the first Epistle exhibited two memorable corrections. At first, the poet and his friend

> Expatiate free o'er all this scene of man,
> A mighty maze *of walks without a plan.*

For which he wrote afterwards,

> A mighty maze, *but not without a plan:**

for, if there were no plan, it was in vain to describe or to trace the maze. The other alteration was of these lines;

> And spite of pride, *and in thy reason's spite*,
> One truth is clear, whatever is, is right:

but having afterwards discovered, or been shewn, that the *truth* which subsisted *in spite of reason* could not be very *clear*, he substituted

> And spite of pride, *in erring reason's spite.**

To such oversights will the most vigorous mind be liable, when it is employed at once upon argument and poetry.

The second and third Epistles were published; and Pope was, I believe, more and more suspected of writing them; at last, in 1734, he avowed the fourth, and claimed the honour of a moral poet.

In the conclusion it is sufficiently acknowledged, that the doctrine of the *Essay on Man* was received from Bolingbroke,* who is said to have ridiculed Pope, among those who enjoyed his confidence, as having adopted and advanced principles of which he did not perceive the consequence, and as blindly propagating opinions contrary to his own. That those communications had been consolidated into a scheme regularly drawn, and delivered to Pope, from whom it returned only transformed from prose to verse, has been reported, but hardly can be true. The Essay plainly appears the fabrick of a poet: what Bolingbroke supplied could be only the first principles; the order, illustration, and embellishments must all be Pope's.

These principles it is not my business to clear from obscurity, dogmatism, or falsehood; but they were not immediately examined; philosophy and poetry have not often the same readers; and the Essay abounded in splendid amplifications and sparkling sentences, which were read and admired, with no great attention to their ultimate purpose; its flowers caught the eye, which did not see what the gay foliage concealed, and for a time flourished in the sunshine of universal approbation. So little was any evil tendency discovered, that, as innocence is unsuspicious, many read it for a manual of piety.

Its reputation soon invited a translator. It was first turned into French prose, and afterwards by Resnel into verse. Both translations fell into the hands of Crousaz, who first, when he had the version in prose, wrote a general censure, and afterwards reprinted Resnel's version, with particular remarks upon every paragraph.*

Crousaz was a professor of Switzerland, eminent for his treatise of Logick, and his *Examen de Pyrrhonisme*, and, however little known or regarded here, was no mean antagonist. His mind was one of those in which philosophy and piety are happily united. He was accustomed to argument and disquisition, and perhaps was grown too desirous of detecting faults; but his intentions were always right, his opinions were solid, and his religion pure.

His incessant vigilance for the promotion of piety disposed him to look with distrust upon all metaphysical systems of Theology, and all schemes of virtue and happiness purely rational; and therefore it was not long before he was persuaded that the positions of Pope, as they terminated for the most part in natural religion, were intended to draw mankind away from revelation, and to represent the whole course of things as a necessary concatenation of indissoluble fatality; and it is undeniable, that in many passages a religious eye may easily discover expressions not very favourable to morals, or to liberty.

About this time Warburton began to make his appearance in the first ranks of learning. He was a man of vigorous faculties, a mind fervid and vehement, supplied by incessant and unlimited enquiry, with wonderful extent and variety of knowledge, which yet had not oppressed his imagination, nor clouded his perspicacity. To every work he brought a memory full fraught, together with a fancy fertile of original combinations, and at once exerted the powers of the scholar, the reasoner, and the wit. But his knowledge was too multifarious to be always exact, and his pursuits were too eager to be always cautious. His abilities gave him an haughty confidence, which he disdained to conceal or mollify; and his impatience of opposition disposed him to treat his adversaries with such contemptuous superiority as made his readers commonly his enemies, and excited against the advocate the wishes of some who favoured the cause. He seems to have adopted the Roman Emperor's determination, *oderint dum metuant*;* he used no allurements of gentle language, but wished to compel rather than persuade.

His style is copious without selection, and forcible without neatness; he took the words that presented themselves: his diction is coarse and impure, and his sentences are unmeasured.

He had, in the early part of his life, pleased himself with the notice of inferior wits, and corresponded with the enemies of Pope. A Letter was produced, when he had perhaps himself forgotten it, in which he tells *Concanen*,* "Dryden *I observe borrows for want of leasure, and* Pope *for want of genius:* Milton *out of pride, and* Addison *out of modesty*." And when Theobald published *Shakespeare*, in opposition of Pope, the best notes were supplied by Warburton.

But the time was now come when Warburton was to change his opinion, and Pope was to find a defender in him who had contributed so much to the exaltation of his rival.

The arrogance of Warburton excited against him every artifice of offence, and therefore it may be supposed that his union with Pope was censured as hypocritical inconstancy; but surely to think differently, at different times, of poetical merit, may be easily allowed. Such opinions are often admitted, and dismissed, without nice examination. Who is there that has not found reason for changing his mind about questions of greater importance?

Warburton, whatever was his motive, undertook, without solicitation, to rescue Pope from the talons of Crousaz, by freeing him from the imputation of favouring fatality, or rejecting revelation; and from month to month continued a vindication of the *Essay on Man*, in the literary journal of that time called *The Republick of Letters*.

Pope, who probably began to doubt the tendency of his own work, was glad that the positions, of which he perceived himself not to know the full meaning, could by any mode of interpretation be made to mean well. How much he was pleased with his gratuitous defender, the following Letter evidently shews:

"SIR, March 24, 1743.

I have just received from Mr. R.* two more of your Letters. It is in the greatest hurry imaginable that I write this; but I cannot help thanking you in particular for your third Letter, which is so extremely clear, short, and full, that I think Mr. Crousaz ought never to have another answer, and deserved not so good an one, I can only say, you do him too much honour, and me too much right, so odd as the expression seems; for you have made my system as clear as I ought to have done, and could not. It is indeed the same system as mine, but illustrated with a ray of your own, as they say our natural body is the same still when it is glorified. I am sure I like it better than I did before, and so will every man else. I know I meant just what you explain; but I did not explain my own meaning so well as you. You understand me as well as I do myself; but you express me better than I could express myself. Pray accept the sincerest acknowledgements. I cannot but wish these Letters were put together in one Book, and intend (with your leave) to procure a translation of part, at least, of all of them into French; but I shall not proceed a step without your consent and opinion, &c."

By this fond and eager acceptance of an exculpatory comment, Pope testified that, whatever might be the seeming or real import of the principles which he had received from Bolingbroke, he had not intentionally attacked religion; and Bolingbroke, if he meant to make him without his own consent an instrument of mischief, found him now engaged with his eyes open on the side of truth.

It is known that Bolingbroke concealed from Pope his real opinions. He once discovered them to Mr. Hooke,* who related them again to Pope, and was told by him that he must have mistaken the meaning of what he heard; and Bolingbroke, when Pope's uneasiness incited him to desire an explanation, declared that Hooke had misunderstood him.

Bolingbroke hated Warburton, who had drawn his pupil from him; and a little before Pope's death they had a dispute, from which they parted with mutual aversion.

From this time Pope lived in the closest intimacy with his commentator, and amply rewarded his kindness and his zeal; for he introduced him to Mr. Murray,* by whose interest he became preacher at Lincoln's Inn, and to Mr. Allen, who gave him his niece and his estate, and by consequence a bishoprick. When he died, he left him the property of his works; a legacy which may be reasonably estimated at four thousand pounds.

Pope's fondness for the *Essay on Man* appeared by his desire of its propagation. Dobson,* who had gained reputation by his version of Prior's *Solomon*, was employed by him to translate it into Latin verse, and was for that purpose some time at Twickenham; but he left his work, whatever was the reason, unfinished; and, by Benson's invitation, undertook the longer task of *Paradise Lost*. Pope then desired his friend to find a scholar who should turn his Essay into Latin prose; but no such performance has ever appeared.

Pope lived at this time *among the great*,* with that reception and respect to which his works entitled him, and which he had not impaired by any private misconduct or factious partiality. Though Bolingbroke was his friend, Walpole was not his enemy; but treated him with so much consideration as, at his request, to solicit and obtain from the French Minister an abbey for Mr. Southcot,* whom he considered himself as obliged to reward, by this exertion of his interest, for the benefit which he had received from his attendance in a long illness.

It was said, that, when the Court was at Richmond, Queen Caroline had declared her intention to visit him. This may have been only a careless effusion, thought on no more: the report of such notice, however, was soon in many mouths; and, if I do not forget or misapprehend Savage's account, Pope, pretending to decline what was not yet offered, left his house for a time, not, I suppose, for any other reason than lest he should be thought to stay at home in expectation of an honour which would not be conferred. He was therefore angry at Swift, who represents him as *refusing the visits of a Queen*,* because he knew that what had never been offered, had never been refused.

Beside the general system of morality supposed to be contained in the *Essay on Man*, it was his intention to write distinct poems upon the different duties or conditions of life; one of which is the Epistle to Lord Bathurst (1733) on the *Use of Riches*, a piece on which he declared great labour to have been bestowed[1].

Into this poem some incidents are historically thrown, and some known characters are introduced, with others of which it is difficult to say how far they are real or fictitious; but the praise of *Kyrl*, the *Man of Ross*,* deserves particular examination, who, after a long and pompous enumeration of his publick works and private charities, is said to have diffused all those blessings from *five hundred a year*. Wonders are willing told, and willingly heard. The truth is, that *Kyrl* was a man of known integrity, and active benevolence, by whose solicitation the wealthy were persuaded to pay contributions to his charitable schemes; this influence he obtained by an example of liberality exerted to the utmost extent of his power, and was thus enabled to give more than he had. This account *Mr. Victor** received from the minister of the place, and I have preserved it, that the praise of a good man being made more credible, may be more solid. Narrations of romantick and impracticable virtue will be read with wonder, but that which is unattainable is recommended in vain; that good may be endeavoured, it must be shewn to be possible.

This is the only piece in which the author has given a hint of his religion, by ridiculing the ceremony of burning the pope, and by mentioning with some indignation the inscription on the Monument.

When this poem was first published, the dialogue, having no letters of direction, was perplexed and obscure. Pope seems to have written with no very distinct idea; for he calls that an *Epistle to Bathurst*, in which Bathurst is introduced as speaking.

He afterwards (1734) inscribed to Lord Cobham his *Characters of Men*, written with close attention to the operations of the mind and

[1] Spence.

modifications of life. In this poem he has endeavoured to establish and exemplify his favourite theory of the *Ruling Passion*, by which he means an original direction of desire to some particular object, an innate affection which gives all action a determinate and invariable tendency, and operates upon the whole system of life, either openly, or more secretly by the intervention of some accidental or subordinate propension.

Of any passion, thus innate and irresistible, the existence may reasonably be doubted. Human characters are by no means constant; men change by change of place, of fortune, of acquaintance; he who is at one time a lover of pleasure, is at another a lover of money. Those indeed who attain any excellence, commonly spend life in one pursuit; for excellence is not often gained upon easier terms. But to the particular species of excellence men are directed, not by an ascendant planet or predominating humour, but by the first book which they read, some early conversation which they heard, or some accident which excited ardour and emulation.

It must be at least allowed that this *ruling Passion*, antecedent to reason and observation, must have an object independent on human contrivance; for there can be no natural desire of artificial good. No man therefore can be born, in the strict acceptation, a lover of money; for he may be born where money does not exist; nor can he be born, in a moral sense, a lover of his country; for society, politically regulated, is a state contradistinguished from a state of nature; and any attention to that coalition of interests which makes the happiness of a country, is possible only to those whom enquiry and reflection have enabled to comprehend it.

This doctrine is in itself pernicious as well as false: its tendency is to produce the belief of a kind of moral predestination, or overruling principle which cannot be resisted; he that admits it, is prepared to comply with every desire that caprice or opportunity shall excite, and to flatter himself that he submits only to the lawful dominion of Nature, in obeying the resistless authority of his *ruling Passion*.

Pope has formed his theory with so little skill, that, in the examples by which he illustrates and confirms it, he has confounded, passions, appetites, and habits.

To the *Characters of Men* he added soon after, in an Epistle supposed to have been addressed to Martha Blount,* but which the last edition has taken from her, the *Characters of Women*. This poem, which was laboured with great diligence, and in the author's opinion with great success, was neglected at its first publication, as the commentator supposes, because the publick was informed by an advertisement, that it contained *no Character drawn from the Life*; an assertion which Pope probably did not expect or wish to have been believed, and which he soon gave his readers sufficient reason to distrust, by telling them in a note, that the work was imperfect, because part of his subject was *Vice too high** to be yet exposed.

The time however soon came, in which it was safe to display the Dutchess of Marlborough* under the name of *Atossa*; and her character was inserted with no great honour to the writer's gratitude.

He published from time (between 1730 and 1740) Imitations of different poems of Horace, generally with his name, and once as was suspected without it. What he was upon moral principles ashamed to own, he ought to have suppressed. Of these pieces it is useless to settle the dates, as they had seldom much relation to the times, and perhaps had been long in his hands.

This mode of imitation, in which the ancients are familiarised, by adapting their sentiments to modern topicks, by making Horace say of Shakspeare what he originally said of Ennius, and accommodating his satires on Pantolabus and Nomentanus to the flatterers and prodigals of our own time, was first practised in the reign of Charles the Second by Oldham and Rochester, at least I remember no instances more ancient. It is a kind of middle composition between translation and original design, which pleases when the thoughts are unexpectedly applicable, and the parallels lucky. It seems to have been Pope's favourite amusement; for he has carried it further than any former poet.

He published likewise a revival, in smoother numbers, of Dr. Donne's Satires, which was recommended to him by the Duke of Shrewsbury* and the Earl of Oxford. They made no great impression on the publick. Pope seems to have known their imbecillity, and therefore suppressed them while he was yet contending to rise in reputation, but ventured them when he thought their deficiencies more likely to be imputed to Donne than to himself.

The Epistle to Dr. Arbuthnot, which seems to be derived in its first design from Boileau's Address *à son Esprit*,* was published in January 1735, about a month before the death of him to whom it is inscribed. It is to be regretted that either honour or pleasure should have been missed by Arbuthnot; a man estimable for his learning, amiable for his life, and venerable for his piety.

Arbuthnot was a man of great comprehension, skilful in his profession, versed in the sciences, acquainted with ancient literature, and able to animate his mass of knowledge by a bright and active imagination; a scholar with great brilliancy of wit; a wit, who, in the crowd of life, retained and discovered a noble ardour of religious zeal.

In this poem Pope seems to reckon with the publick. He vindicates himself from censures; and with dignity, rather than arrogance, enforces his own claims to kindness and respect.

Into this poem are interwoven several paragraphs which had been before printed as a fragment, and among them the satirical lines upon Addison, of which the last couplet has been twice corrected. It was at first,

> Who would not smile if such a man there be?
> Who would not laugh if Addison were he?

Then,

> Who would not grieve if such a man there be?
> Who would not laugh if Addison were he?

At last it is,

> Who but must laugh if such a man there be?
> Who would not weep if Atticus were he?*

He was at this time at open war with Lord Hervey,* who had distinguished himself as a steady adherent to the Ministry; and, being offended with a contemptuous answer to one of his pamphlets, had summoned Pulteney to a duel. Whether he or Pope made the first attack, perhaps cannot now be easily known: he had written an invective against Pope, whom he calls, *Hard as thy heart, and as thy birth obscure*;* and hints that his father was a *hatter*. To this Pope wrote a reply in verse and prose: the verses are in this poem; and the prose, though it was never sent, is printed among his Letters, but to a cool reader of the present time exhibits nothing but tedious malignity.

His last Satires, of the general kind, were two Dialogues, named from the year in which they were published *Seventeen Hundred and Thirty-eight.* In these poems many are praised and many are reproached. Pope was then entangled in the opposition; a follower of the Prince of Wales, who dined at his house, and the friend of many who obstructed and censured the conduct of the Ministers. His political partiality was too plainly shewn; he forgot the prudence with which he passed, in his earlier years, uninjured and unoffending through much more violent conflicts of faction.

In the first Dialogue, having an opportunity of praising Allen of Bath, he asked his leave to mention him as a man not illustrious by any merit of his ancestors, and called him in his verses *low-born Allen.** Men are seldom satisfied with praise introduced or followed by any mention of defect. Allen seems not to have taken any pleasure in his epithet, which was afterwards softened into *humble Allen.*

In the second Dialogue he took some liberty with one of the *Foxes,** among others; which *Fox*, in a reply to Lyttelton, took an opportunity of repaying, by reproaching him with the friendship of a lampooner, who scattered his ink without fear or decency, and against whom he hoped the resentment of the Legislature would quickly be discharged.

About this time Paul Whitehead, a small poet, was summoned before the Lords for a poem called *Manners*, together with Dodsley his publisher.* Whitehead, who hung loose upon society, sculked and escaped; but Dodsley's shop and family made his appearance necessary. He was, however, soon dismissed; and the whole process was probably intended rather to intimidate Pope than to punish Whitehead.

Pope never afterwards attempted to join the patriot with the poet, nor drew his pen upon statesmen. That he desisted from his attempts of reformation is imputed, by his commentator, to his despair of prevailing over the corruption of the time. He was not likely to have been ever of opinion that the dread of his satire would countervail the love of power or of money; he pleased himself with being important and formidable, and gratified sometimes his pride, and sometimes his resentment; till at last he began to think he should be more safe, if he were less busy.

The *Memoirs of Scriblerus*, published about this time, extend only to the first book of a work, projected in concert by Pope, Swift, and Arbuthnot, who used to meet in the time of Queen Anne, and denominated themselves the *Scriblerus Club.* Their purpose was to censure the abuses of learning by a fictitious Life of an infatuated scholar. They were dispersed; the design was never completed; and Warburton laments its miscarriage, as an event very disastrous to polite letters.

If the whole may be estimated by this specimen, which seems to be the production of Arbuthnot, with a few touches perhaps by Pope, the want of more will not be much lamented; for the follies which the writer ridicules are so little practised, that they are not known; nor can the satire be understood but by the learned: he raises phantoms of absurdity, and then drives them away. He cures diseases that were never felt.

For this reason this joint production of three great writers has never obtained any notice from mankind; it has been little read, or when read has been forgotten, as no man could be wiser, better, or merrier, by remembering it.

The design cannot boast of much originality; for, besides its general resemblance to *Don Quixote*, there will be found in it particular imitations of the History of Mr. *Oufle*.*

Swift carried so much of it into Ireland as supplied him with hints for his *Travels*; and with those the world might have been contented, though the rest had been suppressed.

Pope had sought for images and sentiments in a region not known to have been explored by many other of the English writers; he had consulted the modern writers of Latin poetry, a class of authors whom Boileau endeavoured to bring into contempt, and who are too generally neglected. Pope, however, was not ashamed of their acquaintance, nor ungrateful for the advantages which he might have derived from it. A small selection from the Italians who wrote in Latin had been published at London, about the latter end of the last century, by a man who concealed his name, but whom his Preface shews to have been well qualified for his undertaking.* This collection Pope amplified by more than half, and (1740) published it in two volumes, but injuriously omitted his predecessor's preface. To these books, which had nothing but the mere text, no regard was paid, the authors were still neglected, and the editor was neither praised nor censured.

He did not sink into idleness; he had planned a work, which he considered as subsequent to his *Essay on Man*, of which he has given this account to Dr. Swift.

"March 25, 1736.

"If ever I write any more Epistles in verse, one of them shall be addressed to you. I have long concerted it, and begun it; but I would make what bears your name as finished as my last work ought to be, that is to say, more finished than any of the rest. The subject is large, and will divide into four Epistles, which naturally follow the *Essay on Man*, viz. 1. Of the Extent and Limits of Human Reason and Science. 2. A View of the useful and therefore attainable, and of the unuseful and therefore unattainable Arts. 3. Of the Nature, Ends, Application, and Use of different Capacities. 4. Of the Use of *Learning*, of the Science of the *World*, and of *Wit*. It will conclude with a satire against the Misapplication of all these, exemplified by Pictures, Characters, and Examples."

This work in its full extent, being now afflicted with an asthma, and finding the powers of life gradually declining, he had no longer courage to undertake; but, from the materials which he had provided, he added, at Warburton's request, another book to the *Dunciad*, of which the design is to ridicule such studies as are either hopeless or useless, as either pursue what is unattainable, or what, if it be attained, is of no use.

When this book was printed (1742) the laurel had been for some time upon the head of Cibber; a man whom it cannot be supposed that Pope could regard with much kindness or esteem, though in one of the Imitations of *Horace* he has liberally enough praised the *Careless Husband*. In the *Dunciad*, among other worthless scribblers, he had mentioned Cibber; who, in his *Apology*, complains of the great poet's unkindness as more injurious, *because*, says he, *I never have offended him*.*

It might have been expected that Pope should have been, in some degree, mollified by this submissive gentleness; but no such consequence appeared. Though he condescended to commend Cibber once, he mentioned him afterwards contemptuously in one of his Satires, and again in his Epistle to Arbuthnot; and in the fourth book of the *Dunciad* attacked him with acrimony, to which the provocation is not easily discoverable. Perhaps he imagined that, in ridiculing the Laureat, he satirised those by whom the laurel had been given, and gratified that ambitious petulance with which he affected to insult the great.

The severity of this satire left Cibber no longer any patience. He had confidence enough in his own powers to believe that he could disturb the quiet of his adversary, and doubtless did not want instigators, who, without any care about the victory, desired to amuse themselves by looking on the contest. He therefore gave the town a pamphlet,* in which he declares his resolution from that time never to bear another blow without returning it, and to tire out his adversary by perseverance, if he cannot conquer him by strength.

The incessant and unappeasable malignity of Pope he imputes to a very distant cause. After the *Three Hours after Marriage* had been driven off the stage, by the offence which the mummy and crocodile gave the audience, while the exploded scene was yet fresh in memory, it happened that Cibber played *Bayes* in the *Rehearsal*; and, as it had been usual to enliven the part by the mention of any recent theatrical transactions, he said, that he once thought to have introduced his lovers disguised in a Mummy and a Crocodile. "This," says he, "was received with loud claps, which indicated contempt of the play." Pope, who was behind the scenes, meeting him as he left the stage, attacked him, as he says, with all the virulence of a *Wit out of his senses*; to which he replied, "that he would take no other notice of what was said by so particular a man than to declare, that, as often as he played that part, he would repeat the same provocation."

He shews his opinion to be, that Pope was one of the authors of the play which he so zealously defended; and adds an idle story of Pope's behaviour at a tavern.

The pamphlet was written with little power of thought of language, and, if suffered to remain without notice, would have been very soon forgotten. Pope had now been enough acquainted with human life to know, if his passion had not been too powerful for his understanding, that, from a contention like his with Cibber, the world seeks nothing but diversion, which is given at the expence of the higher character. When Cibber lampooned Pope, curiosity was excited; what Pope would say of Cibber nobody enquired, but in hope that Pope's asperity might betray his pain and lessen his dignity.

He should therefore have suffered the pamphlet to flutter and die, without confessing that it stung him. The dishonour of being shewn as Cibber's antagonist could never be compensated by the victory.

Cibber had nothing to lose; when Pope had exhausted all his malignity upon him, he would rise in the esteem both of his friends and his enemies. Silence only could have made him despicable; the blow which did not appear to be felt, would have been struck in vain.

But Pope's irascibility prevailed, and he resolved to tell the whole English world that he was at war with Cibber; and to shew that he thought him no common adversary, he prepared no common vengeance; he published a new edition of the *Dunciad*, in which he degraded *Theobald* from his painful pre-eminence, and enthroned *Cibber* in his stead. Unhappily the two heroes were of opposite characters, and Pope was unwilling to lose what he had already written; he has therefore depraved his poem by giving to Cibber the old books, the cold pedantry and sluggish pertinacity of Theobald.

Pope was ignorant enough of his own interest, to make another change, and introduced Osborne* contending for the prize among the booksellers. Osborne was a man intirely destitute of shame, without sense of any disgrace but that of poverty. He told me, when he was doing that which raised Pope's resentment, that he should be put into the *Dunciad*; but he had the fate of *Cassandra*; I gave no credit to his prediction, till in time I saw it accomplished. The shafts of satire were directed equally in vain against Cibber and Osborne; being repelled by the impenetrable impudence of one, and deadened by the impassive dulness of the other. Pope confessed his own pain by his anger; but he gave no pain to those who had provoked him. He was able to hurt none but himself; by transferring the same ridicule from one to another, he destroyed its efficacy; for, by shewing that what he had said of one he was ready to say of another, he reduced himself to the insignificance of his own magpye, who from his cage calls cuckold at a venture.

Cibber, according to his engagement, repaid the *Dunciad* with another pamphlet,* which, Pope said, *would be as good as a dose of hartshorn to him*; but his tongue and his heart were at variance. I have heard Mr. Richardson* relate, that he attended his father the painter on a visit, when one of Cibber's pamphlets came into the hands of Pope, who said, *These things are my diversion*. They sat by him while he perused it, and saw his features writhen with anguish; and young Richardson said to his father, when they returned, that he hoped to be preserved from such diversion as had been that day the lot of Pope.

From this time, finding his diseases more oppressive, and his vital powers gradually declining, he no longer strained his faculties with any original composition, nor proposed any other employment for his remaining life than the revisal and correction of his former works; in which he received advice and assistance from Warburton, whom he appears to have trusted and honoured in the highest degree.

He laid aside his Epick Poem, perhaps without much loss to mankind; for his hero was *Brutus* the Trojan, who, according to a ridiculous fiction, established a colony in Britain. The subject therefore was of the fabulous age; the actors were a race upon whom imagination has been exhausted, and attention wearied, and to whom the mind will not easily be recalled, when it is invited in blank verse, which Pope had adopted with great imprudence, and, I think, without due consideration of the nature of our language. The sketch is, at least in part, preserved by Ruffhead; by which it appears, that Pope was thoughtless enough to model the names of his heroes with terminations not consistent with the time or country in which he places them.

He lingered through the next year; but perceived himself, as he expresses it, *going down the hill.* He had for at least five years been afflicted with an asthma, and other disorders, which his physicians were unable to relieve. Towards the end of his life he consulted Dr. Thomson,* a man who had, by large promises, and free censures of the common practice of physick, forced himself up into sudden reputation. Thomson declared his distemper to be a dropsy, and evacuated part of the water by tincture of jalap; but confessed that his belly did not subside. Thomson had many enemies, and Pope was persuaded to dismiss him.

While he was yet capable of amusement and conversation, as he was one day sitting in the air with Lord Bolingbroke and Lord Marchmont,* he saw his favourite Martha Blount at the bottom of the terrace, and asked Lord Bolingbroke to go and hand her up. Bolingbroke, not liking his errand, crossed his legs, and sat still; but Lord Marchmont, who was younger and less captious, waited on the Lady; who, when he came to her, asked, *What, is he not dead yet*? She is said to have neglected him, with shameful unkindness, in the latter time of his decay; yet, of the little which he had to leave, she had a very great part. Their acquaintance began early; the life of each was pictured on the other's mind; their conversation therefore was endearing, for when they met, there was an immediate coalition of congenial notions. Perhaps he considered her unwillingness to approach the chamber of sickness as female weakness, or human frailty; perhaps he was conscious to himself of peevishness and impatience, or, though he was offended by her inattention, might yet consider her merit as overbalancing her fault; and, if he had suffered his heart to be alienated from her, he could have found nothing that might fill her place; he could have only shrunk within himself; it was too late to transfer his confidence or fondness.

In May 1744, his death was approaching[1]; on the sixth, he was all day delirious, which he mentioned four days afterwards as a sufficient humiliation of the vanity of man; he afterwards complained of seeing things as through a curtain, and in false colours; and one day, in the presence of Dodsley, asked what arm it was that came out from the wall. He said that his greatest inconvenience was inability to think.

Bolingbroke sometimes wept over him in this state of helpless decay; and being told by Spence, that Pope, at the intermission of his deliriousness, was always saying something kind either of his present or absent friends, and that his humanity seemed to have survived his understanding, answered, *It has so*. And added, *I never in my life knew a man that had so tender a heart for his particular friends, or more general friendship for mankind*. At another time he said, *I have known Pope these thirty years, and value myself more in his friendship than*—his grief then suppressed his voice.

Pope expressed undoubting confidence of a future state. Being asked by his friend Mr. Hooke, a papist, whether he would not die like his father and mother, and whether a priest should not be called, he answered, *I do not think it essential, but it will be very right; and I thank you for putting me in mind of it*.

In the morning, after the priest had given him the last sacraments, he said, "There is nothing that is meritorious but virtue and friendship, and indeed friendship itself is only a part of virtue."

He died in the evening of the thirtieth day of May, 1744, so placidly, that the attendants did not discern the exact time of his expiration. He was buried at Twickenham, near his father and

[1] Spence.

mother, where a monument has been erected to him by his commentator, the Bishop of Gloucester.*

He left the care of his papers to his executors, first to Lord Bolingbroke, and if he should not be living to the Earl of Marchmont, undoubtedly expecting them to be proud of the trust, and eager to extend his fame. But let no man dream of influence beyond his life. After a decent time Dodsley the bookseller went to solicit preference as the publisher, and was told that the parcel had not been yet inspected; and whatever was the reason, the world has been disappointed of what was *reserved for the next age*.*

He lost, indeed, the favour of Bolingbroke by a kind of posthumous offence. The political pamphlet called *The Patriot King** had been put into his hands that he might procure the impression of a very few copies, to be distributed according to the author's direction among his friends, and Pope assured him that no more had been printed than were allowed; but, soon after his death, the printer brought and resigned a complete edition of fifteen hundred copies, which Pope had ordered him to print, and to retain in secret. He kept, as was observed, his engagement to Pope better than Pope had kept it to his friend; and nothing was known of the transaction, till, upon the death of his employer, he thought himself obliged to deliver the books to the right owner, who, with great indignation, made a fire in his yard, and delivered the whole impression to the flames.

Hitherto nothing had been done which was not naturally dictated by resentment of violated faith; resentment more acrimonious, as the violator had been more loved or more trusted. But here the anger might have stopped; the injury was private, and there was little danger from the example.

Bolingbroke, however, was not yet satisfied; his thirst of vengeance incited him to blast the memory of the man over whom he had wept in his last struggles; and he employed Mallet,* another friend of Pope, to tell the tale to the publick, with all its aggravations. Warburton, whose heart was warm with his legacy, and tender by the recent separation, thought it proper for him to interpose; and undertook, not indeed to vindicate the action, for breach of trust has always something criminal, but to extenuate it by an apology. Having advanced, what cannot be denied, that moral obliquity is made more or less excusable by the motives that produce it, he enquires what evil purpose could have induced Pope to break his promise. He could not delight his vanity by usurping the work, which, though not sold in shops, had been shewn to a number more than sufficient to preserve the author's claim; he could not gratify his avarice; for he could not sell his plunder till Bolingbroke was dead; and even then, if the copy was left to another, his fraud would be defeated, and if left to himself, would be useless.

Warburton therefore supposes, with great appearance of reason, that the irregularity of his conduct proceeded wholly from his zeal for Bolingbroke, who might perhaps have destroyed the pamphlet, which Pope thought it his duty to preserve, even without its author's approbation. To this apology an answer was written in a *Letter to the most impudent man living*.

He brought some reproach upon his own memory by the petulant and contemptuous mention made in his will of Mr. Allen, and an affected repayment of his benefactions.* Mrs. Blount, as the known friend and favourite of Pope, had been invited to the house of Allen, where she comported herself with such indecent arrogance, that she parted from Mrs. Allen in a state of irreconcileable dislike, and the door was for ever barred against her. This exclusion she resented with so much bitterness as to refuse any legacy from Pope, unless he left the world with a disavowal of obligation to Allen. Having been long under her dominion, now tottering in the decline of life, and unable to resist the violence of her temper, or, perhaps with the prejudice of a lover, persuaded that she had suffered improper treatment, he complied with her demand, and polluted his will with female resentment. Allen accepted the legacy, which he gave to the Hospital at Bath; observing that Pope was always a bad accomptant, and that if to 150*l.* he had put a cypher more, he had come nearer to the truth.

THE person of Pope is well known not to have been formed by the nicest model. He has, in his account of the *Little Club*,* compared himself to a spider, and by another is described as protuberant behind and before. He is said to have been beautiful in his infancy; but he was of a constitution originally feeble and weak; and as bodies of a tender frame are easily distorted, his deformity was probably in part the effect of his application. His stature was so low, that, to bring him to a level with common tables, it was necessary to raise his seat. But his face was not displeasing, and his eyes were animated and vivid.

By natural deformity, or accidental distortion, his vital functions were so much disordered, that his life was a *long disease*.* His most frequent assailant was the headach, which he used to relieve by inhaling the steam of coffee, which he very frequently required.

Most of what can be told concerning his petty peculiarities was communicated by a female domestick of the Earl of Oxford, who knew him perhaps after the middle of life. He was then so weak as to stand in perpetual need of female attendance; extremely sensible of cold, so that he wore a kind of fur doublet, under a shirt of very coarse warm linen with fine sleeves. When he rose, he was invested in boddice made of stiff canvass, being scarce able to hold himself erect till they were laced, and he then put on a flannel waistcoat. One side was contracted. His legs were so slender, that he enlarged their bulk with three pair of stockings, which were drawn on and off by the maid; for he was not able to dress or undress himself, and neither went to bed nor rose without help. His weakness made it very difficult for him to be clean.

His hair had fallen almost all away; and he used to dine sometimes with Lord Oxford, privately, in a velvet cap. His dress of ceremony was black with a tye-wig, and a little sword.

The indulgence and accommodation which his sickness required, had taught him all the unpleasing and unsocial qualities of a valetudinary man. He expected that every thing should give way to his ease or humour, as a child, whose parents will not hear her cry, has an unresisted dominion in the nursery.

C'est que l'enfant toûjours est homme,
*C'est que l'homme est toûjours enfant.**

When he wanted to sleep he *nodded in company*;* and once slumbered at his own table while the Prince of Wales was talking of poetry.

The reputation which his friendship gave, procured him many invitations; but he was a very troublesome inmate. He brought no servant, and had so many wants, that a numerous attendance was scarcely able to supply them. Wherever he was, he left no room for another, because he exacted the attention, and employed the activity of the whole family. His errands were so frequent and frivolous, that the footmen in time avoided and neglected him; and the Earl of Oxford discharged some of the servants for their resolute refusal of his messages. The maids, when they had neglected their business, alleged that they had been employed by Mr. Pope. One of his constant demands was of coffee in the night, and to the woman that waited on him in his chamber he was very burthensome; but he was careful to recompense her want of sleep; and Lord Oxford's servant declared, that in a house where her business was to answer his call, she would not ask for wages.

He had another fault, easily incident to those who, suffering much pain, think themselves entitled to whatever pleasures they can snatch. He was too indulgent to his appetite; he loved meat highly seasoned and of strong taste; and, at the intervals of the table, amused himself with biscuits and dry conserves. If he sat down to a variety of dishes, he would oppress his stomach with repletion, and though he seemed angry when a dram was offered him, did not forbear to drink it. His friends, who knew the avenues to his heart, pampered him with presents of luxury, which he did not suffer to stand neglected. The death of great men is not always proportioned to the lustre of their lives. Hannibal, says Juvenal, did not perish by a javelin or a sword; the slaughters of Cannæ were revenged by a ring.* The death of Pope was imputed by some of his friends to a silver saucepan, in which it was his delight to heat potted lampreys.

That he loved too well to eat, is certain; but that his sensuality shortened his life will not be hastily concluded, when it is remembered that a conformation so irregular lasted six and fifty years, notwithstanding such pertinacious diligence of study and meditation.

In all his intercourse with mankind, he had great delight in artifice, and endeavoured to attain all his purposes by indirect and unsuspected methods. *He hardly drank tea without a stratagem.** If, at the house of his friends, he wanted any accommodation, he was not willing to ask for it in plain terms, but would mention it remotely as something convenient; though, when it was procured, he soon made it appear for whose sake it had been recommended. Thus he teized Lord Orrery till he obtained a screen. He practised his arts on such small occasions, that Lady Bolingbroke used to say, in a French phrase, that *he plaid the politician about cabbages and turnips.** His unjustifiable impression of the *Patriot King*, as it can be imputed to no particular motive, must have proceeded from his general habit of secrecy and cunning; he caught an opportunity of a sly trick, and pleased himself with the thought of outwitting Bolingbroke.

In familiar or convivial conversation, it does not appear that he excelled. He may be said to have resembled Dryden, as being not one that was distinguished by vivacity in company. It is remarkable, that, so near his time, so much should be known of what he has written, and so little of what he has said: traditional memory retains no sallies of raillery, nor sentences of observation; nothing either pointed or solid, either wise or merry. One apophthegm only stands upon record. When an objection raised against his inscription for Shakspeare was defended by the authority of *Patrick*, he replied—*horresco referens*— that *he would allow the publisher of a Dictionary to know the meaning of a single word, but not of two words put together.**

He was fretful, and easily displeased, and allowed himself to be capriciously resentful. He would sometimes leave Lord Oxford silently, no one could tell why, and was to be courted back by more letters and messages than the footmen were willing to carry. The table was indeed infested by Lady Mary Wortley,* who was the friend of Lady Oxford, and who, knowing his peevishness, could by no intreaties be restrained from contradicting him, till their disputes were sharpened to such asperity, that one or the other quitted the house.

He sometimes condescended to be jocular with servants or inferiors; but by no merriment, either of others or his own, was he ever seen excited to laughter.

Of his domestick character, frugality was a part eminently remarkable. Having determined not to be dependent, he determined not to be in want, and therefore wisely and magnanimously rejected all temptations to expence unsuitable to his fortune. This general care must be universally approved; but it sometimes appeared in petty artifices of parsimony, such as the practice of writing his compositions on the back of letters, as may be seen in the remaining copy of the *Iliad*, by which perhaps in five years five shillings were saved; or in a niggardly reception of his friends, and scantiness of entertainment, as, when he had two guests in his house, he would set at supper a single pint upon the table; and having himself taken two small glasses would retire, and say, *Gentlemen, I leave you to your wine*. Yet he tells his friends, that *he has a heart for all, a house for all, and, whatever they may think, a fortune for all.*

He sometimes, however, made a splendid dinner, and is said to have wanted no part of the skill or elegance which such performances require. That this magnificence should be often displayed, that obstinate prudence with which he conducted his affairs would not permit; for his revenue, certain and casual, amounted only to about eight hundred pounds a year, of which however he declares himself able to assign one hundred to charity.

Of this fortune, which as it arose from publick approbation was very honourably obtained, his imagination seems to have been too full: it would be hard to find a man, so well entitled to notice by his wit, that ever delighted so much in talking of his money. In his Letters, and in his Poems, his garden and his grotto, his quincunx and his vines, or some hints of his opulence, are always to be found. The great topick of his ridicule is poverty; the crimes with which he reproaches his antagonists are their debts, their habitation in the Mint, and their want of a dinner. He seems to be of an opinion not very uncommon in the world, that to want money is to want every thing.

Next to the pleasure of contemplating his possessions, seems to be that of enumerating the men of high rank with whom he was acquainted, and whose notice he loudly proclaims not to have been obtained by any practices of meanness or servility; a boast which was never denied to be true, and to which very few poets have ever aspired. Pope never set his genius to sale; he never flattered those whom he did not love, or praised those whom he did not esteem. Savage however remarked, that he began a little to relax his dignity when he wrote a distich for *his Highness's dog*.*

His admiration of the Great seems to have increased in the advance of life. He passed over peers and statesmen to inscribe his *Iliad* to Congreve, with a magnanimity of which the praise had been compleat, had his friend's virtue been equal to his wit. Why he was chosen for so great an honour, it is not now possible to know; there is no trace in literary history of any particular intimacy between them. The name of Congreve appears in the Letters among those of his other friends, but without any observable distinction or consequence.

To his latter works, however, he took care to annex names dignified with titles, but was not very happy in his choice; for, except Lord Bathurst,* none of his noble friends were such as that a good man would wish to have his intimacy with them known to posterity: he can derive little honour from the notice of Cobham, Burlington, or Bolingbroke.*

Of his social qualities, if an estimate be made from his Letters, an opinion too favourable cannot easily be formed; they exhibit a perpetual and unclouded effulgence of general benevolence, and particular fondness. There is nothing but liberality, gratitude, constancy, and tenderness. It has been so long said as to be commonly believed, that the true characters of men may be found in their Letters, and that he who writes to his friend lays his heart open before him. But the truth is, that such were simple friendships of the *Golden Age*, and are now the friendships only of children. Very few can boast of hearts which they dare lay open to themselves, and of which, by whatever accident exposed, they do not shun a distinct and continued view; and, certainly, what we hide from ourselves we do not shew to our friends. There is, indeed, no transaction which offers stronger temptations to fallacy and sophistication than epistolary intercourse. In the eagerness of conversation the first emotions of the mind often burst out, before they are considered; in the tumult of business, interest and passion have their genuine effect; but a friendly Letter is a calm and deliberate performance, in the cool of leisure, in the stillness of solitude, and surely no man sits down to depreciate by design his own character.

Friendship has no tendency to secure veracity; for by whom can a man so much wish to be thought better than he is, as by him whose kindness he desires to gain or keep? Even in writing to the world there is less constraint; the author is not confronted with his reader, and takes his chance of approbation among the different dispositions of mankind; but a Letter is addressed to a single mind, of which the prejudices and partialities are known; and must therefore please, if not by favouring them, by forbearing to oppose them.

To charge those favourable representations, which men give of their own minds, with the guilt of hypocritical falshood, would shew more severity than knowledge. The writer commonly believes himself. Almost every man's thoughts, while they are general, are right; and most hearts are pure, while temptation is away. It is easy to awaken generous sentiments in privacy; to despise death when there is no danger; to glow with benevolence when there is nothing to be given. While such ideas are formed they are felt, and self-love does not suspect the gleam of virtue to be the meteor of fancy.

If the Letters of Pope are considered merely as compositions, they seem to be premeditated and artificial. It is one thing to write because there is something which the mind wishes to discharge, and another, to solicit the imagination because ceremony or vanity requires something to be written. Pope confesses his early Letters to be vitiated with *affectation and ambition*: to know whether he disentangled himself from these perverters of epistolary integrity, his book and his life must be set in comparison.

One of his favourite topicks is contempt of his own poetry. For this, if it had been real, he would deserve no commendation, and in this he was certainly not sincere; for his high value of himself was sufficiently observed, and of what could he be proud but of his poetry? He writes, he says, when *he has just nothing else to do*; yet Swift complains that he was never at leisure for conversation, because he *had always some poetical scheme in his head*. It was punctually required that his writing-box should be set upon his bed before he rose; and Lord Oxford's domestick related, that, in the dreadful winter of Forty, she was called from her bed by him four times in one night, to supply him with paper, lest he should lose a thought.

He pretends insensibility to censure and criticism, though it was observed by all who knew him that every pamphlet disturbed his quiet, and that his extreme irritability laid him open to perpetual vexation; but he wished to despise his criticks, and therefore hoped that he did despise them.

As he happened to live in two reigns when the Court paid little attention to poetry, he nursed in his mind a foolish disesteem of Kings, and proclaims that *he never sees Courts*. Yet a little regard shewn him by the Prince of Wales melted his obduracy; and he had not much to say when he was asked by his Royal Highness, *how he could love a Prince while he disliked Kings?*

He very frequently professes contempt of the world, and represents himself as looking on mankind, sometimes with gay indifference, as on emmets of a hillock, below his serious attention; and sometimes with gloomy indignation, as on monsters more worthy of hatred than of pity. These were dispositions apparently counterfeited. How could he despise those whom he lived by pleasing, and on whose approbation his esteem of himself was superstructed? Why should he hate those to whose favour he owed his honour and his ease? Of things that terminate in human life, the world is the proper judge; to despise its sentence, if it were possible, is not just; and if it were just, is not possible. Pope was far enough from this unreasonable temper; he was sufficiently *a fool to Fame*,* and his fault was that he pretended to neglect it. His levity and his sullenness were only in his Letters; he passed through common life, sometimes vexed, and sometimes pleased, with the natural emotions of common men.

His scorn of the Great is repeated too often to be real; no man thinks much of that which he despises; and as falsehood is always in danger of inconsistency, he makes it his boast at another time that he lives among them.

It is evident that his own importance swells often in his mind. He is afraid of writing, lest the clerks of the Post-office should know his secrets; he has many enemies; he considers himself as surrounded by universal jealousy; *after many deaths, and many dispersions, two or three of us*, says he, *may still be brought together, not to plot, but to divert ourselves, and the world too, if it pleases*; and they can live together, and *shew what friends wits may be, in spite of all the fools in the world*. All this while it was likely that the clerks did not know his hand; he certainly had no more enemies than a publick character like his inevitably excites, and with what degree of friendship the wits might live, very few were so much fools as ever to enquire.

Some part of this pretended discontent he learned from Swift, and expresses it, I think, most frequently in his correspondence with him. Swift's resentment was unreasonable, but it was sincere; Pope's was the mere mimickry of his friend, a fictitious part which he began to play before it became him. When he was only twenty-five years old, he related that *a glut of study and retirement had thrown him on the world*, and that there was danger lest *a glut of the world should throw him back upon study and retirement*. To this Swift answered with great propriety, that Pope had not yet either acted or suffered enough in the world to have become weary of it. And, indeed, it must be some very powerful reason that can drive back to solitude him who has once enjoyed the pleasures of society.

In the Letters both of Swift and Pope there appears such narrowness of mind, as makes them insensible of any excellence that has not some affinity with their own, and confines their esteem and approbation to so small a number, that whoever should form his opinion of the age from their representation, would suppose them to have lived amidst ignorance and barbarity, unable to find among their contemporaries either virtue or intelligence, and persecuted by those that could not understand them.

When Pope murmurs at the world, when he professes contempt of fame, when he speaks of riches and poverty, of success and disappointment, with negligent indifference, he certainly does not express his habitual and settled sentiments, but either wilfully disguises his own character, or, what is more likely, invests himself with temporary qualities, and sallies out in the colours of the present moment. His hopes and fears, his joys and sorrows, acted strongly upon his mind; and if he differed from others, it was not by carelessness; he was irritable and resentful; his malignity to Philips, whom he had first made ridiculous, and then hated for being angry, continued too long. Of his vain desire to make Bentley contemptible, I never heard any adequate reason. He was sometimes wanton in his attacks; and, before Chandos, Lady Wortley, and Hill, was mean in his retreat.*

The virtues which seem to have had most of his affection were liberality and fidelity of friendship, in which it does not appear that he was other than he describes himself. His fortune did not suffer his charity to be splendid and conspicuous; but he assisted Dodsley with a hundred pounds, that he might open a shop; and of the subscription of forty pounds a year that he raised for Savage, twenty were paid by himself. He was accused of loving money, but his love was eagerness to gain, not solicitude to keep it.

In the duties of friendship he was zealous and constant: his early maturity of mind commonly united him with men older than himself, and therefore, without attaining any considerable length of life, he saw many companions of his youth sink into the grave; but it does not appear that he lost a single friend by coldness or by injury; those who loved him once, continued their kindness. His ungrateful mention of Allen in his will, was the effect of his adherence to one whom he had known much longer, and whom he naturally loved with greater fondness. His violation of the trust reposed in him by Bolingbroke could have no motive inconsistent with the warmest affection; he either thought the action so near to indifferent that he forgot it, or so laudable that he expected his friend to approve it.

It was reported, with such confidence as almost to enforce belief, that in the papers intrusted to his executors was found a defamatory Life of Swift, which he had prepared as an instrument of vengeance to be used, if any provocation should be ever given. About this

I enquired of the Earl of Marchmont, who assured me that no such piece was among his remains.

The religion in which he lived and died was that of the Church of Rome, to which in his correspondence with Racine he professes himself a sincere adherent. That he was not scrupulously pious in some part of his life, is known by many idle and indecent applications of sentences taken from the Scriptures; a mode of merriment which a good man dreads for its profaneness, and a witty man disdains for its easiness and vulgarity. But to whatever levities he has been betrayed, it does not appear that his principles were ever corrupted, or that he ever lost his belief of Revelation. The positions which he transmitted from Bolingbroke he seems not to have understood, and was pleased with an interpretation that made them orthodox.

A man of such exalted superiority, and so little moderation, would naturally have all his delinquences observed and aggravated: those who could not deny that he was excellent, would rejoice to find that he was not perfect.

Perhaps it may be imputed to the unwillingness with which the same man is allowed to possess many advantages, that his learning has been depreciated. He certainly was in his early life a man of great literary curiosity; and when he wrote his *Essay on Criticism* had, for his age, a very wide acquaintance with books. When he entered into the living world, it seems to have happened to him as to many others, that he was less attentive to dead masters; he studied in the academy of Paracelsus, and made the universe his favourite volume. He gathered his notions fresh from reality, not from the copies of authors, but the originals of Nature. Yet there is no reason to believe that literature ever lost his esteem; he always professed to love reading; and Dobson, who spent some time at his house translating his *Essay on Man*, when I asked him what learning he found him to possess, answered, *More than I expected.* His frequent references to history, his allusions to various kinds of knowledge, and his images selected from art and nature, with his observations on the operations of the mind and the modes of life, shew an intelligence perpetually on the wing, excursive, vigorous, and diligent, eager to pursue knowledge, and attentive to retain it.

From this curiosity arose the desire of travelling, to which he alludes in his verses to Jervas, and which, though he never found an opportunity to gratify it, did not leave him till his life declined.

Of his intellectual character, the constituent and fundamental principle was Good Sense, a prompt and intuitive perception of consonance and propriety. He saw immediately, of his own conceptions, what was to be chosen, and what to be rejected; and, in the works of others, what was to be shunned, and what was to be copied.

But good sense alone is a sedate and quiescent quality, which manages its possessions well, but does not increase them; it collects few materials for its own operations, and preserves safety, but never gains supremacy. Pope had likewise genius; a mind active, ambitious, and adventurous, always investigating, always aspiring; in its widest searches still longing to go forward, in its highest flights still wishing to be higher; always imagining something greater than it knows, always endeavouring more than it can do.

To assist these powers, he is said to have had great strength and exactness of memory. That which he had heard or read was not easily lost; and he had before him not only what his own meditation suggested, but what he had found in other writers, that might be accommodated to his present purpose.

These benefits of nature he improved by incessant and unwearied diligence; he had recourse to every source of intelligence, and lost no opportunity of information; he consulted the living as well as the dead; he read his compositions to his friends, and was never content with mediocrity when excellence could be attained. He considered poetry as the business of his life, and however he might seem to lament his occupation, he followed it with constancy; to make verses was his first labour, and to mend them was his last.

From his attention to poetry he was never diverted. If conversation offered any thing that could be improved, he committed it to paper; if a thought, or perhaps an expression more happy than was common, rose to his mind, he was careful to write it; an independent distich was preserved for an opportunity of insertion, and some little fragments have been found containing lines, or parts of lines, to be wrought upon at some other time.

He was one of those few whose labour is their pleasure: he was never elevated to negligence, nor wearied to impatience; he never passed a fault unamended by indifference, nor quitted it by despair. He laboured his works first to gain reputation, and afterwards to keep it.

Of composition there are different methods. Some employ at once memory and invention, and, with little intermediate use of the pen, form and polish large masses by continued meditation, and write their productions only when, in their own opinion, they have completed them. It is related of Virgil, that his custom was to pour out a great number of verses in the morning, and pass the day in retrenching exuberances and correcting inaccuracies. The method of Pope, as may be collected from his translation, was to write his first thoughts in his first words, and gradually to amplify, decorate, rectify, and refine them.

With such faculties, and such dispositions, he excelled every other writer in *poetical prudence*; he wrote in such a manner as might expose him to few hazards. He used almost always the same fabrick of verse; and, indeed, by those few essays which he made of any other, he did not enlarge his reputation. Of this uniformity the certain consequence was readiness and dexterity. By perpetual practice, language had in his mind a systematical arrangement; having always the same use for words, he had words so selected and combined as to be ready at his call. This increase of facility he confessed himself to have perceived in the progress of his translation.

But what was yet of more importance, his effusions were always voluntary, and his subjects chosen by himself. His independence secured him from drudging at a task, and labouring upon a barren topick: he never exchanged praise for money, nor opened a shop of condolence or congratulation. His poems, therefore, were scarce ever temporary. He suffered coronations and royal marriages to pass without a song, and derived no opportunities from recent events, nor any popularity from the accidental disposition of his readers. He was never reduced to the necessity of soliciting the sun to shine upon a birth-day, of calling the Graces and Virtues to a wedding, or of saying what multitudes have said before him. When he could produce nothing new, he was at liberty to be silent.

His publications were for the same reason never hasty. He is said to have sent nothing to the press till it had lain two years under his inspection: it is at least certain, that he ventured nothing without nice examination. He suffered the tumult of imagination to subside, and the novelties of invention to grow familiar. He knew that the mind is always enamoured of its own productions, and did not trust his first fondness. He consulted his friends, and listened with great willingness to criticism; and, what was of more importance, he consulted himself, and let nothing pass against his own judgement.

He professed to have learned his poetry from Dryden, whom, whenever an opportunity was presented, he praised through his whole life with unvaried liberality; and perhaps his character may receive some illustration, if he be compared with his master.

Integrity of understanding and nicety of discernment were not allotted in a less proportion to Dryden than to Pope. The rectitude of Dryden's mind was sufficiently shewn by the dismission of his poetical prejudices, and the rejection of unnatural thoughts and rugged numbers. But Dryden never desired to apply all the judgement that he had. He wrote, and professed to write, merely for the people; and when he pleased others, he contented himself. He spent no time in struggles to rouse latent powers; he never attempted to make that better which was already good, nor often to mend what he must have known to be faulty. He wrote, as he tells us, with very little consideration; when occasion or necessity called upon him, he poured out what the present moment happened to supply, and, when once it had passed the press, ejected it from his mind; for when he had no pecuniary interest, he had no further solicitude.

Pope was not content to satisfy; he desired to excel, and therefore always endeavoured to do his best: he did not court the candour, but dared the judgement of his reader, and, expecting no indulgence from others, he shewed none to himself. He examined lines and words with minute and punctilious observation, and retouched every part with indefatigable diligence, till he had left nothing to be forgiven.

For this reason he kept his pieces very long in his hands, while he considered and reconsidered them. The only poems which can be supposed to have been written with such regard to the times as might hasten their publication, were the two satires of *Thirty-eight*; of which Dodsley told me, that they were brought to him by the author, that they might be fairly copied. "Almost every line," he said, "was then written twice over; I gave him a clean transcript, which he sent some time afterwards to me for the press, with almost every line written twice over a second time."

His declaration, that his care for his works ceased at their publication, was not strictly true. His parental attention never abandoned them; what he found amiss in the first edition, he silently corrected in those that followed. He appears to have revised the *Iliad*, and freed it from some of its imperfections; and the *Essay on Criticism* received many improvements after its first appearance. It will seldom be found that he altered without adding clearness, elegance, or vigour. Pope had perhaps the judgement of Dryden; but Dryden certainly wanted the diligence of Pope.

In acquired knowledge, the superiority must be allowed to Dryden, whose education was more scholastick, and who before he became an author had been allowed more time for study, with better means of information. His mind has a larger range, and he collects his images and illustrations from a more extensive circumference of science. Dryden knew more of man in his general nature, and Pope in his local manners. The notions of Dryden were formed by comprehensive speculation, and those of Pope by minute attention. There is more dignity in the knowledge of Dryden, and more certainty in that of Pope.

Poetry was not the sole praise of either; for both excelled likewise in prose; but Pope did not borrow his prose from his predecessor. The style of Dryden is capricious and varied, that of Pope is cautious and uniform; Dryden obeys the motions of his own mind, Pope constrains his mind to his own rules of composition. Dryden is sometimes vehement and rapid; Pope is always smooth, uniform, and gentle. Dryden's page is a natural field, rising into inequalities, and diversified by the varied exuberance of abundant vegetation; Pope's is a velvet lawn, shaven by the scythe, and levelled by the roller.

Of genius, that power which constitutes a poet; that quality without which judgement is cold and knowledge is inert; that energy which collects, combines, amplifies, and animates; the superiority must, with some hesitation, be allowed to Dryden. It is not to be inferred that of this poetical vigour Pope had only a little, because Dryden had more; for every other writer since Milton must give place to Pope; and even of Dryden it must be said, that if he has brighter paragraphs, he has not better poems. Dryden's performances were always hasty, either excited by some external occasion, or extorted by domestick necessity; he composed without consideration, and published without correction. What his mind could supply at call, or gather in one excursion, was all that he sought, and all that he gave. The dilatory caution of Pope enabled him to condense his sentiments, to multiply his images, and to accumulate all that study might produce, or chance might supply. If the flights of Dryden therefore are higher, Pope continues longer on the wing. If of Dryden's fire the blaze is brighter, of Pope's the heat is more regular and constant. Dryden often surpasses expectation, and Pope never falls below it. Dryden is read with frequent astonishment, and Pope with perpetual delight.

This parallel will, I hope, when it is well considered, be found just; and if the reader should suspect me, as I suspect myself, of some partial fondness for the memory of Dryden, let him not too hastily condemn me; for meditation and enquiry may, perhaps, shew him the reasonableness of my determination.

THE Works of Pope are now to be distinctly examined, not so much with attention to slight faults or petty beauties, as to the general character and effect of each performance.

It seems natural for a young poet to initiate himself by Pastorals, which, not professing to imitate real life, require no experience, and, exhibiting only the simple operation of unmingled passions, admit no subtle reasoning or deep enquiry. Pope's Pastorals are not however composed but with close thought; they have reference to the times of the day, the seasons of the year, and the periods of human life. The last, that which turns the attention upon age and death, was the author's favourite. To tell of disappointment and misery, to thicken the darkness of futurity, and perplex the labyrinth of uncertainty, has been always a delicious employment of the poets. His preference was probably just. I wish, however, that his fondness had not overlooked a line in which the *Zephyrs* are made *to lament in silence.**

To charge these Pastorals with want of invention, is to require what never was intended. The imitations are so ambitiously frequent, that the writer evidently means rather to shew his literature than his wit. It is surely sufficient for an author of sixteen not only to be able to copy the poems of antiquity with judicious selection, but to have obtained sufficient power of language, and skill in metre, to exhibit a series of versification, which had in English poetry no precedent, nor has since had an imitation.

The design of *Windsor Forest* is evidently derived from *Cooper's Hill*, with some attention to Waller's poem on *The Park*;* but Pope cannot be denied to excel his masters in variety and elegance, and the art of interchanging description, narrative, and morality.

The objection made by Dennis is the want of plan, of a regular subordination of parts terminating in the principal and original design. There is this want in most descriptive poems, because as the scenes, which they must exhibit successively, are all subsisting at the same time, the order in which they are shewn must by necessity be arbitrary, and more is not to be expected from the last part than from the first. The attention, therefore, which cannot be detained by suspense, must be excited by diversity, such as this poem offers to its reader.

But the desire of diversity may be too much indulged; the parts of *Windsor Forest* which deserve least praise, are those which were added to enliven the stillness of the scene, the appearance of Father Thames, and the transformation of *Lodona*. Addison had in his *Campaign* derided the *Rivers* that *rise from their oozy beds* to tell stories of heroes, and it is therefore strange that Pope should adopt a fiction not only unnatural but lately censured. The story of *Lodona* is told with sweetness; but a new metamorphosis is a ready and puerile expedient; nothing is easier than to tell how a flower was once a blooming virgin, or a rock an obdurate tyrant.

The *Temple of Fame* has, as Steele warmly declared, *a thousand beauties*. Every part is splendid; there is great luxuriance of ornaments; the original vision of Chaucer* was never denied to be much improved; the allegory is very skilfully continued, the imagery is properly selected, and learnedly displayed: yet, with all this comprehension of excellence, as its scene is laid in remote ages, and its sentiments, if the concluding paragraph be excepted, have little relation to general manners or common life, it never obtained much notice, but is turned silently over, and seldom quoted or mentioned with either praise or blame.

That the *Messiah* excels the *Pollio** is no great praise, if it be considered from what original the improvements are derived.

The *Verses on the unfortunate Lady* have drawn much attention by the illaudable singularity of treating suicide with respect; and they must be allowed to be written in some parts with vigorous animation, and in others with gentle tenderness; nor has Pope produced any poem in which the sense predominates more over the diction. But the tale is not skilfully told; it is not easy to discover the character of either the Lady or her Guardian. History relates that she was about to disparage herself by a marriage with an inferior; Pope praises her for the dignity of ambition, and yet condemns the unkle to detestation for his pride; the ambitious love of a niece may be opposed by the interest, malice, or envy of an unkle, but never by his pride. On such an occasion a poet may be allowed to be obscure, but inconsistency never can be right.

The *Ode for St. Cecilia's Day* was undertaken at the desire of Steele: in this the author is generally confessed to have miscarried, yet he has miscarried only as compared with Dryden; for he has far outgone other competitors. Dryden's plan is better chosen; history will always take stronger hold of the attention than fable: the passions excited by Dryden are the pleasures and pains of real life, the scene of Pope is laid in imaginary existence; Pope is read with calm acquiescence, Dryden with turbulent delight; Pope hangs upon the ear, and Dryden finds the passes of the mind.

Both the odes want the essential constituent of metrical compositions, the stated recurrence of settled numbers. It may be alleged, that Pindar is said by Horace to have written *numeris lege solutis*:* but as no such lax performances have been transmitted to us, the meaning of that expression cannot be fixed; and perhaps the like return might properly be made to a modern Pindarist, as Mr. Cobb received from Bentley, who, when he found his criticisms upon a Greek Exercise, which Cobb had presented, refuted one after another by Pindar's authority, cried out at last, *Pindar was a bold fellow, but thou art an impudent one.**

If Pope's ode be particularly inspected, it will be found that the first stanza consists of sounds well chosen indeed, but only sounds.

The second consists of hyperbolical common-places, easily to be found, and perhaps without much difficulty to be as well expressed.

In the third, however, there are numbers, images, harmony, and vigour, not unworthy the antagonist of Dryden. Had all been like this—but every part cannot be the best.

The next stanzas place and detain us in the dark and dismal regions of mythology, where neither hope nor fear, neither joy nor sorrow can be found: the poet however faithfully attends us; we have all that can be performed by elegance of diction, or sweetness of versification; but what can form avail without better matter?

The last stanza recurs again to common-places. The conclusion is too evidently modelled by that of Dryden; and it may be remarked that both end with the same fault, the comparison of each is literal on one side, and metaphorical on the other.

Poets do not always express their own thoughts; Pope, with all this labour in the praise of Musick, was ignorant of its principles, and insensible of its effects.

One of his greatest though of his earliest works is the *Essay on Criticism*, which, if he had written nothing else, would have placed him among the first criticks and the first poets, as it exhibits every mode of excellence that can embellish or dignify didactick composition, selection of matter, novelty of arrangement, justness of precept, splendour of illustration, and propriety of digression. I know not whether it be pleasing to consider that he produced this piece at twenty, and never afterwards excelled it: he that delights himself with observing that such powers may be so soon attained, cannot but grieve to think that life was ever after at a stand.

To mention the particular beauties of the Essay would be unprofitably tedious; but I cannot forbear to observe, that the comparison of a student's progress in the sciences with the journey of a traveller in the Alps, is perhaps the best that English poetry can shew. A simile, to be perfect, must both illustrate and ennoble the subject; must shew it to the understanding in a clearer view, and display it to the fancy with greater dignity; but either of these qualities may be sufficient to recommend it. In didactick poetry, of which the great purpose is instruction, a simile may be praised which illustrates, though it does not ennoble; in heroicks, that may be admitted which ennobles, though it does not illustrate. That it may be complete, it is required to exhibit, independently of its references, a pleasing image; for a simile is said to be a short episode. To this antiquity was so attentive, that circumstances were sometimes added, which, having no parallels, served only to fill the imagination, and produced what Perrault ludicrously called *comparisons with a long tail.** In their similies the greatest writers have sometimes failed; the ship-race, compared with the chariot-race, is neither illustrated nor aggrandised; land and water make all the difference: when Apollo, running after Daphne, is likened to a greyhound chasing a hare, there is nothing gained; the ideas of pursuit and flight are too plain to be made plainer, and a god and the daughter of a god are not represented much to their advantage, by a hare and dog. The simile of the Alps has no useless parts, yet affords a striking picture by itself; it makes the foregoing position better understood, and enables it to take faster hold on the attention; it assists the apprehension, and elevates the fancy.

Let me likewise dwell a little on the celebrated paragraph, in which it is directed that *the sound should seem an echo to the sense*;* a precept which Pope is allowed to have observed beyond any other English poet.

This notion of representative metre, and the desire of discovering frequent adaptations of the sound to the sense, have produced, in my opinion, many wild conceits and imaginary beauties. All that can furnish this representation are the sounds of the words considered singly, and the time in which they are pronounced. Every language has some words framed to exhibit the noises which they express, as *thump, rattle, growl, hiss*. These however are but few, and the poet cannot make them more, nor can they be of any use but when sound is to be mentioned. The time of pronunciation was in the dactylick measures of the learned languages capable of considerable variety; but that variety could be accommodated only to motion or duration, and different degrees of motion were perhaps expressed by verses rapid or slow, without much attention of the writer, when the image had full possession of his fancy; but our language having little flexibility, our verses can differ very little in their cadence. The fancied resemblances, I fear, arise sometimes merely from the ambiguity of words; there is supposed to be some relation between a *soft* line and a *soft* couch, or between *hard* syllables and *hard* fortune.

Motion, however, may be in some sort exemplified; and yet it may be suspected that even in such resemblances the mind often governs the ear, and the sounds are estimated by their meaning. One of the most successful attempts has been to describe the labour of Sisyphus:

> With many a weary step, and many a groan,
> Up a high hill he heaves a huge round stone;
> The huge round stone, resulting with a bound,
> Thunders impetuous down, and smoaks along the ground.*

Who does not perceive the stone to move slowly upward, and roll violently back? But set the same numbers to another sense;

> While many a merry tale, and many a song.
> Chear'd the rough road, we wish'd the rough road long.

The rough road then, returning in a round,
Mock'd our impatient steps, for all was fairy ground.

We have now surely lost much of the delay, and much of the rapidity.

But to shew how little the greatest master of numbers can fix the principles of representative harmony, it will be sufficient to remark that the poet, who tells us, that

When Ajax strives—the words move slow.
Not so when swift Camilla scours the plain,
Flies o'er th' unbending corn, and skims along the main;*

when he had enjoyed for about thirty years the praise of Camilla's lightness of foot, tried another experiment upon *sound* and *time*, and produced this memorable triplet;

Waller was smooth; but Dryden taught to join
The varying verse, the full resounding line,
The long majestick march, and energy divine.*

Here are the swiftness of the rapid race, and the march of slow-paced majesty, exhibited by the same poet in the same sequence of syllables, except that the exact prosodist will find the line of *swiftness* by one time longer than that of *tardiness*.

Beauties of this kind are commonly fancied; and when real, are technical and nugatory, not to be rejected, and not to be solicited.

To the praises which have been accumulated on *The Rape of the Lock* by readers of every class, from the critick to the waiting-maid, it is difficult to make any addition. Of that which is universally allowed to be the most attractive of all ludicrous compositions, let it rather be now enquired from what sources the power of pleasing is derived.

Dr. Warburton, who excelled in critical perspicacity, has remarked that the preternatural agents are very happily adapted to the purposes of the poem. The heathen deities can no longer gain attention: we should have turned away from a contest between Venus and Diana. The employment of allegorical persons always excites conviction of its own absurdity; they may produce effects, but cannot conduct actions; when the phantom is put in motion, it dissolves; thus *Discord* may raise a mutiny, but *Discord* cannot conduct a march, nor besiege a town. Pope brought into view a new race of Beings, with powers and passions proportionate to their operation. The sylphs and gnomes act at the toilet and the tea-table, what more terrifick and more powerful phantoms perform on the stormy ocean, or the field of battle, they give their proper help, and do their proper mischief.

Pope is said, by an objector, not to have been the inventer of this petty nation; a charge which might with more justice have been brought against the author of the *Iliad*, who doubtless adopted the religious system of his country; for what is there but the names of his agents which Pope has not invented? Has he not assigned them characters and operations never heard of before? Has he not, at least, given them their first poetical existence? If this is not sufficient to denominate his work original, nothing original ever can be written.

In this work are exhibited, in a very high degree, the two most engaging powers of an author. New things are made familiar, and familiar things are made new. A race of aerial people, never heard of before, is presented to us in a manner so clear and easy, that the reader seeks for no further information, but immediately mingles with his new acquaintance, adopts their interests, and attends their pursuits, loves a sylph, and detests a gnome.

That familiar things are made new, every paragraph will prove. The subject of the poem is an event below the common incidents of common life; nothing real is introduced that is not seen so often as to be no longer regarded, yet the whole detail of a female-day is here brought before us invested with so much art of decoration, that, though nothing is disguised, every thing is striking, and we feel all the appetite of curiosity for that from which we have a thousand times turned fastidiously away.

The purpose of the Poet is, as he tells us, to laugh at *the little unguarded follies of the female sex*.* It is therefore without justice that Dennis charges the *Rape of the Lock* with the want of a moral, and for that reason sets it below the *Lutrin*,* which exposes the pride and discord of the clergy. Perhaps neither Pope nor Boileau has made the world much better than he found it; but if they had both succeeded, it were easy to tell who would have deserved most from publick gratitude. The freaks, and humours, and spleen, and vanity of women, as they embroil families in discord, and fill houses with disquiet, do more to obstruct the happiness of life in a year than the ambition of the clergy in many centuries. It has been well observed, that the misery of man proceeds not from any single crush of overwhelming evil, but from small vexations continually repeated.

It is remarked by Dennis likewise, that the machinery is superfluous; that, by all the bustle of preternatural operation, the main event is neither hastened nor retarded. To this charge an efficacious answer is not easily made. The sylphs cannot be said to help or to oppose, and it must be allowed to imply some want of art, that their power has not been sufficiently intermingled with the action. Other parts may likewise be charged with want of connection; the game at *ombre* might be spared, but if the Lady had lost her hair while she was intent upon her cards, it might have been inferred that those who are too fond of play will be in danger of neglecting more important interests. Those perhaps are faults; but what are such faults to so much excellence!

The Epistle of *Eloise to Abelard* is one of the most happy productions of human wit: the subject is so judiciously chosen, that it would be difficult, in turning over the annals of the world, to find another which so many circumstances concur to recommend. We regularly interest ourselves most in the fortune of those who most deserve our notice. Abelard and Eloise were conspicuous in their days for eminence of merit. The heart naturally loves truth. The adventures and misfortunes of this illustrious pair are known from undisputed history. Their fate does not leave the mind in hopeless dejection; for they both found quiet and consolation in retirement and piety. So new and so affecting is their story, that it supersedes invention, and imagination ranges at full liberty without straggling into scenes of fable.

The story, thus skilfully adopted, has been diligently improved. Pope has left nothing behind him, which seems more the effect of studious perseverance and laborious revisal. Here is particularly observable the *curiosa felicitas*,* a fruitful soil, and careful cultivation. Here is no crudeness of sense, nor asperity of language.

The sources from which sentiments, which have so much vigour and efficacy, have been drawn, are shewn to be the mystick writers by the learned author of the *Essay on the Life and Writings of Pope*;* a book which teaches how the brow of Criticism may be smoothed, and how she may be enabled, with all her severity, to attract and to delight.

The train of my disquisition has now conducted me to that poetical wonder, the translation of the *Iliad*; a performance which no age or nation can pretend to equal. To the Greeks translation was almost unknown; it was totally unknown to the inhabitants of Greece. They had no recourse to the Barbarians for poetical beauties, but sought for every thing in Homer, where, indeed, there is but little which they might not find.

The Italians have been very diligent translators; but I can hear of no version, unless perhaps Anguillara's Ovid* may be excepted, which is read with eagerness. The *Iliad* of Salvini* every reader may discover to be punctiliously exact; but it seems to be the work of a linguist skilfully pedantick, and his countrymen, the proper judges of its power to please, reject it with disgust.

Their predecessors the Romans have left some specimens of translation behind them, and that employment must have had some credit in which Tully and Germanicus* engaged; but unless we suppose, what is perhaps true, that the plays of Terence were versions of Menander,* nothing translated seems ever to have risen to high reputation. The French, in the meridian hour of their learning, were very laudably industrious to enrich their own language with the wisdom of the ancients; but found themselves reduced, by whatever necessity, to turn the Greek and Roman poetry into prose. Whoever could read an author, could translate him. From such rivals little can be feared.

The chief help of Pope in this arduous undertaking was drawn from the versions of Dryden. Virgil had borrowed much of his imagery from Homer, and part of the debt was now paid by his translator. Pope searched the pages of Dryden for happy combinations of heroic diction; but it will not be denied that he added much to what he found. He cultivated our language with so much diligence and art, that he has left in his *Homer* a treasure of poetical elegances to posterity. His version may be said to have tuned the English tongue; for since its appearance no writer, however deficient in other powers, has wanted melody. Such a series of lines so elaborately corrected, and so sweetly modulated, took possession of the publick ear; the vulgar was enamoured of the poem, and the learned wondered at the translation.

But in the most general applause discordant voices will always be heard. It has been objected by some, who wish to be numbered among the sons of learning, that Pope's version of Homer is not Homerical; that it exhibits no resemblance of the original and characteristick manner of the Father of Poetry, as it wants his awful simplicity, his artless grandeur, his unaffected majesty. This cannot be totally denied; but it must be remembered that *necessitas quod cogit defendit*;* that may be lawfully done which cannot be forborn. Time and place will always enforce regard. In estimating this translation, consideration must be had of the nature of our language, the form of our metre, and, above all, of the change which two thousand years have made in the modes of life and the habits of thought. Virgil wrote in a language of the same general fabrick with that of Homer, in verses of the same measure, and in an age nearer to Homer's time by eighteen hundred years; yet he found, even then, the state of the world so much altered, and the demand for elegance so much increased, that mere nature would be endured no longer; and perhaps, in the multitude of borrowed passages, very few can be shewn which he has not embellished.

There is a time when nations emerging from barbarity, and falling into regular subordination, gain leisure to grow wise, and feel the shame of ignorance and the craving pain of unsatisfied curiosity. To this hunger of the mind plain sense is grateful; that which fills the void removes uneasiness, and to be free from pain for a while is pleasure; but repletion generates fastidiousness; a saturated intellect soon becomes luxurious, and knowledge finds no willing reception till it is recommended by artificial diction. Thus it will be found, in the progress of learning, that in all nations the first writers are simple, and that every age improves in elegance. One refinement always makes way for another, and what was expedient to Virgil was necessary to Pope.

I suppose many readers of the English *Iliad*, when they have been touched with some unexpected beauty of the lighter kind, have tried to enjoy it in the original, where, alas! it was not to be found. Homer doubtless owes to his translator many *Ovidian* graces not exactly suitable to his character; but to have added can be no great crime, if nothing be taken away. Elegance is surely to be desired, if it be not gained at the expence of dignity. A hero would wish to be loved, as well as to be reverenced.

To a thousand cavils one answer is sufficient; the purpose of a writer is to be read, and the criticism which would destroy the power of pleasing must be blown aside. Pope wrote for his own age and his own nation: he knew that it was necessary to colour the images and point the sentiments of his author; he therefore made him graceful, but lost him some of his sublimity.

The copious notes with which the version is accompanied, and by which it is recommended to many readers, though they were undoubtedly written to swell the volumes, ought not to pass without praise: commentaries which attract the reader by the pleasure of perusal have not often appeared; the notes of others are read to clear difficulties, those of Pope to vary entertainment.

It has however been objected, with sufficient reason, that there is in the commentary too much of unseasonable levity and affected gaiety; that too many appeals are made to the Ladies, and the ease which is so carefully preserved is sometimes the ease of a trifler. Every art has its terms, and every kind of instruction its proper style; the gravity of common criticks may be tedious, but is less despicable than childish merriment.

Of the *Odyssey* nothing remains to be observed: the same general praise may be given to both translations, and a particular examination of either would require a large volume. The notes were written by Broome, who endeavoured not unsuccessfully to imitate his master.

Of the *Dunciad* the hint is confessedly taken from Dryden's *Mac Flecknoe*; but the plan is so enlarged and diversified as justly to claim the praise of an original, and affords perhaps the best specimen that has yet appeared of personal satire ludicrously pompous.

That the design was moral, whatever the author might tell either his readers or himself, I am not convinced. The first motive was the desire of revenging the contempt with which Theobald had treated his *Shakspeare*, and regaining the honour which he had lost, by crushing his opponent. Theobald was not of bulk enough to fill a poem, and therefore it was necessary to find other enemies with other names, at whose expence he might divert the publick.

In this design there was petulance and malignity enough; but I cannot think it very criminal. An author places himself uncalled before the tribunal of Criticism, and solicits fame at the hazard of disgrace. Dulness or deformity are not culpable in themselves, but may be very justly reproached when they pretend to the honour of wit or the influence of beauty. If bad writers were to pass without reprehension, what should restrain them? *impune diem consumpserit ingens Telephus*;* and upon bad writers only will censure have much effect. The satire which brought Theobald and Moore* into contempt, dropped impotent from Bentley, like the javelin of Priam.

All truth is valuable, and satirical criticism may be considered as useful when it rectifies error and improves judgement; hc that refines the publick taste is a publick benefactor.

The beauties of this poem are well known; its chief fault is the grossness of its images. Pope and Swift had an unnatural delight in ideas physically impure, such as every other tongue utters with unwillingness, and of which every ear shrinks from the mention.

But even this fault, offensive as it is, may be forgiven for the excellence of other passages; such as the formation and dissolution of Moore, the account of the Traveller, the misfortune of the Florist, and the crouded thoughts and stately numbers which dignify the concluding paragraph.

The alterations which have been made in the *Dunciad*, not always for the better, require that it should be published, as in the last collection, with all its variations.

The *Essay on Man* was a work of great labour and long consideration, but certainly not the happiest of Pope's performances. The subject is perhaps not very proper for poetry, and the poet was not sufficiently master of his subject; metaphysical morality was to him a new study, he was proud of his acquisitions, and, supposing himself master of great secrets, was in haste to teach what he had not learned. Thus he tells us, in the first Epistle, that from the nature of the Supreme Being may be deduced an order of beings such as mankind, because Infinite Excellence can do only what is best. He finds out that these beings must be *somewhere*, and that *all the question is whether man be in a wrong place*. Surely if, according to the poet's Leibnitian* reasoning, we may infer that man ought to be, only because he is, we may allow that his place is the right place, because he has it. Supreme Wisdom is not less infallible in disposing than in creating. But what is meant by *somewhere* and *place*, and *wrong place*, it had been vain to ask Pope, who probably had never asked himself.

Having exalted himself into the chair of wisdom, he tells us much that every man knows, and much that he does not know himself; that we see but little, and that the order of the universe is beyond our comprehension; an opinion not very uncommon; and that there is a chain of subordinate beings *from infinite to nothing*, of which himself and his readers are equally ignorant. But he gives us one comfort, which, without his help, he supposes unattainable, in the position *that though we are fools, yet God is wise.**

This Essay affords an egregious instance of the predominance of genius, the dazzling splendour of imagery, and the seductive powers of eloquence. Never were penury of knowledge and vulgarity of sentiment so happily disguised. The reader feels his mind full, though he learns nothing; and when he meets it in its new array, no longer knows the talk of his mother and his nurse. When these wonder-working sounds sink into sense, and the doctrine of the Essay, disrobed of its ornaments, is left to the powers of its naked excellence, what shall we discover? That we are, in comparison with our Creator, very weak and ignorant; that we do not uphold the chain of existence, and that we could not make one another with more skill than we are made. We may learn yet more; that the arts of human life were copied from the instinctive operations of other animals; that if the world be made for man, it may be said that man was made for geese. To these profound principles of natural knowledge are added some moral instructions equally new; that self-interest, well understood, will produce social concord; that men are mutual gainers by mutual benefits; that evil is sometimes balanced by good; that human advantages are unstable and fallacious, of uncertain duration, and doubtful effect; that our true honour is, not to have a great part, but to act it well: that virtue only is our own; and that happiness is always in our power.

Surely a man of no very comprehensive search may venture to say that he has heard all this before; but it was never till now recommended by such a blaze of embellishment, or such sweetness of melody. The vigorous contraction of some thoughts, the luxuriant amplification of others, the incidental illustrations, and sometimes the dignity, sometimes the softness of the verses, enchain philosophy, suspend criticism, and oppress judgement by overpowering pleasure.

This is true of many paragraphs; yet if I had undertaken to exemplify Pope's felicity of composition before a rigid critick, I should not select the *Essay on Man*; for it contains more lines unsuccessfully laboured, more harshness of diction, more thoughts imperfectly expressed, more levity without elegance, and more heaviness without strength, than will easily be found in all his other works.

The *Characters of Men and Women* are the product of diligent speculation upon human life; much labour has been bestowed upon them, and Pope very seldom laboured in vain. That his excellence may be properly estimated, I recommend a comparison of his *Characters of Women* with Boileau's Satire;* it will then be seen with how much more perspicacity female nature is investigated, and female excellence selected; and he surely is no mean writer to whom Boileau shall be found inferior. The *Characters of Men*, however, are written with more, if not with deeper, thought, and exhibit many passages exquisitely beautiful. The *Gem and the Flower* will not easily be equalled. In the women's part are some defects; the character of *Attossa* is not so neatly finished as that of *Clodio*; and some of the female characters may be found perhaps more frequently among men; what is said of *Philomede* was true of *Prior*.

In the Epistles to Lord Bathurst and Lord Burlington, Dr. Warburton has endeavoured to find a train of thought which was never in the writer's head, and, to support his hypothesis, has printed that first which was published last. In one, the most valuable passage is perhaps the Elogy on *Good Sense*, and the other the *End of the Duke of Buckingham*.

The Epistle to Arbuthnot, now arbitrarily called the *Prologue to the Satires*, is a performance consisting, as it seems, of many fragments wrought into one design, which by this union of scattered beauties contains more striking paragraphs than could probably have been brought together into an occasional work. As there is no stronger motive to exertion than self-defence, no part has more elegance, spirit, or dignity, than the poet's vindication of his own character. The meanest passage is the satire upon *Sporus*.

Of the two poems which derived their names from the year, and which are called the *Epilogue to the Satires*, it was very justly remarked by Savage, that the second was in the whole more strongly conceived, and more equally supported, but that it had no single passages equal to the contention in the first for the dignity of Vice, and the celebration of the triumph of Corruption.

The Imitations of Horace seem to have been written as relaxations of his genius. This employment became his favourite by its facility; the plan was ready to his hand, and nothing was required but to accommodate as he could the sentiments of an old author to recent facts or familiar images; but what is easy is seldom excellent; such imitations cannot give pleasure to common readers; the man of learning may be sometimes surprised and delighted by an unexpected parallel; but the comparison requires knowledge of the original, which will likewise often detect strained applications. Between Roman images and English manners there will be an irreconcileable dissimilitude, and the work will be generally uncouth and party-coloured; neither original nor translated, neither ancient nor modern.

Pope had, in proportions very nicely adjusted to each other, all the qualities that constitute genius. He had *Invention*, by which new trains of events are formed, and new scenes of imagery displayed, as in the *Rape of the Lock*; and by which extrinsick and adventitious embellishments and illustrations are connected with a known subject, as in the *Essay on Criticism*. He had *Imagination*, which strongly impresses on the writer's mind, and enables him to convey to the reader, the various forms of nature, incidents of life, and energies of passion, as in his *Eloisa, Windsor Forest*, and the *Ethick Epistles*. He had *Judgement*, which selects from life or nature what the present purpose requires, and, by separating the essence of things from its concomitants, often makes the representation more powerful than the reality: and he had colours of language always before him, ready to decorate his matter with every grace of elegant expression, as when he accommodates his diction to the wonderful multiplicity of Homer's sentiments and descriptions.

Poetical expression includes sound as well as meaning; *Musick*, says Dryden, *is inarticulate poetry*;* among the excellences of Pope, therefore, must be mentioned the melody of his metre. By perusing the works of Dryden, he discovered the most perfect fabrick of English verse, and habituated himself to that only which he found the best; in consequence of which restraint, his poetry has been censured as too uniformly musical, and as glutting the ear with unvaried sweetness. I suspect this objection to be the cant of those who judge by principles rather than perception: and who would even themselves have less pleasure in his works, if he had tried to relieve attention by studied discords, or affected to break his lines and vary his pauses.

But though he was thus careful of his versification, he did not oppress his powers with superfluous rigour. He seems to have thought with Boileau, that the practice of writing might be refined till the difficulty should overbalance the advantage. The construction of his language is not always strictly grammatical; with those rhymes which prescription had conjoined he contented himself, without regard to Swift's remonstrances, though there was no striking consonance; nor was he very careful to vary his terminations, or to refuse admission at a small distance to the same rhymes.

To Swift's edict for the exclusion of Alexandrines and Triplets he paid little regard; he admitted them, but, in the opinion of Fenton, too rarely; he uses them more liberally in his translation than his poems.

He has a few double rhymes; and always, I think, unsuccessfully, except once in the *Rape of the Lock*.

Expletives he very early ejected from his verses; but he now and then admits an epithet rather commodious than important. Each of the six first lines of the *Iliad* might lose two syllables with very little diminution of the meaning; and sometimes, after all his art and labour, one verse seems to be made for the sake of another. In his latter productions the diction is sometimes vitiated by French idioms, with which Bolingbroke had perhaps infected him.

I have been told that the couplet by which he declared his own ear to be most gratified was this:

> Lo, where Mœotis sleeps, and hardly flows
> The freezing Tanais through a waste of snows.*

But the reason of this preference I cannot discover.

It is remarked by Watts,* that there is scarcely a happy combination of words, or a phrase poetically elegant in the English language, which Pope has not inserted into his version of Homer. How he obtained possession of so many beauties of speech, it were desirable to know. That he gleaned from authors, obscure as well as eminent, what he thought brilliant or useful, and preserved it all in a regular collection, is not unlikely. When, in his last years, Hall's Satires* were shewn him, he wished that he had seen them sooner.

New sentiments and new images others may produce; but to attempt any further improvement of versification will be dangerous. Art and diligence have now done their best, and what shall be added will be the effort of tedious toil and needless curiosity.

After all this, it is surely superfluous to answer the question that has once been asked, Whether Pope was a poet? otherwise than by asking in return, If Pope be not a poet, where is poetry to be found? To circumscribe poetry by a definition will only shew the narrowness of the definer, though a definition which shall exclude Pope will not easily be made. Let us look round upon the present time, and back upon the past; let us enquire to whom the voice of mankind has decreed the wreath of poetry; let their productions be examined, and their claims stated, and the pretensions of Pope will be no more disputed. Had he given the world only his version, the name of poet must have been allowed him: if the writer of the *Iliad* were to class his successors, he would assign a very high place to his translator, without requiring any other evidence of Genius.

The following Letter, of which the original is in the hands of Lord Hardwicke, was communicated to me by the kindness of Mr. Jodrell.*

"To Mr. Bridges, at the Bishop of
London's at Fulham.

"Sir,

"The favour of your Letter, with your Remarks, can never be enough acknowledged; and the speed, with which you discharged so troublesome a task, doubles the obligation.

"I must own, you have pleased me very much by the commendations so ill bestowed upon me; but, I assure you, much more by the frankness of your censure, which I ought to take the more kindly of the two, as it is more advantageous to a scribbler to be improved in his judgment than to be soothed in his vanity. The greater part of those deviations from the Greek, which you have observed, I was led into by Chapman and Hobbes;* who are (it seems) as much celebrated for their knowledge of the original, as they are decryed for the badness of their translations. Chapman pretends to have restored the genuine sense of the author, from the mistakes of all former explainers, in several hundred places: and the Cambridge editors of the large Homer, in Greek and Latin, attributed so much to Hobbes, that they confess they have corrected the old Latin interpretation very often by his version. For my part, I generally took the author's meaning to be as you have explained it; yet their authority, joined to the knowledge of my own imperfectness in the language, over-ruled me. However, Sir, you may be confident I think you in the right, because you happen to be of my opinion: (for men (let them say what they will) never approve any other's sense, but as it squares with their own.) But you have made me much more proud of, and positive in my judgement, since it is strengthened by yours. I think your criticisms, which regard the expression, very just, and shall make my profit of them: to give you some proof that I am in earnest, I will alter three verses on your bare objection, though I have Mr. Dryden's example for each of them. And this, I hope, you will account no small piece of obedience, from one, who values the authority of one true poet above that of twenty criticks or commentators. But though I speak thus of commentators, I will continue to read carefully all I can procure, to make up, that way, for my own want of critical understanding in the original beauties of Homer. Though the greatest of them are certainly those of the Invention and Design, which are not at all confined to the language: for the distinguishing excellences of Homer are (by the consent of the best criticks of all nations) first in the manners, (which include all the speeches, as being no other than the representations of each person's manners by his words:) and then in that rapture and fire, which carries you away with him, with that wonderful force, that no man who has a true poetical spirit is master of himself, while he reads him. Homer makes you interested and concerned before you are aware, all at once; whereas Virgil does it by soft degrees. This, I believe, is what a translator of Homer ought principally to imitate; and it is very hard for any translator to come up to it, because the chief reason why all translations fall short of their originals is, that the very constraint they are obliged to, renders them heavy and dispirited.

"The great beauty of Homer's language, as I take it, consists in that noble simplicity, which runs through all his works; (and yet his diction, contrary to what one would imagine consistent with simplicity, is at the same time very copious.) I don't know how I have run into this pedantry in a Letter, but I find I have said too much, as well as spoken too inconsiderately; what farther thoughts I have upon this subject, I shall be glad to communicate to you (for my own improvement) when we meet; which is a happiness I very earnestly desire, as I do likewise some opportunity of proving how much I think myself obliged to your friendship, and how truly I am, Sir,

Your most faithful, humble servant,

A. Pope."

The Criticism upon Pope's Epitaphs, which was printed in *The Visitor*, is placed here, being too minute and particular to be inserted in the Life.*

EVERY Art is best taught by example. Nothing contributes more to the cultivation of propriety than remarks on the works of those who have most excelled. I shall therefore endeavour, at this *visit*, to entertain the young students in poetry, with an examination of Pope's Epitaphs.

To define an epitaph is useless; every one knows that it is an inscription on a tomb. An epitaph, therefore, implies no particular character of writing, but may be composed in verse or prose. It is indeed commonly panegyrical; because we are seldom distinguished with a stone but by our friends; but it has no rule to restrain or modify it, except this, that it ought not to be longer than common beholders may be expected to have leisure and patience to peruse.

I.

On CHARLES *Earl of* DORSET,* *in the Church of Wythyham in Sussex.*

Dorset, the grace of courts, the Muse's pride,
Patron of arts, and judge of nature, dy'd.
The scourge of pride, though sanctify'd or great,
Of fops in learning, and of knaves in state;
Yet soft in nature, though severe his lay,
His anger moral, and his wisdom gay,
Blest satyrist! who touch'd the mean so true,
As show'd, Vice had his hate and pity too.
Blest courtier! who could king and country please,
Yet sacred keep his friendships, and his ease.
Blest peer! his great forefathers every grace
Reflecting, and reflected on his race;
Where other Buckhursts, other Dorsets shine,
And patriots still, or poets, deck the line.

The first distich of this epitaph contains a kind of information which few would want, that the man, for whom the tomb was erected, *died*. There are indeed some qualities worthy of praise ascribed to the dead, but none that were likely to exempt him from the lot of man, or incline us much to wonder that he should die. What is meant by *judge of nature*, is not easy to say. Nature is not the object of human judgement; for it is vain to judge where we cannot alter. If by nature is meant, what is commonly called *nature* by the criticks, a just representation of things really existing, and actions really performed, nature cannot be properly opposed to *art*; nature being, in this sense, only the best effect of art.

The scourge of pride—

Of this couplet, the second line is not, what is intended, an illustration of the former. *Pride*, in the *Great*, is indeed well enough connected with knaves in state, though *knaves* is a word rather too ludicrous and light; but the mention of *sanctified* pride will not lead the thoughts to *fops in learning*, but rather to some species of tyranny or oppression, something more gloomy and more formidable than foppery.

Yet soft his nature—

This is a high compliment, but was not first bestowed on Dorset by Pope. The next verse is extremely beautiful.

Blest satyrist!—

In this distich is another line of which Pope was not the author. I do not mean to blame these imitations with much harshness; in long performances they are scarcely to be avoided, and in shorter they may be indulged, because the train of the composition may naturally involve them, or the scantiness of the subject allow little choice. However, what is borrowed is not to be enjoyed as our own, and it is the business of critical justice to give every bird of the Muses his proper feather.

Blest courtier!—

Whether a courtier can properly be commended for keeping his *ease sacred*, may perhaps be disputable. To please king and country, without sacrificing friendship to any change of times, was a very uncommon instance of prudence or felicity, and deserved to be kept separate from so poor a commendation as care of his ease. I wish our poets would attend a little more accurately to the use of the word *sacred*, which surely should never be applied in a serious composition, but where some reference may be made to a higher Being, or where some duty is exacted or implied. A man may keep his friendship *sacred*, because promises of friendship are very awful ties; but methinks he cannot, but in a burlesque sense, be said to keep his ease *sacred*.

Blest peer!

The blessing ascribed to the *peer* has no connection with his peerage: they might happen to any other man, whose ancestors were remembered, or whose posterity were likely to be regarded.

I know not whether this epitaph be worthy either of the writer or of the man entombed.

II.

On Sir WILLIAM TRUMBUL, *one of the principal Secretaries of State to King* WILLIAM III. *who, having resigned his place, died in his retirement at Easthamsted in Berkshire*, 1716.

A pleasing form, a firm, yet cautious mind,
Sincere, though prudent; constant, yet resign'd;
Honour unchang'd, a principle profest,
Fix'd to one side, but moderate to the rest:
An honest courtier, yet a patriot too,
Just to his prince, and to his country true.
Fill'd with the sense of age, the fire of youth,
A scorn of wrangling, yet a zeal for truth;
A generous faith, from superstition free;
A love to peace, and hate of tyranny;
Such this man was; who now, from earth remov'd,
At length enjoys that liberty he lov'd.

In this epitaph, as in many others, there appears, at the first view, a fault which I think scarcely any beauty can compensate. The name is omitted. The end of an epitaph is to convey some account of the dead; and to what purpose is anything told of him whose name is concealed? An epitaph, and a history, of a nameless hero, are equally absurd, since the virtues and qualities so recounted in either, are scattered at the mercy of fortune to be appropriated by guess. The name, it is true, may be read upon the stone; but what obligation has it to the poet, whose verses wander over the earth, and leave their subject behind them, and who is forced, like an unskilful painter, to make his purpose known by adventitious help?

This epitaph is wholly without elevation, and contains nothing striking or particular; but the poet is not to be blamed for the defects of his subject. He said perhaps the best that could be said. There are, however, some defects which were not made necessary by the character in which he was employed. There is no opposition between an *honest courtier* and a *patriot*; for an *honest courtier* cannot but be a *patriot*.

It was unsuitable to the nicety required in short compositions, to close his verse with the word *too*; every rhyme should be a word of emphasis, nor can this rule be safely neglected, except where the length of the poem makes slight inaccuracies excusable, or allows room for beauties sufficient to overpower the effects of petty faults.

At the beginning of the seventh line the word *filled* is weak and prosaic, having no particular adaptation to any of the words that follow it.

The thought in the last line is impertinent, having no connexion with the foregoing character, nor with the condition of the man described. Had the epitaph been written on the poor conspirator[1] who died lately in prison, after a confinement of more than forty years, without any crime proved against him, the sentiment had been just and pathetical; but why should Trumbul be congratulated upon his liberty, who had never known restraint?

III.

On the Hon. Simon Harcourt,* *only Son of the Lord Chancellor* Harcourt, at *the Church of Stanton-Harcourt in Oxfordshire*, 1720.

To this sad shrine, whoe'er thou art, draw near,
Here lies the friend most lov'd, the son most dear:
Who ne'er knew joy, but friendship might divide,
Or gave his father grief but when he dy'd.

How vain is reason, eloquence how weak!
If Pope must tell what Harcourt cannot speak.
Oh, let thy once-lov'd friend inscribe thy stone,
And with a father's sorrows mix his own!

This epitaph is principally remarkable for the artful introduction of the name, which is inserted with a peculiar felicity, to which

[1] Bernardi.

chance must concur with genius, which no man can hope to attain twice, and which cannot be copied but with servile imitation.

I cannot but wish that, of this inscription, the two last lines had been omitted, as they take away from the energy what they do not add to the sense.

IV.

On JAMES CRAGGS, *Esq;*
in Westminster-Abbey.

JACOBUS CRAGGS,
REGI MAGNAE BRITANNIAE A SECRETIS
ET CONSILIIS SANCTIORIBVS
PRINCIPIS PARITER AC POPULI AMOR ET
DELICIAE:
VIXIT TITULIS ET INVIDIA MAJOR,
ANNOS HEV PAVCOS, XXXV.
OB. FEB. XVI. MDCCXX.

Statesman, yet friend to truth! of soul sincere,
In action faithful, and in honour clear!
Who broke no promise, serv'd no private end,
Who gain'd no title, and who lost no friend;
Ennobled by himself, by all approv'd,
Prais'd, wept, and honour'd, by the Muse he lov'd.

The lines on Craggs were not originally intended for an epitaph; and therefore some faults are to be imputed to the violence with which they are torn from the poem that first contained them. We may, however, observe some defects. There is a redundancy of words in the first couplet: it is superfluous to tell of him, who was *sincere*, *true*, and *faithful*, that he was *in honour clear*.

There seems to be an opposition intended in the fourth line, which is not very obvious: where is the relation between the two positions, that he *gained no title* and *lost no friend?*

It may be proper here to remark the absurdity of joining, in the same inscription, Latin and English, or verse and prose. If either language be preferable to the other, let that only be used; for no reason can be given why part of the information should be given in one tongue, and part in another, on a tomb, more than in any other place, on any other occasion; and to tell all that can be conveniently told in verse, and then to call in the help of prose, has always the appearance of a very artless expedient, or of an attempt unaccomplished. Such an epitaph resembles the conversation of a foreigner, who tells part of his meaning by words, and conveys part by signs.

V.

Intended for Mr. ROWE.*
In Westminster-Abbey.

Thy reliques, Rowe, to this fair urn we trust,
And sacred, place by Dryden's awful dust:
Beneath a rude and nameless stone he lies,
To which thy tomb shall guide inquiring eyes.
Peace to thy gentle shade, and endless rest!
Blest in thy genius, in thy love too blest!
One grateful woman to thy fame supplies
What a whole thankless land to his denies.

Of this inscription the chief fault is, that it belongs less to Rowe, for whom it was written, than to Dryden, who was buried near him; and indeed gives very little information concerning either.

To wish, *Peace to thy shade*, is too mythological to be admitted into a christian temple: the ancient worship has infected almost all our other compositions, and might therefore be contented to spare our epitaphs. Let fiction, at least, cease with life, and let us be serious over the grave.

VI.

On Mrs. CORBET,*
who died of a Cancer in her Breast.

Here rests a woman, good without pretence,
Blest with plain reason, and with sober sense:
No conquests she, but o'er herself desir'd;
No arts essay'd, but not to be admir'd.
Passion and pride were to her soul unknown,
Convinc'd that Virtue only is our own.
So unaffected, so compos'd a mind,
So firm, yet soft, so strong, yet so refin'd,
Heaven, as its purest gold, by tortures try'd,
The saint sustained it, but the woman dy'd.

I have always considered this as the most valuable of all Pope's epitaphs; the subject of it is a character not discriminated by any shining or eminent peculiarities; yet that which really makes, though not the splendor, the felicity of life, and that which every wise man will choose for his final and lasting companion in the languor of age, in the quiet of privacy, when he departs weary and disgusted from the ostentatious, the volatile, and the vain. Of such a character, which the dull overlook, and the gay despise, it was fit that the value should be made known, and the dignity established. Domestick virtue, as it is exerted without great occasions, or conspicuous consequences, in an even unnoted tenor, required the genius of Pope to display it in such a manner as might attract regard, and enforce reverence. Who can forbear to lament that this amiable woman has no name in the verses?

If the particular lines of this inscription be examined, it will appear less faulty than the rest. There is scarce one line taken from common places, unless it be that in which *only Virtue* is said to be *our own.* I once heard a Lady of great beauty and excellence object to the fourth line, that it contained an unnatural and incredible panegyrick. Of this let the Ladies judge.

VII.

On the Monument of the Hon. ROBERT DIGBY, *and of his Sister* MARY, *erected by their Father the Lord* DIGBY,* *in the Church of Sherborne in Dorsetshire*, 1727.

Go! fair example of untainted youth,
Of modest wisdom, and pacifick truth:
Compos'd in sufferings, and in joy sedate,
Good without noise, without pretension great.
Just of thy word, in every thought sincere,
Who knew no wish but what the world might hear:
Of softest manners, unaffected mind,
Lover of peace, and friend of human kind:
Go, live! for heaven's eternal year is thine,
Go, and exalt thy moral to divine.

And thou, blest maid! attendant on his doom,
Pensive hast follow'd to the silent tomb,
Steer'd the same course to the same quiet shore,
Not parted long, and now to part no more!
Go, then, where only bliss sincere is known!
Go, where to love and to enjoy are one!

Yet take these tears, Mortality's relief,
And till we share your joys, forgive our grief:
These little rites, a stone, a verse receive,
'Tis all a father, all a friend can give!

This epitaph contains of the brother only a general indiscriminate character, and of the sister tells nothing but that she died. The difficulty in writing epitaphs is to give a particular and appropriate praise. This, however, is not always to be performed, whatever be the diligence or ability of the writer; for the greater part of mankind *have no characters at all*, have little that distinguishes them from others equally good or bad, and therefore nothing can be said of them which may not be applied with equal propriety to a thousand more. It is indeed no great panegyrick, that there is inclosed in this tomb one who was born in one year, and died in another; yet many useful and amiable lives have been spent, which yet leave little materials for any other memorial. These are however not the proper subjects of poetry; and whenever friendship, or any other motive, obliges a poet to write on such subjects, he must be forgiven if he sometimes wanders in generalities, and utters the same praises over different tombs.

The scantiness of human praises can scarcely be made more apparent, than by remarking how often Pope has, in the few epitaphs which he composed, found it necessary to borrow from himself. The fourteen epitaphs, which he has written, comprise about an hundred and forty lines, in which there are more repetitions than will easily be found in all the rest of his works. In the eight lines which make the character of Digby, there is scarce any thought, or word, which may not be found in the other epitaphs.

The ninth line, which is far the strongest and most elegant, is borrowed from Dryden. The conclusion is the same with that on Harcourt, but is here more elegant and better connected.

VIII.

On Sir GODFREY KNELLER.*

In Westminster-Abbey, 1723.

Kneller, by heaven, and not a master taught,
Whose art was nature, and whose pictures thought;
Now for two ages, having snatch'd from fate
Whate'er was beauteous, or whate'er was great,
Lies crown'd with Princes honours, Poets lays,
Due to his merit, and brave thirst of praise.

Living, great Nature fear'd he might outvie
Her works; and dying, fears herself may die.

Of this epitaph the first couplet is good, the second not bad, the third is deformed with a broken metaphor, the word *crowned* not being applicable to the *honours* or the *lays*, and the fourth is not only borrowed from the epitaph on Raphael, but of very harsh construction.

IX.

On General HENRY WITHERS.*
In Westminster-Abbey, 1729.

Here, Withers, rest! thou bravest, gentlest mind,
Thy country's friend, but more of human kind,
O! born to arms! O! worth in youth approv'd!
O! soft humanity in age belov'd!
For thee the hardy veteran drops a tear,
And the gay courtier feels the sigh sincere.

Withers, adieu! yet not with thee remove
Thy martial spirit, or thy social love!
Amidst corruption, luxury, and rage,
Still leave some ancient virtues to our age:
Nor let us say (those English glories gone)
The last true Briton lies beneath this stone.

The epitaph on Withers affords another instance of common places, though somewhat diversified, by mingled qualities, and the peculiarity of a profession.

The second couplet is abrupt, general, and unpleasing; exclamation seldom succeeds in our language; and, I think, it may be observed that the particle O! used at the beginning of a sentence, always offends.

The third couplet is more happy; the value expressed for him, by different sorts of men, raises him to esteem; there is yet something of the common cant of superficial satirists, who suppose that the insincerity of a courtier destroys all his sensations, and that he is equally a dissembler to the living and the dead.

At the third couplet I should wish the epitaph to close, but that I should be unwilling to lose the two next lines, which yet are dearly bought if they cannot be retained without the four that follow them.

X.

On Mr. ELIJAH FENTON.

At Easthamsted in Berkshire, 1730.

This modest stone, what few vain marbles can,
May truly say, Here lies an honest man:
A poet, blest beyond the poet's fate,
Whom Heaven kept sacred from the Proud and Great:
Foe to loud praise, and friend to learned ease,
Content with science in the vale of peace.
Calmly he look'd on either life; and here
Saw nothing to regret, or there to fear;
From Nature's temperate feast rose satisfy'd,
Thank'd heaven that he had liv'd, and that he dy'd.

The first couplet of this epitaph is borrowed from *Crashaw*. The four next lines contain a species of praise peculiar, original, and just. Here, therefore, the inscription should have ended, the latter part containing nothing but what is common to every man who is wise and good. The character of Fenton was so amiable, that I cannot forbear to wish for some poet or biographer to display it more fully for the advantage of posterity. If he did not stand in the first rank of genius, he may claim a place in the second; and, whatever criticism may object to his writings, censure could find very little to blame in his life.

XI.

On Mr. GAY.

In Westminster-Abbey, 1732.

Of manners gentle, of affections mild;
In wit, a man; simplicity, a child:
With native humour tempering virtuous rage,
Form'd to delight at once and lash the age:
Above temptation, in a low estate,
And uncorrupted, ev'n among the Great:
A safe companion, and an easy friend,
Unblam'd through life, lamented in thy end.
These are thy honours! not that here thy bust
Is mix'd with heroes, or with kings thy dust;
But that the Worthy and the Good shall say,
Striking their pensive bosoms—Here lies GAY.

As Gay was the favourite of our author, this epitaph was probably written with an uncommon degree of attention; yet it is not more successfully executed than the rest, for it will not always happen that the success of a poet is proportionate to his labour. The same observation may be extended to all works of imagination, which are often influenced by causes wholly out of the performer's power, by hints of which he perceives not the origin, by sudden elevations of mind which he cannot produce in himself, and which sometimes rise when he expects them least.

The two parts of the first line are only echoes of each other; *gentle manners* and *mild affections*, if they mean any thing, must mean the same.

That Gay was a *man in wit* is a very frigid commendation; to have the wit of a man is not much for a poet. The *wit of man*, and the *simplicity of a child*, make a poor and vulgar contrast, and raise no ideas of excellence, either intellectual or moral.

In the next couplet *rage* is less properly introduced after the mention of *mildness* and *gentleness*, which are made the constituents of his character; for a man so *mild* and *gentle* to *temper* his *rage*, was not difficult.

The next line is unharmonious in its sound, and mean in its conception; the opposition is obvious, and the word *lash* used absolutely, and without any modification, is gross and improper.

To be *above temptation* in poverty, and *free from corruption among the Great*, is indeed such a peculiarity as deserved notice. But to be a *safe companion* is praise merely negative, arising not from the possession of virtue, but the absence of vice, and that one of the most odious.

As little can be added to his character, by asserting that he was *lamented in his end*. Every man that dies is, at least by the writer of his epitaph, supposed to be lamented, and therefore this general lamentation does no honour to Gay.

The first eight lines have no grammar; the adjectives are without any substantive, and the epithets without a subject.

The thought in the last line, that Gay is buried in the bosoms of the *worthy* and the *good*, who are distinguished only to lengthen the line, is so dark that few understand it; and so harsh, when it is explained, that still fewer approve.

XII.

Intended for Sir ISAAC NEWTON.
In Westminster-Abbey.

ISAACUS NEWTONIUS:
Quem Immortalem
Testantur, *Tempus, Natura, Cœlum:*
Mortalem
Hoc marmor fatetur.*

Nature, and Nature's laws, lay hid in night,
God said, *Let Newton be!* And all was light.

Of this epitaph, short as it is, the faults seem not to be very few. Why part should be Latin and part English, it is not easy to discover. In the Latin, the opposition of *Immortalis* and *Mortalis*, is a mere sound, or a mere quibble; he is not *immortal* in any sense contrary to that in which he is *mortal*.

In the verses the thought is obvious, and the words *night* and *light* are too nearly allied.

XIII.

On EDMUND *Duke of* BUCKINGHAM,* *who died in the 19th Year of his Age*, 1735.

If modest youth, with cool reflection crown'd,
And every opening virtue blooming round,
Could save a parent's justest pride from fate,
Or add one patriot to a sinking state;
This weeping marble had not ask'd thy tear,
Or sadly told, how many hopes lie here!
The living virtue now had shone approv'd,
The senate heard him, and his country lov'd.
Yet softer honours, and less noisy fame
Attend the shade of gentle Buckingham:
In whom a race, for courage fam'd and art,
Ends in the milder merit of the heart;
And chiefs or sages long to Britain given,
Pays the last tribute of a saint to heaven.

This epitaph Mr. Warburton prefers to the rest, but I know not for what reason. To *crown* with *reflection* is surely a mode of speech approaching to nonsense. *Opening virtues blooming round*, is something like tautology; the six following lines are poor and prosaick. *Art* is in another couplet used for *arts*, that a rhyme may be had to *heart*. The six last lines are the best, but not excellent.

The rest of his sepulchral performances hardly deserve the notice of criticism. The contemptible *Dialogue* between HE and SHE should have been suppressed for the author's sake.

In his last epitaph on himself, in which he attempts to be jocular upon one of the few things that make wise men serious, he confounds the living man with the dead:

Under this stone, or under this sill,
Or under this turf, &c.

When a man is once buried, the question, under what he is buried, is easily decided. He forgot that though he wrote the epitaph in a state of uncertainty, yet it could not be laid over him till his grave was made. Such is the folly of wit when it is ill employed.

The world has but little new; even this wretchedness seems to have been borrowed from the following tuneless lines:

Ludovici Areosti humantur ossa
Sub hoc marmore, vel sub hac humo, seu
Sub quicquid voluit benignus hæres
Sive hærede benignior comes, seu
Opportunius incidens Viator;
Nam scire haud potuit futura, sed nec
Tanti erat vacuum sibi cadaver
Ut urnam cuperet parare vivens,
Vivens ista tamen sibi paravit.
Quæ inscribi voluit suo sepulchro
Olim siquod haberetis sepulchrum.*

Surely Ariosto did not venture to expect that his trifle would have ever had such an illustrious imitator.

GRAY

THOMAS GRAY, the son of Mr. Philip Gray, a scrivener of London, was born in Cornhill, November 26, 1716. His grammatical education he received at Eton under the care of Mr. Antrobus, his mother's brother, then assistant to Dr. George;* and when he left school, in 1734, entered a pensioner at Peterhouse in Cambridge.

The transition from the school to the college is, to most young scholars, the time from which they date their years of manhood, liberty, and happiness; but Gray seems to have been very little delighted with academical gratifications; he liked at Cambridge neither the mode of life nor the fashion of study, and lived sullenly on to the time when his attendance on lectures was no longer required. As he intended to profess the Common Law, he took no degree.

When he had been at Cambridge about five years, Mr. Horace Walpole,* whose friendship he had gained at Eton, invited him to travel with him as his companion. They wandered through France into Italy; and Gray's Letters contain a very pleasing account of many parts of their journey. But unequal friendships are easily dissolved: at Florence they quarrelled, and parted; and Mr. Walpole is now content to have it told that it was by his fault. If we look however without prejudice on the world, we shall find that men, whose consciousness of their own merit sets them above the compliances of servility, are apt enough in their association with superiors to watch their own dignity with troublesome and punctilious jealousy, and in the fervour of independance to exact that attention which they refuse to pay. Part they did, whatever was the quarrel, and the rest of their travels was doubtless more unpleasant to them both. Gray continued his journey in a manner suitable to his own little fortune, with only an occasional servant.

He returned to England in September 1741, and in about two months afterwards buried his father; who had, by an injudicious waste of money upon a new house, so much lessened his fortune, that Gray thought himself too poor to study the law. He therefore retired to Cambridge, where he soon after became Bachelor of Civil Law; and where, without liking the place or its inhabitants, or professing to like them, he passed, except a short residence at London, the rest of his life.

About this time he was deprived of Mr. West,* the son of a chancellor of Ireland, a friend on whom he appears to have set a high value, and who deserved his esteem by the powers which he shews in his Letters, and in the Ode to *May*, which Mr. Mason has preserved, as well as by the sincerity with which, when Gray sent him part of *Agrippina*, a tragedy that he had just begun, he gave an opinion which probably intercepted the progress of the work, and which the judgement of every reader will confirm. It was certainly no loss to the English stage that *Agrippina* was never finished.

In this year (1742) Gray seems first to have applied himself seriously to poetry; for in this year were produced the *Ode to Spring*, his *Prospect of Eton*, and his *Ode to Adversity*. He began likewise a Latin poem, *de Principiis cogitandi*.

It may be collected from the narrative of Mr. Mason, that his first ambition was to have excelled in Latin poetry: perhaps it were reasonable to wish that he had prosecuted his design; for though there is at present some embarrassment in his phrase, and some harshness in his Lyrick numbers, his copiousness of language is such as very few possess; and his lines, even when imperfect, discover a writer whom practice would quickly have made skilful.

He now lived on at Peterhouse, very little solicitous what others did or thought, and cultivated his mind and enlarged his views without any other purpose than of improving and amusing himself; when Mr. Mason,* being elected fellow of Pembroke-hall, brought him a companion who was afterwards to be his editor, and whose fondness and fidelity has kindled in him a zeal of admiration, which cannot be reasonably expected from the neutrality of a stranger and the coldness of a critick.

In this retirement he wrote (1747) an ode on the *Death of Mr. Walpole's Cat*; and the year afterwards attempted a poem of more importance, on *Government and Education*, of which the fragments which remain have many excellent lines.

His next production (1750) was his far-famed *Elegy in the Church-yard*, which, finding its way into a Magazine, first, I believe, made him known to the publick.

An invitation from lady Cobham* about this time gave occasion to an odd composition called *a Long Story*, which adds little to Gray's character.

Several of his pieces were published (1753), with designs, by Mr. Bentley;* and, that they might in some form or other make a book, only one side of each leaf was printed. I believe the poems and the plates recommended each other so well, that the whole impression was soon bought. This year he lost his mother.

Some time afterwards (1756) some young men of the college, whose chambers were near his, diverted themselves with disturbing him by frequent and troublesome noises, and, as is said, by pranks yet more offensive and contemptuous. This insolence, having endured it a while, he represented to the governors of the society, among whom perhaps he had no friends; and, finding his complaint little regarded, removed himself to Pembroke-hall.

In 1757 he published *The Progress of Poetry* and *The Bard*, two compositions at which the readers of poetry were at first content to gaze in mute amazement. Some that tried them confessed their inability to understand them, though Warburton* said that they were understood as well as the works of Milton and Shakspeare, which it is the fashion to admire. Garrick wrote a few lines in their praise. Some hardy champions undertook to rescue them from neglect, and in a short time many were content to be shewn beauties which they could not see.

Gray's reputation was now so high, that, after the death of Cibber, he had the honour of refusing the laurel, which was then bestowed on Mr. Whitehead.*

His curiosity, not long after, drew him away from Cambridge to a lodging near the Museum, where he resided near three years, reading and transcribing; and, so far as can be discovered, very little affected by two odes on *Oblivion* and *Obscurity*, in which his Lyrick performances were ridiculed with much contempt and much ingenuity.*

When the Professor of Modern History at Cambridge died, he was, as he says, *cockered and spirited up*, till he asked it of lord Bute, who sent him a civil refusal; and the place was given to Mr. Brocket, the tutor of Sir James Lowther.*

His constitution was weak, and believing that his health was promoted by exercise and change of place, he undertook (1765) a journey into Scotland, of which his account, so far as it extends, is very curious and elegant; for as his comprehension was ample, his curiosity extended to all the works of art, all the appearances of nature, and all the monuments of past events. He naturally contracted a friendship with Dr. Beattie,* whom he found a poet, a philosopher, and a good man. The Mareschal College at Aberdeen offered him the degree of Doctor of Laws, which, having omitted to take it at Cambridge, he thought it decent to refuse.

What he had formerly solicited in vain, was at last given him without solicitation. The Professorship of History became again vacant, and he received (1768) an offer of it from the duke of Grafton.* He accepted, and retained it to his death; always designing lectures, but never reading them; uneasy at his neglect of duty, and appeasing his uneasiness with designs of reformation, and with a resolution which he believed himself to have made of resigning the office, if he found himself unable to discharge it.

Ill health made another journey necessary, and he visited (1769) Westmoreland and Cumberland. He that reads his epistolary narration wishes, that to travel, and to tell his travels, had been more of his employment; but it is by studying at home that we must obtain the ability of travelling with intelligence and improvement.

His travels and his studies were now near their end. The gout, of which he had sustained many weak attacks, fell upon his stomach, and, yielding to no medicines, produced strong convulsions, which (July 30, 1771) terminated in death.

His character I am willing to adopt, as Mr. Mason has done, from a Letter written to my friend Mr. Boswell, by the Rev. Mr. Temple, rector of St. Gluvias in Cornwall; and am as willing as his warmest well-wisher to believe it true.*

"Perhaps he was the most learned man in Europe. He was equally acquainted with the elegant and profound parts of science, and that not superficially but thoroughly. He knew every branch of history, both natural and civil; had read all the original historians of England, France, and Italy; and was a great antiquarian. Criticism, metaphysics, morals, politics, made a principal part of his study; voyages and travels of all sorts were his favourite amusements; and he had a fine taste in painting, prints, architecture, and gardening. With such a fund of knowledge, his conversation must have been equally instructing and entertaining; but he was also a good man, a man of virtue and humanity. There is no character without some speck, some imperfection; and I think the greatest defect in his was an affectation in delicacy, or rather effeminacy, and a visible fastidiousness, or contempt and disdain of his inferiors in science. He also had, in some degree, that weakness which disgusted Voltaire so much in Mr. Congreve: though he seemed to value others chiefly according to the progress they had made in knowledge, yet he could not bear to be considered himself merely as a man of letters; and though without birth, or fortune, or station, his desire was to be looked upon as a private independent gentleman, who read for his amusement. Perhaps it may be said, What signifies so much knowledge, when it produced so little? Is it worth taking so much pains to leave no memorial but a few poems? But let it be considered that Mr. Gray was, to others, at least innocently employed; to himself, certainly beneficially. His time passed agreeably; he was every day making some new acquisition in science; his mind was enlarged, his heart softened, his virtue strengthened; the world and mankind were shewn to him without a mask; and he was taught to consider every thing as trifling, and unworthy of the attention of a wise man, except the pursuit of knowledge and practice of virtue, in that state wherein God hath placed us."

To this character Mr. Mason has added a more particular account of Gray's skill in zoology. He has remarked, that Gray's effeminacy was affected most *before those whom he did not wish to please*; and that he is unjustly charged with making knowledge his sole reason of preference, as he paid his esteem to none whom he did not likewise believe to be good.

What has occurred to me, from the slight inspection of his Letters in which my undertaking has engaged me, is, that his mind had a large grasp; that his curiosity was unlimited, and his judgement cultivated; that he was a man likely to love much where he loved at all, but that he was fastidious and hard to please. His contempt however is often employed, where I hope it will be approved, upon scepticism and infidelity. His short account of Shaftesbury I will insert.*

"You say you cannot conceive how lord Shaftesbury came to be a philosopher in vogue; I will tell you: first, he was a lord; secondly, he was as vain as any of his readers; thirdly, men are very prone to believe what they do not understand; fourthly, they will believe any thing at all, provided they are under no obligation to believe it; fifthly, they love to take a new road, even when that road leads no where; sixthly, he was reckoned a fine writer, and seems always to mean more than he said. Would you have any more reasons? An interval of above forty years has pretty well destroyed the charm. A dead lord ranks with commoners: vanity is no longer interested in the matter; for a new road is become an old one."

Mr. Mason has added, from his own knowledge, that though Gray was poor, he was not eager of money; and that, out of the little that he had, he was very willing to help the necessitous.

As a writer he had this peculiarity, that he did not write his pieces first rudely, and then correct them, but laboured every line as it arose in the train of composition; and he had a notion not very peculiar, that he could not write but at certain times, or at happy moments; a fantastick foppery, to which my kindness for a man of learning and of virtue wishes him to have been superior.

GRAY's Poetry is now to be considered; and I hope not to be looked on as an enemy to his name, if I confess that I contemplate it with less pleasure than his life.

His ode on *Spring* has something poetical, both in the language and the thought; but the language is too luxuriant, and the thoughts have nothing new. There has of late arisen a practice of giving to adjectives, derived from substantives, the termination of participles; such as the *cultured* plain, the *dasied* bank; but I was sorry to see, in the lines of a scholar like Gray, the *honied* Spring. The morality is natural, but too stale; the conclusion is pretty.

The poem on the *Cat* was doubtless by its author considered as a trifle, but it is not a happy trifle. In the first stanza *the azure flowers* that *blow*, shew resolutely a rhyme is sometimes made when it cannot easily be found. *Selima*, the *Cat*, is called a nymph, with some violence both to language and sense; but there is good use made of it when it is done; for of the two lines,

> What female heart can gold despise?
> What cat's averse to fish?

the first relates merely to the nymph, and the second only to the cat. The sixth stanza contains a melancholy truth, that *a favourite has no friend*; but the last ends in a pointed sentence of no relation to the purpose; if *what glistered* had been *gold*, the cat would not have gone into the water; and, if she had, would not less have been drowned.

The *Prospect of Eton College* suggests nothing to Gray, which every beholder does not equally think and feel. His supplication to father *Thames*, to tell him who drives the hoop or tosses the ball, is useless and puerile. Father *Thames* has no better means of knowing than himself. His epithet *buxom health* is not elegant; he seems not to understand the word. Gray thought his language more poetical as it was more remote from common use: finding in Dryden *honey redolent of Spring*,* an expression that reaches the utmost limits of our language, Gray drove it a little more beyond common apprehension, by making *gales* to be *redolent of joy and youth*.

Of the *Ode on Adversity*, the hint was at first taken from *O Diva, gratum quæ regis Antium*;* but Gray has excelled his original by the variety of his sentiments, and by their moral application. Of this piece, at once poetical and rational, I will not by slight objections violate the dignity.

My process has now brought me to the *wonderful Wonder of Wonders*, the two Sister Odes; by which, though either vulgar ignorance or common sense at first universally rejected them, many have been since persuaded to think themselves delighted. I am one of those that are willing to be pleased, and therefore would gladly find the meaning of the first stanza of the *Progress of Poetry*.

Gray seems in his rapture to confound the images of *spreading sound* and *running water*. A *stream of musick* may be allowed; but where does *Musick*, however *smooth and strong*, after having visited the *verdant vales, rowl down the steep amain*, so as that *rocks and nodding groves rebellow to the roar?* If this be said of *Musick*, it is nonsense; if it be said of *Water*, it is nothing to the purpose.

The second stanza, exhibiting Mars's car and Jove's eagle, is unworthy of further notice. Criticism disdains to chase a schoolboy to his common places.

To the third it may likewise be objected, that it is drawn from Mythology, though such as may be more easily assimilated to real life. Idalia's *velvet-green* has something of cant. An epithet or metaphor drawn from Nature ennobles Art; an epithet or metaphor drawn from Art degrades Nature. Gray is too fond of words arbitrarily compounded. *Many-twinkling* was formerly censured as not analogical; we may say *many-spotted*, but scarcely *many-spotting*. This stanza, however, has something pleasing.

Of the second ternary of stanzas, the first endeavours to tell something, and would have told it, had it not been crossed by Hyperion: the second describes well enough the universal prevalence of Poetry; but I am afraid that the conclusion will not rise from the premises. The caverns of the North and the plains of Chili are not the residences of *Glory* and *generous Shame*. But that Poetry and Virtue go always together is an opinion so pleasing, that I can forgive him who resolves to think it true.

The third stanza sounds big with *Delphi*, and *Egean*, and *Ilissus*, and *Meander*, and *hallowed fountain* and *solemn sound*; but in all Gray's odes there is a kind of cumbrous splendor which we wish away. His position is at last false: in the time of Dante and Petrarch, from whom he derives our first school of Poetry, Italy was over-run by *tyrant power* and *coward vice*; nor was our state much better when we first borrowed the Italian arts.

Of the third ternary,* the first gives a mythological birth of Shakspeare. What is said of that mighty genius is true; but it is not said happily: the real effects of this poetical power are put out of sight by the pomp of machinery. Where truth is sufficient to fill the mind, fiction is worse than useless; the counterfeit debases the genuine.

His account of Milton's blindness, if we suppose it caused by study in the formation of his poem, a supposition surely allowable, is poetically true, and happily imagined. But the *car* of Dryden, with his *two coursers*, has nothing in it peculiar; it is a car in which any other rider may be placed.

The Bard appears, at the first view, to be, as Algarotti* and others have remarked, an imitation of the prophecy of Nereus. Algarotti thinks it superior to its original; and, if preference depends only on the imagery and animation of the two poems, his judgement is right. There is in *The Bard* more force, more thought, and more variety. But to copy is less than to invent, and the copy has been unhappily produced at a wrong time. The fiction of Horace was to the Romans credible; but its revival disgusts us with apparent and unconquerable falsehood. *Incredulus odi.**

To select a singular event, and swell it to a giant's bulk by fabulous appendages of spectres and predictions, has little difficulty, for he that forsakes the probable may always find the marvellous. And it has little use; we are affected only as we believe; we are improved only as we find something to be imitated or declined. I do not see that *The Bard* promotes any truth, moral or political.

His stanzas are too long, especially his epodes;* the ode is finished before the ear has learned its measures, and consequently before it can receive pleasure from their consonance and recurrence.

Of the first stanza the abrupt beginning has been celebrated; but technical beauties can give praise only to the inventor. It is in the power of any man to rush abruptly upon his subject, that has read the ballad of *Johnny Armstrong*,

Is there ever a man in all Scotland—

The initial resemblances, or alliterations, *ruin*, *ruthless*, *helm nor hauberk*, are below the grandeur of a poem that endeavours at sublimity.

In the second stanza the *Bard* is well described; but in the third we have the puerilities of obsolete mythology. When we are told that *Cadwallo hush'd the stormy main*, and that *Modred* made *huge Plinlimmon bow his cloud-top'd head*, attention recoils from the repetition of a tale that, even when it was first heard, was heard with scorn.

The *weaving* of the *winding sheet* he borrowed, as he owns, from the northern Bards; but their texture, however, was very properly the work of female powers, as the art of spinning the thread of life in another mythology. Theft is always dangerous; Gray has made weavers of his slaughtered bards, by a fiction outrageous and incongruous. They are then called upon to *Weave the warp, and weave the woof*, perhaps with no great propriety; for it is by crossing the *woof* with the *warp* that men *weave* the *web* or piece; and the first line was dearly bought by the admission of its wretched correspondent, *Give ample room and verge enough*. He has, however, no other line as bad.

The third stanza of the second ternary is commended, I think, beyond its merit. The personification is indistinct. *Thirst* and *Hunger* are not alike; and their features, to make the imagery perfect, should have been discriminated. We are told, in the same stanza, how *towers* are *fed*. But I will no longer look for particular faults; yet let it be observed that the ode might have been concluded with an action of better example; but suicide is always to be had, without expence of thought.

These odes are marked by glittering accumulations of ungraceful ornaments; they strike, rather than please; the images are magnified by affectation; the language is laboured into harshness. The mind of the writer seems to work with unnatural violence. *Double, double, toil and trouble*. He has a kind of strutting dignity, and is tall by walking on tiptoe. His art and his struggle are too visible, and there is too little appearance of ease and nature.

To say that he has no beauties, would be unjust: a man like him, of great learning and great industry, could not but produce something valuable. When he pleases least, it can only be said that a good design was ill directed.

His translations of Northern and Welsh Poetry deserve praise; the imagery is preserved, perhaps often improved; but the language is unlike the language of other poets.

In the character of his Elegy I rejoice to concur with the common reader; for by the common sense of readers uncorrupted with literary prejudices, after all the refinements of subtilty and the dogmatism of learning, must be finally decided all claim to poetical honours. The *Church-yard* abounds with images which find a mirrour in every mind, and with sentiments to which every bosom returns an echo. The four stanzas beginning *Yet even these bones*, are to me original: I have never seen the notions in any other place; yet he that reads them here, persuades himself that he has always felt them. Had Gray written often thus, it had been vain to blame, and useless to praise him.

APPENDIX

In his essay on *Rochester* Johnson quotes a Latin poem by Jean Passerat (pp. 119-20). This English translation is kindly provided by Leofranc Holford-Strevens.

Poem by the famous man JEAN PASSERAT,
Regius Professor in the University of Paris.
To the most talented man HENRI DE MESMES.

January is here, the festive Kalends demand their gifts; but I have no present that I can offer on the festive Kalends. Has the water of the Castalian spring [poetic inspiration] so dried up for me? Are my mental faculties so exhausted that the doorkeeper of the returning year should see them without a gift? Rather, that which is nowhere I shall seek by a new path.

But lo! while turning in all directions my muse has found NOTHING, do not despise the gift. For NOTHING is more precious than jewels, NOTHING than gold. Hither therefore turn your attention, turn your well-disposed countenance: a new subject is being spoken of heard by none of our predecessors; the Roman and Greek bards said the rest, but NOTHING was unsaid by the Roman and Greek Muse.

Wherever Ceres looks from the sky at her fields, or Father Ocean embraces the world in his liquid arms, NOTHING is without death and beginning, NOTHING immortal, NOTHING fortunate in all respects. But if from this the divine majesty and might are judged, shall we deem anything worthy of the honours we give the gods, or their altars? NOTHING is pleasanter than the sight of life-giving light, NOTHING than spring, NOTHING more beautiful than a watered garden, more flowery than meadows, gentler than the West Wind's breeze; NOTHING is protected in war, and the uproar of Mars; NOTHING is just in peace, NOTHING is secure in a treaty. Happy is he that has nothing (this was Tibullus' wish); he does not fear deceit; he scorns thieves and fires; he pursues worrisome lawsuits before no judge. Even that sage of Zeno's who submits all things to the unconquerable fates wonders at and desires NOTHING. And of old this was the knowledge of the Socratic crew, that they knew NOTHING, which is now the only object sought, nor does youth in school prefer to learn anything else, since it leads to great wealth and the height of honours. Recognize NOTHING, and you will recognize what is said to adhere to the seed of the Pythagorean bean, to which is attached the voice of the denier. [Latin *nihil* was said to come from *hilum*, understood as a by-form of *filum*, 'thread', with a negative prefix; Pythagoreans, according to most authorities, refused to eat beans.] Many, relying on Mercury [i.e. Hermes Trismegistus] for a leader, melt the pure entrails of the earth, pouring in their inheritances, intent on the secret work [of alchemy] and black coal; in the end, worn out by losses and broken by toil, they find NOTHING and having found it look everywhere for it. No surveyor's pole can measure it, nor could he count it who knew the number of the African sands; even to Phoebus is NOTHING unknown, NOTHING is higher than the stars. And you, though you have outstanding sharpness of mind, penetrating all nature and the secrets of nature, by your leave, de Mesmes, you appear ignorant of NOTHING. But NOTHING is brighter than the sun, and pure fire. Touch NOTHING, and you will say that NOTHING is touched without body. See NOTHING, and you will say that NOTHING is seen without colour. NOTHING is deaf but hears, and speaks without a voice, and flies without the help of wings, and walks without any legs. NOTHING wanders through the void without place and motion. NOTHING is more useful to the human race than the art of healing. Therefore, let him whose empty breast has been pierced by an Idalian arrow [i.e. Cupid's dart] not try bullroarers, or the Thessalian noises [the clash of cymbals], nor pick Dictaean herbs on the summit of Mt. Ida; NOTHING relieves the wounds of cruel love. And whomever the boatman has transported across the gloomy waters, NOTHING will recall to those above from the depths of Hades. NOTHING sways the breast of the king below, and the spindles of the Fates and their inexorable spinning. The Titan youth, smothered on the Phlegraean Fields, learnt that NOTHING is more powerful than the striking of a thunderbolt; NOTHING extends beyond the walls of the great universe; and the gods fear NOTHING. Why should I mention more things to extend my poem? NOTHING is superior to virtue itself, NOTHING is more glorious; lastly, nothing is GREATER than Jupiter. But it is time to put an end to these clever trifles: lest, if I take much paper to praise my poetry, from NOTHING my verses produce boredom with NOTHING.

EXPLANATORY NOTES

In preparing these notes I have relied extensively on Roger Lonsdale's marvellously detailed annotations to his OUP edition of Johnson's *Lives* (hereafter Lonsdale). Many of these constitute short, self-contained essays on aspects of Johnson's thought. Readers who wish, for instance, to explore Johnson's sources, or the relations between individual *Lives* and the rest of Johnson's *oeuvre*, are recommended to the notes in Lonsdale's edition.

ADVERTISEMENT

3 *like those ... Miscellanies*: this is a somewhat obscure reference to a French compilation, *Recueil des plus belles pieces des poëtes francois tant anciens que modernes, avec l'histoire de leur vie*, republished in 1752, and probably written by Bernard de Fonyenelle. The point is that these were brief biographical accounts followed by even briefer critical assessments.

Langbaine: Gerard Langbaine (1656–92) was author of *An Account of the English Dramatick Poets* (1691) (hereafter Langbaine), a biographical dictionary of English playwrights and a survey of their plays.

Dryden's Remarks on Rymer: Thomas Rymer (1642/3–1713) debated the status of Shakespeare with Dryden. Dryden responded to Rymer's *The Tragedies of the Last Age Consider'd* (1678) with his unpublished 'Heads of an Answer to Rymer'.

Mr. Steevens: Shakespeare commentator and editor George Steevens (1736–1800) collaborated with Johnson on his edition of Shakespeare.

Mr. Spence's Collections: one of Johnson's main sources, particularly for his 'Pope', was the manuscript of *Anecdotes and Characters of Books and Men, Collected from Conversation*, compiled by Joseph Spence (1699–1768). It was finally published in 1820.

COWLEY

5 *Dr. Sprat*: Thomas Sprat (1635–1713) was a clergyman and man of letters, who eventually became bishop of Rochester. He is best known for his celebratory *History of the Royal Society* (1667). As a young man and a would-be poet Sprat had befriended Cowley. In 1668, the year after Cowley's death, he published an edition of Cowley's *English Works*, in accordance with the poet's wishes. Prefixed to this was 'An account of the life and writing'. He also composed Cowley's epitaph in Westminster Abbey. Sprat was himself one of the authors included in Johnson's *Lives*.

sectary: a Protestant Dissenter, who did not belong to the Church of England. There is no evidence for this.

Wood: Anthony Wood in his *Athenae Oxonienses* (2 vols., 1691–2).

Sir Joshua Reynolds: as well as the most renowned portrait painter of the age, Reynolds (1723–92) was a friend of Johnson's and a fellow member of 'the Club'.

6 *"to lisp in numbers"*: see Alexander Pope, *Epistle to Dr Arbuthnot*, l. 128.

Sir Kenelm Digby: Digby (1603–65) was an author, diplomat, and keen natural philosopher. He was a patron of poets, notably of Ben Jonson.

7 *Dr. Comber*: Thomas Comber (1575–1654) was Master of Trinity College, Cambridge, from 1631 to 1644.

prevalence: influence.

St. John's College in Oxford: Oxford was a Royalist stronghold and the King had been established there since late 1642.

Lord Falkland: Lucius Cary, second Viscount Falkland (1610–43), was the centre of a literary coterie based at his home at Great Tew, near Oxford. Amongst those whose company he cultivated were Ben Jonson, the poets Sir John Suckling and Edmund Waller, and the philosopher Thomas Hobbes. He was killed fighting for Charles I at the battle of Newbury in September 1643.

Lord Jermin: Henry Jermyn, Earl of St Albans (1605–84), was Lord Chamberlain to Charles I's wife, Queen Henrietta Maria. He accompanied her when she left Oxford for France in April 1644 and helped her raise money for the Royalist cause.

Laura: Francesco Petrarca (1304–74) celebrated 'Laura' in his love poetry, but her true identity is unknown.

8 *Barnes*: the Latin preface of the 1705 edition of Anacreon by Joshua Barnes (1654–1712), professor of Greek at Cambridge.

"airy nothing": see *A Midsummer Night's Dream*, v. i. 16.

"dream of a shadow": from Cowley's own poem 'Life and Fame'.

Mr. Bennet . . . Brown: Henry Bennet, secretary to Charles II's brother, James, Duke of York, from 1649 to 1658, and from 1665 earl of Arlington. He had been at school with Cowley. 'Brown' is Thomas Brown, who published his collection *Miscellanea Aulica; or, A Collection of state treatises, never before publish'd* in 1702.

9 *the Virgilian lots*: *sortes Virgilianae*, the selection by chance of lines from Virgil supposed to foretell the future. It was common in the Middle Ages, when Virgil was often thought to have prophetic status.

9 *Dr. Scarborow*: Charles Scarburgh (1615–94) was a physician and natural philosopher. He was a notable Royalist and was knighted by Charles II in 1669.

10 *the death of Oliver*: Oliver Cromwell died on 3 September 1658.

11 *Dr. Birch*: Thomas Birch (1705–66), author of a *History of the Royal Society* (1756–7).

May's poem: this refers to Thomas May's 1630 continuation in Latin of Lucan's *Pharsalia*, a work that he had already translated. May (1596–1650) was a noted Latinist who also translated Virgil's *Georgics* and Martial's epigrams.

a Song of Triumph: Cowley's *Ode, upon the Blessed Restoration and Returne of His Sacred Majesty, Charles the Second*, published on 31 May 1660.

the Mastership of the Savoy: the Savoy was a charity hospital in the Strand. The Mastership was a remunerative sinecure.

12 *Downes the prompter*: Thomas Downes (d. 1712?) was prompter to the Duke's Company from the 1660s, and a member of Betterton's Company from 1694 until his retirement in 1706. He produced the most thorough and detailed history of Restoration theatre, *Roscius Anglicanus* (1708).

Suckling: Sir John Suckling (1609–41), courtier and poet. His 'Session of the Poets', composed around 1637 and published posthumously in his *Fragmenta Aurea* (1646), seems to have originated the satirical genre of imagined competitions between named poets.

13 *the duke of Buckingham*: George Villiers, second Duke of Buckingham (1628–87), a leading courtier during the reign of Charles II, an author and a patron of poets.

To Dr. THOMAS SPRAT: for the provenance of this letter, see Lonsdale, i. 320.

14 *Monstri simile*: monstrous behaviour.

the Dean: William Fuller, Dean of St Patrick's Cathedral from 1660.

Verbum sapienti: a shortened version of the Latin saying *Verbum sapienti satis est*: 'a word is enough to the wise'.

15 *the metaphysical poets*: this was an established usage by Johnson's day. The *OED* records William Drummond, as early as 1641, describing the attempts of some poets to reform poetry by trying 'to abstracte her to Metaphysical Ideas'. See Introduction, p. xxiv, for further discussion of the term.

the father of criticism: Aristotle. His theory of imitation is outlined in ch. 8 of his *Poetics*, though he does not use the actual phrase that Johnson cites.

Dryden confesses: see Dryden's 'Discourse of Satire' (1693), where he says that 'if we are not so great wits as Donne, yet certainly we are better poets', in John Dryden, *Of Dramatic Poesy and Other Critical Essays*, ed. George Watson, 2 vols. (1962), ii. 144.

"that which ... never before so well expressed": Pope, *Essay on Criticism*, ll. 297–8.

16 *discordia concors*: harmonious discord. The phrase inverts the phrase *concordia discors*, which has a similar meaning and is associated with the doctrines of the Greek philosophers Pythagoras and Heraclitus. The actual phrase was first used by Horace in his *Epistles*, bk. 1, ep. 12.

Epicurean deities: a reference to the belief of the philosopher-poet Lucretius that the gods are indifferent spectators of human actions.

17 *Marino*: Giambattista Marino (1569–1625), an Italian poet renowned for his ornate style.

ruggedness: irregular rhythm.

his lines upon Hobson the Carrier: Milton's two poems 'On the University Carrier'.

18 *The sacred tree ... outshine*: from 'The Tree of Knowledge', ll. 1–8.

Love was ... rage: 'Elegie upon Anacreon', ll. 33–8.

Variety I ask not ... in it: 'Resolved to be beloved', ll. 21–4.

19 *In every thing ... or said*: John Donne, 'To the Countess of Bedford I', ll. 21–8.

This twilight ... shew'd me you: 'To the Countess of Bedford IV', ll. 1–10.

If men be worlds ... soul is: 'To Mr. R.W. III', ll. 29–32.

To a lady ... wit: 'To a lady who made poesies for rings', ll. 25–32.

20 *Five years ago ... forbid*: 'Inconstancy', ll. 1–14.

Hast thou not found ... stone: 'The Welcome', ll. 13–24.

The fate of Egypt ... heart below: 'Sleep', ll. 10–14.

21 *And yet this death ... breath*: 'The Concealment', ll. 23–8.

Th' ungovern'd parts ... arose: *Davideis*, bk. 1, in Abraham Cowley, *Poems*, ed. A. R Waller (Cambridge, 1905), 253. All subsequent references to the *Davideis* in this edition are to *Poems*.

On a round ball ... so: Donne, 'A Valediction of Weeping', ll. 10–18.

Here lies a she sun ... owe: 'An Epithelamium ... on the Lady Elizabeth', ll. 85–8.

22 *Though God be … near*: 'Obsequies to the Lord Harrington', 35–8.

Since 'tis my doom … Gregorian: John Cleveland, 'To Julia to expedite her promise', ll. 1–4 and 10–18. Cleveland (1613–58) was renowned for use of far-fetched conceits, a habit which became known as 'Clevelandism' (a word coined by Dryden). He was, however, widely read and admired in the seventeenth century.

By every wind … get to you: 'Friendship in Absence', ll. 39–42.

In tears I'll waste … punished: 'The Despair', ll. 4–6.

All arm'd in brass … bright: *Davideis*, bk. III (*Poems*, 333–4).

23 *His bloody eyes … sound*: ibid., bk. I (*Poems*, 258).

Of his Mistress … set there: 'Bathing in the River', ll. 1–7.

My name … it was: 'A Valediction: of my name in the window', ll. 1–4.

On an inconstant woman … May: 'Ode. In Imitation of Horaces Ode Lib. I Od. 5', ll. 19–24.

24 *Nothing yet … rows*: 'Written in Juice of Lemmon', ll. 31–6.

Physick and Chirurgery … grow: 'Counsel', ll. 1–6.

The World … part: *Davideis*, bk. I (*Poems*, 260–1).

25 *The moderate value … our sun*: 'News from Newcastle: Upon the Coal-Pits about Newcastle-upon-Tyne', ll. 21–36. Though printed in early editions of Cleveland's works, this is now attributed to Thomas Winnard.

Death … share: 'Elegie on the L.C.', ll. 13–16.

A Lover … in me?: 'The Despair', ll. 25–36.

26 *A Lover's heart … take*: 'The given Heart', ll. 9–16.

The poetical Propagation … desire: 'Eclogue. 1613. December 26', ll. 23–32.

Thou in my fancy … thee: 'Against Fruition', ll. 17–20.

In none but us … that's none: 'To the Countesse of Bedford III', ll. 43–7.

27 *That which I should … post*: 'To Mr. B.B.', ll. 10–14.

Think in how … now: 'The Second Anniversarie', ll. 173–84.

Thou tyrant … me: 'Beauty', ll. 34–6.

Thou who … man: 'The Parting', ll. 21–4.

28 *Though in thy thoughts … sleep*: 'The Innocent III', ll. 12–19.

The true taste ... mine: 'Twicknam Garden', ll. 19–22.

As the sweet sweat ... defiles: 'Elegie VIII', ll. 1–7.

As men in hell ... thee: 'The Usurpation', ll. 33–6.

It gave a piteous groan ... Venice-glass: 'The Heartbreaking', ll. 1–4.

29 *Dryden's Night*: in Dryden's play *The Indian Emperor*, III. ii. 1 ff.

Thou seest me ... seest me: Donne, 'Obsequies to the Lord Harrington', ll. 15–25.

30 *Hope ... waste*: 'Against Hope', ll. 1–20.

Our two souls ... I begun: 'A Valediction: forbidding mourning', ll. 21–36.

31 *Yet 'tis not ... galaxy*: Cowley, 'Ode. Of Wit', ll. 33–40.

lord Falkland: see note to p. 7, above.

Sir Henry Wotton: Sir Henry Wotton (1568–1639) was a diplomat and author, a cousin of Francis Bacon and a close friend of John Donne.

Hervey: William Hervey (d. 1642) was a close friend of Cowley at Trinity College, Cambridge. He was a naval commander in actions against the Spanish under Elizabeth I.

32 *Davenant*: see note to p. 77, below.

two metrical disquisitions: Cowley's 'The Tree of Knowledge' and 'Reason. The use of it in Divine Matters'. He quotes ll. 33–40 of the latter.

Bentley: Dr Richard Bentley (1662–1742), classical scholar, Fellow of the Royal Society and, from 1700, Master of Trinity College, Cambridge. The poem that Johnson refers to is 'A Reply to a Copy of Verses made in Imitation of Ode II. Book III. of Horace'.

34 *Addison*: the passage quoted is assembled from different comments, including some from the *Spectator*, 62 (1711).

35 *Sanazarro ... meas*: Giacomo Sannazaro (1458–1530) was a Neapolitan poet. The quotation is from his *Epigrammata*, i. 64, 'Ad Vesbiam'. 'See how torn apart I am with cares, Vesbia: I burn, and alas! fluid pours from my fire. I am Nile, and I am Etna; quench my flames, O tears, or, flame, drink up my tears' [trans. L. Holford-Strevens].

Pancirolus: Guido Panciroli (1523–99), author of *Rerum Memorabilium iam Olim Deperditatum* (1599), cited by Cowley in his Preface to his 'Pindarique Odes'.

36 *the Nemeæan ode*: 'The First Nemean Ode of Pindar', ll. 5–6 and 54–6.

the Olympionick: 'The Second Olympique Ode', ll. 180–7.

37 *Begin the song ... sound*: from Cowley's 'The Resurrection'. Johnson quotes from several different parts of the poem.

38 *secundine*: placenta or afterbirth.

Casimir ... in annos: Mathias Casimir (1595–1640), a Polish poet. The lines quoted are from his *Lyricorum* (1625), Od. I. iii. 'In every hour the Lord of the world fits on wings to be driven through the void; some are still hidden in the nest, and grow for future years' [trans. L. Holford-Strevens].

new dies the waters name: 'The Plagues of Egypt', st. 17.

Albion no more... white: 'To Dr. Scarborough', l. 6.

the noblest and highest ... verse: Preface to 'Pindarique Odes'.

39 *Nay, if thou lov'st ... without it*: 'To the New Year', ll. 37–48.

cry out with Prior... style!: see Matthew Prior, *An English Ballad* (1695), ll. 95–6. Prior (1664–1721) was a diplomat and successful poet, noted for burlesques, occasional verses, and mild satires. He was included in Johnson's *Lives*.

the highest and noblest ... verse: Johnson quotes again from Cowley's 'Preface' (see note to p. 38, above).

40 *a poem on the Sheldonian Theatre*: Corbett Owen's Lattin ode *Carmen Pindaricum in Theatro Sheldonia* (1669), which was recited at the opening of the Sheldonian Theatre in Oxford, designed by Christopher Wren. *Musae Anglicanae* was a miscellany of poems published in 1692.

the third part: in his Preface to this epic poem retelling the Old Testament story of David, published in 1656, Cowley explains that he completed only four of the twelve books that he originally planned.

Rymer: Thomas Rymer (1642/3–1713), critic and historian. He was an advocate of strict neoclassical decorum and was often dismissive of Shakespeare's drama. He is best known for Dryden's dispute with him on this issue.

41 *He spake the word, and they were made*: Psalm 148: 5.

Saul was troubled ... spirit: 1 Samuel 16: 14.

42 *Saxum circumspicit ... arvis*: Virgil, *Aeneid*, xii. 896–8. 'Then looking around he sees a giant stone, an ancient giant stone, which by chance lay on the plain, set as a landmark, to prevent dispute over the fields.'

45 *Rymer has declared ... pedantry*: from Rymer's preface to Rapin's *Reflections on Aristotle's Treatise of Poesie* (1674).

46 *Denham in his elegy*: Denham, 'On Mr Cowley His Death', ll. 7–8.

Clarendon represents him ... before him: Edward Hyde, first Earl of Clarendon (1609–74), politician and historian. After the Restoration of Charles II he became Lord Chancellor and his daughter married the King's brother, James, Duke of York. For these particular comments, see *The Life of Edward Earl of Clarendon* (1759), 16.

47 *the noble epigram of Grotius upon the death of Scaliger*: Hugo Grotius, 'In Mortem Scaligeri Epicedia' (1617). The scholar and critic Julius Caesar Scaliger (1484–1558) was famous for his encyclopedic learning. Hugo Grotius (1583–1645) was a Dutch philosopher and statesman, best known for his treatise on the philosophy of law *De jure Belli ac Pacis* (1625). He wrote mostly in Latin.

Although I think ... way: 'Maidenhead', ll. 25–32.

Some that have ... night: 'Love's Alchymie', ll. 1–12.

Dr. Hurd: Richard Hurd (1720–1808), clergyman and literary critic. His most important work was his *Letters on Chivalry and Romance* (1762), which stimulated a new interest in medieval and Renaissance literature. He eventually became Bishop of Worcester. For the comments on Donne and Jonson, see Hurd, *Select Works* (1722), i. 63.

48 *His spear ... should be*: *Davideis*, bk. III (*Poems*, 334).

His spear ... walk'd with: *Paradise Lost*, i. 292–5.

49 *One flings ... with't*: *Davideis*, bk. III (*Poems*, 333).

50 *Where honour ... knell*: 'Ode upon Liberty', ll. 95–110.

Round the whole earth ... found: *Davideis*, bk. II (*Poems*, 305).

Yet bid him ... back: *Davideis*, bk. I (*Poems*, 252).

Nor can the glory ... endless space: bk. I (*Poems*, 251). For the note see *Poems*, 273.

51 *quis musas colunt severiores*: Cowley's adaptation of a line from Martial's *Epigrams*, IX. xi. 17: 'who court Muses more unbending'.

52 *Begin, be bold ... run on*: from Cowley's translation of Horace's *Epistle* I. ii. 40 ff.

May and Sandys: for May, see note to p. 11, above. George Sandys (1578–1644) was best known for his translation of Ovid's *Metamorphoses*, published in 1626. It was written in heroic couplets and enjoyed considerable esteem in the seventeenth and early eighteenth centuries.

53 *Felton*: Henry Felton (1679–1740), clergyman and theological writer, published his *Dissertation on Reading the Classics, and Forming a Just Style* in 1709. It is to this work that Johnson refers: see 2nd edn. (1715), 31.

MILTON

54 *Mr. Fenton's elegant Abridgement*: Elijah Fenton (1683–1730), poet and translator, wrote a short biography of Milton that was prefaced to the 12th edition of *Paradise Lost* (1725). He is best known as a collaborator with Pope, and the translator of bks. I, IV, XIX, and XX of Pope's *Odyssey*.

literature: defined by Johnson in his *Dictionary* as 'Learning; skill in letters'.

secondary: a deputy.

55 *Thomas Young*: Thomas Young (*c.*1587–1655) was a Church of England clergyman. He had Puritan sympathies and would go on to collaborate with others in published attacks on the rule of bishops under the name 'Smectymnuus'. In 1644 he became Master of Jesus College, Cambridge. Milton addressed his Latin 'Elegy IV' to Young.

Mr. Gill: Alexander Gill (1565–1635) was appointed high master of St Paul's School, London, in 1608.

a sizar: an undergraduate who received an allowance from the College which allowed him to study and in return for which he had to perform some menial duties for other students. Milton was not in fact a sizar but a 'lesser pensioner'.

Politian: Angelo Poliziano (1454–94) , named after his birthplace of Montepulciano in Tuscany, was a classical scholar and translator, renowned in his youth for his prodigious learning. He went on to compose his own Latin and Greek verse.

Mr. Hampton, the translator of Polybius: James Hampton (1721–78) was a clergyman and scholar whose translation of Polybius' *General History* was widely admired.

Haddon and Ascham: Walter Haddon (1515–72) was a scholar and courtier, employed as an adviser by Elizabeth I. In his own day his Latin verses were much admired. Roger Ascham (1515–68), an author and tutor to Princess Elizabeth, the future Elizabeth I, was a friend of Haddon's. A noted classicist, he was Latin secretary to Queen Mary. He is best known for his educational book *The Scholemaster*, written in English and published posthumously in 1570.

Alabaster's Roxana: *Roxana* (1632), a tragedy in Latin by William Alabaster (1568–1640). Alabaster was celebrated by contemporaries for his Latin verse.

56 *his own verses to Diodati*: Milton's 'Elegy I', addressed to schoolfriend Charles Diodati.

Me tenet … fruor: 'I am in the city which the Thames washes with its tides, and I am happy to be detained in the dear place where I was born. At present

I feel no inclination to return to the reedy Cam and no longing for forbidden quarters there.... It is hateful constantly to be subject to the threats of a stern tutor, and other things which my spirit cannot endure. If this be exile—to be back in my paternal home and to be free of cares and enjoying welcome leisure—then I do not object to the name or the condition of a fugitive and am glad to enjoy my banishment.'

His scheme of education ... Hartlib: Milton's *Of Education* (1644). Its dedicatee was Samuel Hartlib (*c.*1600–62), an educational reformer with strong Puritan sympathies.

his Discourse: *On the Likeliest Means to remove Hirelings* (1659).

57 *"subscribe slave ... forswearing"*: Johnson quotes from Milton's *The Reason of Church Government* (1642).

the Articles: the Thirty-Nine Articles of Religion of the Church of England. These Articles, first laid down in 1563, listed the key doctrines of the Anglican faith. Subscription to the Articles meant swearing adherence to them, a necessity for any individual taking Holy Orders.

58 *Homer's Circe*: see Homer, *The Odyssey*, bk. x.

a quo ... aquis: Ovid, *Amores*, III. ix. 25–6: 'from whom as from a perennial plant the lips of poets are bedewed with Pierian waters.'

Mr. King: Edward King (1611/12–37), a Fellow of Christ's College, Cambridge, was a friend of Milton's who drowned when the ship on which he was travelling to Ireland struck rocks off the coast of Anglesey. He was commemorated in a collection of poems published in Cambridge in 1638. Some of these were in Latin or Greek; others were in English, and the last of these in the book was Milton's 'Lycidas'.

Harefield ... entertainment: Milton's 'Arcades' was an entertainment, composed of songs and a poetic address, with music contributed by Milton's friend Henry Lawes. It was presented by Milton to Alice, Dowager Countess of Derby, who was in her seventies and had often before been addressed by poets (Spenser's *Tears of the Muses* (1591) had been dedicated to her). Her second husband was Sir Thomas Egerton, Lord Keeper; her daughter by her first marriage married his son, who later became the earl of Bridgewater, for whom *Comus* was written. Harefield was 12 miles from Milton's home at Horton.

Sir Henry Wotton's directions: for Sir Henry Wotton, see note to p. 31, above.

Lord Scudamore: John, Viscount Scudamore (1601–71), the English ambassador in Paris.

Grotius: see note to p. 47, above. Grotius was the Swedish ambassador in Paris at this time.

59 *"by labour . . . it die"*: Johnson quotes from Milton's *The Reason of Church Government* (1642).

Carlo Dati . . . Francini: Carlo Dati and Antonio Francini both became friends of Milton during his stay in Florence. Dati, who had studied under Galileo and was only 18 when Milton met him, was the secretary of a private Florentine academy called the *Apatisti*, or 'the passionless'. Francini was another member. Dati continued to correspond with Milton after his return to England. Both men are commemorated in Milton's Latin poem 'Epitaphium Damonis', l. 137.

59 *Holstenius . . . Cardinal Barberini*: Hortensius was the Latinized name of Lucas Holste or Holstein (1596–1661), German scholar and man of letters. He was librarian in the household of Cardinal Francesco Barberini (1597–1678), before taking charge of the Vatican Library. A convert to Roman Catholicism, he sometimes acted as a diplomat on behalf of the Vatican. Barberini was papal nuncio; his was the greatest private library in Rome. He was one of the two members of the tribunal judging Galileo who refused to sign the condemnation of him.

Selvaggi . . . Salsilli: Salsilli is Giovanni Salzilli; about him and Selvaggi little is known. Milton composed a Latin poem to Salzilli, 'Ad Salsillum poetam Romanum aegrotantem' (To Salzilli, a Roman poet, in his illness).

non tam de se, quam supra se: 'not so much about him as above him'. Johnson is quoting from Milton's own preface to the Latin poems in his *Poems* of 1645.

60 *a hermit . . . Manso*: an eremite friar accompanied Milton and introduced him to Giovanni Batista Manso, Marquis of Villa (1560?–1645), who had been a patron of Tasso. Manso himself wrote poems, dialogues on love and beauty, and a *Life of Tasso*. Milton's Latin poem addressed to him was 'Mansus', composed in 1639 and published in the *Poems* of 1645.

visiting Galileo: Milton mentions his meeting with Galileo in *Areopagitica* (Milton, *Complete Prose Works*, ed. D. M. Wolpe et al. (New Haven, 1953–82), ii. 538) and refers to him with apparent admiration as a pioneer of the telescope in *Paradise Lost*, i. 288 and v. 262. At the time of their likely meeting, Galileo was under house arrest outside Florence.

John Diodati and Frederick Spanheim: Jean Diodati was a Protestant theologian and the uncle of Milton's friend Charles Diodati. Friedrich Spanheim (1600–49) was a philologist and Calvinist theologian. He was rector of the Academy of Geneva at the time of Milton's visit to the city.

Charles Diodati: Charles Diodati (1609/10–38) was a schoolfriend of Milton's at St Paul's. He moved to Geneva in 1630 where he studied theology. He returned to England, where he died in 1638, while Milton was in Geneva. Milton wrote a commemorative poem in Latin, *Epitaphium Damonis*, privately printed *c.*1640. It is a pastoral elegy.

61 *Georgick*: the genre of classical poetry describing husbandry and agriculture. The most famous example is Virgil's *Georgics*.

projectors: innovators.

62 *Ὅττι τοι ἐν μεγάροισι κακόν τ' ἀγαθόντε τέτυκται*: Homer, IV. 392: 'whatever good or evil has come about in royal halls'.

its only genuine product: in fact, both of Milton's nephews were fairly prolific authors. The work to which Johnson refers appears to be an essay in Latin on the history of poetry appended to Phillips's edition of Johann Buchler's *Sacrarum profanarumque phrasium poeticarum thesaurus* (1669).

a treatise of Reformation: Milton's *Of Reformation Touching Church-Discipline in England* (1641).

63 *Hall bishop of Norwich*: Joseph Hall (1574–1656), whose *Humble Remonstrance*, defending the powers of bishops, was published in 1641. Five ministers contributed to the rejoinder.

the learned Usher: James Ussher (1581–1656), Archbishop of Armagh, wrote a series of works designed to demonstrate that episcopacy—the rule of bishops—was authorized by the practice of the early Christian Church. The first of these works was *The judgement of Doctor Rainolds touching the original of episcopacy* (1641), which provoked Milton to *Of Prelatical Episcopacy* (1641).

"This ... expectation": Johnson quotes from *The Reason of Church Government*, see *Prose Works*, i. 820–1. He might have found the passage in Thomas Birch's 1738 edition of Milton's *Works*, vol. i, p. xx.

two more pamphlets: Milton attacked Hall bitterly in *Animadversions upon the Remonstrant's Defence Against Smectymnuus*. The second pamphlet, from which Johnson quotes rather loosely, was Milton's *An apology against a pamphlet called 'A modest confutation of a scandalous and scurrilous libel entitled Animadversions'*, a rejoinder to an anonymous pamphlet attacking him personally. It included the charge that he had been expelled from Cambridge.

64 *hell grows darker at his frown*: see *Paradise Lost*, ii. 719–20.

Reading was taken by Essex: the town of Reading was taken by the Parliamentary force of Robert Devereux, Earl of Essex, on 26 April 1643.

he married Mary, the daughter of Mr Powel: in fact Milton married Mary Powell in July 1642, when he was 33 and she was 17.

as Philips relates: Johnson found Edward Phillips's account in Thomas Birch's 1738 edition of Milton's *Works* (hereafter Birch), vol. i, p. xxii.

Lady Margaret Leigh: Lady Margaret Ley, the daughter of James, Earl of Marlborough, was the addressee of Milton's 'Sonnet X'.

65 *"but that house ... dismiss him"*: Johnson took the words of Anthony Wood from Birch, vol. i, p. xxiii.

a Serving man turned Solicitor: Milton applied such a description to the anonymous author of an *Answer* to his *Clasterion.*

65 *Howel in his letters*: James Howell, *Epistolae Ho-Elianae. Familiar Letters Domestic and Forren*, mostly written when the author was in the Fleet Prison, and published in varying editions during the 1640s and 1650s. A moderate Anglican, Howell was an antagonist of Puritan reform.

two sonnets: Milton's Sonnets XI and XII.

66 *Areopagitica ... unlicensed Printing*: Milton's *Areopagitica*, published in November 1644, was a response to the Act for the Licensing of the Press, introduced in June 1644.

67 *he removed ... Fields*: in fact Milton did not move to this house until August or September 1647.

a treatise to justify it: *The Tenure of Kings and Magistrates*, published a fortnight after Charles I's execution on 30 January 1649.

Icon Basilike: the title means 'the image of the king'. Subtitled 'The True Portraiture of His Sacred Majesty in his Solitudes and Sufferings', this collection of Charles I's purported prayers and meditations was published in 1649 and rapidly became very popular. It was issued in more than thirty editions within a year of first appearing. Milton's *Eikonoklastes* was a rejoinder to it, composed at the behest of Parliament. The authorship of *Eikon Basilike* was disputed from the first, including by Milton. In *Eikonoklastes* he rightly identified one of the King's own prayers in a later edition of the *Eikon* as a plagiarism from Sidney's *Arcadia*. Johnson appears to follow the suggestion, made from the late seventeenth century, that Milton inserted the plagiarism in order to discredit the work, but this is rejected by modern scholars. The main author of the *Eikon* is now thought to be the Royalist clergyman John Gauden, 1599/1600–62).

68 *Dr. Juxon*: William Juxon (1582–1663) was bishop of London when he attended Charles I at his execution. In 1660 the newly restored Charles II made him archbishop of Canterbury.

Salmasius: Claude de Saumaise (1588–1653), French classical scholar and author of *Defensio Regii Carlo I* (1649). It provoked Milton to reply in his *Defensio pro Populo Anglicano* (1651).

Tu es ... gallinaceus: 'you are yourself a Gallic cock and said to be rather cocky'. *Gallus* means both 'Frenchman' and 'cock'.

69 *Ker*: John Ker, author of *Selectarum de Lingua Latina Observationem* (1708–9).

Christina: Queen Christina of Sweden, daughter of Gustavus Adolphus, had invited Saumaise to Sweden in 1650, but is reputed to have believed that Milton's rejoinder had out-argued him. It was said that his withdrawal from the Swedish court in 1651 was caused by his mortification at her preference.

Quid agis ... est?: Juvenal, *Satires*, iv. 14–15. 'What can you do when the man himself is more foul and monstrous than any charge you can bring against him?'

70 *About this time ... sonnet*: Milton's first wife Mary died on 5 May 1652 aged 27. Her three daughters were Anne, Mary, and Deborah, the latter born only three days before her death. Milton married the 28-year-old Katherine Woodcock not 'after a short time' but more than four years later, on 12 November 1656. She died of consumption on 3 February 1658; her baby daughter died a little over a month later. The 'poor sonnet' is Sonnet XIX, 'Methought I saw my late espoused saint'.

the author was not known: in his reply, *Ioannis Phillipi Angli Responsio* (1652), Milton assumed that this author was Dr John Bramhall (1594–1663), Archbishop of Armagh. In fact it was the clergyman John Rowland (1605/6–60), who had fled to the Netherlands in 1643 and published a series of tracts defending the Church of England against Puritanism.

71 *Defensio Secunda*: Milton's *Defensio Secunda* (1654) was a reply to *Regii Sanguinis Clamor ad Coelum* by Pierre du Moulin (1601–84). The full title of Milton's pamphlet, translated into English, is 'The second defence of John Milton, Englishman, on behalf of the English people, against an infamous anonymous libel entitled A cry to heaven of the king's blood against the English parricides'. Milton took the author to be Alexander More, a minister of the Reformed Church, who had contributed a preface. His reply is therefore in part a personal attack on More, notably for his supposed sexual indiscretions. It makes considerable use of puns on More's name, which in Greek and Latin can mean 'fool' or 'mulberry tree'.

"Deserimur ... salutaris.": see *Prose Works*, iv. 671–2.

72 *Poma ... Morus*: Ovid, *Metamorphoses*, iv. 51–2. 'Morus, from bearing white fruit, afterwards bore black.'

almost ... press: see Birch, vol. i, p. xxxiv.

73 *long chusing, and beginning late*: *Paradise Lost*, ix. 26.

in his verses to Mansus: see 'Mansus', ll. 80–4.

sketches of poetical projects left in manuscript: Johnson provides reasonably reliable transcriptions of Milton's MS, containing drafts of an outline for a tragedy based on the story of the Fall. The manuscript, written around 1640, is held by Trinity College, Cambridge.

προλογίζει: 'delivers the prologue'.

76 *seemly arts and affairs*: from Milton's *The Reason of Church Government*. Johnson has already quoted the passage containing this phrase, see p. 63, above.

76 *He sent … the Church*: in 1659 Milton published the manuscript of *The Cabinet Council*, attributed to Sir Walter Raleigh, and his own *Considerations touching the likeliest means to remove hirelings out of the church, wherein is also discoursed of tithes, church-fees, church revenues, and whether any maintenance of ministers can be settled by law*. This argued against any form of taxation, such as tithes, that required individuals to support the state Church.

Richard was constrained to resign: Richard Cromwell abdicated on 25 May 1659.

bated no jot of heart or hope: see Milton's sonnet 'To Mr Cyriack Skinner upon His Blindness', ll. 7–8.

both seriously and ludicrously answered: 'seriously' in George Starkey's *The Dignity of Kingship Asserted* (1660); 'ludicrously' in the anonymously published *The Censure of the Rota upon Mr Milton's Book* (1660).

Harrington: James Harrington (1611–77) was best known for his complex work of political theory *Oceana* (1656), in which he advocated a modernized version of classical republicanism. From 1659 he was the leading member of a gentlemanly debating society called 'the Rota', which did discuss, among other issues, the best constitution for a commonwealth. It ceased to meet after the Restoration.

Milton, kicking … Guides: Milton's *Brief Notes upon a Late Sermon* was a rejoinder to *The Fear of God and the King*, a Royalist sermon preached by Matthew Griffith, a former chaplain of Charles I, and published in April 1660. L'Estrange's reply was published later in the same month.

77 *Goodwin's Obstructors of Justice*: this work by John Goodwin (1594?–1665), published in 1649, was a vindication of the trial and execution of Charles I.

Dalrymple's observation: Sir John Dalrymple, *Memoirs of Great Britain and Ireland*, i (1771), 34.

Marvel, Morrice, and Sir Thomas Clarges: Andrew Marvell (1621–78), Sir William Morrice (1602–76), and Sir Thomas Clarges (1619?–95). All three were politicians with strong Parliamentarian sympathies who nevertheless prospered after the Restoration.

Richardson ... *Betterton* ... *Davenant*: Jonathan Richardson (1694–1771), art theorist, friend of Pope and devotee of *Paradise Lost*; Thomas Betterton (1635–1710), the leading actor of the late seventeenth century; Sir William Davenant (1606–68), playwright and theatre manager. Davenant, knighted by Charles I, was a keen Royalist and was imprisoned in 1650. He was released in 1652. The story of Milton's intercession is unproven.

78 *Dr. Paget* ... *Elizabeth Minshul*: Nathan Paget (1615–79) was a physician with strong Puritan sympathies and a friend of Milton's. Elizabeth Minshul (1638–1727), to whom he introduced Milton, was his cousin. She was 24 years old when she married Milton in February 1663.

79 *"You* ... *an honest man"*: the story is in Birch, vol. i, p. xxxvi.

Elwood the quaker: Thomas Ellwood (1639–1713) was introduced to Milton in 1662 by Nathan Paget. At the Restoration he had suffered imprisonment for his religious and political beliefs, and would do so again, interrupting his employment as a reader to Milton. Ellwood described their conversations in a memoir published posthumously in 1714.

80 *Voltaire tells* ... *Heaven*: Voltaire's story is given in Birch, vol. i, p. li.

long ... *late*: *Paradise Lost*, ix, 26; see p. 73, above.

before ... *quality*: for Jonathan Richardson, see note to p. 77, above. The account is taken from Birch, vol. i, p. xxxviii, as is the account in the next paragraph.

81 *"to remember* ... *therein"*: in Birch, vol. i, p. xlv.

redeunt in carmina vires: Milton, 'Elegy V' (1629), l. 5; 'my powers of song revive'.

82 *Sapiens dominabitur astris*: Robert Burton, *Anatomy of Melancholy*, I. II. i. 4; 'a wise man will rule the stars'.

possunt quia posse videntur: *Aeneid*, v. 231; 'they are capable who believe themselves capable'.

an age too late: *Paradise Lost*, ix. 44–5.

83 *they should not willingly let die*: taken from a passage from Milton's *The Reason of Church Government* (1642) already quoted above on p. 59.

unpremeditated verse: *Paradise Lost*, ix. 24.

84 *fallen on* ... *round*: *Paradise Lost*, vii. 25–7.

Elwood: see n. to p. 79, above. The story is in Birch, vol. i, pp. xxxviii–xxxix.

a chaplain of the archbishop of Canterbury: by law, all publications had to be licensed by a state-appointed official. The Printing Act of 1662 prohibited publications 'contrary to the principles of the Christian faith or to the doctrine of government or governors in Church or State'. The licenser of books to whom Johnson refers was Thomas Tomkins (1637?–75), chaplain to Gilbert Sheldon, Archbishop of Canterbury.

85 *Brabazon Aylmer ... Jacob Tonson*: the bookseller Brabazon Aylmer (1645–1719?) specialized in the publication of religious works, both Anglican and Non-conformist. He published Milton's *Epistolarum familiarum liber* (1674) and *Brief History of Muscovia* (1682), but sold the copyright of *Paradise Lost* without having published an edition. Jacob Tonson (1655/6–1736) became the leading bookseller of the late seventeenth century and helped to make *Paradise Lost* a revered monument of English poetry.

86 *only two editions of the works of Shakspeare*: Johnson refers to the First (1623) and Second (1632) Folios. The third Folio was in fact published in 1663.

the Revolution: the Glorious Revolution of 1688.

87 *"that though ... or silver"*: in Birch, vol. i, p. lxi.

the earl of Anglesea: Arthur Annesley (1614–86), first Earl of Anglesey. He was an influential politician after the Restoration, but a sympathizer with Puritanism. He was a friend and protector to Andrew Marvell.

88 *Ramus*: Peter Ramus (1515–72) was the usual name given to the French humanist philosopher and grammarian Pierre de la Ramée.

89 *Mr. Benson*: William Benson (1682–1754), Whig politician and writer. His inclusion of his own name and qualifications on the monument is mocked in Alexander Pope's *Dunciad*, iii. 325.

90 *When the inscription ... its walls*: 'Philips' is the poet John Philips (1676–1709), an imitator of Milton, notably in his burlesque poem *The Splendid Shilling* (1701). He himself was included in Johnson's *Lives*. For Sprat, see n. to p. 5, above. The High Church Francis Atterbury succeeded Sprat as bishop of Rochester and dean of Westminster in 1713. 'Dr Gregory' is Dr David Gregory (1697–1767), Dean of Christ Church, Oxford.

91 *Mr. Cradock's kindness*: the writer Joseph Cradock (1742–1826), a friend of both Garrick and Goldsmith, lent Johnson his copy of Milton's Euripides.

Arminianism: a follower of Arminius (1560–1609), who denied the Calvinist doctrine of predestination.

92 *what Badius says of Erasmus ... sequeretur*: Dominic Baudius, *Epistolae* (1615), II. xxvii ('He was more disposed to flee than to follow').

a popular government ... commonwealth: the quotation derives from John Toland's life of Milton (1698), as cited in Thomas Newton's edition of *Paradise Lost* (1749), vol. i, p. li.

93 *His brother ... Grosvenor-street*: in fact Christopher Milton (1615–93) had three daughters and two sons.

unideal: 'expressing no idea'. Johnson appears to have coined the word, the earliest use of which is found by the *OED* to be a *Rambler* essay of 1751.

94 *Comus was played for her benefit*: the benefit was staged by David Garrick at Johnson's instigation, when he discovered from Thomas Newton (see n. to p. 92, above) that she was in want. 'Tonson' is Jacob Tonson (1714–67), great-nephew of the Jacob Tonson who purchased the copyright of *Paradise Lost*.

nothing satisfied with what he had done: Johnson quotes from Milton's concluding note to 'The Passion' (1630).

95 *a Lion ... dandling the Kid*: see *Paradise Lost*, iv. 344.

Passion plucks ... cloven heel: see *Lycidas*, ll. 2–3, 34, and 85–6.

Cowley ... together: see Cowley's 'On the Death of Mr William Hervey'.

96 *We drove ... of night*: *Lycidas*, ll. 27–9.

what Theobald has remarked: Lewis Theobald, *Works of Shakespeare* (1733), vol. i, pp. xix–xx.

97 *not unseen*: 'L'Allegro', l. 57.

glowing embers: 'Il Penseroso', l. 79.

towered cities: 'L'Allegro', l. 117.

100 *Bossu*: René Le Bossu, author of *Traité du poème épique* (1675), translated into English in 1695.

to vindicate the ways of God to man: Johnson misquotes *Paradise Lost*, i, 26 ('justify the ways of God to men') but follows Pope's witty travesty of the line in the opening of his *Essay on Man*, i. 16: 'But vindicate the ways of God to man'.

101 *of which ... their regions*: *Paradise Lost*, vi, 221–3.

as Addison observes: see the *Spectator*, 303 (1712). 'Clarke' is educationalist John Clarke (1687–1734). Johnson refers to his *Essay upon Study* of 1731.

102 *Θεὸς ἀπο μηχανῆς*: Aristotle, *Poetics*, xv. 10 ('the god in the machine', *deus ex machina*).

103 *Dryden ... overcome*: see Dryden's 'Discourse concerning Satire' (1692).

Cato ... to decide: Cato is celebrated in Lucan's *Pharsalia*, bk. IX; Quintilian's comments are in his *Institutes*, X. i. 90.

105 *through the spectacles of books*: the quotation is from a passage in Dryden's *Of Dramatick Poesie* (1667) in which Shakespeare is praised for not needing 'the spectacles of books to read nature' (Dryden, *The Major Works*, ed. Keith Walker (Oxford, 1987), 110).

pravity: defined in Johnson's *Dictionary* as 'Corruption; badness; malignity', and illustrated with a quotation from *Paradise Lost*, xii. 288.

106 *the port of mean suitors*: see *Paradise Lost*, xi. 8–9.

107 *Bentley*: see note to p. 32, above. Classical scholar Richard Bentley (1662–1742) was infamous for his edition of *Paradise Lost* complete with 'emendations upon Milton'. These were rewritten passages of the poem, licensed by Bentley's groundless theory that a meddlesome editor had corrupted the original text.

108 *burning marle ... starts up in his own shape ... spear and a shield*: *Paradise Lost*, i. 296; ii. 819; iv. 990.

109 *incorporeal spirits ... at large, though without number ... crushed in upon their substance, now grown gross by sinning ... the sooner for their arms, for unarmed they might easily as spirits have evaded by contraction or remove*: *Paradise Lost*, i. 789; i. 790–1; vi. 656–61; vi. 595–7.

110 *a mole of aggregated soil, cemented with asphaltus*: *Paradise Lost*, x. 293–8.

timorous deer: see *Paradise Lost*, vi. 857.

flats among his elevations: see Dryden's Preface to *Sylvae* (1685).

the Paradise of Fools: *Paradise Lost*, iii. 440–97. Milton's depiction of limbo imitates Ariosto's *Orlando Furioso*, xxxiv. 73 ff.

111 *nice*: 'discriminating, exact'.

112 *Our language ... sunk under him*: see the *Spectator*, 297 (1712).

he wrote no language: Ben Jonson, *Discoveries*; see *Ben Jonson*, ed. Ian Donaldson (Oxford, 1985), 569.

a Babylonish Dialect: Samuel Butler, *Hudibras*, I. i. 93. Butler is referring to the manner of speaking of Sir Hudibras, his absurd Puritan protagonist.

The measure ... without rhyme: from Milton's prefatory note to *Paradise Lost* on 'The Verse'.

The Earl of Surrey ... Raleigh himself: Henry Howard, Earl of Surrey (1516/17–1547), translated the *Aeneid*, bks. II and IV into English blank verse. The blank verse poem about Raleigh was 'De Guiana, Carmen Epicum' (1596) by George Chapman.

Italia Liberata: *Italia liberata dai Goti* (1547–8), by Giangiorgio Trissino (1478–1550), an epic poem narrating the sixth-century campaign of the Christian general Belisarus to free Italy from the Goths.

113 *Rhyme ... true poetry*: from Milton's 'The Verse'; see note to p. 112, above.

Blank verse ... the eye: William Locke (1732–1810), a patron of writers and artists, as quoted in Boswell's *Life of Johnson*, 1096.

ROCHESTER

115 *John Wilmot ... Oxfordshire*: in fact he was born on 1 April 1647. His father, Henry Wilmot (1612?–58) was a Royalist general, and thus features in Clarendon's *History of the Rebellion*, his account of the English Civil War (for Clarendon, see note to p. 46, above). Clarendon was Chancellor of the University of Oxford.

In 1665 ... of shot: Johnson derives this account, and much of the biographical information in 'Rochester', from Gilbert Burnet's *Some Passages of the Life and Death of ... John, Earl of Rochester* (1680), published soon after the poet's death. 'Sandwich' is Edward Montagu, Earl of Sandwich (1625–72), admiral of the English fleet in the naval action off Bergen, in Norway, during the Second Anglo-Dutch War. Sir Edward Spragge (*c.*1629–73) was captain of the English flagship the *Dreadnought* during the Four Days' Battle of June 1666. Rochester had volunteered for service on this ship.

Sheffield Duke of Buckingham: John Sheffield, first Duke of Buckingham and Normanby (1647–1721), formerly titled the third earl of Mulgrave. A courtier and wit, who, like Rochester, had fought in the navy against the Dutch, he challenged Rochester to a duel in 1669 because he believed that he was the author of a satire written against him.

Dr. Burnet: see note to p. 115, above. The clergyman Gilbert Burnet (1643–1715), later to be bishop of Salisbury and a noted historian, met Rochester frequently in the last year of his life and attended him on his deathbed. His biography of Rochester included records of their conversations, in which the former libertine repents his misdeeds and his religious freethinking. Burnet has often been accused of inventing these exchanges.

116 *Woodstock Park*: a few miles north of Oxford. Rochester's country estate was at Ditchley in Oxfordshire.

Wood: see note to p. 5, above.

117 *The first ... Antwerp*: Rochester's *Poems on Several Occasions* was published in the autumn of 1680, soon after his death.

His imitation ... unhappy: Rochester's poem usually entitled 'An Allusion to Horace'.

Passerat: Jean Passerat (1534–1602). As well as being a poet he was Professor of Latin at the Collège de France in Paris.

Molliter ... malis: 'My bones will sleep peacefully, provided they are not burdened with mad songs'.

118 *In one ... positive*: see Boileau, *Satires*, ii. 62.

In this ... prior: Johnson quotes Johann von Wower (1576–1635), *Dis Aestiva, sive de Umbra Paegnion* (1610), p. 130. 'Now look round first at the earth, all suspended between strong clasps, the wondrous beauty of the world, and the lands and the stretches of the sea, and the clear fields of the air and the ceilinged palaces of the vasty heaven—darkness is earlier than all' [trans. L. Holford-Strevens].

118 *He who can ... of the town*: from 'On the Suppos'd Author of A late Poem in Defence of Satyr' (1677), by poet and courtier Sir Carr Scroope (1649–80), a frequent butt of Rochester's satire.

buffoon conceit: probably Rochester's 'To the Post Boy'.

every Man would be a Coward if he durst: a slight misquotation of Rochester's 'A Satyre against Reason and Mankind', l. 158.

Thou canst ... thy sword: Scroope's 'Answer by Way of Epigram', ll. 5–6.

119 *Of the satire ... taken away*: Rochester's 'A Satyre against Reason and Mankind' is an imitation of Boileau's *Satire* VIII.

120 *Poema ... versus*: See Appendix, pp. 462–3.

DRYDEN

121 *Derrick*: Samuel Derrick (1724–69) published an edition of Dryden's *Works, with a Life and Notes* in (1760). Johnson assisted him with the biography that was prefixed to this.

Anabaptist: a member of a Protestant sect that disagreed with many items of Anglican doctrine, in particular believing that only adults, and not children, should be baptized.

Dr. Busby: Richard Busby (1606–95), famous headmaster of Westminster from 1638 until his death aged 85.

Lord Hastings: Henry Hastings (1630–49). Dryden's 'On the Death of Lord Hastings' appeared in a collection of elegies, *Lachrymae Musarum* (1649).

122 *In the Life ... riper age*: for his 'grateful' acknowledgement of his education at Trinity College in his 'Life of Plutarch' (1683), see Dryden's *Works*, ed. H. T. Swedenborg, Vinton A. Dearing, et al., 20 vols. (Los Angeles, 1956–2000), xvii. 269. The lines of verse are from 'Prologue to the University of Oxford' (1676; pub. 1684), ll. 35–8.

... a second poem on his restoration: Dryden's *To His Sacred Majesty, A Panegyrick on His Coronation* (1674).

An horrid stillness ... fear: *Astraea Redux*, ll. 7–8.

123 *the Wild Gallant*: first performed on 5 February 1663; published in a revised version in 1669.

Earl of Orrery... and a statesman: Roger Boyle, first Earl of Orrery (1621–79), was a politician and writer. As well as an active statesman he was a playwright.

124 *Sir Robert Howard*: like Orrery (see previous note), Howard was both politician and playwright. In 1663 Dryden had married Howard's sister, Elizabeth.

the Rehearsal ... plot: *The Rehearsal* was a satirical drama written by George Villiers, Duke of Buckingham, in collaboration with others. First performed in 1671, and published in 1672, it featured a self-regarding author called 'Bayes' who shared some characteristics with Dryden.

In this play ... other poets: see *The Indian Emperour*, III. ii. 1 ff. The critic Thomas Rymer (see note to p. 40, above) praised the lines in his Preface to Rapin's *Reflections on Aristotle's Treatise of Poesie* (1674).

"*I am satisfied ... elocution*": Johnson's quotation is inexact. Dryden refers to Prince Rupert (1619–82), Charles II's cousin, and General George Monk, Duke of Albermarle (1608–70), because the two men had shared command of English naval forces in naval battles against the Dutch, which are described in Dryden's poem.

125 *the Gondibert of Davenant*: *Gondibert* (1651) was an uncompleted verse epic by Sir William Davenant (see note to p. 77, above).

Dryden, in his dedication ... his opinion: Dryden's dedication to *The Rival Ladies* (1664); Howard's preface to *Four New Plays* (1665).

Dialogue on Dramatick Poetry: Johnson refers to Dryden's *Of Dramatick Poesie: An Essay* (1667).

Langbaine: see note to p. 3, above.

tierce: a cask holding one-third of a pipe, i.e. 14 gallons.

126 *"whom ... other man"*: Johnson quotes from Dryden's Preface to *The Tempest*, performed in 1667 and published in 1670.

Elkanah Settle: Settle (1648–1724) had a considerable success with *The Empress of Morocco*, a heroic tragedy in rhyming couplets. It won Settle a post at court and was published in an expensive edition with prologues by Rochester and the Earl of Mulgrave.

127 *"He's an animal ... justly!"*: this and the following quotations are from *Notes and Observations on the Empress of Morocco* (1674), whose main author was John Crowne. Dryden contributed only its preface and postscript.

130 *sculptures*: copperplate engravings.

131 *the illustrious duke of Newcastle*: William Cavendish, Duke of Newcastle (1593–1676), author of a variety of literary works, including plays. He collaborated with Dryden on *Sir Martin Mar-All* and possibly on the lost comedy *The Heiress*, performed for Charles II in 1669. 'His lady' was Margaret Cavendish, Duchess of Newcastle (1623–73), herself a noted author of plays, poems, and philosophical speculations.

131 *Cinthio*: Giambattista Giraldi Cinthio (1504–73), author of *Hecatommithi*, a collection of a hundred tales in imitation of Boccaccio's *Decameron*. The plots of both *Othello* and *Measure for Measure* derive from these.

"He only desired ... mine": see John Dryden, *Of Dramatic Poesy and Other Critical Essays*, ed. George Watson, 2 vols. (1962), i. 151–3 (hereafter Watson).

The rants ... the writer: Maximin is the Tyrant of Rome in Dryden's *Tyrannick Love*. His extravagant speeches became notorious, and Dryden seemed to repent such 'rants' in his dedication to *The Spanish Fryar* (1681).

132 *"I considered ... prose"*: Johnson quotes from Dryden's Preface to *The Conquest of Granada*.

All the rays ... concentration: Almanzor is the hero of the two-part *Conquest of Granada*. He is a warrior who fights for the Moors against the Spanish.

Martin Clifford: Clifford (*c*.1624–77) was secretary to the Duke of Buckingham and may have had a hand in *The Rehearsal* (see note to p. 124, above). He charged John Dryden with plagiarism in letters circulated in manuscript. These were published posthumously as *Notes upon Mr. Dryden's Poems in Four Letters* (1687).

133 *Dr. Percy*: the antiquarian and clergyman Thomas Percy (1729–1811), a friend of Johnson.

134 *I'll to the turrets ... sphere*: *The Conquest of Granada I*, III. i. 261–7.

The goodly London ... waves: Settle quotes *Annus Mirabilis*, ll. 601–12.

135 *Two ifs ... not live*: Johnson here conflates three separate passages from *The Conquest of Granada I*, II. i. 130 and 226–7 and IV. ii. 278–8.

Move swiftly ... thy race: *The Conquest of Granada II*, V. iii. 339–40.

If I could ... it down: *The Conquest of Granada I*, III. i. 510–14.

136 *The People ... course*: ibid., IV. i. 11–14.

But can ... flow: ibid., IV. i. 4.

137 *Old father ... those within*: Settle compares *Annus Mirabilis*, ll. 925–8 with a passage from Cowley's *Davideis*, bk. I.

Who, like a tempest ... join'd: *The Conquest of Granada I*, III. i. 43–4.

Sir Charles Sedley: Sedley (1639–1701) was a courtier and writer who was a close associate of Charles II and had a reputation as a libertine.

138 *Troilus ... occasion*: *Troilus and Cressida*, first produced in 1679, does not belong here chronologically. In fact, the section of Johnson's survey from here to *Albion and Albania*, produced in 1685, has been misplaced by Johnson, probably because he read the volumes of his edition of Dryden in the wrong order.

Lee: Nathaniel Lee (1653?–92), playwright and poet.

he happened ... the fifth: Johnson quotes from Dryden's pamphlet *The Vindication of the Duke of Guise* (1683).

This was a play ... the controversy: the Duke of York is Charles II's brother, James (later to be James II), a Roman Catholic. The Duke of Guise was alleged to be a defamatory portrait of Charles II's illegitimate son the Protestant Duke of Monmouth, who was opposed to the Duke of York's succession. The play drew a parallel between the Holy League in sixteenth-century France and the recently formed Protestant Association in England.

139 *Or if a work ... in a play*: from Andrew Marvell's 'On Mr Milton's Paradise Lost', ll. 17–24, which was prefixed to the 1674 edition of Milton's poem.

for remoteness ... of time: Johnson refers to Racine's preface to his play *Bajazet* (1672).

140 *This play ... a critick*: see note to p. 115, above.

the only play which he wrote for himself: Dryden says this in 'A Parallel betwixt Painting and Poetry' (1695). See Watson, ii. 207.

so much . . . the town: see Langbaine, 164.

141 *Cleomenes . . . no hero*: Johnson found the anecdote told by Richard Steele in the *Guardian*, 45 (1713).

When this . . . no more: Charles II died on 6 February 1685. The Duke of Monmouth, Protestant challenger to the new Roman Catholic King James II, landed with three ships at Lyme Regis in Dorset on 11 June.

the earl of Salisbury: James Cecil, Earl of Salisbury (1666–94). In 1687 he had visited Rome and been converted to Roman Catholicism. He was a strong supporter of James II and was imprisoned for a while after he was deposed by William of Orange.

142 *The first . . . Rowe*: it had become the custom by the eighteenth century for the dramatist to be given the takings for the third night of a new production. The playwrights mentioned here are Thomas Southerne (1659–1746) and Nicholas Rowe (1674–1718). Rowe was to be included in Johnson's *Lives*.

Swift . . . easily satisfied: see Swift's *A Tale of a Tub*, ed. A. C. Guthkelch and D. N. Smith (Oxford, 1958), 131. In fact this seems a joke about the frustrations of authorship rather than a true recollection of a real conversation.

The price . . . cheap: slightly different versions of this anecdote were to be found in several sources. See Lonsdale, ii. 325 n. 90.

143 *Lopez de Vega*: Lope Felix de Vega (1562–1635) was a prolific Spanish playwright. Several hundred of his plays survive.

Butler the author of Hudibras: Samuel Butler (1613–80) is best known for his satirical narrative poem *Hudibras* (1662–80). A burlesque version of *Don Quixote*, it mocks Puritanism and was immensely popular in the late seventeenth century. Butler was the subject of one of Johnson's *Lives*.

Buckingham . . . his chaplain: see note to p. 5, above.

144 *as Lamotte . . . the poet*: Charles Lamotte, *An Essay on Poetry and Painting* (1730), 103.

Rochester . . . the town: see Lonsdale, ii. 327 n. 101.

145 *the dutchess of Portsmouth*: Louise Renée de Kéroualle, the Duchess of Portsmouth (1649–1734), was the acknowledged mistress of Charles II and a powerful figure at court.

He prefixed . . . French: Sir Henry Sheeres's translation of Polybius' *History* was published in 1693; Dryden's lives of Lucian and Plutarch appeared in, respectively, the *Works of Lucian* (1711) and *Plutarch's Lives*

(1683). In his *Works of Tacitus* (1728), Thomas Gordon claimed that Dryden's *Annals and History of Cornelius Tacitus*, bk. 1 (1698) was translated from a French translation, not directly from the Latin.

146 *The authority of ... different practice*: Johnson mentions a series of noted translators of classical verse. These include Ben Jonson, translator of Horace's *Ars Poetica* (1640), George Sandys, translator of *Ovid's Metamorphoses* (1621–6), and Barten Holyday, translator of *Juvenal and Persius Translated* (1673). Sir Richard Fanshaw had translated Guarini's *Pastor fido* (1647), while Denham, Waller, and Cowley (all included in Johnson *Lives*) had pioneered free translation ('paraphrase') and imitation.

In 1681 ... at its head: during the so-called Exclusion Crisis of 1681, a powerful Parliamentary faction led by the Earl of Shaftesbury tried unsuccessfully to exclude Charles II's Roman Catholic brother James from succession to the throne in favour of the Duke of Monmouth, the King's illegitimate son. For the Duke of Monmouth, see notes to pp. 138 and 141, above.

Sacheverell's trial: the clergyman Henry Sacheverell (1674–1724) was a popular and controversial preacher. In 1710, after one particularly incendiary sermon in which he attacked Dissenters and impugned the motives of the organizers of the Glorious Revolution of 1688, he was tried for sedition before the House of Lords. Numerous pamphlets were published for and against him. He was eventually found guilty but given the lenient sentence of a three-year ban from preaching.

One of these ... Chancellor: 'Somers' is the powerful politician John, Lord Somers (1651–1716). Pope rejects the attribution in his *Epistle to Dr Arbuthnot*, l. 141 n.

147 *the ignoramus of a grand jury of Londoners*: an 'ignoramus' was a jury's verdict that the evidence for a prosecution was insufficient to justify pursuing a case. Shaftesbury was being prosecuted for treason after the Exclusion Crisis, but a sympathetic jury thwarted the state's efforts to convict him. The news prompted bonfire celebrations in London.

judge Jefferies: George Jeffreys (1645–89) was a notoriously brutal Lord Chief Justice, who made his reputation presiding over the so-called 'Bloody Assizes' in which the participants in Monmouth's Rebellion of 1685 were tried and punished. Settle's *Panegyrick* (1683), praising Jeffreys, pre-dates this.

148 *Sir Kenelm Digby ... the two Rainolds ... Chillingworth*: the courtier and natural philosopher Sir Kenelm Digby (1603–35) was brought up a Roman Catholic and remained such throughout his life. The story of John (1549–1607) and William (1544?–94) Rainolds' mutual conversion is told in Thomas Fuller's *Church-History* (1655), bk. x. The theologian

William Chillingworth (1602–44) converted temporarily to Catholicism in the 1630s.

They engaged ... Stillingfleet: Edward Stillingfleet, Bishop of Worcester and Charles II's former chaplain, had replied to the publication of papers purporting to show that Charles II had converted to Catholicism on his deathbed. The publication had been ordered by James II. Dryden was engaged to publish *A Defence of the Papers* (1686).

employed to translate ... with a large introduction: Dryden in fact translated *The History of the League* (1683) by French Jesuit Louis Maimbourg in 1684, before his conversion to Catholicism.

149 *His name ... the translator*: *The Life of St Francis Xavier* (1688), translated from the French of Dominic Bouhours, was printed with Dryden's name on its title page and at the end of the dedication.

The version ... to flatter: see Tom Brown, *The Late Converts Exposed* (1690), 33.

Varillas's History of Heresies: Antoine Varillas, *Histoire des revolutions arrives dans l'Europe en matière de religion* (1686–9), a Roman Catholic history of the Reformation.

"I have been informed ... employment": the passage is taken from Burnet's *Defence* (1687) of his earlier *Reflections on Mr. Varillas' History* (1686). Johnson probably took it from a secondary source, such as Thomas Birch et al., *A General Dictionary, Historical and Critical* (1734–41).

150 *A fable ... his abilities*: 'Montague' is Charles Montagu (1661–1715), who became earl of Halifax in 1700. With Matthew Prior (1664–1721) he composed a popular parody of Dryden's *The Hind and the Panther*, entitled *The Hind and the Panther Transvers'd to the Story of the Country-Mouse and the City-Mouse* (1687). Halifax and Prior were both included in Johnson's *Lives*.

Thomas Brown: see note to p. 8, above. Tom Brown (1663–1704) was a comic and satirical writer who frequently attacked Dryden in his early works.

151 *Next year ... the Prince*: James II's son, James Francis Edward, was born in June 1688. Dryden celebrated the event in his *Britannia Rediviva*, published a fortnight later.

The revenue ... Og: playwright and poet Thomas Shadwell (*c.*1640–92) had collaborated with Dryden in the 1670s, but later quarrelled with him and features as Og in *The Second Part of Absalom and Achitophel* (1682). Shadwell's appointment as Poet Laureate in 1688 was partly a consequence of his strong Whig sympathies.

152 *Lord Dorset*: Charles Sackville, sixth Earl of Dorset, poet and politician. He was made Lord Chamberlain on 14 February 1689.

153 *as Boileau observes ... than terror*: Boileau's opinion is taken from his *L'Art poétique* (1674), iii. 205–16. Rinaldo enters 'the enchanted wood' in Tasso's *Gerusalemme liberata*, canto XVIII.

This plan ... to manage: Dryden made this accusation in the Preface to his *Fables* (1700).

Fresnoy's Art of Painting: *De Arte Graphica* (1695) by the French painter and art theorist Charles Alphonse du Fresnoy (1611–65).

the lord Clifford ... the earl of Chesterfield ... the earl of Mulgrave: Hugh, Lord Clifford (1663–1730), was a Roman Catholic whose father had been a patron of Dryden; Philip Stanhope, Earl of Chesterfield (1633–1713), politician and courtier, served under Charles II, but refused offers of employment under William III; for the Earl of Mulgrave, see note to p. 115, above.

This translation ... condemned: Johnson refers to Luke Milbourne's *Notes on Dryden's Virgil* (1698), sarcastically praised by Pope in his *Dunciad*, ii. 349 n.

154 *Dr. Birch*: see notes to pp. 11 and 149, above.

first of May 1701: in fact it was 1 May 1700.

a biographical dictionary: Johnson has taken the account from Birch et al.'s *General Dictionary* (see note to p. 149, above). The original author was Elizabeth Thomas (1675–1731) and the story was first published in the *Memoirs of William Congreve* (1730), published by Edmund Curll, a bookseller who specialized in unauthorized lives. For a discussion of the account, see Lonsdale, ii. 336 n. 153.

156 *Farquhar*: the playwright George Farquhar (1676/7–1707) attended Dryden's funeral.

He was buried ... DRYDEN: in 1721 a monument to Dryden was finally erected by John Sheffield, Duke of Buckinghamshire.

157 *the satire imputed to lord Somers*: *Satyr, To His Muse* (1682) claimed that Dryden's wife-to-be had already borne him two children before they were married.

"He was ... mistakes": Johnson paraphrases from Congreve's 'Dedication' to Dryden's *Dramatick Works* (1717).

158 *He is accused ... given him*: Thomas Creed (1659–1700) had translated Lucretius' *De Rerum Natura* to widespread admiration in 1682. His translation of Horace (1684) was less admired. The accusation about

Dryden's role originated with Tom Brown's *The Late Converts Exposed* (1690), 53–4.

Nor wine ... to say: from Dryden's *Satyr, To His Muse* (1682).

159 *His thoughts ... to reject*: adapted from Dryden's Preface to *Fables* (1700).

It is related ... consorted: in Thomas Carte, *History of the Life of James, Duke of Ormonde* (1736), ii. 554.

160 *an address to Eleanor Gwyn*: Aphra Behn dedicated *The Feigned Curtezans* (1679) to Nell Gwyn, Charles II's mistress.

he has ... Englishmen: from Dryden's dedication to *Eleonora* (1692).

161 *Collier*: Jeremy Collier (1650–1726), whose notorious attack on contemporary theatre, *A Short View of the Immorality and Profaneness of the English Stage, together with the Sense of Antiquity upon this Argument*, appeared in 1698. Johnson paraphrases Dryden's response from his Preface to his *Fables*.

Blackmore: Sir Richard Blackmore (1654–1729) was a poet and physician with strong Whig sympathies who wrote a number of epic poems, which included *King Arthur* (1697). Blackmore attacked Dryden in the preface to this work, and in the preface to his *Fables* (1700) Dryden accused Blackmore of stealing his own plans for an epic about King Arthur. Blackmore was included in Johnson's *Lives*.

Milbourne: see note to p. 153, above.

162 *Trapp*: Joseph Trapp (1679–1747), clergyman and critic. Johnson cites his preface to his translation of Virgil's *Aeneid* (1718).

163 *the late amiable Mr. Tonson*: this is Jacob Tonson (1714–67), great-nephew of the Jacob Tonson who was Dryden's bookseller.

165 *Lord Bolingbroke*: Henry St John, Viscount Bolingbroke (1678–1751), Tory politician and man of letters. He was a close associate of Alexander Pope and figures largely in Johnson's 'Pope'.

Dr. King of Oxford: Dr William King (1685–1763), Principal of St Mary Hall, Oxford, whom Johnson had met in 1755.

Mr. Derrick: see note to p. 121, above.

the dutchess of Ormond: Lady Mary Somerset (1664/5–1733), wife of James Butler, Duke of Ormond.

Moyle: Walter Moyle (1672–1721), politician and writer.

Will's Coffee-house: a coffeehouse in London's Covent Garden, famous as a resort of wits.

166 *The utmost malice ... succeed*: from Dryden's *Annus Mirabilis*, ll. 1161 and 1165–8.

Two Arts ... Puttenham: William Webbe, *A Discourse of English Poetrie* (1586) and George Puttenham, *The Arte of English Poetrie* (1589).

168 *It was said ... other*: the sixteenth-century dispute was between Justus Scaliger and Christopher Clavius, and concerned adjustments to the Gregorian Calendar. The saying is adapted from Cicero, *Tusculanae Disputationes*, I. xvii. 39.

Novimus ... occupatur: from Joseph Trapp's *Praelectiones Poeticae* (1711–19), iii. 122.

169 *Spence ... Odyssey*: Joseph Spence, *Essay on Pope's Odyssey*, i (1726), 121–2.

His parallel ... colosso: remarks by Dryden in his preface to *Sylvae* (1685) were censured by George Sewell in his preface to *Metamorphoses* (1717). Johnson also refers to comments made by Dryden in 'A Parallel betwixt Poetry and Painting' (1695) before quoting the first line of Statius' *Achilleis*.

Gorbuduc: a blank verse tragedy (1563) by Thomas Sackville and Thomas Norton.

Chapman's versification: George Chapman translated both the *Iliad* (1598–1611) and the *Odyssey* (1615?). In his preface to *Annus Mirabilis*, Dryden says that Chapman used 'verses of six feet' to translate Homer, which is true of neither poem.

170 *He might ... be found*: see Quintilian, *Institutio Oratoria*, IX. ii. 9 and VIII. v. 6.

171 *His conversation ... only less*: *Threnodia Augustalis*, ll. 337–45.

another and the same: Dryden, 'Of the Pythagorean Philosophy', ll. 580–1.

173 *Translation ... metaphrase*: from Dryden's dedication to his translation of the *Aeneid* (1697).

174 *Sir Edward Sherburne*: Sir Edward Sherburne (1618–1702) was author of 'A Brief Discourse concerning Translation' in *The Tragedies of Seneca* (1702).

What had been ... appears: *Don Sebastian*, II. iii. 586.

176 *He, toss'd by Fate ... pilgrimage*: *Astraea Redux*, ll. 51–4. The next six passages are quoted from the same poem.

178 *"Though this ... remember it"*: François de Malherbe (1555–1628) was a French poet and translator. For the provenance of the comment, see Lonsdale, ii. 355 n. 239.

You have already . . . Cæsar make: *To His Sacred Majesty* (1661), ll. 79–84.

Nor is it . . . fruition: ibid. 69–70.

In open . . . come between: *To My Lord Chancellor Presented on New-years-day* (1662), ll. 31–42. The next four passages quoted are taken from the same poem.

180 *Waller had described a sea-fight*: see Waller's 'Of a War with Spain, and a Fight at Sea'.

Orbem jam totum, &c.: Petronius, *Satyricon*, 119. 1 ('[The conquering Roman] now held the whole world').

It seems . . . the sea: *Annus Mirabilis*, ll. 57–60.

181 *And now . . . seas and wind*: ibid. 93–120.

182 *The night . . . no more*: ibid. 269–84.

and certainly . . . their ignorance: from Dryden's Preface to *Annus Mirabilis*.

183 *So here . . . stiffness notes*: ibid. 617–64.

Instructed ships . . . allied: ibid. 649–50.

184 *The diligence . . . quiet*: ibid, 861–5.

Omnia . . . quiete: 'All things were laid to rest in the calm quiet of the night.' This is not by Virgil; it is to be found in Seneca's *Controversiae*, VII. i. 27.

to which . . . inclined me: from Dryden's 'A Discourse Concerning Satire', see Watson, ii. 91.

Harte: Walter Harte (1708/9–74), clergyman, writer, and Oxford tutor, was a friend of Pope. It is likely that Johnson cites here an 'opinion' that he heard first-hand in conversation with Harte.

he settled . . . exactness: in fact *Aureng-Zebe* is later than the other two plays Johnson mentions here.

185 *Henceforth . . . began*: see *Absalom and Achitophel*, l. 1028.

186 *written by Tate*: Dryden did write significant parts of *The Second Part of Absalom and Achitophel* (1682), including the satirical characters of Settle ('Doeg') and Shadwell ('Og').

Power was his aim . . . wicked means: *The Medall*, ll. 50–64.

neither authorized nor analogical: the title couples a Greek word (*Threnodia*) with a Latin one (*Augustalis*).

187 *The sons . . . play'd*: *Threnodia Augustalis*, ll. 160–4.

With him . . . was deferr'd: ibid. 97–106.

Fervet immensusque ruit: '[thus does Pindar] seethe and, brooking no restraint, rush on', from Horace, *Odes*, IV. ii. 7.

188 *From harmony ... in man*: *A Song for St Cecilia's Day* (1687), ll. 1–15.

As from ... the sky: ibid. 55–63.

189 *Though all ... to repeat*: *Eleonora* (1692), ll. 270–90.

As when ... became: ibid. 1–11.

190 *And this ... prose*: *Religio Laici*, ll. 453–4.

This absurdity ... Prior: see note to p. 39, above.

191 *A milk-white Hind ... to die*: *The Hind and the Panther* (1687), i. 1–8.

to give ... poesy: ibid., 'To the Reader'.

More haughty ... ears: ibid. i. 16–5.

192 *These are ... the same*: ibid. i. 308–26.

For when ... began: ibid. 554–72.

193 *Of Juvenal ... poetical*: Sir Robert Stapylton, *Juvenal's Sixteen Satyrs* (1647), and Barten Holyday, *Juvenal and Persius Translated and Illustrated* (1673).

Creech: Thomas Creech (1659–1700), scholar and translator, contributed to Dryden's *The Satires of Decimus Junius Juvenalis: Translated into English Verse*, published in 1692.

194 *the most noble ... language*: from Pope's preface to the *Iliad* (1715).

Milbourne ... attacked it: see note to p. 153, above.

195 *His criticism ... version*: Johnson quotes from Luke Milbourne's *Notes on Dryden's Virgil* (1698).

197 *Dr. Brady*: Nicholas Brady (1659–1726), poet and clergyman, launched a scheme in 1713 to publish a blank-verse English translation of Virgil's *Aeneid* by subscription. The first six books (Latin and English texts, with notes) were published between 1714 and 1716, but the rest of the work did not appear until 1726 and was little noticed.

With not much better ... Georgicks: for Trapp, see notes to pp. 162 and 168, above. His *Aeneid* appeared between 1718 and 1720; his version of the rest of Virgil's works was published in 1731.

mellifluence: 'flowing sweetness, honied flow'.

198 *Thus the old poem ... Berni*: Matteo Maria Boiardo's *Orlando inamorato* (1480) was modernized by Ludovico Domenichi (1545) and Francesco Berni (1541).

Of the three ... Beroalds: all three of these verse narratives from Dryden's *Fables* (1700) are adapted from stories in Boccaccio's *Decameron*. Filippo Berealdo (1453–1505) translated 'Cymon' into Latin in 1505.

Congreve's remark: see Congreve's 'Dedication' to Dryden's *Dramatick Works* (1717).

The ode for St. Cecilia's Day: better known by Dryden's original title, *Alexander's Feast; Or The Power of Musique* (1697).

199 *Love various minds ... it glows*: *Tyrannick Love*, II. i. 292–7.

200 *he looked on Otway ... beauty*: the playwright Thomas Otway (1652–85), who was included in Johnson's *Lives*, was renowned for the pathos of his drama. Dryden's comment is adapted from 'A Parallel betwixt Poetry and Painting'.

verbaque provisam rem: Horace, *Ars Poetica*, l. 311 ('Once that is provided, words will follow').

201 *Move swiftly ... edge of day*: *Conquest of Granada II*, V. iii. 339–40; *Tyrannick Love*, IV. i. 154–6.

Then we ... securely pry: *Annus Mirabilis*, ll. 653–6.

'Tis so ... as well?: see Cowley, 'To Mr Hobbes', l. 188.

202 *I am as free ... Sebastian reigns*: *Conquest of Granada I*, I. i. 207–9; *Tyrannick Love*, V. i. 238–41, I. i. 245–50, and *Don Sebastian*, I. i. 361–7.

No, there is ... miss: *Conquest of Granada I*, IV. ii. 455–61.

What precious ... your feet: *Conquest of Granada II*, III. i. 59–61 and III. iii. 86, 92–1.

These bursts ... I wrote them: see Dryden's Preface to *The Spanish Fryar* (1681).

203 *as when ... veer starboard*: Dryden's *Aeneid*, iii. 526–7.

virtue spooming before the wind: *The Hind and the Panther*, iii. 96.

They Nature's king ... their eyes: ibid. i. 57–8.

A hollow ... strove: *Annus Mirabilis*, ll. 1121–4.

When rattling bones ... the sky: 'To the Memory of Mrs. Anne Killigrew', ll. 184–5.

No sooner ... the scale: 'Heroique Stanzas', ll. 89–91.

204 *Waller was smooth ... energy divine*: Pope, *Imitations of Horace, Ep. II. i* (1737), ll. 267–9.

Phaer's Virgil ... death of Elizabeth: Johnson refers to Thomas Phaer's translation of the *Aeneid*, published in parts between 1558 and 1573, and Joseph Hall's *Virgidemiae* (1597–8).

205 *Relentless Time ... new decay*: Thomas Parnell, 'An Imitation of Some French Verses', ll. 1–4.

Drayton's Polyolbion: Michael Drayton, *Polyolbion* (1612–22).

206 *Together ... fair Italy*: see Pope, 'Epistle to Mr. Jervas', ii. 25–6.

Laugh all ... the sky: 'Palamon and Arcite', iii. 671–2.

And with ... his throne: see *The Hind and the Panther*, ii. 537.

207 *Of Dryden's works ... supply*: unidentified. See Lonsdale, ii. 374 n. 356 for a discussion of the possible sources.

lateritiam ... marble: Suetonius, *Divus Augustus*, 29.

THE *invocation ... he censures*: Johnson quotes from Milbourne's *Notes on Dryden's Virgil*, 206–9.

208 *Mr. Dryden ... may be lost*: the notes that follow were written on the endpapers of a copy of Thomas Rymer's *The Tragedies of the Last Age* (1678), which was owned by David Garrick. Johnson took the text from the original, though versions had been printed before. See Lonsdale, ii. 374–5 n. 358.

210 *Aristotle's rules*: see *Poetics*, vii.

quoad ... fundamentum: '[not] on account of its dignity, but its priority'. See *Poetics*, vi. 12.

213 *these plays*: Rymer discusses three plays by Beaumont and Fletcher, *A King and No King* (1619), *The Maides Tragedy* (1619), and *The Bloody Brother* (1639). 'Rollo', see p. 215, below, is the protagonist of the last of these.

215 *Dr. Vyse*: Dr William Vyse (1742–1816), Canon of Lichfield, who knew Johnson and showed him the following letter from Dryden to his sons.

216 *Sir William Bowyer's*: Bowyer (1639–1722) of Denham Court, Uxbridge, was related to Dryden's wife.

Mr. Bridgman: Orlando Bridgeman, a subscriber to Dryden's *Virgil*. His father had been Chief Justice under Charles II.

CONGREVE

218 *if the inscription ... in 1672*: Congreve was in fact born in 1670 at Bardsey, near Leeds.

Southern: Thomas Southerne (see note to p. 142, above).

Jacob: Giles Jacob, in *The Poetical Register*, 2 vols. (1723).

219 *his defence against Collier*: from Congreve's *Amendments of Mr. Collier's False and Imperfect Citations* (1698), 39–40. For Collier, see note to p. 161, above.

Mr. Maynwaring: Arthur Maynwaring (1668–1712) was a Whig politician and author, and a leading member of the Kit-Cat Club. He met the young Congreve through Dryden. As well as recommending *The Double Dealer* he helped revise it.

Halifax: see note to p. 150, above.

220 *o'er- informs its tenement*: from Dryden's *Absalom and Achitophel*, l. 158.

de gustibus non est disputandum: 'there is no disputing in matters of taste'.

Congreve testified ... nothing is new: *The Mourning Muse of Alexis: A Pastoral* (1695).

221 *Shaftesbury ... predictions*: for Shaftesbury, see note to p. 456, below. The point of Johnson's example is that Shaftesbury was a rational deist who represented himself as above all mere superstition.

Betterton the tragedian: for Betterton, see note to p. 77, above.

Prynne published Histrio-mastix: William Prynne's *Histrio-mastix: The Players Scourge* (1633) was a vehement diatribe against stage drama.

Nonjuror: one who refused to take required oaths of loyalty to the King, William III (implying that he was not the rightful monarch). Later nonjurors refused to swear loyalty to the Hanoverian monarchs.

222 *Durfey*: the prolific dramatist Thomas D'Urfey (1653?–1723) who was specifically attacked by Jeremy Collier.

Vanburgh: Sir John Vanbrugh (1664–1726), playwright and architect. His response to Collier was *A Short Vindication of the Relapse and the Provok'd Wife* (1698).

a specimen: *Love for Love*, v. ii, followed by Collier's comment from *A Short View* (1698). 76.

223 *the earl of Oxford*: see notes to pp. 324 and 330, below.

"Non obtusa ... ab urbe": Virgil's *Aeneid*, i. 567–8 ('Not so dull are our Punic hearts, and not so far from this Tyrian city does the sun yoke his steeds').

224 *twelve hundred pounds a year*: it was in fact £700 p.a.

his Miscellany: Richard Steele's *Poetical Miscellanies* (1714).

224 *when he received ... visit him*: this account can be found in Voltaire's *Letters concerning the English Nation* (1733), though Johnson may have taken it from one of several secondary sources.

Henrietta dutchess of Marlborough: Henrietta Godolphin, Duchess of Marlborough (1681–1733) was the eldest surviving child of the Duke of Marlborough and a noted patron of the arts. It is possible that she and Congreve were lovers at one time.

225 *Antæus*: in mythology a giant whose mother was the Earth and who gained new strength whenever he was in contact with her. Heracles defeated him by lifting him from the ground as they fought.

an exclamation in The Mourning Bride: Congreve's *The Mourning Bride*, II. ii. 1–17.

226 *lines like these*: *The Mourning Muse of Alexis*, ll. 139–58.

this was his song: *The Tears of Amaryllis for Amyntas: A Pastoral* (1703), ll. 134–45.

227 *of William he will sing*: *A Pindarique Ode, Humbly Offer'd to the King on his taking Namure* (1695), ll. 18–19 and 44–57.

The concluding verses are these: *The Birth of the Muse*, ll. 267–72.

228 *Mrs. Arabella Hunt*: 'On Mrs. Arabella Hunt Singing'.

lady Gethin: 'Verses to the Memory of Grace Lady Gethin'. Grace, Lady Gethin (1676–97) had been a young woman of noted learning.

the cure of our Pindarick madness: in his 'Discourse on the Pindarique Ode' (1706) Congreve argued that Pindar's odes had a regular structure.

GAY

229 *born in 1688*: in fact Gay was born on 30 June 1685.

Mr. Luck: Robert Luck was headmaster of Barnstaple Grammar School from 1698. His poems were published by Edward Cave, Johnson's employer on the *Gentleman's Magazine*.

The dutchess of Monmouth: Anna Scott, Duchess of Monmouth (1651–1732), was the widow of the Duke of Monmouth, who had led the abortive uprising against James II (see note to p. 141, above) and was beheaded. She had been estranged from her husband, who testified that she had not known of his plot, and so after his execution retained her title and possessions. She lived to be accepted in the courts of both Queens Mary and Anne, and to be a patron of writers, especially for the theatre.

230 *Steele ... and Spenser*: the author of the *Guardian* papers on pastoral (April 1713) was, in fact, Thomas Tickell. Pope's response was an ironic

essay in *Guardian*, 40 (1713), which absurdly praised Philips's pastorals above his own.

the earl of Clarendon: Edward Hyde, Earl of Clarendon (1661–1723), cousin of Queen Anne.

he had dedicated ... Hanover: Lord Bolingbroke (see note to p. 165, above) had fled possible prosecution after Queen Anne's death and the accession of George I. By 1715 he was in France as secretary of state to the Old Pretender, James II's son.

231 *Griffin a player ... a knave*: the work is attributed to the actor and playwright Benjamin Griffin (1680–1740) and the critic and translator Lewis Theobald (1688–1744), who would later win renown through his disputes with Pope over the editing of Shakespeare and his enthronement in Pope's *Dunciad*.

Dr. Woodward the Fossilist: John Woodward (1665?–1728) was a physician, natural historian, and antiquary. He was known for his collection of fossils. He developed a theory of the earth which married biblical accounts to the discovery of fossils. These were supposedly destroyed by the biblical flood and preserved in the strata according to their weight.

The earl of Burlington ... Pope's Letters: for Burlington, see note to p. 411, below. 'Mr Pulteney' is the wealthy Whig politician William Pulteney, who made his name opposing the ministry of Robert Walpole. Simon Harcourt, Viscount Harcourt (1661?–1727), had been Lord Chancellor under Queen Anne and, despite his Tory sympathies, continued to be an influential political figure under George I.

Lewis, the steward of lord Oxford: for Erasmus Lewis, see note to p. 330, below.

232 *Gay in that ... thousand pounds*: on the South Sea Bubble, see note to p. 247, below.

Fenton: see note to p. 54, above.

the young duke of Cumberland: Prince William, Duke of Cumberland, was the second surviving son of George, Prince of Wales, the future George II. He was 6 years old at the time.

Mrs. Howard: see note to p. 335, below.

233 *Rich*: John Rich (1692–1761), theatre manager and impresario. At the Lincoln's Inn Fields theatre, where he staged *The Beggar's Opera*, he specialized in pantomime and *commedia dell'arte*.

Pope's words: Joseph Spence, *Observation, Anecdotes and Characters of Books and Men*, ed. James M. Osborn (Oxford, 1996), i. 107–8.

notes to the Dunciad: *Dunciad* (1729), iii. 326.

234 *Dr. Herring*: Thomas Herring (1693–1757) was chaplain to George II and made the remarks in a sermon in March 1728.

234 *prohibited by the Lord Chamberlain*: *Polly* was banned by the Duke of Grafton, the Lord Chamberlain, at the behest of Robert Walpole. It was published by subscription a few months later.

*The** publication ... the second: Johnson indicates with stars on this page where he has obtained information from Spence's *Anecodotes* (see note to p. 3). The first three refer to i. 108, and the fourth to i. 105–6.

the duke and dutchess of Queensberry: Charles Douglas, Duke of Queensberry (1698–78) was a courtier and politician. The Duchess was his second wife, Lady Catherine Hyde (1701–77), a noted patron of writers. She was outraged at the banning of *Polly*, and the affair led to her and her husband retiring from the court.

236 *Phædrus*: Phaedrus (*c*.15 BC–*c*.AD 50) wrote books of fables.

arbores loquuntur, non tantum feræ: from Phaedrus' 'Prologue', i. 6 ('trees are speaking, not to mention beasts').

dignus vindice nodus: Horace, *Ars Poetica*, i. 191. Johnson's translation follows the quotation.

patten: 'a kind of overshoe worn to raise an ordinary shoe above wet or muddy ground, consisting (from the 17th cent.) of a thick wooden sole mounted on an oval iron ring or similar base, and secured to the foot by a leather loop passing around the instep' (*OED*).

SAVAGE

239 *In the year 1697 ... Colonel Brett*: Johnson relied on the anonymous *Life of Mr Richard Savage* (1727) for his information about the Countess of Macclesfield's 'confession'. In fact, when Charles Gerard, Earl of Macclesfield (*c*.1659–1701), began divorce proceedings against his wife, Anne (*c*.1667/8–1753), from whom he had been separated for some years, she denied the accusation. She had been living with Richard Savage, Earl Rivers (*c*.1654–1712) but claimed that she had been turned out of her marital home by her husband. The divorce was granted by the House of Lords on 3 March 1698 and the Countess married Col. Henry Brett in 1700.

While the Earl ... an event: the account given by Johnson reflects his own knowledge of Savage, and the story that Savage told him. The truth is more difficult to discern and is still disputed by scholars. Lady Macclesfield did give birth to a son by Rivers in January 1697, having already borne him a daughter in 1695. He was baptized as 'Richard Smith', with Rivers attending as godfather. He was entrusted to the care of nursemaids, and Lady Macclesfield was to claim that he, like her daughter, had died young.

Savage claimed to have been brought up by his 'godmother', Mrs Lloyd, and said that Lady Mason, his supposed maternal grandmother, had provided for him. Lady Macclesfield persuaded Rivers that Savage was not their son and should not be bequeathed any money. Savage, however, appears to have been convinced that he was their son. He managed to convince others, and to get this claim into print, notably in his Preface to his *Miscellaneous Poems and Translations* (1726) and his autobiographical poem *The Bastard* (1728). Contemporaries disputed his story, which appears to have been believed by some of Rivers's own relations.

241 *The Author to be let* ... *The Wanderer*: *An Author to be Lett* (1729) was a satire on Grub Street; *The Wanderer: A Vision* (1729) was a long poem containing reflections on murder and suicide.

amused: deceived, bamboozled.

243 *At this time* ... *disputants*: in 1717 the Bishop of Bangor Benjamin Hoadly (1676–1761), an ardent Whig, provoked controversy with a sermon and a series of pamphlets arguing that private conscience was more important to the good Protestant than ecclesiastical authority. The sermon was delivered before King George I and was printed at his command. Hoadly was close to several government ministers, and his doctrine, with its strong sympathy for Protestant Dissenters, aroused fierce opposition from High Church Anglicans. A shower of pamphlets and sermons followed over the next few years.

244 *He then attempted* ... *the profit*: the truth of this story too is difficult to discern: see Lonsdale, iii. 393 n. 27. It is possible that Savage and the actor and playwright Christopher Bullock (1691?–1722) adapted different plays by Pedro Calderón de la Barca. *A Woman is a Riddle*, based on Calderón's *La dama duende*, was certainly performed under Bullock's name in 1716, and was indeed his most successful play, revived and then adapted several times over the next fifty years.

from the Spanish: it is also from an original by Calderón, *Peor está que estaba* and was performed at Drury Lane on 17 June 1718.

Sir Richard Steele, and Mr. Wilks: Richard Steele (1672–1729) is now best known as the co-author (with Joseph Addison) of *The Tatler* and *The Spectator*. He was also a playwright, political controversialist, and contributor to numerous periodicals. Robert Wilks (*c*.1665–1732) was a leading actor of his day and joint manager, for almost twenty years, of the Drury Lane Theatre.

Sir Richard Steele ... *his father*: this and the anecdotes about Steele that follow are all likely to have been told to Johnson by Savage himself.

247 *the South Sea traffic*: the so-called South Sea Bubble of 1720, in which a speculative frenzy drove up the value of shares in the South Sea Company, which then collapsed. Many lost their fortunes.

Mrs Oldfield: Anne Oldfield (1683–1730) was, by the time she met Savage, a celebrated and highly paid actress, whose performances were often the main attraction of productions at the Drury Lane Theatre.

248 *a benefit*: a theatrical performance whose proceeds were paid to him.

the Duke of Dorset: Lionel Cranfield, Duke of Dorset (1688–1765), who was praised by Savage in his *The Authors of the Town* (1725).

249 *Sir Thomas Overbury*: Sir Thomas Overbury (1581–1613) was poisoned in the Tower of London after opposing the marriage of his patron Robert Carr, Earl of Somerset, to the divorced Countess of Essex.

250 *Mr. Cibber*: Colley Cibber (1671–1757), co-manager of the Drury Lane Theatre.

Mr. Hill: Aaron Hill (1685–1750). The *ODNB* describes him as 'writer and entrepreneur', for as well as being a prolific dramatist and writer for periodicals, he pursued numerous commercial ventures. He was a patron and promoter of various writers, of whom Savage was one.

251 *Mr. Theophilus Cibber*: Theophilus Cibber (1703–58) was the son of Colley Cibber and also an actor and playwright.

252 *Lady Mary Wortley Montague*: Lady Mary Wortley Montagu (1689–1762) was a wit and a friend of men and women of influence. She was famous in the 1720s for having introduced inoculation against smallpox, which she had observed on her travels to Turkey, into Britain.

253 *On the 20th of November . . . till morning*: Johnson bases his account on the 1727 *Life* (see note to p. 239, above) and one of the several published accounts of Savage's trial.

255 *Mr. Page*: Sir Francis Page (1660/1–1741) acquired a reputation as a 'hanging judge'. He is represented as brutal and unjust not only by Johnson but also by Pope in *The Dunciad* (1743), iv. 30, and by Fielding in *Tom Jones*, VIII. xi.

256 *Mr. Savage . . . his mother*: the 1727 *Life* ended with Savage's eventual fate undecided, so, for the account of the petition to the Queen and the supposed intervention of the woman Savage believed to be his mother, Johnson must have relied on what Savage told him.

257 *the Countess of Hertford*: Frances Seymour, Countess of Hertford (1699–1754), who was the patron of Savage's friend, the poet James Thomson.

259 *The peculiar circumstances . . . lessened*: in his note Johnson attributes this anonymous work to the poet and dramatist Charles Beckingham (1699–1731). For debate about its authorship, see Lonsdale, iii. 400 n. 89.

260 *a poem . . . afterwards*: the poem to which Johnson refers is *The Bastard*, though this was in fact published in 1728, a few months after Savage's trial.

261 *Lord Tyrconnel*: Sir John Brownlow, Viscount Tyrconnel (1690–1754), was the nephew of Mrs Brett, the former countess of Macclesfield, and thus, if Savage's claims about his parentage were true, Savage's first cousin. His temporary support for Savage has been taken as evidence that he accepted these claims.

263 *addressed by Mr. Savage ... great satisfaction*: the 'true author', Johnson believes, was Alexander Pope, to whom Savage supplied information for his *Dunciad Variorum* (1729).

Mr. Savage ... random: 'the Bathos' is Pope's *The Art of Sinking in Poetry* (1728). This ridiculed passages of poetry whose authors were identified by initials. The dedication that Johnson mentions claimed that these were arbitrary.

264 *Dennis*: John Dennis (1657–1734), poet and critic. He was a noted foe of Pope and target of his satire.

a panegyrick on Sir Robert Walpole: *An Epistle to the Right Honourable Sir Robert Walpole* (1732).

265 *I fly ... mind*: *The Wanderer*, i. 13–18.

266 *By woe ... and caress*: ibid. ii. 245–50.

274 *for many years*: this may have been the impression that Savage gave Johnson, but the two men seem not to have fallen out until 1735.

278 *No Mother's care ... restrain'd*: *The Bastard.* ll. 89–92.

Eusden: Laurence Eusden (1688–1730) had been Poet Laureate since 1718. He was satirized by Pope as a drunkard as well as a dunce in several poems, including *The Dunciad.*

The Lord Chamberlain: Charles Fitzroy, Duke of Grafton (1683–1757).

Volunteer Laureat: Savage published a series of seven poems on the Queen's birthday (1 March), beginning in 1732.

279 *the following letter*: Johnson believed that the letter had been written by Savage. When it appeared in the *Gentleman's Magazine* it was signed 'T.B.', indicating Savage's (and Johnson's) friend Thomas Birch.

281 *When the Princess ... her departure*: Princess Anne was George II's second child and eldest daughter. In March 1734 she married William IV, Prince of Orange-Nassau (1711–51). Soon after the wedding she left with her husband for the Netherlands. Savage's poem was *On the Departure of the Prince and Princess of Orange* (1734).

The Daily Courant: a subsidized pro-Walpole newspaper.

282 *The dispute ... political conversation*: the dispute was between Edmund Gibson, Bishop of London, and Charles Talbot, the Lord Chancellor.

It concerned the appointment, proposed by Talbot, of the theologically contentious Thomas Rundle to the bishopric of Gloucester.

Mr. Foster and Mr. Thomson: Dr James Foster (1697–1753), a noted Dissenter, and the poet James Thomson.

284 *Sir Philip Yorke*: Yorke (1690–1764) was a successful lawyer who became attorney general, and later Lord Chancellor and earl of Hardwicke.

286 *Lord Bolingbroke*: see note to p. 165, above. Bolingbroke had been a leading Tory.

289 *But what ... their praise?*: *Of Public Spirit*, ll. 79–86.

291 *a bulk*: a framework projecting into the street from a shop.

a glass-house: premises where glass was made, and where the ashes would remain warm at night.

Though misery ... to name: *The Wanderer*, iii. 265–6 and 269–72.

293 *Among these ... then wore*: *The Coffee-House* (1737), a ballad-opera by James Miller, featured an impecunious poet called Bays.

294 *Duck*: the so-called 'thresher-poet' Stephen Duck (1705?–56), who rose from humble origins and work as an agricultural labourer to become a fashionable poet. When his *Poems on Several Occasions* was published in 1736, the subscribers included royalty and nobility. The Queen became his major patron.

295 *the Duke of Chandos*: James Brydges, Duke of Chandos (1674–1744), one of the wealthiest men of the age and a noted patron of the arts.

296 *a friend*: unidentified, though this may have been Solomon Mendes, a Jewish merchant with literary interests.

299 *one of them wrote a letter to him*: this was Alexander Pope, who gave Savage significant financial support after 1738.

300 *the liberties of the Fleet*: debtors were frequently incarcerated in the Fleet Prison, on the east bank of the Fleet River. Debtors could not be arrested in the area around the prison—'the liberties'.

301 *Sir William Lemon*: Sir William Leman (1685–1741), son-in-law of Mrs Brett, the former countess of Macclesfield.

303 *he has celebrated Mr. Powel and Mrs. Jones*: John Powell (1705–69) was a prominent Swansea barrister and Bridget Jones (1713–80) an attractive widow.

308 *Newgate*: the main prison in Bristol.

309 *Mr. Nash at Bath*: Richard Nash (1674–1761) was master of ceremonies at Bath and more commonly known as 'Beau Nash'. He helped establish

Bath as the nation's most fashionable resort, and by the 1740s, when he assisted Savage, was a notable public figure.

311 *his friend*: almost certainly Edward Cave, editor of the *Gentleman's Magazine*.

313 *Henley ... Savage*: Dissenting minister John Henley (1692–1756) was better known as 'Orator Henly' because he was a noted preacher who charged admission to his sermons at his self-styled 'Oratory' in London. He was the butt of many satirists, notably Pope in his *Dunciad*. In May 1743 the *Daily Advertiser* announced that Henley was to preach a sermon on Pope's 'Cruelty' to Savage.

SWIFT

318 *An Account ... our friendship*: John Hawkesworth (1720–73), originally a co-worker on the *Gentleman's Magazine*, was a close friend of Johnson. In 1755 he published an edition of *The Works of Jonathan Swift*, 6 vols. (hereafter Hawkesworth). A life of Swift was prefixed to it. Johnson clearly advised Hawkesworth, perhaps on his use of existing sources. Hawkesworth's account says very little about Swift's writings and emphasizes his activities as a clergyman. It is a largely admiring narrative. Johnson's account often closely follows Hawkesworth's, paragraph by paragraph, though subtly altering details to achieve a more negative impression of Swift's character traits.

an account ... himself: the autobiographical fragment 'The Family of Swift', which had been printed in Deane Swift's *An Essay upon the Life, Writings, and Character, of Dr. Jonathan Swift* (1755).

the University of Dublin: i.e. Trinity College Dublin.

319 *Sir William Temple*: the author and former diplomat Sir William Temple (1628–99) had been active as a statesman in the 1660s and 1670s, but by 1688 lived in retirement at his Moor Park estate in Surrey.

the Earl of Portland: Hans Willem Bentinck (1649–1709) was a Dutch nobleman who had accompanied William of Orange to England in 1688.

320 *Cyprian and Irenæus*: early fathers of the Christian Church.

Lord Orrery: John Boyle, Earl of Cork and Earl of Orrery (1707–62), had been friendly with Pope and acquainted with Swift. He was the author of *Remarks on the Life and Writings of Dr Jonathan Swift* (1751), written in the form of letters to his son. It was one of Hawkesworth's main sources and therefore influenced Johnson's account.

320 *being recommended ... a year*: a *prebend* is the tenure of parish and its revenue. Henry, Lord Capel (1639–96) was one of the three Lord Justices of Ireland.

321 *the Athenian Society*: this was the supposed literary club that published the *Athenian Gazette, or, Casuistical Mercury*, a periodical begun in 1691 by the bookseller and miscellaneous author John Dunton. The journal invited readers to send questions which would be answered by the club of learned men, which in fact consisted of Dunton and a couple of friends.

Cousin Swift: Dryden was Swift's second cousin once removed.

the Earl of Berkeley: in 1699 Swift became chaplain to Charles, Earl of Berkeley (1649–1710), who had been appointed Lord Justice of Ireland. He retained this position when Arthur Bushe was made Berkeley's secretary.

Soon after ... for her life: Stella was Esther Johnson (1681–1728), the daughter of Temple's steward. She came to Ireland with Rebecca Dingley (*c*.1665–1743), a dependent relative of Temple who had become her companion.

322 *Archbishop Sharpe ... a bishoprick*: *A Tale of a Tub*, like all of Swift's satires, was published anonymously. Hawkesworth was Johnson's source for the story about John Sharp, Archbishop of York (1645–1717), and Elizabeth Seymour, Duchess of Somerset (1667–1722).

Sacheverell ... Smalridge: for Sacheverell, see note to p. 146, above. George Smalridge (1663–1719) was Dean of Christ Church, Oxford, and Bishop of Bristol.

Wotton and Bentley: William Wotton (1666–1727) and Richard Bentley (1662–1742) had both challenged Sir William Temple's arguments, in his essay 'Of Ancient and Modern Learning', for the superiority of the ancients over the moderns.

The Battle ... disowned: Johnson's accusation of plagiarism is almost certainly unjust. See Lonsdale, iii. 435 n. 29.

323 *The attention ... reader's notice*: Swift's anonymous series of Bickerstaff papers mocking astrology in general and the astrologer John Partridge in particular appeared in 1708 and 1709. When he began the *Tatler* Steele adopted the name 'Bickerstaff' as its supposed author.

324 *Soon after ... for pardon*: Swift was sent to London by William King, Archbishop of Dublin (1650–1720), to negotiate for the remission of ancient fees paid by the clergy to the crown. Robert Harley (1661–1724), who was to become a friend and associate of Swift, was Lord Treasurer.

the name of Brother: 'The Brothers' was a Tory dining club.

those by which Addison opposed him: in reply to the Tory periodical the *Examiner*, Adddison produced the *Whig Examiner*.

the Earl of Oxford: this was Robert Harley's new title.

326 *the General*: this is John Churchill, Duke of Marlborough (1650–1722), who had made his name as commander of British troops in a series of victories over the French in the War of the Spanish Succession, beginning with Blenheim in 1704. Swift's *Conduct of the Allies* includes an attack upon him.

Burnet: see note to p. 378, below.

328 *multa gemens, with many a groan*: *Aeneid*, i. 465.

329 *Aislabie*: John Aislabie (1670–1742) was a politician who became influential after George I came to the throne in 1714, and who became Chancellor of the Exchequer in 1718.

Dr. Delany: Patrick Delany (1685?–1768), author of *Observations upon Lord Orrery's Remarks* (1755), a rejoinder to Orrery's account of Swift.

330 *Dr. Lucas*: Charles Lucas (1713–71), a physician and political radical.

old Mr. Lewis: Swift's friend Erasmus Lewis (1670–1754). Lewis had been secretary to Robert Harley, Earl of Oxford, to whom he had introduced Swift. *The Journal to Stella* records Swift dining frequently with Lewis, who had become Harley's confidant. Lewis was friendly with Pope, Gay, and Arbuthnot (whose will he witnessed). In the negotiation with the bookseller Benjamin Motte over *Gulliver's Travels*, Lewis was Swift's representative.

Mr. Worral: John Worral (*c.*1666–1751) was master of the choirs of St Patrick's Cathedral.

Soon after ... in the garden: the true nature of the relationship between Swift and 'Stella' has always been a subject for speculation and dispute. Dr St George Ashe (1658–1718) was Swift's tutor at Trinity College Dublin and the two men became friends. At the time of the supposed wedding, Ashe was bishop of Clogher. The story of Swift's marriage was repeated by all his eighteenth-century biographers. Samuel Madden (1686–1765) was a clergyman and author, and had been a close friend of Swift. In the 1740s he came to know Johnson, who in his thirties edited some of Madden's work.

331 *Mrs. Van Homrigh*: Hester Vanhomrigh (1688–1723), whom Swift met in London in 1707 and with whom he had a close relationship, the nature of which is still a matter of biographical speculation. It appears to be dramatized in his poem *Cadenus and Vanessa*.

men are but men: Swift's disdain for this explanation is unidentified.

thus related by Delany: Delany, *Observations*, 57–8.

332 *upon a broomstick*: see Swift's *Meditation upon a Broomstick* (1710).

332 *The great acquisition ... without change*: William Wood (1671–1730), a Wolverhampton ironmaster, obtained, via George I's mistress the Duchess of Munster, a patent to supply coinage worth over £100,000 for use in Ireland. The brass content was low, and the imposition of the coinage without regulation of its quality, or any consultation, alienated Irish opinion.

one Whitshed, then Chief Justice: William Whitshed (*c.*1656–1727), Lord Chief Justice of the King's Bench in Ireland. He tried Edward Waters, the printer of one of *The Drapier's Letters*.

333 *Lord Carteret ... the Fourth Letter*: John Carteret, Earl Granville (1690–1763), arrived in Dublin as Lord Lieutenant in October 1724. He was an acquaintance of Swift's. By the time that he arrived the Drapier's identity was public knowledge. Carteret himself shared the knowledge (his secretary, Thomas Tickell, identified Swift in his correspondence). Yet, despite the huge reward being offered, Swift was never officially identified as the author. It was the printer, Harding, who was arrested, on Carteret's orders, and who subsequently died in prison.

334 *Archbishop Boulter*: Hugh Boulter (1672–1742), Archbishop of Armagh and Lord Justice of Ireland. Boulter (along with Carteret) had advised the government to withdraw Wood's coinage, which they did.

the king's death: George I died 11 June 1727.

335 *Mrs. Barber*: Mary Barber (*c.*1685–1755), the wife of a Dublin woollen draper. Barber was an acquaintance of Lord Carteret, through whom she became known to Swift, who was impressed by her poetry. Swift supported the subscription to her *Poems* (1734). Despite Johnson's imputations, there is no reason to doubt his assertions that the signature on the letter to Queen Caroline was indeed forged, and that he knew nothing of it.

Mrs. Howard ... Mrs. Masham: Henrietta Howard, Countess of Suffolk (*c.*1688–1767), was a mistress of George II, though her influence over the King seems to have been negligible. She cultivated the company of leading writers, including Pope and Gay. Abigail Masham (1670?–1734) was a lady-in-waiting to Queen Anne who became her confidante and adviser.

two sick friends cannot live together: adapted from a letter from Swift to Pope, 12 Oct. 1727.

assurance double sure: *Macbeth*, IV. i. 83.

336 *In some ... Life of Swift*: 'Biographical Anecdotes of Dean Swift' by John Lyon (1710–90), included in Philip Nichols's *Supplement to Dr. Swift's Works* (1779). Lyon might have been supposed to write with authority. Swift had been his patron when he was a young clergyman, and he had

been appointed a minor canon at St Patrick's. In 1740 he had moved into the deanery to serve as Swift's secretary. He inherited a number of Swift's papers.

Dr. Sheridan: Thomas Sheridan (1687–1738), a clergyman and schoolmaster, and friend of Swift. He impressed Swift with his learning and gave him lessons in Greek.

but if not … have parted: from a letter from Swift to Pope, 12 Oct. 1727.

337 *In a short poem … contempt*: the poem was 'On the Words—Brother Protestants and Fellow Christians' (1733). It mocked Irish MP Richard Bettesworth (*c.*1689–1741).

339 *Mrs. Whiteway*: from the mid-1730s Martha Whiteway (1690–1768), Swift's widowed cousin, helped look after him.

was his debtor: see *Verses on the Death of Dr Swift*, l. 483.

341 *rather with … than harmonious*: from Hawkesworth, i. 39.

he could only preach pamphlets: from Delany, *Observations*, 41–2.

342 *a story … a specimen*: Spence, i. 53–4. See note to p. 3, above.

345 *Dr. Delany … in these terms*: Johnson quotes from the conclusion to Delany's *Observations*, 289–91.

346 *proper words in proper places*: from Swift's *A Letter to a Young Gentleman* (1720).

POPE

347 *gentle blood*: Johnson is quoting Pope himself, in his *Epistle to Dr Arbuthnot*, l. 388. The rest of the paragraph is based on Pope's own biographical note to l. 381 of the same poem.

Mr. Tyers … Mrs. Racket: Thomas Tyers (1724/5–87) was joint proprietor of Vauxhall Pleasure Gardens, which his father had made famous, and a friend of Johnson. His *Historical Rhapsody on Mr Pope* (1781) was a collection of biographical vignettes of Pope. Johnson added this information to his *Lives* in 1783. Mrs Magdalen Racket was Pope's half-sister, his father's daughter by a previous marriage.

the little Nightingale: Pope was apparently so called by the dramatist Thomas Southerne. Johnson found the story in Owen Ruffhead's *Life of Alexander Pope* (1769), one of his main sources for his life of the poet.

Taverner, a Romish priest: 'Edward Taverner' was the alias of the priest John Banister, who became master of a Roman Catholic school at Twyford, Hampshire, which Pope briefly attended.

Ogylby's ... Ovid: John Ogilby (1600–76) published, among many translations, versions of both Homer's *Iliad* (1660) and *Odyssey* (1665). For Sandys's *Ovid*, see note to p. 146, above.

348 *he lisp'd in numbers*: see *Epistle to Dr Arbuthnot*, l. 128.

the bees swarmed about his mouth: there are several sources for this story that Pindar was set on the course of poetry when, as a boy, a swarm of bees found him asleep in the fields and fed him with honey.

the Revolution: the Glorious Revolution of 1688.

Tully's Offices: Tully is the writer better known as Cicero.

349 *the Thebais*: Statius' *Thebaid*.

350 *Sir William Trumbal*: Sir William Trumbull (1639–1716) had been a diplomat and government official, rising to become a secretary of state in the 1690s. He retired from politics to his home at Easthampstead, near where Pope was living at Binfield, in Windsor Forest, and came to cultivate the young poet.

351 *Wycherley*: William Wycherley (1641–1716) was a former Restoration dramatist, notorious for his comedies of the 1670s such as *The Country Wife*. Pope met him in 1705 and pursued the acquaintance. The two men met frequently afterwards and took up a correspondence. Pope helped Wycherley revise his poems for publication, though the older writer appears to have resented the young man's suggestions as to necessary revisions.

Dennis: see note to p. 264, above. Dennis, ever Pope's antagonist, claimed that Wycherley's admiring poem 'To my friend Mr. Pope, on his Pastorals', published in Tonson's *Poetical Miscellanies*, vi (1709), had been written by Pope himself.

Mr. Cromwell: Henry Cromwell (1659–1728) was a poet and translator who became a friend and correspondent of the young Pope.

Mrs. Thomas ... to Curll: the author Elizabeth Thomas (1675–1731) met Pope through Henry Cromwell. Cromwell gave her some letters between himself and Pope. Years later, in severe financial difficulties, she sold these to Edmund Curll (1675–1747), a notoriously unscrupulous bookseller, who published them in *Miscellanea* (1726). In revenge, Pope savagely satirized both Thomas and Curll in *The Dunciad*.

Walsh: William Walsh (1662–1708) was an MP and poet who had been one of Dryden's circle at Will's Coffee House. Pope stayed at his Worcestershire home and Walsh commented on and suggested revisions to his early pastorals. Pope subsequently celebrated him as 'the Muse's Judge and Friend' in his *An Essay on Criticism*, l. 729.

352 *Tonson's Miscellany*: the bookseller Jacob Tonson published several anthologies of new work by contemporary poets. The miscellany of 1709 in which Pope first published his poetry was Tonson's sixth such collection.

353 *"who ... magnanimity"*: a version of a passage from Dennis's *Reflections Critical and Satyrical, upon ... An Essay upon Criticism* (1711): see *The Critical Works of John Dennis*, ed. E. N. Hooker, 2 vols. (Baltimore, 1939–43), i. 396–7.

There are ... at strife: *An Essay on Criticism*, ll. 80–2.

terms too elegant to be forgotten: Dennis, *Works*, i. 404.

354 *the passage*: Pope silently conceded Dennis's point by revising these lines. See *An Essay on Criticism*, ll. 500–3.

"For his acquaintance ... understanding": Dennis, *Works*, i. 416–17.

355 *Dr. Warburton ... by the author*: William Warburton (1689–1779) was a clergyman and ambitious man of letters who wrote an elaborate commentary on Pope's *Essay*. He would later become known to the poet after defending in print the Christian orthodoxy of Pope's *Essay on Man*. See note to p. 391, below. The translations were by Anthony Hamilton (1644/5?–1719), John Robethon (d. 1722), and Jean-François Du Bellay Du Resnel (1692–1761).

It is possible ... inferred: Richard Hooker, *Of the Laws of Ecclesiastical Polity* (1593–7), II. i. 2.

Mr. Ruffhead: see note to p. 347, above.

356 *Mr. Caryl*: Pope's friend and correspondent was John Caryll (1667–1736), one of a circle of genteel Roman Catholic acquaintances near his then home in Windsor Forest. Caryll encouraged Pope's poetic ambitions and provided the poet with the story on which *The Rape of the Lock* is based. Johnson confuses him with his uncle, also called John Caryll (1625–1711), whose heir he was.

357 *Sir George Brown*: Sir George Browne (d. 1730) apparently spoke in a blustering manner, which is suitably parodied in the poem.

at Paris ... her family: in 1775 Johnson travelled for the first time to France and in Paris met Mrs Fermor, abbess of an English convent and niece of the Arabella Fermor who was the original of Pope's Belinda in *The Rape of the Lock*.

merum sal: 'pure wit', from Lucretius, *De Rerum Natura*, iv. 1162.

Berkeley: the philosopher and clergyman George Berkeley (1685–1753).

358 *the Peace*: the Treaty of Utrecht (1713), which ended the War of the Spanish Succession.

Lord Lansdowne: George Granville, Baron Lansdowne (1666–1735), was a leading Tory politician during the reign of Queen Anne. As a minor poet and dramatist he is included in Johnson's *Lives*.

359 *Cato*: Joseph Addison's 1713 tragedy *Cato* was widely admired when it was first staged. It owed its notoriety partly to the fact that both Whigs and Tories appropriated its story of the virtuous Roman republican who commits suicide rather than submit to the tyrannical Caesar. It was a great commercial as well as critical success.

to revenge ... Dennis: Dennis published his *Remarks upon Cato*, a critique of Addison's tragedy, in 1713. Pope's response was a mock-dialogue in which Dennis raves about the play to his nurse.

a Letter to him: this letter addressed to Addison and dated 20 July 1713 was in fact fabricated by Pope from an actual letter that he had written to Caryll the year before.

This year ... Pope: see note to p. 230, above.

Jervas: the portrait painter Charles Jervas (1675–1739). Amongst the subjects of his portraits were Pope's intimate friends Martha and Theresa Blount, and Jonathan Swift. Pope wrote an 'Epistle to Mr Jervas' in 1716.

Lord Mansfield: William Murray, Earl of Mansfield (1705–93), was a judge and politician who had been a friend of Pope's as a young man in the 1730s. The portrait remains in the possession of Mansfield's descendants.

Betterton: for Betterton see note to p. 77, above.

360 *Fenton*: see note to p. 54, above.

361 *Bernard Lintot*: the leading bookseller Bernard Lintot (1675–1736) was a rival of Jacob Tonson and, like him, specialized in poetry and translation. The first version of Pope's *The Rape of the Lock* was published in one of his miscellanies. He paid generously for Pope's *Iliad* but, despite being undercut by piracies, still made a substantial profit from the work. He and Pope later quarrelled over the latter's *Odyssey* translation.

363 *If more help was wanting ... Ogylby*: Johnson refers to translations of Homer by Helius Eobanus Hessus (1540) (into Latin), the Abbé de la Valterie (1681), and Anne Lefebvre Dacier (1711) (both into French prose), and George Chapman (1616), Thomas Hobbes (1676), and John Ogilby (1660–5), all into English.

Eustathius: Eustathius (*c.*1110–1198) was archbishop of Thessalonika and a celebrated annotator of Homer.

Broome: William Broome (1689–1745) was a poet and translator who was introduced to Pope in 1714. He was employed by Pope to extract annotations from the writings of Eustathius. He would later translate eight books of Pope's version of the *Odyssey*.

364 *Thirlby ... Jortin*: Styan Thirlby (1691–1753), a fellow of Jesus College, Cambridge, recommended John Jortin (1698–1770) to Pope. Thirlby was Jortin's tutor. Jortin translated Eustathius' commentary on Homer for Pope's use in his notes to the *Iliad*, though the two men never met.

The terms ... mercantile: Johnson refers to a letter from Fenton to Pope in September 1718.

Parnell: the Irish-born Thomas Parnell (1679–1718) was a poet and essayist, an associate of Swift, and a member of the Scriblerus Club. He assisted Pope with his translation of Homer, staying at Binfield and later at Bath with him in 1714. His 'Essay on the life, writings and learning of Homer' was included in Pope's *Iliad*.

365 *Mr. Craggs*: James Craggs, the younger (1686–1721), a prominent Whig politician, who became secretary of state in 1718.

The Duke of Buckingham: see note to p. 115, above.

descended from ... Museum: Johnson was able to borrow the manuscripts of Pope's *Iliad* translations during the composition of the *Lives*. Dr Matthew Maty (1718–76) was librarian of the British Museum. David Mallet (1701/2–65) was a friend of Pope and was Bolingbroke's literary executor.

366 *From the first ... their variations*: in 1780 the Homer manuscripts were sent to the Thrales' home at Streatham where Johnson transcribed them.

372 *Garth*: Sir Samuel Garth (1660/1–1719) was a renowned physician and also a poet, author of the mock-heroic account of a conflict between physicians and apothecaries, *The Dispensary* (1699). Despite his Whig allegiances he had been a friend of Dryden and was an early mentor to Pope.

373 *"I am obliged ... yours &c."*: Johnson derived Pope's letter from Spence. It is in fact dated 3 December 1714.

374 *nothing but ... knowledge*: *Iliad*, ii. 486.

375 *Kennet*: White Kennett (1660–1728) was an historian and clergyman, eventually bishop of Peterborough. He was a dedicated Whig.

376 *Tickell*: see note to p. 230, above.

Maynwaring: see note to p. 219, above.

377 *quincunx*: a pattern of trees arranged in a group of five, with four occupying the corners of a square or rectangle and the fifth its centre.

378 *Burnet*: Thomas Burnet (1694–1753) was eventually a judge. As a young man he published *Homerides* (1715), a satire on Pope subtitled *A letter to*

Mr. Pope, occasion'd by his intended translation of Homer; by Sir Iliad Doggrel. It was written with his friend and literary collaborator George Duckett. It earned both of them a place in *The Dunciad*.

Ducket: George Duckett (1684–1732), author and Whig MP, collaborated with Thomas Burnet (see note above).

378 *the South Sea*: see note to p. 247, above.

379 *Tonson*: i.e. Jacob Tonson the younger (1682–1735), who approached Alexander Pope to compose a new edition of Shakespeare's plays.

Theobald . . . a haughty character: for Theobald, see note to p. 96, above. Theobald's *Shakespeare Restored, or, A specimen of the many errors as well committed, as unamended, by Mr. Pope in his late edition of this poet* (1726) attacked Pope's 1725 edition of Shakespeare for its sloppy textual scholarship.

380 *Bishop Atterbury*: Francis Atterbury, Bishop of Rochester (1663–1732), was accused of Jacobite conspiracy and tried for treason before the House of Lords in 1723. Pope testified on his behalf. He was found guilty and sentenced to banishment. On the continent he joined the court of the Old Pretender, the self-styled James III.

381 *Spence*: see note to p. 169, above. His *Essay on Pope's Odyssey* (1726) won for its author Pope's friendship.

Burnet's importance in his own History: Pope and Gay were satirizing the manner of Gilbert Burnet's *History of his Own Time* (1724, 1734), which is often accused of overstating the author's own historical significance.

Mr. Fortescue: William Fortescue (1687–1749), a future judge, met Pope through his friend John Gay and became a member of the Scriblerus Club.

382 *Ralph*: James Ralph (1705?–62) attacked Pope in his blank verse satire *Sawney, an Heroic Poem Occasion'd by the Dunciad* (1728). This earned him a place in the second edition of *The Dunciad*.

383 *a Dedication . . . Savage*: see note to p. 263, above.

385 *pious passion . . . friendship*: *Dunciad*, iii. 176.

Aaron Hill: see note to p. 250, above.

Cleland: William Cleland (1673/4–1741), a friend of Pope's. A letter written by Pope, but signed William Cleland (dated 22 December 1728 from St James's), was prefixed to the enlarged edition of *The Dunciad*.

the Duke of Chandos: James Brydges, Duke of Chandos (1673–1744), became massively wealthy after acting as paymaster to the British forces during the War of the Spanish Succession. He was an ambitious patron of the arts, particularly music. He bought an estate at Cannons at

Edgware, north of London, which he improved and adorned in ostentatious fashion.

386 *There is nothing ... favour*: see Juvenal, *Satires*, iv. 70–1.

387 *Lintot, the son of Bernard*: Henry Lintot (1703–58) was son of the famous bookseller Bernard Lintot and himself became a bookseller. He bought the copyright to *The Dunciad* when it became available.

388 *Mr. Allen*: Ralph Allen (1693–1764) made himself wealthy through the innovative operation of postal services. Once established, he became a notable philanthropist.

James Worsdale: the portrait painter James Worsdale (*c*.1692–1767) began as Sir Godfrey Kneller's apprentice and had considerable success as a painter of royalty and of society figures. He also had a dramatic career, acting in London and Dublin theatres.

389 *Howel indeed ... or friend*: Johnson refers to James Howell, *Epistolae Ho-Elianae*, 4 vols. (1645–55) (see note to p. 65, above); Daniel George Morhoff, *De Ratione Conscribendarum Epistolarum Libellus* (1716); Robert Loveday, *Letters, Domestick and Forrein* (1659); George Herbert's letters in Izaak Walton's *Life* (1670); and Sir John Suckling's *Last Remains* (1659).

390 *A mighty maze ... plan*: Pope, *An Essay on Man*, i. 6.

And spite ... spite: ibid. 293.

391 *the doctrine ... from Bolingbroke*: Bolingbroke was a deist (see note to p. 165, below) and privately scornful of Christian faith. Though a Roman Catholic, Pope had written a poem that was interpreted by some as being deistic.

It was first turned ... paragraph: Johnson refers to Étienne de Silhouette, *Essai sur l'homme* (1736), and J. F. Du B. Du Resnel, *Les Principes de la morale* (1737). The religious implications of the *Essay on Man* were analysed in a hostile fashion by the Swiss theologian Jean Pierre de Crousaz (1663–1750) in his *Examen de l'Essai de M. Pope sur l'homme* (1737). He identified the poem's doctrine with the writings of the deistic German philosopher Leibniz. William Warburton won Pope's friendship by defending the theology of the *Essay on Man* in a *Vindication* published in 1740.

392 *oderint dum metuant*: Suetonius's judgement on Caligula in *De Vita Caesarum*, IV. xxx ('he was content to be hated as long as he was feared').

Concanen: Matthew Concanen (1701–49) had been a friend and collaborator of William Warburton, who might even have contributed to his anonymous attack on Pope, *A Supplement to the Profound* (1728). Concanen was probably also the editor of *A Complete Collection* (1728), a republication of satirical replies to the Pope–Swift *Miscellanies*. He is duly mocked in *The Dunciad*. Concanen was also a friend of Pope's foe Lewis Theobald. Pope appears to have remained ignorant of Warburton's early involvement with both men.

393 *Mr. R.*: Jacob Robinson, bookseller and publisher of *History of the Works of the Learned*. It was in this periodical that parts of Warburton's defence of Pope's *Essay on Man* first appeared.

394 *Mr. Hooke*: the translator and historian Nathaniel Hooke (d. 1763). He was a Roman Catholic and Pope became one of his patrons. It was Hooke who brought a priest to Pope's deathbed.

Mr. Murray: William Murray, later Earl of Mansfield. See note to p. 359, above.

Dobson: William Dobson, who had published a Latin translation of Prior's *Solomon* (1734–6). He completed his translation only of the first two epistles of the poem.

among the great: see Pope's *Imitations of Horace, Satire II. i*, l. 133. 'The great' are those with worldly power, officially scorned by any self-respecting satirist.

Mr. Southcot: the Roman Catholic priest Thomas Southcott (1670–1748).

395 *refusing the visits of a Queen*: see Swift's poem *A Libel on Doctor Delany*, ll. 73–4.

the praise ... Ross: see *An Epistle to Bathurst*, ll. 249–80, where Pope gives an admiring vignette of the philanthropic John Kyrle (1634–1724), sometimes known as 'the Man of Ross'. Kyrle lived in Ross-on-Wye, Herefordshire, and Pope found out about him from Jacob Tonson, who had a house nearby at Ledbury. Pope did not know Kyrle personally.

Mr. Victor: author and theatre manager Benjamin Victor (d. 1778).

396 *Martha Blount*: Pope met Martha Blount (1690–1763) and her elder sister Teresa when he was about 20, and Martha in particular remained his close friend for the rest of his life. There were contemporary rumours that she was his mistress, and there has been much biographical speculation since, but there is no good evidence of this. She belonged to a genteel but impecunious Roman Catholic family living near Pope when he was in Binfield. Pope addressed to Martha his satirical *Epistle to a Lady* (1735).

397 *Vice too high*: see Pope's *Imitations of Horace, Satire II. i*, ll. 59–60.

the Dutchess of Marlborough: the character of Atossa in the *Epistle to a Lady* was widely believed to be based on Sarah Churchill, Duchess of Marlborough, (1660–1744), widow of the Whig hero, the Duke of Marlborough, and, during the reign of Queen Anne, a powerful courtier in her own right.

the Duke of Shrewsbury: Charles Talbot, Duke of Shrewsbury (1660–1718). The point is that the suggestion must have been made to Pope years before it was taken up.

derived ... Esprit: Johnson refers to Boileau's 'Épitre X' ('A mes vers').

398 *Who but ... were he?*: *An Epistle to Dr Arbuthnot*, ll. 213–14.

Lord Hervey: John, Lord Hervey (1696–1743), was a leading Whig politician and courtier. He was a confidant of Walpole. He quarrelled with his former friend and fellow Whig politician William Pultney and, after an exchange of insults in pamphlets, the two men duelled with swords in Green Park, London, each wounding the other. He won the enmity of Pope partly for political reasons, but more because, with Pope's former intimate Lady Mary Wortley Montagu, he viciously satirized the poet in *Verses Address'd to the Imitator of Horace* (1733).

Hard as ... obscure: *Verses Address'd to the Imitator of Horace* (1733), l. 20.

399 *low-born Allen*: see note to p. 388, above. Allen's Cornish father had been either a labourer or an innkeeper, perhaps both.

one of the Foxes: the politician Henry Fox (1705–74).

About this time ... his publisher: the satirist Paul Whitehead (1710–74) was summoned before the House of Lords because of a contemptuous reference to Thomas Sherlock, Bishop of Salisbury, in his anti-Walpolean satire *Manners* (1739).

400 *the History of Mr. Oufle*: Laurent Bordelon's *The History of the Ridiculous Extravagances of Mr. Oufle* (1711).

A small selection ... undertaking: Johnson refers to *Anthologia* (1684), a collection of Latin verse by Italian poets which was thought to be edited by Francis Atterbury (see note to p. 380, above).

401 *I never have offended him*: see Cibber's autobiographical *Apology for his Life* (1740), 22–3.

402 *a pamphlet*: *A Letter from Mr. Cibber, to Mr. Pope* (1742).

403 *Osborne*: the bookseller Thomas Osborne (1704–67). In the early 1740s Johnson himself had famously quarrelled with Osborne, who was employing him on the Harleian catalogue. After Osborne abused him for time-wasting, Johnson felled him with a folio volume.

another pamphlet: Cibber wrote several more pamphlets; this one is *Another Occasional Letter from Mr. Cibber to Mr. Pope* (1744).

I have heard Mr. Richardson: since Jonathan Richardson (see note to p. 77, above) was born in 1694 this cannot have been a boyhood memory as here implied. However, Johnson did certainly talk to Richardson about his memories of Pope, whom Johnson himself never encountered.

404 *Dr. Thomson*: Dr Thomas Thompson (d. 1763) was a well-known quack.

Lord Marchmont: the source for this story was Pope's friend Hugh Hume Campbell, Earl of Marchmont (1708–94). Boswell organized a meeting between him and Johnson in May 1779, at which Johnson heard Marchmont's recollections of the poet.

406 *the Bishop of Gloucester*: William Warburton (see note to p. 355, above).

reserved for the next age: see Pope's *Imitations of Horace, Satire II. i*, ll. 59–60.

The Patriot King: Bolingbroke's *Letters on the Spirit of Patriotism* (1749).

Mallet: see note to p. 365, above.

407 *He brought ... benefactions*: Johnson follows Ruffhead's account, but Pope's reference to Ralph Allen in his will was not as Johnson describes.

his account of the Little Club: Pope's account is in the *Guardian*, nos. 91 and 92 (1713).

408 *a long disease*: from Pope's *Epistle to Dr Arbuthnot*, l. 132.

C'est que ... enfant: Johnson had used the lines before in a letter to Hesther Thrale of 4 July 1780. They have various sources: see Lonsdale, iv. 305 n. 259.

nodded in company: see Pope's *Imitations of Horace, Satire II. i*, l. 13.

409 *Hannibal ... a ring*: Juvenal, *Satires*, x. 164–6. Having been betrayed to the Romans, Hannibal took poison which he had concealed in a ring.

He hardly drank tea without a stratagem: one of Johnson's best-known *bon mots* in the *Lives* is in fact adapted from a line by Edward Young in his *Love of Fame*, vi. 190.

he plaid ... turnips: from Lord Marchmont, see note to p. 404, above.

410 *When an objection ... put together*: Pope had composed a Latin inscription for Shakespeare's monument, which was criticized by Samuel Patrick (1684–1748), editor of a Latin dictionary. The Latin quotation is from Virgil's *Aeneid*, ii. 204 ('I shudder as I mention it') and is a joke about the occupation of dictionary-making that Johnson shared with Patrick.

Lady Mary Wortley: see note to p. 252, above.

411 *his Highness's dog*: 'I am his Highness' Dog at *Kew*; | Pray tell me Sir, whose Dog are you?'

Lord Bathurst: Allen, Earl Bathurst (1684–1775), was a Tory politician who cultivated literary men, including Pope. Pope addressed one of his *Moral Essays*, 'On the Use of Riches', to Bathurst.

Cobham, Burlington, or Bolingbroke: two of Pope's *Moral Essays* were addressed respectively to Richard Temple, Viscount Cobham (1675–1749), owner of the house and landscaped gardens at Stowe, and Richard Boyle, Earl of Burlington (1694–1753), architectural connoisseur and literary patron. Bolingbroke was the addressee of Pope's *Essay on Man*.

414 *a fool to Fame*: *Epistle to Dr Arbuthnot*, l. 127.

415 *Of his vain desire ... in his retreat*: Pope satirized the classical scholar Richard Bentley in *The Dunciad* (1743), iv. 199–274. For Bentley, see note to p. 32, above.

421 *Zephyrs ... in silence*: see *Pastorals*, 'Winter', ll. 49–50.

The design ... The Park: Johnson refers to Denham's *Cooper's Hill* (1642) and Waller's *A Poem on St James's Park* (1661).

422 *the original vision of Chaucer*: i.e. Chaucer's *The House of Fame*.

the Pollio: Virgil's 'Eclogue IV'.

423 *Pindar is said ... solutis*: in his *Odes*, IV. ii. 11–12 Horace describes Pindar as writing 'in measures free from rule'.

as Mr. Cobb ... an impudent one: Samuel Cobb (1675–1713), who published several Pindaric odes, was a student at Trinity College, Cambridge, when Bentley was Master there.

424 *what Perrault ... long tail*: from Charles Perrault, *Parallèle des anciens et des modernes* (1693), ii. 41.

425 *the sound ... the sense*: *An Essay on Criticism*, l. 365.

With many ... the ground: Pope's *Odyssey*, xi. 735–8. Though Brome translated Book XI, Pope wrote or approved these lines.

426 *When Ajax ... the main*: *An Essay on Criticism*, ll. 370–3.

Waller was ... energy divine: *Imitations of Horace, Epistle II. i*, ll. 267–9.

427 *to laugh at ... sex*: from Pope's prefactory dedication to Arabella Fermor.

the Lutrin: Boileau's anticlerical satire *Le Lutrin* (1674).

428 *curiosa felicitas*: Petronius, *Satyricon*, 118 ('studied felicity').

the learned author ... of Pope: Joseph Warton (1722–1800), whose *An Essay on the Writings and Genius of Pope* (1756) was an influential reconsideration (and diminution) of Pope's status.

429 *Anguillara's Ovid*: Giovanni Anguillara's 1584 translation of Ovid's *Metamorphoses* into Italian.

Salvini: Antonio Salvini's Italian version of the *Iliad* appeared in 1723.

Germanicus: the Roman general Nero Claudius Germanicus (15 BC–AD 19), like Cicero, translated Aratus' *Phaenomena*.

the plays of Terence ... Menander: all but two of the Latin plays of Terence were adapted from Greek plays by Menander.

430 *necessitas quod cogit defendit*: Seneca Rhetor, *Controversiae*, IX. iv. 5. Johnson provides his own translation.

431 *impune ... Telephus*: Juvenal, *Satires*, i. 4–5. The lines refer to having had to watch a tedious tragedy about the mythological Telephus: 'Shall I have no revenge on one who has taken up the whole day with an interminable Telephus?'

432 *Moore*: James Moore Smythe (1702–34), mocked in *The Dunciad*, ii. 35–50 and 109–20.

Leibnitian: see note to p. 391, above.

433 *from infinite ... is wise*: *An Essay on Man*, i. 17–32, 207–58, and ii. 294.

434 *Boileau's Satire*: Boileau, *Satire* X.

435 *Musick ... poetry*: Dryden, Preface to *Tyrannick Love*.

436 *Lo, where ... of snows*: *Dunciad*, iii. 87–8.

Watts: Isaac Watts, *The Improvement of the Mind* (1741), 357–8.

Hall's Satires: see note to p. 204, above.

437 *The following letter ... Mr. Jodrell*: Pope's letter to Ralph Bridges dated 5 April 1708 was owned by the Earl of Hardwicke (1720–90) and was obtained for Johnson by the dramatist Richard Jodrell (1745–1831).

Hobbes: see note to p. 363, above.

439 *The Criticism ... the Life*: what follows is Johnson's 'Dissertation on the Epitaphs Written by Pope', which was first published in Christopher Smart's *Universal Visiter* (May 1756), pp. 207–19, and reprinted in a revised version in the collected edition of the *Idler* (1767), ii. 287–324.

CHARLES Earl of DORSET: see note to p. 152, above.

442 *the Hon. SIMON HARCOURT*: Simon Harcourt (1684–1720), Tory MP and occasional Jacobite.

444 *Mr. ROWE*: see note to p. 142, above.

Mrs. CORBET: Elizabeth Corbett (d. 1725), daughter of Sir Uvedale Corbett.

445 *the Hon. ROBERT DIGBY ... Lord DIGBY*: Robert Digby was a friend and correspondent of Pope's who died in 1726. His sister Mary died in 1729.

446 *Sir GODFREY KNELLER*: Sir Godfrey Kneller (1646–1723) was the leading portrait painter of his age.

447 *General HENRY WITHERS*: Withers (1651?–1729) had a long military career, ending with service under Marlborough throughout the War of the Spanish Succession.

450 *Quem ... fatetur*: 'Isaac Newton, whose immortality is witnessed by Time, Nature and the Heavens, whose mortality is confessed by this marble'.

EDMUND, Duke of BUCKINGHAM: the third son of Pope's friend the Duke of Buckingham, see note to p. 115, above to Rochester.

451 *Ludovici ... sepulchrum*: Ariosto, 'Ludovicii Aerosti Epit.', ll. 1–11. 'The bones of Ludovico Ariosto are buried under this marble, or under this earth, or under whatever pleases his kind heir, or a kinder friend, or a traveller happening upon him more fittingly; for he could not know the future, nor did his empty corpse matter enough to him to make him prepare an urn while he was alive; but while still alive he prepared these lines he wished to be inscribed on his tomb, if he should ever have such a tomb.'

GRAY

452 *Dr. George*: Dr William George (1697–1756), later provost of King's College, Cambridge.

Mr. Horace Walpole: Horace Walpole (1717–97) was the son of Sir Robert Walpole and later to be a noted author, connoisseur, and letter writer.

453 *Mr. West*: Richard West (*c*.1691–1726) was a close friend of Gray at Eton and a minor poet. He is included in Johnson's *Lives*.

Mr. Mason: William Mason (1725–97) became a lifelong friend of Gray and would eventually be his literary executor. After Gray's death he published *The Poems of Mr Gray, to which are Prefixed Memoirs of his Life and Writings* (1775) (hereafter Mason), which helped establish Gray's reputation. Though he claimed a low opinion of Mason's admiring memoir, Johnson is often reliant on it for facts.

lady Cobham: Anne Temple, Viscountess Cobham, was the widow of Lord Cobham, to whom Pope had addressed a poetic epistle. She lived in the Manor House at Stoke Poges, in Buckinghamshire, where Gray often visited his uncle and aunt.

454 *Mr. Bentley*: Richard Bentley (1708–82) was an associate of Walpole who helped to model his 'Gothic' house at Strawberry Hill in Twickenham. At Walpole's behest, he produced illustrations for the first collection of Gray's poems, *Designs by Mr R. Bentley, for Six Poems by Mr T. Gray* (1753).

Warburton: see note to p. 355, above.

Mr. Whitehead: William Whitehead (1715–85), a playwright as well as a poet.

two odes ... much ingenuity: these parodies of Gray's vatic style were written by George Colman (1732–94) and Robert Lloyd (1733–64).

When the Professor ... James Lowther: Gray's self-description is taken from Mason. He applied to the prime minister, John Stuart, Earl of Bute (1713–92), but the post was given to Lawrence Brockett (1724–68), the tutor of Bute's son-in-law.

455 *Dr. Beattie*: James Beattie (1735–1803) was a poet and Professor of Moral Philosophy at Aberdeen University. When Gray met him he had published *Original Poems and Translations* (1760), which included translations of Virgil's eclogues as well as two Pindaric odes modelled on Gray's own. He would later become best known for his long narrative poem *The Minstrel* (1771 and 1774).

the duke of Grafton: Augustus Henry Fitzroy, Duke of Grafton (1735–1811), was prime minister and Chancellor of Cambridge University.

His character ... believe it true: William Temple (1739–96) was a friend of Boswell who had known Gray in Cambridge. Temple sent this account to Boswell, who published it without authorization.

456 *His short account ... insert*: Gray's comments are taken from Mason, pp. 263–4. Anthony Ashley Cooper, third Earl of Shaftesbury (1671–1713), was the author of *Characteristicks* (1711), a collection of essays and dialogues on philosophy and aesthetics. It was widely read in the eighteenth century and influenced some poets, notably James Thomson. Shaftesbury was a deist, believing that the only necessary religious belief could be inferred by the observation and admiration of Nature. Johnson believed that his influence was pernicious.

458 *honey redolent of Spring*: in Dryden's 'Of the Pythagorean Philosophy', l. 110.

O Diva ... Antium: Horace, *Odes*, i. xxxv ('Goddess, who rule over lovely Antium').

459 *third ternary*: the final part of a three-part poetic unit.

Algarotti: the Italian polymath Francesco Algarotti (1712–64) made the comparison with Horace's *Odes*, I. xv in a letter quoted in Mason, ii. 83.

Incredulus odi: Horace, *Ars Poetica*, i. 188 ('I disbelieve and therefore detest').

epodes: the epode is the last part of a Pindaric ode, after the strophe and antistrophe.

A SELECTION OF **OXFORD WORLD'S CLASSICS**

	Travel Writing 1700–1830
	Women's Writing 1778–1838
William Beckford	Vathek
James Boswell	Life of Johnson
Frances Burney	Camilla Cecilia Evelina The Wanderer
Lord Chesterfield	Lord Chesterfield's Letters
John Cleland	Memoirs of a Woman of Pleasure
Daniel Defoe	A Journal of the Plague Year Moll Flanders Robinson Crusoe Roxana
Henry Fielding	Jonathan Wild Joseph Andrews and Shamela Tom Jones
William Godwin	Caleb Williams
Oliver Goldsmith	The Vicar of Wakefield
Mary Hays	Memoirs of Emma Courtney
Elizabeth Inchbald	A Simple Story
Samuel Johnson	The History of Rasselas The Major Works
Charlotte Lennox	The Female Quixote
Matthew Lewis	Journal of a West India Proprietor The Monk
Henry Mackenzie	The Man of Feeling

A SELECTION OF OXFORD WORLD'S CLASSICS

Alexander Pope	**Selected Poetry**
Ann Radcliffe	**The Italian** **The Mysteries of Udolpho** **The Romance of the Forest** **A Sicilian Romance**
Clara Reeve	**The Old English Baron**
Samuel Richardson	**Pamela**
Richard Brinsley Sheridan	**The School for Scandal and Other Plays**
Tobias Smollett	**The Adventures of Roderick Random** **The Expedition of Humphry Clinker**
Laurence Sterne	**The Life and Opinions of Tristram Shandy, Gentleman** **A Sentimental Journey**
Jonathan Swift	**Gulliver's Travels** **Major Works** **A Tale of a Tub and Other Works**
John Vanbrugh	**The Relapse and Other Plays**
Horace Walpole	**The Castle of Otranto**
Mary Wollstonecraft	**Mary and The Wrongs of Woman** **A Vindication of the Rights of Woman**

A SELECTION OF OXFORD WORLD'S CLASSICS

JANE AUSTEN	Emma Persuasion Pride and Prejudice Sense and Sensibility
MRS BEETON	Book of Household Management
ANNE BRONTË	The Tenant of Wildfell Hall
CHARLOTTE BRONTË	Jane Eyre
EMILY BRONTË	Wuthering Heights
WILKIE COLLINS	The Moonstone The Woman in White
JOSEPH CONRAD	Heart of Darkness and Other Tales The Secret Agent
CHARLES DARWIN	The Origin of Species
CHARLES DICKENS	Bleak House David Copperfield Great Expectations Hard Times
GEORGE ELIOT	Middlemarch The Mill on the Floss
ELIZABETH GASKELL	North and South
THOMAS HARDY	Jude the Obscure Tess of the d'Urbervilles
WALTER SCOTT	Ivanhoe
MARY SHELLEY	Frankenstein
ROBERT LOUIS STEVENSON	Strange Case of Dr Jekyll and Mr Hyde and Other Tales
BRAM STOKER	Dracula
WILLIAM MAKEPEACE THACKERAY	Vanity Fair
OSCAR WILDE	The Picture of Dorian Gray